PROMETHEUS
The Life of Balzac

ARIEL
BYRON
CAPTAINS AND KINGS
DISRAELI
MAPE
LYAUTEY
THE SILENCE OF COLONEL BRAMBLE
GENERAL BRAMBLE
DICKENS
PROPHETS AND POETS
THE THOUGHT READING MACHINE
RICOCHETS
THE MIRACLE OF ENGLAND
CHATEAUBRIAND
THE ART OF LIVING
TRAGEDY IN FRANCE
I REMEMBER, I REMEMBER
THE MIRACLE OF AMERICA
WOMAN WITHOUT LOVE
FROM MY JOURNAL
THE MIRACLE OF FRANCE
PROUST: *Portrait of a Genius*
LÉLIA: *The Life of George Sand*
OLYMPIO: *The Life of Victor Hugo*
THE ART OF BEING HAPPILY MARRIED
THE TITANS: *A Three-Generation Biography of the Dumas*
SEPTEMBER ROSES

PROMETHEUS
The Life of Balzac

ANDRÉ MAUROIS

translated by
NORMAN DENNY

CARROLL & GRAF PUBLISHERS, INC.
New York

to Simone

Contents

TRANSLATOR'S NOTE, 9
AUTHOR'S FOREWORD, 11

Part One
THE UPWARD CLIMB

I Bernard-François Balzac, or Tours under
  Bonaparte, 17
II The Precocious Philosopher, 29
III From Tours to the Marais, 38
IV Apprenticeship of a Genius, 51
V First Novels and First Love, 72
VI Interlude in Bayeux, 91
VII The Literary Trade, 101
VIII Dreamer in Action, 114
IX Return to Serious Matters, 129
X First Breath of Fame, 141

Part Two
FAME

XI The Years of Growth, 155
XII The Ass's Skin, 172
XIII Follies and Retreats, 186
XIV The Reluctant Lady, 207
XV Enter *l'Étrangère*, 218
XVI In Search of the Absolute, 237
XVII The Grand Design, 254
XVIII Rue des Batailles, 265
XIX The Lily in the Valley, 276
XX *Illusions Perdues*, 289

8 CONTENTS

Part Three

THE HUMAN COMEDY

XXI The Contessa, 305
XXII Strange Escapade, 314
XXIII The Death of Madame de Berny, 322
XXIV The Myth of Sisyphus, 335
XXV Treasure Hunt, 345
XXVI Les Jardies, 358
XXVII Rearguard Battles, 371
XXVIII The Secret House, 387
XXIX *La Comédie humaine* (1), 398
XXX *La Comédie humaine* (2), 413

Part Four

SWAN-SONG

XXXI The Torment of Tantalus, 429
XXXII Reunion in St Petersburg, 441
XXXIII Chorus of Wolves, 458
XXXIV Perrette and the Milk-Pail, 470
XXXV The World Around Him, 482
XXXVI Swan-Song, 493
XXXVII Body Without Soul, 502
XXXVIII Wonderland, 510
XXXIX Alarms and Excursions, 517
XL A Ship Befogged, 529
XLI The Race to Death, 543
Epilogue, 551
BIBLIOGRAPHY, 563
CHRONOLOGICAL LIST
AND INDEX OF WORKS, 565
INDEX OF NAMES, 569

Translator's Note

SOME IDEA of the difficulties confronting the French author of this book may be gathered from his Foreword and the bibliography. Balzac literature in France, already extensive, has been very considerably added to since 1950, the centenary of Balzac's death. The biographer setting out to write a new Life, embodying the latest researches, had to use meticulous care if he was to face the intent scrutiny of the countless devotees of the *culte balzacien*. The French edition contains source-notes on nearly every page, as well as a *bibliographie sommaire* occupying nine closely-printed pages.

Where the English-speaking world is concerned this problem does not arise. Our knowledge of Balzac is comparatively remote. We know him largely by hearsay, and directly through a handful of major novels, authentic masterpieces but not his only ones, which are no more than chapters in the huge complex of inter-related long and short novels and short stories constituting the unfinished *Comédie humaine*. (There are also the *Contes drolatiques*, but they are a separate matter.) The close documentation of the original, which in any case refers very largely to sources not available in English, was not thought to be necessary to the English edition. André Maurois's book also contains a certain amount of peripheral matter—names, dates, places, topical allusions—more interesting and intelligible to French than to English readers, and some of this has been omitted.

In short, this may be termed an 'edited' translation, although in a very minor sense. The editing has been carried out by the translator in close conjunction with the author, whose friendly comments and suggestions have greatly helped him in his task and made it a particularly pleasant one.

NORMAN DENNY

Author's Foreword

THIS IS A life of Balzac. A life, not a critical study. Philippe
Bertault has dealt with the subject of Balzac and religion;
Curtius, Alain and Gaëtan Picon with Balzac's thought; Bernard
Guyon, Donnard and Wurmser with Balzac and society; Jean
Pommier, Maurice Bardèche and Pierre Laubriet with Balzac
and literary creativity; Pierre Abraham, Félicien Marceau and
Dr Fernand Lotte with Balzac's characters; Roger Pierrot and
Jean A. Ducourneau with his letters. Marcel Bouteron has
covered everything. A regiment of well-informed lovers of
Balzac, Marie-Jeanne Durry, Pierre-Georges Castex, Pierre
Moreau, Antoine Adam, Maurice Regard, Suzanne J. Bérard,
Madeleine Fargeaud, Marie-Anne Meininger and twenty others
whom I shall cite in their place, have written prefaces to the
novels or examined hitherto little-known aspects of his work and
life. No writer other than Shakespeare has been the object of so
much study, or has more deserved to be. Balzac has been
explored, and will continue to be explored, like a world, because
that is what he is.

The existing lives of Balzac (some of them remarkable, like
those of André Billy and Stefan Zweig) were written before the
recent great flowering of Balzac scholarship. I have sought to fill a
gap. There are those who argue, 'Why worry about Balzac's life?
Only his work matters.' This very old dispute has always seemed
to me meaningless. We know that the works cannot be accounted
for by the life, and that the greatest events in the life of a creative
artist are his works. But the life of a great man is a matter of
profound interest in its own right. Balzac himself, whose fundamental belief was in the unity of the world, would remind us
that 'the mysterious laws of flesh and spirit' shape the works as
they shape the life. However difficult it may be to knit into one
piece the demi-god who gave birth to a world and the fat man
who revelled in childish puns, the effort must be made. By a
ceaseless process of osmosis, the acts and thoughts and encounters of Monsieur Honoré de Balzac nourished the *Comédie*

humaine. We shall seek to discern some aspects of that mysterious alchemy.

Balzac set out to be the chronicler of society; I am simply the chronicler of Balzac. That I do not share all his political and religious views is both obvious and irrelevant. Whether he was right or wrong in any given situation is a matter for the moralist. 'We do not argue with great writers,' wrote Alain, 'we are simply grateful for what they give us.' How is one to pass judgement on Proteus? Balzac was by turns a saint, a criminal, an honest judge, a corrupt judge, a minister, a fop, a harlot, a duchess, and always a genius. We shall see him in his moments of creative ecstasy as well as in those when 'like a sailor on shore-leave' he walks through the streets of the town. 'The tissue of our life is woven of mixed threads, good and bad together.' It is as true of Balzac as it is of the rest of us.

The English reader will find an indication of my major sources in the Bibliography, and there are frequent references in the text and occasional footnotes. I owe particular expressions of gratitude to Madeleine Fargeaud, who read this book in manuscript and to whom I am indebted for numerous unpublished documents; to Maurice Bardèche, whose admirable edition of Balzac, published by the *Club de l'Honnête Homme*, has been of the greatest value to me; and to my wife, who has sustained me throughout this long task, and who certainly deserves to be numbered among the Balzac scholars. Finally, I must pay tribute to two men now dead without whom this book would never have been conceived: to Marcel Bouteron, because it was he who introduced me to the riches of the Collection Spoelberch de Lovenjoul; and to Alain, my master, who in the days when he was unfolding the world and all things to my eyes flung me neck and crop into the *Comédie humaine.* I have never escaped from it. Age does not allow me to embark upon any more large undertakings or very extensive researches. This biography is the last I shall write. I am happy that the subject is Balzac.

A.M.

PROMETHEUS
The Life of Balzac

Part One

THE UPWARD CLIMB

*Parlons un peu de Balzac,
cela fait du bien.*

GÉRARD DE NERVAL

I

Bernard-François Balzac,
or Tours under Bonaparte

Il n'y a pas deux familles comme la nôtre.
BALZAC

IN 1799, THE year of Honoré Balzac's birth, France was in the
state of a convalescent after a serious illness. Ten years of fever
had left the country sick, uneasy and flaccid. The constitution
under the Consulate was endorsed by an almost unanimous
plebiscite. France was not ravished; she gave herself. The
Catholics hoped to be allowed to practise their religion in peace;
the avowed Jacobins accepted the readmittance of the cult, not
without sarcasm, on the understanding that they would keep
their own establishments. In Tours, a provincial capital elegantly
spread along the bank of its beautiful river, the act of appease-
ment was well received. In 1801 Bonaparte sent them General
de Pommereul as Prefect, an artillery officer under the Ancien
Régime and a contributor to the Encyclopedia, who was to prove
himself a competent administrator, and to whom the First
Consul owed a debt of gratitude for the good marks he had
awarded him when he took his first army examinations at
Brienne.

The Prefect had to conform to the new religious policy. He
opened the Cathedral of Saint-Gatien to the priests who wished
to celebrate with a *Te Deum* of thanksgiving and installed an
archbishop, Monseigneur de Boisgelin, to whom he handed the
keys while at the same time delivering a patriotic oration on the
Concordat. The Archbishop was content to reply, coldly enough,
with a few words having no bearing on the subject.

The two men were often to find themselves at odds. The
Archbishop called for the return of the cathedral bells, which
had been confiscated by the Mayor, and further demanded the
removal of the 'caps of liberty' affixed to the towers and their

replacement by crosses. The Prefect, after consulting his Minister and the Government, who were more tolerant than the local Jacobins, returned their bells to all the communes, because 'they were making the same fuss everywhere'. The Ministry of Justice reproved Pommereul for having suspended a priest: 'His conduct was deserving of reprimand, but it would have been more correct and more fitting if you had deferred to His Grace the Archbishop of Tours, with whom it is important, having regard to the general harmony and the proper influencing of public opinion, that you should act in concert in such cases.' These disputes were to have a profound influence on the career of Bernard-François Balzac, the father of Honoré and the friend and favourite of the Prefect.

The views of General de Pomereul are pleasantly reflected in an episode concerning Agnès Sorel, the mistress of Charles VII. Her tomb, which had at first been placed in the choir of a church at Loches, had been removed by the canons after the King's death and relegated to a side chapel, where it was partly destroyed during the Revolution. The Prefect issued an order for its restoration and, to do honour to 'la Dame de Beauté', had it installed in a tower of the Château de Loches. He himself devised the inscription:

THE CANONS OF LOCHES, ENRICHED BY HER GIFTS,
ASKED LOUIS XI
TO REMOVE HER TOMB FROM THEIR CHOIR.
'I WILL DO SO,' HE SAID, 'IF YOU WILL RETURN THE
ENDOWMENT.'
THE TOMB STAYED WHERE IT WAS.
AN ARCHBISHOP OF TOURS, LESS HONOURABLE,
HAD IT REMOVED TO A CHAPEL.
DURING THE REVOLUTION IT WAS DESTROYED.
MEN OF FEELING RECOVERED THE REMAINS OF AGNES.
AND GENERAL POMMEREUL, PREFECT OF INDRE-ET-LOIRE,
RESTORED THE MAUSOLEUM OF THE ONLY ROYAL MISTRESS
WHO DESERVED WELL OF OUR COUNTRY,
IN THAT SHE DEMANDED, AS THE PRICE OF HER FAVOURS,
THE EXPULSION OF THE ENGLISH FROM FRANCE.

Carved on the entablature are the words: '*Je suis Agnès. Vive France et l'Amour!*' Such was the manner of Prefect Pommereul, soldier, sceptic and libertine; such too, with less elegance, was the manner of his protégé, Bernard-François Balzac. The latter, although a lover of Rabelais, could not call himself a son of Touraine. His real name, Balssa, was that of a peasant family from the hamlet of Nougayrié, in Tarn. The root *bals*, in the *langue d'Oc*, means a 'craggy rock'. In Auvergne there are Balsacs, Balssas and Balsans. Bernard-François, being given to self-glorification, preened himself on belonging to the conquered race, the aboriginal Gauls, who had resisted all invasions and from whom sprang the Balzacs of Entragues, a very noble family. It is more probable that, under barbarian pressure, the serfs of the village of Balsac, near Brioude, emigrated to Tarn. The Balzacs' forebears were hard-bitten peasants, 'tenacious, half-starved, scratching their barley-fields with primitive ploughs'. The tides of war flowed frequently over them: crusades against the Albigenses, bands of marauders, English, they suffered from them all. Nevertheless, thanks to their fierce stubbornness, a number of families belonging to the tribe of Balssa survived and prospered.

The grandfather of our Balzac, Bernard Balssa (1716–78), inherited a little land at Nougayrié and became the owner of pastures and vineyards, acquired a piece at a time. The family brought up eleven children who slept on straw mattresses along the walls. The eldest, Bernard-François, helped his father in the fields, and in the evening they discussed secret hiding-places for the family savings, and talked about their friends, the Curé Vialar and the Notary Albar. Bernard-François, intelligent and ambitious, reflected, 'Why not become a priest or a notary?' The Curé taught him to read and write French, and he became a clerk in the chambers of Maître Albar, at Canezac, near Monesties. Here he picked up common law, procedure and the drafting of conveyances. 'The play of interwoven interests, so complex and so cut-throat, was starkly revealed to him, in all its unrelenting harshness.' In about 1765 his signature disappears from the documents issuing from the chambers. Did he go from there to Rodez, to Albi, to Toulouse? What is certain is that, while still very young, he 'went up' to Paris, owning nothing but his hobnailed shoes, a peasant jacket, a flowered waistcoat and three shirts of coarse material, but endowed with boundless ambition and abundant energy.

A self-teacher, interested in science and history, he had read a great deal, and he contrived to make himself useful wherever he went by his knowledge of civil Procedure. That he should later have looked back on his career with pride is understandable. For a son of poor peasants to arrive in Paris with no other fortune than a knapsack on his back, and thereafter become clerk to the Public Prosecutor, rising stage by stage, even at a subordinate level, to the King's Council, where he assisted the Court of Common Pleas in a great variety of matters—this astonishing progress bears witness to a sound intelligence, wide knowledge and invincible determination. The gulf between the lower and the middle class was bridged within the lifetime of a single man.

For a time Bernard-François was private secretary to Bertrand de Molleville, the Secretary for the Navy. He helped Joseph d'Albert, the Master of Common Pleas, to draw up reports on problems as diverse as the liquidation of the French India Company and the signing of extradition treaties between France and the German principalities. A document exists whereby 'His Majesty appoints the Sieur Balzac, secretary attached to his Council, to fulfil the duties of Recorder'. This contact with greatness imbued Bernard-François for the rest of his life with a mingling of respect and envy of the nobility. He dreamed of particles (the 'de' before the surname which is the hall-mark of nobility), although this did not prevent him, in 1791, from treating Madame d'Albert, the widow of his former employer, with the arrogance of an 'active citizen'. Later on, when a newly appointed Prefect of Indre-et-Loire asked for his credentials he replied: 'Secretary to the *ci-devant Conseil d'Etat* for sixteen consecutive years; *Commissaire de Section* in Paris on the 21st June, 1791, the day of the flight of the ci-devant King. I was successively appointed *Président de Section, Député à la Commune, Officier Municipal,* commissioner on the Police Tribunal, and President of this Tribunal, which at the time was in sole charge of the Paris police.' He had been skilful in negotiating the dangerous bend of the Revolution.

It seems nevertheless that at the time of the flight to Varennes doubts were cast upon his loyalty. An opportunist by necessity, but generous by nature, he was believed to have saved a number of royalists, his former protectors and friends. A member of the Convention who was friendly towards him advised him to leave

Paris. He took refuge in Valenciennes and in the end turned the situation to advantage. 'Someone reliable was needed,' he wrote, 'to safeguard the funds and to direct the supply services for the Army of the North. . . . The choice fell upon me. I was appointed at one and the same time director of (1) food distribution; (2) fodder; (3) heat and light; (4) the victualling of Paris; (5) the siege provisioning of the armies. . . . Until the victory of Fleurus I alone was in charge of these five services. . . . So strictly and justly were they supervised that not one of my subordinates was imprisoned or arrested. . . . My five balance-sheets have been presented and I hold their legal acquittance.'

So much conscious rectitude, such protestations of honesty! But it is a fact that he played a part in the partly civilian administration of army supplies, under the orders of Daniel Doumerc, a financier who had 'a finger in all the supply-markets'. After the battle of Fleurus, Bernard-François was appointed to posts in Brest and then in Tours, 'a key-position', he said, 'since it was the sole centre of the funds allocated to the campaign against the Chouans and the Vendée'. So in 1797 he went to live in Tours, responsible for supplies, very comfortably off without being rich, and an impressive figure in a handsome blue, silver-embroidered uniform, the upturned points of the collar enclosing a white cravat. At the age of fifty-one he was still a bachelor, but then his chief, Doumerc, got him married to a very pretty girl thirty-two years younger than himself—Laure Sallambier.

Her parents came of a solid bourgeois family of drapers and manufacturers of brocade, highly respected in the Marais, the Paris quarter of well-to-do merchants and shopkeepers. They had many connections in the mercantile world, and were allied by numerous marriages to the Sedillots, who counted orientalists, surgeons and a leading astronomer among their number. The Marais was a gateway to the Institute.

Madame Sallambier, an intense, very active woman, had drawn up a strict set of rules for the instruction of her daughter: 'I recommend to my daughter, Laure, that she shall give thought to the position of her body when writing, and take pains to hold her pen correctly so that her handwriting may be well-formed. . . . I shall say nothing regarding her general conduct, since she has promised me that she will deal kindly with everyone,

and especially with Her Mother. . . .' The capitals are Sophie
Sallambier's own. There follows:

DAILY TIME-TABLE FOR MY DAUGHTER LAURE

Monday
Rise at 7
7–8, cleanliness
8–9, breakfast and
recreation
9–10, writing
10–12, useful work

Notes
Clean teeth; wash hands and face; tidy
bedroom.

By useful work I mean dressmaking,
knitting, hemming, embroidery. Clothes
for her dolls are recreation.

The programme covers every day and hour of the week: 'On
Sunday after lunch the record of conduct for the past week will
be reviewed.' This severity accepted, Madame Sallambier could
be 'adorable'; but she left her daughter greatly prone to nervous
agitation.

The position of the Sallambiers in the social scale was
decidedly higher than that of Bernard-François Balzac. Why,
then, did they bestow their young and beautiful daughter on
a man of lesser standing, aged fifty? It may have been because
the career of Bernard-Francois was very similar to that of Joseph
Sallambier. Both had belonged to the supply service and both
were Freemasons. There was a sense of comradeship and com-
plicity between them. The bride received as her dowry the
farm of Volaille, 'in the parish of Gazeran, a league from Rambouillet', valued at 30,000 francs in the marriage contract (to
reduce costs) but in fact worth over 120,000. The bridegroom
guaranteed a marriage settlement of 1,800 francs a year.
Bernard-François in fact possessed little or no fortune, nothing
but his several salaries, a few investments and a share in the
Tontine Lafarge. A *tontine* was a form of private investment
trust of which the members agreed to share the income during
their lives but to leave the capital to the survivors after their
death. The last survivors might come in for very large sums.

Bernard-François, such was his confidence in the soundness
of his constitution, had no doubt that he would live to be a
hundred. Because he came of a mixture of Gallic, Roman and

Gothic stock, he believed that he possessed the attributes of all three races: health, courage and patience. A disciple of Rousseau, he lived a life of healthy moderation; he liked milk and the sap of trees; he had a passion for walking. He rose and went to bed early, and prided himself on never having been to a doctor or put ten sous in an apothecary's pocket. He walked like a conqueror with his head held high, and was given to saying: 'Je suis beau comme un marbre et fort comme un arbre.'

A member of the Tours Masonic Lodge and a great reader of the Bible, he was also a student of the papacy, of Catholic schisms and heresies, and of Chinese civilization. Politically he was a supporter of the Empire. He did not repudiate the Revolution, but condemned the disorders and acts of revenge which had followed it.

My father [his daughter Laure wrote] had something of Montaigne, Rabelais and Uncle Toby in his philosophy, his eccentricity and his goodness of heart. Like Uncle Toby, he was possessed by a dominant idea, in his case that of *health*. He fitted so well into life that he wanted to live as long as possible, and he reckoned, basing his estimate on the number of years that a man needs to achieve the *perfect state*, that his life would last a hundred years *and more*. . . . He took extraordinary care of himself and was constantly on the alert to establish what he called the *equilibrium of the vital forces*. . . .

His eccentricity, which became proverbial in Tours, was displayed as much in his speech as in his actions; he neither said nor did anything like other men; Hoffmann might have used him as a character in one of his fantastic tales. My father often talked derisively of men in general, saying that they worked incessantly for their own unhappiness; he could never encounter a human failure without inveighing against the parents, and above all against governments, which cared less about the improvement of the human stock than it did about that of animals. On this very ticklish subject he had singular theories which he arrived at in a no less singular fashion. . . .

'But what would be the point of publishing my ideas?' he would say as he strode up and down the room in his quilted silk gown, his head half-buried in the big cravat which he had retained from Directoire fashions. 'They'd simply say I was an *original*—' the word infuriated him '—and there would be not one half-starved or ricketty person the less. . . .'

His wife was a sore trial to his patience and philosophy. Beautiful, fine-featured, vain, often stiff and disdainful, she was a remarkable woman but with little warmth. She had been well-educated at the convent of the Dames de Saint-Servan, in Paris. Like her mother she believed in the occult sciences, in witches and clairvoyants.

The Balzacs lived in style. When a subscription was opened for the founding of a lycée in Tours, Citizen Balzac contributed 1,300 francs, the Prefect 1,000 francs and the Archbishop 600 francs. Apart from his *rentes* and the income from his wife's farm, Bernard-François drew salaries from several sources. Pommereul, who had known him 'at the Court and in the camps', had had him appointed deputy-mayor of Tours and administrator of charitable institutions.

The family lived first in a rented house in the Rue de l'Armée d'Italie. On 20 May 1798, fifteen months after her marriage, Laure Balzac gave birth to a son (Louis-Daniel) whom she insisted upon feeding herself and who lived only twenty-three days. Accordingly, when the second child, Honoré, was born on 20 May 1799, the Balzacs put him out to nurse with the wife of a gendarme at Saint-Cyr-sur-Loire. He was joined there the following year by his sister, Laure, who was born on 29 September 1800.

Honoré never forgave his mother for letting him be thus separated from her: 'Who can say how much physical or moral harm was done me by my mother's coldness? Was I no more than the child of marital duty, my birth a matter of chance . . . ? Put out to nurse in the country, neglected by my family for three years, when I was brought home I counted for so little that people were sorry for me . . .' (Balzac, *Le Lys dans la vallée*). The truth is that Madame Balzac, appalled by the death of the child fed at her own breast, had simply followed the custom of the time. But it must be added that, although her children were at no great distance from her, she seldom visited them.

The wet-nurse was a good woman. Unfortunately her husband drank and grew violent in his cups. However, Honoré retained a strangely tender memory of that hill overlooking the Loire, of whole days passed in building 'miniature Louvres of pebbles and mud' and above all of his 'assistant builder', his little sister, Laure, 'pretty as a Raphael virgin'. The remoteness of their parents favoured brotherly affection.

I was only two years younger than Honoré,* and in the same position as he where our parents were concerned. Brought up together, we loved each other dearly, and my memories of his tenderness go back a long way. I do not forget the haste with which he would run to prevent me falling down the three steep steps, of unequal height and without a rail, leading from our nurse's room to the garden! His touching protectiveness continued at home, where more than once he let himself be punished on my account rather than give me away. When I arrived in time to confess he would say, 'Don't own up another time. I like being scolded for you.' (Laure Surville)

He stayed for some years in that village of white houses flanking the Loire, 'bordered with magnificent poplars whose rustling we could hear'. The broad river flowed between sandbanks and leafy islands, and the child was happy in that charming countryside where 'neither audacity nor magnificence prevailed, but the simple beauties of nature'. On the opposite bank ran the line of hills, 'velvety, broken with white splashes' of the châteaux built on their slopes. 'It was beneath your pure sky that my eyes first followed the flight of the first clouds.' That Touraine landscape was to remain an ideal for him throughout his life, the setting of his most tender love.

He was four when he was brought back to Tours. His mother was a woman who did not know how to win affection. Honoré was 'a charming child'; his happy nature, his well-shaped, smiling mouth, his brown eyes, at once shining and gentle, his high forehead and rich, dark locks, attracted notice when they went out walking. But the pretty little boy, impulsive and warm-hearted, encountered 'the devouring flame of a stern eye'. Madame Balzac 'knew nothing of caresses, kisses, the simple joys of living and creating a happy home for others'. A taste for luxury, and the desire to live up to her station in life, soured her character.

A second daughter, Laurence, was born on 18 April 1802, and on the occasion of her baptism the Balzacs dignified themselves with the particle 'de', which however was only inter-

* In fact, sixteen months (20 May 1799-29 September 1800).

mittently used. Their rise in status seems to have been rapid. Bernard-François, under the protection of the Prefect, had become a leading figure in the town. As deputy mayor he felt the need to own property in Tours, and accordingly, having sold the Gazeran farm, the property of his wife, he bought a handsome house with old timbering, stables and garden at 29 Rue d'Indre-et-Loire—'an imperial street, a street with pavements on either side; a well-surfaced, well-built street, well-washed and clean as a mirror; the queen of streets, the only street in Tours'. A week later he bought the Saint-Lazare farm, on the road from Tours to Saint-Avertin. This farm was alienated Church property, and he was able to get it at a bargain price.

More ambitious than ever, and being persuaded that all things were possible to a man with back-stairs influence, Bernard-François passed his time in intrigues and had little leisure to spare for his children. His too-young, too-pretty wife 'plunged delightedly into the social whirlpool' and 'kept under her spell' the landed gentry of the district and the English, who were at that time in enforced residence at Tours, by the Emperor's decree.

Much later, in her old age, she said to her daughter: 'An elderly husband forced me to maintain a certain reserve and keep my distance with people who were disposed to like me; and my rather serious cast of countenance helped me to appear more unforthcoming than amiable.' But her precautions were in vain. The local ladies found her over-dressed and concluded that her husband was doing rather *too* well in his affairs. She contrived, by her successes and her conquests, to get on the wrong side of all the virtuous members of her sex. 'Your father, because of his age, had the tact to say nothing.' Nor did he say anything when there were whispers of a liaison between his wife and Monsieur de Margonne, owner of the Château de Saché. In the view of Bernard-François a peaceful home-life was essential to longevity.

The Margonne family were on the border-line between the middle-class and the lesser nobility. By general consent they were allowed the particle, but Jean de Margonne signed himself plain 'Margonne'. Born in 1780, this handsome and elegant young man had in 1803 married his rather unattractive cousin, Anne de Savary, who brought him the Saché estate with three manor houses two farms and six mills. Her father, Messire Henri-Joseph de Savary, squire and former cavalry officer, had

in 1791 bought a wine-growing property at Vouvray. He wore
the perruque, kept a mistress-housekeeper and 'concealed a
deep peasant shrewdness beneath a deceptive appearance of
simplicity'. His son-in-law, Margonne, too much a 'townsman'
to bury himself in the country, until 1815 lived far more in
Tours than at Saché. He had provided himself with a reason
for staying in the town by accepting a commission in the
Cohorte Urbaine, the élite of the *Garde Nationale*, and on
Sundays he led the march of his Grenadiers along the Mail and
the Rue Royale. Perhaps it was the sight of him in his splendid
uniform, stern-faced, virile and self-pleased, which caused
Laure Balzac, if family gossip and probability are to be believed,
to fall in love with him. All love-affairs are absorbing. When her
son and daughter were brought home from Saint-Cyr-sur-
Loire their mother scarcely saw them except on Sundays.

Honoré, Laure and Laurence were placed in the charge of a
formidable governess, Mademoiselle Delahaye, and lived in a
state of constant apprehension, both of the stony, blue-eyed
gaze of their mother, and of the lies the governess told. She
maintained that Honoré detested his home and that he was not
stupid but sly; and she mocked him for his interest in the stars,
which he studied with a curious intensity. Child though he was,
he invented stories to amuse his sisters. 'For hours on end,'
Laure wrote, 'he would scratch away at a little red violin, and
his rapturous expression showed that he believed he was hearing tunes. He was astonished when I begged him to stop.
"Can't you hear how pretty it is?" he would say.' He had the
gift of living in an imaginary world and hearing celestial
harmonies that sounded for his ears alone.

The greatest event of his childhood was a trip with his mother
to Paris in 1804. The Sallambier grandparents wanted to get to
know their grandson. They were delighted with the pretty child,
whom they thoroughly spoilt, and he returned home with
countless tales to tell his sisters about their grandparents' house
with its fine garden, and Mouche, the watch-dog. Madame
Sallambier delighted to tell the following story, which his sister,
Laure Surville, later repeated:

One evening when she had had the magic-lantern brought
out for him, Honoré, not seeing his friend Mouche in the

audience, stood up and cried, "Wait!" in a commanding voice. (He knew he was master in his grandfather's house.) He left the drawing-room and came back with the dog, to whom he said, "Sit down and watch, Mouche. It won't cost you anything. Grandpapa is paying!"

Children's utterances are all too often the echo of thoughts their parents suppose to be secret. There was far too much talk in the Balzac household of money and legacies. A few months after that visit to Paris, Grandpapa died of a stroke. It was a great grief to Honoré. A little later Grandmamma came to live with her daughter. She contributed an income of 5,000 francs to the family budget, but made the mistake of entrusting some of her capital to her son-in-law, who risked it in a 'dazzling' speculation and lost 40,000 francs. Madame Sallambier would gladly have indulged her grandchildren, had her daughter's strictness not prevented her from doing so. Honoré trembled, literally, when his mother talked of taking charge of his education. On the other hand, he enjoyed his father's disquisitions and idiosyncratic outbursts, even if he did not understand them. Madame Balzac sent her daughters to the Pension Vauquer, and her son as a day-boy to the Pensionnat Le Guay, at six francs a month. A pew-holder at the Cathedral of Saint-Gatien, Madame Balzac herself took her son to church, becoming the more strict in her behaviour as she felt herself the more open to reproach.

When Honoré was eight she decided to send him as a boarder to the Collège de Vendôme. At the time she was expecting another child, which rumour attributed to Jean de Margonne. Honoré was deeply distressed at being parted from Laure, the companion 'of his misery and his tears'. No doubt over-sensibility caused him to exaggerate the unhappiness of his childhood. Later he was to say, 'I never had a mother.' This was a cruel exaggeration, written in a moment of anger. But a child's feelings are none the less acute for being in part unwarranted. There are bastards of the imagination, born in wedlock, who nevertheless feel themselves to be rejected by their parents, without knowing why. These more than others long for worldly triumphs, to compensate for their deep-rooted sense of loss.

II

The Precocious Philosopher

*Comme l'enfant qui dit son propre prénom en parlant de
lui, le romancier se désigne lui-même à travers une infinité
de troisièmes personnes.*

ROLAND BARTHES

THE COLLÈGE DE VENDÔME, which Honoré Balzac entered in
1807, at the age of eight, was one of the most unconventional
schools in France. It had been founded by the Oratorians who,
like the Jesuits, devoted themselves to education, and who
passed for liberals, which must have pleased Bernard-François.
Indeed, the joint headmasters of the college in Balzac's time,
Mareschal and Dessaignes, had both taken an oath of allegiance
to the nation and were both married. But these married priests
kept their Catholic faith and maintained an almost monastic
discipline. The boys left the school only when they had completed their studies. 'Our pupils never have holidays,' the headmasters wrote to the Rector of Orléans. 'They never go into the
town. Parents are asked not to invite their children home.' All
letters, both in- and out-going, were opened by a member of
the staff. The parents renounced all authority.

The Oratorians of Vendôme taught respect for the Emperor,
without which their establishment would not have survived;
but they were opposed to the military spirit of the high schools
under the Empire. It was a bell, not a drum, which summoned
the boys to class. Ordinary high school regulations prescribed
reading aloud during meals, a precaution against dangerous
thoughts. The Oratorians allowed conversation in the refectory,
and when reproached with this they replied: 'For the sake of
good conduct and discipline, and to preserve the progress made
during the year, we allow no holidays, and thus deprive ourselves
of rest and of the financial saving which holidays would represent;
yet we are blamed for the small pleasures we allow our pupils.'
These small pleasures consisted of: 'Occasional country excur-

sions organized as follows: a leader, three masters and forty-two boys. The senior parties set out at four o'clock in the morning and walk perhaps ten miles to visit a foundry, a glass-works or an observatory; they dine frugally in the open and come back tired out.' It may be conceded that these were manly and rustic diversions. The college led an austere life. A picture of a mathematics class is to be seen in the Vendôme town library. Although the room is heated by a stove of sorts, the master in charge has his head covered and the collar of his tail-coat turned up. Punishments included extremely painful chastisement over the knuckles with a leather rod, numerous impositions and long periods of confinement in a sort of dungeon situated beneath the stairs which the boys called 'the alcove', or in what were known as the *culottes de bois*, boxlike cells six feet by six installed in every dormitory for wrongdoers.

Honoré, when he joined the junior class at Vendôme, was a round-faced, red-cheeked little boy, but gloomy and silent, obsessed with unhappy recollections of his family life. Later he was to write a great deal about guilty mothers who preferred the child of adultery to their legitimate offspring. He came to the school with the cringingly distrustful air of a whipped dog, endowed with neither grace nor self-reliance.

Anyone who will trouble to picture the isolation of that big school with its monastic buildings set in the middle of a small town, and the four grades (very small, Small, Medium and Big) into which we were hierarchically divided, will have some idea of the interest which the arrival of a *newcomer* aroused in us, truly a new passenger in the ship. . . . (Balzac: *Louis Lambert*)

The child Balzac seemed little qualified to make any impression on that schoolboy community. Being almost entirely deprived of pocket-money by the parsimony of his mother, he could rarely share in the games or in such purchases as were allowed. Other boys' parents came to Vendôme for the prize-giving; his own never did. In six years, he tells us, from 1807 to 1813, his mother visited him only twice, perhaps to conform to the spirit of the College. The first letter written by him which has been preserved was addressed to Madame Bernard-François Balzac:

Vendôme, 1 May

My dear Mother,

I think Papa was very unhappy when he heard that I had been put in the alcove. To console him please tell him that I have got an *accessit*. I do not forget to clean my teeth with my handkerchief. I have a new exercise-book in which I make fair copies of my exercises and I get good marks and that is how I hope to please you. I embrace you warmly and all the family and the gentlemen of my acquaintance. These are the names I know of boys who have won prizes and come from Tours:

Boislecompte

He is the only one I can remember.

Balzac Honoré,
Your obedient and affectionate son.

The *accessit* (consolation prize) for a speech in Latin, which was to reassure Papa, consisted of a poor little volume bound in rough sheepskin, a History of Charles XII of Sweden, bearing the inscription in gilt letters: *Prix à Honoré Balzac, 1808*.

Did he find among his masters the affection which his parents denied him? One of them, Père Lefebvre, played a large part in his youthful life. According to the report on his noviciate, this teacher showed 'talent, intelligence, a good memory, more imagination than judgement, and a taste for marvels and philosophical systems'. He had, in short, something in common with the peculiar little boy who also had a taste for marvels. Feeling himself to be an exile upon earth, Honoré looked to Heaven for a miracle. One of Père Lefebvre's tasks was the cataloguing of the immense school library, a part of which came from the looting of châteaux during the Revolution. He gave Honoré extra lessons in mathematics, since his father hoped to send him later to the École Polytechnique; but, more poet than mathematician, he did not restrain the boy from reading what he liked during those periods of private tuition. 'So, by a tacit understanding between us, I did not complain of learning nothing and he said nothing about the books I borrowed.'

The borrowings were very numerous, and the priest imposed no censorship on the works chosen by young Balzac, who read in the recreation periods, sitting under a tree, while his school-fellows played games. He often got himself confined in the *cachot* so as to be able to read undisturbed. Thus he developed a passion for reading, and he picked up a great deal of haphazard knowledge which, by its very untidiness, lent a precocious originality to his thinking. 'From childhood I tapped my forehead, saying like André Chenier, "There's something there!" I seemed to feel within myself a thought to be expressed, a philosophy to be propounded, a science to be explained. . . .' But in those days he was the only one to envisage a great future for himself. To his teachers and schoolfellows he was a very commonplace boy, remarkable only for his absorption in the printed word and for a good opinion of himself which nothing seemed to justify.

Also like André Chenier he tried to write poetry:

Impelled by this immoderate passion I neglected my studies in order to compose poems which can certainly have shown little promise, if I may judge by an over-long line which became famous among my schoolfellows, the beginning of an epic on the Incas:

O Inca! O roi infortuné et malheureux!

I was derisively nicknamed 'the poet'; but this teasing did not deter me. I went on pouring out poetry, despite the sound advice of Monsieur Mareschal, our headmaster, who tried to cure me of what was, alas, an inveterate addiction by telling me the fable of the fledgling that fell out of its nest through trying to fly before its wings were grown. I went on reading. I became the least active, the most idle and the most dreamy pupil in the junior division, and the one most often punished. . . .

Those are the words of one of his characters, but the testimony of those who knew him at the time makes it clear that there was a close affinity between the fictional Louis Lambert and his creator. That thirteen-syllable line about the Inca was actually written by the schoolboy Honoré Balzac. But his deeper instinct at that time drew him towards neither poetry nor the pursuit of knowledge, but rather to the formulation of an ingenuous occult philosophy. His knuckles bruised by the rod, his affections rebuffed, 'he took refuge in the heavens conjured up by his imagination'. He may have been less precocious than Louis Lambert, but, like him, while he was still very young he read mystical writers who 'familiarized him with those vivid movements of the soul of which ecstasy is both the means and the end'.

'He would have hated to be mistaken for a devoutly religious pupil'; for him the period of evening prayer was passed 'in recounting or hearing the incidents of the day'; and his thoughts during Sunday Mass were concerned with balancing the scant pocket-money that remained to him against 'the hankerings aroused by the miscellany of goods offered in the school shop'. In the Collège de Vendôme irreligion was more than a habit among the pupils; it was a matter for emulation. The son of Bernard-François, that disciple of Voltaire, never gave any sign of the spontaneous acceptance manifest in children who, without effort or reasoning, achieve faith. He took a hard-headed line, and even disputed with the college chaplain.

When I grew older and, on the occasion of my first communion, asked the good old man who was instructing us where God found the Word, he did not exactly say, 'In a cabbage-patch' but he answered in the beautiful words of St John, 'In the beginning was the Word, and the Word was with God.' No one of my age could have understood that sentence, on which all philosophies are based and which perhaps sums them all up. In any case, like all sceptics, I wanted something positive, not simply notions but facts. I asked him where the Word came from. 'From God,' he replied. . . . 'But if everything comes from God,' I said, 'how can there be evil in the world?' The poor man was not strong in debate; he understood religion in terms of feeling and accepted dogma without being able to explain it. But he was no saint. Being unable to argue with me he flew into a temper and sentenced me to two days' imprisonment for having interrupted him during religious instruction. . . .

But however questionable the orthodoxy of the young Balzac, and although he was irked by all dogmatic restrictions, he nevertheless displayed at the time of his first communion a longing for *la chose divine*. A skinny boy, with shining dark eyes, 'he went on his knees in an ecstasy of happiness, thanked God, was joyful, light-hearted and content. . . . That evening he felt himself to be worthy of the angels because he had passed the day without sinning in thought, word or deed. . . .' Despite a family upbringing which his father's ideas and his mother's coldness had largely deprived of religious feeling, after Vendôme he held himself to be 'dedicated to intimate commerce with heavenly spirits'. Angels were to occupy a surprisingly large place in his thoughts.

The headmasters of the college were not the men to encourage any kind of childish mysticism mingled with arrogance. Jean-Philibert Dessaignes reasoned more like a scientist than a churchman. 'Possessed of an encyclopedic mind,' his great-grandson wrote of him, 'he could pass without effort from the teaching of rhetoric or philosophy to the natural sciences, physics or chemistry. He even touched on the study of physiology, writing an elementary textbook on the subject for the use of his philosophy pupils.' As an observer and researcher, author of some remarkable studies on phosphorescence, he would have been disposed to look for a physiological explanation of the state of ecstasy; he was preparing a large work designed to show that feelings and passions are related to bodily processes.

Dessaignes taught that the observation of facts, and their analysis, was worth more than any ideology; but his pupil, Balzac, more given to theorizing than to systematic research, secretly evolved his own cloudy scheme of metaphysics. When undergoing confinement in the *culottes de bois*, or under the stairs, the infant philosopher passed his time seeking the *unity of the world* in the concept that Thought and Will were possessed of real substance, fluids analogous to electricity. Dessaignes had propounded the thesis, at that time daring and novel, that all the 'imponderable fluids', heat, light, electricity and magnetism, were but manifestations of a single ethereal fluid actuated by different impulses. Did he discuss the matter with that peculiar child? Did he talk to him about the physiology of thought? It is possible, because when he was recovering from an illness Balzac stayed for a time at La Lezonnière, the country house of the headmasters, and went on plant-collecting excursions with them. But Dessaignes, a detached scientist, had little communication with the boys. 'He lived apart from us,' wrote Edouard de Vasson, 'and his remoteness added to his authority.'

Did Balzac, while still a schoolboy, write a *Thesis on Willpower*, and was it torn up by Père Haugoult? That particular episode seems to have been an invention; but there can be little doubt that he pondered, even at that age, on the nature and functioning of the will. When he was under the stairs in company with an intelligent schoolfellow, such as Barchou de Penhoën, they would discuss philosophical problems. Barchou de Penhoën was inclined to scepticism; Balzac believed in the almost limitless power of will and in the physical action of thought. Perhaps in later life he exaggerated his early precocity, but it is clear that at that time his sluggish appearance concealed an astonishing intelligence and boundless ambition. 'I shall be famous,' he would proclaim; and the others would laugh at this vainglory and he would laugh with them, for he was a good-humoured boy.

Reading, from his childhood, was 'a kind of hunger which could never be stayed', and what he later wrote of Louis Lambert was true of himself:

He devoured books of every kind, indiscriminately gulping down religion, history, philosophy and physics. . . . He grasped seven or eight lines at a time, and his mind absorbed their meaning as rapidly as his eyes moved; often a single word in a sentence was enough to tell him its content. . . . His memory was as retentive of what he read as it was of the notions inspired by his own reflections or in conversation. . . .

'At the age of twelve his imagination, stimulated by the constant exercise of his faculties, had developed to such a point that the things he learned through reading were as vividly imprinted on his mind as if he had actually seen them; whether because he proceeded by analogy or was endowed with a kind of second-sight, by means of which his mind encompassed all created things. . . .'

At a very early age the word *seer* became a part of his vocabulary. The gaze of the seer embraces past, present and future simultaneously. Why should this be impossible? In my dreams, as I lie stretched on my bed, I journey through time and space; therefore time and space in their entirety exist in my mind. Moreover, since the mind can travel in this fashion, and since thought can cover any distance, thought-reading is possible, as well as second-sight, which in imagination observes distant objects. Will-power can be concentrated and projected beyond the self, which enables it to act at a distance upon others, by

magnetic force. . . . Thus did his thinking run; and he, Honoré
Balzac, of the Collège de Vendôme, believed himself to possess
this power. . . .

Dessaignes's co-director, Lazare-François Mareschal, was a
less original thinker than Dessaignes but possessed of a goodness
of heart which endeared him to the boys. He wrote light, erotic
verse which he was careful not to let them see. However, they
used a Latin grammar of his composition which contained some
odd examples. '*Di, facultatem concedite huic pariendi atque non
peccandi*—God grant this woman the faculty of childbearing
without sin; *Puella post carectes* [sic] *latebat*—The girl hid behind the bushes; *Venus, nuda pedes*—Venus barefoot.' It was
to the Latin poets that Chateaubriand owed his first sexual
stirrings. Balzac, with his intensely vivid imagination, was no
doubt also visited by fleshly, pagan images when he repeated
sentences such as these. In his *Balzac et la Religion*, Philippe
Bertault asks: 'Is is too much to surmise that from between the
lines of those modest classical works there emerged the first
shadowy figures of Honoré Balzac's dreams?'

He rose to the second grade; too much reading and the
visions it evoked, and his days of solitary confinement, had induced in him a strange state of 'absence', a sort of lethargy which
was the more disturbing to his masters since they did not understand its cause. In fact, he was absent because his spirit was
elsewhere, in the world conjured up by his reading. To the
Oratorians of Vendôme young Balzac was a lazy pupil who did
little work and could not endure mental fatigue. His sister wrote:
'Grown thin and sickly, Honoré was like those somnambulists
who sleep with their eyes open. He did not hear most of the
questions put to him, and did not know what to answer when
he was abruptly asked, "What are you thinking about? Where
are you?" '

This odd condition, of which he later became aware, was due
to a sort of mental congestion. At the age of puberty, when the
excess of physical energy demands an outlet, he lived a purely
cerebral life and gave an impression of extreme sluggishness.
The worthy Mareschal became alarmed and wrote to Madame
Balzac, and on 22 April 1813, in the middle of the school year,
Honoré was taken back to Tours. His fathers and sisters were
horrified at his condition.

'So this,' said Grandmother Sallambier, 'is how the college returns the healthy boys we send them.'

But change of environment, fresh air and contact with his family soon restored Honoré's natural vitality, and Bernard-François was reassured.

III

From Tours to the Marais

TO RETURN HOME after six years' absence is to undergo a strange and vivid experience. People and affairs are seen in a new light. Bernard-François was now in serious difficulties. His friend, General-Prefect Pommereul, had gone elsewhere after quarrelling with two successive archbishops. The Emperor wanted no disagreements between *his* prefects and *his* bishops. Civil functionaries were under orders to attend religious services. However, still grateful to Pommereul for those examination results at Brienne, Napoleon appointed him Préfet du Nord and later Directeur Général de la Librairie: there are falls from grace which lead to advancement. Deprived of their protector, Bernard-François and his fellow Commissioners of Charitable Institutions soon found themselves in trouble with the new Prefect, Baron Lambert, who joined forces with Monseigneur de Barral, the second of the archbishops. They were charged with financial irregularities in the administration of the hospitals, and an old business of assignats was brought to light, in which Bernard-François was said to have defrauded the State. Nothing was proved, but the atmosphere became oppressive and the town was divided into two camps, Catholics versus Freemasons, the latter rendered cautious from fear of displeasing the Emperor.

The Ministry was moved to reply to Prefect Lambert's repeated denunciations of the Commissioners with a 'Moral Assessment', concerning which the Prefect wrote, 'The General Council and myself are referred to in this species of manifesto, if not as though we were seeking to demolish the most valuable public body in the Department, at least as though we were

refusing for no valid reason to allocate the necessary funds.'
He urged the Minister to reconstitute the hospital administration; but the Minister refused: 'I by no means share your
views, Monsieur, as to the necessity of entirely replacing the
Commission. . . . I feel obliged to point out that, to pass balanced
judgement on the conduct of the charity administrators, it is
necessary for you to put yourself in the position in which circumstances may have placed them.' In short, His Excellency
defended le Sieur Balzac against the local hostility which his
lofty manner, his scepticism, his apparent opulence and the
fashionable elegance of his wife had aroused.

Bernard-François lost none of his Rabelaisian good humour.
While privately manœuvring to get himself appointed away from
Tours, he read voraciously, discoursed volubly and published
some resounding pamphlets. In 1807, in a *Memorandum on the
Means of Preventing Thefts and Assassinations*, he spoke up on
behalf of men released from prison. They were given a ticket-of-
leave card, a badge of infamy; and since no one would then
employ them, they were forced to return to a life of crime.
Recidivism must be forestalled by setting up special workshops
for ex-convicts, where they would be properly fed and clad and
paid a reasonable wage. Their work would profit the State and
there would be less crime.

In 1808 he produced a *Memorandum on the Scandalous Disorders brought about by Young Girls being Betrayed and Left
Entirely Destitute*. In the past unmarried mothers had been
entitled to claim a subsistence allowance from the father; but
under the Code Napoléon inquiry into the paternity of the child
was forbidden. This, wrote Bernard-François in his ornate style,
had in no way diminished 'the over-riding charms of reproduc-
tion'. And a pregnant girl could not hope to get a job. A shocking
state of affairs! Such corruption! There were twenty thousand
victims to be saved. All charitable institutions should reserve
special posts for unmarried mothers. The author himself had
done this with success at the Hospice de Tours.

And in May 1809, came *Of the Grandeur of Nations and how
they may Bequeath to the Centuries Indestructible Evidence of their
Greatness*. This pamphlet was less altruistic. It was important to
Bernard-François, at a time when he was in troubled waters,
to be assured of the Emperor's good will. Imperishable monu-

ments to the great regime which had begun in 1799 must be created for the benefit of posterity—but what form were they to take? Written testimony could be disputed; only edifices were unassailable. The Great Wall of China and the Pyramids of Egypt had endured through the ages. There followed numerous other examples, the fruit of his extensive reading. And what other monument was worthy of the ruler who had repaired the altars of France, restored her finances, drawn up a lucid Code of Laws and renovated the Army? A prodigious statue must be erected to him, or a pyramid higher than those of Egypt, to stand between the Tuileries and the Cour du Louvre, or at the Porte de Neuilly or on the Champ de Mars.

Honoré, as he gradually emerged from his torpor in 1813, enjoyed listening to the paternal harangues, deriving from them a taste for large-scale projects, pseudo-scientific theory and Rabelaisian rhetoric. Books had a large place in that house. Bernard-François's library included all the great classical authors, as well as works of philosophy and history, a collection of the fables of Touraine and illustrated books on China; and Madame Balzac collected the works of a wide variety of mystics. Honoré would cut short 'long hours of labour in the classroom to slip into his father's study and read Voltaire, Rousseau or Chateaubriand'.

Silent, attentive and sardonic, he observed his family. 'Bonne-maman', Grandmother Sallambier, overflowed with vitality although she constantly complained of feeling ill. generally for no reason, and was always visiting clairvoyants. She detested her son-in-law for having gambled away a part of her fortune. (In 1813 Bernard-François himself had to sell his fine house.) Despite her rigid ideas on the bringing-up of daughters, she had not been very successful with her own. Laure Balzac still shocked the more strait-laced ladies of Tours. She talked with too much complacency of her 'old husband'. Inflexible and arrogant, she was capable of a limitless devotion to her own brood, but not of tenderness. She had inherited from her parents a liking for strict rules—for example, in the matter of cleaning the teeth. 'My father was like that; he gave orders and had them carried out more quickly than other men.' She had read Mesmer and she dabbled in hypnotism, another form of power. Her daughter, Laure, who had come to terms with her, called her *Ti-mère*, a childish abbreviation of *petite mère*. Honoré was terrified of her, knowing that she preferred his brother Henry, and he was all too familiar with the stern, hard gaze which she directed at the children when they annoyed her.

Laure and Honoré adored one another. As children he had let himself be punished on her account, but now she was the universal favourite. Even their mother confided in her. Without being really pretty, Laure was attractive—bright-eyed, bubbling with life and with a charming expression. 'You're a mischievous imp,' said Honoré. 'I come to you whenever I want to laugh.' Laurence, whom they called Laurençot, 'fat Laurence' and 'Milady Plumpudding', was less vivacious than Laure, 'but when one got to know her one found that she had a natural, spontaneous sense of fun'. The whole family effervesced with stories, plans, grievances and gossip. They were all humorous, outspoken and idiosyncratic, and all proud of being Balzacs. Among the children there existed a teasing companionship based on deep affection. They shared their parents' love of books and all talked a family jargon in which gossip and chatter was called 'tra-la-la', a sulk was *de la grogne* and an affected young person *un petit brisquet*. All the Balzacs had critical minds and did not spare each other, yet felt themselves to be solidly a clan. Or rather, this may be said of the trio, Laure, Laurence and Honoré. Those 'bitter fruits of conjugal duty', as Honoré called them, had more scorn than affection for Henry, the love-child.

If Bernard-François had been master in his own house he would have sent Honoré to the Collège de Tours directly after his return from Vendôme in 1813. But Madame Balzac wanted 'moral guarantees'. She made amends for her husband's un-belief by being assiduous in her attendance at the cathedral, where she took Honoré, who became very familiar with the old houses round Saint-Gatien, the beautiful flying-buttresses bestriding the street, and the quarrels of the priests with the aged spinsters who let them lodgings. At Saint-Gatien he breathed 'a scent of Heaven', and he often wandered by himself in the Cloister of La Psalette, 'enveloped in damp shadow and profound silence'. At home he had a room on the third floor and no clothes other than his 'wretched boarding-school outfit'. 'Our mother,' wrote Laure, 'considered hard work to be the basis of all education, and was wonderful at planning the time-table; she did not allow her son an idle moment.'

She may have sent him to Paris for a few months, as a boarder at the Institution Beuzelin et Ganser; and perhaps she brought him back to Tours in March, 1814, from fear of the Allied occupation of the capital. In any event he had private lessons at home from March to July of that year, and made some progress in Latin.

In April 1814, the defeated Napoleon was exiled to Elba. The event was a great shock to the Balzac children, brought up in the climate of Imperial splendour. Their whole world was plunged in darkness. Before long the Duc d'Angoulême made his entry into Tours, 'in an outburst of enthusiasm'. Never had so many weather-cocks turned so rapidly. The Staff of the 22nd Division (of which Bernard-François was a member) held a banquet and ball for His Royal Highness, and all the *ci-devant* nobility emerged from their châteaux. Jean de Margonne, lieutenant of the *Cohorte Urbaine*, gave a reception. Honoré, now fifteen, was sent to represent his father, who was away, and moved in rapture among the crowd of women, dazzled by the lights, the red hangings, the diamonds and above all the white shoulders. He never forgot that scene or the scent of femininity.

In July 1814 he entered the Collège de Tours as a day-boy to take his third-grade examinations. He was awarded the decoration of the Lily, assigned to 'Honoré *de* Balzac'. It testified less to the excellence of his work than to the need of the restored but not unopposed Monarchy to win over the younger generation. At Tours as at Vendôme he suffered from the unwitting parsimony of his mother, who was a lavish spender but mean in small matters. While his schoolfellows enjoyed the delicious *rillettes* (a paté of finely chopped pork and fat which was a local speciality) supplied by their families, he had to make do with dry bread. 'Is that all you can afford?' they jeered. Long afterwards one of them still referred to him as 'poor Balzac'. Aggrieved and humiliated, he swore that he would dazzle them some day with his fame. What form was it to take? He had no notion, but he felt the stirring of great things within him. The precocity of his judgements astonished even his mother. 'You certainly don't know what you're saying, Honoré,' she would snap; and he would smile slyly, mocking and good-humoured. His knowing grin exasperated Madame Balzac. She found it hard to live in daily contact with this perspicacious youth who saw too much. His sisters laughed when he told them that one of these days *ce petit brisquet d'Honoré* would surprise the world. While waiting to do so, he observed it.

He had an astonishing memory for scenes and people. The soft Touraine landscape, the rich beauty of its poplar-fringed valleys, the villages scattered among the hills, the majestic Loire studded with sails, the gothic towers of the Cathedral, the old stained glass, the faces of the priests, the talk of family friends— his mind recorded them all. Not only did he remember these things, but he could conjure them up at will, alive and breathing, just as he had seen them. 'He collected materials,' his sister Laure wrote, 'without knowing what he was going to make of them.'

His father, who still had a vague notion of sending him to the Polytechnique, arranged for him to have lessons in science. That lively intelligence was becoming an astonishing mixture of factual knowledge, paternal paradoxes, grandmotherly super-stitions and the mysticism dear to his mother. At the end of the holidays he was invited by Jean de Margonne to visit the Château de Saché. The poplars were losing their leaves and the woods sinking into the hues of winter. To his delight he re-encountered some of the ladies he had so greatly admired at the ball in Tours. He was thirsty for everything, for love no less than fame.

Bernard-François, meanwhile, was anxious to get away from Tours as soon as possible. Shortly after the Emperor's abdica-tion he had published a pamphlet entitled *On the Equestrian Statue which the French People desire to Erect to perpetuate the Memory of Henri IV*—evidently to offset that Imperial Pyra-mid. There is no limit to opportunism in times of upheaval, and the thinking of an army supplier is likely to be in concrete terms; but how, in the city of Tours, could the glaringly new coat of royalism, adopted by the Bonapartist of yesterday, be passed off as his authentic colouring? Fortunately for Bernard-François his friend Auguste Doumerc, the son of his first employer, was still in office and had him appointed Director of Victualling to the First Military Divisions, in Paris. In Novem-ber 1814 the whole family, including Grandmamma, removed to 40 Rue du Temple in the Marais quarter, the cradle of the Sallambiers. It was a homecoming.

Honoré was sent to the Pension Lepître, a private boarding-establishment conducted on Royalist and Catholic lines by a fat, club-footed man who walked with a crutch and looked like Louis XVIII. During the Terror Jacques-François Lepître had been involved in the Royalist plot to rescue Marie-Antoinette from the Temple. This gave him a certain prestige when the Bourbons returned, and he was rewarded with the *Légion d'honneur*. In fact, Lepître, like Bernard-François, had manoeuvred as craftily as he could during the difficult years. The pupils at his establishment attended courses at the Lycée Charlemagne. The house was a former noble residence, the Hôtel Joyeuse, 9 Rue de Turenne. The porter, 'a real smuggler', was 'the defender of misdeeds, the accomplice of late-comers, the hirer of forbidden books'; also the purveyor of *café au lait*, which had been rendered fashionable for breakfast by the high price of colonial products under Napoleon. Honoré, ill-supplied with pocket-money, got into debt with him. He could afford only to dream of the brothels in the Palais-Royal, that Eldorado of Love, where his richer and bolder comrades gained their first experience of sex 'and where the most virgin doubts were resolved'; although, if one may believe Michelet, certain of the boarders showed a pronounced fondness for 'very pretty boys'.

During the Hundred Days, Lepître had much difficulty in restraining his anti-Monarchist boarders. Not all his threats, or even the brandishing of his crutch, could intimidate the fanatical adherents of the Emperor. After the 'wave of the wand' of the Second Restoration a good many of these were expelled. Honoré did not leave until 29 September 1815, with a report testifying to his industry and good conduct. It is probable that, like his comrades, he had followed Napoleon's last campaign with hope and enthusiasm. General de Pommereul, an over-zealous Bonapartist, was exiled when the King returned. The more prudent Bernard-François emerged unscathed.

Honoré then went as a boarder to the 'austere but paternal' Abbé Ganser, a priest of German origin and a saintly man, who presided over an establishment in the Rue de Thorigny where the pupils also attended courses at the Lycée Charlemagne. He spent a year there and came thirty-second in Latin, which earned him a blistering letter from his mother and a period of house detention. On Sundays he was taken, 'under good escort', to the Rue du Temple for his dancing lesson. Madame Balzac, who would have liked her son to be a genius but feared he was a dunce, treated him the more sternly because she loved him, after her fashion. He was beginning to show an aptitude for writing, and for the benefit of the family archives Laure preserved one of his compositions, a speech addressed by the wife of Brutus to her husband after the condemnation of their sons. It was no more than an exercise in conventional rhetoric, high-flown but conscientious. At the Lycée Charlemagne Balzac again met his best friend at Vendôme, Barchou de Penhoën, and made a new friend, the plump Auguste Sautelet. Villemain was probably his teacher for some months, but he would have been more concerned with the brilliant pupils such as Jules Michelet than with the miserable thirty-second in Latin, buried in the ranks of mediocrity.

In 1816, having concluded his studies without distinction, Honoré returned to the family dwelling, which he found unchanged. Bernard-François was still being careful of his health and 'inner tranquility', while his wife worked herself into a fever over everything and nothing. Laure and Laurence were boarders at a School for Young Ladies, where they received instruction in English, piano-playing, dressmaking, embroidery and whist, with a few bursts of classical oratory and 'a whiff of chemistry'. Laure was at the top of her class. Henry, the too-much-loved, went from school to school, working very badly, but none the less cossetted by his mamma. The Marais was still the most respectable quarter in Paris, a place of sombre streets where everybody was in bed by nine; while the aristocratic Faubourg Saint-Germain kept it up all night. Drinking-water was brought to the Marais by Auvergnat water-carriers; its houses were warmed with log-fires and lighted with candles and oil; and rent was paid to the concierge, a despot fully capable of turning an elderly rentier in a threadbare perruque out into the street if his political opinions displeased her.

Life could be lived comfortably in the Marais on an income of ten thousand *livres*, which was about what the Balzacs had. Around them lived their friends of the middle bourgeoisie, artisan and trading families, active or retired—the whole clan of the Sallambiers, drapers and embroiderers; the Malus family; the Sedillots; and little 'père Dablin', bachelor, former hardware merchant at the sign of the Cloche d'Or, wealthy collector and great reader, whose 'probity and goodness of heart' won him many friends. Honoré was fond of these people. Later, like all the artists of his day, he was to deride the 'bourgeoisie' and to depict the vices of the class, which was his own; but he did so with 'profound tenderness and a secret admiration'.

Baron Doumerc had died in 1816. The Balzacs kept up their friendship with his daughter, Josephine Delannoy, the widow of an army contractor and a lady of influence. Another friend was Jean-Baptiste Nacquart, the family doctor and author of a remarkable work on the human brain, based on the theories of Gall, the German phrenologist. Dr Nacquart stressed the relationship between psychology and physiology. The soul, he maintained, was an expression of the physical and chemical forces of the body. Honoré read his books, from which he derived a 'philosophy of unitary man' in which morality was reduced to the level of social science, politics to expediency.

The people of the district were cautious in their views. The private mansions in the Marais, those of Rambouillet and Sevigné, were no longer occupied by great families. The quarter still contained representatives of the petty nobility, but they were bourgeois, well-to-do and respectable. After so many changes of regime those merchants and functionaries preferred harmless platitudes to ideas, which were always compromising. Many had witnessed the growth and decline of Louis XVI, the Revolution and the Emperor. In politics they followed the path of prudence, keeping a clear conscience in readiness for the next upheaval. Nearly all went to the café to read the newspapers, because a man was dangerously marked if he subscribed to any one in particular. The *Quotidienne* and the *Gazette de France* indicated royalist sympathies; the *Constitutionnel* and the *Débats* were liberal. The best way to cover one's tracks was to read them all.

The Balzacs' notary, Maître Passez, lived in the same house as they, and so did an old friend of the dowager Madame Sallambier, Mademoiselle de Rougemont, a lady of distinction in the days of the Ancien Régime who had known Beaumarchais.

Honoré took pleasure in getting her to talk about that sparkling writer. The fabulous life of Beaumarchais was like something out of the Thousand and One Nights, and he enjoyed fables. Why should not he become a dramatist? But Madame Mère, his mother, had other ideas. Maître Passez had offered to take him as a clerk-in-chambers and later make the practice over to him. What could be better? Bernard-François, his mind forever bubbling with new projects, wondered whether science did not offer greater chances of success. However Madame Mère, mindful as ever of the passing of time, was determined not to allow her son a moment's idleness and thrust him promptly into Law.

His name was entered on the rolls on 4 November 1816, with a view to his becoming a Bachelor of Law in three years. At the same time he was to have private lessons in science, follow courses at the Sorbonne and embark upon 'higher literary studies'. His professors at the Sorbonne, Guizot and Cousin, were celebrated men and wholehearted opponents of the extreme Monarchists, the 'ultras'. Victor Cousin in particular, still a very young man, was passionately admired by the students in general and on terms of friendly intimacy with his own. Two opposed tendencies were at work in Balzac's mind. On the one hand, he could not accept orthodox Christianity, having been too much influenced by his atheist, materialist father who treated it as though it were no more than a chapter of zoology; but on the other hand, ever since Vendôme he had been strongly repelled by pure materialism. He was haunted by a fixed idea, that of the unity of the world. All things, whether spiritual or material, were linked together. Cousin's doctrine of eclecticism consisted in the reconciliation of factual knowledge, the basis of observation and research, with self-knowledge, the fruit of direct intuition. Balzac listened and learned, but concluded, in his youthful arrogance, that 'this professor had made a great name for himself by saying things that anyone can find out by reading a few books'.

Being interested in everything he also attended lectures at the Muséum d'Histoire Naturelle. One teacher there was Geoffroy Saint-Hilaire, a zoologist and anatomist who had set up as a philosopher. Science could not be simply a matter of observation and classification, he maintained: to reason and draw conclusions, this was its real aim. He founded the *school of ideas*, as opposed to the *school of facts* fostered by his colleague, Georges Cuvier. Balzac preferred Cuvier, but Saint-Hilaire had propounded a doctrine of 'the unity of composition' which could not fail to fascinate a mind so given to grandiose speculations: 'It would seem that Nature is confined within certain limits, and has shaped all living creatures after a single plan, essentially the same in principle, although she varies it in countless ways. . . .' In short, the germs of all the organs exist in every species, but differing requirements develop particular characteristics in one species which they suppress in another. In his celebrated *Mémoire sur les poissons*, for example, Saint-Hilaire pointed out the relationship between the fins and tail of fishes and the limbs of vertebrate animals. This principle of analogy, and of the balance of organs (since Nature operates on a fixed budget, over-expenditure in one direction calls for retrenchment in another) constitutes the essence of his theory of unity.

Attracted as he was by the ingenuity of such theories, young Balzac confusedly envisaged the possibility of extending them to the social field. He had an irresistible urge to discover reasons. He needed causes and effects. As he pondered these matters he began to have glimpses of a sublime conception of life. What was he to make of it? A philosophy? Works of art? He did not know, but he had no doubt as to his own powers. Whether Cousin and Saint-Hilaire were right or wrong, it was intoxicating to discuss these vast, vague concepts with his fellow-students of law (fat Sautelet, for example, whom he had run into again at the Faculty) or with young medical students over an eighteen-sous lunch *chez Flicoteaux*, that 'temple of hunger and poverty'; or to dazzle the family with his discourses. Formerly so shy, he was now becoming as voluble as his father. The family, unimpressed, considered that he talked too much. After lecturing them on magnetism, or the occult, or the unity of the world, he would amuse himself by talking nonsense, like a child.

His parents kept him strictly disciplined. Bernard-François considered that the theoretical law he was learning at the Sorbonne should be improved without delay by its practical application. So Honoré had to spend part of his three years at Law School in the chambers of an advocate and a notary. The advocate was a friend of the family, Jean-Baptiste Guillonnet-

Merville, an excellent jurist and a cultivated man with a taste for letters.

Those years of apprenticeship under Guillonnet-Merville were to be highly fruitful. It was to them that Balzac owed his knowledge of Civil Procedure, one of the several Codes promulgated under the Empire which still play a large part in the daily lives of the French. It was to have a great influence upon his way of thinking and his approach to life. All the domestic dramas are unfolded in an advocate's chambers. He saw a wife bring charges of total incapacity against her husband; a colonel under the Empire returning like a ghost from Germany to find that his wife had remarried; a thousand living dramas shedding their light upon the baser and, less often, the nobler aspects of mankind. He lived with the other clerks-in-chambers, greedy and penniless young demons who respected nothing but still often shared their monthly hundred francs with an aged mother living in an attic. While they engrossed pleas and conveyances, the lively, sardonic youths tore the clients to shreds. The dark and dust-laden room where they worked contained no other adornment than the big yellow notices of property-sales, huge, stuffed filing-cabinets and fly-blown articles of furniture. The air was thick with the odours of cheese and chops and chocolate, mingled with the musty smell of documents. An advocate's chambers were, 'of all social premises, one of the most horrible'; but it was here that young Balzac learnt the grim poetry of life. He was so given to exuberance, and so amusing, that he often had an unsettling effect upon his fellow-clerks. The head clerk on one occasion sent him a note: 'Monsieur Balzac is requested not to come today because there is a great deal of work to be done.'

In the evenings he played cards with Grandmamma who, mellowed by age, showed an increasing fondness for her grandson and by intentionally losing enabled him to win the small sums he needed to buy books. His passion for reading was greater than ever, and he had an especial liking for rare, obscure and unusual books; also, though there was nothing to warrant it, he believed more firmly than ever that he was destined to be famous, wealthy and beloved. We know, if we may accept the testimony of his sister Laure, that despite his lack of money, Balzac, even in adolescence, had brief successes with women:

'He wanted to please as well, and some very intriguing adventures came his way; but they are too lively to be described. I can only affirm that no man ever had more right to be conceited, from the beginning of his life. . . .' And she goes on to relate how Honoré won a bet with his grandmother by winning the favours of one of the prettiest women in Paris, whom the old lady had rashly named, being certain that she would not lose the hundred crowns she staked. But Honoré won. Despite his untidy hair and the big mouth which had already lost some of its teeth, his readiness of speech, his bright, intelligent eyes, and perhaps also his youth, gained the victory. Grandmamma was far from straitlaced, and they played strange games in that 'most excellent' family.*

* They liked to call themselves '*la céleste famille*', like the family of the Emperor of China. *Trs.*

IV

Apprenticeship of a Genius

THE YEAR 1819 brought great changes. Bernard-François, then
aged sixty-three, was suddenly retired. He lost his handsome
salary of 7,800 francs a year, and despite his efforts to get his
pension increased by invoking his years of service as clerk on
the King's Council, he received only 1,695 francs per annum.
To this modest stipend there was nothing to be added except his
wife's small income (she owned a house in Paris as well as the
farm near Tours), the dividends from a few invested savings
and his share in the Tontine Lafarge. The value of this depended on longevity, and here Bernard-François had no misgivings. He possessed a hundred recipes for ensuring long life,
and was fond of citing the case of a Signor Cornaro, of Venice,
who died a centenarian after ruining his health at the age of
forty. The subject was one on which he discoursed at great
length, with sardonic references to those shareholders who had
already died, whom he called 'the deserters'.

But pending the Lafarge benefaction the family was in low
water, and they could no longer afford to live the life of wealthy
bourgeoisie in the Marais. Rather than lose face, they preferred
to move outside Paris, where rents, food and domestic service
all cost less. A relative, Claude-Antoine Sallambier, agreed to
buy a house at Villeparisis and rent it to them. This was a
village of 500 inhabitants midway between Paris and Meaux,
a staging-point for coaches, its unadorned, rough-cast houses
lining the royal road from Paris to Metz. The village possessed
six inns offering accommodation for man and beast, which
were used by carriers, commercial travellers and other nomads.
The main street echoed with the clatter of vehicles and the

shouts of postillions and fair-buskers with performing animals. The mail was brought on foot from the neighbouring town of Craye.

Among the local notables were the Comte d'Orvilliers, who lived in a decidedly modest 'château' opposite the Balzacs' house, a Monsieur Gabriel de Berny and his wife, Parisians who came there only for the summer, and a retired colonel. The Balzacs' house had a five-window front and two upper storeys, one of attics, and a garden of which the vegetable-plot and orchard were hidden from the road by shrubs. On the first floor were three bedrooms with fireplaces, those of Madame Sallambier, Madame Balzac and Laure. The shareholder in the *tontine*, that man of iron, was content to sleep in an unheated room, and the children hated 'the draught that came from father's door'. Laurence slept in an annex to Laure's room, and Honoré, when he was there, in one of the attics. The domestic help consisted of a rather deaf neighbour, Marie-Françoise Pelletier, known as 'la mère Comin', a cook, Louise Laurette, and a gardener.

The people of the neighbourhood welcomed the arrival of this colourful family, 'all of them intelligent, cultivated, talkative, literary, sensitive and highly-strung'. Bernard-François, still clad after the fashion of the Directoire and 'bursting with health', dined on fruit at five (one of his prescriptions for longevity) and went to bed when the hens did. He had a large bookcase in his bedroom, of which he kept the key in his pocket, and he spent his days reading. Tacitus and Voltaire helped him to weather his wife's nervous crises and the caustic remarks of his mother-in-law, who referred to him as a 'Gascon dog' and envied his perennial youth. 'His good humour was rarely affected except when, despite his strictly ordered life, his theories of longevity seemed to be at fault. An aching tooth was a disaster that plunged him in despair.' But he soon recovered. 'All matter is subject to decay,' he said, 'but inner serenity is invulnerable.' When he had an attack of gout he pointed to the aristocratic nature of the malady, which went back to King David. His great regret was that, unlike that monarch, he did not live in the bosom of 600 young wives.

His mother-in-law paid frequent visits to Paris to consult doctors and clairvoyants, fearing lest she should 'stumble into eternity'. Laurence remained at boarding-school for some months, more interested in dances than schoolwork. Laure practised the piano, learnt English and by her happy nature did much to relieve the family tensions. One such drama, which fortunately did not come to the ears of the neighbours, was the sentencing to death, at the Tarn assizes, of Louis Balssa, Bernard-François's brother, for the murder of a farm girl whom he was alleged to have seduced. The girl, who was pregnant, had been strangled. It is possible that Louis Balssa was innocent, and that the real murderer was a notary named Albar, a connection of the one under whom Bernard-François had made his start in life. Nevertheless Louis Balssa went to the guillotine. No mention of the tragedy is to be found in the Balzac family correspondence, and no attempt was made by his brother to save the condemned man. The event seems to have been passed over in silence, regard for the family reputation triumphing over family loyalty and even the sense of justice. The Balzacs were good bourgeois citizens, but they did not overdo the goodness.

Honoré could not leave Paris at the time of the move, nor did he wish to do so. He had passed his law examinations in January, and his parents looked to him to restore the family fortunes. Bernard-François indulged in an orgy of pipe-dreams. Maître Passez had agreed to accept Honoré, after a long probationary period, as a partner in his practice. A wealthy marriage would enable him to pay the premium. To have a well-established notary for a son, and daughters married to graduates of the École Polytechnique (preferably with 'de' before their names), this was success as the Marais understood it. But Honoré had set his face against a legal career and was not to be shaken. He too, as ambitious as he was vainglorious, had his dreams of success; but it was literary success that he wanted. His omnivorous reading, tales of the brilliant life of Beaumarchais, and his father's pamphlets were no doubt partly responsible for putting the idea in his head. In any event, the whole family had a taste for writing. But could literature lead to fortune? That was the question, as Madame Balzac saw it; and it was a matter of vigorous family discussion. Dablin, the retired hardware-merchant, 'le petit père Dablin', a person of high standing in Marais circles, where he was held to be a model of culture and good taste, declared roundly that Honoré was only fit to be a commission-agent. Bernard-François knew his son better than that. To him Honoré, whose intelligence he did not under-rate, was their supreme hope; and since the boy believed himself to possess literary talent, he must have a chance to prove it. They would give him two years, during which his parents would allow him 1,500 francs a year.

The generosity of this offer deserves to be underlined. The money represented a substantial part of their income, and they gave it, not to enable Honoré to pursue further studies which might be regarded as an investment for the future, but simply so that he could write plays and novels. Such an act of faith is touching, and because of it Madame Balzac may be forgiven much petty parsimony and the cold severity of her gaze. She found Honoré an attic room at 9 Rue Lesdiguières, an old house near the Bibliothèque de l'Arsenal, at a rent of sixty francs a year. There Honoré was to show what he was made of. However, since they did not like admitting to their Paris friends that they were keeping a son 'in idleness', it was agreed that, for public consumption, he would be understood to have gone to live with a cousin in Albi. He must therefore show himself as little as possible in Paris, and only go out after dark. Contact would be maintained between him and Villeparisis by means of their servant and neighbour, 'la mère Comin', who often came on errands to Paris. Honoré and his sisters christened her Iris, the messenger of the gods.

His attic, according to Balzac, was 'a hole worthy of the stews of Venice'. It was on the fifth floor, a dark, low-ceilinged room reached by a dirty, creaking staircase. 'Nothing could be more horrible than that garret with its dirty yellow walls reeking of poverty . . . ,' he wrote in *La Peau de chagrin*. 'The sky could be seen through the gaping tiles of the roof. . . . My rent was three sous a day, I burnt three sous' worth of oil a night and made the bed and cleaned the room myself. Two sous for laundry and two for coal; I was left with two sous a day for emergencies.' But if the garret reeked of poverty, it was the artificial poverty of a young man who had only to go to Villeparisis to live in comfort.

Honoré bought and cooked his own food. Because of the agreement with his parents the only people he saw were little Dablin, whom he called 'Pylade Dablin' and who at too rare intervals climbed the five flights of stairs to shower advice upon him and bring him news of the outside world, the people on the second floor, who had a pretty daughter, and the owner of the house, to whom he paid his rent. He made himself a screen of blue paper as a protection against draughts. The great occasions were the visits of Mère Comin, bringing funny and affectionate and sometimes scolding letters from Laure, who passed on their mother's rebukes:

Papa told us that the first thing you did when you were on your own was to buy a mirror in a gilt frame and a picture for your room. Mamma and Papa are not pleased. My dearest brother, you are free to do what you like with your money, and so you should spend it sensibly on rent and laundry and food. When we think how much eight francs is, out of what Mamma is able to give you in our present difficult circumstances, she is terrified at the thought of how little will be left for you to live on. She wants you to know that you have not been clever in your first purchase because you have made her feel that her own was superfluous, and that those five francs, which were more than she could afford, were ill spent, and she asks you to give it back to Mère Comin, because two mirrors in a room like yours are certainly unnecessary. Dear Honoré, please try not to put yourself in the wrong like this. I only want to be able to write fondly to you, and at the most to pass on Mamma's advice. I don't like carrying out these orders at all, not at all. . . .

The fact was that their highly susceptible Mamma could not bear to think that her son had preferred another mirror to the one she had chosen for him. Laure also gave the latest news from Villeparisis:

The holiday season will liven things up, you know how necessary that is in the country. . . . People think you are on your way to Albi, and they pray for the safety of travellers. . . . We don't yet know if we shall like the Bernis [sic] ladies. . . . Grandmamma has made us a present of three stitched straw hats, the kind that are being worn now; they're marvellous, you can guess how proud we are. . . . The country round Villeparisis is altogether charming, the woods are pretty. I practise the piano every morning from six to eight and while I'm doing scales, and my mind isn't occupied, I visit you in the Rue Lesdiguières. . . .

This chatter delighted Honoré, and he answered at length. Like his sister, he poured out words unreflectingly on paper, 'as his thoughts ran'. It was a welling up of talk between fresh, youthful hearts:

To Mademoiselle Laure, 12 August 1819: You ask, my dearest sister, for details of my household and way of life. Well, here you are. I've written to Mamma about the purchases. But now I'm going to make you tremble. This is worse than any purchase. I've taken on a servant! ! ! !

'A servant, my dear brother? How could you dream of such a thing?'

'Dr Nacquart's servant is called Tranquille. Mine is called Myself. When I wake in the morning I ring for Myself and he makes my bed.

'Myself.'

'Sir?'

'I was bitten in the night. Look and see if there are any bugs.'

'There are no bugs, Monsieur.'

'Good.'

He then starts sweeping, although he's not very clever at it. . . . Still, he's not a bad youth, all things considered. He has arranged my underclothes neatly in the chest of drawers beside the fireplace, after wrapping them in white paper, and he fixed his own lock on it. With six sous' worth of blue paper and a frame which was given him he made me a screen; and he has painted the room white, from the bookcase to the fireplace.

If he seems displeased with his situation, which hasn't happened so far, I shall send him to Villeparisis to buy fruit, or perhaps to Albi, to see how my cousin's getting on. . . .

As for Honoré's work, alas, there was not much to be said about it: 'Do you know, I've spent a whole week ruminating and broodulating and eatulating and strollulating without doing anything useful? *Coquecigrue** seems to me too difficult and beyond my scope. I'm still studying and forming my taste.' A wise policy. He was reading furiously, both French and foreign authors, verse and prose.

Laurence, then aged seventeen, also wrote to Honoré; but she believed herself, wrongly, to be stupid. 'I irritate Grandmamma, I annoy everyone and they're quite right. . . . Mamma is absolutely fair between Laure and me, but her impartiality must cost her something because my sister is worth so much more than

---

* A plan for a novel in letters.

I. . . . Why should one of us be so sweet-natured and the other so given to sulks?' (The word she uses is *bousarderie*, another example of the Balzac family vocabulary; there is no *bousarderie* in the French dictionary.) Laurence professed to be jealous of her 'good sister's' piano-playing, but the truth is that they loved each other dearly. The romantically inclined Laurence would retire to her private corner of the garden, among the lilacs, there to dream of future husbands. She had already dismissed seven in her mind, among them the Sallambier cousin, an embroiderer who embarrassed her when he addressed her as 'cousin' in public and talked about his shop.

Like all the Balzacs, Laurence was a worshipper of Voltaire and forthright in her speech. After being taken to High Mass in Paris she wrote to Laure: 'I don't know who wouldn't have felt caught out and damned after that sermon. But me, my legs were so cold that I knew I couldn't be in Hell yet. So you see, I'm quite ready to continue my wrongdoing and go to theatres, balls, concerts, all the worldly and perverse places where innocence and modesty—etc. . . . etc. . . .' The Balzac children were merciless in deriding the platitudes of orthodoxy.

From his attic window Honoré gazed over the roofs of Paris, brown, grey and red, of slate and tile'. He discovered 'singular beauties: luminous streaks escaping from badly closed shutters, the yellow glow of street-lamps in the mist; a girl at her toilet in the shabby framework of a garret window, nothing to be seen of her but the long tresses raised in the air by a white, pretty arm . . .'. He soaked in the poetry of Paris, strolling after dark through the Faubourg Saint-Antoine or the Père-Lachaise cemetery. In the faubourg he studied the workmen, joined their groups and grew heated with them in their grievances against the foreman. At times he would follow some couple and, listening to their talk, would have a sense of entering into the lives of that particular man and woman. It was in this that he practised his gift of seeing:

With me observation had already become intuitive, penetrating to the soul without disregarding the body; or rather, it so quickly noted outward details that it went instantly beyond them. It endowed me with the faculty of living the life of the person upon whom it was exercised, so that I could substitute myself for him like the dervish in the Thousand and One Nights who took possession of the body and soul of persons over whom he spoke certain words. . . . Listening to people talking I could enter into their lives, feel their tattered clothes on my back, walk with my feet in their shoes; their desires, their needs, all passed into my soul, or my soul passed into theirs. It was the dream of a man awake. . . .

Whatever the nature of this power, he had possessed it from childhood.

Standing on the hillside between the tombs of Père-Lachaise, he gazed at Paris, 'tortuously sprawled' along the banks of the Seine, enveloped in the bluish haze of its smoking chimneys as the lights began to gleam in the town, his eyes intent upon those forty thousand houses. Between the Place Vendôme and the Invalides there lived a world of fashion which he longed to know, and into which he hoped, in his sanguine moments, to force his way by the power of genius.

His family had given him two years in which to prove his talent. How was he to do it? His inclination was towards philosophy. He wanted to understand society, the world, human destinies. He had derived from his father a taste for 'enlightened despotism' (the political creed of Voltaire, not far removed from that of Bonaparte) and scientific materialism. Young men at that time were reading Bichat's *Anatomie générale* and Gall's *Anatomie du cerveau*. But at Vendôme and Tours, and now in Paris, Honoré studied the works of less mechanistic thinkers—Descartes, Spinoza, Leibnitz. He borrowed Malebranche's *La Recherche de la vérité* from the Bibliothèque de Monsieur, near the Rue Lesdiguières. He was feeling his way towards a metaphysical creed. The philosophical notes he jotted down between 1817 and 1820 have been preserved. They show a resolve to establish his own personal belief, 'to tear down the last veils'; and they point to a reading-list as abundant and haphazard as that of Bernard-François—Plato, Bayle, Diogenes, Aristotle, St Bernard, Rabelais, the Lateran Councils, Hindu philosophers, Lamarck, Hobbes' *Leviathan* and many others. He was always to have a fondness for compiling lists of great names. He had a notion of writing a *Treatise on the Immortality of the Soul*, in which he did not believe. 'The waning of mental faculties proves that the soul is subject to the same laws as the body; it is born, grows and dies. . . . There can be no doubt that memory fails, and that intelligence and courage may vanish, although the man continues to exist. . . .' In short, it was really to be a treatise on non-immortality. 'We have still no convincing proof of the existence of the soul. How can we treat it as immortal when we do not even know if it exists? There is nothing immortal in us except the memory we leave behind, and this only on the supposition that the world is eternal. . . .' Moreover the garret philosopher had discovered that the dogma of the immortality of the soul dated only from the First Lateran Council—'It comes to us not from Christ but from Plato.'

What is important is not his young man's philosophy, which in any event underwent changes, but the need he felt to have one. 'He did not believe that any outstanding talent could exist without profound metaphysical knowledge. . . . He plundered all the philosophical riches of ancient times so that he might absorb them.* Later, dictating an autobiographical preface to a friend, he recalled the time when, 'Monsieur de Balzac, sheltering in an attic near the Bibliothèque de l'Arsenal, toiled ceaselessly at comparing, analysing and summarizing the works which the philosophers and doctors of antiquity, of the Middle Ages and of the last two centuries have left on the subject of the human brain. This tendency of his mind is a predilection. . . .' The words are no mere self-adulation. Ample traces have survived of his immense labours. The philosophy underlying the Balzac novels came before their writing. During those years in his garret he laid the foundations upon which later he was to build.

He looked everywhere for the books he needed, asking Père Dablin for a Latin Bible with a French introduction and Laure for their father's Tacitus. 'Oh, darling Laure whom I love so much, why can't you swipe the Tacitus? Who has the key of the bookcase? Is Papa always in his room?' Meanwhile he read other classics. He wrote to Dablin: 'I am meditating a Ciceronian objurgation upon you, petit père. A whole month and you have not put your nose inside the Rue Lesdiguières! . . .' But he was only too aware that philosophy would not get him a living. The theatre offered more substantial rewards. He asked Père Dablin to get him Casimir Delavigne's *Vêpres siciliennes* and Pierre Lebrun's *Marie Stuart*. There was a former lawyer's clerk, Eugène Scribe, whose plays were constantly performed; but he

* *Illusions perdues.*

wrote farces, and Balzac aimed higher. Why not a five-act tragedy in verse? At an earlier stage he had written one or two poems which he himself now laughed at, and which proved only one thing, his 'lack of talent for versification'. The fact is that he was almost unbelievably lacking in the sense of poetic rhythm. Nevertheless, after reading the two volumes of Villemain, who had made Cromwell fashionable, he decided to use the Protector as the central figure of a tragedy. He roughed out a scenario.

To Laure Balzac, 6 September 1819: But tremble, my dearest sister! It will take me at least seven or eight months to turn it into verse and contrive the scenes, and *longer still* to polish it! The main ideas are on paper, with a line of verse here and there; but I shall have to gnaw down my nails seven or eight times before I have erected my first monument. (Oh, if you realized the difficulty of a work of this kind!) It's enough for you to know that the great Racine spent two years polishing *Phoedre* [*sic*]. The desperate labours of poets! Two years, I ask you! Two years!

It is very sweet to me as I wear myself out (soon it will be night and day) to associate my work with those who are dear to me. I feel that if Heaven has granted me any talent my greatest delight will be to spread the fame it may win me over you and our dear mother. Think how I shall rejoice if I should make the name of Balzac illustrious! How wonderful to conquer obscurity! ... So when, having trapped a splendid thought, I set it down in sonorous verse, I seem to hear your voice exclaiming, 'Well done!' and then I bend over my task with renewed vigour. ...

Needless to say, he wanted to write not for the moment but for posterity. The writer's calling was clearly difficult. He made strange statistical calculations. A tragedy contained roughly two thousand lines, and this required from eight to ten thousand thoughts. 'Ah, my dear sister, the torments that are the other face of fame! Long live all grocers! How happy they are! But then again, they pass their lives between the cheese and the soap. So down with the grocers and long live the writers!' Now and then he took a rest from Cromwell 'by dashing off a little tale in the classical manner. ... I seldom go out, but when I feel myself flagging I go and cheer myself up in Père-Lachaise ... and while seeking out the dead I see nothing but the living.' The living occasionally penetrated even to the Rue Lesdiguières. Mamma brought some pork which made a useful addition to his daily diet. Père Dablin continued to visit him, and Honoré enjoyed discussing the theatre, books and politics with that well-read and broad-minded ironmonger. 'Faithless petit Père, I haven't seen you for sixteen whole days. It's unkind when I have only you to console me. . . . For the past week I've been living as though in the depths of the Inferno. I haven't seen or heard anything, and no one has written to me. I haven't even seen Mère Comin. . . .'

He was already weary of his English regicides, and yet he struggled on, day and night, to turn them into French alexandrines. 'I'm determined to get to the end of *Cromwell* even if it kills me, to finish something before Mamma comes and asks me to give an account of my time. . . .' But the theatre was to be only a first step. He wrote to Laure that the French revolution was far from over, and that in future political crises writers would be needed because they understood the human heart; in short, if he was man enough (and he hoped he was) he might not only achieve literary renown but also that of a great citizen. 'I'm a real *Perrette au pot au lait**. . . . If genius should be on sale in Villeparisis you must buy me as much as you can.' He longed to have a piano in his garret, so as to relieve his feelings by playing his favourite piece, 'Le Songe de Rousseau' by Cramer. The need to stay in hiding oppressed him. He wrote to Dablin in October 1819: 'I have not yet seen a single play by my old general Corneille. It's hard on a young recruit. I so much want to see *Cinna* that I've been wondering if I might not do so in a screened *loge*. Who on earth would recognize me from the stalls?' At that time he was thin, pale, hollow-eyed and bearded, and looked as though he had just come out of 'hospital or a melodrama'. Although he suffered from toothache he refused to have his teeth seen to, saying that 'wolves don't go to dentists, and men should be like wolves'. It was this attitude, worthy of his father, which made him gap-toothed while he was still young.

His heart was in Villeparisis. One could not so easily detach oneself from the 'most excellent family'. Grandmamma, 'suffer-

---

* The milkmaid in the La Fontaine fable who carried the pail of milk to market on her head, skipped with delight at the thought of the money it would bring in, and spilt it. *Trs.*

ing greatly from her wretched nerves', secretly paid his book-
binder's bill. Mère Comin brought him letters in which Laure
urged, 'Write, write, write!' He did so, marvelling at the erudi-
tion of his sister, who quoted Montesquieu—'Happy the
brothers whose sisters are like Laure!' She teased him about his
flirtation with the girl on the second floor, whom he scarcely
knew, and with some other girl. 'That Laure! She would like
me to be a Lovelace—but why, I ask you? All very well if I were
an Adonis or a Celadon, but a Chinese image doesn't get into
ladies' beds, only on to their mantelpieces.' He asked her to
picture him at night in the ice-cold room, wrapped in an old
cape over a quilted waistcoat, and asked her to send him 'a red
merino hood lined with cotton-wool—like Papa's'. The cost of
oil for his lamp made him tremble, and he was beginning to be
worried about a certain Monsieur Surville to whom Laure
referred rather frequently. This was a young civil engineer, a
product of the Polytechnique, who had a job under the department of Bridges and Highways. He was engaged upon the repair
of the Ourcq Canal and was stopping at one of the inns in Villeparisis. Having made the acquaintance of the Balzac girls he was
becoming very attentive.

You talk about M. de Surville. Shove him off on Laurence;
he seems to visit you pretty often. Make yourselves agreeable,
but keep your distance like the girls of the Marais in the song.
A conquest is always useful. When one wants to catch pigeons
doesn't one put one near the trap? Not that I think you're a trap,
but marriage! . . . Marriage is another thing. . . .

Eugène-Auguste-Louis, known by the name of Surville, was
the illegitimate son of Catherine Allain, a provincial actress who
had adopted Surville as her stage name, and 'a deceased father'.
A wealthy citizen of Rouen, Louis-Emmanuel Midy d'Andé, a
'ci-devant squire', had recognized the child in 1791 as being
'among the works of his late brother' and by legal covenant had
endowed mother and child with a modest income. A Rouen
journalist with a sentimental interest in the mother later secured
the boy's legal right to use his natural father's name. Eugène,
however, continued to call himself 'Allain *dit* Surville', and was
admitted to the École Polytechnique under this name in 1808.
He passed in twentieth, a very high rating. Later he went to the

Imperial School of Bridges and Highways, and when, in 1817, he was appointed to the Ourcq canal he elected to live in Ville-parisis. Throughout his life he had an especial, and unfortunate, fondness for canals.

Laure at first considered him too small game: 'I was still in the stage of day-dreams. If only I could be rich, if I could marry an English milord, if—if—if—' In vain did Surville bring her chocolate on New Year's Day; his undistinguished offerings were despised. But in May, 1820, he was able to proclaim his right to his father's name, Midy de la Greneraye, and to the paternal inheritance. Catherine Allain, learning of her son's matrimonial hopes, had told him the secret of his birth. In a letter addressed to the Comte de Becquey, Director-General of Bridges and Highways, Eugène declared that, his mother having neglected to implement the ruling of the court, he had had to go to Rouen to have his civil status confirmed. He requested that in future he might be officially designed 'Midy de la Greneraye, *dit* Surville'. This, and the private income, com-pletely changed the situation in the eyes of the Balzac parents. A graduate of the Polytechnique, with a particle to his name, was not to be disdained. Pressure was brought to bear on Laure. Surville, who often went to Rouen on duty, undertook to send off the letters she wrote her brother, of which the following is a charming example:

VILLEPARISIS COURT CIRCULAR

Yesterday the King went to Mass. No, I'm wrong, His Majesty never goes. Yesterday the King signed the marriage-contract of Mademoiselle ... No, he didn't sign anything because his daughters the princesses aren't getting married. Yesterday the King's legs were cold. Well, that's true, his room's icy and there's no padding round the door.

Yesterday the Queen had a very sore shoulder; the doctors say it's because of the draught through the windows of her drawing-room, but they hold out hopes of an early recovery. There are a great many geese in these parts, and they come and quack in the castle stream which is very upsetting to the Queen; they woke her up this morning with a start. Since she has no Capitol to save Her Majesty was extremely cross at having her slumbers disturbed.

22 *October*—Birthday of Her Majesty Queen Anne-Char-

lotte-Laure Sallambier. Always thoughtful for the happiness of her subjects, Her Majesty wished to hold a feast, but the King, intent upon the welfare of the State, ordained that so notable an anniversary should be celebrated in silence. This was heart-breaking for the princesses who had to put on their Sunday dresses to pay a call on the de Bernis [sic] ladies. The feast was to be as follows, so that you may at least have a sniff of it: Princess Laurette, the life and soul of the family, having dis-patched a prose missive to Cousin Sallambier begging him to convert the bouquet of artificial flowers into delicious things to eat [boustifailles, a Balzac word], the said cousin was to bring a brioche warm from the oven of the renowned Carpentier, a Savoy cake and roasted Lyons chestnuts; after which there were to be pastoral dances. . . .

The fascinating princesses were enraptured at the prospect of thus stretching their legs; but alas the plan was lost in the mists of the Seine.

In any case the feast couldn't have happened because Cousin Sallambier, who plays so large a part at Court, was at that moment in Elbeuf, visiting his textile mills. The happy day was accordingly passed *en famille*, and after dinner Princess Laurence vanished for a moment down the cellar stairs, which are extremely steep, to reappear with the remains of a bottle of Bordeaux wine. So the health of the illustrious Queen was drunk with the dessert. . . .

Monsieur de Surville comes every evening; he is a young nobleman who conducts himself admirably. According to the Queen he takes no interest in the princesses (a pity, for he has a poetic nature); yet the match would be of great benefit to France. . . .

And here is Honoré:

Fire broke out in this quarter, at 9 Rue des Lesdiguières, in the head of a young man on the fifth floor. The fire brigade have been working on it for a month and a half, but there's no putting it out. The young man is consumed with a passion for a beautiful woman whom he has not met. She is called Fame. . . .

I know now that riches do not mean happiness and I promise you that the three years I shall pass here will be for me a source of felicity and memories for the rest of my life. To sleep in com-fort, to live as I choose, to work at what pleases me and do nothing when it suits me, to pay no heed to the future, to have only persons of wit and intellect for company, including Père Dablin, and to take leave of them when they annoy me; to observe fools in passing and pass by at the sight of fools; to dream of Villeparisis only in the knowledge that you are happy there; to have La Nouvelle Héloïse for mistress, La Fontaine for a friend, Boileau for a judge, Racine for an example and Père-Lachaise to walk in. . . . Ah, if only it could last for ever! . . .

The tragedy of *Cromwell* was painfully taking shape. In November 1819 he sent Laure a detailed outline.

Be respectful, Mademoiselle, it is Sophocles who addresses you. Try to imagine, dearest sister, from the small, gay, comical fancies which you conceive in your own small, gay, comical head, the effort required for the composition of a stage piece which must observe the unities, avoid implausibilities, etc., etc. . . . If you have any happy notions, send them to me. You can keep the gay ones; it is the sublime ones that I want. I want my Tragedy to be a Chronicle of kings and peoples; I mean to start with a masterpiece or die in the attempt. . . .

As for Laurence, suffering from growth-pangs and languour, she had become very thin. 'The plump Laurençot' was scarcely recognizable. The 'Queen' took her to Paris, where the miraculous Dr Nacquart restored her to health. She too kept a Court Circular:

Princess Laure is as charming as ever, as warm-hearted, happy and gentle as an angel; we love each other very much. I admire her greatly; she was born on a day of feasting, and her heart came flawless from the hands of Nature. I take her as my model. I *mean* to be like her, even if it kills me. . . .
Monsieur de Surville visits us constantly. He has plenty of intelligence and good sense, and he does not think about us at all. He does not want anyone to rule over him. His motto is, 'Long live Liberty!—and, in consequence, bachelordom. . . .'

Honoré, wrapped in his old cape, with his head enveloped in a 'Dante-esque hood', shivered in his garret and considered the purchase of an old armchair which would at least protect 'his back from the cold and his bottom from piles'. The work progressed slowly. 'I wrote a verse-monologue in the manner of

Chapelain, which verses I thought superb. But reading them over I found that they were nearly all artificial. What a comedown!...' At the beginning of December Madame Balzac climbed his steep, dark staircase, and was horrified. 'If he on whom I counted above all to safeguard my family has, in a few years, lost the greater part of the gifts Nature showered on him, it is because no one listened to what I said.' Instead of making strides along the road to success, instead of having achieved the high status of a master-clerk, Honoré had let himself become intoxicated with the theatre and the names of actresses. He was now punished for it, said his mother. *All* master-clerks were launched upon the road to fortune; they might become ministers or generals. Honoré, more talented than any, was living on bread and milk in a squalid room furnished with a threadbare chair, a ricketty table and a truckle-bed. Such were the fruits of his obstinacy.

But still *Cromwell* progressed, sustained by a great deal of coffee. The piece was like a tracing made from the Latin classics combined with the works of Corneille and Racine. Honoré noted: 'For the curse at the end of Act Five I must study Dido's curse in Virgil, and Camille's in Corneille.' The effect of his studies was all too apparent. As Camille cursed Rome, so did Henriette curse England:

> Exécrable Albion, je puis donc te haïr!...
> Je renonce à régner où l'on m'a pu trahir!
> Je redeviens Française et je lègue à la France
> Ma couronne et mes fils, mes droits et ma vengeance!...
> Puisse de mon pays s'élever un vengeur
> Qui, de l'orgueil anglais rabaissant la hauteur,
> De vingt siècles de haine accepte l'héritage,
> Et sous une autre Rome engloutisse Carthage!...*

---

* A not unfair English rendering of this passage might run as follows:
> Abominable England, on you I breathe my hate!...
> Where I have been betrayed, my rule I abdicate!
> I become French again, and I bequeath to France
> My crown and my sons, my rights and my vengeance....
> May from my land a new Avenger ride
> Who, in tearing down the growth of English pride,
> Of twenty centuries of hate accepts the heritage
> And from another Rome wreaks havoc on Carthage!...
>
> *Trs.*

Bossuet, the Scriptures and Honoré joined forces to produce the line, Ô rois! Instruisez-vous à gouverner le monde.' The magnanimity of Charles I was modelled on that of Augustus in Corneille's *Cinna*. In short, the piece was the work of a student of rhetoric, well-read but with little talent for poetry, who had had a gallant shot at a decidedly awkward subject. But such as it was, *Cromwell*, when finally it emerged from the garret, delighted Madame Mère. To have brought into the world the author of a five-act tragedy in verse, however boring, greatly flattered her self-esteem. In January 1820 Laure wrote to her brother, 'Mamma is happy about you and enthusiastic about your work.' So enthusiastic, indeed, that she undertook the task of copying the whole thing in her beautiful handwriting.

To rest from his labours Honoré spent a few days at L'Isle-Adam, in the delightful valley of the Oise, with his father's old friend, Louis-Philippe de Villers-La Faye. Monsieur de Villers, a priest and canon without religious convictions, had from 1782 to 1790 held the comfortable post of 'Master of the Oratory' to the Comte d'Artois. After the Revolution he shed his cassock and returned to the world, which indeed he had never left. Always fortunate with women, he was ending his days in company with a well-born widow who 'kept house' for him, Aimée Amat de la Plaine. Villers 'lavished gallant attentions upon ladies'. He had always liked young Honoré and the feeling was reciprocated. When he went to live in his garret, Balzac had written to Laure:

I feel really conscience-stricken at not letting M. de Villers, who is so fond of me, into our secret. He knows no one to whom he might reveal it, his adventures with ladies have taught him discretion, and you must agree that the laborious winter I have ahead of me will call for a fortnight's rest when the fine weather comes. As you know, L'Isle-Adam is my terrestrial paradise and it has a great influence on me. You mustn't think it's because I'm afraid of having bitten off more than I can chew, because I'm happier than ever. But poor M. de Villers who's so fond of me! You must write and send him my love. Well, we shall see. . . .

The former Abbé's influence on Honoré was opposed to religion and the practice of virtue. Not that he had the bad taste to decry the Church to which he owed so much. But his gallantries were in themselves 'a demonstration of the relativity of religion and morals'.

Upon his return from L'Isle-Adam, Honoré was summoned by his father to Villeparisis. They would invite a few friends and he would read them his play. Confidently expecting a triumph, Honoré insisted that Père Dablin, who had said that he was only fit to be a commission-agent, should be one of the party. But Laure wrote later: 'The friends arrived and the solemn ordeal began. The reader's enthusiasm steadily diminished as he felt how little impression he was making and saw the frozen or disconsolate faces of those who sat listening.' As soon as it was over Dablin delivered his opinion with his customary forthrightness. 'Honoré protests,' wrote Laure. 'He repudiates the critic; but the other members of the audience, although more tactful, agree in finding the work far from perfect.' Madame Mère was wounded in her pride, Laure and Laurence in their affection. Bernard-François, the kindly man, was afflicted by his son's distress. He suggested that *Cromwell* should be read by a competent and impartial authority, and Surville, anxious to be of service, because he was now in love with Laure, offered to send the manuscript to Andrieux, a dramatist and member of the Académie who had been his professor of literature at the Polytechnique.

Honoré agreed and hastily smothered the manuscript with ingenuous footnotes—'There are occasional faults of French, but these are intentional. . . .' Laure made a fresh copy, and in August, 1820, *Cromwell* was delivered to the great man. He read it with care, but when Madame Balzac and Laure called on him to ask his opinion he suggested that the author's time might be better employed than in the writing of stage pieces. He added that he did not wish to discourage a young man and was quite ready to suggest to him 'how he should approach the study of belles-lettres'. The sheet of paper on which he had noted his private opinion of the play was lying on his desk. Laure got hold of it and passed it on to Honoré. It was a good deal more blunt: 'The author would be well-advised to try anything *except literature*. . . .'

'Honoré,' noted Laure, 'received this body-blow without wincing or turning a hair, because he did not admit defeat.

"Verse tragedies aren't my line, that's all," he said; and he went on writing. . . .'

He made a last attempt to save *Cromwell*. Père Dablin had a friend who owned a house in the Rue de Richelieu, opposite the Théâtre-Français, and who knew the actor Lafon, a member of the Comédie-Française company. Dablin promised to get the piece read by Lafon, but on the understanding that Balzac would accept his verdict, whatever it was. 'Let your children be judged by those who ask nothing better than to find them charming, if they really are.' This advice was not followed. When Lafon rejected the play Balzac called him 'an idiot, incompetent to judge'. In his heart he knew very well that *Cromwell* was a failure, and that if he wanted to go on writing he must try some other line.

But he was not unduly depressed. His faith in himself was unshaken. Romantic despair had never been a habit of the Balzac family. They were more given to laughter, to jesting with love while they waited hopefully for fame and fortune. On 18 May 1820, Laure was married to Surville at the Church of Saint-Merry in Paris, in the presence of a great gathering of Sallambiers. The bridegroom's mother is designated in the marriage-contract as 'Dame Catherine Allain Surville, spouse of the late Midy de la Greneraye, now his widow', and the best man was the bridegroom's guardian, 'Jean-Gabriel Milsan, man of letters'. The professed widow and the guardian were presumably living together, since they gave the same address. Another illegitimate child of Catherine Allain, her daughter Théodore, was living there too; but it may well be that Surville did not mention this to the Balzacs until the wedding was safely over.

And what did it matter? Face was saved, and Eugène Midy de la Greneraye Surville was a very satisfactory-sounding son-in-law. He was, alas, less brilliant than he sounded. When he went with his wife to Bayeux, to take up a new post, he had nothing but his salary as a second-grade engineer—260 francs a month. This was far below the terms of the marriage contract and Laure's ambition. But she was a Balzac, her head full of visions of a glorious future to make amends for present short-comings. And full of plans. She would use her connections to advance her husband's career and secure the concession for all the canals in France. The 'most excellent family' owned vast estates in their imaginary world.

Meanwhile Laure invited any and all of them to Bayeux. 'Grandmamma will be beautifully looked after, if she's the one to come. I have a handmaiden who will serve her faithfully, and I myself will see to the details—the bed-warmer, the rug for her feet, a walk when she feels like one, music, sewing, etc. . . . If it's Papa, he will be entirely undisturbed in his room, and there will be music, the newspaper after dinner, etc. . . . And that brother of mine, instead of going to Touraine why doesn't he take the road to Bayeux?' As for her poor mamma, so given to melancholy, she chided her gently: 'You'll say when you read this, "Oh, my dear girl, one can see that you're used to happiness. Your philosophy and high spirits have not yet been undermined by misfortune. The past inspires you only with hopeful dreams for the future." To which I reply that I have had my troubles, but with me the clouds soon pass . . . but you, dearest Mamma, you have to be always looking back at them.' The charming Laure proved herself wise in counsel, and if, despite her equable humour, she sometimes found her husband a little difficult, it is because that is what he was.

Madame Mère admonished her daughter in her turn: 'I'm going to go on playing the mother to you, high and noble lady that you now are, by warning you, my dearest, to be on your guard against the flatteries men lavish on you. Happiness is very fragile; a breath suffices to blow it away.' It was a matter on which Madame Balzac was entitled to speak, since she had so thoroughly ruined her own happiness. Later, when Laure had prudently discouraged a gentleman's advances and reassured the agitated Surville, she wrote: 'You are right, my love, to humour a heart that would be less jealous if it loved you less.' Honoré had ample reason for going to Villeparisis: there was plenty of subject-matter there, and models for his pen.

As to his ultimate aims, these had not changed: 'Shall I ever fulfil my only but immense desires, to be famous and to be loved?' Later, in portraying a young man, he was to recall himself at the age of twenty. 'How many Arabian Nights tales are contained in adolescence? . . . How many Wonderful Lamps must one have rubbed before discovering that the real Wonderful Lamp is chance, or work, or genius? With some men, these dreams of the awakening spirit last but a little while; mine still endure! When I fell asleep in those days I was always the Grand-Duke of Tuscany—a millionaire—the beloved of a princess—or famous!' Did he ever cease to sigh for that Wonderful Lamp, even when toil and genius had brought him both princess and fame?

V

First Novels and First Love

. . . Une femme qui se fût devouée à m'expliquer les écueils de chaque route . . . et à me conseiller sans révolter mon orgueil.

BALZAC

THE ATTIC WAS abandoned before the end of 1820. His parents were anxious to bring the prodigal home to Villeparisis, and now that Laure was married there was a room available. Honoré gave way, although—'. . . Nature always surrounds roses with thorns and pleasure with a host of drawbacks. Mamma follows Nature's example. . . . So long as I am there, my dear sister, I shall follow father's example and say nothing. . . . ' But the tedium need not be unrelieved. The Balzacs still had a *pied-à-terre* in the Marais; their son could take the coach now and then and spend a day or two in Paris. He had a standing invitation to Villers-La Faye's home at L'Isle-Adam, and these visits, when he read Buffon, worked, played backgammon and listened to the old gentleman's reminiscences, were a great pleasure to him. Monsieur de Savary, the father-in-law of Jean Margonne, also took a fancy to him and invited him to the Château de Moncontour, in Touraine. Life, in short, was tolerable, and Honoré was fond of his father, who so equably took each day as it came. It was true that he was not independent and had no position, and his sister Laurence talked of him as living in 'Empty-pocket Street'. 'However,' he wrote to Laure, 'in the past fortnight I have had the wit to assure myself of a hundred thousand crowns to be drawn from the pockets of the public, and I shall receive payment in full in return for a few novels for which I shall have a good sale in Bayeux.'

The drama having failed him, he was now thinking of novels as a source of fame and fortune. He had already attempted one, when he was still very young, based in part on a sheaf of philosophical notes reflecting the atheistic rationalism of Bernard-

François. But Honoré's ideas were more complex than his father's. Although he did not believe in Providence, a God brooding over men and concerned with the individual destinies of those specks on a grain of sand, he liked to think that there were human beings who, by concentrating their will, could acquire a magical power over Nature. He was obsessed with the desire for omnipotence, whether it was born of strength of character or of occult knowledge shared by a few initiates. Some time in 1820 he wrote to a friend, 'Before long I shall possess the secret of that mysterious power. I shall compel all men to obey me and all women to love me.'

In the draft of a novel, *Falthurne*, several times abandoned and resumed, of which the action took place in Italy at about the time of Canossa, he embodied this magical quality in a very beautiful girl of enormous stature, endowed with supernatural powers, whose strange name signified 'tyranny of light'. Like all adolescent writings it was filled with echoes of his reading. There were sonorous periods borrowed from Bossuet, imagery from Homer and Virgil, and Fénelon's *Télémaque* had lent colour and gloss to the style. The tale was attributed to an imaginary Abbé Savonati, a great man culled from Walter Scott and Rabelais, and a translator, Monsieur Matricante, an elementary schoolteacher. Savonati, the spiritual hero, was contrasted with Matricante, a sort of Sancho Panza, the lover of material things—two aspects of Balzac himself.

The appetite for power and the magnetic power of the will, both heightened in this apprentice work, embodied his secret obsessions, and a well-drawn minor character, the ex-monk Bongarus, owed something to Rabelais and Cervantes. He was later to write part of a new version of *Falthurne* in which a mysterious girl called Minna nurses a crusader afflicted with leprosy in an airy valley surrounded by blue-tinted mountains. *L'Homme de désir* by Saint-Martin, one of Madame Balzac's collection of mystical works, had inspired him with the notion of ending the story by having Minna borne up to Heaven 'seated on a cloud of good deeds'. A belief in divine spirits, although it scarcely suited his temperament, seems to have haunted him since Vendôme.

In 1820 and 1821, after finishing *Cromwell*, he started a novel in letters, *Sténie ou les erreurs philosophiques*. Jacob del Ryès, a young man of twenty, returns to Tours where he has left a childhood friend, his foster-sister, Sténie de Formosand. The story begins with a rescue. Del Ryès saves two of Sténie's cousins from drowning in the Loire. But during his absence Sténie's parents have married her to a man from la Vendée, Monsieur de Plancksey. When he hears this del Ryès nearly dies of grief, but revives in the arms of Sténie. While they are walking together in Saint-Cyr-sur-Loire (the village where Balzac himself was put out to nurse) they meet Plancksey and the men fight a duel. 'The young wife is in despair, the lover irresistible, the husband brutal and cynical'—a tale of romantic love recalling Goethe's *Werther*. Del Ryès is the embodiment of what the young Balzac wanted to be, attractive to women and rich in the promise of future fame. He reads poetry and is greatly admired; he writes philosophical letters to Sténie and a friend about the non-existence of God, about dreams and the material power of thought. In short, *Sténie* was a first attempt at a kind of work that appealed to Balzac—a novel laden with high thinking. But he lacked the skill to achieve the difficult feat of reconciling romance with philosophical digressions, and it was never finished.

The margins are filled with his self-reproving comments: 'To be done again . . . to be corrected . . .' Yet, considering his age, the work shows great promise. When he writes about the banks of the Loire and the landscape of Touraine, Balzac conveys something of his own enchantment to the reader. He lovingly describes the paths of Saint-Cyr, where he took his own first steps, and especially the spot where he and Laure built miniature Louvres. All this was invested for him with a nostalgic charm. Jacob tenderly recalls 'his little foster-sister, pretty as a Correggio cherub'. Balzac was thinking of Laure far more than of Sténie. The lifelong affection between brother and sister lends a touch of enchantment to those early rhapsodies. But he was still not mature enough to produce a good book.

In any case he had to relieve the family anxieties by earning money. Through his friend, Sautelet, he had made the acquaintance in Paris of a group of accommodating young writers who were in close contact with the theatrical and publishing worlds. Auguste Lepoitevin, or Le Poitevin de l'Égreville, the son of a well-known actor, had made a very early start with slapdash but ably contrived novels which he produced under the name of Vieillerglé. He had formed a team of bright young men whom he drilled in the art of giving the public what it wanted. Étienne Arago, brother of the celebrated astronomer, was one of them. The starry-eyed young Balzac seemed full of ideas, and they offered him a job in their novel-factory.

They went in for mass-production. To them writing was not an art but a trade with its own skills and devices. They imitated the fashionable novels of the day, in the Empire-Restoration style, which themselves were inspired by English writers—the sentimental novels of Maria Edgeworth and Mrs Opie, peopled with aristocratic characters; the 'black' novels of Ann Radcliffe and Maturin and Monk Lewis, in which fantasy was mingled with terror. There had always to be an innocent victim, a villain and a righter of wrongs, roles as ancient as humanity itself. An insatiable public devoured fiction of this kind, as it did the light novels of Pigault-Lebrun and Paul de Kock; and numerous bookseller-publishers, in the Palais-Royal and the Marais, were on the look-out for new authors. Large output mattered more than talent, and a Byronic shade haunted the market-place. For Honoré, with his lofty aspirations, it was a decided come-down; but what penniless youth would not have been attracted by this prospect of good money and a back-stage entry into the popular theatre?

He went through the phase, perilous for an artist, of despising his art. The wonder is that for him parody became the mistress of truth. Amid the banalities one catches glimpses of a young man very conscious of the tremendous class-upheavals brought about by the Revolution and the Empire, and the shuffles to which so many men of his time owed their careers. He did not lack examples, even in his own family. At moments the seer peers through the mask of the hack.

Auguste Le Poitevin became a regular visitor at Villeparisis. Balzac wrote to Laure that 'milady Plumpudding' (Laurence) thought he came to see her, and he had great difficulty in persuading her 'that all authors are thoroughly bad bargains, financially of course'.

To Laure Surville, 2 June 1821: If you want a properly laid-out situation-report, you should devote the first column to

Papa, who is pacing up and down his room after reading the newspaper. The second column should be horizontal because Mamma is ill in bed with an imaginary congestion of the lungs which has caused such an upset in the next two columns, headed Laurence and Honoré, that we have postponed writing so as to be able to tell you the worst and the best at the same time. As for the Remarks, Cash-in-Hand, Prospective Husbands and General Gossip column, there is plenty to fill it, but this will have to wait until things are calmer. . . .

When you read this letter you must try to picture Mamma's room, the garden of Monsieur d'Orvilliers, that man of duty, coming and going with his son as they water it, and your beloved brother seated writing opposite the fireplace at the small table which used to carry your writing-case; you must imagine the sound of my voice and all our silliness, because today is Saturday, the day before Sunday. Are you doing it? Come, come, an effort, please. That's better. . . .

A few days later:

Laurence Balzac to Laure Surville, 10 June 1821: Honoré is definitely going to Touraine, but first he has to finish a novel of which the first volume is very cleverly written, with plenty of wit and imagination. He and his friend have also to finish the work in four volumes which they are doing together.

So far the plot is working out well and the characters are beautifully drawn; they have cunningly brought in two humorous characters to stem the tears of sensitive ladies who might be over-affected by the truly dramatic plot. I should perhaps tell you what it's about; but as I'm sure it will be sold all over Europe and indeed throughout the world, starting with Bayeux, I won't spoil it for you. As soon as it's published we'll let you know the title so that you can go and read the riot act in all the bookshops that haven't got it in stock. . . .

They all missed Laure:

Balzac to Laure Surville, June 1821: You feel the separation from your family; but do you think we don't suffer from not having you with us, laughing, skipping, arguing, teasing, romping? . . . I may say, moreover, that I don't like the idea of you shopping in the market. Because the Bayeux people are simple, is that a reason for being simple yourself? If one adapts oneself to every place one goes to, one becomes as flexible as silk. It's quite enough to conform in essential matters, like breathing air, drinking cider and eating Bayeux bread. . . . Do you propose to attend Mass and go on your knees before prejudice and church stucco? Only yesterday I watched the moulding of a hundred plaster saints who will receive the homage of a hundred thousand dupes. Oh, that town of Bayeux with its devout population must be a wonderful place for an author to use; it must be bursting with secret love-affairs and intrigues, because religious devotion is the hallmark of that sort of thing. . . .

Laurence told Laure about their family life in Villeparisis: 'We aren't madly gay and we aren't unhappy; we're good bourgeois, avoiding all extremes. In the evenings it's whist or boston, or sometimes écarté, or cousin-hunting, and stew . . . A few funny remarks by Honoré, and then we go to bed.' Balzac asked Laure to ransack Bayeux for a rich widow for him to marry:

You can praise me to the skies—twenty-two years old, nice manners, docile, bright-eyed, ardent, the best husband-material that Heaven ever produced. I'll give you 5% of the dowry and a packet of pins.

He was glad to get away from Villeparisis:

I may tell you, very confidentially, that our poor Mamma is getting to be like Grandmamma and worse. I hoped that the state of life she has reached would affect her whole constitution and change her character; but not a bit of it. Oh, Laure, watch out for yourself, we must all watch out for ourselves, we're highly-strung and when we're young we deceive ourselves: that particular disease creeps on gradually. What amuses me is that *asinus asinum fricat*. Mamma exclaims, 'Oh, poor Grandmamma, how tiresome she is! . . . What a wretched malady, etc. . . .' and only yesterday I heard her grumbling like Grandmamma, fussing about the canary like Grandmamma, scolding first Laurence and then Honoré, changing her mind in a flash and only remembering the things that suited her latest point of view. And the exaggerations! Perhaps it's the fear of seeing our mother go that way that makes me see things as I do. Anyway, I pray for the opposite, for her and for us. What dismays me most is the touchiness of this family. We're like a little town of three or four inhabitants; we watch each other like Montecuculli and Turenne. . . . Oh, there can't be another family like ours anywhere on earth, and I believe we're all unique in our own way. . . .

That particular letter ended with a flourish:

Well, good-bye, my dear sister. Get out of your easy chair to accompany your brother, who is staying with you, to the door.
'How very nice your lamps look!'
'Yes, don't they?'
'And the clock is in such good taste.'
'You must be back in time for dinner. Mind you don't get lost in Bayeux.'
'If I do you'll have to send the watchman after me.'
'Five o'clock, don't forget.'
'I won't.'
'Hullo!' says Surville, meeting me, 'Are you out for a stroll?'
'Yes.'
'Good. Wait a minute and I'll come with you.'
But, *goddam*, it's only a dream. . . . Good-bye then, I embrace you fondly and am your down-at-heels brother who still loves you.

In the lively turn of phrase, the penetrating remarks on Madame Mère, the swift imagination always ready to take flight in dialogue, a critical reader might have discerned the novelist trying his wings.

Laurence was in a desperate hurry to get married. Her family did not do her justice. She suffered by contrast with the greater maturity, wit and intelligence of her elder sister. Yet she had 'flashes of wit and judgement which would have been the pride of a mother whose only daughter she was'. Her letters were 'full of charm, freshness and spontaneity'. She even dared to attack Dr Nacquart, who was sacred in the eyes of the family:

This Monsieur Nacquart, with his long words, his loud laughter, his grand airs and grand pretentions, his small talent and great show of devotion, seems to me a doctor like any other. He cares precious little about his patient, and when he has run out of talk he sends you into the country or orders you back to your native air or tells you to go on a journey, it amounts to the same thing. . . .

After Laure's departure, Laurence had to be given her chance.

Balzac to Laure, July 1821: Besides, you know that Laurence is fit to be painted, that she has the prettiest arms and hands you could hope to see, and a very white skin and two beautifully placed breasts; and that when you get to know her you find her very intelligent, but, as one can't help realizing, with a natural wit which has still to be developed. She has beautiful eyes, and as for her pallor, it is a tint that a great many men like. I have no doubt at all that marriage would do her a lot of good. . . .

Her father did not allow her time to develop, or to choose. On 19 July 1821, he wrote to Laure that he had 'fixed a marriage' for Laurence. A marriage after his own heart. The prospective husband was Amand-Désiré de Saint-Pierre de Montzaigle—double particle; double distinction. He came of a family of authentic but very recent nobility which had formerly owned a château and some farms in Villeparisis. These were no longer in their possession; but Bernard-François had been friendly with the father, first on the King's Council and then in the Supply Service. To him this amounted to a guarantee. The young man, aged twenty-three, was an official in the Octroi de Paris, the toll-office. 'What more do you want, unless you're going after the Devil's carillon?' His past, it was true, gave rise to some misgivings: 'He's one of those Paris youngsters who have made the most of their chances, but without doing anything dishonourable.' And, having sampled everything that a life of dissipation could offer the ardours of youth, what else was there for him to do but settle down and become a good husband? He was, perhaps, a little overbearing. 'But surely,' wrote Madame Balzac, 'this is only because he is so expert with pistols and foils. That is the catalogue of his faults. Let us pray there are no others.' Honoré, irritated by the assertive manner of his future brother-in-law, whom he nicknamed *Il Troubadouro*, wrote sarcastically, 'He writes verse, he's such a terrific marksman that when he's out shooting he brings down twenty-six birds with twenty shots. . . . He's an expert at billiards; he does gymnastics, he shoots, he hunts, he drives, he . . . he . . . he . . .' Laurence accepted the pretentious match without delight. The troubadour did not seem to be in love with her, and this was scarcely surprising. A police-report described him as much given to debauchery, a frequenter of gaming-houses and women of the town.

Bernard-François hurried the business on, afraid lest the eagle of Montzaigle should find a better bargain. Two sets of cards were sent out, the first announcing that Monsieur Balzac, former clerk on the King's Council, ex-Director of Supplies, and Madame Balzac, were marrying their daughter, Laurence; the second stating that Monsieur and Madame *de* Balzac had pleasure in announcing the marriage of Mademoiselle Laurence *de* Balzac to Monsieur Amand-Désiré Michaut de Saint-Pierre de Montzaigle. The marriage-contract was signed on 12 August 1821. The Balzacs gave their younger daughter a dowry of 30,000 francs. 'Mamma thinks a financial sacrifice is worth more than a century of good humour,' remarked Honoré; and, describing the grand reception held in Villeparisis to celebrate the signing, he wrote, 'There were ices, relations, friends, even acquaintances, cakes, nougat and other delights. . . .' Bernard-François was less dandified than usual. A coachman had damaged his eye with a clumsy flourish of his whip, a dreadful thing to befall a man so mindful of his sight and health. 'Nothing is more heartrending than the pain of a woman or an old man,' wrote his sympathizing son.

Honoré himself, at this time, was terrified that Dr Nacquart, from ill-considered benevolence, would find him a job. In which case he would become

. . . a clerk, a machine, a riding-school hack doing its thirty turns a day and eating, drinking and sleeping at fixed hours. I shall be like everyone else. And that's what they call living, that life at the grindstone, doing the same thing over and over again. If only someone could invest that dismal existence with some sort of charm. I have not yet smelt the flowers of life and I'm in the only season when they blossom. What good will wealth and pleasure be to me when I'm sixty? Is it when one has nothing better to do than watch the lives of others, and need only pay for one's seat in the stalls, that one needs the actor's wardrobe? An old man is one who has had his dinner and watches the new arrivals dine. But my plate is empty, with no gilt on it; the cloth is dingy and the food tasteless. I'm hungry and nothing is offered to appease my appetite. What do I want? . . . I want ortolans: for I have only two passions, love and fame, and nothing has happened to satisfy either, and never will. . . .

'Two passions, love and fame . . .' It was his favourite phrase; a phrase uttered by every aspiring young man, but this one knew himself to be insatiable. He was thirsty for life and in terror of frustration. But that October brought him some comfort. He was saved from the office job by his collaboration with Le Poitevin, which began to produce results. A bookseller in the Galeries de Bois, Hubert, paid them eight hundred francs for a novel entitled *L'Héritière de Birague* which they had written under the name of Vieillerglé and Lord Rhoone (anagram of Honoré). 'A piece of literary offal,' said Balzac. The story was about a plot to secure an inheritance, a family secret and a noble defender; but there were two ex-soldiers, comedy characters borrowed from Scott, who had a gleam of life. It must have sold reasonably well because its successor, *Jean-Louis, ou La Fille trouvée*, fetched 1,200 francs. Distressing though it might be to publish this rubbish, it was delightful to be able to say to the family, 'I'm earning my living.' And anyway, was it entirely rubbish? The herculean Jean-Louis had a touch of Pantagruel. Balzac's skill at devising elaborate plots was almost worthy of Beaumarchais. With all the absurdities, the vitality of the story-telling gave promise of better things. This bogus stuff was helping the development of a born writer who unconsciously put his own imprint on the work. But the constant urge for money stultified his gifts by driving him to work at breakneck speed. His head was full of calculations. 'If I sell *Clotilde de Lusignan, ou Le Beau Juif*, which I'm writing by myself, for 2,000, and if I publish four novels a year, I shall be rich.' Indeed, he would have been earning a bigger income than his father when he was Director of Supplies. But it was another pipe-dream.

Honoré gave Laure the latest news of the Montzaigle household, which was far from happy. Laurence, who had been ill ever since her marriage, had frequent nervous crises and was losing her beautiful dark hair. Her husband spent his time hunting and left her a great deal alone. Unwell and separated from the 'most excellent family', she read *L'Esprit des lois* in 'a big salon which seems to be pitch-dark'. Her husband's creditors were already swarming round them, for Montzaigle was heavily in debt. Laurence came in tears to Villeparisis with her tale of woe, and Grandmamma Sallambier declared that the 'eagle' was a scoundrel, no better than a crook, and that 'he would ruin the Grand Mogul himself'—like her son-in-law and grandson, Grandmamma had a fondness for large-scale imagery. 'As for Papa, he's like the pyramids of Egypt, immovable amid all convulsions and getting younger all the time.' Madame Mère, in excellent health, was driven to Paris in the 'handsome barouche' of her neighbour, Madame de Berny, and made bad jokes all the way. 'The reward of kindness!' concluded Honoré, who was sorry for her companion.

For the 'ladies at the other end' had come to assume a large place in the thoughts of the Balzac family. The Bernys owned two houses in Villeparisis, one next door to the Balzacs, which was let to a retired colonel, and the other, bought in 1815 from the ruined Montzaigle, situated at the far end of the village, which they occupied themselves. This latter house, the last in the village, differed from the rest only in its size and the number of its small-paned windows. By no means princely, but very large and comfortable, it looked over a sanded courtyard flanked with orange-trees and pomegranates in tubs. Bernard-François had long been acquainted with Gabriel de Berny, a Counsellor at the Royal Court (and formerly at the Imperial Court). The families had been near neighbours in the Marais, but there was a hint of condescension in the attitude of the Berny ladies to Madame Balzac, and a hint of respect in that of the Balzac ladies. Laure and Laurence put on their Sunday dresses when they invited them to any kind of 'beano'. The 'de' of the Bernys was more authentic than that of the Balzacs and they ranked far higher in the social scale.

Madame de Berny, whom her husband had married during the Terror, had been Laure Hinner, the daughter of a musician of German extraction and Louise de Laborde, a lady-of-the-bedchamber to Marie-Antoinette. King Louis XVI and the Queen had stood godparents to their daughter, who was born at Versailles in 1777, and so she had been given the impressive name of Louise-Antoinette-Laure. She had grown up in the intimacy of the Court and still retained its polished manners. After Hinner's death his widow had married the Chevalier de

Jarjayes, a faithful retainer of Marie-Antoinette who had tried to organize her escape from the Prison du Temple. He was to serve Alexandre Dumas as a model for the character of the Chevalier de Maison-Rouge. In the tragic climate of the time Laure Hinner, then barely sixteen, was married in haste to the Comte de Berny. The newly-weds were almost immediately arrested, and only the fall of Robespierre saved their lives. In 1799 Gabriel de Berny entered the administration of Subsistances Militaires, which made him a colleague of Bernard-François. In 1800 he became Deputy-Chief of Personnel in the Ministry of the Interior, and in 1811 a counsellor at the Cour de Paris.

The couple had had nine children, of whom one son and one daughter had died. There was no great harmony between them. Gabriel de Berny, who suffered from chronic ill-health, looked an old man at fifty. Peevish and atrabilious, an incessant grumbler, he was losing his sight, and he left his wife a free hand in the management of their estate, which she 'cut and pruned as she thought fit'; but he was not sparing in complaints and recriminations. Their past was overshadowed by a strange, unhappy episode. From 1800 to 1805 they had lived apart. Laure de Berny, having fallen in love with 'an abominable Corsican who stole her youth', bore him a daughter, Julie. The Corsican, Campi, had eventually disappeared, husband and wife had been reconciled, and from time to time Berny permitted Julie Campi to visit Villeparisis—'a ravishing beauty, a flower of Bengal'.

Since he had come to live in Villeparisis, Honoré had frequently met Madame de Berny and her children. The young ladies in white and the young Messieurs de Berny in black were to be seen at village festivities, and they attended the baptism of the child of Louise Brouette, the Balzacs' cook. The 'ladies at the other end' played the part of a squirearchy in the village.

Balzac to Laure Surville, February 1822: I may tell you that Mademoiselle de Berny nearly smashed herself to bits in a fall, that Mademoiselle Elisa is not as stupid as we thought, having a talent for painting and in particular for caricature and being also a musician . . . that Madame de Berny, having discovered after forty years of reflection that money is everything, has gone into the corn-and-fodder business. Monsieur de Berny can't see any better this year than he did last and he has thinned out his brood of offspring (they say that Monsieur Manuel was at the bottom of it) by sending two of them to boarding-school. One got a scholarship. . . . Madame Michelin* has borne a Micheline of which Monsieur Michelin is the titular parent. For the rest, the Berny children are the only ones anywhere who know how to laugh, dance, eat, sleep and talk in a civilized manner; and their mother is, as always, a very agreeable, very devoted woman. . . .

The light-hearted tone concealed a deeper interest. Honoré, having been engaged by the 'house at the other end' to act as tutor to the Berny children, had fallen in love with their mother. It was not her doing. She made no attempt to hide her forty-five years, admitted to being a grandmother, and had certainly no thought of seducing a youth of twenty-two. Greatly given to banter, and even to sarcasm, she teased Honoré about his uncouth manners, his boastfulness and high-flown ambitions. But she also perceived the exceptional intelligence, the quickness of wit and ardour in all things which made it easy to overlook his faults. He talked to her about his childhood and his mother's neglect 'in the sharp tones of a young man whose wounds are still not healed' and questioned her endlessly about the world of the Ancien Régime, acutely conscious of the gulf between this god-daughter of a queen and the people of the Marais, his father's friends. He took especial delight in the richness of her voice: 'The *ch* as she pronounced it was like a caress. . . . In this way she unconsciously enhanced the meaning of words, translating the spirit into a higher sphere. . . .'
He came by gradual stages to desire her, for she was still desirable. Her face, although not strikingly beautiful, radiated kindness and warmth. The skin of her neck and shoulders was like a girl's. He came to feel that this woman, and only she, could bring him the things he lacked—good taste, knowledge of the world—and satisfy the itch for a love-affair rendered acute by his age, his reading and his father's freedom of speech. 'Love has its intuitions, just as genius has.' He was suddenly plunged in love, still knowing very little about it.

* Madame de Berny's eldest daughter.

For an awkward youth, dealing with a woman he deeply respected, to make the giant stride from light-hearted flirtation to physical possession seemed an impossible feat. He would ask himself when he left the house, 'Can I hope to win her?', and the next day would say nothing, more tender than bold. Yet he knew she was unhappy and constantly distressed by the ill-temper and insignificance of her husband. Seven years earlier she had lost a son who would now have been Honoré's age. This created a bond between them. And he knew that she had had a lover. At some time in the autumn of 1821, or possibly the spring of 1822, he ventured to declare himself. 'At first you will think this one of the best jokes that ever was, a fitting subject for your kind of humour . . .'

Balzac to Madame de Berny, March (?) *1822*: Think, Madame, that far from you there exists a being whose spirit, greatly privileged, covers all distances, flies to you through the air and is constantly near you; who delights to share in your life and your sentiments; who now pities you, now desires you, but always loves you with that ardour and freshness of love which flowers only in youth. A being to whom you are more than a friend, more than a sister, almost a mother but still more than all this; a kind of visible divinity to whom his every action is referred. Indeed, if I dream of grandeur and fame it is that I may use them as a stepping-stone to bring me nearer to you; if I attempt great things it is in your name. To me, though you do not know it, you are truly a protectress. Think finally of everything that is tender, loving, delicate and glowing in the human heart. I believe these things to be in my heart when I think of you. . . .

It was all true; a very young man nearly always believes his own love-letters. She went on laughing at him, his sighs, his novels, his clothes, his letters; but he would not give up. 'What pleasure can a generous heart find in tormenting someone who is unhappy? . . . I realize more and more that you don't love me, that you will never love me . . . that it is folly to persevere. And still I persevere.' She replied that he would never see her except surrounded by her children, that she was forty-five and old enough to be his mother. In fact, Madame Balzac was a year younger than she. 'Heavens!' retorted Honoré. 'If I were a woman, even of forty-five, and still pretty, I would behave very differently from you! I would surrender to love and seek to rediscover the delights of youth, its innocent illusions, its simplicities and exquisite privileges. . . .' He knew that he had none of the graces or the audacity of a lover; but 'I am like those girls who seem awkward, foolish, shy and gentle, but who conceal a fire within them . . . capable of consuming the domestic hearth and the whole house . . .'. He compared himself to the Rousseau of the *Confessions*. Was he not the same kind of lover, in search of another Madame de Warens who would be both mistress and mother to him? And was not Madame de Berny's name Laure, like that of his own mother and favourite sister? His sister's place was now only in his memories and his heart. It was to this new Laure that all his thoughts were directed, 'the vagabond troop of loves, the hope of all delights'.

While this was going on, Laurence, pregnant and living alone at Saint-Mande with her heavily indebted troubadour, had found her way to the pawn-shop, 'which swallowed up for ever her diamonds and her beautiful cashmere shawl'. Montzaigle asked his father-in-law to guarantee a loan of 5,000 francs, but Bernard-François bluntly refused. It led to a quarrel which nearly caused Laurence a miscarriage, and Madame Mère declared herself to be 'in hell' at finding her daughter so ill-cared-for—'A girl of eighteen and a doctor of twenty-four with no reputation, and whom one only has to look at to see that one wouldn't trust him with a cat!' However, the crisis passed and in April, 1822, Madame Mère left for Bayeux.

Honoré stayed in Villeparisis with his father and grandmother, and now that his comings and goings were less closely supervised spent all his days in 'the house at the other end'. He was kindly received, but friendship was not enough. 'The first time I set eyes on you my senses were aroused. . . . Your forty-five years don't exist for me, or if I notice them for an instant I see them as proof of the strength of my passion. . . . So your age, which would render you ridiculous in my eyes if I did not truly love you, becomes a bond between us, a particularity which, by its very oddness and contradiction of accepted notions, draws me closer to you. . . . I alone am the judge of your beauty. . . .' He threatened that if she continued to reject him, and to offer no more than friendship, he would give up seeing her. What was she afraid of—morality?—convention?—becoming unworthy in her own eyes? He knew that she had 'philosophical principles', meaning that she shared the moral outlook of the eighteenth century. But if she was sincere in this, 'it follows that we die entirely, that there is neither vice nor virtue nor Hell nor Paradise, and that our lives should be guided solely by this axiom, "Take all the pleasure you can" . . .'. Not only would they incur no dishonour in becoming lovers, but they would be honouring each other.

The letters poured out day after day, passionate and often moving. Young Balzac always wrote them in draft and, having made a fair copy, kept the originals. He talked to her of his own philosophical preoccupations, knowing her to be intelligent and hoping to interest her in his account of the chain of thought which, according to Leibniz, led from matter to man: 'He says that even marble, by the very fact of being born and growing, has thoughts, but extraordinarily confused.' Laure de Berny listened smiling, but enjoined the philosopher to talk no more of love or she would have to send him away for good.

Balzac to Madame de Berny: I think I have understood your letter. It is an ultimatum. Farewell. I have lost all hope, and I prefer the torments of exile to those of Tantalus. Since you will feel no suffering I conclude that whatever may happen to me is to you a matter of indifference. May you come to believe that I never loved you! Farewell. . . .

Naturally he did not want to break it off—but did she? It is not displeasing, at the age of forty-five, to find oneself adored, even if the young man is a little uncouth and his rather ill-bred parents scarcely to the taste of a god-daughter of Marie-Antoinette. After all, a flower can grow on a dung-heap, and she had too much perception not to know that the author of those letters was no mediocrity. He was writing bad novels, but were they altogether bad? She might help him to write better ones, more worthy of his talents, by teaching him a knowledge of the world and of women. So they both made a series of false exits, like the lovers in a Molière comedy who reappear, one from up-stage and one from the wings, and smile when they meet again. After taking leave of her one evening he went back and found her in a pensive mood. They sat together on a garden bench in the deepening twilight and she granted him his first kiss.

Balzac to Madame de Berny: Do you think of me as often as I think of you? Do you care for me as much as you say? . . .

How pretty you were yesterday! I have often dreamed of you brilliant and adorned with every grace, but I must confess that yesterday you outshone your rival, that figment of my imagination, and, excepting only the sweet smile I dreamed of, you glowed with all the ideal beauties I endowed you with, never believing that I should see you attain them. You must never mention your age to me again, because I should laugh, but it will be a foolish joke. . . .

Admit that the dress you wore was the one you kept back on Sunday, and that you put it on yesterday because no one could say you were doing so for me, and you wanted to please me and console me for those curling-papers! But to make me utterly happy you should have welcomed me when I arrived with a 'good day' as tender as your 'good night'. . . .

She held him off a little longer, alternating promises with last-minute refusals. 'But nothing can prevent me,' he wrote, 'from being at the gate at ten and lingering in the thought of her whom I hoped to find there. I shall be happy to be there, even without hope.' Then one night, after another false exit, he went back and found her in the garden, and this time she gave way.

Balzac to Madame de Berny, early May 1822: Oh, Laure, I am writing to you in the middle of a night that is filled with you, in the heart of its silence, haunted by the memory of your impassioned kisses! What thoughts can I have? You have swept them all away. My very soul is bound to yours, and henceforth you will never walk without me at your side.

Oh, I am bathed in the tenderest of spells, enchanted and magical; I can see nothing but the bench, feel nothing but your soft touch; and the flowers before my eyes, faded though they are, still have their intoxicating scent.

You are afraid, and you tell me your fears in a voice that wrings my heart. Alas, I am sure now of what I swore to you, for your kisses have altered nothing—or rather, I am altered, for I love you to madness. . . .

Obsessed with the memory of Rousseau, he called her, 'My poor Mamma . . .' He had great difficulty in tearing himself away from her. Sometimes, after leaving her in the evening, he would return by himself to 'the beloved bench', to sit there dreaming in moody solitude. His own home seemed to him dismal and colourless. 'Grandmamma's smile annoyed me, my father's voice had lost its charm and I read the newspaper with tears in my eyes. . . .' Even the full-throated laughter of the good Mère Comin, reading his *Jean-Louis* and exclaiming, 'Ah, monsieur, it's a very funny book!' gave him no pleasure. He wrote to Laure, 'I wish to God I had never been born. . . . One is so wretched alone, so wretched with other people. . . .'

Passion soon throws caution to the winds. He spent too much time in the 'house at the other end'. The young Bernys saw what was going on and disapproved. 'I fear we cannot escape the fact that the girls, with their clear-sighted gaze, have guessed our secret. I can never look at E. without her blushing. As for A., her disdain and a great many other feelings are beginning to show. J. knew long ago, and they all surround us with a wall of feelings which they no longer hide. . . .'

Madame de Berny was now the one who ran risks, while her youthful lover begged her to be prudent. But young men are easily seen through. Madame Mère, back from Bayeux, very quickly grasped the situation and was outraged. It was bad enough that Honoré should be having a love-affair with a woman her own age; but on top of this he was doing no work. She promptly decided to send him to the Survilles in Bayeux.

How could he refuse to go, confronted by that cold, blue gaze that always petrified him? In any case, however painful it might be to leave his mistress, he longed to see his sister and her husband in their home. But first he must 'visit the bench' again, for the last time; indeed, he wanted more—that Madame de Berny should come to Paris. He would be spending a few days there, in his parents' lodging. 'Couldn't you manage to be there too? . . .' He proposed a time-table: Wednesday, 8 May, last visit to the bench; Sunday, the 12th, together in Paris; and he would leave for Bayeux on the 14th.

His parents were greatly relieved by the prospect of his departure:

Bernard-François to Laure Surville, 18 May: We are sending Honoré to you. . . . He is daily adding to his knowledge of the world. . . . But he is gaining nothing, or almost nothing, in the most important matter of all—the care of his health. He has not learned how to organize this. If he thinks of it from time to time, after receiving some forcible physical reminder, I am afraid he always puts off any good resolution he may make. . . .

Honoré managed to postpone the trip until the 21st. Madame de Berny gave him a bottle of *Eau de Portugal* for the journey, 'his amulet' and a volume of André Chénier's poems, which they had read together, and he made her promise to write him a weekly letter, 'in very small handwriting with no white spaces', addressed to Monsieur Honoré, chez Monsieur Surville, Rue Teinture, à Bayeux. The separation must have been a great wrench, but there was no avoiding it: 'The fateful journey is so thoroughly decided upon that Mamma talks as though I had already left. . . .' Madame Balzac wrote to Laure that Honoré was in a 'pitiable state' and that the parting between them had been painful, in which she exaggerated. Louise Brouette, who put Honoré on the coach, returned with the news that her young master would be travelling in company with a 'very amiable countess' and that he had got into conversation with her by the time the coach started. The anguish was evidently less severe than his parents had feared. The truth is that Honoré so loved life, and transformed it so easily into fiction, that it could never make him unhappy for long.

VI

Interlude in Bayeux

*Moi, j'ai souvent été général, empereur; j'ai été Byron,
puis rien. Après avoir joué sur le faîte des choses humaines,
je m'apercevais que toutes les montagnes restaient à gravir.*

BALZAC

HE WAS MET BY his brother-in-law at the coach-stage in the
little Normandy town of Bayeux and escorted by him to the
house in the Rue Teinture. The green paint was flaking off the
porte cochère. A young maid-servant in a cotton cap made a bob.
The apartment, with polished walnut panelling, was dark, 'with
tapestry-upholstered chairs and antique armchairs symmetri-
cally arranged'. Three windows overlooked a big garden. 'From
the well-polished floor to the green check window-curtains,
everything shone with a monastic cleanliness.' Laure was
proving herself a good housewife. It was a joy to Honoré to see
her again, 'Ti-Laure', the sister who was so close to him.

As for her, she was delighted by his visit. Although she loved
her husband, as a good daughter of the Marais was bound to do,
she was not much in love with Bayeux. Upon their first arrival
her vivacity and aplomb had caused a sensation; but Surville
was still a rank-and-file engineer of Bridges and Highways, at
260 francs a month. Despite his training and qualifications, he
was only concerned with such things as the surfacing and paving
of roads, the digging of gutters, maintenance of verges and
clearing of ditches. These routine tasks bored him, and his
modest status disappointed his wife. She dreamed of luxury, he
of vast civil works—above all, of canals, which he loved. However, he was plump and good-humoured, given to humming as
he worked. The arrival of a brother-in-law bubbling over with
plans and ready to be enthusiastic about other people's made a
pleasant change.

Honoré talked to Laure about his books. He insisted that
L'Héritière de Birague was 'tripe', but that *Clotilde de Lusignan*,

which was shortly to be published, would be hailed as a masterpiece. He had brought his work with him, the beginning of a
novel entitled *Wann-Chlore* and the outline of another to be
called *Le Vicaire des Ardennes*. Laure was also full of ideas. The
three of them would write the *Vicaire* together, and they would
all be rich; after which they would have a go at the theatre.
Honoré lolled on a couch in knee-breeches, without stockings or
necktie, while he and his sister laughed and talked endlessly
about Mamma, the family connections, poor Laurence, *Clarissa
Harlowe* and *La Nouvelle Héloïse*. Surville took him on trips to
Caen and Cherbourg, Laure showed him the countryside; and
so the novelist gathered grist for his mill, mentally recording
scenes of town and country, the mysterious glow of candles in
the cathedral, the sad tale of a great lady (the Comtesse de
Hautefeuille) deserted by her lover. It has been said that Honoré
attempted the conquest of that forlorn lady, but was heavily
defeated. In any event, he studied the local society, being, as
always, interested in everything. His remarkable aptitude for
distinguishing between species, like a naturalist, enabled him to
discern social patterns common to the small towns of Restoration France—a quasi-royal household, living in obscurity but
allied to the most illustrious families in Paris; a wealthier class of
less ancient aristocracy; some elderly spinsters of high estate,
and a few middle-class families who, being known for their
royalist sympathies, were condescendingly received in the
Faubourg Saint-Germain.

Clotilde de Lusignan was published, to be followed by one of
those shattering letters which Madame Mère knew so well how
to write:

Madame Balzac to Laure Surville, 5 August 1822: During
the past few days, my dear Laurette, I have had a new cause of
distress. . . . It is Honoré, the good, the excellent Honoré who has
unintentionally thrust a dagger in my heart. You have yet to
experience, dear child, the strength and delicacy of a mother's
pride, and how readily it is stirred by the desire of all good
mothers to see their children amount to something. That is my
feeling for Honoré, but my hopes are far from being fulfilled.
You will ask what is troubling me? Why am I saying this? I
will tell you. I wanted, before writing this letter, which I hope
you will make use of in the manner I desire, I wanted Honoré to

finish the work he tells me he has now completed while staying with you. I am sure your comments will have been heeded by him far more than the things I said to him about the unfortunate *Clotilde*. . . .

What it came to was that Madame Mère, having listened to the reading of *Clotilde* while it was in progress, and told the author that he must revise it, had now discovered that Honoré had taken no notice of what she said. The published work filled her with horror. What did the Survilles think of such things as a *slender* ray of light, the word *suave* repeated every other line, *silky movements, seminal humours*? Many faults had been overlooked during the reading because Honoré read with such fire and spirit; but 'reading in cold blood' his parents found that the work had grave defects. The construction was good and the story interesting, but the author tried to show off, he lectured the reader, he was guilty of bad taste. 'I hoped to hear it praised everywhere. Nothing of the kind.' For Madame Mère the general opinion was all that mattered. Their friends agreed that Honoré possessed imagination, but they also said that he lacked judgement. Rabelais had been bad for him, Sterne even worse, and he had done himself no good by mixing with young men who, consorting in cliques, ruined each other's sense of values. 'In short I am in despair, that is the gist of the matter.' But she dared not say so to her son, who was so easily cast down. 'Honoré either thinks himself *everything* or *nothing*.' She hoped the Survilles would say it for her, using what tact was required.

You should also talk to Honoré about another thing, no less important. Honoré has a belief in his own superior knowledge which offends everyone. Monsieur Dablin, who is very fond of him, accuses him of being capricious in his opinions. . . . Honoré does not keep a sufficient check on himself when he is with other people; his humour is two-edged. Madame de Berny, who takes a great interest in him because her son would have been the same age, told me the other day that when he was with them Honoré often made himself ridiculous, and that he was not liked. . . . 'I am very attached to him,' she said, ' and I would give a great deal to see him pay more attention to his speech, his bearing and his manners.'

In addition, he had promised his publisher that when *Clotilde* appeared he would see that it was well noticed in the papers. By this, said his mother, he simply meant these friends of his, 'little *brisquets* who have only been around for two days' and who had no standing whatever. 'One needs a great deal of influence.' But people who might have spoken for him preferred not to do so because of the book's shortcomings. Dr Nacquart had said, 'Why did not Honoré, who knows how much I like him, come and read me the beginning? There are errors on the very first page!'

Madame Mère went on to tell of other grievances. She had bought the first copy of *Clotilde* as a present for her husband on his sixty-seventh birthday. That was good of her, was it not? But Honoré had not even bothered to thank her. All this was having a disastrous effect on her nerves. Well, she hoped that before he left them the Survilles would give Honoré a good talking-to, without discouraging him, of course, but enough to make him feel, in the kindest way, that he needed to keep a better watch on himself and to think himself less wise and learned. And above all not to forget that the 15th was Mamma's birthday.

Laure replied consolingly: 'Poor *ti-mère*, when I read your letter tears came into my eyes as I thought how ti-sad it is to be a mother! . . .' She could understand that the four Balzac children were a great worry to *ti-mère*, but in principle she was always an optimist and did her best to look on the bright side. She did not think *Clotilde* was really such a bad book; certainly it was far better than *L'Héritière de Birague* and *Jean-Louis*, which had 'horrified' her. There were repetitions and pieces of slipshod writing, but these were due to the fact that Honoré had written four volumes in two months. Whole chapters were good, and much was to be expected from so rich an imagination. Honoré would feel the force of the criticism. Indeed, instead of being tactful about it, Laure had read him the whole of their mother's 'wise, just and well-considered' letter. 'He didn't say anything, except to murmur that it was true, and then he looked very distressed and unhappy, and went and sat on the ottoman while I talked about it. If I'd looked at him I shouldn't have been able to say another word because his eyes were so hurt; I should have burst into tears and left the room . . .'

One can reach Honoré only through his heart. He can be led anywhere by kindness. And, my dear, he must only be scolded for big things, and left entirely free in small ones. What do details of dress matter, or failures in minor courtesy and even in minor duties? Are you not sure of his heart? Where will you find anyone who equals him in kindness? Honoré is changeable in his moods, it is true, sometimes sad, sometimes gay, but what does that matter? Everyone has their weaknesses. You must pay no attention to these ups and downs. If you make him happy you will be happy yourself. . . .

In short, Laure considered that *ti-mère* was taking altogether too gloomy a view of things. The book was not signed with the name of Balzac, and so the honour of the family was not affected. It might sell very well. Could a novel be expected to be a masterpiece when it had been written simply to make money? 'Honoré does not aspire to be a Richardson or Fielding or Walter Scott; that is not in his line. . . . You have attached more importance to the book than he does himself.'

This was certainly true. Honoré at the time was far more concerned with making money than with writing masterpieces. Moreover, although he had a very real sense of literary values and feeling for style, since he did not yet know how to live up to it, he pretended not to care. He was to become a genius in his own despite.

Laure went on to talk of her husband's affairs and his wish to move nearer to Paris. It was a great grief to them both that Honoré was to leave the next day (9 August): 'We have so enjoyed these two months. We shall feel lost without him, our good and gentle brother, but perhaps we shall see him again soon. I console myself with that thought.'

Meanwhile in Villeparisis, Madame Balzac had taken a relation to live with them, her nephew, Edouard Malus, a young man of twenty-two, rich and orphaned and consumptive, who by night was coughing up the last of his lungs in Honoré's bedroom and by day on a camp-bed in the garden. During Honoré's absence Grandmamma, always the devoted ally of her grandson, had smuggled messages between him and Madame de Berny. 'We continue as usual to see our neighbours from the other end,' she wrote. 'They show our young invalid a thousand attentions . . . and are always interested in hearing your news.'

Offerings of butter from her farm, for poor Edouard, were among Madame de Berny's means of keeping in touch with Honoré. 'Your letter has been "forwarded",' wrote his obliging Grandmamma.

Before he left Bayeux, Honoré had written Madame de Berny a most melancholy screed: 'I dare not say that you sadden me in enclosing no more flowers in your letters. My *eau de Portugal* is finished, and were it not for my Chénier I should have no talisman. . . . There are beings who are born to unhappiness and I am one of them.' The fanciful youth was going through another Werther crisis. So many lost illusions on the subject of himself and his art! 'Would to God that I had never been born!' In vain did Madame de Berny assure him that she had 'regained her liberty of choice', in other words, that her husband would henceforth leave her entirely free. 'Of my own will I renounce seeing you,' wrote Honoré, plunged in gloom by the reception of *Clotilde*.

Balzac to Madame de Berny, 30 July 1822: I think I have been deluded about myself, and moreover I have deluded myself about life. . . . Content henceforward to live on in your heart, if I have the place in it that you have in mine, I shall sustain myself with memories, illusions, dreams, and my life will be wholly one of the imagination, as it has been in the past. . . .

Madame Sallambier to Laure Surville: So your brother is returning to us. God grant that all his splendid schemes will not vanish into air as they generally do, because he does not always make his best of mothers happy.

What Grandmamma did not understand was that the 'splendid schemes' were Honoré's way of compensating himself for the blows of fortune and forgetting his disappointments in real life. Facts destroy illusion, but literary creation revives them. 'Amid these illusions, elegant daughters of a too lively imagination,' he wrote to Madame de Berny, 'there will be a fixed star, always brightly shining, which will serve me as a compass. It will be you, my dearest friend.' But he feared that he would have to content himself with no more than the distant contemplation of his star:

When one is a mediocrity, possessed only of a spirit without fire or ferment, one must bow to destiny. Mediocre means yield no high reward. Lacking the power to communicate great emotions and to dispense the riches of renown, talent and greatness, one is under an obligation to withdraw one's heart from the stage, for no one must be deceived. To do otherwise is to commit a moral fraud, like praising a house that is falling down. The fruits of genius and the privileges of great men are the only things that cannot be usurped. A dwarf cannot lift the club of Hercules.

I have said that I shall die of despair the day I am forced to recognize that my hopes are impossible of fulfilment. Although it has not happened yet, I feel that the time is near. I shall be the victim of my own imagination. Therefore I beseech you, Laure, do not attach yourself to me; I beg you to break all bonds between us. . . .

Were these a lover's scruples, or a vague presentiment of the fragility of a love that time must inevitably spoil? He was to write much later: 'The sudden revelation of the poetry of the senses is the powerful link which attaches young men to women older than themselves; but it is like the prisoner's chains, it leaves an ineffaceable imprint on the soul, an implanted distaste for fresh and innocent loves. . . .' In the meantime, desire vanquished scruple. Ten lines farther on he was bombarding her with affectionate questions. Did she often go into the meadow and the vegetable-garden, did she sit on *the* bench? Had she given up the piano? While he was writing, Surville, somewhere close at hand, was singing, '*Que le jour me dure*'. Heavens, how badly he sang! And how cold was the Normandy sky!

On his way through Paris Balzac was button-holed by Charles-Alexandre Pollet, a bookseller-publisher who got him to sign a contract for two novels, *Le Centenaire* and *Le Vicaire des Ardennes*, printings of a thousand copies each, against a payment of 2,000 francs, 600 in cash and the balance in eight-monthly bills. Things were not going so badly. But he had to deliver both works by 1 October, and he had left the manuscript of the *Vicaire* with the Survilles who, never doubting their own talent, were to continue working on it.

Balzac to Laure Surville, Villeparisis, 14 August 1822: So we have the month of September in which to get the *Vicaire* finished. I don't think it will be possible for you to do two chapters a day each, so that I can have it by 15 September; and even that will only leave me a fortnight to revise it. Talk it over. . . . If you have any pity for me you'll send me that blasted *Vicaire*, and if you think I'm telling you a tale I'll send you the Pollet contract and you'll see that there's a deduction if it isn't printed by November. . . . This rush of work is more than you can manage, Laure. I don't believe you'll be able to write sixty pages a day. If you think you can, and if you'll promise to send it off to me on 15 September, then go ahead; but because of that infernal deduction, if the manuscript hasn't reached me by the 17th I shall get on with it myself, and as you know one can do a novel for Pollet in a month. . . .

The family was preparing to leave Villeparisis. Madame Balzac's cousin, Antoine Sallambier, the owner of their house, had sold it to another cousin, Charles Sallambier, who was asking a higher rent. The indignant Balzacs decided to return to Paris. They had found a 'hole' in the Rue du Roi Doré, with a room for Honoré. But the dying Edouard Malus could not be moved; seated in his invalid chair the poor boy was learning embroidery. Bernard-François was in excellent spirits, convulsing Honoré with his witticisms. Madame Mère, business-like and in high excitement, made a trip to Paris to persuade their influential friend, Madame Delannoy, to procure a post for Laure's husband at Montargis or Pontoise, so that they would be nearer the capital. She scolded Honoré severely for having left a 'face-towel with red stripes and a handkerchief' in Bayeux—an unforgiveable domestic crime. He read the beginning of the novel he had written in Normandy—*Wann-Chlore* (or *Jeanne la Pâle*)—to his Villeparisis audience and it was not badly received, although he had drawn a slightly ridiculous picture of his mother. He went to meet every arrival of the mail-coach in the hope of getting *Le Vicaire des Ardennes*: 'I embrace Surville with all my heart, and you as tightly as I can without hurting. . . . Edouard is busy dying, Grandmamma is busy with her ailment, Mamma in Paris is busy exaggerating, Papa is busy with eternal health, Louise is busy at the door, Louis with stupidity, Henry with imbecile jokes and me, I don't know what I'm busy at . . . *Le Vicaire—le Vicaire—le Vicaire*! . . . Mail after mail! Because I've got to get on with it. . . .'

As for Laure de Berny, he had only needed to see her for his Werther crisis to be swept away in a torrent of love renewed.

Balzac to Madame de Berny, 4 October 1822: Every day I find new beauties in you. . . . I tell you, Laure, the Consecration of the bench, that festival of a love which we thought dying, has re-inspired it, and far from being a tomb the enchanted spot now seems to me an altar. . . .

There would be some greatness in concealing how much we love one another, but there is more still in persisting in our love. I leave the decision to you, my darling. Today as four months ago I place my destiny in your hands, my whole being, my soul, swearing that it has only gained by contact with yours. . . .

Now that all barriers were down between them he was learning better to understand his mistress's wisdom. He could not hide his love, and Madame Balzac talked severely of it to Laure. After writing to Surville about Edouard, whose death was imminent, she continued (12 October):

For Laurette's eyes alone. Honoré leaves the house at midday and comes back at five; he goes off again after reading the paper and comes back at ten. Although Edouard is so ill, those men leave me here alone. Honoré does not see how indiscreet of him it is to be visiting that house twice a day. He doesn't see that she's trying to *get him*. I wish we were a hundred miles from Villeparisis. He isn't writing a line. He has only twenty pages to do to finish *Le Centenaire*; but he has only one thing in his head, and he doesn't see that by giving himself too much to it he'll end by growing tired of it; but by then his conduct will have made it impossible for him to treat it reasonably. I have shown him how necessary my prudent and tactful attitude was. You must write to him, perhaps he'll listen to you. If I leave tomorrow I'll write again, more *fully*. . . .

Edouard Malus died on 25 October, leaving Madame Balzac the considerable sum of 90,000 gold francs. The combination of family devotion and bourgeois realism had made charity profitable. In November they returned to the Marais, 7 Rue du Roi Doré, having given up the lodging in the Rue Portefoin. The rent of the new apartment was 730 francs per annum, including extras. On 1 November a curious agreement was signed between Honoré and his father. He agreed to pay his father a hundred francs a month for board and lodging. 'Monsieur Honoré will be charged separately for his light, fire-wood and laundry, the sum of twelve hundred francs covering board and lodging alone.' It was Honoré's pride, not his father's meanness, which dictated these terms.

VII

The Literary Trade

Nous arrivâmes à Paris croyant a l'aisance et au bonheur.
MADAME BALZAC

MADAME SALLAMBIER did not live long to enjoy their return to her favourite part of Paris. She died in January, 1823, and Honoré lost a devoted friend. Her children gave her a handsome and costly funeral: status had to be maintained: but she left only a small legacy, having been partly ruined by her son-in-law's speculations. However, the family finances were now much improved. In addition to the proceeds of the sale of the Saint-Lazare farm and the money left by Edouard Malus, the annuity from the Tontine Lafarge was rapidly increasing as the 'deserters' became more numerous. The Survilles, by favour of 'Bridges and Highways', had moved nearer to Paris. They were now at Champrosay, but he was angling for the post of civil engineer for Seine-et-Oise, at Versailles. Laurence, in growing misery, was confined while she and her husband were under distraint for debt. Her letters were filled with girlhood memories —'I'm sure you'll make some beautiful marmalade and roast chestnuts in the fire. . . .' As for 'Henry le trop aimé', he was turning out to be as extravagant as Honoré and as light-headed as Laurence but, unlike the other Balzacs, entirely devoid of enterprise.

Honoré was working extremely hard. He finished *Le Vicaire des Ardennes* for Pollet and *Wann-Chlore* for Hubert. His mother praised his industry—'He never has a minute to spare'. But the *Vicaire*, alas, was suppressed on publication. It was the story of a marquise who believes herself to be in love with the new vicar, whereas her feeling for him is in fact maternal (he turns out to be her son, born of an affair with a bishop), and the theme greatly shocked the authorities. Its sale was forbidden.

Yet it began not too badly, somewhat in the manner of

Dickens or Sterne. There were portraits of village worthies—a schoolmaster soaked in Latin, a grocer-mayor, an elderly curé as full of homespun wisdom as Sancho Panza—which had some life, although they were over-drawn. But the whole thing collapsed into high-flown melodrama. A Byronic pirate invades the Ardennes; the vicar marries despite his cassock, only to discover that his wife is his sister, and later that she is not. The Censor's disapproval probably did more good than harm to Horace de Saint-Aubin, the name under which Balzac wrote the book.

Another novel followed only a fortnight later. *Le Centenaire, ou Les Deux Beringheld*, also signed Horace de Saint-Aubin (*bachelier ès lettres*) was evidently inspired by Maturin's *Melmoth*, translated from the English in 1821, which had made a great impression on Balzac. The character of a centenarian was, in any case, bound to attract him, since he had been hearing about longevity all his life. The aged Beringheld, like Melmoth, has made a pact with the Devil: his life can be extended to several lives provided he now and then kills a young girl, whose blood he pumps into his veins to renew his youth. He is a gigantic, monstrous old man, and his adventures are described in a series of episodes, 'boldly interwoven without regard for chronology'. In the end the last descendant of the Beringheld family, General Tullius Beringheld, rescues his fiancée from the vampire's clutches just as he is getting ready to murder her.

Balzac to Laure Surville, 2 April 1822: Now that I'm beginning to know what I can do I hate having to waste the best of my energies on this nonsense. There are things stirring in my mind, and if only my means were assured—that is to say, if I had no obligations to fulfil, and enough to live on and an Armide to inspire me—I would do serious work. But for this one has to keep aloof from the world, and I always come back to it. . . .

Like so many young men, he was torn in different directions. He was involved with a group of literary tradesmen who made a mock of everything, especially high thinking. They contributed to popular pamphlets such as *Le Pilote* and *Le Corsaire*, which specialized in scurrilous gossip, steering a middle course between satire and blackmail; and they ran up farces and melodramas for actresses of easy virtue. In addition to Auguste le Poitevin and Etienne Arago, who boasted of having been a member of the *Vente Bleue*, a republican secret society, the group included Horace Raisson, a young man whose father, like Bernard-François Balzac, had skipped nimbly from Royalism to Jacobinism and back. Raisson was connected with the painter Delacroix, who said of him, 'He's a liar and a coxcomb. . . . Under the skin of an idler he's more Gascon than anyone I know. . . .' Henry Monnier relates that one day, when he was in the Café Minerva with Raisson, the latter rose suddenly saying, 'Let's get out of here. Here comes the boring Saint-Aubin.' It was Balzac, who in those days, according to Monnier, looked like a monk or peasant. Raisson would seem to have been ungrateful and spiteful, as well as a liar and a coxcomb.

These young men all devilled for better-known dramatists. Balzac, who had hopes of making his fortune in the theatre, wrote a harrowing melodrama entitled *Le Nègre* which was rejected by the Théâtre de la Gaîté, although not without a few kind words.

But although he was playing the same game as the rest of them, in his heart he hated it. He was too sensitive and sincere for this kind of cynical commercialism, and he felt that he had it in him to do better things. Here and there in his pot-boilers he slipped in a penetrating comment on the laxity of the age, the sexual promiscuity and general corruption. His father's theories on the relationship between the physical and the spiritual, not badly reasoned and by no means stupid, were still very much in his mind, and in 1822, on the advice of Dr Nacquart, he bought the works of Johann Lavater and had them bound at considerable expense. The Swiss theologian, who was greatly esteemed by Goethe, had written a work on 'physiognomy' (the reading of character from facial characteristics), in which 'with shrewd and enlightening observations' he described six thousand human types, their outward aspects and inner nature.

For Balzac this became a sort of Bible. 'People of perception, diplomats and women who are the rare and fervent disciples of these two celebrated men [Lavater and Gall] have frequent occasion to note other outward indications of the workings of men's minds. Bodily habits, handwriting, tone of voice, manners, etc., have often enlightened the woman in love, the scheming diplomat, the astute administrator and the sovereign (Napoleon)

—all those who need to know true from false. . . .' The remark contains the seed of a widespread study of social groups. Balzac, the disciple of Buffon and Geoffroy de Saint-Hilaire, was fascinated by detailed classifications of this kind. But would it not be far better to express them in fiction, instead of simply imitating writers like Victor Ducange and Pigault-Lebrun? The more he read, the more he came to think so. But he had no time. He was harrassed by immediate needs, and the work he was one day to do, hazily taking shape in his mind, was still beyond his means.

He dreamed of a series of Platonic dialogues in which he would propound his philosophy, but his *Phaedo Up-to-date* was never written. However, there is a later work, *Les Martyrs ignorés*, published in 1843, which gives some idea of the conversations he may have had with his more intelligent friends in the Café Voltaire, near the Odéon Theatre, round about 1824. The central character, Raphaël, recalls Balzac himself, 'face flushed with health, dark hair, eyes of a hawk'. The other members of the symposium are an Irishman, Théophile Osmond, a fanatical follower of the Christian philosopher, Ballanche; Tschoern, a German, fair-haired, liberal and a poet; Dr Physidor from Touraine, a young man of twenty-seven who practises phrenology; Dr Phantasma from Dijon, aged sixty-three, a disciple of Mesmer; and Grodninsky, mathematician, chemist and inventor. They play dominoes at what is known to the other habitués of the café as 'the philosophers' table'.

'Double six—it's my start!' says Dr Phantasma; but while they play they talk in a manner that sheds light on the thinking of the youthful Balzac. Physidor, who is Balzac's mouthpiece, relates how an elderly physician, an adept in the occult sciences, once confided to him: 'I'm going to tell you a secret. It is this. Thought is more powerful than the body; it devours, absorbs and destroys it.' A thought can kill. . . . Every member of the circle has tales to tell of mysterious tragedies in which unregarded victims die of imaginary poisoning, or some disease which they haven't got, or are driven mad by the tyranny of an idea. For thought is a material force. The dead can manifest themselves to the living because the life of ideas is more enduring than that of the body. 'We must believe in the occult sciences! . . .' The alchemists, far from being concerned only with the making of gold, were seeking other and higher things. They were seeking to discover the basic atom, the principle of movement reduced to terms of the infinitely small, the secret of universal life. . . . 'That is *Magism*, which is not to be confused with *magic* and is the highest of all sciences. . . .

Thus one may conceive of purely moral crimes, impossible of punishment. In the bosom of the family, in utter secrecy, the persecutor can drive his victim to madness and death by purely mental torture, the gentler spirit being destroyed by the harsher, which puts it to the question with lethal words. Conversations such as these furnished the budding novelist with new and strange themes.

He read a great many books on these matters. The medical profession at the time was divided into three schools: the vitalists, who believed that man possessed a 'life force', which was another name for the soul; the mechanistic-chemical school which scorned all metaphysical concepts and saw only organs, actions and reactions; and the 'eclectic' school which advocated the empirical approach. There was a Dr Virey, a vitalist, whose theories broadly corresponded with Honoré's beliefs—that longevity was to be attained by husbanding the vital forces; that these were squandered no less by intellectual labour than by dissipation, and that chastity led to the accumulation of a reserve of energy which, concentrated in thought, produced physical results. To these principles Balzac added the one with which he had always been obsessed, namely that man is able, by the use of his will, to control his own vital force and project it beyond himself. Hence the magnetic healing which he practised, like his mother, by the laying-on of hands.

But there was a third man in Balzac, kept deeply hidden. He had a friend whom he valued far more than any of the Raisson set. This was Jean Thomassy, the Catholic and Royalist whom he had met at the Faculty of Law, if not earlier. Thomassy was as far removed from the irreligious liberalism of Bernard-François as he was from the brashness of the young ink-slingers at the Café Flicoteaux. 'There's only one thing for him to do,' wrote Sautelet, 'and that is to take the cassock. Between ourselves, I think that's how he'll end.' Among their common acquaintance, Thomassy had no high opinion of plump Sautelet or the arrogant Le Poitevin, but he was attracted by Balzac's generous nature and intellectual gifts. In politics they seemed to be wholly on opposite sides. Like his father, Honoré was a monarchist by expediency, an opportunist by necessity, a Bonapartist by admiration and a Voltairian by temperament. One of his novels, *Jean-Louis*, had been taken to task for 'seditious warmth' and sympathy for the Revolution. The fact was that although he despised the existing order of society he had no wish to destroy it. Any other would be as bad.

Although primarily an atheist, after reading Swedenborg and Saint-Martin Balzac tended towards Illuminism. The wise men of India and the hermits of the Egyptian deserts had always fascinated him. He dreamed of the ecstasies of infinite beatitude, the peace of forgetfulness, the rapture of perfect love. He was not a Catholic and found it easier to believe in an Eternal Principle, impassively letting things take their course, than in a providential God, intervening in the affairs of men. Nevertheless Swedenborgian mysticism opened a door in his mind through which Christian spirituality was able to enter. Man is neither angel nor beast, but in refusing to behave like the beasts he may become an angel, that is to say, conserve the best of himself, the inner being, and so 'rise to higher spheres in the depths of the Infinite'.

Was he an initiate of Martinism? This has been affirmed without being proved; but in the draft of a 'Treatise on Prayer' he expressed the desire to convey to wounded souls 'how sweet was my initiation, how easy my progress along that path once I had overcome the first obstacles, what rich fruits refreshed my jaded palate. . . . Those who read this book are asked to bring to it the serenity requisite for the discovery of the meaning of the Word. . . .' This is the obscure, exalted style of Louis-Claude Saint-Martin, philosopher and illuminist. Chateaubriand, after meeting him, spoke jestingly of that 'philosopher of Heaven', who 'talked as though he were an archangel'. The visionary irritated Chateaubriand; Balzac believed he had found in him a guide towards what he called the religion of St John, the mystical Church. He owed to Saint-Martin and Swedenborg one aspect of his conception of the world.

He talked to Thomassy in 1823 about his projected 'Treatise on Prayer', but Thomassy, who by then had left Paris to become secretary to the Prefect at Bourges, persuaded him against it:

'You cannot conceive how greatly your talent will grow if it is nourished with moral and religious ideas. . . . But you must not think that a "Treatise on Prayer" can be written under the influence of the senses.' Thomassy was mistrustful, and rightly so, of the mystical-erotic style in which Honoré described his profane loves:

Jean Thomassy to Balzac, 7 January 1824: Tell me about your 'Treatise on Prayer'. It is not enough, in order to write it, to have a noble spirit and a rich imagination. It calls for the regular practice of religion; it calls for prolonged communion with the Deity; and finally it calls for a spirituality rich in growth and tenderness. . . . If you have never trembled upon suddenly hearing the solemn strains of the organ; if you have never been deeply moved at hearing a young priest invoke the blessing of the God of Abraham upon a bride and groom as youthful as himself . . . then abandon your 'Treatise on Prayer'. Rousseau himself would have failed at it because he lacked the religious habit of mind of which I speak. It is one thing to write ten or thirty lines in an inspired moment, but quite another to sustain the impulse throughout a book. . . .

Pending the 'Treatise on Prayer', Balzac published a pamphlet on *The Right of Primogeniture* and an *Impartial History of the Jesuits* both of the most surprising orthodoxy. The former was not lacking in force. He reminded his readers that vineyards and woodlands called for long cultivation and, therefore, security of tenure; and he drew attention to the danger of the equal sharing of estates among a number of heirs, since it 'multiplies ambitions in a country which, unlike England, does not possess vast outlets for its youth'. The pamphlet was probably a task imposed on him by Raisson, an opponent of the régime who aimed at making the Government appear even more reactionary than it really was. There was nothing those young men would not do for 'real money' as Balzac called it, greatly preferring the ring of currency to the notes-of-hand issued by the book-publishers, which were always subject to discount charges and delay.

'My children,' said Finot, 'the Liberal Party will have to liven up its invective, because at present it has nothing to say against the Government, and you know how embarrassing that is for the Opposition. Which of you would care to write a pamphlet demanding the restoration of the Right of Primogeniture, so as to raise an outcry against the secret designs of the Court? It will be well paid'.

'I'll do it,' said Hector Merlin. 'It fits in with my views.'

'Your Party would say you were compromising youself,' said Finot. 'Félicien, you take it on. Dauriat will publish it and we'll keep the author a secret.'

'How much?' asked Vernon.

'Six hundred francs. You can sign it, Count G——.'

(Balzac: *Illusions perdues*)

Balzac played the part of Devil's advocate with skill, and who can say that he did not convince himself? He found it very easy to get inside his adversary's skin. Needless to say he did not send his parents a copy of the pamphlet, but he sent one anonymously to his brother-in-law. As it happened, Bernard-François was visiting the Survilles when it arrived. He read it and, outraged by these reactionary views, at once sat down to write a refutation. Laure, who had little doubt where the pamphlet came from, was greatly amused.

In June, 1824, the Balzacs, having some capital to spare, bought the house they had rented in Villeparisis from their cousin, Charles Sallambier, for 10,000 francs. Village life was not displeasing to Bernard-François, who could cut more of a figure in the country than he did in Paris. Maintaining that an open-air life and sexual diversions were favourable to longevity, he continued, at the age of seventy-eight, to indulge his taste for rustic encounters with the local wenches. Madame Balzac had hoped that Honoré would accompany them to Villeparisis, but he refused and rented a modest lodging on the fifth floor of 2 Rue de Tournon. 'So that he can work', pleaded the faithful Laure. Their mother did not believe it. She was convinced that Honoré simply wanted a place where Madame de Berny could visit him.

Madame Balzac to Laure Surville, 29 August 1824: Now we come to Honoré's desertion. Like you, I say 'Bravo!' if it is really to settle down to work in a straightforward manner; but I fear this breakaway is no more than a pretext, so that he may be entirely free to indulge a passion that is destroying him. He went off with her; she spent three whole days in Paris, and I did not see Honoré at all, although he knew that I had come on his account. I fancy they went round hunting for lodgings together, to make it look as though she were a relation, and I think he deliberately avoided me so as not to have to tell me where he was. All this leads me to suspect that complete freedom was all he really wanted. I pray I may be mistaken and that his eyes will be opened! . . .

The lady from the other end overwhelms me with visits and attentions. You can imagine how flattered I am! She makes a point of walking through the village to call. I'm fuming! She came today to invite me to dinner and I refused as politely as I could. . . .

In a letter a few days later she reminded Laure that Honoré had always been free to draw on his parents for money:

Only recently I offered to pay all his debts if this should be necessary to allow his talents free play, so that he may at last produce something we can all acknowledge. But it seems that it would worry him to be under this added obligation, and he refused. I suggested that we should allow him enough to live on, more than which we should not do for his own sake. But he would not accept. He has repaid our kindness with scandalous behaviour almost under our own roof. He has placed us, despite our anxiety to see nothing, he has placed us, I say, beyond the possibility of doubt! Our position in the eyes of the world has become embarrassing. A dignified attitude on my part, even a stern glance, was not enough to restrain a number of grins in the village, when I walked down the street with her. . . .

But Laure must not suppose (she went on, after this outburst) that she was antagonistic to her son. Her arms and her purse were always open to him. If he proved his talent it would be a cause of great rejoicing to his parents. And if he treated his passion in the way it deserved, as a source of pleasure and not a hindrance to his work, they would be delighted to find it of value to him; but it was high time . . .

Since he left here the lady has paid frequent visits to Paris. She always stays two days, which leads me to fear that I was right and that Honoré left home only in order to be free. . . .

Madame Mère's bitterness at finding herself robbed of her son by a woman older than herself, a grandmother, is not surprising. As for Madame de Berny, she was more in love than ever:

> Why must it be, my darling, that being so happy in *ourselves* we should be so troubled by what goes on around us? . . . Indeed I love you! You are more to me than the air to the birds, water to the fishes, sunshine to the earth, all Nature to the soul. By simply repeating after him, 'Darling, I love you, I adore you' I wanted to delight his ear, failing the birds of spring; by asking him to take his beloved to his heart and go for a delightful walk with her I wanted to make him believe it was the loveliest of summer days. But this happiness was denied me, because I feared that my letter might cause unkind things to be said to my dearest, and thus be a disturbance to him and spoil his pleasure. . . . Your gifts are immense, but your sweetheart feels and knows them all. Oh, why am I not a thousand women, to be able to give you all I long to give as I would wish to give it? But, my dearest, if my whole being suffices you, in all its parts and its entirety, enriched with everything that the most perfect love can add to it, then I am content, for nothing of myself belongs to me. . . .

At the beginning of their liaison she had been maternal and light-hearted; but after four years her attachment to this youth whose genius she had been the first to perceive had become a consuming passion. It distressed her to see him forced to accept the shoddy commissions offered by Raisson, who was simply exploiting his overflowing gifts. Balzac was far more than a hack, even if he was a remarkable hack; but he was less clever than Raisson at catching the ear of publishers. At one of the regular meetings of their circle, at the Café Voltaire or the Café Minerva, near the Théâtre Français, Raisson proposed that they should produce a series of 'Codes' in the flippant, cynical style that was then in vogue—a Civil Code, a Code for Honest Men, a Commercial Traveller's Code, a Code for Literary Men and Journalists, a Code of Gallantry. Balzac had no equal when it came to knocking off a slim volume in a few nights. Fortified by Lavater he scribbled a *Code de la toilette*, as brilliant as it was trivial.

Le Code des gens honnêtes was first published anonymously and then under Raisson's name, but it was largely the work of Balzac, as Raisson himself acknowledged. Its ostensible purpose (part

Balzac, part Swift) was to warn honest men against the dangers threatening their precious money, which all the prowling Redskins of Paris had their eye on. Not that the author had anything against thieves. The whole working of society depended on rogues, and without them life would be a comedy without Figaros: 'Where should we be without them? How would the gendarmes get their living, the magistrates, the police, the locksmiths, the porters, the gaolers, the advocates?' In any case, everybody stole. The army-contractor (Balzac was coming near home) who cooked the accounts and supplied inferior goods was stealing no less than the man who destroyed a will, the trustee who fiddled the trust-funds, or the organizer of a tontine.

Drawing upon his time in chambers, Balzac denounced the stratagems of lawyers and notaries, the art of spawning costly legal documents, the false mortgages. He gives the honest man sage advice: 'Let us lay down as a first principle that the worst out-of-Court settlement is better than the best lawsuit. . . . If you are forced to go into Court, reject costly petitions and the calling of unnecessary witnesses. . . . Stand the lawyer's clerk dinner without worrying about his boss; lavish truffles and rich wines on him, observing that three hundred francs spent in this way will save you a thousand crowns.' The little book is shot through with caustic irony: 'Generally speaking your man-of-the-world, assuming him to be reasonably educated, will only renounce probity in exchange for enough money to set him up for life. . . .' Trifling though it is, it is important in relation to Balzac. It is like a book of jottings, full of the seeds of novels concerned with the law and legal and financial chicanery, and revealing the author's amused indulgence for his most deplorable characters.

Then, the vogue changing from Codes to 'Physiologies', he sketched out a *Physiology of Marriage*. He had listened for years to his father's startling views on eugenics and the physical side of love, and his old friend, Villers-La Faye, had talked to him a great deal about women, their stratagems and conjugal diplomacy. Other friends had made him read Stendhal's *De l'amour*, of which he thought highly. His parents had taught him something at first hand about the perils of adultery. Madame Balzac's excessive fondness for Henry, the intruder she had thrust on a family which rejected him, had been one of the great griefs of

Honoré's youth. The Berny household, the Survilles, the Mont-zaigles, afforded other lessons. In short, young as he was Balzac already knew a great deal about matrimonial problems and was disposed to write about them. He searched for a title—*A Marital Code, or the art of keeping a wife faithful: The art of keeping one's wife*; and finally, *Physiologie du mariage*. One of his favourite authors, Laurence Sterne, had set the tone, in the words of Maurice Bardèche, 'by affecting to treat marriage as a clinical situation periodically manifest in a physical act'. The *Physiologie du mariage* was not to appear until later, but it seems that an earlier version was produced at about this time, perhaps in collaboration with Bernard-François, because a copy is in existence which Honoré had bound with another of his father's pamphlets, *Histoire de la rage*.

This string of minor works called for very extensive reading. He browsed in the bookshops, and pored over foreign authors, bringing Napoleonic energy to the performance of his many tasks. But he was now twenty-five and success still eluded him. He thought nothing of the novels of Horace de Saint-Aubin, written with his tongue in his cheek, at times with a sense of shame. He believed himself to be a thinker and philosopher. Those pot-boilers had taught him a few tricks of the trade, but he wanted to make better use of his skill. Raisson and Le Poitevin might be content to remain mere literary men-of-all-work, but it did not suit him! Everything in him aspired to what was big and rejected what was small:

I was consumed with ambition, I believed myself to be destined for great things, and I felt that I was getting nowhere. . . . Like all grown-up children, I secretly longed for wonderful love-affairs. Among the young men of my acquaintance there was a dandified clique who walked with their heads held high, talked trivialities, seated themselves without a tremor beside the women whom I found most unapproachable, addressed them boldly, chewing the ends of their canes and simpering, had their will of the most charming creatures, laid or pretended to have laid their heads on every pillow, and all with an air of being surfeited with pleasure, treating the most virtuous and the most prudish women as though they were easy of access, ripe for conquest at a word, at the smallest bold gesture, the first insolent glance. . . . I learned later that women do not like to be too humbly wooed. I have seen many whom I worshipped from afar, ready to offer them a heart proof against all trials, a soul to be torn asunder, a devotion not to be dismayed by sacrifices or torments; but they all belonged to boors whom I would not have employed as porters. . . .

Meanwhile he had to earn his keep. He was now living alone in the Rue de Tournon, the umbilical cord cut. Occasionally his mother paid his rent in secret. He is known to have been ill in 1824. He was overworking. To make the name of Balzac famous was still his dream. But thus far he had only written under pseudonyms, from lack of confidence in his work. At the beginning of his career as a novelist his parents had looked for a miracle. The benevolent and optimistic Bernard-François still wrote to their cousins, 'Honoré is unremitting in his literary labours, writing good and interesting things which sell well.' Honoré took a sterner view; disgusted with himself, he even thought of suicide, or so Étienne Arago related.

One evening Étienne Arago, crossing one of the bridges over the Seine, saw him standing motionless with his elbows on the parapet looking down at the river.

'What are you doing, my dear fellow? Are you imitating the character in *Le Misanthrope* and spitting in the water to make rings?'

'I'm looking at the Seine,' said Balzac, 'and wondering whether to lay myself to rest in that watery bed.'

Étienne Arago was horrified.

'Suicide!' he exclaimed. 'But this is madness! Come with me. Have you had supper? We'll sup together.'*

It seems unlikely that the engaging, well-loved youngster, his head teeming with plans, can have thought seriously of killing himself. The question was far more whether the whole of his brief life, the only one he had, was to be spent in doing publishers' chores.

---

* Quoted by L.-J. Arrigon in *Les Débuts littéraires d'Honoré de Balzac.*

VIII

Dreamer in Action

*On ne doit jamais juger les gens qu'on aime. L'affection
qui n'est pas aveugle n'est pas.*

BALZAC

DURING THE EARLY part of 1825 Balzac saw Madame de
Berny nearly every day. She had sold the house in Villeparisis
and taken lodgings in Paris not far from his own in the Rue de
Tournon, and here, with her devoted love, she brought him the
memories and shrewd wisdom of a woman of experience who
viewed the world of men and affairs without illusions but also
without malice. She was mother and passionate mistress,
counsellor, companion, protectress and confidant. She lighted
the world for him.

Balzac was intently following the course of events in the Paris
of Restoration France, absorbed in the drama of a world in
transition. The energies which under the Empire had found
their outlet in martial enterprise were now dangerously
accumulating. At the summit two social orders were intermingled—that of the former aristocracy in the Faubourg Saint-
Germain, decimated by the Terror but grown strong again with
the return of the King, and rashly seeking to restore its power
and privilege while pursuing its revenges; and the *parvenu*
society of the Empire and high finance, many of whom had kept
their footing by going over to the monarchy, from expediency
if not from inclination. Two conflicting worlds, both almost
inaccessible to Honoré.

On a lower level there was a section of the bourgeoisie, stifled,
cautious, hiding its resentments, which deplored the reactionary
attempt to abolish the gains of the Revolution. As a bourgeois
himself, the son of an Empire official, Balzac could only detest
the 'ultras', the extreme royalists. Everything testifies to his
Bonapartist fervour. He sympathized with the anger of the

liberals and the bitterness of the out-of-work heroes, the half-pay officers who, incapable of adapting themselves to civil life, passed their time playing billiards in the cafés and plotting against the régime.

King Louis XVIII, clearly perceiving the danger, was seeking to bridge the gulf between the two hostile groups, and Balzac commended his wisdom: 'The last head of the House of Bourbon was as anxious to placate the Third Estate and the people of the Empire as the first Napoleon had been to attract the great aristocrats and to endow the Church.' In his obscurity he studied the scene both as an artist and as a lover of life 'from below, as one of the crowd, amid the hardships and the struggle, with all the huge demands of his talent and his extravagant nature, which meant that what was denied him was guessed a thousand times over, imagined, penetrated, before being eventually possessed and known'.*

The world of Paris as he came to know it seemed to him piti-less and even barbarous. Every kind of skulduggery was practised in the pursuit of money and success. He was too generous by nature, and too high-minded, to be sufficiently wary of the young sharks surrounding him. Although he had witnessed the tribulations of his own family, the quarrels over money, and accustomed as he was to the cheap witticisms of his literary colleagues, living in that seedy atmosphere of down-at-heel journalists and threadbare publishers, he remained in-genuously trustful. But he was beginning to despair of literary success, or even of earning a living by his pen (the publishers were lavish in promises, but their notes-of-hand often went unredeemed) when a friend of his father, Jean-Louis Dasson-villez de Rougemont, suggested that he should go into business. Another adviser, Jean Thomassy, wrote: 'Concentrate on some-thing practical and treat writing as a side line. We need to make sure of two solid courses for dinner before we worry about the dessert. That is the way to sleep in peace and with a clear conscience. Literature, as a means of achieving success, is an intractable instrument which often wounds those who are rash enough to adopt it. Besides, the whole-time man of letters is always tainted with envy; whereas those with other resources

* Sainte-Beuve, *Causeries du Lundi.*

are only light-heartedly envious, having achieved other things.' Why should not business and letters go hand-in-hand?

Honoré had all his father's fondness for bold undertakings. In his dreams he was a man of action, and his enthusiasm for anything new was easily aroused. When he saw the first daguerreotypes he had instantly grasped the possibilities of the invention and was heartbroken because he could not have a share in exploiting it. He saw nothing but ultimate success, impatiently dismissing all thought of the slow labours which must precede it. It happened that the bookseller who was to publish *Wann-Chlore*, Urbain Canel, of the Place Saint-André-des-Arts, was planning to publish the complete works of La Fontaine and Molière, each in a single volume, printed in double-column and in very small type. Balzac, when he heard of this, was delighted with the idea. There must be countless educated readers who would want to acquire the classics in so handy a form. If he joined in the enterprise his fortune would be made, and it would call for very little work and leave him plenty of time for writing.

Accordingly he entered into a contract with Canel whereby they were to share the profits, costs and risks of the Molière volume. To do so, of course, he had to raise money. Dassonvillez de Rougemont advanced 6,000 francs and later another 3,000, at a high rate of interest. Madame de Berny, at her own suggestion, lent him 9,250 francs for the La Fontaine: she thought well of the project and hoped it might render Honoré independent of his parents. The family also approved. Honoré was now twenty-six and had still not made a name for himself. If he could not achieve literary success he had better try commerce!

The only one to counsel prudence was poor Laurence, who was wasting away, worn out by her many troubles. Her blackguard of a husband was trying to get her to sign her money over to him, and Madame Mère had forbidden her to do so. Consumptive and in the last stages of a painful pregnancy, Laurence had fled for refuge to her parents' apartment in the Rue du Roi-Doré, where her mother tormented her with wounding remarks. 'I shall always do everything possible for my daughter,' she said, 'but I can no longer love her.'

Laurence de Montzaigle to Balzac, 4 April 1825: I am worried about your three or four commercial enterprises, my dear Honoré; an author should have enough to do in the service of his Muse. Immersed as you are in literature, in a calling which has demanded the whole lives of men who became famous as writers, how can you find time to adopt a new career and plunge into trade, about which you know nothing? . . . To make a fortune in business, if you start with nothing behind you, you must have only one thought in your head from the moment you get up to the moment you go to bed—to make a show, to praise your wares and sell them at a profit. . . . You're associated with people who will make you see everything in the rosiest light. Your imagination will run away with you, you'll think you have an income of 30,000 a year, and when one starts day-dreaming like that judgement and good sense fly out of the window. . . . You have a goodness and honesty which will never protect you against the shabbiness of other people. . . . It is because I care for you that I am saying these things, dear Honoré, and I would rather see you surrounded by manuscripts, serious works, and not a penny in your pocket, living the life of an artist in a top-floor garret, than loaded with money and business success. . . . With which I take leave of you, my dear promoter. Keep a shrewd eye on your undertakings if you do not want to be yourself undertaken! If you make your fortune, don't ever marry, because you already have two nice nephews and a niece. All this, my dear, is in jest. I command you not to let your Muse slumber too long; I await your works, I long to read them. . . .

Laurence was all too clear-sighted; but Honoré flung himself heart and soul into the new venture. Urbain Canel was looking for an engraver of modest pretensions to illustrate his cheap classics. There was one in Alençon, a bookseller called Pierre-François Godard. Balzac took the coach and found him installed in a cluster of gabled houses and small shops which his alert eye and unfailing memory instantly recorded. He stopped at the Hotel du Maure, a traditional Normandy inn with stables at the end of the yard and a kitchen off the main-entrance. This, too, was registered.

Directly he got back he had to write Introductions to the Molière and the La Fontaine, finish the novel *Wann-Chlore* (or *Jeanne la Pâle*) and set about soliciting press notices to herald the publication of the Molière. He was counting on one from Philarète Chasles, an intelligent and busy reviewer and a friend of Raisson, who after spending two years in England was now making a name for himself as a literary journalist. Balzac needed all the help he could get. He had to succeed. Madame de Berny and Dassonvillez were both gambling heavily on his prospects.

Surville, having got the appointment he had been hoping for, that of Civil Engineer to the Department of Seine-et-Oise, had moved to Versailles. Balzac went there frequently to see Laure and their friend, Madame Delannoy. Her daughter, Camille, was at school with the daughter of the widow of General Junot, created Duc d'Abrantès by Napoleon. Laure Surville had made the acquaintance of the Duchesse, Laure d'Abrantès, who was renowned for her many love-affairs, among others with Prince Metternich, the Austrian Chancellor. In 1825 she admitted to being forty-one.

Like so many others Madame d'Abrantès had discovered monarchist sympathies after the Restoration, and Napoleon, her former idol, had become 'a monstrous usurper'. After Waterloo she had tried to resume her 'little dinner-parties', but the debts on the Junot estate amounted to about a million, and finding herself penniless she had been forced to sell her jewels, her furniture and the contents of her cellar. Pauline Borghese, who had been left extremely rich, had an eye on her old friend's sapphires and Spanish wines.

With her pension finally fixed at 6,000 francs, the Duchesse settled down modestly at Versailles, in a small house in the Rue de Montreuil, hoping to eke out her slim resources by writing. She was still an attractive woman, bright-eyed and full-lipped, with jet-black hair. Honoré was distinctly interested. She had lived at the Court of the Tuileries: '. . . She saw Napoleon when he was still young and unknown. She knew him in everyday life and she watched him grow and rise in the world until it resounded with his name. To me she is like some rare being who has come to seat herself at my side after living in Heaven, near to God himself. . . .

The Duchesse found the lively, inquisitive, well-read young man not without charm. Knowing him to be in contact with the literary world she showed him a translation she had done. Balzac thought she should do better than this. Why not write her memoirs? He tried to seduce her, but she refused and he accused her of letting 'hardness prevail over sensibility'. There were, he told her, two kinds of women, those who were all grace and submission and those in whom masculine ideas and bold concepts were weirdly mingled with the weaknesses of their sex. He propounded the following axiom: 'A woman is never so moving and so beautiful as when she humbles herself before a master.' But Laure d'Abrantès was no serving-wench of love. She offered friendship instead.

Friendship [replied the dejected Balzac] is a mirage that I still pursue despite many disappointments. Since my schooldays I have sought not for friends but for one friend. I share the view of La Fontaine, and I have not yet found what my romantic and exigent imagination depicts to me in such glowing colours. . . . Yet I like to think that there are souls that know and understand one another at a glance. Your proposal, Madame, is so pleasing and flattering that I cannot but clasp your extended hand. . . .

Some one had warned the Duchesse that Honoré was already 'in silken fetters', meaning the liaison with Laure de Berny. He rejoined: 'If I have any quality it is that of energy. . . . To be dominated is intolerable to me. I have refused every offer that would place me in a subordinate position. In this respect I am a real creature of the wild.' Women were attracted by creatures of the wild, and he hoped that this proclamation of independence might tempt the lady to try to enslave him. He went on to describe himself:

In my five feet three inches I contain every possible inconsistency and contrast, and those who find me vain, extravagant, obstinate, frivolous, illogical, fatuous, negligent, idle, unpurposeful, unreflective, inconstant, talkative, tactless, crude, unpolished, crotchety and of uneven temper are no less right than those who would say that I am economical, modest, courageous, tenacious, energetic, neglected, hard-working, constant, reserved, full of finesse, polite and always cheerful. The man who calls me a poltroon will be no more wrong than the man who says I am extremely brave. In short, learned or ignorant, talented or inept, I am astonished by nothing more than myself. I conclude that I am simply an instrument played upon by circumstance. . . .

Does this kaleidoscopic state arise out of what Chance has installed in the souls of those whose aim is to depict every condition of the human heart, to paint all feelings so that by the power of imagination they may themselves experience the feelings they paint; and is the gift of observation simply a kind of memory designed to assist this striving of the imagination? I begin to think so. . . .

In August 1825 the unfortunate Laurence died at her parents' home, exhausted by the birth of her second son. The family displayed a shocking indifference. Laurence had always been the unloved. Shortly before her death Bernard-François wrote to his nephew: 'My second daughter, Madame de Montzaigle, aged twenty-two and the mother of two sons, will have passed into the next world by the time you get this letter; it is a desolating event. Her elder sister, Madame Surville, is at the beginning of her second pregnancy. Madame Surville's husband has drawn the plans of a new canal, to cost seventeen millions, and these have been approved by the Government, who have appointed him engineer-in-chief to this great project. The company is raising funds to start the work. . . .' The Essonne canal, to which Bernard-François so casually referred in the same breath as the death of his daughter, was to play an important part in the life of the family. They all expected to make fortunes out of it, and Honoré had undertaken to draft a prospectus. Meanwhile Surville, too preoccupied with his personal ambitions and his passion for canals to attend properly to his routine duties, was incurring the rebukes of the Director of Bridges and Highways. It is characteristic of Honoré that while as a brother-in-law he shared all Surville's hopeful dreams, as a novelist he noted the harm that an obsession was doing him.

At the time of Laurence's death he was staying with the Survilles in Versailles. Laure was undergoing a difficult pregnancy, and at first he kept the news from her. But he told the Duchesse d'Abrantès:

The sufferings of my poor sister are over. An express letter has just arrived and I am leaving at once, not knowing how long my sad duties will keep me in Paris. I shall return to Versailles as soon as possible. I hope you will have some compassion for me, failing all other feeling, and will not crush me at a moment

when every grief seems to be descending on my head. Good-bye.
Keep your friendship for me, I beg you. It will sustain me in
this new trial.

My sister has not been told. Please keep the secret of this
tragic death. I am going with Surville. Good-bye, good-bye.

The friendship of August became the love-affair of September.
In a letter written from Saché, Balzac addresses the Duchesse as
tu and calls her his 'dear Marie'. Her name was in fact Laure,
like that of Madame Balzac, Madame Surville and Madame de
Berny; but perhaps after his many impassioned avowals to *La
Dilecta* (his pet-name for Laure de Berny) he found it embarrassing to use the same Christian name in a letter to another
woman. Scruple has its quirks which constancy does not know.

The Duchesse wanted him in Versailles, and he promised to
hurry back from Touraine as soon as possible:

I forgive you all your scoldings, my beloved angel, and I hope
soon to be intoxicated by that dear gaze and to see that heavenly
face. I cannot leave here before 4 October, and so there is time
for another sweet letter from my Marie to reach me—but not
the scolding Marie, Marie the adored, the Marie I love. I do
not want to fly to you, my dearest, without having had a letter of
love and reconciliation. I shall come to you in gratitude, and you
can now count upon my return. . . .

Sleeping with a duchess, addressing her as *tu*, the *petit
brisquet*, Honoré Balzac, was not doing so badly in the matter
of women! And in the world of letters he also had a ray of hope.
Urbain Canel, when he published *Wann-Chlore* in September
1826, mentioned it to another of his authors, Henri de Latouche,
who had some standing as a critic: 'This is the work of a
courageous young man with a great future. With your influence
you should do him the service of writing about him.' Latouche
was a cultivated man who had tried everything, plays, novels
and journalism, without ever 'taming the monster', that is to say,
achieving real success. He was soured in consequence, and quick
to take offence, but he was a good critic. 'I have made more
novelists than novels,' he said bitterly. He read *Wann-Chlore*
and saw that with all its weaknesses it showed genuine promise.
One scene in particular pleased him, in which a provincial lady,

an ageing coquette, hearing a visitor at the door sends her daughter to practise the piano in another room, thus ridding herself of a potential rival—a dart aimed at Madame Mère.

'Amid the flood of books that drown us, this one is worthy of attention,' Latouche wrote. 'A strong and gripping plot, dramatic scenes and warm, vigorous descriptive passages will recommend it to readers, especially feminine readers, who look for observation and vividness in a novel.' A few days later he was visited by a pale, thin, frail-looking young man, dark-haired and bright-eyed, clad in a frock-coat and cape, trousers whose under-straps failed to hold them down to ground level and a hat glistening with rain. It was Balzac come to thank his critic, to whom in his gratitude he promised a wonderful pony bred by an Indian snake-charmer.

The princely gift existed only in his imagination; but Latouche took a fancy to him and wrote a second article about him in the review *Pandora*: 'A play by Goethe, dramatic in subject, impressive in some of its details and absurd in others, undoubtedly supplied the idea for the novel *Wann-Chlore. . . .* It is a work of lively, bizarre interest, the product of a distinguished mind, written in a style that is sometimes happy and often careless. In any event, *Wann-Chlore* has achieved success as a tearjerker and is in its second edition. . . .' Latouche was proclaiming success in the hope of promoting it. The truth was that the book was simply collecting dust on Urbain Canel's shelves and Balzac was in despair. In the family's eyes he was coming to be regarded as 'an incompetent', an author of unsaleable novels. In charity they took him in at Villparisis.

Bernard-François Balzac to Laure Surville, 14 January 1826: Honoré arrived here last week in what seemed to me, although I did not say so, a really desperate state, quite without resources. He spent four days resting, without being able to write a word. On the fifth day he began a new book, and after doing about forty pages left on Wednesday for Paris, to return here the next day and go on working. Your mother and I have paid his rent, and I gave him the receipt as a New Year gift. That is for your private ear. Will he come back here? What does he want to do? What is he going to do? I know nothing except that at the age of twenty-seven he has used up perhaps forty years of his energies without making any progress in the world. . . .

Nor did his business interests fare any better. The edition of
La Fontaine, a printing of 3,000 copies, was selling badly.
Balzac's associates had persuaded him to buy them out, and
were thankful to have done so. He was now sole proprietor, but
he had had to borrow more money. A bookseller named
Baudouin bought the entire edition, which had cost 16,741
francs, for 24,000. On the face of it, Balzac had made a profit;
but Baudouin's payment took the form of bills on concerns
that were on the edge of bankruptcy. To unload doubtful
securities, on which the discounters might not pay even 30%, on
an over-trusting creditor was a common swindle in those days.

Dassonvillez advised him to retrieve his losses by setting up
as a printer himself, and Balzac was charmed by the idea. To do
his own printing would be an immense economy. He would
bring out editions not only of Molière, but of Corneille and
Racine. A foreman-printer named Barbier arranged for him to
buy a printing works in the Rue des Marais-Saint-Germain.
The price was 60,000 francs, of which Balzac did not possess
even a tenth. Madame Delannoy, now the accredited patroness
of the family, advanced 30,000 which Honoré's parents agreed
to guarantee. By this time Madame de Berny had heard about
his affair with the Duchesse d'Abrantes (very likely from
Madame Mère, who had been told of it when she was visiting the
Survilles and was certainly capable of a calculated indiscretion);
nevertheless, she continued to help him, thereby winning the
gratitude of Bernard-François. The Balzacs were prepared to
forgive the sins atoned for by the sleeping partner. However,
being acutely distressed by Honoré's infidelity, Laure de Berny
forbade him to go on seeing the other Laure. It was a cruel
dilemma. The love of a duchess was highly gratifying to him,
and her connections might be useful. But his *Dilecta* gained
the day. Being commanded to choose he kept away (for a time)
from Madame d'Abrantès, who reacted with a bitter and scornful letter:

Your distaste for coming here is more than ridiculous. To
put your fears at rest I may tell you without anger that the most
complete indifference has succeeded anything that may once
have existed between us. And since the word 'indifference' is to
be interpreted literally you need not have any fear of scenes or

reproaches. But I must see you. However strange this may be, *it is the case*. If the interests of my family and my future were not involved, and even your own interests, I assure you that I should treat all relations between us, past, present and future, as though they did not exist.

Will you therefore remember for the last time that I am a woman, and simply accord me the strict courtesy that any man owes to the humblest of creatures. If you are still so weak as to be on the defensive, poor soul, then you are even more pitiable than I thought!

Will you be kind enough to return the books which the Versailles librarian has asked me for more than ten times, and which were only lent to you in my name. . . .

Before acquiring a printer's licence he had to undergo a police investigation. The verdict was highly favourable. Monsieur Honoré de Balzac was found to be 'a young man of good conduct, correct thinking and well-to-do family who has been properly educated, has qualified in law, and is moreover a man of letters'. On 4 June 1826, he left the Rue de Tournon to take up residence at 17 Rue des Marais-Saint-Germain, now the Rue Visconti. It was more an alleyway than a street, but situated in a picturesque corner of Paris which in the eighteenth century had been a quarter of writers and actors. The big printer's shop, on the ground floor, had windows looking on to the street. An iron circular staircase led up to Balzac's living quarters—lobby, sitting-room, bedroom with alcove. Latouche, who had good taste and enjoyed bargain-hunting, helped him to furnish the last of these rooms, of which the walls were draped with blue muslin. Altogether it made a charming setting for the visits of Madame de Berny.

Those daily visits were the only thing that enabled him to endure what was in fact a squalid life, attended by the incessant clatter of the printing-presses and recurrent crises when bills became due. In the days when he lived in the Rue Lesdiguières he had challenged Paris ('A nous deux maintenant!') believing that he would one day conquer the city with his pen; now he found himself trueing-up type-panels and filing accounts amid the smell of paper and ink. He printed historical memoirs for Canel and Sautelet, advertising leaflets for 'anti-catarrhal pills ensuring long life' (longevity seemed to haunt him!) and a register of the shop-signs of Paris. He also printed the third impression of Alfred de Vigny's *Cinq-Mars*, and Vigny has left us the following account of him: 'A very dirty young man, very thin and very voluble, who got into a muddle with everything he said and spluttered when he talked, because all the upper teeth were missing from his over-moist mouth,' But his *Dilecta* did not desert him. 'An angel sustained me in that horrible war,' he was to write ten years later. 'Madame de Berny was like a goddess to me. She was mother, mistress, family, friend and counsellor; she made the writer and consoled the man; she wept and laughed with me like a sister, and came every day like healing slumber to ease my tribulations. . . .'

There was no shortage of the latter. The business had very few customers and they paid badly. Balzac did not know how to cost the different jobs, or how to prevent wastage, always enormous under an incompetent manager who does not keep a close eye on what goes on; and he had a fatal habit of confusing personal with business expenditure. Nevertheless in 1827 he expanded further, acting on the principle of allied trades. Having become a printer so as to do his own publishing, he now became a type-founder so as to remain a printer. The Company of 'Balzac & Barbier', with a third partner, Jean-François Laurent, purchased a type-foundry, again with money provided by Madame de Berny.

In February 1828, seeing that they were headed for a crash, Barbier pulled out, leaving Balzac in sole charge of the printing-works. 'Balzac & Barbier' was dissolved and a new Company was formed, that of 'Laurent, Balzac & de Berny'. It was a time when the impatience of her over-youthful lover, kicking against the pricks of fidelity, caused Laure de Berny great unhappiness, but still she came to his rescue:

Madame de Berny to Balzac: If you had ever in your life known the sufferings which I have undergone since yesterday, you would not have been so harshly and pointlessly cruel. As for what you said about women, I scarcely understand it, but if you are looking for a heart that can love you like a god and yet detach itself from your own without pain, well, that is a new philosopher's stone, worthy of an unjust egoist . . . Arrange the business as you choose; it makes no difference to me whether my name appears or not. . . .

She contributed 9,000 francs in cash to a total capital valuation of 36,000, of which 18,000 took the form of stock and equipment supplied by Jean-François Laurent.

It was an act of rash generosity, for Honoré's financial position at the time was worse than precarious. He was personally indebted to the Company to the extent of 4,500 francs, incurred by far too lavish spending on clothes and the decoration of his apartment. And he allowed the Company's largest debtor, a bookseller in Rheims, to settle his account in books, thus adding to his private library at the expense of the balance-sheet. Disaster seemed unavoidable. Yet Bernard-François, as much given to fantasy as his son, wrote in triumph:

Honoré is going ahead like lightning. In less than fifteen months he has set up a printing-works with fifteen presses, secured a licence for the bookshop which was already established next door and started a type-foundry for the use of other printers. If he doesn't get ill he will have made his fortune in five or six years, thanks to his talent, his extraordinary energy and the 50,000 francs which I advanced him. You see to what lengths I am prepared to go, to help my children. . . .

But facts are stubborn things.

Balzac to Théodore Dablin, March 1828: All is lost, *mon petit père*, if you don't help me. My last resource, my own bill for a thousand francs, went out today to meet an unexpected demand. My monthly accounts are settled at the time of writing, but only at the expense of tomorrow's pay-roll. I have just eight hours' respite, and that is all. I beseech you to think of me and see what you can do to raise those wretched 1,500 francs. It's only half what I need, but let me have it. I scraped the bottom of the barrel yesterday. I'll call at half-past six this evening. You have so many connections that you may possibly be able to find . . .

In March, harassed by creditors and unpaid work-people, Balzac took refuge with Latouche. The type-foundry, the only profitable business in the group, was sold. Balzac's place was taken by Alexandre de Berny, Madame de Berny's son, and she gave him a receipt for 15,000 francs of his debt to her. The printing-works had to go into liquidation. Balzac's parents were anxious at all costs to save him from legal bankruptcy, which would have entailed, among other things, the loss of civil rights. To be exact, his mother, at times heartless but always loyal in emergencies, acting without the knowledge of his father (he was then eighty-three), begged her cousin, Charles Sedillot, a man of probity and experience, to perform the difficult operation without bringing them to dishonour. Sedillot persuaded Barbier to repurchase the printing works at a capital valuation of 67,000 francs, which sum was to be passed on to the creditors. Honoré's parents undertook to settle the remaining debts. Thus Balzac, after a three-year incursion into the real world, was left without publishing-house, printing-works, type-foundry or anything else, and in addition owed his parents 45,000 francs, an enormous sum in those days and at that level of society. On the other hand he had gained first-hand knowledge that was to be invaluable to him—of money-matters, of the nightmare existence of a trades-man on the run and of the feeling of impending disaster. The experience marked him for life.

Another drama caused an upheaval in the most excellent family. The octogenarian Bernard-François was believed in Villeparisis to have got one of the village girls in the family way. This at least was what the girl herself said, and Madame Balzac, although she cared little enough about the event in itself, was afraid that the over-vigorous old gentleman might be black-mailed. Did he remember having written a *Memorandum on the Scandalous Disorders brought about by Young Girls' being Betrayed and Left Entirely Destitute*? She appealed to Laure Surville for help:

I am very cautiously preparing to sell the house, but your father has proudly changed his mind. It will call for all your cunning to work him into a new state of enthusiasm for Ver-sailles. We must see to it that he is afraid of going back to Villeparisis, and has no wish to set foot there again. By all means an anonymous letter, from Melun or Meaux. But should he get it before leaving for Versailles? I think *yes*. At Versailles it wouldn't affect him; on the other hand, it ought to arrive too late for him to be able to see the woman again before leaving, to avoid argument. Apart from this, your father's idea is to stay here till 10 July; but this doesn't give me much time to find a buyer. What other way is there of getting him out of Ville-parisis? If he's here when she's confined they'll all be at him, and he'll do anything they want, partly from vanity and partly from fear. . . .

So the Balzacs went to live in Versailles to be near the Survilles. Their son was afforded a further subject for his meditations, that of love and old men. His years of apprenticeship had been hard but instructive. 'His reverses had in no way diminished his pride.' He still retained 'the ability to defy the tempest'. His dark eyes were like spots of coal gleaming in a face rendered haggard by anxiety, and if at times he had a melancholy expression, induced by the sense of his poverty, he still had reserves of exuberance and hopefulness. One day when he was crossing the Place Vendôme in company with Monsieur Pépin-Lehalleur and little père Dablin, he paused at the foot of Napoleon's column and talked about what he would someday become. He had abandoned none of his high hopes. Dablin remarked that honours and wealth change men's hearts, and he replied that nothing would ever alter his affections. In defeat he thought only of future victories. He lived in the future, a triumphant future teeming with houris and riches.

Hence his material setbacks. His thoughts travelled faster than life. How could he worry about a few wretched creditors when his mind sped through the centuries as he read history, and through millennia when he studied the geology of Cuvier? In those exalted moments he truly believed himself to be endowed with supernatural powers. He believed more than ever in the oneness of the world. If the effects of a pistol-shot on the Mediterranean coast could be felt as far away as China, then even more must the human will be able to work physically upon the people and things surrounding it. Nothing less than the omnipotence of an Arabian Nights magician could appease his secret longings. As Madame Mère had said, 'Honoré either thinks he's everything or nothing.' When he paused to cast a sidelong glance at the ruin he had caused during his brief sojourn in the world of action, he was inclined, for a brief, humble moment, to think himself nothing. For a man who knew himself to be everything it was intolerable.

IX

Return to Serious Matters

Les ouvrages se forment dans les âmes aussi mystérieuse-
ment que les truffes dans les plaines parfumées du Périgord.

BALZAC

BALZAC IN 1828 was gasping like a hunted animal. He fled
from the Rue des Marais-Saint-Germain, which was besieged
by his creditors, leaving his cousin Sedillot to attend to the
liquidation of the business—petty tasks for petty minds!
Latouche gave him shelter, proving a friend in misfortune,
hospitable and affectionately sardonic. They tried in vain to sell
the securities loaned by Madame de Berny, who was in despair
at the disaster.

Madame Mère sharply admonished her son, and this time
with justice. He must go and see Cousin Sedillot, 'at least' to sign
documents. And Surville found him an apartment in the Rue
Cassini, near the Observatory, and paid the first quarter's rent.

The *Observatoire* district seemed like the end of the world,
cut off on one side from Paris by the tree-nursery of the Luxem-
bourg, which was the size of a considerable wood. The Boulevard
du Montparnasse, running through fields, was lined with
drinking-booths, arbours and fair-ground attractions. 'Here
Paris is no more, and yet it still exists. This place is like a
mixture of public square, street, boulevard, fortification, garden,
avenue, province and capital; there's something of all these in it,
and yet it is none of them. It's a desert.' Thus did Balzac
describe it in the *Histoire des treize*. Heartbroken, and needing
silence and solitude if he was to work, he came to bury his
despondency in those remote, rutted byways. The Rue Cassini
was little more than a lane at the end of the Allée de l'Observatoire, and the house, No. 1, consisted of two small villas. Surville
had rented the upper floor of one of these. The villas, situated
between an outer courtyard and a garden, were linked by a

windowed passageway which served as an entrance-hall. A low wall surmounted by flower-pots divided the courtyard from the garden, and the whole was enclosed in an iron grill.

Latouche, with his love of furniture, materials and knick-knacks, again offered to help with the decoration. He and Balzac and another friend, Auger, covered the walls with a shiny blue calico which looked like silk. After being submerged, Balzac was rapidly surfacing again. The debts were forgotten; his present thoughts were all for the elegance of his new establishment. He had a partition shifted and the woodwork scrubbed. He bought three rugs at the *Renard-Bleu* for forty francs, a clock on a brown marble pedestal for four hundred, a mahogany bookcase for his study, and a number of handsome books, including Bayle's dictionary and a bound edition of *The Thousand and One Nights*. 'There is no luxury here,' he wrote to his sister, Laure, 'but there is a good taste which renders everything harmonious.'

Why worry, in that bright setting, about Cousin Sedillot and his wretched accounts? A small door concealed by a curtain gave access from the bedroom to a bathroom whose white stucco walls and bathtub were lighted from above by a big skylight with frosted-glass panes which bathed them in a pink glow. It might have been a woman's bathroom. As for the bedroom, flooded with white and pink light and glittering with gilt, Werdet wrote in his *Scènes de la vie littéraire*, 'It was like a bridal chamber for a fifteen-year-old duchess'. At the head of the bed, behind a curtain of pink and white muslin, was a door leading by way of a flight of steps to the garden. The study was furnished with the mahogany bookcase, filled with volumes bound in red morocco and decorated with the coat-of-arms of the Balzacs of Entragues, a thick blue-and-black carpet and an ebony filing-cabinet with red folders initialled in letters of gold, on which stood a plaster statuette of Napoleon. Attached to his sword-scabbard was a slip of paper bearing the words, 'What he did not achieve by the sword I shall achieve by the pen. HONORÉ DE BALZAC.'

Finally, lest he be unworthy of so much elegance, he ordered from the tailor Buisson, in the Rue de Richelieu, 'on 29 April, a pair of black dress-trousers, price 45 francs, and a white quilted waistcoat, 15 francs; on 23 May, a blue tailcoat of fine Louviers cloth, 120 francs, a pair of pepper-and-salt drill trousers, 28 francs, and a pleated waistcoat of chamois leather, 20 francs'. There was a kind of heroism in these follies. 'My creditors scream their heads off,' Balzac seems to say, 'my cousin struggles to pacify them, my family ruins itself, and I spend.' Never mind about paying. At least where Buisson was concerned there was no problem; that exemplary tradesman was content to accept notes-of-hand however many times renewed, gambling on the future prospects of his gifted customer. As for the furniture-shops, Latouche endorsed similar notes, thus incurring debts for the sake of his 'brother', as he called him. He also disposed of the articles Honoré wrote, doing it all with a curious mixture of generosity, coyness and toughness:

Man, you promised to come and see your sick brother; you haven't done so, and you're running true to form. To put myself in line with you I hereby notify you that the manuscript you left with me has been handed to M. Canel, who came to fetch it in your interest. . . . Good-bye, man. Health and happiness. . . .

Seated in that handsome study released from business cares by his remarkable talent for escape, Balzac was again filled with a burning eagerness to write. But to write what? He began innumerable books and did not finish any. He thought of a history of the Primitive Church, and also of a novel. He believed himself to be so constituted that, 'to start his imagination working it needed some author, even a second-rate one, to set the tone'. In the past the other authors had been Maturin or Pigault-Lebrun or Ducray-Dumesnil, all bad exemplars. They had moved him to write melodramatic fantasies on stereotyped lines, besides giving him a taste for haunted castles with horrific dungeons. It is said to have been Latouche who steered him in the direction of Scott and Fenimore Cooper. But did Balzac really need any steering? Publishers known to him had brought out translations of Fenimore Cooper, whose work he greatly admired. 'Oh, to live the life of a Mohican!' he wrote. 'Oh, how I feel for the Red Indian. How well I understand pirates, adventurers, the lives of all rebels! . . .'

The Waverley Novels, with their evocation of the Scottish past, people, customs and everyday life, had broken new ground. They were social studies as well as historical novels. 'The local

colour was simply a background,' Maurice Bardèche has written.
'In the foreground were characters of significance, such as Balzac
was later to call 'social types' . . . not merely fictitious characters
but representatives of the different orders of society . . . necessary for the understanding of Scottish life.' Nothing more
fascinated Balzac, the student of the great naturalists, than to see
a novelist at work on similar lines. In a moment of illumination
he saw the possibility of evoking the whole history of France in a
series of novels.

But he was not content to be merely an imitator of Scott. He
expressed his view of the matter some years later in the words of
Daniel d'Arthez, talking to Lucien de Rubempré in *Illusions
perdues*:

If you don't want to be Walter Scott's shadow you must find
other methods, instead of simply imitating him. Like him you
begin with long conversations to establish your characters; and
after they have talked you set the scene and start the action. The
clash which is essential to any dramatic work comes last. Why
don't you reverse the proceeding? Replace the opening dialogue,
which is magnificent in the hands of Scott but colourless in
yours, with a descriptive passage of the kind to which our
language lends itself so well. Let the dialogue be the natural
outcome of your preliminaries. Start at once with a scene of
action. Attack your subject now in the flank, now from the rear;
in short, vary your approach so that you are never twice the same.
You will produce something fresh, while at the same time adapting the Scotsman's form of drama-with-dialogue to the history
of France. Walter Scott is entirely lacking in [sexual] passion,
either because he did not know what it was, or because the
hypocritical habit of his country prevented him from depicting
it. To him every woman is duty incarnate. With a few rare
exceptions, his heroines are all the same, drawn with the same
brush, to use a painter's expression. They all grew out of
Clarissa Harlowe. By making them all conform to the same
principle he could only produce a series of reproductions of a
single type, with slight variations of colouring. But women create
disorder in society through passion, and passion is infinite in its
range and possibilities. Paint the passions and you will enter
the immense field which that great genius denied himself for
the sake of being read in every household in puritanical England. . . .

For Balzac the principle was sound. He was not good at 'general conversation', and to sustain his characters he needed the solid structure of a house, a town or a doctrine. The novelist's problem is very different from that of the dramatist. The latter has living actors, chosen by himself, to bring his characters to life. Balzac achieved realism by the depth and clarity of his descriptive writing. A staircase as he saw it was not just the picture of a staircase but the sum of all the causes that had made it what it was. He described the physical appearance of a man or woman with the meticulous exactitude of a disciple of Lavater, but he sought to illumine the formal image in the reader's mind by investing it with emotion. He was to show how a town was formed and grew, and why each of its districts had acquired its own character, shaped by historical events and the nature of the ground on which it stood.

He was destined to become a prodigious innovator, a historian of the contemporary scene; but at the outset he tried his luck, not surprisingly, with the historical novel, which was then so fashionable. Vigny's *Cinq-Mars* had appeared in 1826, and Balzac himself had printed the third edition. Victor Hugo had promised the publisher, Gosselin, a novel about the cathedral of Notre Dame. Balzac made notes for two historical novels, one, *Le Capitaine des Boute-Feu*, with a fifteenth-century setting, and the other, *Le Gars*, set in the very recent period of the royalist insurrection known as the *Chouannerie*. Latouche had nothing to do with the choice of the second subject, which had long occupied Balzac's mind, and about which a large number of non-fiction works, historical and autobiographical, had already been written. He had bought a good many of them and borrowed others from the Bibliothèque Nationale. He thought at first of making a play of it; but what a splendid subject for a novel—the 'Blues', the republicans who later became Bonapartists, on one side, and on the other side the 'Whites', the *Chouans*, half-savage peasants clad in goatskins, led by royalist emigrés returned from England! For background the shrub-grown countryside, its woods so favourable to ambushes and its old castles a setting for councils of war and love-affairs with intrepid amazons. As a secondary theme there was the conflict between the country nobility fighting to recover their estates from the bourgeois townspeople who wanted to hang on to them.

The more he read—in that tranquil and charming garden-house in the Rue Cassini, interrupted only by the fond visits of Madame de Berny, who came on foot from her lodging in the Rue d'Enfer-Saint-Michel—the more he felt that this was the subject he had been looking for. For a period to become matter for an historical novel it needs to have lapsed a little into the past; but 'a nation sometimes grows more in a decade than in a century'. The collapse of the Empire had caused a whole epoch to become a part of history, yet the *Chouannerie* was close enough to have its living witnesses. Bernard-François himself had had a post in Brest in 1795, and later, from Tours, he had supervised the accounts of the army in Vendée. Honoré had started jotting down episodes some years previously—an attack on a coach, a love story intermingled with war, the kidnapping of a senator. A manuscript and preliminary announcement of *Le Gars* were in existence in 1827.

The latter is headed with a quotation from Rivarol: 'We have seen so many great men pass and be forgotten that in these days a man must attempt something monumental if he is to live in men's memory.' Prophetic words which show that even in the midst of failure Balzac was thinking in terms of an enduring monument. There followed a biographical note on the pseudonymous author, for he did not intend to publish the novel under his own name. He called himself Victor Morillon. The reader was informed that the young writer, born in the region of Vendôme, had received his schooling under the rod of an ex-Oratorian, which would not have got him very far had he not possessed an inordinate taste for reading and meditation. In short, we are offered a picture of Balzac himself, endowed, like his creator, with visionary powers.

Victor Morillon tells his schoolmaster that out in the fields, or under the thatch of his humble dwelling, he enjoys all the luxuries of wealth: 'He pictured the delights of opulence with an astonishing vividness, the fashionable balls where his gaze was ravished by the bare shoulders of women, their dresses, flowers and jewels, their dancing, their glowing eyes; he described in meticulous detail the homes they lived in . . . the carriages they drove in . . . without having seen any of it. . . .' It was Balzac's own vision of oriental luxury, the palace and harem of a Parisian sultan, lacking none of the things, even to the thick carpets and jewel-studded walking-sticks, which the penniless young man so ardently desired. But Victor Morillon never saw the light of day. Balzac finally decided to sign *Le Gars* with his own name.

He had his subject-matter. What he lacked, if the thing was to be brought to life, was first-hand knowledge of the country-side and its people. As it happened, he had friends in the *Chouan* country. The Balzacs, it will be remembered, had been on intimate terms with General-Prefect Pommereul when they lived in Tours. The latter had died in 1823, but his son Gilbert, also a retired general, lived in Fougères, where the family owned a handsome town house, as well as two country châteaux and vast estates. Fougères was in the very heart of the *Chouannerie*. His affairs having been straightened out by honest Cousin Sedillot, Balzac wrote to the Baron de Pommereul on 1 September 1828:

I have been cast down from the height of my small fortune. The financial happenings which have disturbed the Paris business world have brought me to a standstill. Thanks to the devotion and generosity of my father and mother our honour and good name have been saved at the cost of my fortune and theirs. . . . By the terms of my liquidation all my debts have been settled, and I am left, on the verge of thirty, with courage and an unstained reputation.

I acquaint you with this sad story, my dear General, only because of a circumstance that has grown out of my latest resolve. I am going to take up writing again, and the agile quill of the crow or the goose must help me to gain a living and repay my mother. For the past month I have been occupied with historical works. . . . By pure chance a historical fact from the year 1798 has become known to me, relating to the campaign of the *Chouans* and the *Vendéens*, which furnishes me with a subject easy of execution. It calls for no research, except a study of the scene.

I thought at once of you, and I was about to beg your hos-pitality for some three weeks. My Muse, my inkwell, my sheaf of paper and myself would certainly not take up much room. Nevertheless it seemed to me, on second thoughts, that you would be found to find me burdensome. . . . But consider, General, that a truckle-bed and a single mattress, a table, pro-vided it is truly four-legged and not ricketty, and a roof over my head, are all I ask, together with your own most delightful company. . . .

An agreeable letter, sparkling with youth and confidence. General de Pommereul replied, 'I await you'. Balzac promptly boarded the coach for Brittany, stopping a night at the Hotel du Maure in Alençon, which he already knew. He walked round the town, taking note of an old house in the Rue du Val-Noble which seemed to reflect the whole timeless history of the province. It was another picture permanently imprinted on his mind; and on the way from Alençon to Fougères he observed the countryside with the same unfailing eye. When he reached the home of the Pommereuls the Baronne, very much younger than her husband, received him with the greatest kindness. They were both rather startled at first by the visitor's seedy appearance and 'really awful' hat. However, the shock passed. The removal of the hat revealed a face full of high spirits and gaiety, a forehead glowing 'like the reflection of a lamp', and dark-brown eyes with flecks of gold. Honoré told the tale of his journey with so much gusto that the General and his wife were soon convulsed with laughter.

They were friends at once. Madame de Pommereul and her housekeeper set about fattening him up, and Balzac christened his hostess 'Lady *Bourrant*' (or stuffing). There was always a dish of biscuits and butter beside his plate at mealtimes. He had a pleasant room with a small green table to work at, and the sweet nature of Madame de Pommereul did much to salve his wounds. Every morning his host took him out to explore the surrounding country, the heathland covered with gorse and broom, the woods blazing with autumn gold, and the slope of the hill called La Pèlerine, scene of a famous ambuscade during the civil war.

He visited the people in their dwellings and studied the local customs. A novelist may and must invent, but only on a foundation of truth. The General told him stories of the war, in particular of the attack on Fougères by the insurgent peasants, and introduced him to some of the survivors. He also told him about the two fanatical priests, Abbé Bernier and Abbé Duval, and Balzac ran them together to make the character of the ferocious Gudin in his book. He spent every afternoon re-shaping and re-writing *Le Gars*, filling it out with what he had seen and heard. Madame de Pommereul, who did not like the title, persuaded him that it should be changed. He thought first of *Les Chouans, ou La Bretagne il y a trents ans*; and then of *Le Dernier Chouan, ou La Bretagne en 1800*, which was the title of the first impression. He worked happily, feeling that at last he was contriving to blend romance with realism, history with fiction; but snowed under as he was with pictures, anecdotes and characters, the construction of the story gave him great trouble.

Latouche wrote indignantly about his long absence from Paris:

'Fougères—town of 7,200 souls, seat of the local Assizes, mill producing rough cloth, tanneries on the Couesnon, longitude 3.36, latitude 48.20—and that is the romantic solitude where my mad friend has chosen to bury himself, far from the Rue d'Enfer and the Rue Saint-Honoré! Travel expenses, nights spent on the leather seat of a coach, headache and blistered arse —is it worth it? For heaven's sake come back with or without a masterpiece! I haven't laughed since you went away. . . . May the gods of inspiration visit their curse on you!

Madame de Berny also missed him.

Good night, darling Minet, it will soon be ten and I like to think that at this moment you are writing the word which is a caress, *Min-min*, which I so love to hear or to read. . . . My precious one, take your Minette on your knee and let her put her arm round your neck while you rest your head on her shoulder. But you are not to fall asleep, and to make sure you don't I give you one of those kisses we know so well. What a pretty picture! If only the reality would be as kind to me! I'm afraid you may stay away a long time. Still, if you're happy and working hard I should be content. Dearest, my head will do whatever you wish, but my heart is too much a spoilt child to be able to accept with a good grace the privations you impose on it. . . .

He returned to the Rue Cassini at the end of October and asked Latouche to bring round some of his novel *Fragoletta* to read to him. This was the strange tale of a Neapolitan hermaphrodite on which Latouche had long been working. In return, Balzac promised to read him a scene from *Les Chouans*. 'All right, I'll come,' said Latouche. 'But only between five and six. I hope that after ten minutes of *Fragoletta* you will serve me the new fruit, a slice of that pear which was ripe when it had scarcely flowered. . . .' The occasion was a great success for Balzac. Not only did the difficult Latouche like his book, but he said so, which was still more remarkable. Of course there was still room for improvement, things that caused the man of taste to raise an eyebrow, but these were unimportant. The thing now was to publish it.

Latouche to Balzac: As for your book, *exeat*, a hundred times *exeat*! Why do you make me go on saying the same thing? God knows, I'm not refusing to listen to you read it—there's always pleasure and profit; but give me something new. Don't spend your whole time declining *Musa*, the Muse. I'm always ready to consult anyone whose talent I respect, and afterwards I tell them in the way of gratitude of the use I have made of this or that piece of advice; but once I've cooked the joint I don't start re-cooking it. It's high time you stopped, child that you are! If I knew the formulae of exorcism I'd use them here, because from the absolutely unexpected, absolutely inexplicable time which the overflowing Honoré, that volcano of novels who can turn one out in six weeks, is taking over his *Chouans* makes me feel that that book must be possessed of a devil. You must stop it! It is in four volumes that I want to see your Marquis, with his titles in gilt on a nice blue jacket! Haven't you been fondling the pampered infant long enough? We shall sell it like hot cakes. . . .

'*We* shall sell it . . .' Latouche had undertaken to fix up terms for the book with Urbain Canel. Balzac knew Canel well and had a great liking for his wife, whom he called La Miss, or Miss Anna, and whose glossy hair he stroked. But Canel did not want to undertake the printing costs, and it was Latouche who put up the money for this. We do not know if he was to have a share in the profit or if he was merely underwriting Canel against loss. In any event, Balzac was to receive only 1,000 francs for the first edition, which was, however, to be only 1,000 copies, the rights to revert to him when they were sold. Latouche wrote to Balzac: 'And now, if you're not the most Gascon of Gascons, a builder of castles in Spain, come along with your work in your hand, or at least with a promise on your lips. We're ready to sign the contract. . . .'

But signing a contract with Balzac was not easy. Latouche even went to the Rue Cassini, at the other end of Paris, only to find that he was away. He was spending most of his time at Versailles, at his parents' home or that of his sister, where he could always count on a bed and free meals. So what was to be done—follow him down there, or console oneself by writing insulting messages on the cottage wall? And then he complained about his lack of money!

Latouche to Balzac, 30 November 1828: Your situation is no different today from what it was on the 15th. Why worry about it? You're still the man who chose to live in the Rue Cassini without even being there, and who goes everywhere except to the places where money may be found; the man who fits himself out with luxurious carpets, mahogany bookshelves, expensive books, pictures and useless clocks; the man who has me running all over Paris with torches which he never lights, and who hasn't even enough money in his pocket to visit a sick friend! Anyone who mortgages himself to a decorator for two years ought to be in prison! A man can be happy in a creaking attic living on a crust, with friends who don't have to come ten miles to bring him courage, praise and laughter. That's what you really want. . . .

But was it what he wanted? What did he want? He no longer knew. He wrote to Latouche: 'My dear friend, I leave it to you. I give you *carte blanche* to negotiate on my behalf. . . . Do what you think best'. In his confused state of mind he went so far as to propose that he should come and live with Latouche near Aulnay, to which Latouche replied, 'And who is to pay the costs of this establishment of two people living in the backwoods? Who is to make the beds and cook lunch and dinner for two working men? Will you? The day wouldn't be long enough to get the housework done. . . . God help us, the next day we should be blacking each others' eyes! . . . Rue d'Enfer, Fougères, Versailles, Aulnay—what a devil of a lot of moving about! You'd be kicked out of a tribe of nomads for not staying still. Even the Wandering Jew wouldn't want you for a travelling-companion.'

This letter ended with an offer to buy any manuscript which Balzac had completed, 'cheap, but for cash'. Latouche had too much good sense not to realize that Honoré had none, and too much literary judgement not to know that he possessed outstanding talents. But the gifted young man caused him great vexation.

Finally, on 15 January 1829, the contract was signed and the advance paid. It only remained to persuade the author to part with his manuscript, which he obstinately clung to in the hope of making it into a masterpiece.

X

First Breath of Fame

Les feux de l'amour ne sont pas si doux que les premiers regards de la gloire.

VAUVENARGUES

Le Dernier Chouan (later *Les Chouans*) was a mysterious book. The Whites and the Blues, royalists and republicans, fought with a savage ferocity and 'shot each other down like rabbits'. As to which side Balzac favoured, he should by family and up- bringing have been a supporter of the Blues. General Pom- mereul, the former Bonapartist, must certainly have been sym- pathetic to them. The Blues had been regular troops led by trained officers, whereas the Whites fought like Red Indians. But Balzac made no attempt to pass judgement, he simply described the event. For him, as for Hegel, *Vendée* was an instance of the tragic workings of history. The Chouans were heroes born too late, inspired by high but outmoded motives. Amid the thickets and the wastelands the reader catches a glimpse of formidable shadows. The police-agent, Corentin, seeks to make use of a woman of ill-fame, Marie de Verneuil, who falls in love with the man she has promised to betray and goes with him to his death, after the most passionate and des- pairing of bridal-nights. The story ends with the picture of a peasant peacefully leading his cow across the market-place. He was the renowned Marche-à-Terre, the most ferocious of the *Chouans*, whom Pommereul may have pointed out to Balzac during one of their morning excursions. The most touching epilogues may be born of such chance encounters.

Balzac knew that he had written his first real novel. The career of Horace de Saint-Aubin was over, and Victor Morillon was never to be born. *Le Chouan* was signed Honoré Balzac. But he lacked all facility as a writer, or so he believed, and his first drafts were never good. He smothered the proofs with alterations and additions, and Latouche, who would have to foot the bill, was decidedly worried about the extra expense: 'What the devil has got into you. Forget about the black mark under your mistress's left tit, it's only a beauty-spot. . . .' Balzac had asked for a month in which to finish the book, but six weeks later he was still at it. He also wanted additional copies to give to his family, Madame de Berny and the Pommereuls. This was natural enough, but Latouche foamed: 'If I'd known you were going to add 500 copies to the cost, which I've got to get back on 1,000 copies, do you think I'd ever have gone into the business? . . .' Worst of all, he now never saw Balzac. 'I can only suppose you're sulking. An honest man flies into a rage, he doesn't sulk. . . .' The honest man was busy announcing the work to his friends:

Balzac to the Baron de Pommereul, 11 March 1829: But what am I saying?—my work. . . . It is partly yours, because the truth is that it is composed of the tales you so admirably and generously told me, over buttered biscuits and that excellent little wine of Graves. Everything, from the song '*Allons! Partons, belle!*' to the Tower of Melusine grew out of our talks. It is all yours, together with the author's heart and his pen and his remembrance. . . . I hope Madame de Pommereul will laugh at some of the details I have included—the ewers, the resin candles, the hedges, the stiles and the difficulty of getting to the ball—if indeed she is able to read so far without falling asleep. I have not forgotten your pretty wife's dislike of the title, *Le Gars*, and this has been changed. . . .

The book appeared in March 1829, and Latouche praised it in a review in *Le Figaro* and promoted other favourable reviews. But in spite of this it did not sell.

Latouche to Balzac, 15 April 1829: Praises are being showered on you in the press, thanks to our zeal. Perhaps it will sell in the end. For the present we have no more money and no advice to offer you. We don't see each other any more! You're running true to form. Was I wrong, my friend, when I told you my maxim, *The man who is not a misanthrope by the age of thirty was born heartless*? Good-bye, my dear egotist.

At the end of eight months, Urbain Canel had sold only 450 copies, and Latouche drew up his balance-sheet. He had not even got his money back. When his own novel, *Fragoletta*, appeared a little later Balzac reviewed it in the *Mercure* in a manner that was to say the least unenthusiastic, if not actually hostile. He discoursed on Naples, Vesuvius and the eighteenth Brumaire, but conveyed no idea of the novel itself. Of Latouche he said: 'It is the bitter laughter of a man who believes neither in happiness nor in liberty. . . . There are traces in him of Voltaire and Lord Byron. . . . Let those who are brave enough attempt to analyse this book. For myself, I do not dare. . . . M. Latouche's laconic style strikes like lightning. The reader is dazzled and does not know which way he is facing. Whatever my personal views may be, it is a book that will make a great impression, and it will be not a little praised and not a little blamed. . . .' In the fulsome atmosphere of the time, these were words that might have been written by an enemy, and Latouche was outraged. A prince of egotists, that Balzac! To say nothing of the fact that Charles Sedillot, the punctilious liquidator, was collecting the last debts owed to his cousin with 'a rather brutal conscientiousness', even from Monsieur de Latouche. 'It's really carrying things too far! For God's sake, Monsieur Sedillot!' And in a lyrical outburst Latouche wrote:

May the Devil take the Rue Cassini! May those living there be forever afflicted with aged mistresses, stale bread, iron forks, loathsome plots and prefaces full of apologies! . . .

The fact is that the two men had come to dislike one another. Latouche, fastidious, careful of his person and punctilious, was constantly exasperated by Balzac's casualness, his uncouth manners and bulky physique. Balzac enjoyed coarse jokes and dirty stories, to which Latouche responded with pursed lips. George Sand, who knew them both well, said: 'I have always thought that Latouche wasted too much of his real talent in talk, whereas Balzac wasted nothing but folly. He threw away the surplus and kept his deeper wisdom for his work.' Latouche told Balzac that his literary vanity was a form of clowning. Balzac retorted:

Because one has ideas which one can't dress up as gracefully and wittily as you do, it follows that one is vain. My God, what a lot of vain people there must be, because I have plenty of colleagues who can't express themselves any better than I. . . .

As for the *Chouan*, I once published a book at my own expense and lost a lot of money on it. I wasn't able, by myself, to procure the sale of a single copy, but the printer, without a line of advertising, sold 400. You're even more unfortunate than me, because you've had reviews but still sold only 300. To sell a book you *must* have favourable reviews in three papers, and they must be in a good position on one of the main pages. That is how *Le Chouan* will sell and in no other way, and may the Devil take me if my vanity has anything to do with it. . . .

But if *Le Chouan* had thus far earned no money, it had found its way into the hands of a few discriminating readers and it marked the beginning of Balzac's reputation.

Surville, the former student at the École Polytechnique, had put him in touch with other polytechnicians, instructors at the Military Academy of Saint-Cyr, near Versailles. There were very capable men among them, some of whom had read and enjoyed *Le Chouan*, and they had much to tell him of warfare and captivity. In particular there was Major Carraud, the Director of Studies, whose wife Zulma, a woman of great character, was to become one of Honoré's closest friends. She was a woman entirely without coquettishness, slightly deformed but with a warm and vivid face. He made her small presents, hoping that they would find a place in her family home at Issoudun: 'To be remembered by a rich spirit is one of my fondest illusions.' But it was no illusion. Zulma Carraud, truly a rich spirit, had the perception to see in Balzac a great man swamped in trivialities who came from time to time to forget his troubles at Saint-Cyr.

Madame Carraud had inherited the liberal principles of the eighteenth century from her father, Rémy Tourangin, deputy-mayor of Issoudun and a man of means. All her well-to-do bourgeois family had been republicans. Two of her brothers became deputies. Her husband had refused to vote for the Consulate, and his career had suffered in consequence. Both were generous in their friendship for Balzac.

Things were not going well with the Balzac family. His up-rooting had disagreed with Bernard-François. Sundered from Villeparisis and his old-man love-affairs, he was ageing rapidly, and self-doctoring and drugs had made him thoroughly ill. The doctors found at the end of April that he had a large abscess above the liver which needed draining; in fact, that his condition was serious. Madame Mère upbraided Honoré for his extravagance, money squandered on expensive furniture and other non-essentials when he was so heavily in debt, particularly to her. Laure defended him. It was true that he had bought a mahogany bookcase and had some of his books bound in full morocco, and at a pinch he would sell these and pass the money on to his mother. But in that case he would have to borrow the books from the Bibliothèque Nationale, and the cost of transport would be more than the proceeds of the sale. What else was there? A few yards of brocade, a few hangings, a carpet or two —mere trifles. Honoré himself did not feel in any way at fault and he was distressed by these constant reproaches. He needed peace and freedom from disturbance if he was to get any work done, and if now and then he briefly exchanged asceticism for luxury, surely this was natural? During his working hours the artist needed nothing but an attic and a crust of bread: 'But after these long flights of fancy, after dwelling in that peopled solitude, those enchanted palaces, he of all men most greatly stands in need of everything that civilization has devised for the distraction of the rich and leisured. . . .'

Only Laure, and perhaps her husband, really understood him. The attachment between brother and sister was as close as ever, and he wrote to her in February 1829:

When I am in trouble it is something on which I let my thoughts dwell as though on a mistress. Just now, sitting by my fire, I found myself making that fluttering movement with my arms, rather like the wings of a bird, which you make when you are pleased with yourself—with something you have said, or a thought, or a feeling, whatever it may be. So that made me think of you and I said, 'I must write and tell her how much I love her, and Surville too.' And so . . .

That relationship was as tender as any love-affair; but the real love-affairs were less easy to manage. After two years of the separation insisted upon by Madame de Berny he had returned to the Duchesse d'Abrantès, being no more capable than other men of resisting temptation. He visited her secretly at her small house in Versailles, and side by side at the window, during those summer nights so dear to lovers, they gazed at the stars and felt the 'pervading silence which fills the soul'. And, like all women with their first youth behind them, she talked of her tribulations, of hopes deceived, of a life withered before the coming of age. Melancholy is a telling form of coquetry. Honoré consoled her after the fashion of young men by saying, without believing it, that many women older than she had entered on a new lease of life. She scolded him for having sacrificed her to 'that old entanglement', and he made solemn false vows, promising to visit her more often—'but my sister mustn't know'. It was Madame de Berny he was really thinking of. Her generous treatment of him in his financial difficulties had restored her to favour with all the Balzac family, and she regularly visited Laure Surville in Versailles. She was fifty-two, but still the most passionate of mistresses:

Oh, my dear divinity, all I can do is live in ecstacy, entranced with memories. How can I make you feel my happiness? You would need to know yourself, which is impossible, and it is even more impossible for you to know what you mean to me. If I had longed in a wild dream for a heavenly lover, and if it had really happened, it would be nothing compared with what you have given me. Oh, what am I to do? Where shall I find the strength, the power, all that I seek, everything I need to deserve so great a love? Last night alone was like ten centuries. . . . Glory to you, honour, love . . .'

On another occasion she wrote: 'Glory to my darling with the first light of dawn, Glory to my sweet master! . . .' But she could not understand how so rich a heart could conceal something from one so adoring. She *knew* he was seeing the Duchesse again. Seated on her sofa, 'in that sacred place', he replied: 'Dearest Laure, how am I to break it off so abruptly? Must I not pay my debt to someone who seems to offer me everything?' But did he not owe a still greater debt to the woman who had sustained him in misfortune with her presence, her embraces and her money? She wrote: 'I must say again, in good faith, my dearest, that I do not believe that woman can be or wishes to be of any service to you. . . .'

Seated on the 'sacred sofa' he promised everything; but directly he was free he went back to Versailles, where he overhauled his duchess's writings and was rewarded after her fashion. Poor 'Dilecta' went on foot to the Rue Cassini, only to find him gone. She punished him by addressing him formally as *'vous'*: 'Will you be good enough to let me know if, regardless of sun or rain, I may venture to come to the Rue Cassini at three o'clock? . . .' But then she lapsed into tenderness—*'Adieu Didi . . . Adieu toi. . . .'*

Moralists may condemn these falsehoods and infidelities, but Balzac defends them: 'The man accustomed to make of his soul a mirror reflecting the whole world must necessarily lack that particular kind of logic and obstinacy which we call "character". He has a touch of the strumpet. . . . He longs like a child for everything that takes his fancy. . . . He will love to idolatry and then desert his mistress for no apparent reason. . . .' Among primitive peoples those possessing second sight, the singers and tellers of tales, were held to be privileged; but in these days, 'when a light shines too brightly everyone rushes to put it out, because they think the house is on fire'. Thus did he assert his right to inconstancy.

For him there were two kinds of love, to which he added a third compounded of the other two. His café friends had infected him with a taste for sexual promiscuity: 'Nature has given me an appetite, we should try to fast as little as possible . . . make love as the laws of society require, observe the code and follow the etiquette, acquit ourselves of our duty, as with dancing, fencing or singing. . . .' Love of this sort was of its nature trivial, something to be gratified by any white and pink expanse of flesh that came within reach. But neither desire nor passion was the whole of love: 'Men and women may, without doing themselves dishonour, indulge in many loves—it is natural to go in pursuit of happiness! But in every life there is only one true love.' He believed he had found this in Laure de Berny. At once sensual, wise and tender, she had been for him 'an angel descended from Heaven'. She had shaped and guided and revealed him to himself, and without her his genius would perhaps never have flowered. He knew it well.

His love for her was a mingling of physical passion and deep affection, fickle only where the first was concerned. Beyond all earthly love Balzac looked for something wholly angelic, a woman who would play the part of a sublime sister of mercy, content to nurse his genius without making physical demands. But no woman is all angel. Laure de Berny's touching devotion could not stifle her bodily needs. It could not abolish the antagonism, inherent in human nature, between profane and spiritual love; or that other antagonism, special to the creative artist, between the woman and his work. Every woman who loves an artist is condemned sooner or later to suffering.

Bernard-François died on 19 June, at the age of eighty-three. He too became a 'deserter' from the Tontine Lafarge; and having put everything he could into annuities, since he believed himself to be immortal, he left his widow very badly off. The announcement of his death was signed by Surville and Mont-zaigle. Honoré seems to have been away. Possibly he was working at La Bouleaunière, near Nemours, a house which Madame de Berny had rented, having sold the one in Ville-parisis. He probably returned to Paris for the funeral, which took place at the Église Saint-Merry.

But it was becoming a different Paris from the one he had hitherto known, the circumscribed world of the Marais families, the seedy world of lawyers, impecunious writers, publishers, discounters and money-lenders. It was growing larger. The friendship of Latouche, and the *succès d'estime* of *Les Chouans* had opened a few distinguished doors. On Wednesday nights he went to the studio of François Gérard, man-about-town as well as painter, and here met a select circle which included Delacroix, David d'Angers, and Ary Scheffer, as well as poets, scholars, statesmen, 'fashionables' and pretty women. He has left us an account of these gatherings. There would be one or two painters with their subject ready made, working by the light of the lamps while they listened to the talk. Balzac, waiting for the moment 'when brilliant controversy gave way to anecdote', heard many interesting tales.

Ideas for novels and short stories came to him without effort: 'The artist himself does not know the secrets of his own mind. . . . He does not belong to himself. He is at the mercy of an impulse that is eminently capricious. . . . On some days he does not write a line, and if he attempts to, it is not he who holds the pen but his double, his other self, the man who enjoys riding or making jokes . . . but has not the wit to invent anything except foolery. . . . And then one evening when he is walking down the street, or one morning when he is getting up, a glowing ember lights his brain, his hands, his tongue. . . . His work is there with all its fires ablaze. . . . This is the ecstacy of conception, hiding the agonizing pangs of birth. . . .' A man may contain both clown and poet within the sack which is his skin, and Balzac was well aware of the duality.

Without being a part of the new romantic movement, he rubbed shoulders with it. In July 1829 he was invited to the reading of *Marion de Lorme*. The author, Victor Hugo, then aged twenty-seven, with a charming wife and three children, was already a master in the eyes of the younger generation. Alfred de Vigny, the author of *Éloa* and *Cinq-Mars*, who was then adapting Shakespeare's *Othello* for the French stage, was also present, and Prosper Mérimée, Sainte-Beuve and Alfred de Musset were other young men who encircled Hugo with their growing reputations. The illustrious Alexandre Dumas flourished his huge arms in delight. But Balzac, 'poor Balzac', who had only just buried Horace de Saint-Aubin, had no followers. Sainte-Beuve, that little monkey of a man, a zealous supporter of the great Victor, had never even heard of the author of *Le Chouan*. For fear of weeping, Balzac hastened to make fun of those Scenes of Literary Life:

Miserable newcomer admitted for the first time to that social mystery, what manner are you to adopt? Are you to applaud, to cry 'Bravo!' What shallow praise! You are lost if you do anything of the kind. There is only one safe course for you, an attitude of suffocated silence because your rapture is so great that the words stick in your throat. Or, if you have been introduced by a close friend you may approach the reader with tears of gratitude in your eyes, and clasping him warmly by the hand exclaim in broken accents:
'Thank you! Thank you!'
This is sound policy. It attracts notice and is not lacking in elegance. . . . The reading proceeds, and the comments begin to be heard:
'How very Moorish!' says one.
'Truly African!' says another.
'But with a touch of Spain!' says a third.
'You can positively see the minarets in that verse!'
'The whole Orient!'

Upon my sacred oath, I have heard those words spoken in my presence, referring to Africa and Spain—'The whole Orient!'

'Miraculous' and 'immense' are the mildest adjectives that can be applied to an ode of fifteen lines. . . . And when it comes to an entire play, then—'The whole of history portrayed in action . . . The unveiling of the future . . . The world! . . . The Universe . . . God! . . .'*

The Duchesse d'Abrantès had acquired a lodging at the Abbaye-aux-Bois, a peaceful and secluded spot where, in a hostel separate from the convent, the nuns gave shelter to ladies of quality who wished to go into semi-retreat. Madame Récamier lived there, ruined but still great in beauty, constancy and a reputation extending beyond the bounds of Europe.

It was an immense honour to be received by the 'divine Juliette' in her small apartment on the third floor, where a magical spell seemed to diminish the steepness of the stairs. People of all shades of opinion met and mingled there. Chateaubriand chatted to Benjamin Constant and Lamartine, Madame la Duchesse du Faubourg Saint-Germain exchanged courtesies with Madame la Duchesse Impériale, and Madame d'Abrantès introduced Balzac.

'Look closely at that dark-eyed, dark-haired young man. Look at his nose and above all his mouth when a sly thought causes it to turn up at the corners. You may catch a gleam of scorn, even of malice, in his eyes, which nevertheless show kindness for his friends. He is Monsieur de Balzac. Although he is only thirty, many books have already issued from his pen.'

Étienne Delécluze, a member of the Académie, who was present on the day Balzac was first 'received', never forgot his naïve, almost childish gratification: 'He had to keep a tight hold on all the wits that were left to him to avoid flinging himself into the arms of his fellow-guests.' This excessive rapture might have looked absurd, but Delécluze was touched by the young man's spontaneity, and sitting down beside him found him to be highly intelligent. The intensity of his longing, and the long period of waiting, may perhaps excuse his too-manifest delight.

* Balzac, *Des salons littéraires et des mots élogieux*. An essay published in the review *La Mode*, November, 1830

At about the same time he made the acquaintance of Fortunée Hamelin, one of the *Merveilleuses* in the days of the Directory, who could tell him a thousand romantic tales. Sophie Gay, whose salon was frequented by the young writers of the romantic school, also received him. She had once scored a point off the Emperor himself:

'Has no one told you that I don't like clever women?'

'Yes, Sire, but I didn't believe it.'

It was said of Sophie Gay that she did everything well—books, children and preserves. In her salon and that of the Comtesse Merlin, the mistress of his friend Philarète Chasles, Balzac began to meet the 'world'—that is to say, the two or three thousand people who knew each other, visited each other and, having nothing else to do, cultivated their finer feelings. But his frank pleasure at being accepted and invited by these exclusive beings was mitigated by the realization that they only tolerated him: 'I suffered in every way in which one can feel suffering. Only women and those who are slighted know how to observe, because everything touches their feelings and observation is born of wounds.' The young fashionables in their yellow gloves, the lovers of those goddesses, looked down their noses at the badly-dressed or over-dressed newcomer; and he, taking the measure of the blockheads they were, both envied and despised them.

As for the women, adorable and inaccessible, he could only worship from afar. Yet, how he longed for them!

How glorious is love arrayed in silks, reclined on cashmere, surrounded with marvels of luxury which marvellously adorn it, perhaps because it is itself a luxury. I love to titillate my senses with ravishing *toilettes*, to crush flowers, to plunge a devastating hand into the elegant structure of a flawless *coiffure*. . . . I am enchanted by aristocratic women with their remote smiles, their distinguished manners, the value they put on themselves. When they set up barriers between themselves and the world, they flatter all those vanities in me which are halfway to love. My felicity seems to have more savour when it is desired of all men. In doing none of the things done by other women, not walking or living like them, in swathing herself in a cloak that other women cannot possess, in breathing a scent that is all her own, my mistress seems all the more mine. The more remote she is

from earth, even in the more earthly moments of love, the more
exquisite does she become in my eyes. . . .

Was he capable of pleasing those rare creatures? More than he
thought. He amused them, which was half the battle. His voice
was attractive, and there was warmth and goodness in his face.
He might play the lecherous monk or the boisterous commercial
traveller among his friends, but in the fashionable salons he
knew how to control his tongue, to interest and to charm. He
said one day to a young acquaintance: 'You find it surprising no
doubt that delicate concepts and subtle thoughts should come
out of this crude outer shell.' It may have been surprising; but
the women who listened to him knew that it was true.

When he saw their eyes grow gentle he felt the approach of
triumphs. Only two years previously he had had to go into
hiding after the most lamentable of failures. He had known
neither 'happy childhood nor fruitful springtime'. But he was
beginning to have faith in himself. He would write great books
and compel Paris, indifferent and formidable, to accept him.
The worshipping, faithful Laure de Berny still sustained him.
He was making progress, for all his defeats. He knew his weaknesses, the touch of vulgarity, the lack of taste which he derived
from his family, the childish love of luxury. But he also knew his
strength, the tremendous creative energy, the fire and imagination, the wit and high intelligence. He was long to look back on
this stage of his life as a period of indomitable growth which,
often though he was assailed by feelings of apprehension and
shaken confidence, by its very impetus enabled him to conquer
them; and he was to enrich the finest of his novels with the
memories, painful and marvellous, of his youth and lost illusions.

Part Two

FAME

*Après cet âge rapide comme
une semaison, vient celui de
l'exécution. Il est en quelque
sorte deux jeunesses, la jeunesse
durant laquelle on croit, la
jeunesse pendant laquelle on
agit; souvent elles se con-
fondent chez les hommes que la
nature à favorisés et qui sort,
comme César, Newton et
Bonaparte, les plus grands
parmi les grands hommes.*

BALZAC

XI

The Years of Growth

N A SHORT time Balzac's success was established. *La Physio-
ogie du mariage*, 'by a young bachelor', appeared in December
1829. The brilliant, uninhibited book revealed an astonishing
knowledge of women. It owed much to the author's own
experience, to the confidences of Madame de Berny and the
Duchesse d'Abrantès, to Fortunée Hamelin and Sophie Gay, to
his father, who had never ceased to discourse vigorously and
humorously on the subject of marriage, and finally to Villers-La
Faye, the retired philanderer and sceptical pundit of the Ancien
Régime. In the mingled lyricism, humour and cynicism of its
style it recalled both Rabelais and Sterne, as Balzac had hoped
it would, and here and there it foreshadowed the romantic tales
of Alfred de Musset and Théophile Gautier. But beneath the
flippant surface and eighteenth-century bawdiness it had serious
things to say. Balzac used it to propound his whole philosophy of
creative energy and the unity of the world.

The basic theme is that 'marriage is not born of Nature', that
there is little connection between romantic love and the reproductive instinct, and that most husbands play on their
wives' feelings like a monkey playing the violin, and are in
consequence 'minotaurized'—that is to say, betrayed by better
musicians. The stratagems resorted to by wives, the precautions
available to a husband, the signs heralding his downfall, the
functioning of the marital police-system, the pitfalls awaiting the
adulterous wife, the means whereby the adroit husband may
steer her into safe channels—these are among the matters it
discourses upon. Marriage, says the 'young bachelor', is a
battle, a civil war requiring weapons and strategy, in which

victory (meaning personal liberty) goes to the better general.

Balzac was on the side of the wife. He confessed to having been advised by two ladies, one of whom was 'among the most humane and intelligent at the Court of Napoleon' and both of whom had talked to him with great frankness. He showed women to be scheming and dishonest, but forgave them; they were not to be held responsible for their shortcomings, which were due to the state imposed on them by society and to their husbands' blindness. To some extent his ideas on the equality of the sexes were borrowed from Saint-Simon, whose doctrines he had first heard of from little Père Dablin, who had corresponded with him; and later he had printed the review, *Le Gymnase*, the organ of the 'Saint-Simoniens', on his presses in the Rue des Marais-Saint-Germain. 'A woman's heart is given, it is not sold,' said *Le Gymnase*. And so, things being what they were, marriage became a conflict. But in war one fights with whatever weapons are available, and the husband is the enemy, unless . . . Unless, instead of abusing the 'rights' which the law allows him, he seeks to win his wife's affection and obeys the law of the heart, which requires that possession shall be knit with love. 'It follows that, if he is to be happy, a man must conform to certain rules of honour and delicacy.'

Women devoured the book, which, in setting forth their grievances, expressed what many of them thought and few dared to say. Some were shocked by it. Zulma Carraud wrote an indignant letter from Saint-Cyr, to which Balzac replied:

Your feeling of revulsion, Madame, after reading the first pages of the book which I brought you, does you too much honour and is too sensitive for anyone, even the author, to be offended by it. It proves that you do not live in a world of falseness and perfidy, that you do not know the kind of society that sullies everything, and that you are worthy of that solitude in which men always grow great and noble and pure.

It is perhaps the author's misfortune that you did not overcome the first indignation which assails every innocent-minded person when they hear a tale of crime or disaster, or when they read Juvenal or Rabelais or Perse or Boileau, for I believe that later you would have been reconciled to him, when you came to read certain strong strictures and vigorous arguments on the side of virtue and of women; but how shall I reproach you for a repugnance deserving of praise? . . .

What is admirable is that the 'seer' understood it all, the genuine high-mindedness of Madame Carraud no less than the silk-smooth scheming of the Duchesse d'Abrantès.

The *Physiologie du mariage* contained endless matter for works of fiction, an immense store of scenes and embryonic plots. While he was writing his *Codes*, Balzac had started a day-book of notes and observations, rather on the lines of Lavater or Gavarni. The present trend in fiction was away from the historical novel and towards the novel of middle-class life. Why should he not write short tales which would be studies of contemporary life and morals? Why spend his time in lengthy, erudite research when he could dramatize the history of his age? He proceeded to do this, using settings and social groups of which he had first-hand knowledge. *La Maison du chat qui pelote*, was based on the draper's shop of the Sallambier family, in the Rue Saint-Denis. The rotunda in *Le Bal de Sceaux* was a dancing-hall which he and his sisters had often visited. *La Vendetta*, based on a story told him by the Duchesse d'Abrantès, started at the Imperial Court and moved on to an artist's studio where young ladies from the Marais, like Laure and Laurence, and others from the Faubourg Saint-Germain came to take lessons in painting. *Une Double Famille* began in Bayeux.

These 'Scenes of Private Life', penetrating deeply into the homes and privacies of everyday families, represented a sharp departure from the extravagant melodrama of his early writings, both in the realism of their settings and characters and in their subtlety of feeling. He found that the time he was living in had its own melodrama, arising out of the clash of different strata of society—Ancien Régime, Empire and Restoration—and its great political upheavals, above all the return from Elba and the second Restoration. His stroke of genius was to endow contemporary realism with some of the qualities of the historical novel, filling out broad political and social concepts with vivid and meticulous descriptions of detail. France in that turbulent period was the battleground of an aristocracy that had learnt nothing, a bourgeoisie that was gaining possession of the nation's wealth, and the powers of high finance and industry;

while the working class, still profoundly dissatisfied, harboured future revolts.

Balzac gained the perspective he needed by setting his scene in the very recent past. His picture of Monsieur Guillaume's shop, in *La Maison du chat qui pelote*, illustrated the paternalism as well as the daily routine of a small private business under Napoleon. With instinctive shrewdness he endowed nearly all these tales with the social and moral values of the popular romance. Augustine Guillaume, the draper's daughter, marries out of her class, and it is not long before her husband, a fashionable painter who was infatuated with her beauty, deserts her for a duchess. She dies of despair; whereas her elder sister, Virginie, who makes do with their father's principal assistant, settles down to a life of quiet prosperity, the pair eventually taking over the business. In other stories we meet Gobseck, a remarkable portrait of a money-lender, moon-faced and thin-lipped, whose dealings serve to illustrate, through the misfortunes of his customers, the disasters arising out of social misconduct. The story, *Une Double Famille*, depicts both the ravages caused by bigotry and the dangers of free love.

The theme of nearly all these *Scènes de la vie privée* is happiness or unhappiness in marriage. Nearly all uphold respectable middle-class tradition and marital fidelity, however contrary to natural instincts these may be: 'We are punished sooner or later for not having bowed to the laws of society.' A conformist attitude remarkable in the 'young bachelor' who at the time was deceiving Monsieur de Berny with his wife, and the latter with the Duchesse d'Abrantès. But he had witnessed the unhappy fruits of adultery in his own family circle. His mother had visited the deplorable Henry upon them, and his father had marred the last years of his life with his rustic vagaries.

His family had also taught him the effects of snobbishness and over-ambition in matrimonial matters. Laure for a time had behaved very much like Émilie de Fontaine in *Le Bal de Sceaux*, although in the end she had seen the error of her ways and made a fairly sensible marriage; Laurence, on the other hand, had been sacrificed to a high-sounding name. Wills and inheritances had loomed as large in the lives of the Balzac, Sallambier, Sedillot and Malus families as they did in the chambers of the notary, Maître Guillonnet-Merville. Balzac had no illusions about that bourgeois world and the part played in it by money. His *Scènes* presented a true picture of the customs and morals of a particular social class at that time. It was still not a very extensive class; but what matters to a novelist is not to know *all things* but to know *thoroughly*—to be master of his material, and to penetrate to the heart of the world which actually surrounds him.

A work of particular interest is *La Femme de trente ans*. It was scarcely a novel, rather a series of episodes written separately and afterwards rather clumsily linked. The first episode appeared in 1831 in *La Caricature* with the title, *La Dernière Revue de Napoléon*. It is the story of a girl who drags her father to a military review at the Tuileries because she has fallen in love with a handsome colonel, and it throws a brilliant light on the world of the Empire. It was followed a month later by *Les Deux Rencontres*, in which a general's wife (possibly the colonel of the first story) has a love-affair with another man, whereupon her daughter, learning about it, elopes with a highly improbable 'Parisian pirate' who becomes a Byronic corsair. This extravaganza is all too like the 'black 'novels of his early period. Then, in September and October 1831, he published *Le Rendez-vous*, a novella in five episodes which leaves us in no doubt that the heroine, Julie d'Aiglemont, is the lovelorn girl of the Tuileries. Her husband has been unfaithful to her and she is now in love with an Englishman, Lord Arthur Grenville. The string of tales, slightly modified, were published in one volume under the title *Même histoire*; but it was not until 1842 that the book appeared in its definitive form, and with the title *La Femme de trente ans*. It is one of Balzac's least finished works; the separate parts do not hang together. Yet it has great qualities. The confessions of the ageing, disillusioned Madame d'Aiglemont recall moonlit confidences made to Honoré de Balzac on a garden-bench in Villeparisis. They have a glow of the '*poème* Berny'.

Where his personal life was concerned, after 1829 Balzac had fewer grievances against society. His overflowing energies seemed at last to have found their outlet. Success had partly opened the door to the magic circle of the Romantics, although he remained on the outskirts of that movement and in an anonymous article was cruelly derisive of Hugo's *Hernani*. He felt very much closer to the classical tradition of Corneille, Molière and La

Fontaine. Such leaning as he had towards Romanticism was only due to his fondness for Scott, Byron, Rabelais and all rebels. But heretic though he was, his works were not ill-received. Unknown women wrote to him, seeing themselves in his heroines, and the *Scènes de la vie privée*, decorous without being prudish, were reassuring to feminine readers who had been shocked by the outspokenness of his *Physiologie du mariage*. His books were sought-after in public reading-rooms, and publishers were asking for more. As his reputation grew, former school-fellows at Vendôme, who had not been too kind to him in the past, recalled themselves to his notice. But he had been plunged too deeply in misfortune to be able to forget what it was like. He saw behind the masks: 'Those serene, smiling faces, those smooth foreheads concealed odious calculations; the protestations of friendship were false, and many a man was less mistrustful of his enemies than of his friends.' If vanity was the vice that rotted high society, the bourgeois world had vices of its own, above all the passion for money. 'To have or not to have investments, that is the question.' The more Balzac observed the scene, the more did he come to believe that money, 'the modern god', was the mainspring of contemporary society. The upper class needed it to sustain them in rank and luxury; the middle-class amassed it 'more for the sake of security than from any instinct of enjoyment'; and the money-lender Gobseck loved wealth as an abstraction, for its own sake. 'Gold represents all the forces of mankind,' says Gobseck. 'Is not our life a machine set in motion by money? . . . Gold is the spiritual doctrine of present-day societies.' Gobseck knew all there was to be known about Paris. He kept a close eye on the sons of well-to-do families, on theatre people and women of fashion. Outside business hours he was honest and even generous in his way; but since the struggle between rich and poor was unavoidable it was better to be an exploiter than one of the exploited. 'The little withered old man had grown,' the advocate, Derville, says of him. 'He was transformed beneath my eyes into a fantastic image personifying the power of gold.'

A fantastic image . . . In this sense the money-lender, a typically 'Balzacien' character, at once true and larger than life, recalls the early novels. The *Scènes de la vie privée* still deals in crimes, monsters and gallant protectors, as did the outpourings of Horace de Saint-Aubin; but the crimes are now within the law, the monsters have recognizable faces, the protectors are magistrates. Young though he still is, their creator has seen and suffered a great deal. He is revolted and bitter, but with the intelligence to rise above revolt and bitterness and say boldly: 'That is how it is.' His philosophy pervades his descriptions. He describes not for the sake of describing, but in order to show how the truth of a man's character is manifest in his face, his attire, his house, his unconsidered gestures. Thinking as a philosopher, and above all as a scientific investigator, Balzac seeks to relate the visible effect to the hidden cause. Again and again in his work one comes upon the words, '*Voici pourquoi.*'— 'This is why.'—and then follows the detailed explanation, sometimes startling but always profound.

It was not only in books that he displayed his remarkable knowledge of contemporary life. He was writing countless articles. He, too, needed money, to pay his current debts and run up new ones, and journalism was a quicker way of earning it than books. The periodical press at the time was being considerably enlivened by Émile de Girardin, a young man of enterprise and originality. An illegitimate child brought up in private, without ties or scholastic discipline, he was one of the generation which had been 'radically cured' of Chateaubriand's *René*, and believed in attacking instead of moaning. In 1828 he started a paper called *Le Voleur*, and in 1829 another called *La Silhouette*, illustrated by caricaturists such as Gavarni and Henri Monnier. Balzac was much attracted by their harsh, irreverent drawings. Like him, they created types; and like him Gavarni conveyed 'the impression of a garment, the thought within a dress'. Henri Monnier's 'Monsieur Prudhomme' was the prototype of the *bourgeois balzacien*.

The editor of *La Silhouette* was Victor Ratier, a friend of Balzac who published a first piece by him in January 1830. Later he introduced him to *La Mode*, another publication in the Girardin group. The Goncourt *Journals* contain a description of Balzac as Gavarni first saw him, based on Gavarni's own account: '. . . a plump little man with attractive dark eyes and a slightly bent, turned-up nose, who talked a great deal and very loud. He [Gavarni] mistook him for a bookseller's assistant.' But not for long. Whether the little man talked or wrote, the sparks flew; his zest and humour brought the most common-place subject to life.

It is not easy to establish a list of Balzac's contributions to these reviews because Girardin's team of writers were given to signing their pieces with invented initials or interchangeable pseudonyms. *Étude de moeurs par les gants*, in which a 'small and lively countess' deduces the characters and love-affairs of a number of men from their gloves, was certainly his; he was obsessed with the subject. There is also a piece on *Les Mots à la mode* in which he makes fun of current fashions in words. The word *actualité* (topicality) was then coming into use: 'In these days books, like everything else, must possess *actualité*.' And one could no longer, in that year of 1830, say of an actress, 'She was sublime last night', but 'She was *étourdissante* [stunning]', this being the high peak of praise; and at the other extreme one said, 'It was *outrageously* bad.' When it came to philosophy, the meaning had to be wrapped up in sentences like this: 'The reproductive power of reflection does not extend to certain phenomena, because if reflection is a totality it is a totality that is confused.' A fashion which still persists . . .

But despite his success as a journalist and in the literary salons, Balzac still felt a little lost in the company of men already accustomed to fame. What was he compared with Cuvier, Victor Hugo, de Vigny, Charles Nodier or Eugène Delacroix? His clothes caused dismay, his vitality astonished. 'Monsieur de Balzac is here,' Fontaney noted in his *Journal*, 'and at last I have seen him, this new star of growing renown—plump, bright-eyed, wearing a white waistcoat, the bearing of a herbalist, the clothes of a butcher, the look of a gilder, the whole very impressive.' Delacroix found something inappropriate in his general get-up, adding 'and gap-toothed already!' The Comte de Falloux found him heavy and cumbersome: 'Many people are delighted by his lively imagination and readiness of speech, but disenchanted by his vanity and lack of good sense.' He was more or less accepted by 'the best people', but was not one of them. Fortunately! It enabled him 'to observe society out of the corner of his eyes and so discover the non-appearance of its appearances'.

His own appearance came as a shock—the unkempt, pom-aded hair rising in a tangle on his head, and the plump, flabby-looking face. When he entered a drawing-room, pre-maturely pot-bellied and a little out of breath, his feminine admirers were inclined to ask, 'Can this really be Balzac?' But directly the gold-flecked eyes were turned upon them their doubts vanished. It was as though a tempest, an electric storm, had swept into the room. The little, broad-shouldered man began to talk, and the ladies listened in delight. How could any writer be accused of vulgarity whose mind was so brilliant, whose distinction so undeniable?

But still there were men who kept aloof, either from envy or because they lacked the quality to appreciate his own, and he was too sensitive not to guess what some people thought of his manners and looks. It caused him great distress: 'I realized many things, things which it is grievous to know, so that my heart was filled with disgust for this world. . . . Those people taught me to understand Rousseau.' He consoled himself with the thought that a creative artist needs to be unhappy: 'The man of talent may look like a fool ten times a day, and the men who shine in the *salons* will find it easy to prove that he ought to be a shop-assistant. His thoughts travel farther; he does not notice the trifles to which the world attaches so much importance.' What he found even more intolerable was the fatuous self-satisfaction of the newly-rich middle-class: 'The power of money is bringing us to the most dreary of aristocracies, that of the strong-box.'

But he was no revolutionary. A bourgeois of the Marais, a lover of aristocratic women, he had no wish for violent change. He condemned the extremists on both sides. In the *Scènes de la vie privée* he deplores the follies of the counter-revolutionary and anti-Bonapartist purges. All forms of bigotry shocked him. In the Abbé Fontanon, the confessor of Angélique de Granville (*Une Double Famille*), he gives us a picture of an ambitious, hypocritical priest which might have been drawn by the anti-clerical Stendhal. Two years later, in *Le Curé de Tours*, he was to denounce the hidden influence of the *Congrégation*, that association of priests and laymen for the manipulation of power, by grace of which the chaplain had his say in the promotion of army-officers and the vicar-general in the appointing of Prefects. In *Le Bal de Sceaux* he speaks through the mouth of the Comte de Fontaine, a supporter of the Vendée who refuses to serve under Napoleon and at first condemns Louis XVIII for his opportunism, but later comes to understand that philosophical monarch and to accept his middle-of-the-road liberalism. A compromise had to be found between the post-revolutionary new-rich and the unrepentant emigrés, if the nation was to be spared further upheavals. The essential thing was that the central authority should be strong enough to enforce this compromise: 'Politics is the technique of the balance of forces.'

It has been wrongly said that Balzac became a monarchist for purely self-interested reasons, to gain admittance to some fashionable salon or win the favours of some high-born lady. The truth is that he was never a thorough-going legitimist. Unlike Chateaubriand, he never became sentimentally devoted to *his* King. But on the other hand, he was never wholly a man of the Opposition, like Carraud or Surville. What he looked for were solutions appropriate to the existing state of affairs. Any revolution brought about fundamental changes, so that afterwards one could not act as though it had never taken place: 'Once a revolution has passed into the realm of facts and ideas it is indestructible; it can only be accepted as a fact.' He looked with a clear-sighted sympathy upon 'the noble champion amid the ruins', but he acquiesced in the course of historical evolution, knowing it to be irreversible.

In May 1830, he published in *La Mode* a strange tale entitled *Les Deux Rêves*. A small party is assembled in a salon in the year 1786. It consists of Calonne (finance minister under Louis XVI, whose frauds and extravagance did much to destroy the monarchy), Beaumarchais, the narrator and two unknowns, a surgeon and a provincial advocate, whom the reader at once guesses to be Marat and Robespierre. Each of them recounts a dream. Robespierre tells of his meeting in a dream with Catherine de' Medici, who explains what happened on the night of St Bartholomew. For her it was in no sense a matter of cruelty, religious fanaticism or personal ambition, but simply of political expediency: 'If our power was to be effective at that time it was necessary that the State should have one God, one faith and one master.' The massacre, appalling thought it was, had seemed to be the only way of averting other and worse blood-baths. 'And you, too, who listen to me . . . ,' she says to

Robespierre, and the reader is left to finish the sentence. 'I found,' concludes Robespierre, 'that there was something in me which subscribed to the abominable creed of that Italian woman.' As we know, the advocate from Arras was destined to follow her example and kill in order to preserve the unity of the State. But what did the son of Bernard-François think of those methods, which history shows to have been not altogether successful? It seems that he was not very far from approving of Catherine— and Machiavelli and Robespierre and Metternich. He wrote at about that time: 'He became a great statesman because he despised mankind. Has not this feeling always been the secret of the men we admire? . . .'

The Duchesse d'Abrantès gave him a minor lesson in Machiavellism. She got him to edit her memoirs, and when they were successfully published calmly denied that he had had anything to do with them. 'I had to,' she told him. 'Do you want me to be deprived of the little merit there is in having produced this humble work? . . . I warn you . . . be sensible and *don't say a word.* You want so much to be well thought of; you must surely realize that nothing could make you appear more odious or more vulgar. . . .' At the same time another of his women friends, Zulma Carraud, was playing the part of anti-Machiavelli. Balzac was unable to visit her at Saint-Cyr as often as he would have liked; too much of his time was taken up with writing and proof-correcting: 'The days melt in my hands like ice in the sun. I don't live, I exhaust myself dreadfully—but whether one dies of work or anything else, it comes to the same thing. . . .' Madame Carraud, the staunch Republican, accused him of political opportunism. 'You must not accuse me of unpatriotism,' he replied, 'because my intelligence enables me to cast the exact account of men and affairs. It's like quarrelling with a balance-sheet because it shows a loss. After every revolution, genius in government consists in bringing about a fusion; which is what Napoleon and Louis XVIII did, both men of talent.' Policy in action must be practical, not based on preconceived ideas. Balzac felt this; Zulma Carraud denied it.

But amid all the stresses, the invective and the contradictions, the haven of peace was still Madame de Berny. His Dilecta was perhaps no longer physically desirable, but there was none more ready than she to serve him. She had shaped him, and now he had passed beyond her. She asked no more than 'her humble place at the feet of the child grown big over whom she still watched with a mother's eye'. Her very great merit, from a writer's point of view, was that he always worked well when he was with her. At some time in May or June 1830, he decided that they should go into retirement together in Touraine. They rented a charming old house called La Grenadière at Saint-Cyr-sur-Loire (the village where he had been put out to nurse), from the terrace of which they had a view over the lovely valley, the city of Tours, the islands, church-towers and châteaux. The road to it ran gently uphill, through vineyards. It was the perfect retreat, for work and for love. Before settling in they made a boat-trip down the Loire, visiting Saumur, Le Croisic and Guérande, and all these places were stored away in Balzac's indefatigably retentive mind.

He wrote to Victor Ratier in July:

If only you knew what Touraine is like! . . . It is a place where one forgets everything. I can forgive the inhabitants for being stupid, they're so happy. As you know, people who enjoy life very much are naturally stupid. Touraine admirably explains the *lazzarone*. I have come to regard fame, the Chambre des Deputés, politics, the future and literature as nothing but bullets for the killing of stray dogs . . . and I say, 'Virtue, happiness and life are simply six hundred francs a year on the banks of the Loire. . . .'

Touraine gives me a feeling of being up to the neck in *foie gras*, and its delicious wine, instead of making you drunk, makes you feel drowsy and beatific. So I've rented a cottage until November, because when I shut my windows I can work, and I don't want to see the luxury of Paris again until I'm well stocked with literary goods.

Let me tell you also that I have made the most poetic journey that it is possible to make in France. To travel from here by water to the end of Brittany, to the sea, does not cost much, only three or four sous a league, and you glide between the sunniest river-banks in the world; I felt my thoughts swell with the river, which becomes enormous as it draws near the sea. . . .

Upon my soul, my friend, I believe that writing in these days is a street girl's calling, prostitution at a hundred sous a time! It leads nowhere, and I have an itch to wander, to search, to engage in living drama, to risk my life—for what do they matter, a few wretched years more or less! . . . Oh, when one looks up at this magnificent sky on a fine night one is ready to undo one's flybuttons and piss on the heads of all the royalties! Since seeing these true splendours, like a beautiful, sound fruit, like a golden insect, I have become very philosophical, and in particular when I set my foot on an ant-heap I say with the immortal Bonaparte, 'This, or mankind! . . . What difference between them, seen from Saturn or Venus or the Pole Star? . . .'

Small wonder if this cosmic view of things led him into frivolous writings. Why trouble to be serious when one is writing for an ant-heap? He began a *Traité de la vie élégante*, a light-hearted work in the style of his *Physiologie du mariage*, extolling idlers, Beau Brummell, all foppery and elegance of dress. 'Is it worthy of me?' he asked *La Dilecta*. She was not sure. But he would not listen to criticism—'Ta-ta-ta!' he said. Madame de Berny went to Paris, taking the beginning of this work with her; so that Balzac was alone at La Grenadière when the revolution of 1830 occurred at the end of July. He had heard in May of the suicide of his friend Auguste Sautelet. That unhappy young man had seemed to be on the way to success. Publisher as well as advocate, he had recently joined Girardin and Balzac in launching a literary review, the *Feuilleton des Journaux Politiques*. Stendhal says that he killed himself because of a woman. Balzac grieved for the 'weak and excellent young man' until the events leading to the July Monarchy put him out of his mind.

'Concessions were the downfall of Louis XVI,' said Charles X, the successor of Louis XVIII. 'I must either ride on horseback or in a cart.' He did neither. The three 'Glorious Days' (28, 29 and 30 July) drove him out of France. The people would have voted for a republic if they had had the chance; but Lafayette thrust a *tricolore* flag into the hands of Louis-Philippe, Duc d'Orléans, and had him proclaimed King of the French. France remained smouldering with rage. Balzac, in the calm of La Grenadière, took very little notice of what was happening. He finished his *Vie élégante*, wrote a *Physiologie gastronomique*, and sketched out a series of *Contes drolatiques* in the manner of Rabelais—'that marvellous language of the sixteenth century, lush and juicy and evergreen'. Madame de Berny wrote from

Paris saying nothing about the Glorious Days but much about her love—'*amoureuse folie, sublime exaltation*':

> Oh, sweet and gentle hope, enter my heart that I may caress you; show me my beloved, my adored master, tell me of his coming. If you wish me to burn incense on your altar, I will not weary you with a stream of indiscreet avowals. Only one, and then I am silent: *he* and *he*, and that is all. For the rest, give yourself elsewhere with open hands; I claim nothing of you, nor of your great executor, fortune.
>
> Sweet, the sun today seems in tune with my heart; it is bringing freshness to Nature, as our love does to my whole being. Something lifts me off the earth; a more noble region seems to await me. Do I not hear my angel? . . .

After a rhapsody such as this there was some excuse for the 'Ta-ta-ta!', but so much devotion touched him, and although he had other women, La Dilecta was not wrong when she talked of his 'dear and faithful constancy'.

He wanted to go back to Paris loaded with manuscripts, and he took no interest in the accession to power of his former teachers at the Sorbonne, Villemain, Guizot and Cousin. Every change of régime leads to a rush of place-seeking. His friends were all finding themselves jobs. Girardin became Inspecteur des Beaux-Arts; Stendhal, consul at Trieste; Dumas, the King's librarian; Philarète Chasles, an attaché at the Embassy in London. Balzac asked for nothing and was even scornful, having no desire to become a bureaucrat. He had far loftier ambitions. 'Balzac,' Arsène Houssaye wrote later, 'will not reveal his secret until he becomes a minister. Someone asked him when this would be, and he replied, "The day when France remembers Richelieu".'

He returned in September, Girardin having commissioned a series of 'Paris Letters' for *Le Voleur*, in which he was to keep provincial readers in touch with the situation following the revolution. In addition, his friends the Carrauds had appealed for his protection against the purging wind that was blowing through Saint-Cyr. He asked them to write telling him the exact position: 'I dine tomorrow with the private secretary of the Minister of War, a good friend and comrade who will refuse me nothing.' Moreover he offered to consult his regular clairvoyant (*somnambule*) in whom he had the utmost confidence. But the two oracles, secretary and clairvoyant alike, proved equally ill-informed. 'You should join the École Polytechnique,' Balzac advised Carraud, 'because it is almost certain that Saint-Cyr is to be abolished.' Saint-Cyr was not abolished, but in 1831 Carraud was appointed officer in charge of the Angoulême gun-powder factory, which he rightly regarded as a humiliation.

The Paris Letters seem at first to have been objective and impartial—too impartial, in the view of the ardent Zulma. Balzac replied that their intention was 'less to advocate any opinion than to provide a faithful picture of political develop-ments and the clash of ideas'. His friends had given him lyrical accounts of Liberty on the Barricades, as though it were a picture by Delacroix; but he found Paris cool and sceptical, and said so. He described different attitudes, that of the war-mongers, the Café du Commerce strategists who were ready to declare war on all Europe, and the pacifists, 'the honourable landowner whose property is situated near the frontiers where the war would be fought'. He wrote derisively of the '*curée*', the scramble for jobs. All the 'victors of July' wanted to be sub-Prefects or consuls: 'Comedy begins to raise its head. You meet fashionables who were wounded by bullets through their valets' waistcoats . . . and there are six hundred heroes each of whom was *first* to enter the Louvre.' A friend of his, Dr Ménière, had attended to the wounded at the Hôtel-Dieu. All, without exception, had been working-men. But the bourgeoisie was keeping them out of power and, what was more, treating them as an enemy. The new government, under Thiers and Mignet, was no more liberal than that of Charles X. 'Is not every government,' Balzac wrote, 'obliged to resort to the same kind of thimble-rigging, to juggle the pea in the same way?' The liberal opposition had attacked the former Prime Minister, de Villèle, for ordering civil servants to think like the government; now that they were in power they were sending out circulars to exactly the same effect.

In the first of the Letters, although he was critical Balzac seemed disposed to accept the new régime. But he was soon undeceived, and said so in the pages of *La Caricature*, making fun of Louis-Philippe, of La Fayette, the vain, weak hero, and of Thiers, the unprincipled careerist. He wanted new elections and younger men in power. The present gerontocracy, of old

old men and old young men, was a stronghold of mediocrity. France was still in the hands of small men. *La Caricature* filled its pages with the follies of the triumphant and ridiculous Monsieur Prudhomme, and of the grotesque and bureaucratic Garde Nationale. Who was now governing France? The victors of July? By no means. The grocers had reaped the spoils of victory. Who was responsible for foreign policy? The defenders of the national frontiers and enemies of the Holy Alliance? Again, no. The men in power were all-out pacifists, prepared to stand by while the Belgian and Polish revolutions were crushed.

But if an adventurous foreign policy was not feasible, it was at least possible for internal policy to be bolder. There should be total freedom of the Press: 'A persecuted man of talent is always stronger than the authorities.' The suitability of electoral candidates should not be determined by any property qualification. It should be enough for them to be French citizens and over the age of twenty-five. This last point was no doubt partly a matter of self-interest, since Balzac's own ambitions, boundless though they were, could only be pursued on orthodox lines; but it was also the view of the country as a whole. At heart, the son of the former Empire official still retained his admiration for Napoleon; and the bourgeois of the Marais advocated liberty but not equality. Viewing the world of human society in the way that Cuvier and Geoffroy Saint-Hilaire viewed the animal world, he saw an inexorable tendency to class-division which in his eyes ruled out all utopian dreams.

He did not welcome this harshness in the natural order of things, but simply took note of it: 'I do not construct a nation to please myself, I accept it as it is.' Every organized society, he maintained, was an insurance contract of the rich and established against the poor. The latter rebelled, but oppression always triumphed in the end. Even the Revolution had seen those who made it, having become powerful, rich and leisured, declare it to be subversive and dangerous. It had produced nothing except the despotism of Napoleon. And who had overthrown Napoleon? Metternich and the descendants of the Revolution's victims! Nothing could change the social hierarchy except a slow process of transformation. The business of the novelist must be to depict the structure of social classes. The world was all one, ranging from brute creation to the angels, by way of man.

'Jacob's mystical ladder, the zoological ladder and the social ladder; the spheres, the species, the classes; the upward movement of creation, the evolution of species and the aspirations of men, these are three different aspects of one and the same reality. . . .' Such was the vast concept on which he wished to base a work of fiction. But the birth of such a work is more complex than any system of philosophy.

XII

The Ass's Skin

Le ciel est allégorique.
ALAIN
La vie décroît en raison directe de la puissance des désirs.
BALZAC

THE FAMILY'S FINANCIAL position was getting worse. Madame Balzac had been left almost nothing by her husband. She held Honoré's note-of-hand—a mortgage on the mists of the Seine!—and she had two properties of her own, the farm in Touraine, which she sold in January 1831 for 90,000 francs, and a house of no great value in Paris. She was liable for part of the dowry of Laurence's children. Laure Surville was bringing up two daughters, Sophie and Valentine, who would one day have to be 'established' according to bourgeois custom, and their father was taking great chances in an attempt to increase his income. In 1829 he resigned his safe but poorly paid post under 'Bridges and Highways' to devote himself to the construction of a lateral canal, from Orleans to Nantes, in the province of Loire-Inferieure. 'Surville the official had had his day; Surville the pioneer had now appeared on the scene.'

He and Laure came to live in Paris in 1830, leaving Versailles 'for the road to Eldorado'. But Surville had not yet even secured the official concession for the canal. He floated a 'development company' of which the capital was largely subscribed by the Pommereul family and their friend the Chevalier de Valois, Dr Nacquart and Madame Mère, who could never resist a bad speculation. When he told them that the annual dividend might well equal the amount of their contributions, the magic words so inspired the subscribers that they doubled them. But before long Surville, 'a ferocious republican', was complaining of an entirely imaginary conspiracy against him, conducted by the Jesuits. Honoré, who in times of family crisis was always able to escape into fiction, began *Les Aventures administratives*

172

d'une idée heureuse, and jotted down a good title for future use, *Les Souffrances de l'inventeur*. He was living on terms of fraternal intimacy with the Survilles. They shared expenses, and one day they would share the clean-up. Meanwhile he observed them.

Brother, or half-brother, Henry was a constant disappointment to his mother. In her blind affection she had blamed his teachers for all his failures at school: 'Henry is unhappy! They treat him unkindly. . . . He must go somewhere else.' But the changes made no difference. Industry and application were what he lacked. In 1824, when he was seventeen, he wrote to Laure: 'What have I done since the beginning of the year to make progress in the career I am to adopt? Nothing.' A spoilt child, over-indulged and under-gifted, he toyed for a time with the idea of acquiring a thorough knowledge of several foreign languages and thus securing 'an important post'. He wrote to Laure on another occasion: 'Thinking of your husband I see that if I become a rich English milord I might make him engineer-in-chief', words worthy of Balzac himself. But with Henry, for all his good intentions, 'his progress from aspiration to realization was from infinity to zero'. Affectionate, sluggish and good-for-nothing, he went from job to job just as he had gone from school to school. In March 1831, he embarked in the sailing-ship *Le Magellan* for the colonies, believing that it was the chance of a lifetime. The ship reached Mauritius in June, and Henry stayed there.

Honoré was living a life of enormous industry, bombarded by newspapers and reviews with requests for articles, novellas, short stories. 'You are greatly in demand,' Dr Veron, the editor of the *Revue de Paris*, wrote to him. His *Physiologie du mariage* had earned him the reputation of a rake and playboy, at which he protested: 'Many women readers will be disappointed to learn that the author of the *Physiologie* is young, steadygoing as an elderly departmental manager, sober as an invalid on a diet, a drinker of water and a very hard worker.' While turning out light pieces for *La Caricature* and *La Mode* he was planning something larger, a novel to be called *La Peau de chagrin* (*The Ass's Skin*), which was to contain something of his own life and philosophy.

His day-book contains the following note: 'The discovery of

a skin representing life. An oriental fable.' At the time he thought of it as no more than a fantastic tale in the manner of Hoffmann, and he even referred to it as 'a piece of thorough nonsense in the literary sense, but in which he [the author] has sought to introduce certain of the situations in this hard life through which men of genius have passed before achieving anything'. The story is about a magic talisman, an ass's skin, which makes all its owner's wishes come true. It bears the following inscription 'in Sanskrit':

IF YOU POSSESS ME YOU WILL POSSESS ALL THINGS.
BUT YOUR LIFE WILL BELONG TO ME. GOD HAS
SO WILLED IT. DESIRE AND YOUR DESIRES
WILL BE FULFILLED. BUT MATCH
YOUR DESIRES TO YOUR LIFE.
IT IS THERE. WITH EVERY WISH
I SHALL DIMINISH
LIKE YOUR DAYS.
DO YOU WANT ME?
TAKE ME. GOD
WILL HEAR YOU.
SO BE IT!

So the skin was to shrink with the fulfilment of each wish, and when it had shrunk to nothing its owner would die. The aged and emaciated antique-dealer who sells it to the young man, Raphaël, has lived to be a hundred because he has been careful never to express a wish, or even to desire anything.

The more Balzac pondered the fable, the more depths in it did he discover. He knew all about longevity. Bernard-François had constantly reminded him that the learned Fontenelle, who was incidentally a member of the Royal Society of London, advised old men to economize their activities and their emotions. Miserliness was their wisdom, because they dared have no other; whereas the young desired 'mad extravagance, imprudence, violent passion, restless endeavour', and thus youth headed for disaster. As he hands the talisman to Raphaël de Valentin, the antique-dealer says, 'I will disclose to you in a few words the mystery of human life. Man expends himself in the performance of two instinctive acts which drain away all the sources of his being. All the forms of these two agents of death may be summed up in the two words "will" and "can".'

It was a philosophy that condemned all brilliance in life, luxury, dissipation, every form of action. Bernard-François had favoured retreat to the country and living on the fruits of the earth. There was something of Rousseau in this rejection of social living. 'Human society is the road to death,' said Honoré in his turn. *La Peau de chagrin* was to become much more than a Hoffmannesque fantasy. Balzac set it in his own time and turned it into an allegory. His master, Rabelais, had reacted against medieval asceticism in a vast symbolical tale for the rehabilitation of the body; Balzac, writing after the Empire, that orgy of action, used other symbols to convey another message, the perils of the lust for power. Far from being 'a piece of thorough nonsense in the literary sense', the book became a brilliant and ambitious undertaking, but one which he was capable of carrying out. 'It is the property of a good fable that the author himself does not know all the riches it contains.'

And so, in January 1831, he sold to Messieurs Charles Gosselin and Urbain Canel, for the sum of 1,135 francs, a work in two volumes, to be entitled *La Peau de chagrin*, which he was to deliver by 15 February. He had also promised Canel another book, *Scènes de la vie militaire*. Work never frightened him, and promises even less. *La Peau de chagrin*, in fact, got off to a slow start. He was dining out a great deal, having become friendly with the magnificent Eugène Sue, dandy and novelist, and with Sue's mistress, Olympe Pélissier, a beautiful and intelligent courtesan whose salon was frequented by such distinguished figures as the Duc de Fitz-James, Horace Vernet and Rossini. He also sometimes took pot-luck, in an attic on the Quai Saint-Michel overlooking the river and Notre-Dame, with a young pair of lovers, Aurore Dudevant (better known as George Sand) and Jules Sandeau, for whom he had a great affection. 'Until you have known the fascination of Monsieur Balzac you can understand nothing of the magic of a look or the sympathy of souls,' Aurore wrote to a friend. At the same time he was giving lavish dinner-parties of his own in the Rue Cassini, concerning which a schoolfellow of his Vendôme days wrote ecstatically: 'I shall never forget those delightful hours . . . your wonderful readings . . . your brilliant friends and your champagne, rendered the more intoxicating by the wild, sublime creations of the inimitable Monnier. . . .' In short, Balzac was shrinking his talisman.

To escape the distractions of Paris, and get some work done, he went to stay with the Carrauds in March, and in April moved on to join Madame de Berny at La Bouleaunière. He worked well while he was with her, as he always did; but, insatiable as ever, he was now seized with a new and wild idea. Why should he not stand as a candidate in the forthcoming parliamentary elections? Politics offered a short cut to fame and fortune, and after the 1830 revolution the way seemed open for new men. Lamartine and Victor Hugo had accepted official posts. Barthélemy and Barbier were bringing new lustre to satirical verse. Stendhal, in 1830, had published *Le Rouge et le noir*, a sombre picture of a young man rising from the lowest class. Balzac dreamed of taking part in a national reconstruction. 'We have had enough of great wars,' he wrote. 'I think the time of great peace has arrived.'

To stand as a candidate he needed to pay a statutory deposit of 500 francs, but trifles of this sort never worried him in his flights of fancy. Where should he offer himself? He sent letters in three directions—to Cambrai, where he had a friend who owned the local paper; to the Baron de Pommereul, at Fougères ('My dear General, I must tell you frankly that, in view of the difficulty you are having in finding a suitable parliamentary representative for your constituency of Fougères, I am thinking of proposing myself to your fellow-citizens as a candidate. You know my principles, and you would be a true father to me, in this new order of things, if you would consent to act as my sponsor with the electors. . . .); and finally to a lawyer friend at Tours. He sent each a copy of a political pamphlet, *Inquiry into Two Ministries*, signed Honoré *de* Balzac. His Tours friend replied with high praise for his stories in *La Revue de Paris*, but went on to say that he had no political chance in Touraine: 'Your pamphlet makes the mistake of reaching no conclusion, and in these days one has to come out frankly under a party banner.' Baron de Pommereul was equally discouraging. The pamphlet did not correspond to the views of the majority in Fougères, and, even more important, 'they only want a local man'. The news-paper-owner, less pessimistic, invited him to Cambrai. But by that time Balzac, still at La Bouleaunière, was working feverishly on *La Peau de chagrin*. When did any writer of fiction desert his imaginary world, while it was in full spate, for the disillusions of reality? He gave up the idea of Parliament and never went to Cambrai.

There is a story that he hoped to acquire a fortune, and put himself in the parliamentary income-group, by marrying a Mademoiselle Eléonore de Trumilly, the daughter of an emigré who had been rewarded for his devotion to the royalist cause by Louis XVIII. The Balzacs had known the Baron de Trumilly at Villeparisis, and it has been suggested that Honoré's legitimist sympathies were prompted by the desire to ingratiate himself with him. This is improbable. The marriage could not have affected his electoral eligibility until after the election was over; and as for his political opinions, they were more solidly rooted than the story suggests.

He was surrounded by a youthful generation, influenced by Byron and infected with the *mal du siècle*, whose feeling was one of nostalgia for the warlike triumphs of Napoleon and disgust with the bourgeois Monarchy. Philarète Chasles wrote in his *Mémoires* (1876-77):

What a time! . . . A wonderful epoch thrown away. It asked too much, hoped for too much, counted on its strength, scat-tered its seed on the winds of north and south. It did not stop to hear itself live, but lived. It had fervour, sap and dash. . . . We were wrong, but nobly wrong; we went astray over the paths and on the rocks, but we marched. We were at the heart of a tempest, not of death. . . .

It was this anarchic state of mind which Balzac sought to depict in *La Peau de chagrin*. The first use its hero, Raphaël de Valentin, makes of the talisman is to call for an orgy of feasting and women. No sooner has he expressed the wish than, as he leaves the antique-shop, he runs into a couple of friends, Blondet and Rastignac. They bear him off to a fabulous dinner-party given by a retired banker who, not knowing what to do with his money, wants to make intellectual capital of it—that is to say, to found a newspaper.

'The Government, meaning the aristocracy of bankers and lawyers who today manipulate the nation as the priests once manipulated the monarchy, have found it necessary to mystify the good people of France with new words and old ideas, after the fashion of all the philosophers of every school and the strong men of every period. So we seek to promote a royally national spirit by proving to ourselves that it is better to pay twelve hundred million francs thirty-three centimes to the country as represented by Messieurs So-and-So than to pay eleven hundred million francs nine centimes to a king who said "I" instead of "we".' . . .

'Ah,' said Raphaël naively, 'we're on the way to becoming great rascals.' . . .

'You're perfectly right. Pass the asparagus. For after all, liberty gives birth to anarchy, anarchy leads to despotism and despotism brings us back to liberty. . . .'

'But, my dear fellow, Napoleon did at least leave us glory!'

'Glory! A wretched commodity. You pay a high price for it and it doesn't last. Is it anything but the egotism of great men? . . .'

'You're a Carlist!'

'Why not? I'm in favour of despotism, it proclaims a certain contempt for the human race. . . .'

Having thus derided liberty and monarchy the diners, now completely drunk, summon the women of the town.

With his feet in the lap of a beautiful, half-naked girl, Raphaël tells the story of his life before his purchase of the talisman, and it is the life of Balzac, suitably embellished. He describes how, the son of a great family ruined by his father's extravagance, he shut himself away in a garret to write a book entitled, *The Theory of Willpower*: 'Ignored by women, I remember observing them with all the detachment of love disdained. . . . I wanted to be revenged on society, I wanted to possess the soul of all women . . . and to see all eyes turned towards me when my name was announced by a footman in the doorway of a salon. . . . I saw myself as a great man.'

There was a great deal of Balzac in Raphaël. He, too, wanted everything—fame, wealth and women. He knew that in his genius he possessed a talisman that would bring him all things, but that he was burning up his days and the tale would end badly. Rastignac, the calculating social climber, regards Raphaël as both a man of genius and a fool. According to him the secret of success lies not in work but in intrigue, egotism and extravagance. To squander a fortune is to invest it in friends, pleasures and patrons. If the squanderer loses all he has, he can still make a useful marriage and become the attaché of a minister or ambassador; but he must have the support of a social clique. The next day Rastignac introduces Raphaël to the Comtesse Foedora, the most beautiful woman in Paris, and Raphaël falls violently in love with her.

How can he hope to win her without so much as thirty francs in his pocket? The story now recalls the tribulations of poverty. Only a penniless suitor can realize what romance costs in carriage-fares, in gloves (ah, those yellow or straw-coloured gloves, so expensive and so fragile!), in suits and linen. The ass's skin provides Raphaël with everything he needs, but it is wasted expense, for Foedora is a woman without a heart. One night he contrives to hide behind her bedroom curtains, whence he sees the most exquisite of bodies and discovers the most ignoble of souls. 'I had to forget Foedora, rid myself of this infatuation and return to my studious solitude, or die.'

This bedroom scene is said to have been enacted in real life between Balzac and Olympe Pélissier; but that warm-hearted trollop bore no resemblance to the brilliant, mocking phantom of the story. She would have given herself (as she probably did) without demur—her letters to him were more than friendly. Foedora was certainly not Olympe Pélissier; neither was she Princess Bagration, Mademoiselle Mars or any other single woman, but a symbol conceived in Balzac's mind, born of a dozen women.

Despite the advice of the learned doctors he consults (here Balzac's scientific and medical reading stood him in good stead), the ass's skin shrinks until Raphaël can put it in his pocket. His only chance of survival is to become like the old curio-dealer and want nothing. But seeing his mistress half-naked he desires her—and breathes his last breath.

The book was a fine one, mingling fantasy with realism in a way that struck a new note. Balzac had written the poem of his own avid and frustrated youth, with hints of an underlying philosophy. He hoped for success, and lobbied for support:

Balzac to Charles Gosselin: I can undertake to get something out of (1) *Le Temps*, (2) *La Revue de Paris*, (3) *Le National*, (4) *Le Figaro*, (5) *Le Méssager*, (6) *La Revue des Deux Mondes*, (7) *La Mode*, (8) *La Quotidienne*, (9) *L'Avenir*, (10) *Le Voleur*.

I will see to it that the reviews are good and promptly forth-coming, which will greatly facilitate your task as publisher, at a time when you are having domestic troubles. . . .

To make quite sure of favourable reviews, he wrote some of them himself: 'In these two volumes the talent of M. de Balzac achieves the stature of genius,' (*La Mode*). 'We have as much friendship as admiration for M. de Balzac'—signed, Comte Alex de B——, who was Balzac. He foresaw that the first impression would be rapidly sold out, and urged Gosselin to be ready to reprint at short notice—'otherwise you may lose con-siderable sales, and these chances do not come twice'. The book did indeed rapidly disappear from the bookshops, and there was keen competition to obtain it from the lending-libraries.

Charles Philipon to Balzac, 7 August 1831: My most excellent lord, you will find it easy to believe that there is no getting hold of *La Peau de chagrin*. Grandville had to stop everything in order to read it, because the librarian sent round every half-hour to ask if he had finished, saying, like the ladies, 'You're taking a very long time! Hurry up!' Audibert and I have tried in vain to secure a copy of the devilish work; it is booked long in advance. . . .

Jean de Margonne to Balzac, 10 August 1831: I am writing from Tours, where I arrived yesterday. This morning I asked for *La Peau de chagrin*, having read of its success in the papers. Copies were received here almost as soon as it appeared, but it is so much in demand that I could not get one.

Aurore Dudevant and Jules Sandeau wrote that they had begun to read *La Peau* and found it impossible to put down. The success of the *Physiologie du mariage* and the *Scènes de la vie privée* was strikingly confirmed. The young man from Touraine, unknown three years previously, had with three works become the desired of all publishers, the golden boy of the booksellers, and the women's favourite author. Far-sighted judges saw in him a great writer in the making. *La Peau de chagrin* was not merely a fable but the picture of a decadent society. At the banker's dinner-party writers and artists tear opinions and ideas to shreds in an 'intellectual witches' sabbath', seeing falsity in all things. Power was passing from palaces and national assemblies into the hands of bankers, lawyers and newspaper editors, a dangerous process. In a grasping and unprincipled world strong government was needed. Balzac dreamed of devoting a big romantic novel to the politics of dictatorship.

Everything he wrote at this time reflected the same pessimism. He had promised Gosselin a series of fantastic tales. They had a bitter taste. In *L'Élixir de longue vie*, the father of Don Juan, when he is dying, asks his son to anoint him after death with a mysterious elixir which will restore him to life. Don Juan, who for years has been awaiting his paternal inheritance, does not do so, but keeps the elixir for himself. After a life of dissipation he, too, lies dying and asks his son to do him the service he refused his father. The son obeys, but, horrified by the sight of the reviving corpse, drops the phial before the anointing is complete. The ecclesiastical authorities, having acknowledged the miracle, solemnly canonize Don Juan.

In *L'Auberge rouge* a German passing through Paris dines at the house of a banker and tells the story of a murder committed at Andernach in 1799. He does not know that the murderer, now a rich and respected financier, is among the company, or that his present wealth is due to that undiscovered crime of his youth. He guesses the truth when he sees the murderer on the verge of fainting; but he is in love with his daughter. Can he marry her and in doing so become heir to a fortune so abominably acquired? He puts the case to his friends as a matter of conscience, and they all favour the marriage: 'Where should we be if we had to investigate the origins of every fortune?'

His friend Philarète Chasles wrote a preface to this collection of stories, *Romans et contes philosophiques*, in which he praised Balzac not only as a teller of tales but as a thinker:

He has seen with what a dazzling outward show this valetudinarian society adorns itself, the garments that cover the dying body, the galvanic life that still causes the corpse to twitch. . . . In depicting its spurious agitation and funereal splendours, as opposed to the profound inner void of the body politic, he believes . . . that there is still magic in the contrast, and interest to be found in the greedy play of social impulses concealed behind the elegant façade. . . . A story-teller who bases his tales on the secret criminality, the inertia and unease of his period; a thinker and philosopher who has set out to show the confusion caused by thought—such is Monsieur de Balzac. . . .

Or rather, such was the role which Monsieur de Balzac aspired to play, that of the misanthropic thinker endowed with a lighthearted gusto. By November 1831, his reputation was so widespread that literary vendettas began. Charles Rabou, of the *Revue de Paris*, warned him to be on his guard against professional jealousy and told him that Jules Janin, an influential reviewer, intended to check his meteoric rise to fame: 'He is working to this end in *Journal des Débats*, where they cordially dislike you. It's a kind of revolt. . . . Well, we must close our ranks!' Balzac was beginning to discover that a man's success does not necessarily delight his so-called friends. Another lost illusion.

Malice sought to block his path. The 'de' which he had added to his name was a cause of easy derision. He had not used it to start with. *Le Chouan* and the *Scènes de la vie privée* were simply signed Honoré Balzac. He risked it first on his political pamphlet, but he said later that the addition of 'd'Entragues' was not his own, but the work of ill-wishers seeking to make him look ridiculous. For the rest of his life he was to be the object of the crudest, most scurrilous attacks, personal as well as professional. Jealousy relieves its spleen by stirring up mud. But the greatness that was in him continued to develop. From his very earliest days, even in his garret in 1820, he had peered into a misty future when he would produce a work on an epic scale. While pouring out hack fiction he had thought in terms of Dante and Shakespeare. And when he put his fictitious 'doubles' on paper—Raphaël in *La Peau de chagrin* and Victor Morillon in the announcement of *Le Gars*, he endowed them with the genius he himself aspired to and, from childhood, had believed himself to possess.

A great man, even if he is first and foremost a novelist, cannot remain indifferent to the political life of his country. The riots that had followed the Glorious Days, the looting of the Archbishop's palace in Paris by a raving mob and the profanation of works of religious art, had filled Balzac with abhorrence for the July Monarchy: 'A time will come when, secretly or openly, half the French people will regret the departure of that old man and that child, and will say, "If the 1830 revolution was to be done again it would not happen".' There had been bloody uprisings at Lyons caused by the poverty of the *canuts* (silk weavers), the grasping inhumanity of the merchants and a short-sighted factory system. The followers of Saint-Simon were advocating workers' organizations and the sharing of wealth. Balzac concentrated on the moral aspect. The middle-of-the-road bourgeoisie seemed to him unfit to govern because they thought solely in terms of financial profit and not at all of their responsibilities. 'There is no longer any religion in the State,' he wrote, and went on to specify: 'I'm not talking religious cant, I use the word in the widest political sense.'

His own attitude to religion had long been ambivalent. Under the influence of his father and the eighteenth-century philosophers he had always regarded dogma and ritual as so much accumulated superstition; but from his earliest childhood, in the cathedral at Tours and at Vendôme, he had been moved by church music and the pealing of the bells. He had often gone alone to the cathedral, to experience 'a shiver of religious awe at the unbelievable sublimities of its silence'. After 1830 he came to recognize the political necessity and tactical value of Catholicism. The very word 'religion' implied a bond, and what bond could exist between people of all classes except that of a common faith?

In 1831 he published an allegorical tale entitled *Jésus-Christ en Flandre*, based on an old Brabantine legend. A small sailing-vessel, at some indeterminate period of history, is carrying passengers from the island of Cadzant to Ostend. The wealthy and aristocratic are in the after-part of the ship, the poor in the bows. A gale springs up and those in the stern cry: 'We are lost!' The captain gives the order to man the pumps. The ship capsizes. A Stranger with a luminous profile proclaims: 'Those who have faith shall be saved. Let them follow me.' He walks on the waters and those who trust him do the same. The aristocrats are all drowned. In a characteristically Balzac touch, the captain, a man of action but not of faith, lashes himself to a plank and is saved by his own purely human exertions. 'All very well for this time,' the Stranger says to him. 'But you must not do it again. You would be setting too bad an example.'

Must we then humbly believe? Balzac extends his allegory to embrace the Church. While he is musing in the cathedral built to commemorate this miracle an old woman, a hag, seizes him by the hand, crying, 'Protect me! Protect me!' She leads him to a bedroom with threadbare hangings, full of old clothes and gilded brass. 'I mean to make you happy for ever,' she says. 'You are my son!' Through the ravaged, hideous features he sees the innocent, lovely girl she once was. 'Ah, now I know you!' he says. 'Wretch, why did you prostitute yourself? . . . Contemptuous of man and delighting to see the lengths to which human folly will go, you commanded your lovers to go on all fours, to give you their riches, their treasured possessions, even their wives. . . . For no reason you have devoured millions of men, flinging them from the West upon the East. You have descended from the highest realms of thought to seat yourself at the side of kings. . . . You have called for blood, being sure that you would get it. . . . Why do you exist at all? . . . Where are your riches? What good thing have you done?'

At the question the old woman draws herself erect and grows in stature. A luminous mist envelopes her; she is fair-skinned and young, clad in a linen garment. 'Look and believe!' she says. He sees countless cathedrals with their tracery of stone; he hears ravishing music. Millions of men move through the stately buildings, preserving art and letters, and serving the poor. Then the light dies down, and the beautiful girl is again the old woman in her graveyard rags. 'Men no longer believe,' she says bitterly. And Balzac concludes: 'I found the cathedral buried in shadow like a man wrapped in a cloak. "To believe is to live!" I said to myself. "I have witnessed the funeral procession of a monarchy; I must defend the Church!" '

He added the last words when the story was reprinted in 1845; but it was written in February 1831, and it sufficiently reveals his attitude to Catholicism and Monarchism at that time. In the shipwreck of Charles X, the Church and the Monarchy, he also saw the sinking of the Arts. But although he regretted the departure of the old king, he respected the Republicans. Armand Carrel was to become one of his heroes and was later incorporated in the character of Michel Chrestien. It is one of the signs of greatness, always present in Balzac, that it recognizes and honours greatness in others, even in its adversaries. But had he really any adversaries? His genius lay in understanding: strength in a writer, weakness in a man of action.

XIII

Follies and Retreats

*'Mon avenir, se dit-il, dépend d'une femme qui appartienne
à ce monde.'*

BALZAC

THE YEAR 1831, a year of literary success, should also have
been one of financial ease. Balzac had received 1,125 francs for
La Peau de chagrin, 3,750 for the *Scènes de la vie privée*, 5,250
for the *Romans philosophiques* and the *Contes drolatiques*, and
4,166 francs for newspaper and review articles; making a total
of 14,291 francs, more than enough to enable a bachelor to live
on a lavish scale. Yet his debts had increased by 6,000 francs.
At the end of the year they totalled 15,000 francs, in addition
to the 45,000 francs he owed his mother.

The reason was simply that he was incapable of resisting
temptation. The long years of penury led him into wild
excess. Like Raphaël de Valentin, he had dreamed of life on
a princely scale, and now he could make the dream come
true. His bills for champagne alone were enormous. Under
the influence of Eugène Sue and his friends he saw himself
not as a dandy, for he had a horror of 'the solemn imbecilities
indulged in by the English with their vaunted sangfroid',
but as 'a man of fashion'. The tailor, Buisson, supplied him
with new clothes to the value of 631 francs, including three sets
of his monkish working-attire, the white house-gowns with
gold-tasselled girdles. In payment for a short story he asked
Urbain Canel for a dozen pairs of straw-coloured kid gloves
(gloves were still an obsession) and one of reindeer skin. His
booksellers' and binders' bills, if more excusable, were none the
less ruinous.

In September 1831 he bought himself a horse, a tilbury and
a violet-coloured carriage-rug with his monogram and a coronet
embroidered on it in goat-hair; and a month later, a second

horse. To these were added a groom or 'tiger', a tiny youth called Leclercq, for whom Buisson made a suit of blue livery, a green American waistcoat with red sleeves, and a pair of striped duck breeches. Monsieur de Balzac was now equipped to visit the Opera or the Italiens, or cut a dash at the side of Eugène Sue or Lautour-Mézeray.

Lautour-Mézeray, the reigning king of Paris fashion, had acquired some importance in Balzac's life, as a boon companion and an example to be followed. The son of a notary in Argentan, where he and Émile de Girardin had been at school together, he now had a share in that press-magnate's undertakings, among them *Le Voleur* and *La Mode*. Provincial though he was, his tall figure, sardonic wit and lofty bearing had made him a 'lion' of the town, with the boulevards his empire, Tortoni's his tavern and the Opera his seraglio. Here he and his friends shared a stage-box known as the 'loge infernale'. For a time Balzac also had a seat in it, but he gave up paying his share, although it was demanded of him in an impudent letter addressed to 'Monsieur de Balzac d'Entragues de la Grenadière'. Lautour-Mézeray always wore a white camellia in his buttonhole, an expensive habit which became 'a positive badge of lionhood', such affectations being a surer way to celebrity than either virtue or talent.

In any event he was important to Balzac as an intimate of the distinguished Girardin circle. Émile de Girardin had recently married Sophie Gay's daughter, Delphine, who had been the idol of the young romantics. As Madame de Girardin she presided over a salon where it was a privilege to be received, and where Lamartine, Hugo, Sue, Dumas and Balzac were frequent guests. Balzac, whose growing reputation and brilliant talent for journalism were adding lustre to her husband's periodicals, was among her favourites.

The apartment in the Rue Cassini was fast becoming too small for the rapidly rising young man. He rented another floor of the house, which entailed further expenditure on decorations, furniture and carpets—particularly carpets, thick and soft and ruinous. But why worry, now that he had the wind in his sails? Girardin wrote him a note proposing to call on Urbain Canel, 'the publisher whose fortune you are making . . .'. But those who really cared for him were worried about his debts, his borrowings and his too evident heedlessness. His sister Laure lent him a little money, but exclaimed, 'Go gently!' and 'Do be good!' Zulma Carraud, now exiled to the gunpowder-factory in Angoulême, grieved to see him launching out in a world which she held to be unworthy of him:

Zulma Carraud to Balzac, 8 November 1831: The 20th August, the 20th September and now the 20th October have gone by. I have waited for you in vain, not a line, not even a word of greeting! It isn't kind, Honoré. I have been hurt, although I have not yet added you to the list of my friends who discarded that title as soon as we left school. One thing has consoled me for your neglect; I think it is simply due to the new successes you have doubtless had. . . . You can always come back to me when you feel the need to be yourself. Carraud says that you're afraid of being infected with provincial crudity; but, dear Honoré, though Paris may give you the elegance that suits you, does it also give you the true affection you would have found at Frapesle? . . .

You are so busy describing the feelings of fictitious characters that inevitably you neglect the treasure, so precious in another sense, of those personal to yourself. So I shall refrain from adding to the weight, already too heavy, of the claims of which I speak. I do not want, and have never wanted, the easy friendship you offer women. . . . I look for something higher. Yes, Honoré, you must have sufficient regard for me to hold me in reserve, as it were. If some misfortune should disturb your happiness, if some disappointment should touch your heart, then you will turn to me, and you will see how I shall respond. . . .

The generous Dr Nacquart now and then lent him four or five hundred francs, writing off the loan and exhorting the borrower, 'Go on growing for the greatness of France and the happiness of your friends.' By the end of 1831 Balzac had spent three times as much as in the previous year, but he had had some fun for his money. It was breathlessly exciting for the penniless youth of not so long ago, who had challenged Paris from the heights of Père Lachaise, to find himself among the great figures at Tortoni's, the fashionable writers, brilliant hostesses and dazzling women of the town, and to know that he was esteemed by them.

Olympe Pélissier to Balzac, 2 January 1832: Can I count on you for nine o'clock next Monday? Rossini is coming to dinner, and it will be a good start to the New Year. You must be at your most charming; the rest should have made you more brilliant than ever. . . .

Delphine de Girardin, 9 May 1832: We haven't seen you for centuries. Come and tell us your news tomorrow evening. You'll meet an enthusiastic admirer of your last book, and some old friends who don't forgive you for having neglected them. . . . Till tomorrow? . . .

In the background of this triumphant existence were the nagging embarrassments of unpaid bills, debt-collectors, family complications; but the greater the trouble, the greater the need for distraction. The child at play still lurked in the author of distinction, revelling unrestrainedly in the trappings and dissipations of success. So intense had been his longing for fame, so agonizing his poverty, that now he could not have enough of the heady draught; and when things became too difficult he could always beat a retreat, leaving Madame Mère, scolding but devoted, to take charge of his house and restore a little order in his affairs. He could bury himself at La Bouleaunière with Laure de Berny, or at Saché with Jean de Margonne, or at Angoulême with the Carrauds, and here, safe from his creditors, do work that would endure.

Rabelaisian though he was, he believed, without puritanism, that a writer should live as chastely as possible, since by conserving physical and emotional energy his thinking would rise to greater heights. But still he kept his two mistresses. Laure de Berny remained the Dilecta, adoring and caressing and the invaluable corrector of proofs. The Duchesse d'Abrantès clung to him because he helped her in her literary career, besides amusing her. But his books brought him a great many letters from unknown admirers. He received one in October 1831, signed with an English nom-de-plume, which caught his fancy. It was addressed simply to 'Monsieur de Balzac, à Paris', but the postal service had somehow traced him, first to the Rue Cassini and then to Saché. His anonymous correspondent took him to task for the cynicism of the *Physiologie* and his low opinion of women. But the letter was headed by an address, and thus encouraged he wrote to thank her 'for the compliment implied in your rebukes, since they show that my writings have made an impression on you. . . .

For a woman who has known the tempests of life, the sense of my book is that it attributes the faults committed by married women wholly to their husbands. It is an act of absolution. . . . You must not suppose that your letter, filled with the touching expression of feelings natural to a woman's heart, has left me indifferent. Such sympathy inspired at a distance is my most cherished possession, my whole fortune, my most pure delight. . . .

Touched in her turn by his lavish response (four large pages from an overworked writer!) the lady disclosed her identity. She was the Marquise de Castries, originally Claire-Clémence-Henriette de Maillé, a member of the most exclusive circle in the exclusive Faubourg Saint-Germain.

Her own life might have been the subject of a novel. After the failure of her marriage to the Marquis (later the Duc) de Castries, she had met, in 1822, the son of the Austrian Chancellor, Victor von Metternich, a romantic, delicate and charming young man with whom she fell deeply in love. She left her husband and in 1827 bore the young Count a son, upon whom the Austrian Emperor, at the Chancellor's request, conferred the title of Baron von Aldenburg. Later she was severely injured in a riding accident, and in 1829 Victor von Metternich died of consumption. Heartbroken, crippled in body, and under the stigma of her scandalous love-affair, she took refuge by turns with her father, the Duc de Maillé, at the Château de Lormois, and her uncle, the Duc de Fitz-James, at the Château de Quevillon. Fitz-James, a grandson of the first Duke of Berwick, who was the natural son of James II and Arabella Churchill, had made Balzac's acquaintance in Olympe Pélissier's salon; so Henriette de Castries had known something about the man she was writing to.

In a second letter she invited Balzac to visit her, and he replied:

28 February 1832: It is rare to encounter noble hearts and true friendships. I, more than anyone, am so lacking in disinterested support on which I can rely that, at the risk of losing a great deal by making myself known to you in person, I accept your generous offer. If I were not engaged in an urgent task I should have called upon you already to pay my respects with that openness of heart which you so value; but after many struggles and honourable misfortunes—misfortunes of which one is proud—I have still some work to do before gaining a few hours of leisure during which I need be neither writer nor artist but simply myself; and it is those hours which, with your permission, I hope to devote to you. . . .

The hour came and the meeting overwhelmed him. At the time of her marriage, when she was in her twenties, the Marquise, with her red hair and white skin, had been so radiantly beautiful that 'when she entered a salon, clad in a pale pink gown revealing shoulders worthy of Titian, she literally dimmed the light of the candles'. In 1832 she admitted to the age of thirty-five, and since her accident she could only walk with difficulty; but she still retained her beauty and charm. What rapture for Balzac to drive in the new tilbury with his liveried groom into the courtyard of a great house in the Rue de Grenelle-Saint-Germain! Nevertheless after that first visit he executed a strategic withdrawal: 'However sweet a woman's compassion may be, it is yet more wounding than mockery; when heart and mind are in sympathy they go very far. I can cherish a memory of you that is full of charm. . . .'

Was this the novelist playing a skilled game of coquetry? In any event he went back. He presented the lady with some of his manuscripts, and between March and May he wrote to her:

The author's business has been attended to. Will you now let me express my gratitude to you, a profound gratitude for the hours you have allowed me? They are imprinted on my memory like unwritten poems, like dreams born of an arrangement of clouds in the sky, like the sound of beautiful music. I would tell you that I begin to fear such sweet enchantments, did I not feel that you are above foolish talk of that kind. For you there must be no flattery; nothing but truth and, above all, the most affectionate respect. . . .

He was beginning to indulge in the wildest hopes. To have one of these great, inaccessible ladies for a mistress—what a victory! 'Moved by extremely violent emotions, in which vanity was strangely intermingled with love, he seemed to be bewitched by the woman.'* He had never dreamed of love in a cottage; it was the luxury surrounding his Marquise that went to his head. She for her part was evidently attracted to him; she kept him with her in her boudoir until far into the night, although always at a respectful distance. May 16 was his name-day, the feast of St Honoré, and she sent him a large bunch of flowers. He thanked her repeatedly for the 'delightful hours she gave him' and ended his letter with *Amitié tendre'*. His affairs seemed to have taken a hopeful turn—except that this new conquest cost him precious evenings which might have been spent at his desk.

Was it for the sake of the Marquise that he contributed articles to a new legitimist paper, *Le Renovateur*? Her uncle Fitz-James was one of the leaders of the party. Certainly Balzac took pleasure in putting his talents at the service of friends whose kindness flattered him. Madame de Castries was excitingly skilled at mingling praise with a hint of more to come: 'I may allow myself to miss you, but never to hinder work which I so greatly enjoy. I love to see you in print; *Le Renovateur* delighted me when I awoke this morning. But I think I like you even better when I hear you talk. . . .' No doubt he felt, in the agreeable atmosphere of the Rue de Grenelle-Saint-Germain, that political truth must go naturally hand-in-hand with the genuine distinction of an aristocracy possessing so much charm.

But his political philosophy remained fundamentally what it had always been. He believed in power, a single man in command to concentrate the energies of the nation. Whether the man was Bonaparte or Charles X, emperor, dictator or king, mattered very little to him. His greatest objection to the July Monarchy was that it lacked vigour. Among his new legitimist friends he opposed the extremists, those who advocated the boycotting of elections. The Duc de Fitz-James, more intelligent than these, urged a more flexible approach which would make use of an elected parliament, and was against what he called 'a state of emigration within the country'. He had consented to swear allegiance to Louis-Philippe because the national interest

* Bernard Guyon.

required it. But he had renounced his privileges as a peer, reserving his right to enter the popular assembly as a deputy if the voters in some corner of France were prepared to elect 'a man who has never shirked the telling of a truth'. This shrewd and lofty wisdom suited Balzac's own ambitions.

His 'entanglement with the Right' came as a painful shock to his Liberal friends. Amedée Faucheux protested from Tours: 'So now you are definitely a Legitimist. Believe me, you should not support a bad cause which has no future in the country. Things may go very badly for us, but never so badly as to bring back Henry V and his retinue of clerics and gentry.' Zulma Carraud, because she loved him, was even more outspoken:

3 May 1832: Dear Honoré, are you never going to give up this tempestuous life? . . . Like the alchemist, having squandered your gold you will find nothing at the bottom of your crucible. . . . Honoré, you are a noted author, but you were meant to be more than that. Celebrity is not for you; you should be aiming higher. If I dared I would tell you exactly why you are so fruitlessly wasting such rare qualities of mind. The fashionable life is all very well for those so afflicted with moral weakness that it is necessary to them as a way of forgetfulness. But you, you! . . . I cannot finish what I want to say, because I am afraid to overstep the rights you allow me; but I should be so proud of your fame, if it were fame as I understand it! . . .

I have been told that you are involving yourself in politics. Oh, be careful, be very careful! I am afraid for you. It is not for you to attach yourself to individuals; there can be no glory in that unless one has *lived* in intimacy with the great ones of the earth. Then it may be fidelity in affection. But you, who must outlive your own life, you can only dedicate yourself to a principle, one to which you have applied your intelligence, and which your own way of living has made congenial to you. Leave the defence of individuals to the domestic circle of the Court, and do not sully your just celebrity with any such alliance. . . . My dear, my very dear, keep your self-respect, even if it means sacrificing the English horses and the Gothic chairs. . . .

She was right, and in his heart he knew it. But what man is not the victim of his desires? Balzac, more than any other, was insatiable. One novel must be followed by ten more; one woman by the next; every success by even greater triumph.

There was certainly vulgarity in his obsessive need of pleasures and compensations; in the accounts he was always drawing up of the financial gains of authorship; in his unregulated appetite for carpets, hangings, pictures and furniture. Yet, while coveting everything, he was capable of putting everything aside for the sake of his work. When the urge to create came upon him the man of pleasure was transformed into a recluse. He wrote to Zulma: 'I have not left my desk for a month. . . . I live under the harshest of despotisms, that which we inflict on ourselves. I work day and night. . . . No amusements. . . . I'm a galley-slave of pen and ink, a real idea-monger. . . .'

How much time could there be for recreation when he went to bed at six, had himself called at midnight, and then wrote for twelve or fifteen hours on end? If now and then he spent an evening with the Girardins, or at the Opera or a dinner-party, it was after being shut away for weeks, like a sailor going ashore after a long sea-passage. And the fact that he talked so much about contracts and earnings does not mean that money-making was the main purpose of his work. . . . The endless proof-correcting, the enormous additions and ruthless rewriting, all these point to an artist as self-exacting as any has ever been. The deep and shallow Balzacs lived together in symbiosis. Zulma asked why his letters never showed his deeper side. The answer is that it went into his work.

As for Laure de Berny, more useful to him because she was nearer, her aim was always to get him away from Paris so that he might be more truly himself. She was now aged fifty-five, old indeed for an impassioned mistress. In April or May 1832, she succeeded in bearing him off to Saint-Firmin, on the edge of the forest of Chantilly. Here, in a magnificent burst, he wrote *Le Curé de Tours* and finished *La Femme de trente ans*.

Le Curé de Tours was not only an admirable novella but an act of courage. The story itself is slight, that of an impecunious and simple-minded cathedral priest who is turned out of his lodging by the machinations of a malicious elderly spinster and a scheming canon with an eye on the bishopric; but Balzac made it a study of every aspect of social life in Tours, the secret powers of the Congrégation and the occult influence of the *Grande Aumonerie*. As a document of the Restoration period it is invaluable, and it is remarkable in its understanding of human nature and of the trifles which are the stuff of daily life. It was undoubtedly inspired by Madame de Berny.

Paris, when he returned there, was in a state of great unrest. There was an outbreak of cholera, and the Duchesse de Berry had landed in Vendée. Balzac was highly indignant with the Government for not having consulted clairvoyants, who would at once have diagnosed the cause of the epidemic. He planned to leave again as soon as possible. How wrong people were to think him worldly! All he asked was life in the country with a perfect wife! He was thinking now of a very rich young widow, the Baronne Deurbroucq. He hoped to see her during the summer at the Château de Saché, when he went to stay with the Margonnes. There was nothing like a widow with money of her own and some experience of love! But at the end of May he had a road-accident, the second time his tilbury had overturned. On the first occasion, in April, the sufferer had been Delphine de Girardin.

Balzac to Madame Émile de Girardin, 31 May 1832: We were both destined, Madame, to experience the vicissitudes of the tilbury in all their variety, and not far from the spot where you were so roughly handled I too have come in contact with those heroic cobblestones. . . . This head, this noble head, well anyway, this head . . . was badly dented, and I do not know but that some of the cogs in the mechanism of my brain may have got out of adjustment. . . .

Nothing in his brain was out of adjustment, but Dr Nacquart sent him to bed, put him on a diet, bled him, and forbade him to write or think. In June his longing to be out of Paris increased. For one thing, he wanted to escape from creditors, money-troubles and the nagging of publishers—vexations which he unloaded on his unhappy mother, whom he installed in the Rue Cassini with full power of attorney. He also wanted to get away from the Duchesse d'Abrantès, who was still trying to inflict tasks on him for which he no longer had either the time or the inclination. And finally he wanted to work, because he felt full of novels. The Marquise de Castries had invited him to join her at Aix-les-Bains in August and accompany her on a journey to Switzerland and Italy. 'Well?' wrote Balzac to Madame Mère— '*Hein?*' There is something touching in those *heins* to his mother, his retort to her severe strictures on him in the past.

He could not afford the trip to Aix; so he went to Saché, where he might hope to save a little money. The devoted but hunchbacked Madame Margonne was sometimes tedious, but she gave him a comfortable room, plenty of coffee, a bedside lamp and comparative peace. And he soon had further reason for being thankful that he was out of Paris. There was rioting in the town. Some of the most prominent Legitimists, including Châteaubriand and even the Duc de Fitz-James, were arrested in consequence of the Duchesse de Berry's escapade in Vendée.

They were released after ten days, but the arrests delighted Madame de Berny: 'Because if that party is destroyed you will have to join another.' She abhorred the Legitimists because she associated them with Henriette de Castries. In the intervals of correcting Balzac's proofs, she wrote to him from La Nièvre, where she was staying with an old friend, General Allix:

A mortal fear sometimes clutches my heart. I am afraid that if *a certain lady* should write asking you to join her, you would have the kindness to go. Did not another lady once get you to leave Tours for Versailles, to console her for misfortunes which she selfishly exaggerated for your benefit? This time the circumstances are much more serious, and unfortunately your vanity is still alive and active, and has the greater power over you because you do not realize how strong it is. But my dearest, my friend, my lover-son, you must pay a little heed to the arguments . . . of the most friendly voice that will ever reach your ear. Remember that certain people will not give you a single one of the three or four thousand crowns you so desperately need, and that, even if they should be victorious, they have always been *ungrateful on principle*, and they will not change their ways for you. They have all the defects of egotism, and all the cunning and dishonesty of weakness; a disdain, even to contempt, for all those born of blood other than their own. Beloved friend, for the sake of all that you hold dear, your reputation, your future happiness, my peace of mind (for you love me), do not believe them, do not trust them. . . .

Why, she asked, did he not join her? General Allix would gladly give him a room and he had many tales to tell of secret diplomacy under Bonaparte. How delightful it would be to live together, far removed from a world so little suited to rare and delicate souls! She still had faith in his 'gentle heart', but how could it fail to be corrupted amid so many depravities? The *Scènes de la vie privée* evoked cherished recollections: 'I remember where we were when you read certain passages to me, and what you said about them, and the words of love which followed; and I hurry to rest in your heart as on your dear body when . . . you know? . . .'

She was still so physically in love: 'I think of myself as your beloved and shower on you all our usual caresses. I kiss you everywhere . . .' And a few days later: 'Oh, my dearest Didi, my darling, my adored master, come to me to receive the tribute of a sensuality created by you, the caresses of an adoring woman moulded to your use. Oh, I pray that we shall see each other soon! It would be too terrible to allow others to gather those exquisite flowers whose scent still returns to intoxicate me, whose colours still rejoice my heart. . . .' Did he still love her, or was he now another's? She would sooner die! 'Adored beloved, I know of nothing more inhuman than a life that depends on someone who no longer wants it. . . .' Separated from her husband, torn between her children who were themselves at loggerheads, she had only her lover to live for—'I am broken.'

Complaints of a different order came from Madame Mère, on whom Honoré shamelessly imposed one errand after another. She was to search his papers for the copy of a certain manuscript and send it to the publisher Mame. 'And then, kind Mamma, I need my summer trousers. Buisson should have finished them by now.' . . . 'On Wednesday morning I shall be putting a parcel on the mailcoach containing the story for Gosselin [Louis Lambert]. . . . Having appeased Gosselin I shall press on with *La Bataille*. . . . Tell anyone who comes asking for money that I'm abroad but shall be back on 15 August. . . .' In between these instructions he told her of his matrimonial hopes. The widow Deurbroucq had not, alas, come to Touraine, but Balzac, having sent her a copy of *Scènes de la vie privée*, felt that all was going well: 'She wrote me a very polite note of thanks.' His capacity for wishful thinking knew no bounds.

But that marriage could not in any case have taken place in time for him to settle his more pressing debts. Something had to go; and he wrote to Madame Mère: 'If you can sell the horses, do so; and if you want to get rid of Leclercq, pay him off and dismiss him.' All he needed was six months respite, because 'I have never been in a more hopeful position. Sooner or later literature, politics, journalism, marriage or my grand affair will make my fortune. We have only to hold out a little longer. All would be well if I were the only one to suffer, for I should have left France twenty times over in the past four years were it not for Madame de Berny. But now you are far from well, and necessity forces you to become one of the objects of my deepest concern. . . . You ask me to write to you in detail, but, my poor mother, do you not yet know how I live? When I can write, I produce manuscripts; when I'm not producing manuscripts I think about them. A single page sacrificed to business matters or social obligations, or to affection, is so much time lost from my life. . . .' He was not entirely wrong. How create a world of the imagination if the real world persisted in intruding with embarrassments and recriminations? But all this was very hard on a sick and ageing woman who was doing her best under constant pressure.

Balzac to his mother, 19 July 1832: I was just about to make a brave start on my work this morning when your letter arrived and threw me out completely, because it's enough to make anyone weep. How can I possibly think in terms of art if I am suddenly confronted with the picture of my pennilessness as you have drawn it? Do you suppose that if I did not feel it already I should be working like this? . . . Adieu . . . Adieu . . .

Madame Balzac was so afflicted by the happenings in that madhouse in the Rue Cassini that Laure felt compelled to write to Honoré asking him to treat her more gently. The tender-hearted Balzac was moved to tears—for as long as it took him to write a letter.

Balzac to Laure Surville, 20 July 1832: Poor mother! If only you knew how my heart bleeds at the thought of her ill and hard up! That is what is needed to give me the infernal courage which makes me work. But a time of great happiness and splendour will come which will compensate her for everything. Only she has an imagination like my own, and at moments she sees nothing but the lack of money and the difficulties, just as with other people she sees nothing but their triumphs. I forgive her everything, and I love her today more than ever. You must

tell her, dearest Laure, that as I write these lines there are tears
in my eyes. . . .

His justification was that during the stay at Saché he wrote the
Notice biographique sur Louis Lambert, a work in which he sought
to emulate the Goethe of *Faust* and the Byron of *Manfred*.
Louis Lambert was to be a shattering reply to his enemies and
'produce an effect of incontestable superiority'. It was the
portrait of a youthful prodigy, compounded of the Balzac of
Vendôme and the Balzac of the garret. In his account of Louis
Lambert's childhood, entirely fictitious, he describes him as
reading books which he himself read much later, between the
ages of fifteen and twenty-five, and attributes to him thoughts
which were his own as he sat writing at the age of thirty-three.
But the philosophical framework remains, and *Louis Lambert*
needs to be read with care if we are to understand the forming
of Balzac's mind.

'The Old and New Testaments came into Louis's hands at the
age of five, and it was this book, which contains so many books,
that determined his destiny. . . . From that time on reading
became for him a species of hunger which nothing could allay.'
Louis is strongly attracted to mystical books: 'Our intelligence is
an abyss which delights in abysses.' His secret is the power of
seeing, the power of imaginatively picturing what he reads, or
what is told him, with such vividness that he thoroughly knows
persons and events which he has not seen. Reading an account of
the battle of Austerlitz he hears the thunder of the cannon, the
cries of the combatants, the galloping of the horses; he smells
the powder; he is the witness of an Apocalypse. When he thus
immerses himself in what he is reading he loses all sense of the
outside world. But he is able at certain moments, if he chooses,
to concentrate his whole being on a given point in that world,
and then he is invincible. If he thinks intently of the effect
produced by a knife-blade thrust into his flesh, he feels a sharp
pain: 'A thought causing physical suffering? . . . Well, what do
you say to that?'

Louis Lambert's philosophy was that of Balzac himself, who
followed the esoteric tradition of the Cabbalists, which had been
revived by Saint-Martin and Swedenborg, and which embraced
the occult sciences. For Balzac, as for Swedenborg, every man

was two men—the *outward man*, subject to the laws of Nature, and the *inward man*, possessor of a vital force thus far inaccessible to science, but of the same nature as material force. In certain privileged beings (such as Louis Lambert) the inward man can detach himself from the outward man; this explains apparitions at a distance, the second-sight of clairvoyants, and the heroic detachment of martyrs, who at the time of their physical torment are *elsewhere*.

Ideas and desires emanate from the inward man, who sends out vibrations of varying strength according to the individual. This was what Louis Lambert called 'the material substance of thought', and it explained why a thought or desire could sap the strength of the body. We are back with the theme of the ass's skin. Louis, the child-visionary, is one of those beings, like Balzac himself, who are in intuitive contact with the universe; he feels himself to be on the threshold of a total understanding of creation. But the excessive richness of his inner life destroys the outward man. His spirit recoils from the 'trough of egotism' which is Paris. He prefers thought to action, an idea to a practical undertaking. He might become a power in the land, but he lacks the ability to concentrate on material things which is essential to anyone seeking to win material fortune. Instead his overflowing genius drives him to madness, despite the love of Pauline de Villenoix, a beautiful and generous woman of partly Jewish extraction, and he dies in her arms, 'a centenarian at twenty-five'.

Balzac sincerely believed that *Louis Lambert* was his masterpiece. He put into it all the fruits of his widespread reading of mystics, magi, philosophers, men of learning and science. He rewrote it a number of times, adding long discourses on social and metaphysical themes, and seeking to explain the different stages of creation in terms of the gradual pervasion of matter by thought. The superhuman genius with which he credited Louis Lambert was in some sort his own; but 'God can create everything except another God; genius can re-create everything except genius'. Louis never came to life. Madame de Berny, to whom he sent the first draft, and to whom the book was dedicated (*Et nunc et semper dilectae dicatum*), read it with anguish: 'I think you have attempted the impossible.' She did not believe that the public would put up with being told by any author, no matter how gifted, that he had grasped the whole meaning of the universe, or see in this anything but pretentiousness. Such sentences as, 'The admirable struggle of Thought, having achieved its greatest powers, its fullest possible expression . . . The spiritual world whose boundaries he had extended for himself . . .' would be found intolerable. She wrote to him: 'Let the whole world see you for themselves, my dearest, on the heights on which they place you, but do not cry out to them to admire you, because then the most powerful magnifying glasses will be directed at you, and what becomes of the most exquisite object when it is put under a microscope?' A woman, even in love, may have more sense than a man of genius.

'Consult Madame Carraud,' she advised, having faith in Balzac's only other genuine woman friend. (There is something touching, even sublime, in the attitude of those two high-minded women who, without ever meeting, together kept watch and ward over their poet.) Angoulême was only sixty leagues from Saché. He had enjoyed his first visit to La Poudrerie, the previous December. The residence was small, more farmhouse than country house, but he had been happy with Zulma Carraud and he greatly valued her affection. He was inclined to go there, the more so since he could not afford Aix-les-Bains— 'which,' he wrote to his sister, 'is a great disappointment to Madame de Castries, who shows me much kindness. I may find in her a younger Madame de Berny, more able to serve. . . .' Moreover he was beginning to find Saché oppressive:

Balzac to Zulma Carraud, 10 July 1832: I'm smothered by this *vie de château*. There are always guests, one has to get dressed at a fixed hour, and these provincials would think it very strange to go without dinner for the sake of pursuing an idea. They have cut short a good many for me with their gong. . . .

And not a single person capable of understanding him— imagine Madame de Margonne reading *Louis Lambert*! So he decided to go to La Poudrerie; but Zulma would have to come and pick him up at Angoulême, where the coach stopped. He was like a child in need of a mother's care, as incapable of covering the few miles between the town and the gunpowder-factory as he was of taking himself to China.

It was while he was staying with the Carrauds that he wrote

one of the best of his short novels, *La Femme abandonnée*. Although it is dangerous to attempt to pinpoint the exact source of any work of fiction, in which real life and the author's invention are so mysteriously blended, the elements in this case may be clearly discerned. The novella is dedicated to the Duchesse d'Abrantès, who in her *Mémoires sur la Restauration* tells a very similar tale about people known to have existed. As in Balzac's story, a man breaks off a liaison in order to marry, but cannot forget his former mistress and commits suicide when she refuses to see him again. The details coincide so exactly that there can be no mistaking their origin. Balzac owed a great deal to Laure d'Abrantès' rich store of memories. Moreover, when he was in Bayeux, he had had the opportunity of observing another '*femme abandonnée*', Madame d'Hautefeuille—'as intelligent and witty as any woman in Paris.' And for the emotional climate of the tale he possessed a third source in Laure de Berny.

He never abandoned Madame de Berny; but at that time he was much preoccupied with two alternative plans which caused him to neglect her. Could he raise the money to join the Marquise de Castries at Aix? And could he marry the wealthy Baronne Deurbroucq? A longing for security drew him towards the widow, although he knew very well that the monotony of marriage would do him no good as a novelist, thriving on crisis and emotional upheaval. Where the trip to Aix was concerned, he was torn between the hope of rapture in the arms of Madame de Castries and his fear of driving Laure de Berny to despair and losing her altogether. While he was describing the early stages of the love-affair between Gaston de Neuil and Claire de Beauséant in *La Femme abandonnée* he must surely have looked back on his memories of Villeparisis, when it was Madame de Berny who had been the afflicted woman living in rustic solitude, 'a prey to the shameful memory of a former passion' (the Corsican, Campi) and he himself who had been the writer of impassioned love-letters—of which he had kept copies! He certainly made use of these; and after all, why not? Abrantès, Berny, Hautefeuille—had he not the right to evoke those melancholy shades in order to create a living, breathing woman? Who would remember them now, so long buried in the past, if out of their sorrows and avowals Balzac had not conjured up Claire de Beauséant?

La Poudrerie was a good place to work in. He arrived there exhausted after finishing *Louis Lambert*, and he confessed to Zulma that at moments, like his hero, he had been afraid of going mad. 'If you go mad I will take care of you,' she said, and he never forgot those words or the look which accompanied them. He was in full creative flood, with new books stirring in his mind. Something tremendous was beginning to take shape. He wrote to his sister: 'In these last six months I have made immense strides in every direction.' He admitted in a burst of frankness that he had ruined their mother, although he still looked to the glorious day when everything would be repaid. He wrote to her: 'My dearest mother, I must try to console you a little as I console myself, with dreams. . . .' But for him the dreams were prophecies, and he did not doubt, in his moments of euphoria, that they would all come true.

With the Carrauds he recovered his peace of mind, finding affectionate admiration among friends and, something that to him was always precious, the adulation of strangers. A student at Angoulême University, hearing the name of Balzac, dropped his satchel in his excitement. When he went to have his hair cut women competed for his locks. But he wrote to his mother, with the bluntness characteristic of the family, that enforced continence was upsetting him and robbing him of sleep. This is presumably why he suddenly and surprisingly made advances to Zulma. She must have been tempted. She loved him deeply, and Major Carraud, fifteen years older than she, was rapidly ageing. 'You are naturally sensual,' said Honoré, 'and yet you fight against sensuality,' and he went on to talk of the 'undiscovered delights' into which he would initiate her, the stock formula of every seducer. But Zulma was firm. She knew very well that he only wanted her, at that particular moment, 'because you needed a woman. . . . Because being deprived of intimate relations with my sex had caused you to love it as a whole. . . . But I have too much pride to let myself be chosen for that sort of reason.'

And then the trip to Aix suddenly became possible. The astonishing Madame Mère managed to secure a long-term loan of 10,000 francs from their friend Madame Delannoy. It was enough to appease his more persistent creditors and pay the coach-fare.

Madame Delannoy to Balzac, 27 July 1832: I like your talent and yourself and I would not have it said that the one was hampered and the other distressed when I was in a position to prevent it. A happy chance has served me, since I have just recovered certain funds which have not yet been invested. They will serve to pay your debts and will enable you to undertake the journey you desire, which seems to me a suitable one from every point of view. . . .

So the two elderly ladies had put their heads together and were thrusting Honoré into the arms of Henriette de Castries. He had sent her an exerpt from *Louis Lambert*, a love-letter to Pauline de Villenoix:

Everything has joined in prompting me to make this amorous approach, to claim those first favours which a woman always refuses, no doubt that they may be ravished from her. But you, dear love of my soul, you will never know beforehand how much you mean to grant my love, and you will give yourself perhaps without intending to, for you are true and only obey your heart. . . . Oh, you have sensed those celestial harmonies, you who unite in yourself so many conflicting feelings and so often turned your eyes Heavenward rather than answer me! You, proud and smiling, humble and despotic, giving your whole soul in thought but drawing back from the shyest of caresses. . . .

He did not doubt that this tale of tender withdrawal would pale beneath more positive delights at Aix. At the moment of leaving Angoulême he found that he was short of ready money, and accordingly borrowed 150 francs from Major Carraud, asking his mother to return them, and to forward him another 300 at Lyons. While at La Poudrerie he had written *La Grenadière* (in a single night) and *La Femme abandonnée*. The tide of genius was flowing strongly.

As has already been mentioned, since 1830 Balzac had been amusing himself, between more serious works, by writing a number of *Contes drolatiques*, light-hearted tales of bawdry written in archaic language in the manner of Rabelais and other Touraine story-tellers. He continued with these in 1831 and 1832, and the title he selected for them shows what he had in mind: *Les Cent Contes drolatiques colligez ès Abbaïes de Touraine et mis en lumière par le sieur de Balzac pour l'esbattement des Pantagruelistes et non autres.*

As to why he persevered so long with this series of pastiches, which called for an immense amount of work, it was certainly in part because of the love of Rabelais he had inherited from his father. But they were written even more in protest against the unnatural melancholy of romanticism, 'that ridiculous word', and to revive the French spirit of earthy gaiety, '*l'esprit gauloise*', which had not prevented the publication of Pascal's *Pensées* or Montesquieu's *Esprit des lois*. 'Laughter is a necessity in France, ' he wrote in an article in *La Mode*, 'and the public is clamouring to be let out of the catacombs into which painters, poets and prose-writers are leading it, from one corpse to the next. . . . It is the act of a good citizen to oppose the hypocrisy. . . .' More particularly, it was the act of a *French* citizen, the enemy of English cant and German fantasy.

To which it may be replied that he himself had dipped deeply into the macabre, and that his love-stories, in general, did not offend modesty. But he wanted to be a whole man, to give the body its due as Rabelais had done, and to revive the great French literature of the fifteenth century, 'so sparkling with humour, so racy and alive with words which in those days had not been dishonoured'. His mother had complained when he was twenty of the bad influence Rabelais and Sterne were having on him; he believed, on the contrary, that in becoming the Rabelais of the nineteenth century he would add to his reputation. But he did not intend to let Pantagruelism infect his serious work: 'I have written the *Cent Contes drolatiques* for that small, particular cult.' Priapus was entitled to his statue, but it must be placed at the bottom of the garden.

He borrowed tales from all the old story-tellers, but the method of telling them was his own, and there were here and there accounts of amorous refinements very foreign to Rabelais: 'The thousand gradual advances, dilatory, interlocutory, preparatory, the cossetings, the little pans put in the oven to warm, the branches smoking like incense and gathered twig by twig in the forests of love, the touchings, toyings, pattings, strokings, venturings, murmurings, the sweets tasted together, the licking of the cup as cats do, and the other tiny becks and trafficks of love which rakes know of, which lovers invent and which ladies delight in more than their souls' salvation, because they are more cats than women. . . .' The skilled lover of Laure de Berny shines through the Rabelaisian verbiage. What did she think of it? We do not know, but Zulma Carraud, surprisingly enough, found the stories 'so amusing that they will outlast everything'. The Duc de Fitz-James, another Rabelaisian, praised them warmly. While predicting that Balzac would be 'assailed by the lightnings of humbugs and Academicians' he was ducally amused.

George Sand was among the ladies who disapproved: 'When, against my will, he tried to read some passages to me I nearly threw the book in his face. I remember that when I told him he was disgusting he called me a prude and left, shouting from the stairs, "You're an ass!" But in the end we were better friends than ever, Balzac was so genuinely simple and good.' In Delphine de Girardin's circle, on the other hand, they were much enjoyed. Antoine Fontaney wrote in his *Journal intime* (12 January 1832): 'Balzac, with a strange and unbelievable virtuosity, told us some droll, fantastic stories which greatly amused the ladies. Delphine helped him and gave him ideas. We listened and admired—a remarkable performance.'

The first ten, *Le Premier Dizain*, were published by Gosselin in April 1832. As happened so often to Balzac, they were badly received. 'Are the *Contes drolatiques* amusing?' asked the *Revue des Deux Mondes*. 'Truly they are not. They are obscene and not lascivious. . . .' The *Revue de Paris* said coldly: 'M. Gosselin likens his author to a child who shows himself naked in perfect innocence. We would reply to M. Gosselin that in *literature* children of the age of M. de Balzac have long worn trousers. We regret that it is not the same in the *bookselling* business.' Only Barbey d'Aurevilly approved of the simplicity and high spirits of the author: 'The literary historians of the future who concern themselves with Balzac will, I have no doubt, recognize the truth of an opinion which today I have done no more than suggest, and will not dispute it.' The Constable of Letters, as he was called, proved himself a worthy judge of this nineteenth-century Rabelais. But the fact remains that the *Contes drolatiques*, technical *tour de force* though they were, added nothing to Balzac's reputation. As with Rabelais, his thinking was worth more than his bawdry; but perhaps he needed the occasional spell of bawdry to stimulate his thought.

XIV

The Reluctant Lady

BIANCHON: *On aime parce qu'on aime.*
RASTIGNAC: *Eh bien! Moi, je l'aime par bien d'autres raisons.*

BALZAC

HE SET OFF radiantly for Aix, never doubting that his first 'great lady' was going to be his. She had summoned him, she had insisted that he should come incognito, and her every evening was to be spent with him. During the daytime, of course, he would work as usual. There was *La Bataille* to be written, proofs of *Les Chouans* and *Louis Lambert* to be corrected, and some short stories to be produced for the *Revue de Paris*, which had unexpectedly agreed to a contract guaranteeing him 500 francs a month. He stopped a few hours between stages at Limoges, where he saw Lucile Nivet, Zulma Carraud's sister, whose husband, a manufacturer of chinaware, was to supply him with a dinner-service for the Rue Cassini. Her young son showed him round the town, and, jotting down names and details as usual, Balzac added it to his stock of useful backgrounds.

Between Limoges and Lyons he had a painful accident. He had chosen to sit beside the driver, to get a better view of the countryside. He was climbing back to his seat after the coach stopped at Thiers, and had just let go the straps he had been holding on to, when the horses started with a jerk and he fell. He managed to grab one of the straps, but was flung with his whole thirteen-stone weight against the iron step of the coach, and badly cut his shin. Fortunately the damage was more painful than serious, and reclining on the roof of the coach he was still able to enjoy the rest of the four days' journey. He was always a lover of landscapes. Those of Limousin and Auvergne delighted him.

Madame de Castries had reserved him a small but pleasant

room at the hotel in Aix, and here he passed his days in complete solitude, sending out for his lunch, which consisted of an egg and a glass of milk. At six he went down to dine with the Marquise and remained with her until eleven. Thus (so he told his mother) he was able to spend the whole day working on *La Bataille*, which was to be one of the *Scènes de la militaire*. But the fact is that he had not yet started on *La Bataille*. He was correcting proofs of *La Femme abandonnée* and adding last touches to *Louis Lambert*.

Three medicinal baths at Aix completed the healing of his leg, leaving only a scar. His room cost him two francs a day and his lunch fifteen sous. Henriette de Castries did not allow him to pay for his dinner. 'Well, Mother, even if I am a bit dreamy and poetic you must admit that I'm economical!' He saw no one; his only diversion was the evening tête-à-tête with the lady. She was kindness itself, but she allowed him no greater liberty than a hand-clasp; which finally got on his nerves.

Balzac to Zulma Carraud, early September 1832: I came here hoping for little and much. Much, because I shall never be loved by her. Why did you send me to Aix? . . . She is a woman of the most fastidious kind, Madame de Beauséant and more; but are not these refinements acquired at the expense of the spirit? . . .

To which the heroic Zulma thundered back: 'Poor Honoré! You are suffering and I am not there to look after you!' She had hoped that the view of mountains and lakes would release his spirit from the vanities with which it was encumbered. 'Yes, my lord, it is I, poor creature that I am, who dare to address these words to the idol of the day!' She maintained that he was corrupted not by his own nature, which was noble and good, but by his thirst for the applause of a single class of society ('. . . and they're the only ones you care about; they have to smell of English honey and essence of Portugal'). How could the mind capable of conceiving *Louis Lambert* see nothing but bigotry in any man clad in old-fashioned garments, nothing but a rude mechanical in any working man, nothing but food for the Assizes in any rough-handed tiller of the soil? 'Honoré, it grieves me not to see you great!' It also grieved her to learn that he had come to terms with Pichot of the *Revue de Paris*, a crude individual who had treated him offensively and would now be saying with a grin, 'You can get anything for money!':

Money! And simply because in your fashionable circles one cannot arrive on foot! How I love Raphaël in his garret, how noble he is, and how right Pauline is to adore him! Because, make no mistake about it, she only loves him afterwards because of her memories; she loves him rich because of what she did for him when he was poor. How small he is when he possesses millions! Have you measured your own ass's skin since you had your apartment redecorated and bought that up-to-date tilbury which brings you home from the Rue du Bac at two in the morning? You ask why I sent you to Aix. Because that is the only place where you can find what you want. . . . I let you go because we have not a single thought in common; because I despise the things you revere; because I am ordinary people, people of breeding but always on the side of those who suffer oppression. Because I hate all power, inasmuch as I have not yet found any that is just. . . . You are at Aix because a party wants to buy you, and a woman is the price they are prepared to pay. But I, ugly, small and limping as I am, would never accept a man who can be bought on those terms. . . . You are in Aix because your soul is falsified; because you have rejected true renown for *glamour*; because my heart can never be stirred by the hand-clasp of a man who preens himself when he drives past the walkers in the Bois and arrives first at the Place Louis XV. . . . You are allowing the most frivolous gratifications to take the place of all others. I am saying hard things to you, dear Honoré, but I say them without fear, for I have such a store of good and honest affection for you that I can make amends for all unkindness. When you run out of duchesses I shall still be here, offering you the consolations of a true loyalty. . . .

Perhaps in her heart she regretted having rejected the advances of a man she certainly loved. If she had told him these home-truths to his face the tremor in her voice must have given her away. To end on a magnanimous note, she predicted that he would find his happiness at Aix: 'It could not happen at once. But you dine together and are living under the same roof; vanity and physical attraction will bring you together, and you will get what you want. Besides, believe me, the lady has too much interest in securing you to permit you to indulge in plebeian loves.' But with all her intuition Zulma was wrong, and

Balzac got no farther. Madame de Castries 'had been endowed by nature with all the arts of the coquette. . . . All the delights of love were hinted at in the freedom of her expressive gaze, in the undertones of her voice and the charm of her words. She let it appear that there was the most noble of harlots concealed within her . . . that she would become the most ravishing of mistresses by the act of removing her corset.' Alas, the corset was not removed.

To desire but not possess is to secrete an inner poison. Those delightful but unfulfilled encounters exasperated Balzac to the point of frenzy. If he tried to lay hands on her she grew indignant, pretended to be alarmed, and 'banished him from the sofa at the precise moment when the sofa became perilous'. She had no lack of arguments—religion, the memory of a great love to which she wished to remain faithful, and the physical weakness due to her accident. There may well have been some truth in all of them. She was certainly a sick woman, broken in body and perhaps dead to any feeling of love. Balzac appealed to her by his intelligence and vivacity, he amused her, and his fame as a writer flattered her pride. She admired and was even fond of him, but she had certainly no wish to go to bed with a fat, uncouth man whose real qualities she was far from understanding. She had whistled him to her side like a dog, but she granted him only those favours which by a Jesuitical prescription were tolerated in her own circle 'where they wanted everything of love except that which testified to love'.

But still he hoped. With his usual sentimentality he had asked to be allowed to call her by a private name reserved for him alone. Once again it was 'Marie'. She had consented. So that was a good sign, wasn't it—*hein, ma mère*? She was planning a tour of Switzerland and Italy with her uncle Fitz-James, who had a great liking for Balzac. Honoré was asked to come too. Another good sign, surely; there could not fail to be propitious occasions. And the money problem could easily be solved. The monthly payments from the *Revue de Paris* would keep his mother; the *Contes drolatiques* would be a best-seller; and he was already including *La Bataille* in his calculations, although it was still unwritten. He had made the acquaintance in Aix of James de Rothschild (he always spelt the name Rostchild) who would give him a letter of introduction to his brother in Naples.

How much was he going to need for this Italian trip? A thousand crowns. Madame Mère received her orders. She was to send him 1,200 francs, some top-boots, some pomade and a flagon of Portugal-water, the latter a weapon of seduction as potent, in the Balzac alchemy, as straw-coloured gloves. He further sent her two pieces of flannel that he had been wearing on his stomach. Madame Balzac was to consult her clairvoyant as to the cause of his trouble, taking the flannel *wrapped in paper* so as not to weaken the emanations. And finally: 'Please put half a dozen pairs of yellow gloves in the parcel.'

He accompanied his noble friends on an excursion to the Grande Chartreuse where, side by side with 'Marie', he marvelled at the majestic alpine scene, a stream in torrent, a ruined mill. Madame de Castries seemed also to be deeply moved. It was a solemn day.

I saw the Grande Chartreuse, I walked beneath those ancient, silent vaults and heard, under the cloisters, the water from the spring fall drop by drop. I entered a cell to measure the extent of my nothingness; I breathed the profound peace that my predecessor in that place had known, and read with emotion the inscription he had carved on the door, following the custom of the monastery. All the precepts of the life I wished to live were contained in those Latin words—*Fuge, late, tace. . . .*

This occasion had a profound effect on Balzac. For a month he had been living in the company of a woman he desired, and he had suffered greatly at not being loved in return. The peace of the monastery afforded him a sudden revelation of the feelings of a man who, fleeing the world after a disappointment in love, takes refuge in solitude. A master-phrase occurred to him, '*Aux coeurs blessés l'ombre et le silence*', and he was seized with an idea. It can happen to a writer that in an inspired moment, like a lightning flash illuminating great vistas, he sees a whole book. The work has still to be done, conception is not execution, but the essence is there; and so one can understand why Honoré wrote to his mother: 'I have worked three days and nights and produced an octavo volume entitled *Le Médecin de campagne*.' It was not true; the book was still no more than an idea. But Balzac had seen it in that flashing moment, and for him it was a fact.

Balzac to the publisher, Mame, 30 September 1832: Take careful note, Maître Mame. I have long been struck by, and desirous of achieving, the popular success which consists in selling countless thousands of copies of a small octavo volume like *Atala, Paul et Virginie, The Vicar of Wakefield, Manon Lescaut*, the tales of Perrault and so on.

The numerous reprints compensate for the fact that the work is in only one volume; but it must be suitable for *everyone*, the young girl, the child, the old man, even the nun. Once the book has become known, which may take a longer or shorter time according to the author's talent and the ability of the publisher, it becomes a valuable property. For example, Lamartine's *Meditations*, 40,000 copies, Volney's *Ruines*, etc.

My book is conceived in that spirit, a book that can be read by the doorkeeper or the great lady. I have taken the New Testament and the Catechism as models, both books with an excellent sale. . . . It is a story with a village background, and for the rest, you can read it at a sitting, a thing that does not often happen with me. . . .

At first sight this is a shocking letter. Having undergone a profoundly moving spiritual experience which he wants to express in a novel, he talks of nothing but the book's commercial prospects, citing the New Testament in evidence. Scarcely the approach, one would think, to inspire confidence in a publisher. But we must remember how Balzac's mind worked. To him the book already existed; it was entered in the accounts; it was to pay for the Italian journey. Not for the first or last time, financial necessity was to be the unworthy source of a masterpiece. And perhaps something of the kind is always needed, the urgency, the heightened temperature fusing together the elements pre-existing in the author's mind.

As to the book itself, if he intended it to be short he also meant it to be edifying. A man wounded in spirit takes refuge in 'shadow and silence', and turns his retreat to practical use by civilizing a whole canton in the mountains. It was a simple but splendid theme, recalling the broad frescoes of Goethe. At first Balzac was inclined to take *The Vicar of Wakefield* as a model and make his hero a village priest. But he knew too little about the workings of the religious mind. On the other hand, he knew a good deal about doctors. The village of Voreppe, near the Grande Chartreuse, had been transformed by a doctor. There was his own doctor, Nacquart. There was Dr Buisson, a great local benefactor, whom he had met at L'Isle-Adam. Balzac had also been responsible for printing a book about Pastor Oberlin, the philosopher and philanthropist. No doubt it was of all these, of random reading, childhood recollections and recent impressions, that Dr Benassis was born; but he was destined to live in his own right, infused with the spirit of his creator. 'A writer never invents,' Balzac was fond of saying. He might have added, '—and he never copies.'

He intended also to include among the minor characters some sketches of soldiers under the Empire. Napoleon was still a popular hero, and merely to evoke his memory would assist the sale of the little two hundred-page book. The reader was to learn of the work accomplished in that mountainous region from the conversations between Benassis and a Major Genestas, a character based in part on a close friend of the Carrauds, and there was to be talk of the Emperor among old soldiers returned from the wars. Thanks to his Saint-Cyr friends, Balzac had a great fund of war stories, and there was no greater admirer of Napoleon. But it was all in the future. When he left Aix, on 10 October, *Le Médecin de campagne* was still a dream, and so was *La Bataille*.

Before leaving he wrote to Zulma Carraud:

You are unfair to me. . . . Do you really think I would sell myself to a party for a woman? . . . I who have lived chastely for a year! . . . You make monsters of my flights of fancy. . . . My home is a pleasure to me, and as much a necessity as clean linen and a bath. I have earned the right to live in silk, because if need be I would return without regret, without a sigh, to the author's garret, bare of every luxury, rather than do anything shameful or sell myself to anyone. Oh, do not slander someone who loves you and thinks of you with pride in the difficult moments! Great labours call for great excesses—it is quite simple. . . .

As for his ideas on the subject of government, he assured her that if ever a time came when he could put them into practice they would be liberal in principle:

The abolition of all nobility outside the Chamber of Peers; the separation of the clergy from Rome; the natural boundaries of France; the perfect equality of the middle class; the recognition of genuine superiority; economy in public spending and increased revenue by a better system of taxation; education for all—those are the main points of my policy, to which you will find me faithful. My deeds will be consistent with my words. . . .

But he asked her not to divulge this programme, which would be very ill-received by the Legitimist party. If he allied himself to those people it was because he could not hope to be elected without their help. The Duc de Fitz-James would secure him a seat in the Chambre des Deputés. *Le Médecin de campagne* would win him friends: 'It is a work that will do good, and worthy of the Prix Montyon. . . .

What else was there? Zulma must not suppose that he was the slave of the Marquise de Castries: 'I consider that a life like mine must not be tied to any woman's apron-strings, and that I must follow my destiny in large terms and look a little higher than the waist.'

Balzac to his mother, 23 September 1832: All things carefully reckoned, this money will get me to Rome. I shall travel fourth class, in Madame de Castries' carriage; and the agreed sum, to cover everything—food, carriage and inns—is 1,000 francs from Geneva to Rome, my share being 250. . . . I shall have a pleasant journey with the Duc, who is like a father to me. And everywhere I shall be moving in the highest society. I shall never have such a chance again. He has been in Italy before; he knows the country and will be able to save me all kinds of delays, apart from the fact that his name will open every door to me. The Marquise and he are *very good* to me. . . .

The Duc may have been, but the Marquise continued to send him away every evening, raging with frustration. What he needed, to overthrow that paragon of virtue, was the audacity of the great womanizers, who do not ask but take. He had reached the point where there was only one thought in his mind, to possess her. When they stopped together at the Hôtel de la Couronne, in Geneva, he thought the game was won. But it was not to be. Upon their return from a pilgrimage to the Villa Diodati, where Byron had lived, and after a deceptively warm embrace, she told him that she would never be his mistress. He walked back weeping into the town, in an agony of unfulfilled desire and even more of wounded pride. There was

no point in going on. He did not confess defeat to Zulma
Carraud in so many words, but wrote: 'Once again I am assailed
with bitter trials. . . . I must give up the Italian journey. . . . I'm
so unhappy that I can't tell you about it. . . .

We know that the reason he gave Zulma for not going to Italy
('My mother doesn't want to have to look after my affairs in
Paris any longer') was untrue, because at the same time he
wrote to Madame Balzac: 'Dearest Mother, I think it will be
wiser for me to come back to France for three months. . . . But I
shall not come to Paris, and no one will know of my return. In
February I shall go from Marseilles to Naples on the steam-
packet. . . .' There was no definite break with the Marquise, who
continued to write to him; but he had been most painfully
humiliated. He dashed off a 'Confession of Dr Benassis', to go
into *Le Médecin de campagne*, in which the doctor accounts for
his retirement by his need to escape from a heartless woman:

Such is my story, a horrible story, that of a man who for a
few months rejoiced in all the beauties of Nature, all the
radiance of sunshine in a rich countryside, and then lost his
sight. . . . Yes, Monsieur, a few months' rapture and then
nothing. Why was I so feasted? . . . Why for a few days did she
call me her beloved, if she intended to withdraw that title, the
only one the heart craves? . . . She confirmed it all with a kiss,
that sweet, sacred promise. . . . A kiss can never be effaced. . . .
When was she lying? Was it when she ravished me with her
gaze, murmuring the name I had given her, the token of love
between us; or when she broke the contract binding our hearts
and for ever mingling two thoughts in a single life? She lied at
some time. . . . You ask how the disaster came about. . . . In the
simplest way in the world. On one day I was everything to her,
and on the next day I was nothing. On one day her voice was
melodious and tender, her gaze bright with enchantment; on
the next her voice was harsh, her eyes cold, her manner withdrawn. During the night a woman had died, and it was the one
I loved. Why did it happen? I do not know. . . . For some hours
I was tempted by the demons of revenge. I would make the
whole world hate her, expose her to the public gaze tied to a
stake of infamy. . . .

This 'confession' was written in the fury of the moment. He
did not include it in the final version of that particular book,

but he was to bind the lady to her 'stake of infamy' in another novel which was already taking shape in his mind. 'A writer compensates himself in his own fashion for the unfairness of life.' Meanwhile, where was he to go? Zulma offered the powder-factory and her loving heart, as he had expected: 'How great was my gratitude when I read your good and affectionate letter, upon which I had counted with all the trust of La Fontaine going to Madame d'Hervart! . . .' Certainly he would go to Angoulême; but first he must go to La Bouleaunière, to Laure de Berny, the angel of mercy who had always dressed his wounds.

Here the publisher, Louis Mame, paid him a visit, hoping to be handed the manuscript of *Le Médecin de campagne*. All Balzac could show him were the chapter-titles, less satisfactory to the publisher than they were to the author. To facilitate his work, a young painter named Auguste Borget, a friend of Zulma and great admirer of Balzac, offered to relieve Madame Mère of her burden by going to live in the Rue Cassini and take charge of Honoré's affairs. Before long he too was overwhelmed by the Balzac hurricane. 'You say that the tempests succeed one another with a terrifying rapidity,' he wrote to him. 'What surprises me, my dear friend, is that you did not foresee this. You have done everything possible to attract the lightnings and then you are amazed when the storm breaks. . . .'

It was agreed that Balzac would pay his mother 150 francs a month, very modest interest on the money she had lent him. She still owned a house in the Rue Montorgueil and although badly off was not destitute. Early in December Balzac returned to the Rue Cassini without having been to Angoulême. He had a hankering for Paris, after being away so long. Eugène Sue wrote to him in the airy fashion of the '*loge infernale*':

My good Balzac . . . I will answer your questions in order. 1. Love. I'm keeping a girl and amusing myself, as I have already told you, by treating her abominably. She must be very hungry to put up with me. I also have a lady of fashion whom I worry about no more than she worries about me; but we cling to each other from force of habit; after all, at our age one looks too low and sees too clearly to regard love as an objective, a source of rapture or a matter of faith. . . .

This cynicism was in marked contrast to the cooings of the Dilecta, pathetically recalling Balzac's sojourn at La Grenadière two years before. But what was he to do? Madame de Berny had given him a true love 'which had to end'. She no longer possessed any 'sensual beauty'. Where was he to look for consolation? He had no fondness for strumpets or for kept mistresses: 'A woman of distinction will not make advances, and I, who find eighteen hours a day insufficient for the work I have to do, cannot spare the time to prostitute my nature by simpering and dressing up for the benefit of some easy woman. . . . Marriage would be a rest. But where am I to find a wife? . . .'

Lack of money was the obstacle; there would be no lack of fame. But his figure was not improving. He was growing stouter, and the bulging belly on top of his short legs made him look, in side-view, like the ace of spades. Nevertheless Lamartine, who met him at the Girardins, noted that his gaiety and brilliance of mind caused his physical shortcomings to be forgotten:

There was nothing in him of the man of this century. One might suppose, on seeing him, that one had entered another epoch and was in the soceity of one of those two or three men, by their nature immortal, of whom Louis XV was the centre. . . . Balzac was standing in front of the marble fireplace. . . . A good deal of the fullness of a Mirabeau, but no heaviness. He had so much spirit that he bore it lightly, gaily, like a flexible covering and not at all like a burden. . . . That expressive face, from which one could not detach one's gaze, was entirely charming and fascinating. But its predominant characteristic, even more than its intelligence, was the goodness it communicated. . . . No passion of hatred or envy could have been expressed by that face; it was impossible for it to be anything but kind. But it was not the kindness of indifference or heedlessness as in the epicurean countenance of La Fontaine; it was a loving kindness, aware of itself and of others. . . . That is exactly what Balzac was. I loved him by the time we sat down to dine. . . .

Women could also love him, as Laure de Berny and Zulma Carraud so well knew. But in a wife he needed fortune, beauty, youth and social rank; and all he could offer in return, apart from the genius which notaries do not enter in their accounts, was 100,000 francs of debts.

XV

Enter *l'Étrangère*

---

*Le mythe de la côte d'Adam, c'est qu'il s'était fait une
femme comme tout jeune homme les rêve, aussi lui vient-elle
en dormant.*

BALZAC

FOR SOME MONTHS he had been nursing an exotic, preposterous and delicious dream. Among his huge number of letters
from women there was one which had particularly attracted his
notice. It was signed *l'Étrangère* and had been posted in Odessa
on 28 February 1832. The handwriting and manner suggested
a woman of good position, perhaps even more. After warmly
praising his *Scènes de la vie privée* she reproached him for
having forsaken, in *La Peau de chagrin*, the delicacy of feeling
which had led to their success. The orgy scene, the women
of the town, the heartless Foedora, all these had shocked
her, and so she had decided to write to the author. Balzac, on
the off-chance, acknowledged the letter in an insertion in the
Gazette de France, which, however, the lady did not see. On
7 November she wrote to him again:

Your soul embraces centuries, Monsieur; its philosophical
concepts appear to be the fruit of long study matured by time;
yet I am told that you are still young. I would like to know you,
but feel that I have no need to do so. I know you through my
own spiritual instinct; I picture you in my own way and feel
that were I to set eyes upon you I should exclaim, 'That is he!'

'Your outward semblance probably does not reveal your
brilliant imagination; you have to be moved, the sacred fire of
genius has to be lit, if you are to show yourself as you really are,
and you are what I feel you to be—a man superior in his knowledge of the human heart.

My heart has leapt as I read your works. You elevate woman
to her true dignity; love, in her, is a celestial virtue, a divine

emanation; and I admire in you the admirable sensibility of soul which has enabled you to perceive this.

She did not want to tell him her name: 'For you I am *l'Étrangère* and shall remain so all my life.' But she proposed to write to him from time to time to remind him of his celestial qualities, feeling that he possessed 'the soul of an angel', capable of understanding the fiery soul which she believed herself to be. Although separated from him by a thousand leagues, she hoped to become his conscience and reveal to him eternal truths: 'A word from you in *La Quotidienne* will tell me that you have received my letter and may write to you without misgiving. It should be addressed "*A l'É.*" and signed "H.B." '

The mystery, the mysticism and the exalted style were too much after Balzac's own heart for him to neglect a chance like this. *La Quotidienne* of 9 December contained the following classified announcement: 'M. de B. has received the letter addressed to him; he has only today been able to acknowledge it in the columns of this journal, and regrets not knowing where to address his reply.' Whereupon the lady promptly disclosed her identity. By birth the Countess Éveline Rzewuska, belonging to an illustrious Polish family which had rallied to the cause of Russia, she had in 1819 married Wenceslas Hanski, a member of the Ukrainian nobility twenty-two years older than herself. Her eldest sister, Caroline, a woman of great beauty and an intellectual, had left her elderly husband for the Russian general Witt, with whom she had been living openly for fifteen years. During this *liaison declarée* she had had affairs with the poet Adam Mickiewicz, and with Pushkin, and had brought the two men together. The Tsar held her to be dangerous, as faithless in love as she was in politics. The women of that family had a taste for famous men; but Éveline was considered to be more reliable than Caroline.

Wenceslas Hanski was owner of the castle of Wierzchownia in the Ukraine, and an estate of 21,000 acres, inhabited by 3,035 'souls'. To Balzac this latest prospect was like something out of an eastern fairy-tale, a superb solace to his pride after the Castries affair. She seemed to possess every desirable quality— youth (she was in fact thirty-three at the time, but only admitted to twenty-seven), beauty (he did not doubt it), fabulous wealth and an elderly husband. Because of the latter, certain precautions were needful if the distinguished writer and the romantic countess were to correspond freely. A go-between was found in the person of Henriette Borel, called Lirette, the Swiss governess of Madame Hanska's only surviving child, Anna. She undertook to pass on Balzac's letters, which were sent to her in a double envelope.

A novelist has a hundred guises. For the benefit of *l'Étrangère* Balzac wrote himself a new part, entirely different from the one he was accustomed to play in the company of men like Eugène Sue and Lautour-Mézeray. Yet he was not really cheating. The youthful heart, the fresh imagination, the pure ardours and exaltation which he offered Madame Hanska were a genuine part of himself. There were, he wrote to her, sad exiles from Heaven who instinctively recognized and loved each other; and he and she were of their number:

In the midst of my incessant struggle, amid my labours and endless studies in this turbulent city of Paris where politics or literature absorbs sixteen or eighteen hours out of every twenty-four, unhappy though I am, and very different from the author of everyone's dreams, I have had charming hours which I owe to you. That is why, in gratitude, I dedicated the fourth volume of the *Scènes de la vie privée* to you by putting your initials at the head of the final Scene, the one which I was writing when I received your first letter. But someone who is a mother to me, and whose wishes, and even jealousies, I am bound to respect, has asked that this mute expression of my feelings shall be removed. I do not fear to tell you of the dedication and its deletion because I think you have sufficient greatness of soul not to desire an act of homage which would have pained a person as noble and as great as the one who bore me, for she protected me amid the distresses and disasters which nearly caused me to die young. . . .

The person was, of course, Madame de Berny. The touching filial picture of his relationship with her was, after all, not untrue. 'Bonds eternal and bonds broken.' What was less true was his account of his solitary life and the political perils to which he was exposed: 'Spokesman of a defeated party, soon to be the representative of all noble and religious ideas, I am already an object of bitter hatred. The more that is expected of my voice, the more is it feared.' In his exhausting labours and tribulations, he said, he needed the sympathy of a woman whom he could love and respect, and the part was one which the chatelaine of Wierzchownia might play. She was tempted, but became mistrustful when she received a letter in an entirely different style and handwriting, with a black seal. It was written by Zulma Carraud, at that time in mourning, who sometimes helped Balzac with his fan-mail.

Balzac to Madame Hanska, January 1833: You were afraid you were being laughed at? By whom? By a poor child, the victim yesterday, as he will be again tomorrow, of his feminine modesty, his shyness, his trustfulness. You ask me suspiciously to account for my two different handwritings; but I have as many handwritings as there are days in the year, without being in the least versatile on that account. This changeability is born of an imagination which may conceive anything and still remain pure. . . .

Not the most plausible of explanations; but swiftly changing the subject he went on to talk about *Louis Lambert*, which he held in its present form to be a 'wretched miscarriage' and which he was proposing to rewrite. At the moment he was finishing a work 'wholly evangelical in its nature, and which seems to me like a romanticized *Imitation of Christ*'. This was *Le Médecin de campagne*, which was to be followed by *La Bataille*. He had not yet written a line of the latter, but he described it in masterly fashion:

The reader in his armchair must see the campaign, the details of the terrain, the masses of men, the strategic movements, the Danube, the bridges; he must follow the struggle as a whole and in its parts, hear the gunfire, observe the moves on the chessboard, see everything, feel every joint and muscle of the great body of Napoleon, whom I shall not bring on the scene, except perhaps to show him crossing the Danube one evening in a boat! Not a sign of a woman; cannons, horses, two armies, uniforms. The guns roar out on the first page, and fall silent on the last. You will read through their smoke, and by the time you close the book you should have seen everything with your mind's eye, you should recollect the battle as though you had been there. . . .

Such vast matter to be handled; and how badly did the 'poor child' of genius need a courageous voice to lead him to man's estate, while allowing him 'to pluck the flower of passion at the roadside'. From his first breath he had longed for the love of a young and beautiful woman. The love had been granted him, but the woman, alas, was no longer young. 'I love you, dear Unknown, and this strange fact is no more than the natural outcome of a life that has always been empty and unhappy.' Madame Hanska was prompt to join in the game. She questioned travellers arriving from France about Balzac and was told that he drank ('I only drink coffee'), that he was friendly with depraved characters like Eugène Sue ('Eugène Sue is a goodhearted and amiable young man, who makes a great show of vice'), that he was worldly (it was true that at one time he had sat up till after midnight telling stories to friends; but he had given this up so as not to be considered a mere entertainer). Moreover, 'the bitter disappointment which all Paris is talking about' (his rebuff at the hands of Madame de Castries) had, he said, plunged him in silence, solitude and toil.

He did undoubtedly get through a prodigious amount of work during those first months of 1833. *Louis Lambert* was published on 31 January and torn to shreds by the critics. It was only to be expected. If philosophical abstractions are to evoke any response in the general reader, they need to be embodied in a tale. *Louis Lambert* was pure thinking, unshaped and unadorned. The loyal Zulma placed it 'all affection apart, a thousand miles above Goethe's *Faust*'; but affection may have played a larger part than she knew.

His unexecuted commitments were coming home to roost. The *Revue de Paris* was clamouring for short stories in return for its monthly payments. Balzac hurriedly wrote the first episode of a book to be called *L'Histoire des treize* which he had long been meditating and which suited him admirably: 'Thirteen men come together in Paris under the Empire ... all endowed with sufficient courage to remain faithful to the same beliefs, all having sufficient integrity not to betray each other. ...' Violent action, the will to power, secret societies—these were subjects that Balzac, like his father, had always enjoyed. There were links between the Freemasons, of which Bernard-François had been a member, and the secret workers' organization known as the '*compagnonnage*'. The mutual-assistance network of the '*compagnons*' extended throughout France. And the public had learned about the solidarity of the underworld from the memoirs of Vidocq, an ex-convict who became chief of the Sûreté, the criminal police.

Secret societies correspond to one of man's most ancient needs; initiation ceremonies and magical associations go back to the dawn of history. Balzac especially was fascinated by the idea of a man or group of men, godlike figures, making themselves masters of Paris and the world. He took great delight in creating the character of Ferragus, the chief of the *Devorants*, a cruel, unconquerable superman and one of the Thirteen; and the readers of the *Revue de Paris* were no less pleased by the fantasy, set in their own world and time. The Thousand and One Nights had come to Paris! No one who started to read *Ferragus* could put it down. The Duchesse de Berry, imprisoned in the fortress of Blaye, read it and made her doctor, an acquaintance of Balzac, write and ask him how the tale was going to end. 'She wept and groaned . . . ,' wrote Dr Ménière. 'Thank you, magician, you are the consoler of captives.' Balzac replied: 'To be a consoler of captives, my dear Ménière, is the most wonderful thing in the world, and I attach more value to bringing comfort to those angels called women, when they are suffering for no matter what reason, than to the utmost fame.'

He announced a further episode in the *Histoire des treize* which was to be entitled, *Ne touchez pas à la hache*. It eventually became *La Duchesse de Langeais*, a novel based on the Castries affair, in which he savagely revenged himself on the lady by causing her to be branded with a hot iron, and then rescued her and packed her off to Mount Carmel. (There was a Carmelite convent next door to the Rue Cassini, and he was touched by the singing of the nuns.)

But he felt that the 'fabrication of ideas' was exhausting him. Ever since his garret days he had resorted to stimulants to assist his furious labours, in particular coffee, to keep sleep at bay. With ordinary mortals coffee loses its effect after two or three weeks—'Time enough, fortunately, to write an opera,' Rossini said. Balzac prolonged the effect by making it ever stronger. He found that coffee crushed in the Turkish fashion had more flavour than ground coffee, that it had more virtue if infused in cold water and then heated, and that a week or two might be gained by diminishing the amount of water until it became a concentration as thick as soup. Taken on an empty stomach coffee causes inflammation, griping and other ill-effects—'and then the mind is aroused, ideas pour out like the regiments of the Grand Armée over the battlefield, and the battle begins. Memories come charging in with flags flying; the light cavalry of comparisons extends itself in a magnificent gallop; the artillery of logic hurries along with its ammunition train, and flashes of wit bob up like sharpshooters. . . .'* In short, the paper gets covered with ink like the battlefield with black powder, the books get written and the author's heart suffers.

The life of literary Paris added to his weariness and his disgust. 'How squalid it all is!' He talked to *l'Étrangère* about Victor Hugo, saying of him (quite wrongly) that 'married for love, with delightful children, he has flung himself into the arms of an infamous strumpet'. As for himself, Heaven had saved him from these pitfalls by according him the devotion of a few great hearts —the Dilecta, the lady of Angoulême, the painter Auguste Borget, his sister Laure, and now his beloved Foreign Lady. If only she would write more often!

I beseech you, tell me in that charming, *catlike* style, how your days are spent, hour by hour, make me see it all. Describe the rooms you live in, even to the colour of the furniture. . . . Draw me a picture so that when I turn to you in thought I may meet you; so that I may see the tapestry-frame with the beginning of a flower, see you in all your hours. If you knew how often tired thought needs repose that is in some sort active, and how much good it does me to be able to indulge in a reverie beginning, 'At this moment she is there, she is looking at that'! I who credit thought with the gift of being able to cover distances so completely as to abolish them! Those are my only pleasures amid my ceaseless toil. . . .

And such toil! Spurred on by both the resolve to build himself a deathless monument and the need of publishers' advances, he was no longer signing contracts for single novels but for novels in series. The *Études philosophiques* was for Gosselin, the *Études de mœurs* for Mame. Despite his prodigious capacity, he

* Balzac: *Traité des excitants modernes* (*Treatise on Modern Stimulants*).

could not keep pace. He was committed ten books ahead, and every delivery date found him lagging behind, although he worked day and night. So then he redoubled his efforts.

To Zulma Carraud: 'I must tell you that I am submerged in excessive labour. The mechanics of my life have altered. I go to bed at six or s_ven in the evening, like the hens. I am awakened at one o'clock in the morning and work till eight. At eight I sleep for an hour and a half. Then I have something light to eat and a cup of black coffee, and harness my wagon until four. I receive callers, I take a bath or I go out, and after dinner I go back to bed. I have to live like this for months on end if I am not to be overwhelmed by my obligations. The profits accrue slowly; the debts are inexorable and fixed. It is now certain that I shall make a great fortune; but I need to go on waiting and working for another three years. I have to rewrite, to correct, to make everything worthy of the monument—thankless work that does not figure in the accounts and shows no immediate profit. . . .

To complicate matters, women made claims on his time, although not Madame de Castries: 'A strange chilliness is gradually succeeding what I believed to be love in a woman who came to me with some nobility.' But there was the Duchesse d'Abrantès, writing to ask if he was dead and complaining because he did not visit her more often. And the prudent Zulma warned him against the Girardins. 'He's a speculator. . . . She is frigid. . . . If you spent all your time with simple, sensible people like us, how much happier you would be, even if your stories lost something of their vividness!' A writer's friends always advise him to see no one except themselves. Dr Nacquart again prescribed rest. Balzac spent the last two weeks of April and the first half of May with the Carrauds at Angoulême. When he returned to Paris it was to be met with a storm of rage. A new review, *L'Europe littéraire*, had opened its pages to him. He had bought a share in it and contributed a brilliant essay on the lines of Lavater entitled *Théorie de la démarche* ('A Theory of Behaviour'). Now he was writing something else for it, a 'Scene of Provincial Life' which was to become *Eugénie Grandet*. Gosselin and Mame, outraged by this double-dealing, brandished their unfulfilled contracts in his face, and Mame summoned him to appear before the Tribunal de Commerce. In a childish act of reprisal, Balzac went to Barbier's printing works and broke up the type of the *Médecin de campagne*. It was open warfare, but a war that he could only lose, having the law against him. He appealed to Laure d'Abrantès to intervene, since it was he who had introduced her to Mame, who was now her publisher. She fought on his behalf, so she claimed, 'like a sister defending a beloved brother', telling Mame that *Le Médecin de campagne* would be the most wonderful book that ever was. All she asked in return was that Balzac would come and see her, 'at the hour which is no longer day but not yet night. . . . Come soon, and always count on me as your best friend.' He did not go. He did not even thank her, but with perfect unreason repudiated the good offices he had asked for:

You did me a poor service when you talked about my work to that ignoble butcher who bears the name of Mame, who has a look of blood and bankruptcy, and who can add to the tears of those he has ruined the griefs of a poor, hard-working man. He could not ruin me because I did not possess anything; he tried to sully my reputation and he caused me great distress. If I do not come to see you it is because I do not want to meet that bird of prey. . . .

Extravagant abuse such as this did not better his case, and the arbitrators found against him. He consoled himself with the thought of the success which *Le Médecin de campagne* must bring. It was finally published on 9 September: 'Upon my soul, I think I can die in peace, I have done a great thing for my country. To my mind this book is worth more than laws and victorious battles. It is the Gospels in action.' Certainly it was unlike the usual run of novels. The mysterious Dr Benassis expounds his views on politics, which are Balzac's own. He is opposed to universal suffrage and predicts that the growth of bourgeois liberalism will lead to a long struggle between the bourgeoisie and the working class, who will see in it a sort of spurious aristocracy: 'Allow a hundred peers in France and they will cause merely a hundred disturbances.' But abolish the peerage altogether and the rich would become a privileged class; social inequality would be an endless source of friction.

Balzac here shows himself in a somewhat new light, in no

sense reactionary but progressive. He points to the movement of population from the country to the towns, the dangerous growth of a dissatisfied, uprooted class. 'A writer seeking to paint a true picture of the French society of his period, and to influence its thinking, cannot ignore these phenomena.'* Dr Benassis has revived a corner of France in the first place by facing the facts. Account has to be taken of the nature of the peasants, who are neither angels nor monsters but rendered hard and narrow by the harshness of their lives. A communal spirit has to be fostered in them (and here Balzac was anticipating the thoughts of present-day reformers) but it is a task calling for great patience. In order to succeed, says Benassis, 'one needs to find in oneself every morning a renewed store of what might seem to be the easiest kind of courage, that of a schoolmaster repeating the same things day after day'.

Benassis and his guest, Major Genestas, attend a peasant-gathering, and lying on straw listen to folk-tales. The old soldier, Goguelat, 'tells about the Emperor': 'You must know, my friends, that Napoleon was born in Corsica, which is a French island warmed by the Italian sun. . . .' With a simple lyricism the huge epic is unfolded, in a long digression that has no bearing on the subject of the book. It may even have been originally intended for *La Bataille*; but it had an immense success in its own right and was reprinted separately a number of times. Finally Genestas hears Dr Benassis' 'confession'. One version of this, written at the time of Balzac's rebuff by Madame de Castries, has already been mentioned. In the second version Benassis relates that he has gone into retirement to expiate a misdeed of his youth which ruined the lives of two girls. Loosely thrown together though it is, the book has great charm.

Zulma Carraud praised it warmly: 'Splendid! I love to see you writing like this. . . . There are no *witticisms* in it, and that is what I like.' But it was this that set the public and the critics against it. The women did not find what they were accustomed to look for in Balzac, and his political adversaries had a field-day. He wrote to Madame Hanska: 'All the papers here are attacking *Le Médecin de campagne*. It is like a stab in the back.' The popular reviewers said that Balzac had delivered a lecture on forestry, rural economy and paternal administration, whereas

* Bernard Guyon.

what was expected of him was a *story*, not a mish-mash of social hygiene, politics and morals. Balzac refused to be shaken. He was convinced that one day he would bestride the intellectual world of Europe as Voltaire had done; that readers would find in *Le Médecin de campagne* the Gospels in action, and that the book would be awarded the Prix Montyon. The Académie Française mistakenly decided otherwise.

In a preface which he did not publish Balzac claimed that he had not wished for the Montyon award: 'If he should obtain a sum of money through the working of academic chance . . . his self-esteem would suffer; he would feel that he had written an imbecility, whereas his intention was to warm, here and there, hearts simple enough to be moved by the pedestrian poetry of goodness. . . .' But however scornful he might pretend to be, he was sickened at the reception of a book to which he had devoted such great pains, and he wanted to escape from Paris.

He wanted at last to meet his Foreign Lady. She had persuaded her elderly husband to take her to Neuchâtel in Switzerland, where Henriette Borel, the governess, had been born. In those days the very wealthy Russian families were accustomed to travel with a large retinue. While husband and wife stopped at the Hôtel du Faucon, the daughter Anna, the governess, two elderly relatives and a large domestic staff were installed in a house opposite the hotel. Madame Hanska wrote to Balzac that she was afraid of him. There were so many stories. Was it true that he was a cold and calculating libertine? He wrote back: 'Oh, my unknown love, do not mistrust me, do not believe any harm of me! I am a child, that is all, more frivolous than you thought, but pure as a child and loving as a child. . . . Woman has always been my dream, and I have never opened my arms except to embrace illusions. . . .' He was most certainly coming, he needed rest after so much struggle; and he proposed to call himself the Marquis d'Entragues: 'Everybody would be suspicious of Monsieur de Balzac, but who knows Monsieur d'Entragues?' In a characteristic flight of imagination he described in advance their meeting: 'I see your lake, and my intuition is so strong that I am sure I shall exclaim when I really see you, "It is she!" She, my love, is you. . . .'

As it happened he had a pretext for making the journey. An idea for a large-scale business enterprise had recently occurred

to him: books to be sold by subscription at one franc a volume—
a sort of book-club. One book a month would be issued, and the
printing would be enormous. He already had partners in the
venture; he had offered shares to Zulma Carraud and to Surville. But for these cheap editions a special paper was needed,
thin and strong like India paper, and it was to be made in
Besançon. From there he could very easily slip across the
frontier to Neuchâtel. The meeting itself appeared less simple.
How could he be sure of recognizing Madame Hanska, in spite
of what he had said? Ten years later he recalled the moment
when he saw her in the distance for the first time:

You still do not know what took place in me when, at the end
of that courtyard of which the smallest cobble is imprinted on
my memory . . . I saw a face at the window! I lost all bodily
sensation, and when I spoke to you I was bemused. That state
of bemusement, like a torrent which in its eagerness stays its
course to leap forward with a greater impetus, lasted for two
days. 'What must she be thinking of me?' was a mad phrase
which I repeated to myself in terror. . . .

She was wearing a violet velvet dress, and violet was Balzac's
favourite colour. Directly he arrived in Neuchâtel he had sent
her a note by Henriette Borel:

I shall go for a walk in the town from one o'clock till four. I
shall spend all the time looking at the lake, which I do not know.
I can stay here for as long as you are staying. Please send me a
line to let me know if I can write to you here, poste restante,
with perfect safety, for I fear to cause you the least displeasure,
and I beg you, give me your exact name.
A thousand tendernesses. There has not been a moment,
between Paris and here, which has not been filled with you, and
I gazed at the Val de Travers with you in mind. It is enchanting,
that valley.

Tradition has it that in the course of this walk he saw a lady
reading. She had dropped her handkerchief. Balzac drew near
and saw that she was reading one of his books. It must have
been a dramatic moment when, after so much rarified correspondence, they set eyes on each other in the flesh. Although she had
told him in her first letter that she was sure his appearance

afforded no clue to his true nature, she must have been taken aback by the sight of that plump, gap-toothed little man with untidy hair. But, as always happened, his intelligence and fire, the warmth of his smile and the brilliance of his speech, soon caused her to recover from the shock. Surely there could be no other man alive so vivid and so witty! Balzac, for his part, saw an imposing, richly curved woman with a rounded forehead, a rather fat neck and a sensual mouth. She had 'an air of abandon and dignity, an expression at once lofty and lascivious', and a foreign accent which enchanted him. He would have made a goddess of her whatever she had been like, but in fact he was so delightfully surprised that he had to tell his sister Laure all about it:

Balzac to Laure Surville, 12 October 1833: I found there everything that can gratify the thousand vanities of the animal called man, of which the poet is assuredly the vainest variety; but why do I say vanity, when it is nothing of the kind? I am happy, very happy in thought, honourably happy, if still no more. Alas, there is an infernal husband who did not leave us alone together for an instant in five days. He dodged between his wife's skirts and my waistcoat. Neuchâtel is a small town where a woman, a distinguished foreigner, cannot move a step without being seen. I felt as though I were in a furnace. Restraint does not suit me.

The essentials are that we are twenty-seven years old and beautiful to admiration, that we have the most beautiful black hair in the world, a smooth, deliciously soft brunette skin, an adorable little hand and a twenty-seven-year-old heart, naïve—a real Madame de Lignolle—and imprudent almost to the point of flinging our arms round my neck in sight of all the world. I say nothing about the colossal wealth. What is that by comparison with a masterpiece of beauty which I can only liken to the Princesse de Bellejoyeuse, but infinitely more so? A glancing eye which, when one meets it, acquires a voluptuous splendour. I was intoxicated with love. . . .

God, but the Val de Travers is beautiful and the Lac de Bienne ravishing! This, as you can imagine, is where we sent the husband to order luncheon. But we were exposed to view, and so in the shadow of a great oak-tree we exchanged our first furtive kiss of love. Then, since our husband is getting on for sixty, I swore to wait and *she* to keep her hand and heart for me.

Was it not sweet to have dragged a husband, who looks to me like a tower, all the way from the Ukraine, and travel six hundred leagues to meet a lover who only had to come a hundred and fifty, the monster? . . .

The husband, a bespectacled boyar in a fur collar, had guile-lessly accepted the supposedly accidental presence of the eminent writer, and not unnaturally made much of him. Wenceslas Hanski looked far from well; marriage to his widow in the not-too-distant future seemed by no means impossible. And what a marriage—to a positive monarch ruling over several thousand serfs! So they exchanged their kiss and their vows beneath the oak-tree, and it was agreed that Balzac should meet the Hanskis in Geneva at Christmas. The romance had to be consummated. This time it was the lady, unlike Madame de Castries, who came near to reproaching him for having made do with a kiss:

Villain! Did you not see in my eyes all that I longed for? But have no fear, I felt all the desire that a woman in love seeks to provoke, and if I did not tell you how ardently I hoped for you to come one morning, it was because I was so awkwardly lodged. That house was too risky. Elsewhere it might have been possible. But in Geneva, oh, my adored angel, in Geneva I shall have more talent for our love than ten men need in order to be called talented. . . .

She had found him a little vulgar. She wrote to her brother: 'Do you remember saying that he would eat with his knife and blow his nose in his napkin? Well, if he did not commit the second of these crimes he was certainly guilty of the first.' But she felt that Balzac's huge vitality earned him forgiveness in all things; he was superb in his very gluttony, whether for a beauti-ful woman or a beautiful fruit. The works seemed greater than the man, both loftier and more profound; but this could only be the appearance, since it was the man who had created the works.

His return journey was an uncomfortable one. The coaches did not serve him well; he was handled like a package and got back to Paris covered with bruises, to be instantly assailed, as usual, with financial troubles: 'I have found everything even worse than I feared. The people who owe me money and had promised to pay have not done so. But my mother, whom I know to be in difficulties, has been sublime in her devotion.' A new hope dawned: Madame Charles Béchet, the widow of Pierre-Adam Charlot and daughter of the publisher Béchet, an attractive and wealthy woman who had taken over her father's business, proposed to bring out a collected edition of Balzac's works in a dozen volumes under the general title *Études de mœurs*, to include reprints of the *Scènes de la vie privée* and first impressions of the *Scènes de la vie de province* and *Scènes de la vie parisienne*. She offered between 27,000 and 30,000 francs in payment, an enormous sum. 'Well, this is going to make the sluggards howl, the yapping dogs, the men of letters! ... My dearest love, my Eve—it is settled! They'll die of jealousy!' The magnificent contract would enable him to pay off all his creditors (except, of course, Madame Mère, who agreed to wait) and to settle with the 'butcher' Mame, who was still clamouring for his pound of flesh, *Les Trois Cardinaux*, or the return of the advance.

To complete Volume II of the *Scènes de la vie de province* Madame Béchet needed another eighty pages. Balzac sat down and in a single night wrote a novella entitled *L'Illustre Gaudissart*, to which he attached little importance. It was a sketch of a commercial traveller, another of those 'contemporary types' with which, with an astonishing fecundity, he filled the pages of *La Mode* and *La Caricature*. But Gaudissart (the name was derived from the words '*gaudisserie*' and '*gaudriole*' both meaning broad, loud humour) was destined to have a long life. The commercial traveller had become a figure of importance in the new bourgeois society, the 'link joining the village to the capital', the man who brought the latest products of Paris to the provinces. By 1830 he was dealing not only in hats and linens, 'Paris wares' in general, but also in ideas. *Le Globe*, that high-minded Saint-Simonian journal which published studies of Goethe and numbered Sainte-Beuve among its contributors, owed a large part of its circulation to the puns, jests at the expense of the clergy and Rabelaisian gusto of Gaudissart, the incomparable traveller, paragon of his kind.

This high-spirited anecdote was dedicated, surprisingly, to the Marquise de Castries. After returning from Switzerland, and perhaps under the influence of his kinder treatment at the hands of Madame Hanska, he had written her a venomous letter which greatly upset her.

'What a horrible letter you have written me! One would want to have nothing to do with the woman who deserved it or with the man who could write it! You have hurt me; so am I supposed to apologize? I am wrong to write to you when I am so agitated. You are breaking a heart that is already broken. . . .

His line with Madame Hanska was that he had sacrificed Madame de Castries for her sake. In fact the quarrel between them died down, to be succeeded by a stormy friendship. But in the meantime, since he could never resist temptation, yet another woman had entered his life—in addition, that is to say, to the devoted, ill and unhappy Madame de Berny. He was having a secret affair with 'a sweet person, a most innocent creature who has fallen like a flower from the sky, who visits me in private, asks for no letters, no attentions, but simply says, "Love me for a year and I will love you all my life!" ' She was Marie-Louise-Françoise Daminois, the wife of Guy Du Fresnay, of a respected legal family. In 1833 she was twenty-four years old and was expecting a child by Balzac. He dedicated the novel on which he was then working, *Eugénie Grandet*, *to her*:

TO MARIA. May your name, you whose portrait is the highest adornment of this book, stand here like a sprig of consecrated box, culled from no matter what tree but certainly sanctified by religion and replaced, ever green, by pious hands to protect the house.

If *Eugénie Grandet* is indeed a portrait of Marie Du Fresnay we can readily picture her—'tall and strong, with none of the prettiness that pleases common people'; but possessing, in the writer's eyes, a classic beauty refined by the gentleness of Christian feeling, behind her serene forehead a world of love and inward nobility unconscious of itself. Balzac was never at a loss for embellishments.

Eugénie Grandet, which was to be one of the *Scènes de la vie privée*, is constructed around a remarkable 'Balzacien' character, le père Grandet. Although it has become one of the best-known of Balzac's works, for reasons which are partly aesthetic (simplicity of structure and unity of theme), and partly sentimental

(Eugénie's touching love-story and the devoted servant, Nanon), he himself regarded it as simply 'a good little tale, easy to sell' and not in the same class as *Louis Lambert*. He was quite wrong. Everything in the book attracts the reader—the clear and factual account of Old Grandet's business undertakings; the struggle between two families for the hand of his heiress; the picture of his home-life with its sharp contrasts of light and shade, and between the harshness of the old man, the saintliness of his wife and the self-abnegation of his daughter; above all, the character of Grandet himself, one of those 'new men' whose rise to fortune sheds a light on the history of the time.

'The life of a miser is a constant exercise of human power,' said Balzac. Hence the interest evoked by the picture of a miser when it is ably drawn. But Grandet is far more than a miser. He is a man who knows how to make money, and for whom money-affairs are, as a matter of course, more important than affairs of sentiment. He is unmoved by his nephew's loss of a beloved father, but genuinely sympathizes with his loss of a fortune. As an army-contractor he has acquired, by greasing the palm of a fanatical republican, the land belonging to a religious community. Like Bernard-François Balzac he has a reputation for being 'interested in new ideas', although in fact he is only interested in vineyards. As Mayor of Saumur he has his house and landed property assessed for taxation at a rate highly advantageous to himself. The Restoration offered a new means of money-getting—the Funds. Five-per-cent stock bought for 45 francs in 1814 could be sold six years later for 100 francs. Grandet 'plays the Restoration' just as he 'played the Revolution'. Better than any handbook of economics, so Pierre-Georges Castex has said, the novel describes the process whereby the new bourgeoisie was able to amass huge fortunes. Quick grasp of a situation, prompt action and a minimum of scruple—these talents add up to a kind of inhuman genius.

Balzac set *Eugénie Grandet* in Saumur, but Tours or Vouvray would have suited the story equally well. Attempts have been made to find prototypes of the characters in Saumur; but the fact is that he was only there once, and then only for a few hours. He gives a correct, if superficial, picture of the town; but there are lapses which suggest that the real setting was in the region of Tours. Old Grandet himself may have been based partly on

Monsieur de Savary, the father-in-law of his friend Margonne; but we need not stress again that no character in a novel, if the novelist knows his business, is derived from a single source.

Zulma Carraud found Grandet unconvincing. For one thing, she said, he was too rich; no amount of parsimony or greed could enable a mere cooper to amass such a vast fortune. Balzac replied: 'The facts are against you. There is a grocer with a small shop in Tours who has eight millions; and M. Eynard, an ordinary pedlar, has twenty. . . . However, I will reduce Grandet's fortune by six million in the next edition.' And he wrote to Laure, who raised the same objection: 'But, silly, since the story is true do you want me to improve on the truth?' Zulma also thought that the character was 'too remarkable', adding— 'in the provinces nothing is outstanding'. But Balzac was more concerned with effect than with literal truth. What he had set out to show, not for the first time, was the devastating power of a fixed idea, which leads to the destruction of a family.

The power of thought, and the danger of thought, had always been at the heart of his philosophy, as his former schoolfellow, Barchou de Penhoën, now a respected philosopher, could testify. Inventors (or creators) and misers fascinated him by the intensity of their ruling passion. But hitherto he had followed two distinct paths—that of the philosophical novel (*La Peau de chagrin* and *Louis Lambert*, and that of the *Scènes de la vie privée*. During the years 1832-33 he achieved a synthesis between them. Although each story stands on its own feet, all are part of a larger whole. In the still clouded depths of his mind, Balzac was beginning to catch glimpses of the works to come. He meant to depict all levels and conditions of society. He would place his characters against a strongly drawn social background, in towns whose structure he would analyse, and in a unitary world where the physical and the spiritual were but two aspects of a single reality. Hence his long dissertations on Paris, on country towns and districts, on the bearing of a respectable woman, on a miser's economy of effort. A dramatic and gripping narrative might incidentally harbour a treatise reminiscent of Lavater or an essay on architecture. Cuvier could reconstruct the skeleton of an animal from a single bone; Balzac, starting with a single object, a house, a room, reconstructed men, cities and nations.

What is astonishing is that the most profound writer of his time should have had so much difficulty in persuading the critics to take him seriously. 'It is quite certain,' one of them pontificated, 'that M. de Balzac has never written a good novel.' He could only obtain critical recognition by writing the reviews himself or getting his friends to do so. Saint-Beuve and all the 'important' reviewers treated him with a disdainful condescension. Victor Hugo impressed them by his loftiness of style, his choice of subjects and his Olympian presence. Balzac did not suit the literary climate of the time. Because he wrote about everyday life, money-matters, the drama of the senses, he was held to be trivial and vulgar; and his jovial countenance, his clothes and his excitability seemed to confirm this.

It is noteworthy that he perfected his art as a writer only when he abandoned philosophy. He more than once brought thinkers on to his stage, painters, musicians and others, who wore themselves out in trying to guess the meaning of the Universe, and failed because they attempted too much. The same thing happened to himself when he sought with too much elaboration to expound his philosophical views. He had to come down to earth, and he was saved on the day when he realized that his ideas were best expressed in terms of everyday life. Louis Lambert died young; Old Grandet will live for ever.

XVI

In Search of the Absolute

La vanité, sans laquelle l'amour est très faible, soutenait sa passion.

BALZAC

HE LONGED TO join Madame Hanska in Geneva, there to complete his conquest, a gesture as necessary to his pride as it was to his love. He already addressed her as *tu*, a first step to complete intimacy: 'To our next meeting. Work will make the time pass quickly. How happy we were in Neuchâtel! We'll go on expeditions, won't we? . . .' But before he could be away for any length of time he had to deal with 'squalid matters' in Paris. The Béchet contract had not disposed of everything. He wrote to Madame Hanska on 29 October: 'My beloved Eve, on Thursday I have to pay between four and five thousand francs, and I literally haven't a sou. These are trifling battles to which I am well accustomed. . . .' She diffidently offered him a small sum. (She had nothing but her allowance, all the money being her husband's.) 'My darling angel, bless you a thousand times for your offer of a drop in the ocean. It means everything to me —and nothing. What is a thousand francs to a man who needs ten thousand a month? . . .'

'Let us forget the dismal subject of money. . . .' But if his Eve was cautiously generous in this respect, she was decidedly vigilant in others. Who, in Heaven's name, was she jealous of? Madame de Castries? 'We are on coldly formal terms.' Madame Récamier? What a strange notion! 'Certain courtesies are due to a lady of rank with whom one is acquainted, but I cannot think that a polite call on Madame Récamier comes under the heading of *relations*.' And how could she reproach him with delaying his journey when he was killing himself with the effort to hasten to her side? On 20 November he still had 100 pages of *Eugénie Grandet* to write, *Ne touchez pas à la hache* (later *La Duchesse de Langeais*) to finish, and *La Femme aux yeux rouges*

(*La Fille aux yeux d'or*) to do entirely. 'I shall be dead when I arrive. . . . Yesterday I broke my armchair, the companion of my sleepless nights. It is the second that has collapsed under me since the battle began. . . .' But he had found a wonderful subject to work on while he was in Geneva. Visiting the sculptor Théophile Bra, a cousin of his friend Marceline Desbordes-Valmore, he had seen

. . . the most exquisite masterpiece that ever was 'Mary' with the infant Christ in her arms adored by two angels'. . . . There and then I thought of a wonderful book, a small volume to which *Louis Lambert* would be a preface, to be called *Séraphita*. Séraphita is the two sexes united in a single being, like [Latouche's] *Fragoletta*, but with the difference that I conceive the creature to be an angel arrived at the final stage of its evolution and breaking out of its earthly garment to rise to the heavens. It is loved by a man and a woman to whom it says as it flies upwards that both have loved the love that united them, seeing in it that which is purely angelic; it reveals their passion to them and bequeaths them love as it escapes from our terrestrial woes. If I can I will write this beautiful tale while I am in Geneva, near to you. . . .

Marceline Desbordes-Valmore, a romantic poet, was the wife of an indifferent actor and the mistress of Latouche. She and Balzac had recently become friendly. 'We come from the same country, Madame, the land of tears and sorrow.' He would not have written in those terms to Eugène Sue, but '*à chacun sa verité*'. It was she who had introduced him to Bra, an unimportant sculptor but an astonishing personality who married two clairvoyants in succession. Bra shared Balzac's interest in Swedenborg, hermaphrodites and the hosts of Heaven, and it was under these influences that he had conceived this group of the Virgin and angels, which Balzac regarded as a work of 'sublime genius'.

It certainly inspired Balzac, anxious to please his divine *Étrangère*, with the oddest of ideas for a novel. One of the angels was to be himself, the other Eve, and of their union the twofold Being was to be born, Séraphitus-Séraphita, both man and woman. Joined on earth by love, 'each of us must liberate the angel imprisoned in his carnal being'. The hermaphrodite had always been among Balzac's most cherished myths, the man bringing intelligence, the woman beauty, the man movement, the woman stability; till they become literally one flesh and rise up to Heaven as a single being, having regained their angelic form.

Such was the work he proposed to offer Eve Hanska. But it would not be easy to write. The final ascent would have to resemble a Dantesque canto. To divorce it from everyday life and take the reader into unfamiliar regions he proposed to set the fable in Norway. It was to begin 'on a morning when the sun broke over the countryside, lighting the fires of all the ephemeral diamonds produced by the crystallization of snow and ice. Two beings passed over the gulf, crossing and flying the length of the slopes of the Falberg, rising from height to height towards its summit. Were they living beings? Were they arrows? Anyone seeing them at that height would have supposed them to be two eider-ducks flying in company through the clouds. . . .' In fact they were skiers climbing the 'Bonnet of Ice', a Norwegian peak.

Balzac knew Norway only from books, and Swedenborg only from a French outline of his writings; but Eve would lend him inspiration. Their fondness for the supernatural had been a bond between them from the start. In the case of Madame Hanska it was an inherited taste. Numerous mystical vagabonds had been hospitably received in the Rzewuski manor-houses, and the family annals were filled with legends of ghosts and premonitions. The Poles, in any event, were restless spirits, ardent in their desire to escape the trammels of the flesh. Mesmer had found adepts among them, Swedenborg had found readers. It is fair to add that Madame Hanska's aunt, Countess Rosalie Rzewuska, did not hold with any of this. She regarded her niece as a nice, gentle creature but slightly mad, her mind disordered with too much reading: 'The muddle of ideas coloured by an over-vivid imagination produced a brilliant confusion in her talk, sometimes amusing to her listeners but often wearisome.' Such was Aunt Rosalie's stern conclusion, but Eve's belief in premonitions, her vein of exalted prophecy, delighted Balzac.

He intended, in writing *Séraphita*, to draw largely on the works of the Swedish mystic, in which an appearance of scientific discipline was mingled with biblical lyricism. It was a method that suited his own way of thinking. Swedenborg, like himself, believed in the unity of Nature, maintaining that the material and the spiritual were but different aspects of a single whole. He saw in all organic and spiritual life a related process subject to the mechanical laws governing the universe; but on the other hand he regarded matter as 'the degraded end of the spiritual and divine'. It cannot be said that Balzac derived his unitary philosophy from Swedenborg. It was already present in the 'Notes Philosophiques' of his youth, and he owed it far more to men like Buffon, Cuvier and Saint-Hilaire. But Swedenborg lent him the idea that the physical world is no more than a symbol of the spiritual world, and that between the two 'relationships' may be found. In that obscure lyricism Balzac saw a marvel 'greater in its sublimity than those of Dante and Milton'. He believed, with Hugo, that the material world was heavy with secrets, and it is this that accounts for the mysterious and disturbing element in the 'Balzac labyrinth', where all material objects are symbols. Swedenborg's influence did not transform his thinking; it rather confirmed his view of the world.

Meanwhile letters filled with tender avowals, protests and plans were being secretly conveyed to Madame Hanska by Henriette Borel. There had also to be letters of a more formal kind, for the benefit of the lady's husband, who would have thought it strange not to hear anything from him. These were ceremoniously flippant: 'I do not think, Madame, that the House of Hanski will reject these trifling tokens of the House of Balzac's remembrance of its charming and graceful hospitality.' He had some pebbles, collected by her daughter, made up into a modest article of decoration, and he also sent her Rossini's autograph, solicited from the maestro 'as an offering to Monsieur de Hanski, who so greatly admires him. . . . I beg you, Madame, to present it to him with the expression of my warmest sentiments and remembrances, to kiss Mademoiselle Anna on the forehead in my name, and to accept my most respectful homage. . . .' We may gain an inkling of Madame Hanska's feelings from the letter she wrote to her brother, Count Henri Rzewuski, on 10 December:

We have made a charming acquaintanceship in Switzerland, that of Monsieur de Balzac, the author of *La Peau de chagrin* and so many other delightful works. The acquaintance has ripened into a true friendship which I trust will last throughout our lives. . . . Balzac reminds me very much of you, my dear Henri. He is gay, light-hearted, and loveable. He is even a little like you in appearance, and there is something in both of you that resembles Napoleon. . . . Balzac is a real child. If he likes you he tells you so with the candid frankness of childhood. When you meet him you marvel that so much knowledge and loftiness of spirit can be joined to such freshness, charm and youthful simplicity of thought and feeling. . . .

She also wrote: 'I have never in my life passed two such happy, peaceful months as the July and August we spent in Neuchâtel.' Everything had delighted her, the lake, the excursions, the people. To be in love with everything is to be truly in love.

But love is the thief of time. What with letter-writing, creative writing and quarrelling with publishers, it was not until the second half of December that he was able to leave Paris. As a sort of revenge on the past he would have liked to stay at the Hôtel de la Couronne, the Geneva hotel where he suffered at the hands of Madame de Castries; but Madame Hanska had reserved a room for him at the Auberge de l'Arc, very much nearer the Maison Mirabaud, where she and her husband were stopping, with their retinue. The inn was situated amid trees in the Eaux-Vives quarter, and it had a weather-cock in the form of a bow. When he arrived there, on Christmas Day, Balzac found a ring awaiting him, together with a note asking if he loved her.

Do I love you? But I am near you! I wish it had been a thousand times more difficult and that I had undergone more pains. But at least a whole month has been won, and perhaps two. Not one but a million caresses. I am so happy that I can't write any more than you can. . . .

Yes, my room is perfect, and the ring is like yourself, my love, delicious and exquisite!'

He spent forty-three days there, days of work and love. Since he had now been entirely accepted by the lady's husband, exchanges between the Maison Mirabaud and the Auberge de l'Arc presented no difficulty. Gifts passed between them, quince jelly from Orléans (which Balzac, always lyrical in praise of his

own offerings, held to be infinitely precious and delectable),
coffee, tea, a malachite inkstand and more than daily letters. His
Eve enchanted him beyond words, and she was delighted with
the idea of *Séraphita*. But with the memory of previous events
in Geneva still rankling, he found that he preferred to work on
La Duchesse de Langeais (still called *Ne touchez pas à la hache*).
It was a novel of compensation in which the Duchesse de
Langeais (Madame de Castries) falls in love with a certain
Montriveau (Balzac) and is rejected by him. But although he
might revenge himself on paper, the smart of humiliation was
abating in the warmth of his new love, and his gay and fun-
loving nature reasserted itself. Everything was delightful in the
company of his Countess. He teased her about her French accent
—she pronounced the word '*tilleuls*' (lime-trees) as though it
were written '*tiyeuilles*'. She wrote notes addressed to Monsieur le Marquis (a teasing reference to the 'Marquis d'Entragues')
and he replied with 'Madame la Maréchale', her husband being
Marshal of the Nobility of Volhynia.

To Her Rzewuskian Majesty Madame de Hanska, at Geneva.
Most dear sovereign, sacred Majesty, sublime Queen of
Paulowska and the surrounding country, autocrat of hearts, rose
of the East, star of the North, etc. . . . etc. . . . etc. . . . fairy of
the *tiyeuilles*! . . .

There followed an invitation to drive by carriage to Coppet
with her 'humble mujik'.

This intimacy was charming in itself, but Balzac was determined to have more. She slipped out by moonlight to visit him
in his hotel room wearing a grey dress which 'swept so softly
over the boards'; but still for a few days she held him off, saying
that she was jealous of the Geneva ladies, of her cousin, Countess
Potocka, to whom she had introduced him, and of Laure de
Berny. She accused Balzac of being 'a flighty Frenchman'. . . .
'Forgive me, my love, for what you call my coquetries. . . . I
shall see no other woman.' Not even Madame de Berny? He
certainly did not mean to renounce her, but maintained that she
had never been more than a foretaste of the true Dilecta: 'You
are the Dilecta in youth. . . . Do not complain of this confusion
of sentiments. I like to think that I loved you in her. . . .' There
is no end to the resourcefulness of amorous casuistry.

He demanded everything: 'Our poor kiss still deprived of the ultimate raptures touches only your heart, and I want it to embrace the whole of you. You will find that possession increases and enhances love. . . .' She now professed to fear the opposite, that the act of possession would destroy his love; whereupon he wrote: 'How am I to tell you of my intoxication at your lightest touch, and that if I possess you a thousand times you will find me more intoxicated still, because there will be both hope and memory where now there is only hope. . . . On the road to Diodati I wept that any woman, having permitted all the caresses you allowed, could then, with a single word, destroy the fabric she had seemed to take pleasure in weaving! . . . Judge if I adore you, you who know nothing of odious stratagems, who give yourself in candour and happiness to love, and thus speak to my deepest heart! . . .' And eventually, on Sunday, 19 January 1834, he was able to issue a victory-bulletin:

My beloved angel, I am almost as insane about you as if I were really insane; I can't put two ideas together without your coming between them. In spite of myself, my thoughts fly back to you. I hold you, I clasp you, I kiss you, I caress you, and a thousand amorous caresses take possession of me. . . . Oh, my adored Eve, don't you know? I picked up your card; it is here in front of me, and I am talking to you as though you were here. I see you as I did yesterday, beautiful, admirably beautiful. All yesterday evening I said to myself, 'She is mine!' Oh, the angels are not as happy in Paradise as I was yesterday!'

But he seems to have been even happier on 26 January, which remained for him 'the unforgettable day'. The particular reason—whether, perhaps, there was a promise of marriage—is not known. 'The most that can be said,' writes Pierre-Georges Castex, 'is that he wrote a letter of exceptional fervour after a night filled with delights: "My beloved love, with a single caress you brought me to life. . . ." ' That 'caress of honey and fire' was for him a new initiation in love. From his adolescence he had dreamed of a madly passionate love-affair with a mistress who would be both great lady and courtesan. He believed that the artist, like the man of action, needed violent distractions to compensate for a life far outside the common run. He was allured by debauches; a debauch had been the first desire of

Raphaël in *La Peau de chagrin*. He was evidently skilled in erotic play. But if he wanted women swayed by desire, he also wanted them warm-hearted, intelligent, and able to understand, approve and even inspire his work. Eve Hanska seemed to fulfil every requirement.

For her part she seemed happy. To a woman of her exalted temperament it was intoxicating to share the thoughts of a man of genius, and one, moreover, who did not fail her in physical matters, for which she evidently had a considerable aptitude. 'Only artists are worthy of women, having something of the woman in themselves,' Balzac wrote to her. The enraptured couple made their plans. They might hope for thirty years before the onset of old age. Without wishing harm to Wenceslas Hanski, it was reasonable to suppose that in five years, ten at the most, his wife would be free. 'But by that time I shall be forty,' she said, and he replied, 'To me you will always be beautiful.' How could she suppose that the fashionable salons or fame or other women would ever lure him away from her? *Adoremus in aeternum* was to be the sacrilegious motto of their union. 'Henceforth there will be nothing in my life but you and my work.' He wrote disrespectfully in her autograph-album: 'Great men are like rocks; only limpets can cling to them', and she wrote below in loving humility, 'So I am a limpet.' He was ill for a few days and she came to his hotel and nursed him, with her husband's permission. When at length he had to return to Paris, in February, it was agreed that he would rejoin them a little later in Italy or Vienna, that he was to be invited to spend some months with them in the Ukraine and (the secret clause) that someday they would marry.

Sweet babe, in ten years you will be thirty-seven and I shall be forty-five. At that age one can still love, marry and worship for a lifetime. So let there be never any doubt, my noble comrade, my dear Eve; you have promised. *Séraphita* is both of us. Let us spread our wings in a single movement, and love in that same fashion. . . .

He arrived back in Paris on 12 February, bringing with him a bundle of manuscript—*La Duchesse de Langeais*, nearly finished; part of *Le Cabinet des antiques* and some more *Contes drolatiques*—and the ring she had given him. 'When I start work I put the talisman on my finger.' He had been instructed in the flora of Norway, for *Séraphita*, by the great botanist Pyramus de Candolle, who lived in Geneva. But above all he brought a rich store of memories—Eve at the Auberge de l'Arc; the precautions necessary to avoid making the boards creak; the grey stuff of her dress, fallen at last, from which he had taken a strip to bind the manuscript of *Séraphita*; the face of his beloved in the moment of pleasure: 'There is one of your smiles of happiness, a small, ravishing contraction, a pallor which overtook you at the supreme moment, that fills my heart with ecstasy. . . .'

In an 'open letter' to husband and wife he said: 'You do not know that in twelve or fifteen years those two visits, to Neuchâtel and Geneva, are the only times when it has been permitted me, I know not by what grace of Heaven, to look neither forward nor back, to be alive under the sky without a thought of sorrows or business matters or any unhappiness. . . .' He overflowed with gratitude, even in the open letters: 'There are times when I say the word *tiyeuilles* and laugh like a child.' He hoped that Anna was well, that Monsieur Hanski was not troubled by 'black dragons' and that Mademoiselle Borel was happy; and he gave his adored Eve advice in the matter of health and avoiding stoutness. It was sad that he did not follow it himself.

But in France he encountered 'black dragons' of his own. Madame de Berny was seriously ill and had aged twenty years in a month. 'I concealed my anxiety, which is very great. Until I have been reassured, either by my doctor or a clairvoyant, I shall not be easy in my mind about that life which, as you know, is so precious to me. . . .' Zulma Carraud had lost her father, whom she greatly loved. Now mistress of Frapesle, the family château near Issoudun, she warmly invited Balzac to come there and work. She was expecting her second child, and the pregnancy was not an easy one.

The 'most excellent family' was being an infernal nuisance, as usual. Madame Balzac had engaged in some rash financial transactions and lost the last of her money. Surville, stupidly jealous, was making life difficult for his wife. Poor Laure could not even visit her brother except in secret! Or was it perhaps that Laure herself was making their home life intolerable? Honoré began to wonder. As a brother he forgave everything;

but as a novelist he had glimpses of an ambitious, nagging wife, and among his jottings there is a plan for a story about two sisters, 'one truly superior, calm and resigned, dying young and unhonoured, her husband a coxcomb; the other making a great show of superiority, plaguing her husband, who is simple and modest'. Were these Laurence and Laure, seen ten years later? It may be so. Laure, very career-minded, was driving Surville to attempt too much—canals, of course, but also water-distribution and two bridges, at Andelys and Sully. The poor man could not sleep and his anxieties made him feverish. 'They are half off their heads,' Balzac wrote to Eve. He was afraid at one moment that his mother and sister would arrive penniless to take up residence in the Rue Cassini.

But still there was good news. *Eugénie Grandet* was selling well, and the public was enthusiastic. Delphine de Girardin wrote: 'Eugénie Grandet is adorable, and big Nanon and old Grandet, what talent, what talent! Oh, great Balzac!!! My sister, my mother and I are lost in admiration, we are your fanatical devotees. Never has one of your works had so great a success. You must come and see us very soon so that we can tell you *all* that we think of you. . . .' In the hope of placating the Marquise de Castries, whose anger and influence he feared, he read her the beginning of *La Duchesse de Langeais*. She warmly approved, and indeed the picture he drew of her in the early chapters was not unattractive.

What followed was to please her less. There was a scathing account of the great families of the Faubourg Saint-Germain at the time of the Restoration, who instead of displaying an aristocratic magnanimity had behaved as greedily and shabbily as any parvenu. The nobility had been shameless in the pursuit of wealth and office, the veneer of elegant manners concealing their lack of principle. 'Religion will always be a political necessity,' the Duchesse de Langeais cynically proclaims. 'Would you really want to govern a nation that thinks? Napoleon didn't dare, he persecuted ideologists. . . . We must accept the Catholic religion and all that this entails. If we want Paris to attend Mass we must start by going ourselves. Religion, after all, is at the root of the conservative principles which enable the rich to live in peace. Religion is closely bound up with property.' As a royalist Balzac did not repudiate this order of ideas, but as a novelist he showed mercilessly what it amounted to in the mind of a worldly woman.

Madame Hanska's sister, the Countess Potocka, had advised him to pay his respects to Countess Apponyi, the wife of the Austrian ambassador. The Embassy was one of those that become powerful centres of attraction in the countries to which they are accredited. Count Apponyi and his wife had been in Paris since 1826, and their brilliant receptions and dance-luncheons drew all the fashionable world of Paris—legitimist and Louis-Philippe circles as well as writers and artists. Balzac longed to be invited. Countess Potocka, mistrusting his fondness for improper stories, warned him: 'Mind you behave yourself at Madame Apponyi's. She's an angel. Nothing must mar the atmosphere of purity which surrounds her. . . .'

Angels held no terrors for him. He called at the Embassy on 18 February and was not received, but the Countess wrote a friendly letter of apology: 'I blush to know that my dearest Marie has said so many nice things about me. . . . Will you do me the pleasure of coming this Sunday at three?' Countess Potocka wrote later: 'Are you back in your elegant hermitage? Do you ever leave it to visit Madame Apponyi, who complains of your neglect and despairs of her power to attract you to her house? This is the season when she gives her dance-luncheons. You'll find all Paris there, with its pretty women. . . .' Balzac became a regular visitor at the Embassy. 'It is necessary,' he wrote to Eve, 'that the House of Balzac should be on good terms with the House of Austria.' But Eve was perturbed by the reports she was receiving from her Polish friends of his social successes. Was he again showing 'a French heart'? And why was he corresponding with Countess Potocka?

'You must not be jealous of Madame P——'s letter. She must be on *our side*. I have flattered her, and I hope she thinks you are disdained.' This was not at all what Eve wanted, concerned as she was for her own dignity. She was being told that Balzac had mistresses. He wrote for her reassurance: 'Your bengali is behaving.' Every reader of their correspondence will know what was meant by the 'bengali', for which Eve's '*minou*' was 'a cage of delight'. He was working too hard, he said, to have time for anything else. When one went to bed at six and returned to one's desk at midnight there was no time to play the gallant. He had even had a tiff with the Girardins over a trifling publishing matter. 'Madame Girardin has made several attempts to get hold of me, but your obstinate mujik—if he weren't a mujik he wouldn't know how to say *niet*—has said *niet* with the utmost politeness, because after all he's fairly civilized, your devoted mujik. . . .'

No one can work as he did without paying for it. Early in April he had a sort of collapse. Dr Nacquart talked of the possibility of brain-fever and ordered a change of air and complete rest. This became an annual routine. He left for le Berri and spent a week or so with the Carrauds at Frapesle. But he could never remain idle. He was now working on *César Birotteau* and *La Fleur des pois* (which was to become *La Vieille Fille*). *Séraphita* was progressing only slowly. 'It is a crushing and terrible task,' he had written in March to Madame de Castries. 'I have spent and am spending days and nights on it. I write, un-write and rewrite, but in a few days all will have been said: either I shall have grown greater, or the Parisians will not understand. . . .' The subject was too much for him. He felt (rightly, alas!) that he was adventuring in a too-rarified atmosphere, beyond this earth. But he believed in the book, and *she* expected it of him.

He strolled in the garden at Frapesle with Zulma, now heavy with child, and helped her with the decoration of the house and talked about Eve. With Major Carraud he explored Issoudun, meeting the people and listening to the local tales. This was used later in *Un Ménage de garçon*. In a few days he contrived to know more about the little town than its oldest inhabitants.

He was living on two levels. In real life he consoled Zulma, made love to Eve, manoeuvred Henriette de Castries, discoursed on magnetism at the Austrian Embassy, lunched with Vidocq, the former criminal turned police-chief, and with the executioner Sanson and his son; in his imaginary world he was constructing a whole society in which Issoudun, like Alençon, was to have a place. *César Birotteau* was slowly emerging from his recollections of the Marais, *La Duchesse de Langeais* from his past bitterness. It all went on at the same time, the quick-money writings, the social studies, the philosophical works. The real Balzac was not the man of money-troubles or love-affairs, but the man creating a world.

On 20 April he heard the Fifth Symphony at the Conservatoire and recognized in Beethoven his equal and his brother. 'Ah, how I wished you were there!' he wrote to Eve. 'I was alone in a stall. Quite alone. It was inexpressibly painful. I have a need of self-expression which is cheated by my work, but which any strong emotion causes to break out in tears.... I am jealous only of the illustrious dead, Beethoven, Michaelangelo, Raphael, Poussin, Milton—in short I am moved by all that has been great, noble and solitary. Everything has not yet been said about me; I am still at the minor details of a great work.'

He was like an architect, carrying the design of a cathedral in his head, who lacks the means to execute it and can only concern himself with fragments. The uninitiated, seeing nothing but a few isolated stones, criticize their shape, not knowing where they are meant to go: 'We live only for style, and in France, where one has to hurry to put it all together, before the capitals are carved or the columns finished, you are judged by the uncomplete work, and condemned. . . .' At moments he grew weary: 'I'm afraid I have drawn too heavily on my capital. It would be strange if the author of *La Peau de chagrin* were to die young. I almost despair of completing my life's work.' But then his justifiable pride came uppermost. What a year he was having! *Eugénie Grandet, Les Chouans* (rewritten), *La Fleur des pois*—and *Séraphita, Une Vue du monde* and *Les Mémoires d'une jeune femme* were soon to come. He was anticipating of course, treating the work in gestation as though it were already completed, but what other writer could have piled up works, so many of them masterpieces, in the way he did?

Daily life and family matters persisted in intruding—Henry, for instance, disastrous brother Henry who had landed with such high hopes on the island of Mauritius. He had got a job as a schoolmaster and found lodgings in the house of a widow whose husband had left her with a son and a respectable fortune. Henry married her and, a typical Balzac in his extravagance, speedily ruined her. But it was some time before this became known. Laure Surville, hopeful but ill-informed, wrote to their friend, Madame de Pommereul: 'Henry is doing wonders over there, earning money and behaving well . . . and he has just married a lady who has brought him 150,000 francs. Mamma is

delighted. . . .' Honoré was inclined to be envious of his brother
—a Balzac who had brought off a rich marriage!—and he worked
the envy out of his system by bringing colonial fortunes into his
books. Charles Grandet was sent to the West Indies.

For two years there was no further news of Henry, whose
progress was far from encouraging. The school where he had
been employed was closed and the British authorities made
difficulties about renewing his residential permit. In June 1834,
he wrote to say that he was coming home, and Madame Mère,
now greatly concerned, rented a small apartment for him at 6
Rue Coquenard, where the Survilles were living.

He arrived with a wife considerably older than himself, a
stepson and 150,000 francs of debts. 'Did he really need to go
five thousand miles to find a wife like that?' demanded Honoré.
Surville, loyal as ever to the family, found him a job in connection with the Andelys bridge, in Normandy, the building of
which he was supervising. Henry did no good at it. His wife was
expecting a child. Madame Balzac, with her infinite capacity
for despair, wrung her hands. 'She is punished for her love-
child,' wrote Honoré. The helpful Laure went to the aid of her
sister-in-law, who was brought to bed in Andelys, a far cry from
sunny Mauritius. Honoré stood godfather to the child and
presented it with a curtained bassinet, as lavishly extravagant as
one would expect. Madame Balzac sold the last property she
possessed, the house in the Rue Montorgueil, for Henry's sake.
She now had nothing to live on except the interest on the
money she had lent Honoré.

For his part, Honoré had no doubt of his ability to supply the
needs of the entire family. There was the 'breathtaking' contract
for the *Études de moeurs* which he had signed with Madame
Béchet. The manager of her publishing business, Edmond
Werdet, a plausible and ambitious 'Gaudissart', followed this
up by coming to him with an offer of his own. He proposed to
publish Balzac himself, and he was prepared to sink his life-
savings, a sum of 3,500 francs, in the venture. Arrayed in his
white working gown, with red morocco slippers and a gold
chain round his waist, Balzac received the offer coldly and even
with sarcasm. What, in Heaven's name, was the use of 3,500
francs to an author who had just been paid 27,000 and was
receiving 500 monthly from the *Revue de Paris*! This summary

refusal was his first reaction, and the right one. But then he recalled Werdet. He could never resist ready money. The sum would at least suffice to pay off a few urgent debts, and besides 'intelligent publishers are so rare'. The flattered Werdet acquired in exchange for his savings the right to reprint *Le Médecin de campagne*. It sold so well that he conceived the ambitious notion of henceforth becoming Balzac's sole publisher. After all, why not? Walter Scott had had only one publisher, and the unity of the work would benefit by unity of imprint.

The difficulties were considerable. Rights had to be bought back from Gosselin, Levavasseur and Madame Béchet. Balzac had to share in this, which entailed paying out money he did not possess. But in spite of everything the contracts were signed, and he wrote to Madame Hanska:

Today I have escaped from that nightmare of stupidity. The illustrious Werdet, who is a little like my Illustrious Gaudissart, is buying from me a first edition of the *Études philosophiques*, twenty-five volumes in five deliveries of five volumes each, to appear one a month. . . . You will realize that to carry out this task, and to satisfy Madame Béchet, to whom I owe three more deliveries of the *Études de moeurs*, I need to have a Vesuvius in my head, a body of bronze, good pens, unlimited ink, not the tiniest 'blue devil' and a constant longing to set off in January for Strasbourg, Cologne, Vienna, Brody, etc. . . . doing battle with the snowdrifts. I say nothing about the trifle which is called 'health', or that other trifle which is called 'talent'. . . .

Talent, at least, was not lacking. In June 1834, he had begun a new Philosophical Study—*La Recherche de l'absolu*. Like *Eugénie Grandet* it was the story of an over-riding passion which ends by destroying a family. His first idea, which went back to 1832, had been a book to be called *Les Souffrances de l'inventeur*, of which the central figure was to be Bernard Palissy, based on Eugène Surville. Balzac made a great many notes for Palissy, but real-life characters did not suit him, incomplete as they are bound to be, and he ended by drawing on his imagination. Balthazar Claës, the inheritor of an immense Flemish fortune, takes up chemistry in an attempt to discover the 'absolute', the single element of which all things are composed. In his struggle to '*décomposer l'azote*' (break down the nitrogen atom) he wrecks the lives of his wife, whom he loves, and his children, and sells the ancient and renowned family art-collection. There are times when he seems to be aware of his state of obsessed folly, but he always returns to it, and not even his wife's despair can save him. The house of Claës goes down in ruin: 'The idea of the Absolute had ravaged it like a fire.'

Claës' theories were Balzac's own. He too believed in an Absolute of which, modified by environment, all created things were born. What is noteworthy is that Claës and Balzac were probably right, a century ahead of their time. He wrote to Eve: 'Two members of the Académie des Sciences instructed me in Chemistry to ensure that the book is scientifically correct. They made me revise the proofs ten or twelve times. I have had to read Berzélius, to learn how to hold my own in science and write scientific language, and at the same time not bore unresponsive French readers with chemistry while writing a book based on chemistry. . . .' He had attempted to assimilate Arago as well as Berzélius, and had worked himself to a standstill. Joséphine Claës in the story says to her husband: 'A great man should not have wife or children. You must tread your unhappy path alone. Your virtues are not those of ordinary people. You belong to the world; you can never belong to a wife or family. You drain the soil around you like a great tree!' It was Balzac communing with Balzac.

He continued to keep Eve in touch with events in Paris. She need have no fear of Madame de Castries, or of George Sand-Dudevant either, whose latest novels he considered shallow and false, and whose discarded lover, Jules Sandeau, had come to live in the Rue Cassini, in the rooms formerly occupied by Borget. 'Sandeau will be lodged like a prince; he can't believe in his luck. . . .' Balzac wanted to use 'le petit Jules' to devil for him. He and Emmanuel Arago were to collaborate on plays under his direction, and they would sign them 'San-Drago' and all three would make a fortune.

La Recherche de l'absolu had exhausted him: '. . . no doubt it will enhance my reputation, but there are victories which are too dearly won.' His hair, formerly jet-black, turned grey overnight and came out by handfuls. He went to work 'like a gambler to the gaming table', slept for five hours and then worked fifteen to eighteen at a stretch. 'It calls for the kind of exaltation which only visits those who are disappointed in life.' The 'miraculous' Dr Nacquart, as Laurence had called him, once again prescribed country air. Not an inspired prescription, but what could he hope to do for a man whose greatest malady was his genius? Towards the end of September 1834, Balzac left for Saché to stay with the Margonnes, and here he started work on a new novel, *Le Père Goriot.*

La Recherche de l'absolu was published by Madame Béchet, who in Balzac's view handled it very badly. '*L'Absolu*, ten times greater, I consider, than *Eugénie Grandet*, is destined to have no success.' Like every disappointed author he blamed his publisher; but the fact is simply that the book was far less attractive to the general reader than *Grandet*. It did however bring some rewards. He wrote to Eve: 'My mother is very proud of *l'Absolu*. . . . Madame de Castries has written to tell me that it made her weep. . . .' Moreover she got her Uncle Fitz-James to invite him to the Château de Quévillon. Balzac refused. The 'Duchesse de Langeais' had lost all hold over him, and was somewhat bitter in consequence.

There was another contretemps. Certain letters not intended for his eye came into the hands of Monsieur Hanski. Balzac explained them away by saying that Madame Hanska had once laughingly remarked to him that she longed to know what a real love-letter was like, so he had written a couple, expecting her to realize that it was only a joke. If he had offended her he begged Monsieur de Hanski to intercede for him—'I am most anxious, Monsieur, that this entirely natural explanation should reach you.' What the gentleman thought of the explanation is not known; he said no more. And Balzac had more serious things to think about. He was writing *Le Père Goriot.*

XVII

The Grand Design

*Balzac, jetant sur ses ouvrages le regard à la fois d'un
étranger et d'un père, s'avisa brusquement, en projetant sur
eux une illumination rétrospective, qu'ils seraient plus beaux
réunis en un cycle ou les mêmes personnages reviendraient
et ajouta à son oeuvre, en ce raccord, un coup de pinceau, le
dernier et le plus sublime.*

MARCEL PROUST

ONE DAY IN 1833 Balzac hurried from the Rue Cassini to the
Faubourg Poissonnière, where the Survilles were now living,
to make the following pronouncement: 'Salute me, I am on the
way to becoming a genius!' Striding up and down their living-
room he told them of his plan to group all his novels within a
single framework. There was nothing vague about it. The
following year he described it to Eve Hanska with great precision:

I believe that by 1838 the three sections of this vast work
will be, if not entirely complete, at least super-imposed, so that
the reader will be able to judge it as a whole.

The *Études de moeurs* will be a complete picture of society
from which nothing has been omitted, no situation in life, no
physiognomy or character of man or woman, no way of living,
no calling, no social level, no part of France, nor any aspect of
childhood, old age, middle age, politics, justice or war.

That is the foundation, the story of the human heart traced
thread by thread, social history depicted in all its parts. These
will not be imaginary facts; they will be things that happen
everywhere.

So then the second layer is the *Études philosophiques*, because
after the effects will come the causes. In the *Études de moeurs*
I shall have depicted sentiments and their interplay, life and the
course it takes. In the *Études philosophiques* I shall show the
why of sentiments, the *what* of life; what is the structure, what
are the conditions outside which neither society nor man can

exist; after having surveyed it [society] in order to describe it, I shall survey it in order to judge it. Also, in the *Études de moeurs* there will be *individuals* treated as *types*, and in the *Études philosophiques* there will be *types* depicted as *individuals*. Thus I shall have brought all aspects to life, the type by individualizing it, the individual by typifying him. I shall have invested the fragment with thought and given to thought the life of an individual.

Then, after the *effects* and the *causes*, come the *Études analytiques*, of which the *Physiologie du mariage* is a part, because after *effects* and *causes* the principles must be sought. The *moeurs* are the play itself, the *causes* are the back-stage and the machinery. The *principles* are the author; but as the work spirals upward into the heights of thought it tightens and becomes condensed. If twenty-four volumes are needed for the *Études de moeurs*, only fifteen will be needed for the *Études philosophiques* and only nine for the *Études analytiques*. Thus Man, Society and Mankind will be described, judged and analysed without repetitions in a work which will be like a western Thousand and One Nights.

When all is finished, my Madeleine designed, my pediment carved, my scaffolding removed, my last touches of the brush applied, I shall have been right or I shall have been wrong. But having composed the poem, the exposition of an entire system, I shall propound its scientific theory in an *Essai sur les forces humaines*. And round the foot of this palace, a laughing child, I shall have traced the huge arabesque of the *Cent contes drolatiques*. . . .

The architect had decided on the placing of his masses. He got Félix Davin, a young and talented writer who was a friend of Berthoud, to write lengthy prefaces to the *Études philosophiques* and the *Études de moeurs*. Writing under Balzac's guidance, and sometimes to his dictation, Davin emphasized that Balzac had not at once conceived his grand design, and that it was better so. Perhaps if the vast scheme had been apparent to him from the outset his heart would have failed him at the sheer enormity of the task. It was easier to suppose that he had become gradually aware of it. Its unity was not imposed but had grown out of the work itself. Works of art, like human institutions or like children, were born, not of conscious acts but of the play of natural forces:

May not we suppose that one day, reviewing the different themes running through his work, he behaved like the craftsman who suddenly leaves the reverse side of his tapestry and stands back to look at the design as a whole. Thenceforward, and because the germ of a great synthesis had long been present in his mind, it was the whole that preoccupied him. Suddenly, his mind filling in the gaps in a composition covered with frescoes, imagining a group here, a major figure there, and farther off a deeper level or patch of related colouring, he was carried away by these images and returned to work with a *French fury*, because he was still at the age when one fears nothing. . . .

Davin rightly condemned the critics who, lacking a sense of proportion, had referred to his friend's books as *contes* and *nouvelles*, fables and anecdotes, using the words in a disparaging sense; and to confound them he repeated Balzac's own favourite image:

But do not these supposed trifles exactly resemble the squared stones, the scattered capitals, the tiles half-covered with flowers or dragons, which, seen in the builder's yard between the workman's saw and chisel, appear small and insignificant, but which the architect intends to use in his design to ornament some rich entablature, to create vaulting, to surround the great ogived windows of his cathedral, his château, his chapel, his country house . . . ?

The time had come for the building to be assembled. In September 1834, Balzac left for Saché, resolved while he was there to write, rapidly, a novel which was to be one of the cornerstones, *Le Père Goriot*. We still possess the seed out of which this book sprang, a note in his day-book: 'A worthy man —middle-class boarding-house—600 francs income—stripped himself to the bone for his two daughters, who each have 50,000 a year—dies like a dog.' He wrote to the Marquise de Castries that he wanted to depict 'a sentiment so great in itself that it withstands constant affronts', and to Eve that he had chosen for his leading character 'a man who is a father in the way that a saint or martyr is a Christian'. Once again he was to describe the ravages of a passion pursued to madness: 'Passion does not compromise; it accepts every sacrifice.'

Le Père Goriot was conceived on a very much larger and bolder scale than *Eugénie Grandet*. It contains a number of interwoven stories. There is the tragedy of Goriot himself, ruined and then rejected by his daughters, Anastasie de Restaud and Delphine de Nucingen; the drama of Vautrin, a new incarnation of Ferragus, the ex-convict living under a false name in the Pension Vauquer, who with diabolical skill weaves a network of intrigue until he is unmasked by the police; the story of Rastignac, the young Gascon who, leaving his provincial home still largely uncorrupted, is horrified by the depravities of Paris; and the story of his cousin, Claire de Beauséant, a great lady deserted by the lover she adores (shedding further light on a tale already told in *La Femme abandonnée*). A family boarding-house is the place where these paths cross. Was not the world a '*pension de famille dorée*' and the Court of the Tuileries itself a family boarding-house with a crown over the door?

From that time onward Balzac contained an entire society in himself; but he brought it to life with countless factual details, the fruit of memory and observation. For the purpose of creating Goriot, the former manufacturer of '*pâtes*' (spaghetti, macaroni), he consulted the owner of his house in the Rue Cassini, who was himself a flour-merchant. As for the unforgettable Pension Vauquer, he knew it well. It was not any one boarding-house but an amalgam of '*pensions bourgeoises des deux sexes et autres*', and the name Vauquer came from Tours. A small detail illustrates the workings of the novelist's mind: the dreadful Mother Vauquer pronounces *tiyeuilles* like Eve Hanska. This whimsy gave Balzac great pleasure. In Rastignac he partly (but only partly) depicted himself. Rastignac's aims are very different from those of a writer, but like Balzac he has two sisters, and the elder, whose name is Laure, sends her brother her girlhood savings. Rastignac challenges Paris from the heights of Père-Lachaise, crying, 'Now it is between the two of us!' as Balzac must surely have done when he was living in the Rue Lesdiguières. The mingling of innocence and ambition in Rastignac in that early period of his life is not unlike that of the youthful Balzac.

As for Vautrin, he is partly Vidocq and again partly Balzac. At the age of twenty Balzac had dreamed of magical powers

whereby he would dominate the world, and his first novels had
been filled with pirates, freebooters, outlaws of every kind. Even
in 1834 he was not far from believing, with Vautrin, that 'men
devour each other like spiders in a jar' and that nobody calls the
successful criminal to account: 'No one will ask me, "Who are
you?" I shall be Mister Four-Millions.' Balzac admired Vautrin.
'A great crime is sometimes a poem.' But, like Rastignac, he
still had scruples. Because the world is a jungle there must be
laws, a State, a religion and families.

The father-myth in Balzac touches a deep and sensitive spot.
In the case of Goriot it is a matter of the paternity of the flesh.
'My life is in my two daughters,' Goriot says. 'If they are
enjoying life, if they are happy and bravely clad, what does it
matter what garments I wear or where I sleep at nights? I am
not cold if they are warm, I am never sad if they are laughing.
. . .' His attitude towards them is like God's attitude to creation:
'But I love my daughters more than God loves the world,
because the world is not as beautiful as God and my daughters
are more beautiful than I.' Throughout Balzac's work we come
upon this passionate desire to live a larger, happier life through
another person. There can be no doubt that the theme is ob-
scurely linked with the myth of Promethean creation. The
novelist creates for himself a seraglio of all the women he has
never had; he knows love, power and fame in the semblance of
his characters, just as Goriot knew happiness in his daughters.
Balzac, like Goriot, had to choose between creation and life;
and was destined to kill himself for the sake of his work as the
old man did for his children.

But of all the threads in *Père Goriot* the one closest to the
author is that of Rastignac's apprentice years. Eugène de
Rastignac arrives from the provinces believing in the warmth of
family affection, and everywhere finds baseness and corruption,
daughters who reject their father, wives who deceive their husbands, cynical and callous lovers: 'In three hours, between the
blue boudoir of Anastasie de Restaud and the pink salon of
Claire de Beauséant, he underwent a three-year course in *Paris
Law.*' His cousin, Madame de Beauséant, a proud, passionate
woman, gives him his first set of rules: 'The more coldly you
calculate, the better you will get on. Strike without mercy and
you will be feared. Think of men and women as post-horses to

be left behind at each relay; thus you will reach the peak of your desires. Remember that you can be nothing here without a woman to interest herself on your behalf. She must be young, rich and elegant. But if you have any true feeling hide it like a hoarded treasure; never let its existence be suspected, or you will be lost.'

The formidable Vautrin confirms this: 'I defy you to walk two steps in Paris without encountering the most vile intrigues. . . . That is life as it really is. It is no more beautiful than a kitchen, it stinks as much and you have to dirty your hands if you want to cook anything. . . . There are no principles, but only happenings; there are no laws, but only circumstances. The superior man allies himself to happenings and circumstances so as to make use of them.' Once one has grasped these truths the road is open to vice and success. The apprentice sheds his last young man's tear on Goriot's tomb, and then—'as a first step in his challenge to society, Rastignac went to dine with Madame de Nucingen'.

A striking feature of the book, one which makes it truly a keystone of the arch, is the reintroduction of characters. Balzac had more than once made casual use of a name or character from an earlier book; but the procedure now became deliberate and systematic. He was to have his doctors (Bianchon and Desplein), his policemen (Corentin and Peyrade), his advocates (Derville and Desroches), his financiers (Nucingen and the Kellers), and his money-lenders (Gobseck, Palma and Bidault, alias Gigonnet). Madame de Restaud first appeared in *Gobseck*. We first meet Rastignac as a minor character in *La Peau de chagrin*; later we encounter him at different stages throughout his career, and we watch him change, so that the dimension of Time is added to the picture. Vautrin reappears later in *Splendeurs et misères des courtisanes*, overshadowing the destiny of Lucien de Rubempré as he did that of Rastignac. In the case of Madame de Beauséant we are here told the story of the broken love affair which was the basis of *La Femme aban-donée*. A whole aristocracy—Listomère, Kergarouët, Mau-frigneuse, Grandlieu—passes through her salon. This world of Balzac's creation became more real to him than the world he lived in. He gives news of it in passing, like gossip from the real world: 'Now let us talk of serious matters. Who is to marry

Eugénie Grandet?' . . . 'Do you know whom Félix de Vandenesse is marrying? She's a Mademoiselle de Granville. It's an
excellent match.'

This idea of 'reappearances' seems logical enough. Any great
novelist might use it; all carry in their heads a number of
characters dear to their hearts, whom they portray under
different names and in different guises. In the case of Stendhal,
there is the man he would have liked to be, Fabrice del Dongo
or Lucien Leuwen; the woman he would have liked to love,
Madame de Rênal or Madame de Chasteller; and the cynical,
witty old man, the elder Leuwen or the Marquis de la Mole. In
the same way Balzac produced the composite Ferragus-
Vautrin, both projections of his own lust for power. Monsters
like Vautrin are rare, and he was allowed to escape from
imprisonment so that he could be used again. On the other hand
Balzac had to produce a whole string of foppish careerists, from
Henri de Marsay, who becomes Prime Minister, La Palférine
and Maxime de Trailles to the unhappy Paul de Manerville;
and a string of *grandes coquettes*—la Duchesse de Langeais, la
Princesse de Cadegnan, la Marquise d'Espard.

It was obvious, of course, that if his earlier works were to be
incorporated in the Grand Design they would have to undergo
some modification, occasional changes of names and dates. But
the gain was to be enormous. Trifling episodes open up wide
new vistas. Sometimes it is the future that throws light on the
present; but more often the latest novel springs out of what has
gone before. An after-dinner conversation suddenly affords the
key to a hitherto enigmatic character. Everything happens as it
does in life, which we see bathed in shadow. We get to know
people by chance, through half-open doors and unexpected
confidences. The best example is de Marsay, whom we never
see in action as a politician but still know to be 'the only statesman since Talleyrand'; another is Ronquerolles—'admirably
sketched. . . . We meet him; we scarcely know him, yet we know
all we need to know. He is one of the Thirteen, and nothing
else. . . .'*

Thus there is a reality of the whole hugely transcending that
of the parts. Critics have objected: 'How can a group of players
having limited roles be accepted as a world? How believe that

* Alain, *Les Arts et les dieux.*

all Paris was treated by Bianchon and had Derville for its advocate; or that Serizy, Bauvan and Granville presided for so long over the whole judiciary of France?' But the fact is that at any time countries are managed by a small élite, and that the heroines of resounding love-affairs, in any period, can be counted on the fingers of one hand. Moreover a necessary convention of the novel allows the many to be represented by the few. It is one of the functions of art to bring intelligible order to the spawning confusion of the world. The artist must know how to invest the world he creates with elements of mystery and hazard to create the illusion of life's measureless abundance.

Balzac had never worked with so much assurance. He wrote *Père Goriot* in daily spells of from sixteen to eighteen hours (twenty hours a day during November 1834), first at Saché and then in Paris. 'A master-work,' he told Eve Hanska. He wanted to finish the book quickly so as to be able to join her in Vienna for the anniversary of the 'unforgettable day' (26 January). He had to correct proofs of the beginning while he was still writing the end, since it was due to appear in the *Revue de Paris*. On 15 December he was 'laid low in bed, incapable of doing or understanding anything.' The Duchesse d'Abrantès wrote to reproach him for neglecting her. 'There is a fact which dominates my life,' he replied, 'continuous, incessant work. . . . I can't write to you, my fatigue is too great. . . . Do not think badly of me. Say to yourself, "He works day and night", and be surprised by only one thing, that you have not yet had news of my death. I go to the Opéra or the Italiens to digest. That is my sole distraction, because there I do not have to think or talk, but only to look and listen. . . .'

Zulma Carraud had given birth to a second son, strangely christened Yorick (for love of Sterne, and therefore of Balzac). He 'kissed its forehead', but at a distance—no time to pay a visit to Frapesle: 'Never has the torrent which bears me flowed so fast; never has so majestically terrible a work taken possession of the human mind. I go to work like a gambler to the tables; I sleep only five hours and work eighteen; I should arrive exhausted; but the thought of you sometimes refreshes me. I'm buying La Grenadière and paying my debts. . . .' Madame Mère had been installed in Chantilly with a friend, and Laure and Honoré would have liked to visit her on her fifty-sixth birthday; but how could they manage it, when everything conspired to keep them in Paris? To console her they jointly sent her a watch on a blue ribbon, warning her that she must say nothing to Surville—'for I have a husband,' wrote Laure, 'who understands nothing of these tokens of affection.'

At the instigation of Madame de Castries the Duc de Fitz-James again wrote in the friendliest terms inviting Balzac to Quevillon. But *Goriot* was still unfinished, and moreover he was annoyed by the lady's sudden interest in Sainte-Beuve, a writer whom he detested. The latter's *Volupté* had been published in July 1834, and she had written to him: 'It would be difficult indeed for an unhappy woman ignorant of all things except the sorrows of life to express to you how deeply your beautiful book has moved me. . . .' This well-worn gambit had worked. They had become friendly, and since Sainte-Beuve was less fiery in his demands than Balzac, an intellectual friendship sufficed them, although it evidently had its tender moments, for she presented him with the silver cross which her dead lover, Victor von Metternich, had kissed when he lay dying. This infuriated Balzac, who wrote her a very cold letter in which he addressed her as 'Madame'. For a time she held aloof, but then she sought to win him back.

La Marquise de Castries to Balzac, 29 October 1834: I am not again asking for the friendship you have so often promised. No; if it is not in your heart, you must not wear it on your lips. . . . Last night I was tormented by a cruel dream, and I have an overwhelming need to turn to you. My dear, one breaks with a mistress; but with a friend, a friend who wishes to rejoice in all your happiness and share your sorrows, a friend of three years whose thoughts you have shared, and one so sad and ill! Since only days are left to me, why should I invite another blow and a hurtful one? Your 'Madame' wounded me! Do you remember Aix, and the letter from *Louis Lambert* which you sent me, and the stream, and the ruined mill, and La Chartreuse—am I the only one who remembers? . . . If it is so, then do not write to me; your silence will tell me that all is over. All over! But that cannot be true, can it? You still care for me. I am your friend, your Marie. Good-bye. Do not make me wait too long for the word that will set my heart beating. . . .

It was a great act of self-abasement in so proud a woman. He was very slow to reply; but he could not entirely break away from her and he confessed his weakness: 'You have gradually broken, one by one, the countless bonds I was so happy to accept; but it is your especial privilege that you can renew them with a word. . . .'

Nevertheless, when at the beginning of 1835 he allowed himself a few days' rest, he went to spend them at La Bouleaunière with the ailing Madame de Berny. 'She is sixty,' he wrote to Eve. 'Her sorrows have changed and weakened her. My affection for her is doubled. I say so without pride, for I see no merit in it. It is my nature, which God made forgetful of evil but always alive to kindness. A person who loves me always makes me quiver. Generous feelings are so fruitful; why go in search of the bad . . . ?' He wrote of his distress to Auguste Borget, another devoted friend: 'Madame de Berny is suffering from a fatal illness, an aneurism of the heart, which is incurable. My life is threatened at its source. If that light from Heaven is taken from me, every day will be less sunny. She is, as you know, my conscience and my strength; she prevails over everything like the sky, like the spirit of faith, of hope; I do not know what to do. She does not know what her illness is, but she knows only too well that she is dying. . . .'

And to Madame Hanska: 'You will be, if she should be taken from me, the one and only person who has opened her heart to me. You alone know the *sesame*; for the feeling of Madame Carraud . . . is in some sort the replica of my sister's. . . .' Weeping for the love that death was to dissolve, he turned for support to his other love, younger and, although he did not realize it, the more precious to an overworked man because distance rendered it less demanding. How much power and prestige does a mistress gain by separation! 'A woman means much in our life when she is Beatrice and Laure. . . .' Dante's Beatrice, Petrarch's Laura . . . both models of discretion.

When *Père Goriot* was finished on 26 January (rendering that date doubly memorable) he sent the manuscript, specially bound, to Eve with the following inscription: 'To Madame E. de H. Everything mujiks do belongs to their masters.—DE BALZAC. But I beseech you to believe that even if I did not owe you this by virtue of the laws that govern your poor slaves, I would still lay it at your feet, brought there by the

most sincere of affections. 26 January 1835. The inmate of
the Hôtel de l'Arc, in Geneva.' In short, an 'open' dedication,
fit for the eyes of Wenceslas Hanski.

The readers of the *Revue de Paris* applauded *Le Père Goriot*
no less than Eve. Balzac himself knew it to be an advance on
anything he had written: 'There is only one verdict. *Eugénie
Grandet, l'Absolu*—all are surpassed.' The first printing was
sold out before publication. But the reviewers were not to be
won over. They rebuked Balzac for his exaggerations. 'What a
world! What a society!' the *Courrier Français* piously exclaimed.
'What a caricature of fatherhood! What deplorable morals!
What cynical portraits! What adulterous women!' In vain did
Balzac, in a humorous preface, make a list of his heroines proving
that thirty-eight out of sixty were women of virtue. He had even
carried benevolence to the point of bringing back some of his
earlier sinners, rather than create new ones. It availed him
nothing. Political resentments were aligned against him, phari-
saical protests—above all, intense jealousy.

In December 1834 the review *La Mode*, which had hitherto
been friendly to him, made fun of the 'ubiquity' of M. Balzac,
'whose name flutters incessantly before our eyes like some
fantastic apparition. . . . M. Balzac is the *inévitable* of the booksellers—of the booksellers, be it clearly understood, for bookselling and literature are by no means synonymous. . . . It is not
our fault if this thought has occurred to us in connection with
M. Balzac. . . . M. Balzac, who shares with M. Paul de Kock the
honour of seeing his name in letters four inches high in the
windows of every reading-room in Paris, the suburbs and the
provinces. . . . M. Balzac promises, in the publishers' lists,
matter to satisfy the appetite of even the most voracious con-
sumer of modern writing for ten years to come. May God help
us! . . .' They attacked the man, his name, his luxury, his love-
affairs. When fame goes beyond acceptable bounds, malice dis-
cards all decency. He might have said: 'God defend me from my
friends; from my enemies I can defend myself.' But he preferred
work and silence. 'However violent the attacks and calumnies,
I rise above them. I do not reply. . . . Besides, *Le Père Goriot* is
a sensation. There has never been such a rush to read a book;
the booksellers put up advance notices. This is indeed tremendous. . . .'

XVIII

Rue des Batailles

BEFORE STARTING *Père Goriot*, Balzac had published with Madame Béchet, as a part of his *Scènes de la vie parisienne*, the beginning of a strange and compelling story entitled *La Fille aux yeux d'or*, which he finished in 1835. Although it was comparatively short, an episode in the *Histoire des treize*, it is of great importance in relation to his work as a whole.

It opens with a brilliant discourse on Paris, 'a vast field ceaselessly swept by a tempest of interests' in which one encounters not faces but masks, 'masks of weakness, of strength, of poverty, of happiness, of hypocrisy; all strained, all imprinted with the ineffaceable signs of a breathless avidity. What do they covet? Is it gold or pleasure? . . .' In this cauldron 'where everything fumes, burns, glitters, bubbles, evaporates, goes out', Balzac distinguishes five social categories. There is *the world that owns nothing*, labourers, proletarians, stall-keepers, and the *world that owns something*, traders, government officials, clerks—in a word, the bourgeoisie. What does the bourgeois aspire to? 'The flintlock of the Garde Nationale, a pot simmering on the fire, a decent grave in Père-Lachaise and, for his old age, a little money honestly earned.' The third circle in the inferno 'which perhaps will one day find its Dante' is composed of lawyers, doctors and notaries, all confessors of a society which they despise. The fourth is the world of artists—nobly ravaged faces, but ravaged none the less, destroyed by rivalries and calumnies. Finally there is the fifth circle, the aristocracy, the landed proprietors, the world of wealth and lofty, gilded salons, idle and richly provided for, in which nothing is real. Here polished manners conceal an endless disdain; vanity and tedium prevail, and the emptiness of life shapes faces of card-board—'that countenance of the rich in which impotence grimaces and gold is reflected, and whence intelligence has fled.' In a few pages Balzac draws a vast fresco, sombre but admirable.

The excessive turbulence of Paris, he goes on, benefits a few privileged beings; there are women living in oriental luxury who preserve their looks and young men of great charm: 'To the youthful beauty of English blood they add a meridional firmness of feature, French qualities of mind and purity of form. The glow in their eyes, the delicious redness of lip and lustrous black of their smooth hair, the pale skin, the distinction of countenance, make them beautiful human flowers, magnificent by contrast with the mass of faces, shrunken, ageing, grimacing, distorted. . . .'

The leading character is introduced, an Adonis, the mysterious Henri de Marsay, illegitimate son of Lord Dudley and one of 'the Thirteen': 'A woman had only to set eyes on him to lose her senses.' But de Marsay with his clear gaze and youthful vigour believes neither in man or woman, nor God or Devil. Then, outside the Café des Feuillants, he meets a strikingly beautiful girl, and they fall in love at first sight. Although Paquita Valdès, the girl with the golden eyes, is jealously guarded, he finds his way to her, and in a white boudoir of fantastic luxury she becomes his mistress. He finds her a virgin but adept, skilled in sexual pleasure because she is in love with a woman, the Mar-quise de San-Réal, herself the daughter of Lord Dudley and therefore Henri de Marsay's half-sister. It is the resemblance between them which prompted Paquita to return to the Tuileries in order to see the young man again. She is now in love with the same person in two forms, man and woman, and this leads to a hideous denouement. When Henri, having discovered that Paquita has another lover, comes to exact vengeance supported by his comrades of the Thirteen, the Marquise stabs the girl to death. Brother and sister confront each other in the blood-spattered room. The Marquise enters a convent; Henri be-comes the lover of Delphine de Nucingen.

Such was this 'magnificent and unforgettable tale—' (the words are those of Hugo von Hoffmannsthal) '—wherein volup-tuousness is born of mystery, where, in the sleepless Paris night, the Orient lifts its heavy lids, adventure twines with reality . . .

and the present is illumined with the light of a torch so dazzling that it resembles the great dreams of the remotest times. . . . The beginning might have come from the pen of Dante, the end from the Thousand and One Nights; but the whole could only be the work of the man who wrote it. . . .'

Despite the beauty of the narrative, the subject shocked Eve Hanska, and Zulma Carraud turned away her head. Yet it was not the first time a work of fiction had dealt with lesbianism. Balzac had read all the erotic literature of the eighteenth century, including Diderot's *La Religieuse*. Latouche's *Fragoletta* had touched upon the equivocal friendship between Lady Hamilton and the Queen of Naples. Balzac himself had written, in the *Physiologie du mariage*, 'A girl may leave boarding-school a virgin, but not chaste', and had talked of 'those experiments in pleasure, those fumblings of sensuality, those imitations of rapture'. He had made a note for a story to be called *L'Amour au harem*: 'A wife in love with another wife, and the tricks she uses to keep her away from the master'. And of course he knew about the much-discussed relationship between George Sand and the actress, Marie Dorval. Lodging with him in the Rue Cassini was Jules Sandeau, who had been infatuated with the first of the two women and after separating from her had made the second his mistress, 'because he found in her a perfume of the past'. Moreover Balzac was a close friend of the doctor, Émile Regnault, one of his models for Horace Bianchon and a confidant of Sandeau and Sand when they were together. That he was thinking of Marie Dorval is implied in a postscript to *La Fille aux yeux d'or*: 'If there are some who are interested in the Girl with the Golden Eyes they may see her, when the curtain has fallen on the drama, as one of those actresses who, to receive their ephemeral laurels, pick themselves up in excellent health after being publicly stabbed. . . .'

It was not this recent instance which had caused him to write the story. A novelist setting out to depict the whole society of his time could not disregard the vast field of sexual perversion. The relationship between Vautrin and Eugène de Rastignac was no different from the passion of the Marquise de San-Réal for Paquita Valdès. 'It is because I love you,' Vautrin says to Eugène. Balzac attached a near-mystical value to attachments between men. Théophile Gautier, who knew him well, wrote:

'One of Balzac's dreams was of heroic, devoted friendship, two souls, two courages, two minds fused in a single will.' He had been greatly struck by the figures of Pierre and Jaffier in Otway's *Venice Preserved*, two conspirators ready to die for one another, and he often referred to them. Vautrin says to Rastignac, 'Pierre and Jaffier, those are my passion.'

L'Histoire des treize was the story of such a fusion of will extended to a group of men, but without sexuality. Balzac was so haunted by the idea that later he founded a secret society, 'Le Cheval Rouge', whose members were sworn to support one another in all circumstances, to respond to every summons by the 'stable' and to gain key-positions in publishing, the press and the theatre. Théophile Gautier, Léon Gozlan and the critic, Alphonse Karr, were among 'the horses Balzac assembled round a restaurant table to discuss plans of campaign'. 'The devilish man,' wrote Gautier, 'had such a vivid imagination that he described to each of us, down to the smallest detail, the magnificent and glorious life which the Society would secure for him.' Indeed, the idea of conquering society, 'to end up modestly as a peer of France, a minister and a millionaire' had haunted him from his youth.

He was soon obliged to dissolve his 'Cheval Rouge', concluding when he did so, 'In France associations of men are impossible.' But he continued to be attracted by the idea of acting as protector to some young man, and first Auguste Borget, then Jules Sandeau, lived with him in the Rue Cassini. In the unpublished part of his memoirs Philarète Chasles suggests that these were something more than ordinary friendships: 'He had no liking for women, and the only one of whom he was publicly considered an admirer was Madame Canel (the wife of his publisher) who is said to have pleased him by the beauty of her long hair, which flowed down the length of her body, and through which the naturalist-novelist delighted to run his fingers.'

No liking for women! The known facts and the written word prove the absurdity of the contention. No writer has described better than Balzac the adolescent itch for women. No man ever asked more of women, or gave more in return. In him the friend of women was the equal of the lover. No man ever understood them better. Sainte-Beuve caught the *odor di femina* in his novels. Philarète Chasles might have answered that this in itself pointed to something feminine in his nature. Indeed it did. A major novelist must discover every aspect of humanity in himself, and be able, at need, to feel as a woman does. It is certainly true that when he described a pretty boy Balzac showed himself to be an admirer of masculine beauty. Perhaps now and then he had a suppressed desire for some youth. But that is all. He *guessed* Vautrin; he imagined him; perhaps he envied him; but he did not imitate him.

We have already noted his obsession with hermaphrodites. Séraphitus-Séraphita, the compound of man and woman, re-appears in *La Fille aux yeux d'or* in the form of Henri de Marsay and his sister. The duality corresponds to Balzac's own double nature: the strong, rebellious man who demands everything and fights with unbelievable energy to get it; whose hunger for power causes him to long for magical gifts or the support of a secret society; who shows himself to be both heroic and ferocious in 'that terrible struggle with the angel' which is literary creation: and on the other hand the weak, bruised, confiding '*pauvre enfant*' who cries out to Laure de Berny, Eve Hanska and Zulma Carraud for a mother's protection, and who in his love-affairs resorts to the conventional, sentimental verbiage 'which brings him closer to women'. This is neither inversion nor perversion, but weakness and humility; and both sides were necessary to the creative writer.

There is nothing mysterious about the case of Jules Sandeau. While lunching with Balzac in August 1834, he told him that after parting from George Sand he had come near to committing suicide, that he had lost all confidence in himself and all sense of purpose in life, and that he was penniless. Balzac simply invited him to come and live in the Rue Cassini, in the apartment previously occupied by Auguste Borget. To allay his scruples he proposed to put him to work on a play about La Grande Mademoiselle (the Duchesse de Montpensier, niece of Louis XIII) of which he himself had written the scenario. 'I'm taking Jules Sandeau in with me,' he wrote to Eve. 'I have to furnish his rooms and then pilot him through the literary ocean, poor, warm-hearted, shipwrecked devil that he is. . . .' The furnishing cost a great deal, and the piloting might be difficult. But what matter? 'My Sandeau' would pay it all back when *La Grande Mademoiselle* had made him rich.

On 1 November Sandeau was present at a dinner-party given by Balzac to some of his more eminent contemporaries. 'I'm being lavish beyond reason,' Balzac wrote to Eve. 'I have Rossini coming and Olympe, his *cara dona*, who will preside . . . the most exquisite wines in Europe, the rarest flowers, the most wonderful food. . . .' Salmon-trout, chicken, ices, all on credit. The goldsmith Lecointe supplied five silver platters, three dozen forks, a fish-slice with a heavy silver handle: and the whole glittering array, having made its effect, would go straight to the pawnbroker. Sandeau was appalled by this way of life, and even more by Balzac's industry: 'He says that no amount of fame is worth so much effort, and that he'd sooner die than attempt it.'

Disillusion soon set in. Balzac wanted some research done in connection with the play, and Sandeau did not get on with it fast enough to suit him: 'I scribbled till I was breathless but he was never satisfied. I could count myself lucky if, when I was lying exhausted in my narrow iron bed, that Titan did not wake me up to read me what he had just written, or put me to work correcting one of his innumerable sets of proofs.' And he wrote later to Balzac: 'The battle makes you bigger, but it kills me; you need tempest, but I need calm.' Balzac had by now come to share George Sand's view of '*le petit Jules*'. Laziness amazed and exasperated him: 'One can hardly conceive of so much indolence and nonchalance. He had no energy and no willpower. . . . He breaks the heart of friendship as he did of love. . . .' Nevertheless it was Sandeau who made the break, and Balzac suffered from it 'financially and morally'. Sandeau walked out in March 1836, leaving his unpaid rent and other debts on Balzac's hands, together with an affectionate letter: 'My Mar, I have felt for a long time that there was little dignity in the life I have been living. I have been surrounded by luxury that bears no relation to my work, with my debts mounting up every day, and I have sometimes felt that I was heading for suicide. I tried to work, but I couldn't. . . . Well, I've given up. . . . Good-bye, my dear; your Musch loves you.' And later: 'Beloved Mar, I counted on being able to come and embrace you on the last day. . . .' It is the 'Mar' and 'Musch' which have rendered the friendship suspect. But they were no more than a casual, lunch-time joke, like Vautrin's trick of adding 'rama' to words—he

called Rastignac le Marquis de Rastignacorama. It amused
Balzac to turn the slang suffix 'mar' into a prefix, and he referred
to himself as the '*mar-tyr*' and the '*mar-about*'. Because of the
monkish gown he wore his friends nicknamed him 'Dom Mar'.
In any case, that letter was written long after he had left
Sandeau to his own devices in the Rue Cassini, with only
the cook for company and an 'Apartment to Let' notice on
the garden gate. He had fixed himself up an 'unassailable
retreat' in the Rue des Batailles, in what was then the suburb
of Chaillot.

The need to escape his creditors was certainly one reason for
the move. Although he had earned a great deal of money during
the past four years, he had not paid them off. He now had
46,000 francs of debts, apart from what he owed his family. The
debts have been commonly attributed to the failure of the
printing works, but they were far more due to personal extravagance, his fantastic expenditure on luxuries. He could only work
happily in a handsomely furnished, thickly-carpeted room,
filled with bronzes, bric-à-brac and expensively bound volumes.
Lecointe supplied him not only with silver but with two walking-
sticks, one red cornelian and the other with a knob incrusted
with turquoises. Balzac's 'canes'—of gold or rhinoceros-horn
gleaming with precious stones—became famous. Delphine de
Girardin used *La Canne de Monsieur de Balzac* as the title of
a novel, affecting to believe that his stick had magical properties
whereby he could make himself invisible, the better to study the
private lives of his fellow-men.

All this was background, the dream made real, a fairy-tale
world. He liked to pretend that for an evening the wave of a
wand could abolish all the harsh realities of money, time and
space. But when—for instance, after that dinner-party, which
caused Rossini to declare that he had known nothing better at
the tables of royalty—he went back to work, he was returning to
the real world, the world of the Pension Vauquer and the
Maison Nucingen. Here he was his true self, looking with a cool
head and lucid eye at the extravagances of Old Goriot, describing with a meticulous precision the vast financial transactions of Baron Nucingen. Now and then he tried to apply
his characters' masterly concepts in real life; always without
success, because when life made difficulties he withdrew at

once to the imaginary world. The business venture became a novel, and showed no other profit.

His passion for luxury was not solely due to vanity. It was something more complex, a part of the stupendous work of fiction which was Balzac's own life, enacted both in his head and in the world. For him the frontier between the real and the imaginary was never sharply drawn. When he gave a dinner-party he had a tale to tell about every bottle. The claret had travelled three times round the world; the rum had lain for a century in a barrel at the bottom of the sea; the tea had been plucked by moonlight by the daughter of a Chinese emperor. If someone asked, 'Balzac, is that really true?' he would give his childlike laugh and reply, 'Not a word of it!' His 'unassailable retreat' in the Rue des Batailles included a specially decorated boudoir with a white cashmere divan fifty feet in circumference. He made use of it in *La Fille aux yeux d'or*, where he describes it in the following words:

The back of this immense bed rose several inches above the cushions, which further enriched it by the manner of their trimmings. The divan was covered with red material over which was draped India muslin, ribbed like a Corinthian column with raised and sunken ridges, and adorned at the top and bottom with a band of poppy-red embroidered with black arabesques. Beneath the muslin the poppy turned to rose, the colour of love reflected by the window curtains, which were of India muslin lined with pink taffeta and decorated with fringes of poppy and black. Six silver-gilt arms, each carrying two candles, were fixed to the wall at equal distances over the divan. The ceiling, from the centre of which hung a silver chandelier, sparkled with whiteness, and the cornices were gilt. The carpet was like an Eastern shawl, with designs recalling the poems of Persia, where it had been worked by the hands of slaves. The chairs were upholstered in white cashmere with black and poppy-red adornments. The clock and the candelabra were all of white marble and gold. . . .

The shimmer of the hangings, whose colour changed according to the angle of vision, becoming pure white or pink, harmonized with the play of the light which filtered through the diaphanous ridges of muslin, producing a snowy effect. The soul has I know not what attachment for white; love takes pleasure in red, and gold heightens the passions, having the power to realize their fantasies. Thus everything that is vague and mysterious in man, all his unexplained affinities, were indulged in their unwitting predilections. There was in this perfect harmony a mingling of colours which evoked in the spirit a sensual response, random and undecided. . . .

Such was the fruit of those childhood and adolescent dreams, and the long years of disappointment and frustration—a setting fit for an Arabian Nights Sultan and his fabled wives.

But in addition to the creditors he had another and urgent reason for leaving the Rue Cassini. The Garde Nationale was trying to conscript him for watch-duty, obsessed with the absurd notion that he was a citizen like any other, and he was threatened with imprisonment if he did not obey the summons. He had to disappear. The apartment at 13 Rue des Batailles was not rented in his own name, but in that of a fictitious Madame Durand. No one was allowed in without giving a password which was frequently changed—'The apple-season has begun' or 'I'm bringing lace from Belgium'. And then, above the unoccupied ground and first floors, having passed through two shabby, empty rooms and along a dismal passage, the initiate drew back a heavy curtain and found himself in an oriental palace. Was it Balzac's study or the boudoir of Paquita Valdès? He had had the walls quilted, whether to ensure silence for himself or to stifle the cries of the Golden-eyed Girl. He was hoping that the divan would be shared with a lady who had lately caught his fancy, a young Englishwoman whom he had met at the Austrian Embassy. He may even have still had hopes of Henriette de Castries, from whom he had never detached himself entirely.

Balzac to the Marquise de Castries, March 1835: How could you have supposed that I was still in the Rue Cassini? I am within a stone's throw of you. I do not like to think that you are sad, and I would scold you severely if you were here. I would seat you on a big divan where you would be like a fairy in her palace, and tell you that in this life we must love if we are to live. . . .

He went on to tell her that he was working on a new novel—'the great feminine figure I promised'. It was *Le Lys dans la vallée*, and the heroine's christian name was Henriette, a surprising act of homage to Henriette de Castries after so many ups-and-downs. He was devoting all his energies to it:

That is why I am not 'shut in with my mistress', as the world tells you. If, with all the work I do, I really had the five or six mistresses people credit me with, I should deserve to be publicly decorated. Hercules would be a Lilliputian by comparison. . . . An hour of feminine distraction would perhaps be very good for me, but the white divan awaiting the lily will always be what it is now. For the first time in my life I have surrounded myself with the poetry I always longed for. Jules Sandeau, who came the day I started work, said that it made him think of the view of Palermo Cathedral in *Robert le diable*. It's feminine! But charmingly and graciously feminine. Thank you for the quills; thank you for the briar-rose, a poor flower fallen into an abyss of toil. Why do you not come at the time when I get up, to perch like a bird on the divan, just for an hour? Who in the world would know? Only the two of us. Between eleven and one you would have a moment of poetic, mysterious life; but you grow too old in pleasure for me to believe in such youthful things. . . .

He was visited in the Rue des Batailles by Prince Alfred von Schönburg, ambassador-extraordinary sent to notify King Louis-Philippe of the accession of Ferdinand I to the throne of Austria, and through him he sent Eve Hanska the manuscript of *La Fille aux yeux d'or*. But he confessed that he had not yet finished the difficult *Séraphita*. He was too tired: 'My life is sapping my brain while my body grows thick with inaction. . . . For about twenty days I have worked steadily, twelve hours a day, on *Seraphita*. The world knows nothing of this immense labour; it only sees, and should only see, the outcome. But I have had to devour the whole of mysticism to shape it. *Séraphita* is a devouring work for those who believe. Unhappily, in this dismal Paris, the Angel has chanced to become the subject of a ballet. . . .'

He also told Eve, not without pride, that his turquoise-studded cane was still the talk of Paris, and even of Rome and Naples: 'It threatens to become European. . . . If someone tells you on your travels that I have a magic stick which sets horses galloping, causes palaces to sprout out of the earth and scatters diamonds, do not be surprised but laugh with me. Never did the tail of the dog of Alcibiades wag so briskly! . . .' For a man in love with fame it is no bad policy to make himself a living legend. Popular imagination is more ready to grasp the tail of a dog or the knob of a cane than any philosophy.

And now, good night. It is two in the morning, and *Séraphita* has been robbed of an hour and a half. She is grumbling and calling to me. I have got to finish her because the *Revue de Paris* is also grumbling; it is nineteen hundred francs in advance of me, and *Séraphita* will scarcely square the account. Good night; you may well believe that I think of you as I finish the book that is written for you. It is time it appeared; the literary world here has decided that I will never finish it, that it is impossible. . . .

But for him nothing was impossible. He promised to bring 'Her Rzewuskian Majesty' the manuscript of *Séraphita* before she returned to her Polish domain. What he did not mention was that, with the coming of Spring, he was making frequent trips to Versailles to visit an English lady, the Contessa Guidoboni-Visconti.

Balzac to Zulma Carraud, 17 April 1835: There are several men in me: the financier; the artist fighting against the papers and the public; and the artist wrestling with his own works and themes. Finally, there is the man of sensibility who will lie on a rug at the foot of a flower, to rejoice in its colours and breathe its scent. Here you will say, 'That villainous Honoré!', but no, I do not deserve the epithet. Would you really have me refuse every joy that is offered and lock myself away to go on working? *Cara*, why don't you write to me any more? Do you think that you have lost anything at all of my affection? The vicissitudes of life cause old friendships to grow warmer. So you will be seeing me in a few days. It is an escape to which I look forward with great happiness. . . . But also, during the past few days I have fallen under the spell of a very compelling person, and I do not know how to shake it off, for I am like the poor wenches, powerless against what pleases me. . . .

Alas, Polish friends in Paris told Madame Hanska of this latest diversion. Her letters became terse and scolding. He realized that he would have to go to Vienna to clear himself; but it was difficult for him to leave his desk: 'I'm like a dog on a chain. When will the capricious hand of Fate release me? I don't know.' He was suffering from a liver disorder. 'But stay where you are, Mistress Death! . . . My work is not yet done!'

XIX
The Lily in the Valley

La constance est une des pierres angulaires de mon caractère.

BALZAC

IN THE SPRING OF 1835 he had the following works in hand or in the preliminary stages: *Le Lys dans la vallée* (a reply to Sainte-Beuve's *Volupté*, 'but better'), *La Fleur des pois*, the third set of ten *Contes drolatiques*, *Les Mémoires d'une jeune mariée* and *Sœur Marie des Anges* (which in the event was never written). In addition he was revising *Louis Lambert* and *Séraphita*. Madame Béchet was complaining, Werdet was alarmed and the reviews were thundering. As always, Balzac thought he was within sight of his objective. Why should he doubt his powers? Six years previously he had been a hollow-cheeked hack-writer executing publishers' commissions; now he was read throughout Europe. The fulfilment would come in 1837, when all his books, the rights having reverted to him, would be re-issued as *Les Études sociales*. Then he would be rich. He would pay all his debts, even what he owed his mother, and join his Eve, and the years of toil would be rewarded.

'I sing in my unbeautiful voice, "Diodati, Diodati!" ' he wrote to Eve. He had to see her before she left. Meanwhile he showered manuscripts on her and talked about his present work: 'I'm writing a splendid and noble book called *Le Lys dans la vallée*—a charming, great-souled woman, and virtuous, with a disagreeable husband. It will be a story of earthly perfection in purely human form, just as *Séraphita* will be a story of Heavenly perfection. . . .' But Eve wrote less and less often, and mostly about her jealous misgivings. He waited for a summons, prepared to hurry to her side. 'You know that one of the bengali's virtues is a boundless fidelity. Poor Asian bird without his rose, his Peri, songless, sad but always loving . . .' He longed for

Vienna, '. . . where I shall forget all my vexations. The atmosphere of Paris kills me; it is nothing but work, commitments and enemies! I need an oasis.' He would finish the *Lily* in Vienna, and visit the battlefields of Essling and Wagram, which he needed to see for his *Scènes de la vie militaire*. Before leaving, however, he hoped to buy La Grenadière in Touraine, the house he loved best—another pipe-dream, he had not a penny to spare. In May he suddenly made up his mind. He wrote imploring the Hanskis to postpone their departure; he would come to Vienna for four days: 'I am as happy as a child at the thought! To get away from my treadmill and see new country! *Allons, à bientôt!*'

He went for money to the devoted Werdet, who, being himself out of funds, applied to Baron James de Rothschild. The Baron advanced the necessary sum, remarking as he did so, 'You should be careful with Monsieur de Balzac. He's very irresponsible.' A fair observation. Monsieur de Balzac set off in a hired carriage taking his manservant, Auguste, with him. He called at Schloss Weinheim, near Heidelberg, where Prince Alfred von Schönburg introduced him to Lady Ellenborough, a lady of great beauty who lived an adventurous life crowded with lovers, but could not know, when he departed, that she had given him something of what he needed for the character of Arabella, Lady Dudley, in *Le Lys*. (We shall come in due course to his other English model.) 'What I guessed about Lady Ellenborough, during the two hours we strolled in the park with the silly Schönburg paying court to her, was the exact truth. . . .' The pause at Weinheim was particularly fruitful because, apart from meeting Lady Ellenborough, while he was waiting he composed Louis Lambert's 'letter in italics', a foggy metaphysical discourse which he considered a document of genius. He scribbled it seated on a bench in the park, and later included it in the book.

Then by way of Stuttgart and Munich he went on to Vienna, where the Hanskis had reserved a hotel room for him in the Landstrasse. The encounter was far from being as happy as the one in Geneva. Eve Hanska was full of grievances and could not easily contrive to be alone with him. He snatched hasty kisses, but this was all that could be managed. He wrote her a letter from 'a dirty, untidy man' in reply to some mortifying words she had used: 'Although I am not dirty I am certainly stupid, because I understand nothing of what you have been so good as to say to me. . . .'

The Viennese aristocracy, all readers of Balzac, would gladly have overwhelmed him with hospitality. He accepted what he could, but still tried to save a few hours for work and to maintain his monastic existence, even on holiday. 'It is impossible for me to work when I have to go out,' he wrote to Eve, 'and I never work for as little as one or two hours at a stretch. You arranged matters so that I did not get to bed till one. . . . I want to see the Prater in the early morning, when it's deserted. If you would care to, it would be very kind, because I shan't be going on with *Le Lys dans la vallée* till tomorrow, and then I shall have to work fourteen hours on end to make up for lost time. I have to finish the book in Vienna, or fling myself in the Danube. . . .',

But he was flattered at being received by Prince Metternich, whom he knew at second hand through the Duchesse d'Abrantès and Madame de Castries. The latter had entrusted him with a private message concerning her illegitimate son, Roger von Aldenburg, the Chancellor's grandson.

Extract from the diary of Princess Mélanie von Metternich, 20 May 1835: This morning Clément [her husband] saw Balzac. He opened the conversation as follows:

'Monsieur, I have read none of your works, but I know of you and it is clear that you are mad, or amusing yourself at the expense of other madmen, and that you want to cure them by means of an even greater madness."

Balzac replied that Clément had guessed correctly, that this was his object and that he would achieve it. Clément was delighted with his way of looking at things . . . .'

Balzac's political views were certainly not far removed from those of the Chancellor. As for the Princess, she found him 'simple and good, apart from his dress, which is fantastic'.

Prince Felix zu Schwarzenberg conducted him over the field of Wagram, and the Schönburgs and Kisseleffs entertained him. He also met Baron Joseph von Hammer-Purgstall, an orientalist who translated the inscription on the ass's skin into Arabic for his benefit. It sounded very well in Arabic, because of its 'weighty terseness'. According to the novel it should have been

in Sanscrit, a language with which the Baron was unfamiliar—
but who would know the difference? He presented Balzac with
a talisman, a signet-ring called the Bedouck, saying: 'One of
these days you will realize the value of this small gift.' The seed
fell on fruitful soil. Balzac was soon telling people (in good
faith) that it had belonged to the Prophet, that the English had
stolen it from the Grand Mogul, and that the latter was prepared to give gold and diamonds by the ton in exchange for it.
'Bedouck' became a magic descended directly from Adam, a ring
of invisibility, a love-charm, a panacea for all ills. Well, at least
it was a mystery added to the magical powers which Balzac
already believed himself to possess, not wholly without reason.
Talking of his guest's enormous industry and all the female
characters he had created, the Baron described him as 'a
Hercules despatching fifty virgins in a night'.

Astolphe de Custine, who was in Vienna at the same time, was
struck by Balzac's social success, but wrote to Sophie Gay:
'Our friend greatly embarrassed me by the way he presented me
to a Polish lady, a rare spirit from the solitudes of the Ukraine
and the most learned woman on the banks of the Don, saying
as he introduced us that I was the man whose conversation had
impressed him more than any other in his life. I did not know
what to say, and if I had followed my own inclination I should
have stood there like a flunkey without opening my mouth.
Instead, I did my best, but I felt the whole time that I was
expected to play a part. I seemed to have lost my wits. I could
not be at my ease with the lady, who is nevertheless a very
distinguished person. . . .' Tact and genius are not inseparable
companions.

But the Hanskis had to return to the Ukraine, and everything
called Balzac back to Paris. In any case, he wanted to go: 'A
thousand kisses, for I have a thirst for them that these small
surprises only aggravate. We shall not have an hour together,
not a minute. These obstacles so heighten my longing that,
believe me, I do well to hasten my departure.' He had spent all
his money and needed more to pay his hotel bill and the return
journey. However, this was a trifle—all that was needed was a
bill-of-exchange on Werdet, who had only to charge it to the
Lys, and if he had not sufficient ready money he could borrow
from Laure Surville. The Vienna Rothschilds cashed the bill

without a murmur, and Werdet paid up and was lauded to the skies: 'Believe me, you and I are now friends for life. . . .' And the visit to Vienna had been valuable in one respect: it had taught Balzac the extent of his reputation. As he was leaving a concert a student kissed his hand. Cultivated Europe not only admired but even furnished its homes '*à la Balzac*'. The world he created was spreading far and wide.

Back in Paris he had to resume his burdens. It seems, from his letters to Eve, that he was at once involved in family troubles. Henry, 'incapable of anything', was talking about blowing out his brains, when he needed only to work. Laure seemed to be seriously ill and his 'dear, beloved mother' said that she was half-mad with worry. He probably exaggerated a little in the hope of touching Eve, who had gone back into her shell. He consulted a clairvoyant to find out what was happening: 'She told me that you had written to Paris for news of me. . . . She found that your heart is bigger than it should be . . . but there is no danger. Your heart, like your forehead, is largely developed. I was very moved when she said, with that solemn expression of clairvoyants: "They are people who are very attached to you, they truly love you." '

Shut away in the white-and-pink boudoir he strove with his thoughts, pouring ink over paper in the ceaseless struggle to plug the breaches in his budget. Laure had done something ridiculous. To help Werdet meet the bill-of-exchange she had pawned all Honoré's silver: 'So now I have to work day and night to repair other people's stupidities. I have three or four months of hard labour ahead of me, during which I beg of you to be indulgent. I shan't be able to write to you as often as I would like. I have to deliver *Le Lys dans la vallée* and *Mémoires d'une jeune mariée* almost immediately, the one to Werdet and the other to Madame Béchet. They have all complained horribly about me. But you need feel no remorse; I shall never regret the journey, short though it was, and shorter still the time the world allowed us. . . .'

He needed to produce faster than ever, but the pressure had a stimulating effect. He wrote *La Messe de l'athée*, a short story which is a masterpiece, in one night, and *l'Interdiction* in three. 'Work and again work! Feverish night followed by feverish night, days of meditation followed by days of meditation!'

Officially the house in the Rue des Batailles was still occupied by the fictitious Widow Durand, and his friends wrote notes beginning, 'Dear, estimable widow'. He replied: 'You will be greeted with a cup of *café à la crème* such as only a widow knows how to make. . . .' But he did not really want callers. Work was all he had time for.

Except for an occasional miraculous and happy *tour de force* Balzac worked with great difficulty. From the time of *Les Chouans* he had fallen into the habit of treating his first text as no more than a draft which he worked over in proof-form. Because his handwriting was scarcely legible he had it set at once in galleys, using worn type. The corrections and additions on these galley-slips were so numerous that the publishers had to charge him for them. The compositors did their 'hour of Balzac' as though it were an hour at the treadmill, and then were rested by being given something simpler. Hounded though he was, with the pack of creditors baying at his heels, he allowed himself no compromise where his work was concerned. It had to be as good as he could make it. 'That obstinate founder,' wrote Gautier, 'would remelt the metal ten or twelve times over, if it did not exactly fill the mould.'

After keeping the printer waiting, sometimes for weeks on end, he would suddenly produce two hundred sheets scribbled in five frenzied nights. A contemporary, Édouard Ourliac, wrote:

They know what to expect. It is a scrawl, a chaos, an apocalypse, an Indian poem. The time is short, the handwriting unbelievable. So the monster is transformed, translated more or less into recognizable symbols. . . . The author sends back the first two galley-slips pasted on enormous sheets, like posters, like screens! . . . From every character, every printed word, runs a line of ink soaring out like a rocket and bursting at the end into a luminous shower of phrases, adjectives, nouns, underlined, crossed through, mixed up, altered, overwritten; it is a dazzling sight.

Picture four or five hundred arabesques of this sort, tangled, interwoven, climbing, running from one margin to the other and from south to north. Picture a dozen maps with towns, rivers and mountains all superimposed, a skein of wool that a cat has played with, all the hieroglyphics of the dynasty of the Pharaohs, or the fireworks of twenty feast-days. . . . One deals with it as best one can, trusting in God. . . .

Six or eight or ten sets of proofs would come back like this, crossed out, expanded, smothered with tram-lines and balloons. To produce a number of books a year by these methods called for superhuman resolution. When Balzac had a major work on hand he would vanish for two or three months, like a river going underground, to burst forth suddenly with a masterpiece under his arm, breathless and exhausted but laughing and content. He would drop on to the divan, mash sardines in butter to make a sort of paté which reminded him of the 'rillettes de Tours', eat it on bread and then sleep for an hour. The Titan might seem to be at the end of his strength; but the fire stolen from Jupiter brought a hundred men of clay to life.

The book he had most at heart in 1835, the one he was resolved to finish at all costs, was *Le Lys dans la vallée*. Towards the end of July he went to Madame de Berny at La Bouleaunière, and from there to Zulma Carraud at Frapesle. He had missed the lilacs, but he was in time for the roses. Absorbed in child-bearing and domestic affairs, Zulma was following his achievements with less attention than formerly, but he was always happy with her and her husband and he worked well. Major Carraud talked to him about astronomy in his leisure moments, and another officer, Major Périolas, about warfare, artillery and the Emperor.

He devoted nearly all his nights to the *Lys*, confident that this would be one of his finest novels, 'a beautiful, white statue', its theme 'the overwhelming physical attraction which overtakes two people who are ignorant and virginal in such matters'. The lady of irreproachable morals 'assailed by a college youth hungering for white shoulders', cannot suppress the prickings of desire; but the two of them, Félix de Vandenesse and Henriette de Mortsauf, although they are deeply in love, deny themselves the act of possession out of respect for human and divine law, and so bring disaster upon themselves. Félix has a love affair with a beautiful Englishwoman who gives him pleasure but no happiness; Henriette, the victim of her own destructive virtue, dies tormented by sacrilegious regrets. The story is sublime in itself; and, as always in Balzac, its human passions are deeply involved in the social developments of the time. 'It is the history of the Hundred Days seen from a château on the Loire,' Alain wrote; indeed, Félix has come to Clochegourde as the envoy of the 'roi de Gand'. Politics, and a penetrating view of society as a whole, come into the 'apprentice letter' which Henriette writes for Félix when he is leaving for the Court, an unknown territory whose language he does not speak. It gives her great pleasure, the woman who has renounced the world, to reassemble the scattered fragments of her own bitter experience for the benefit of this youth whom she loves.

Above all, she warns him, he must accept society and morals as they are: 'I say nothing of religious beliefs or of principles; this is a matter of the workings of a mechanism of iron and gold. . . .' She is strangely realistic in her counsel; the very virtues she enjoins upon him are designed to further his worldly success: 'Straightforwardness, honour, loyalty and courtesy are the most sure and speedy instruments of fortune. . . . But true courtesy implies Christian thinking; it is like the flower of charity. . . . When something is asked of you that you cannot do, you should refuse plainly, without encouraging false hopes. . . . You must not be over-confident, or commonplace, or over-eager, these are three traps. Over-confidence diminishes respect; commonplace makes you despised, and excessive zeal makes you easy to exploit. And above all, dear child, remember that you will have only two or three real friends in the course of your life. . . . One of the most important rules in the science of behaviour is to preserve almost complete silence concerning oneself. . . . The young people of today possess a hothouse astuteness, bitter at its source, which leads them to pass harsh judgements on deeds, thoughts and writings; they cut with the edges of knives that have not been tested. Do not make this mistake. . . . Cultivate influential women. Influential women are old women. . . . They will give you their hearts, and protection is the last expression of love. . . .' As for young women, he should choose one and one alone: 'Serve all, but love only one.'

The latter is wonderfully characteristic of Balzac. As always, the book contains elements of autobiography. The melancholy, the shyness, the wild yearnings of Félix de Vandenesse, all are echoes of his own youth, perhaps even to the ball at Tours in

1814, with its perfume of women. But Félix, with wealth and family behind him, could make a career for himself in the great world, whereas Honoré had to do so by his pen. Henriette de Mortsauf, in her practical realism and self-abnegation, has much of Laure de Berny. The one holds back, the other gave herself; both die of it. In a letter to Eve, Balzac referred to Madame de Berny as 'the divine creature of which Madame de Mortsauf is the pale reflection'. He wanted Eve to see in her the double of Séraphita; but also to see herself as both Madame de Mortsauf and Lady Dudley, a combination of purity and sensuality. There may also have been something of Madame de Berny's husband in Monsieur de Mortsauf, although here Balzac was trying to unite 'all the characteristics of the emigré with all the characteristics of the husband'. And he believed that in Lady Dudley he had drawn a faithful picture of an Englishwoman in love: 'I have described the woman of that country admirably in very few words.'

But it is the work itself that matters, not the sources. Balzac had challenged his enemy, Sainte-Beuve, on his own ground, and he beat him hands down. The latter's *Volupté*, although it is not without merit, lacks vitality and strength. Balzac said patronizingly: 'It is weak, cowardly and diffuse, but there are good things in it.' Madame de Berny deplored *Volupté*, being outraged by the passage in which the lover plunges into squalor to purge himself of his desires. She was delighted by the *Lys*, although at first she only said that it was truly the Lily of the Valley. 'That is high praise, coming from her,' he wrote to Eve. 'She is very difficult.' He himself had no doubts about it: 'If the *Lys* is not a breviary of woman, then I am nothing. . . . To make a drama out of virtue, to give it warmth, to use the language and style of Massillon—well, you know, that is a problem which, determined upon at the outset, has called for three hundred hours of revision, costing the *Revue* four hundred francs and me a slight attack of liver. . . .'

The reviews were malicious and unworthy: 'Monsieur de Balzac outrages the conventions with every line. . . . Yet one cannot deny that he possesses a degree of talent. He is the genius of the provinces and the reading-rooms. . . . We may grant him the popularity of Paul de Kock. . . .' The moralists refused to believe that Henriette de Mortsauf could have sighed on her death-bed for the fleshly joys she had rejected. 'They're all against it,' Balzac wrote to Eve. 'They have all abused and spat on it. I have been told that the *Gazette de France* demolished it because I don't go to Mass, and the *Quotidienne* because the editor has a grudge against me. In fact, they all have their private reasons. Instead of selling two thousand, as I hoped for Werdet's sake, it has only gone to thirteen hundred. Our material interests have suffered. There are blockheads who don't realize the beauty of Madame de Mortsauf's death; they don't see in it the conflict between body and spirit which is the basis of Christianity. They see nothing but the naggings of the cheated flesh, the injured physical being, and take no account of the sublime tranquillity of the soul when the Countess has confessed and dies a saintly death.'

Later he went so far as to write: 'The secret battle that takes place, in a valley in the Indre, between Madame de Mortsauf and physical passion, is perhaps as great as any of the great battles known to men.' Madame de Berny wrote: 'I can die in peace, being now sure that you wear the crown I wanted to see on your head. The *Lys* is a sublime work, without fault or flaw. Except that Madame de Mortsauf's death need not have been attended by those horrible regrets; they detract from the beautiful letters she writes.' Accordingly, when the book was reprinted he removed about a hundred of the lines that had offended: 'But I did not regret a single one, and no one has ever been more deeply moved than I when my pen crossed them out.'

Zulma Carraud went deeper: 'With all the clever thinking that has gone into *Le Lys dans la vallée*, a thousand women will say as they read it, "That still isn't right." The fact is, however intimate the confidences you may receive from women, there are some which will never be made to you; because it would be shaming to make them; because there are a thousand shameful things which cannot be spoken, and which would be denied, even to the friend who guessed them. . . .' Poor Zulma! To deny or keep silent was an admission in itself.

In October 1835, Balzac went to La Bouleaunière on what was to be his last visit to Laure de Berny. He worked peacefully on *La Fleur des pois*, which became *Le Contrat de mariage*. 'I have gloriously accomplished what I set out to do,' he wrote to his sister. 'It is the fight between notaries of the new and old school. . . . So an important *Scène de la vie privée* has at last been finished. The winding-up of the estate after death will go into the *Scènes de la vie de province.* . . .' In this technical matter (but in fact the book was never written) he intended to consult the official appraisers with their vast experience of human depravity; in the matter of wills and successions none knew better than they the extent to which infamy was mingled with farce.

He had no suspicion that he would never see La Dilecta again. On the contrary, she was suffering less from palpitations and he thought her health improved. But a month later, despite her enfeebled state, she had to nurse her favourite son, Armand, who was suffering from a serious chest complaint. She had lost four of her children and seen one of her daughters lose her reason. Assailed by so many misfortunes and by vague feelings of remorse, she begged Balzac not to come to her, or even write: 'You know how, when everything within us is in a state of tension, the smallest shock, whether it comes from taxed affection or from inadvertence, may lay us low. A dreadful situation! . . .' Armand died, and she had no further communication with Honoré except by letter. He realized the truth, and wrote to his mother: 'I am drunk with grief. Madame de Berny is dying. There can be no doubt of it. God and I alone know the extent of my despair. And still I have to work! . . .'

He was again being harried. Madame Béchet, who had been so wonderful in 1833, was contemplating remarriage and abruptly changed her tone. She had paid advances on books which had not yet been delivered, and she talked bitterly of her 'commercial anxieties', threatening to suspend all payments if there was any further delay. Balzac, protesting at her 'nagging', promised *Le Cabinet des antiques* and *Illusions perdues*, and on the strength of this she let him have another 5,000 francs. But it meant that he had now been paid nearly the whole of the sum agreed upon for the *Études de mœurs*. He had to write two further books for 500 francs—'work to be done for nothing!' Indeed, his financial position at the end of 1835 would have been catastrophic for anyone but Balzac. He borrowed from Dr Nacquart, from Borget, from the accommodating Madame Delannoy and from little '*père* Dablin'. Werdet had paid for the *Lys* in advance.

And the owner of the house in the Rue Cassini (which he had kept on although he was now living in the Rue des Batailles) was demanding two quarters' arrears of rent. Poor Madame Mère's sole income, the interest he owed her, reached her very irregularly.

But he kept a bold face. There were still ways and means. First—a reprint of all the youthful novels of Horace de Saint-Aubin. He would deny that they had anything to do with Balzac, and who cared if nobody believed him! He was offered 10,000 francs for this. Secondly, he would print a third set of ten *Contes drolatiques* at his own expense and sell them to Werdet at a profit. And thirdly, when Madame Béchet had sold out the *Études de mœurs*, he would place the whole series with another publisher for 45,000 francs.

So after all he was rich, and this being so why should he not buy himself a house? He needed to own one to regain the property qualification necessary to his political career, which he had lost when his mother's house had been sold. Alas, the balance-sheet in December 1835 showed a total debit of 105,000 francs, including the 46,000 he owed his mother. Werdet was at his wits' end. But Balzac still had his magic talisman, the signet-ring, 'Bedouck'—and author and publisher were saved by a stroke of luck. Buloz, who had begun the serial publication of *Séraphita* in the *Revue de Paris*, refused to go on with it, saying that his readers could not understand this 'shapeless rigmarole'. Werdet took it over and included it in a *Livre mystique* with *Louis Lambert* and a story entitled *Proscrits*. The break with the powerful Buloz, who ran the two most important literary journals, looked like madness. But it was valuable publicity, and Werdet advertised the book widely. The first edition sold well, and Balzac was hopeful again: 'One can write a *Goriot* any day, but a *Séraphita* only once in a lifetime'.

Three months later it was another story: 'The *Livre mystique* is not much liked here. The second edition isn't selling.' Madame de Berny took him to task from her retirement: 'She is the only one with the courage to tell me that the angel talks too much like a trollop. What seemed good before the end was known, later looks shabby, and I realize now that I need to *synthesize* the woman, as I have done in the rest of the book. Unfortunately it will take me six months to rewrite that part, and meanwhile discerning readers will blame me for this fault, which they will see all too clearly. . . .'

Nevertheless Thomassy, the Catholic, came to embrace Balzac after reading *Séraphita*, and Geoffroy de Saint-Hilaire, whom he had so greatly admired in his youth, used a quotation from the *Livre mystique* at the head of one of his major works— 'All knowledge is one, and you have shared it'—adding that he owed the words to 'one of the greatest writers of the century'. But Eve Hanska, to whom the book was dedicated, and who had been sent the manuscript bound in the grey stuff of the dress 'which swept so lightly over the boards' in Geneva, was disturbingly silent. Her formidable aunt, Rosalie Rzewuska, always hostile to her French lover, had raised doubts in her mind concerning *Séraphita*'s orthodoxy. She eventually told Balzac of this, to his indignation: 'No sacred writer has more vigorously proved the existence of God!' It was true that Swedenborg did not preach the religion of St Peter or Bossuet, but—'Your aunt seems to me like some poor Christian who, arriving just as Michelangelo is painting a nude on the Sistine ceiling, demands how the popes can allow such horrors to appear in the Chapel of St Peter. . . . *The Road that leads to God* is a very much higher religion that that of Bossuet; it is the religion of St Teresa and of Fénelon, of Swedenborg, of Jakob Boehme and of Monsieur Saint-Martin. . . .'

In short, Eve was a Roman Catholic, whereas Balzac thought of Catholicism as poetry and 'a sublime weapon in the struggle between flesh and spirit'. Did not the *Lys dans la vallée* show that he understood, no less than she, the greatness of the Church of Rome? Thus did he venture to dispute with the châtelaine of Wierzchownia; but not without ceremony and protestations of love.

XX

Illusions Perdues

Il faut toujours bien faire ce qu'on fait, même une folie.
BALZAC

AN ATTRIBUTE COMMON to all the members of the most
excellent family was their almost unbelievable capacity for self-
deception. They preferred their hopes to reality and, like
children, were never able to distinguish clearly between the two.
Of such had been Bernard-François, of such was Laure, and of
such remained Honoré at the age of thirty-seven. He admitted
it, not without a certain complacency. It was an exaggeration, a
convenience, sometimes an excuse. Zulma Carraud, who judged
him with so much clear-sighted affection, said of him: 'Poor boy,
he always saw the will-o-the-wisp he was chasing get away from
him!' His close friends, Gautier, Léon Gozlan, Werdet, all had
wonderful and sometimes farcical tales to tell of his extraordinary
aberrations. He knew it to be a weakness, but sought to defend
it to Eve Hanska, who reproached him with being always a dupe
in practical affairs although in his books he saw and judged with
so much penetration:

Alas, would you still love me if I were never fooled by
anything? . . . When all my strength and faculties are stretched
to breaking-point, day and night, in the effort to compose, to
write, to communicate, to depict and to remember; when I have
to fly on slow and painful and often crippled wings over the
spiritual landscape of literary creation, how can I keep my feet
on the material earth? When Napoleon was at Essling he was
not in Spain. That is what one has to do, dear remote and
solitary Countess, if one is not to be disappointed in life, in
friendship, in business and in every other connection; one has
to be a financier pure and simple, or man of the world, or man
of business. Of course I know that people fool me and will go
on fooling me, that this man or that has cheated me or is going

to cheat me, or will go off, taking something of me with him. But in the very moment of feeling it, or foreseeing or knowing it, I have to go and do battle elsewhere. I see it when I am carried away by the necessities of a book or a moment, by some task which will be ruined if I do not finish it. I often build a cottage by the light of one of my burning houses.

A brilliant and, on the whole, convincing defence. He had golden ideas; nearly all the business ventures in which he failed made a fortune for someone else, not only the type-foundry and the land speculations, but the reprints of the classics and the scent-advertising. But the artist performs his act of creation in a world where he is God; and when he finds himself contending with obstacles and hazards which he cannot shape to his requirements, he retreats into the sphere where his very setbacks become his raw materials. Laure Surville has described her brother coming to see her, grey-faced, exhausted, utterly despondent:

'My dear, I'm done for!'
'Rubbish! No one who writes books like yours can possibly be done for.'
'By God, you're right! Those books would keep anyone alive.... Besides, luck can save a Balzac as well as an imbecile.... It only needs one of my millionaire friends—and I have a few!— or some banker who doesn't know what to do with his money to come along and say, "I know about your immense gifts and your difficulties. You need such-and-such a sum to be free. Accept it without misgiving, you will pay it back, your pen is worth all my millions!..." '

And in an instant Honoré has taken flight. Fantasy has become fact. The banker *has* saved him: 'It's something to be able to say, I saved a Balzac!... Balzac is free!... You will see, my dear friends and my precious enemies, what tremendous things he will do!' And the dream (or the novel) goes running on. He is a member of the Institut, of the Chamber of Peers; he is a Minister; and finally, having succeeded in all his undertakings, he returns to the banker, the man who made it all possible. 'For him it will be glorious! People will say, "That is the man who understood Balzac, advanced him money against his talent, helped him to reap the honours he deserved!" That will be his claim to fame!'

He badly needed some such philanthropist at the beginning of 1836. There had been a disaster. In the previous December the entire stock of the third set of *Contes drolatiques*, printed at his own expense, had been destroyed by fire. It was a heavy blow for a man already in serious difficulties. His quarrel with Buloz was more bitter than ever, and he was suing him for having secretly reprinted *Le Lys dans la vallée* in St Petersburg. Buloz's tame writers were attacking him in the press and in scurrilous leaflets, Madame Béchet was harassing him, and he was looking round for a platform from which he could counter-attack. There was a review for sale, *La Chronique de Paris*, a small, almost reader-less, legitimist journal belonging to a businessman of doubtful reputation, William Duckett. The printers were Béthune and Plon. In December 1835, Balzac formed a company to take it over, in partnership with Duckett and Max de Béthune, the latter to hold an eighth-share each and himself the remaining three-quarters. The transaction cost him only 120 francs in cash, because the *Chronique de Paris*, with no subscribers or funds, was for practical purposes valueless; but he agreed to find 45,000 francs working capital—money which, of course, he did not possess.

On the face of it, it was a preposterous venture; but in Balzac's imagination it at once became a gold-mine. He would contribute a story a month, and this would bring in subscribers. Victor Hugo would write for it. Gustave Planche, who had also quarrelled with Buloz, would do the book-reviewing. Jules Sandeau was asked to bring in Théophile Gautier, whose talent Balzac had noted, and who was to become one of the 'horses' in his stable. The youthful Gautier was in a state of some trepida-tion when he first called on Balzac, who was wearing his white cashmere robe. But the great man received him with the utmost affability, and Gautier was instantly struck by his athlete's neck, round as a column, his strong nose, his broad, magnanimous forehead and above all his eyes—'eyes to outstare an eagle, to see through walls and into hearts; eyes of a ruler, a seer, a lion-tamer'.

Gautier promised to contribute. Buloz, the tycoon, was furious: 'So Planche has gone over to Balzac whom he so admired—you remember?—and he's worshipping Hugo's backside, whom he so venerated! A wonderful alliance! . . . Doesn't it make you laugh?' But Balzac took the *Chronique* very seriously. With the support of this 'powerful review', of which he would be absolute master, he could at last embark on the political career he had so long dreamed of. And above all it would be a steady source of income, at least 20,000 francs a year, because Balzac the owner would pay Balzac the editor a handsome salary, and Balzac the manager would also get his share. It was the solution of all problems—with one small drawback: ready money was needed to get it off the ground. But all was well; the bounteous Madame Delannoy advanced 15,000 francs. 'It's going through,' Balzac wrote to Laure. 'Tell my dear Surville that I have taken the first step on the road to power.' Everything seemed to be working out miraculously. Surville had a scheme for a new canal out of which there was 200,000 francs to be made. Balzac, the powerful politician, would see to it that the plan was adopted and share in the profits. They would all be rich. In Balzac's mind they already were.

The *Chronique de Paris* appeared under its new management on 1 January 1836. Victor Hugo, Gustave Planche, Alphonse Karr, Théophile Gautier and Charles de Bernard formed a brilliant literary team; and Henri Monnier, Granville and Daumier were to be the cartoonists. Balzac, as a prospective minister, reserved to himself the field of foreign affairs. He engaged two assistants to help him in research, young men of good family as penniless as himself, the Marquis de Belloy, whom he called the 'Cardinal', and Comte Ferdinand de Gramont. But in fact he had to carry the whole thing on his own shoulders. Every Saturday his contributors were handsomely dined and wined—*jambon rôti, pluviers au gratin, grenadins de veau, filets d'esturgeon, asperges blanches, beignets d'ananas*—feasts held in a house of which the rent remained unpaid. Like a captain at the head of his crew, the '*patron*' summoned them to produce their copy. It was never ready. They laughed and sang, and Alphonse Karr crowned Honoré with a wreath of paper roses. Finally, the company having departed, he settled down to 'the business of the paper'—that is to say, to writing nearly the whole of it himself.

But there—it had been a wonderful evening. He adored

festivity and delighted in the simplest of jokes. Nothing amused him more than mock proverbs, of which he kept a list: 'Opportunity makes the thief'; 'Flowing beer gathers no foam'; 'Tell me whom you haunt and I will tell you whom you hate.' A new one would be greeted with a gargantuan shout of laughter. Little things for little minds . . . but a man with a world in his head may be allowed to lay down the burden for a few hours. Besides, these trifles found their way, like everything else, into the stockpot of the *Comédie humaine*, and we hear them from the lips of Mistigris in *Un début dans la vie*.

His production during January and February 1836 was feverish but excellent. He contributed a number of stories to the *Chronique*, some specially written, other brought out of store— *La Masse de l'athée* (with a masterly portrait of the great surgeon, Dupuytren, under the name of Desplein); *L'Interdiction*, *Facino Cane*, *Les Martyrs ignorés*. The wonder was that, no matter how great the pressure on him, the work never fell below the highest standard. There was glitter even in the political articles. He replied derisively to the ministerial journalists who wrote about Thiers and Guizot and their ideas: 'M. Guizot and M. Thiers have only one idea, and that is to rule over us. . . . M. Thiers has never had more than one thought, the thought of M. Thiers. . . . M. Guizot is a weathercock which has been affixed to three different monuments; M. Thiers is a weathercock which, for all its spinning, stays on the same building. . . .'

With its brilliance and vigour, the *Chronique* might have succeeded. At first new subscriptions came in with what Balzac, never at a loss for superlatives, called 'a miraculous abundance'. The truth was less impressive. There were 160 new subscribers in January, 40 in February, 19 in March and by July the figure was down to seven. But Balzac was still in the clouds. He wrote to Eve at the end of March:

I have always had in me something which impelled me to do things differently from other men, and with me consistency is perhaps a form of pride. Having nothing but myself to rely on, I have been forced to grow and to strengthen my *self*. My whole life consists of this, a life without common pleasures. None of those around me would want to pay the price 'even for the glory of Napoleon and Byron combined', as de Belloy said.

I'm a gambler, poor in everyone's eyes; but one who gambles his entire fortune once a year, and who picks up what the others scatter. . . . Did I not tell you in Geneva that within three years I should have laid the foundations of my political mastery? Did I not repeat it in Vienna? Well! The *Chronique* is the old *Globe* (the same idea), but on the right instead of on the left; it is the new doctrine of the Royalist party. Our role is that of opposition, and we favour autocratic power; which means that when it comes to business we shall not be found contradicting everything we have said. I am the supreme director of the paper, which appears twice a week in an enormous in-quarto format. . . . My interest is the equivalent of 32,000 francs capital, and this, if the number of subscribers exceeds two thousand, will bring me in an income of 20,000 francs, without counting the high payment for my contributions and my salary as director. We have sufficient capital for two years. . . . Is there not something splendid about this enterprise? Moreover it has gained steadily in esteem and authority during the three months I have been in charge. . . .

But despite his 'greatly improved' financial situation (he expected to sell sixteen of his shares in the *Chronique* for 16,000 francs, while still retaining control; he was to get 3,000 francs for a new edition of the *Contes drolatiques*, and another 24,000 the day he could release himself from Madame Béchet by delivering the last volume of the *Études de mœurs*; making a total of 43,000 francs—very largely in the air) he had to confess that although in theory he was rich, in practice he could not pay his bills at the end of the month or get his silver out of pawn:

This would cost 3,000 francs, and I haven't got 3,000 francs. I owe about 8,400 at the end of the month. To reach this point honourably, and do justice to everyone, I have used up all my resources; everything is gone. This is my Marengo. Desaix will have to arrive, and Kellermann will have to charge, and then all will be well. But the gentlemen who are going to pay 16,000 francs for sixteen shares in the *Chronique* are coming to dine with me. People do not trust or lend money to anyone but the rich. Everything about me must breathe opulence, luxury, the wealth of the successful artist. If there is borrowed silver on my dinner-table everything will collapse. The man conducting the negotiations is a painter, a follower of an observant, malicious calling, his gaze as penetrating as that of

Henri Monnier. He'll see the chink in the armour, he'll guess at the pawnshop, which he knows at first hand only too well. And that will be the end of it! . . . I dare not ask *anyone in Paris* for money, because everyone thinks I'm rich and I would lose prestige and everything would vanish. This business of the *Chronique* is based on my personal credit. I have been able to talk like an owner. Fill in the picture by imagining the ceaseless activity and ardour of a spirit that consumes itself, and tell me—is it not a drama? One needs to be a great financier, a man of cold, shrewd, prudent mind; one needs . . . But I say no more, for yesterday one of my friends said to me, with reason: 'When they put up a statue to you they should make it of bronze, the better to express the man! . . .'

Indeed, it needed a man of bronze or steel to sustain so much effort and so many anxieties. The stories and articles he was writing for the *Chronique* took all his time, so that he had none to spare for Werdet or Madame Béchet. The latter, with her second marriage now imminent, was making a great commotion. In becoming Madame Jean-Brice Jacquillat she wanted 'to give up the book-trade in favour of happiness' and to settle her affairs with Balzac. But she had rashly paid him in advance. Was it to be expected that the 'supreme director' of a review worth 90,000 francs would write a novel for a beggarly 500? Even worse, his associates on the *Chronique* were losing heart. In May Duckett sold his shares, finding no one to buy them but Balzac and Werdet, who paid almost entirely by note-of-hand. A cautionary bond had to be deposited in connection with the lawsuit over *La Lys dans la vallée*. Where was this money to come from? There remained the 16,000 francs he hoped to get for the sixteen shares in the *Chronique*. But although the parties to this transaction came and enjoyed his princely dinner, they, too, were proving difficult.

Balzac to Madame Hanska, 20 March 1836: Never has my solitude been so complete, my labours so cruelly unremitting. My health is so impaired that I no longer attempt to preserve the appearance of youth which formerly I was weak enough to cling to. All has now been said. If at my age one has still not known happiness, pure and unalloyed, Nature will not henceforth allow one to put the cup to one's lips; white hairs may not approach it. Life for me will have been the most bitter of pleasantries. One by one my ambitions are crumbling. Power is a trifle. Nature created in me a being filled with love and tenderness, but circumstances have compelled me to write my desires instead of satisfying them. . . .

The high hopes all were fading. How continue to live in a dream of triumph while the rats left the sinking ship? Duckett's departure was followed by that of his two assistants. Balzac did not know where to turn. Everything had failed, the *Chronique*, the business of the *Contes drolatiques*, Surville's new canal. Only the loyal Dr Nacquart was prepared to lend him small sums—enough to keep him alive. He was worried about Honoré's health, and even feared for his reason. 'I am crushed, more than despairing; I am going mad.'

Balzac was forced to return to the Rue Cassini to escape from the Schönburgs, who much against his wishes planted their son on him in the Rue des Batailles. And in the Rue Cassini the Law caught up with him for his failure to perform his duty as 'a soldier-citizen', and he was borne off to serve the prison sentence inflicted on him by the 'grocers' of the Garde Nationale and 'that ignoble dentist who crowns his hideous profession with the abominable functions of a sergeant-major'. He was taken to the Hôtel Bazancourt (known as the 'Hôtel des Haricots') on the Quai des Bernardins, which served as a house of detention. At first he was highly annoyed, and not without reason. That the great Balzac, the friend of Metternich, a writer read throughout Europe, should be treated like a common criminal! The crowded, squalid place disgusted him. His fellow-inmates consisted largely of workmen who had dodged guard-duty in order not to lose a day's work, and a few artists and writers who had refused as a gesture. But Honoré soon began to enjoy himself. He secured firewood, a room from which he could see 'the blue of the weather', a table, a chair and an arm-chair, and set about recorrecting *Le Lys dans la vallée*. As soon as he could escape in spirit, cut himself off and work, he ceased to worry.

Werdet brought him a little money. Balzac made him stay to dinner, with the manager of the newspaper *La Quotidienne*. It was the gayest of meals. The next day Werdet, acting on his instructions, invited Jules Sandeau, Regnault, Gustave Planche and Alphonse Karr. By now the prison-cell was piled high with provisions, to say nothing of the flowers sent by lady admirers. 'An unknown friend' (the words were in English) sent him a lock of fair hair in a gold ring. Other people sent jewels—and he instructed Lecointe to make them into a seventh walking-stick. His dinners were supplied by the restaurants Chevet and Véfour, and paid for by Werdet. In three days of captivity (he was there just over a week) Balzac spent 575 francs.

His lawsuit with Buloz had not yet come into court: 'We must wait another six days, if it isn't postponed again. The business of the *Cent Contes drolatiques* is still not completed, and the shares in the *Chronique* are proving difficult to sell. So my troubles are doubled. During the two months I've been doing business I have done little else. Two months wasted, which means that the goose that lays the golden eggs is ill. I am not only discouraged, but my exhausted imagination needs a rest. . . .' This was the worst thing of all. His magnificent creative brain, the only capital he possessed, was refusing to function. All he could do was revise the *Lys*. And Béthune, the business manager of the *Chronique*, was hoisting danger-signals. Subscriptions were not being paid and new ones were not coming in. The *Chronique de Paris* had failed.

Balzac to Madame Hanska, 16 May 1836: In the past three days a great change has come over me . . . I no longer want to enter public life as a deputy or through journalism. My immediate object is to get rid of the *Chronique de Paris*. I made up my mind after witnessing two sessions of the Chamber. The stupidity of the speakers, the fatuousness of the debates, the small likelihood of achieving any kind of triumph amid so much wretched mediocrity, made me decide to abandon the attempt and have nothing to do with it except as a minister. So I shall try, within the next two years, to batter down the doors of the Academy, because Academicians can become peers;* and I shall try to earn enough money to be able to enter the Upper Chamber —to achieve power through power itself. . . .

Another day-dream, consoling to Balzac but not to the shareholders and creditors of the *Chronique de Paris*. Harassed by his

---

* The title *pair de France* was the equivalent of an English life-peerage today, carrying with it membership of the Upper House. *Trs.*

staff, who were clamouring for their wages, and threatened with bankruptcy by Duckett, he sighed: 'Life is too burdensome; I take no pleasure in it.' A rare avowal in a man so given to quick recoveries. But one thing turned out well. He won his action against Buloz, the Court finding that the *Revue de Paris* had exceeded its rights in using proofs of the *Lys dans la vallée* which had not been marked *'bon a tirer'* by the author. Balzac, the subject of so many calumnies, was now inundated with letters of congratulation. Moreover, the stir occasioned by the case was excellent publicity. Within two hours Werdet sold 1,800 copies of the 2,000 he had printed.

Another blow fell on 12 June. Madame Béchet, more than ever in a hurry to quit the book-trade for domestic bliss, secured an injunction summoning him to deliver the remaining two volumes of the *Études de mœurs* within twenty-four days, or pay a penalty of fifty francs for each day's delay. This disaster did at least afford him a pretext for getting away from Paris, Béthune and the *Chronique*, to take refuge in Saché— '. . . there to write two volumes for the woman in twenty days and so be rid of her,' as he wrote to Eve. 'I am beginning the dreadful struggle again, the business of commitments and books to deliver. I have got to work off the last of my contracts by appeasing Madame Béchet and at the same time produce a good book. I have twenty days! It shall be done! *Les Héritiers Boisrouge* and *Illusions perdues* will be written in twenty days! . . .'

The first of the two stayed in what he called his 'file of miscarriages', but *Illusions perdues* (Part I) was finished in twenty days and he had never written anything better. Misfortune lent an edge to his gifts, and the story, so close to his heart, afforded an outlet for his mood of bitter melancholy. Its main theme was the contrast between provincial and metropolitan attitudes— provincial illusions in particular—embodied in the tale of a young man who believes himself to be a great poet, and is encouraged in the belief by a wealthy woman who then casts him adrift in Paris, penniless and unprotected. But when Balzac started work on it events and characters sprang in such profusion from his pen that the first part of the novel was enough in itself to fill the two volumes required by Madame Béchet. The second part came later. 'When will the author be able to complete his canvas?' he wrote in a preface to the first part. 'He does not know; but he will complete it.'

Part I of *Illusions perdues* is the story of Lucien Chardon, a young man of extraordinary good looks, the son of impecunious parents in Angoulême, who adopts his mother's maiden-name, de Rubempré. It tells of the boundless devotion to this very attractive, naïve, youthful egotist displayed by his sister, Ève, and his future brother-in-law, the printer, David Séchard; of Lucien's love-affair with Madame de Bargeton, and of his virtual abduction by his mistress, who leaves him to fend for himself far from his native town. Balzac very soon realized that he would have to write a sequel, and that it would be far more important than the first part. This eventually became Part II of the novel, *Un grand homme de province à Paris*, the tale of Lucien's struggles and frustrated ambitions. Balzac did not at first think of it in relation to his own life, but in terms of George Sand and Jules Sandeau, who had so quickly parted in bitter disillusion. But their story was, of course, transformed. There is little of George Sand, a woman of undeniable genius, in Anaïs de Bargeton; she far more resembles Rosa de Saint-Surin, also a writer, artist and poet, a woman who for a time had held a literary salon in Angoulême, and then, being legally separated from her husband, had moved to Paris.

In his account of Lucien's love-affair with a woman fifteen years older than himself Balzac must certainly have thought of Madame de Berny. But he covered his tracks. It is David Séchard, the printer, and not Lucien who bears a physical resemblance to himself—the plump, dark face carried on a thick neck, the broad, flat, turned-up nose, the flashes of genius and the 'ashes surrounding the volcano'. Lucien, who is brilliant and audacious despite his indolent appearance, has a woman's figure and might be taken for a girl in disguise. 'In this friendship there was one who loved to idolatry, and it was David.' He ruins himself for Lucien.

The novel has a solid background of fact. The printer's shop was familiar ground; Zulma Carraud had taught Balzac much about the inner workings of Angoulême society, and his own perception enabled him to discern the especial peculiarities of a community of this kind, divided between an Upper and a Lower Town. Built originally, for strategic reasons, on a hilltop, the ancient town had from feudal times been an administrative and aristocratic centre. But the fortifications surrounding it had prevented it from expanding. The industrialized and wealthy suburb of L'Houmeau, was spreading along the banks of the Charente at the foot of the hill, with its paper-mills, its cannon-foundry, tanneries and laundries: 'Above were Aristocracy and Power, below were Commerce and Money: social diversions that are always and everywhere enemies.' Lucien, the young man from L'Houmeau, embarks upon the conquest of Angoulême proper, and so the drama begins. The pictures teem in Balzac's mind, scenes, events, fragments from the great store of memories accumulated from every period of his life and every place he has ever visited.

He wrote the two volumes in the little room at Saché where so many crucial hours in his life as a writer had been spent. It was here that he had written *Louis Lambert*, dreamed of *Séraphita* and shaped *Père Goriot*: 'Again I contemplate the splendid trees which I have gazed at so often while searching for ideas. I am no farther forward in 1836 than I was in 1829; I'm still in debt and I go on working! I have the same sense of youth in me, the same childlike heart. . . .' But he was wrong to say that he had made no progress. He now carried a world in his head, densely peopled with characters whose destinies he already foresaw. The task was there and it was enormous; and he longed, in order to fulfil it, to rid himself of all the shackles binding him to Paris and retire to a cottage in Touraine, there to labour in peace. He wrote to Laure d'Abrantès, who was, as usual, complaining of neglect: 'The men on the field of battle, you know, have no time to chat, or even to let their friends know whether they are alive or dead. . . .' But he was doing too much. On 26 June, while walking in the park at Saché, he had a seizure and collapsed. He had written half the first part of *Illusions perdues* in a very few days, and the intensity of the effort 'had carried the blood to his head'. But by the next day he had recovered from this ominous attack, except for a singing in his ears. He was able to finish the two volumes and placate Madame Béchet; and the same morning he wrote a Rabelaisian letter to Émile Regnault: 'Whereupon I embrace you from afar and trust that all goes well with you in the low country which you affectionate. . . .'

Since his hero, Lucien de Rubempré, was a poet, he wanted to include a specimen of his work, and accordingly asked Regnault, 'Will you please tell dear Charles de Bernard that for *Illusions perdues* I need a short, sonorous poem in the manner of Lord Byron? . . . It would be very kind of him to do one for me, because I haven't time. I also want something on the lines of 'Beppo' or of de Musset's 'Namouna' or 'Mardoche', a single piece of a hundred lines. The other should be in two stanzas.' Charles de Bernard was a charming writer and a friend and disciple of Balzac, who had introduced him to the *Revue de Paris*—hence the latter's casualness in asking this not inconsiderable favour. But Bernard was incapable of writing in the manner of Byron or de Musset or anyone except himself, and in the end Balzac fell back on some verses of his own, written in 1824 for Julie Campi, the 'flower of Bengal' born of Madame de Berny's love-affair with the 'abominable Corsican'. Like the inventor, the writer uses any bit of old iron that may be lying about the shop.

He applied urgently to Zulma Carraud for topographical details of the places where he wanted to situate the Séchard printing-works and Madame de Bergeton's house: 'If the Major would be so kind as to draw me a large-scale map, that would be all to the good. . . . I'm still working like a drowning man afraid that every breath will be his last.'

On 10 July he returned to Paris to wind up the business of *La Chronique*. When it ceased publication he owed 18,217 francs of short-term debts, as well as 24,000 to Madame Delannoy and 5,000 to Père Dablin. It was a harsh return to earth from the cloud-world in which he had been living; but he brought with him, from that flight in solitude, the beginning of his finest novel.

Part Three
THE HUMAN COMEDY

En somme, voici le jeu que je joue, quatre hommes auront eu une vie immense: Napoléon, Cuvier, O'Connell et je vais être le quatrième. Le premier a vécu la vie de l'Europe; il s'est inoculé des armées! Le second a épousé le globe! Le troisième s'est incarné dans un peuple! Moi, j'aurai porté une societé tout entière dans ma tête.

BALZAC

XXI

The Contessa

Les grandes passions sont rares comme les chefs-d'œuvre.

BALZAC

WHILE CONTINUING TO assure his mystical spouse, the divine Eve, of his unshakable fidelity and rigorous chastity, Balzac had for some time been involved (at first secretly) with another lady possessing all those attributes of beauty, rank and worldly situation which were most gratifying to his self-esteem. The affair may be said to have originated in the letter of introduction to the wife of the Austrian Ambassador given him in Geneva, in February 1834, by Countess Marie Potocka, Madame Hanska's aunt. In the autumn of that year he beheld, at one of the Embassy receptions, a pink and white young woman with ash-blond hair, a supple, swaying figure and the eyes of an oriental princess. He was struck by her *allure provocante de bacchante lascive*, and upon making inquiries he learned that she was Frances Sarah Lovell, (Fanny), the English wife of a member of an illustrious Milanese family, the Conte Emilio Guidoboni-Visconti.

A great deal of information regarding Fanny Lovell, nearly all of it incorrect, is contained in the memoirs of a certain Versailles magistrate, Victor Lambinet. By his account the Lovell family, besides possessing extraordinary powers of seduction, was given to the wildest follies and suffered from suicidal mania, the mother having drowned herself to avoid growing old, one brother having cut his throat and another having hanged himself.

The younger daughter, Julia [writes Monsieur Lambinet], a fantastical, ravishing creature, was given to all manner of hysterical excess, purchasing the favours of barbers' assistants, debauching actors and, like her elder brother, debasing and stupefying herself with alcohol. Her erotic inclinations having diminished under the influence of the divine bottle, she married an elderly Prussian scholar, Dr Biedermann, who took a wife simply in order to have someone to drink with. . . .

The truth is that the Lovells of Cole Park were a highly respected Wiltshire family. Fanny's mother was the daughter of an arch-deacon, himself the son of the Bishop of Bath and Wells. Contrary to what M. Lambinet tells us, Fanny Lovell, before her marriage, had moved in the most exclusive English circles. None of her brothers had committed suicide, and the youngest, who according to Lambinet cut short his life by his debauches, died in 1906 at the age of eighty-five. Her mother did indeed drown herself, but only at the age of seventy-two, twenty-nine years after Fanny's marriage. There was, in short, no reason for the Conte Guidoboni-Visconti to feel any misgivings concerning his bride's 'appalling antecedents', as Lambinet puts it, and he was fascinated by her great beauty and silvery, 'tête-à-tête' voice.

But no sooner was she married than the young Contessa showed herself to be possessed of a passionate temperament incapable of 'resisting an appeal to the senses', and a conscience easily accommodated to its demands. The Countess of Albany and Teresa Guiccioli won her especial admiration by their flaunted love-affairs with two men of genius, the Conte Alfieri and Byron. Her husband, on the other hand, proved far less censorious than the Conte Guiccioli. The Conte Guidoboni-Visconti was a man wholly lacking in unkindness and strength of character whose life was devoted to two hobbies—music (he liked to play in orchestras with professional musicians) and the apothecary's trade. He was never happier than when mixing, bottling and labelling nostrums. 'A gentle soul,' wrote L.-J. Arrigon in his far more balanced account, 'unassuming, moody, rather tedious and tiresome but not stupid, with a mixture of shrewdness and ponderous naivety.' A man, in short, born to be deceived, to know it and to put up with it.

Encouraged by what he heard of her, Balzac had himself introduced to the lady, who had read his books and was anxious to meet him. She was at first disconcerted by his dress—white waistcoat with buttons of coral, green frock-coat with

gold buttons, rings on every finger. She must have mentioned
this to someone who passed it on to Balzac, because he was
more soberly clad at their next meeting. In any case, women
soon revised their first impression of him. A letter to her father
from Sophie Koslowska, a friend of Fanny Visconti, gives an
admirable account of the liaison:

You ask me, 'What is this new passion of M. de Balzac for
Mme Visconti?' It is simply that Mme Visconti is full of wit
and imagination and fresh, bright ideas, and M. de Balzac,
who is also a superior person, enjoys her conversation, and
since he has written a great deal and is still writing he often
makes use of the original fancies which so constantly occur to
her, and so their conversation is always exceedingly interesting
and amusing. That explains the attraction. . . .
    M. de Balzac cannot be called a handsome man, because he is
small, fat, round and stocky, with wide, square shoulders, a big
head, a nose flattened at the end, that might be made of
rubber, a very pretty mouth but almost toothless, and stiff, jet-
black hair in which there is a little white. But there is a fire in
his dark-brown eyes, a look so compelling that, without wanting
to, you are forced to admit that few men are so prepossessing.
    He is kind, overflowing with kindness for the people he likes,
but terrible towards those he dislikes and merciless to pretentious fools. His epigrams do not always impress you at first, but
later you remember them and they haunt you ever after, like
ghosts. He possesses iron will and courage; he forgets himself for
the sake of his friends and his friendship knows no bounds. He
has the greatness and nobility of a lion and the gentleness of a
child . . . .
    That is a very rough sketch of M. de Balzac, whom I like so
much and who is so good to me. He is thirty-seven. . . .

Balzac visited the Guidoboni-Viscontis at their Paris home in
the Avenue de Neuilly (now the Avenue des Champs-Élysées)
and at Versailles, where they had a summer residence. Here
they had friends in common who must have told him of the
Contessa's many adventures, her latest adorer being the Comte
Lionel de Bonneval. The rivalry did not trouble Balzac, nor did
he misjudge the position, for in a short while the warmest
friendship had been established between the lady and himself.
He and the Viscontis shared the expense of a box at the Théâtre

des Italiens three evenings a week, and his friends were quick to notice the ardent court he paid her. Madame d'Abrantès wrote: 'I'm cross with you for not coming to dinner. . . . Do make an effort, and you can go on to the comedy afterwards. . . .'

Was he really in love with Fanny? He was certainly attracted by highly-sexed women, and in this respect she was remarkable. Women of high social station gratified his vanity and were helpful to his ambitions. Finally, he was always on the look-out for women who could be used in his writings. Fanny, with her lively imagination, may be said to have 'posed', with Lady Ellenborough, for the character of Arabella, Lady Dudley, in *Le Lys dans la vallée*. She called Balzac 'Bally', the equivalent of Arabella's 'my Dee'.

And she? Undoubtedly she had a fondness for her great man, whom she helped for a long time in circumstances of the utmost difficulty. He pleased her by his gaiety and gusto, his scabrous anecdotes and his capacity for almost feminine intimacy.

Monsieur de Balzac knows a great deal about women [wrote Sainte-Beuve]; he knows their secrets, whether of sensibility or sensuality. He confronts them in his tales with bold, blunt questions, the equivalent of privacies. He is like a still-youthful doctor who has entry to the bedside and the alcove; he takes it upon himself to talk in veiled words of those mysterious, intimate details which confusedly charm even the most modest. . . .

And what part did he propose for Madame Hanska, his adored Eve, in this new stage-play? Balzac took pleasure in conducting a number of affairs at a time, keeping them in separate compartments, and thereby extended the frontiers of his imaginary world. Had not the creator of a world the right to several lives? From the outset of his affair with Madame Hanska there had been a third party, Marie du Fresnay ('Maria'), of whom she knew nothing. It goes without saying that he made no mention of the Contessa in the letters he wrote to her after his return from Vienna: 'There is no room in my life, I will not say for an infidelity but even for a thought. . . . I have not been inside the Opera for a month. I fancy I have a box at the Bouffons [Théâtre des Italiens]. . . . I so abominate the women of

Paris that I stay bent over my work from six in the morning till six in the evening. . . .' But Madame Hanska knew him well enough to feel assured that the time without her would not be spent in total abstinence. She might put up with an Olympe Pélissier, or wenches of no importance, but she was disposed to be far less indulgent towards a liaison with a woman of fashion, a member of the cosmopolitan circles to which she herself belonged. She also knew that Balzac would be too puffed up with this sort of conquest not to cry it to the housetops, besides writing letters that would go the rounds of Paris.

Balzac to Mme Hanska: Madame de Visconti, of whom you speak, is the most charming of women and one of infinite and exquisite kindness, of a refined and elegant beauty, who does much to help me endure life. She is gentle but very firm, unshakable and implacable in her ideas and her dislikes. She is a person to be trusted. She is not rich, or, rather, her fortune and that of the Count are not appropriate to the splendid name they bear, for the Count is the representative of the first branch of the legitimized sons of the last Duke, the famous Barnabo, who left only bastards, some legitimized and others not. It is a friendship which consoles me for many reverses, but, alas, I see her only rarely. You cannot conceive of the privations to which my work condemns me. Nothing is possible in a life as hard-pressed as mine, and when one goes to bed at six in the evening to rise at midnight. . . . I can perform no social duties. I see Madame de Visconti once a fortnight, and it is a real grief to me, because she and my sister are my only true kindred spirits. My sister is in Paris, Madame de Visconti is at Versailles, and I scarcely ever see either. Can that be called living? You are in the wilds at the other end of Europe; I know no other women in the world. . . .

To be always dreaming, always waiting; to see the brave days pass and youth being plucked from one, hair by hair; to hold nothing in one's arms and then be accused of being a Don Juan! What a fat and empty Don Juan! . . .

Mme de Visconti was slow to yield. Lionel de Bonneval, whom she esteemed as possessing 'the art and science of the life of society', made fun of Balzac's lack of taste, his clothes and untidy hair and 'scribbler's' trade. It looked for a time as though Balzac was in for a repetition of the treatment he had received at the hands of Mme de Castries. After waiting in vain to be visited by the Contessa in the Rue Cassini he renewed his preparations in the Rue des Batailles. The boudoir of the *Fille aux yeux d'or*, with its enormous white divan, was devised largely on her account. And finally, in the spring of 1835, he triumphed. *Le Lys dans la vallée* certainly owes its English-sounding title to Fanny Visconti, and no doubt Balzac took a wry pleasure in contrasting, on the same canvas, his Dilecta and his newest passion—Mme de Mortsauf and Lady Dudley.

Possession was far from killing love. On the contrary, Balzac the lover and connoisseur of women was enchanted by the radiant specimen of Anglo-Saxon womanhood he was now given the opportunity of studying:

The Englishwoman, [he wrote in *Le Lys dans la vallée*] is an unhappy creature, virtuous by force of circumstances and ready to shed her virtue, condemned to perpetual untruth in the depths of her heart, but delightful in her outward seeming because hers is a people to whom form is all-important. Hence the peculiar beauty of the women of that country, the exaltation of a tenderness which for them is what life enforcedly consists of, their exaggerated care for their person and the delicacy of their love, so exquisitely depicted in the famous scene in *Romeo and Juliet*, where Shakespeare's genius sums up all English women. You who envy them for so many things, what can I tell you that you do not know about those white sirens, so impenetrable in appearance and so quickly known, who believe that devotion suffices for love and who infuse tedium into physical pleasures by never varying them, whose soul has but a single note, whose voice a single intonation, who have never bathed in the ocean of love and must be for ever ignorant of some part of the poetry of the senses? . . .

And later:

Have you ever reflected upon the general sense of English morals? Is it not the deification of matter, a circumscribed epicureanism, considered and knowingly applied? Whatever she may do or say, England is materialist, perhaps unconsciously. She has religious and moral principles from which divine spirituality, the Catholic soul, is absent, and its fecundating grace cannot be replaced by any form of hypocrisy, however

well this may be enacted. She possesses in the highest degree
the science of living which adorns the most trifling material
objects, which makes your bedroom-slippers the most beautiful
in the world, which endows your linen with an indescribable
quality, which perfumes the wardrobe and lines it with cedar,
which at a given hour pours out tea, elegantly served, which
banishes dust, nails down carpets from the lowest stair to the
furthest corner of the house, sweeps the cellar walls, polishes the
door-knocker, softens the springs of the carriage; which makes
of all matter a sustaining, fleecy pulp, shining and clean, in the
midst of which the soul expires under the weight of comfort;
which produces the terrible monotony of well-being, affords a
life without irk or hindrance, lacking all spontaneity, and, in a
word, turns you into a machine. . . .

There was something of this comfortable materialism in
Fanny Visconti, but there were also real qualities of character
and intelligence. She was not suspicious or nagging or hot-
tempered, like Eve Hanska. When she gave herself she did so
warmly and candidly. She did not worry about her reputation,
since she showed herself openly with Balzac at the Italiens; but
on the other hand she did not try to keep him to herself. She
fully understood that an artist needs to be free, and his adventures amused her.

We know that on 16 June 1835 Balzac left for Boulogne and
was away six days. On 29 August he again had his passport
visa'd for Boulogne and set off on the 31st in a hired carriage
which he returned to the hirer a week later. He probably escorted
Fanny as far as Boulogne when she went on a visit to England,
and in a renewed burst of passion journeyed to meet her on
her return. With his fondness for private names he called
her by her second name, Sarah, instead of Fanny, like everyone else. In 1836 she gave birth to a son of whom Balzac was
said to be the father. But there is no proof of this, and the child
was baptized Lionel-Richard (Lionel being Bonneval's christian
name). In any event, one would expect Balzac to have made
more of this triumphant paternity, if he had had reason to
believe in it.

Fanny Visconti was Balzac's mistress for a long time, and
showed him great generosity. At the time of the collapse of the
Chronique de Paris, when he had such pressing reasons for

escaping from Paris, she devised a scheme which enabled him to do so without damaging his credit.

Her husband's mother had died, and the Conte had no wish to leave his nostrums and his orchestra in order to travel to Turin and contest his share of the estate. The matter was highly involved. After being left a widow by her first husband, the Conte Pietro Guidoboni, the former Contessa had married a Frenchman and borne him a son, and it was this that gave rise to the complications. Since Balzac had served his time in a lawyer's chambers, Fanny considered him admirably qualified to represent her husband's interests. She arranged for him to go to Turin with power of attorney, at the family's expense, and he was to receive a commission on whatever sum he managed to secure. It was an ingenious way of coming to his rescue.

A small matter may be mentioned in passing. During his liaison with Fanny he was in correspondence with a mysterious lady whom he never met and knew only by her christian name, Louise. She had written to him, as so many women did, by way of his publisher. But since the affair of Mme de Castries he had grown wary of unknown women. He wrote to her:

My childlike credulity has many times been put to the test, and you must have noticed that in animals mistrust is in direct proportion to their weakness. . . . Yet sometimes I write letters like a soldier breaking out of barracks, who is punished for it next day. . . . You may believe that every good thing you think of me is even better; that my capacity for devotion is without end, my sensibilities feminine, and the only thing masculine in me is my energy. But everything that may be good is stifled by the necessities of a man continuously at work. . . . I have all the egotism of enforced labour; I am like a prisoner chained by the leg, and I possess no file. . . . I am fixed in my workroom like a ship lodged in ice. . . .'

He did not reject the extended hand, but could not escape to clasp it: 'Let me go on rolling my stone in my cell and believe that if I were free I should not behave like this.' Only once in his life, he said, had he encountered a devoted love which did not quarrel with his work, that of the angel who, during twelve years, had snatched two hours a day from the world, her family and her duties, to console and sustain him. It would never happen again. He liked to think of his correspondent as young, beautiful and gay, but he wished his feeling for her to remain a secret. And she herself hung back; yet it was she who had the better part. She received wonderful letters for which she need make no return, since he rejected everything. It is true that the presence of Fanny Guidoboni-Visconti as an active factor in his life probably accounted for this restraint.

XXII
Strange Escapade

*Quand, dans ce monde, on n'a plus d'infantes à enlever,
il faut travailler, ou mourir d'ennui.*

EUGÈNE DELACROIX

BALZAC LEFT FOR Turin on 25 July 1836; but he did not
go unaccompanied. He had made the acquaintance, through
Jules Sandeau, of a good-looking young woman of thirty-three
named Caroline Marbouty, who had published in the *Chronique
de Paris*, an autobiographical tale which she wrote under the
name of C. Marcel. From her early youth this romantic, impulsive and ambitious girl had alarmed her respectable family by
proclaiming her scorn for provincial life and bourgeois prejudice. 'The provincial,' she wrote, 'knowing nothing and caring
for nothing except profit and loss, is barren in his relationships
and stereotyped in his ideas, and his life is devoid of poetry.'

Her father, a councillor at the court of Limoges, concluded
that the sooner Caroline was married the better. The husband
hastily selected for her, Jacques-Sylvestre Marbouty, a public
registrar, was the son of a lawyer and small landowner. He
was thirty-three when they married, and she nineteen. As a
girl Caroline had written poetry; as a dissatisfied wife she
wrote novels; and since she kept open house she had soon
formed a literary salon of well-fed admirers who listened to
her poems and christened her 'the Muse of Limoges'. The
poems, largely concerned with her ardours and frustrations,
were not flattering to her husband, and that gentleman was
accustomed to leave the room while she read them aloud.

Despite her many admirers and the nagging of her parents-
in-law, who disapproved of the company she kept, her way of
dress and her habit of 'putting on airs', young Mme Marbouty remained faithful to her registrar for nine years, which

seems heroic. But in 1831 Baron Guillaume Dupuytren
appeared on the scene. This was a doctor of great distinction,
ennobled by Louis XVIII, surgeon-in-chief to the Hôtel-Dieu
in Paris and a member of the Institute. A native of Limousin,
he had come to Limoges to stand as parliamentary candidate for
the constituency of Haute-Vienne, and he stayed for a month
with the Marboutys. It fell to the Muse of Limoges to introduce
him to local society, and she was ravished by his intelligence.
A man of many conquests, he had little difficulty in adding this
one to his list. But he lost the election, greatly to his surprise,
and left Limoges in dudgeon, never to return.

Shortly afterwards Caroline Marbouty made a trip to Paris
'for reasons of health', and from there went to La Rochelle,
where her mother's family owned property, for reasons connected with Jules Sandeau. The romantic example of Aurore
Dudevant (George Sand) was turning the heads of all provincial
blue-stockings at the time, and 'le petit Jules', wearing his
broken heart on his sleeve after his separation from her, was able
to profit by the circumstance. All this had an unsettling effect on
Caroline, who felt that her talents were being wasted in Limoges,
and eventually she persuaded her husband to allow her to live in
Paris, ostensibly for the better education of their two daughters.
She really hoped to retrieve Dupuytren, but that high-minded
man, who had no wish to turn a passing affair into a permanent
liaison, declined the honour, saying that no gentleman would
compromise a married woman. Where was she to go for consolation? Sandeau did not amount to much. She continued on
friendly terms with him, but she was looking for bigger game.
She thought of Sainte-Beuve, and invited him to call. 'He was
short, reedy-voiced, thin and awkward. His weak eyes and
extreme self-consciousness caused him to bear himself in a
curiously mincing way. In short, a caricature. . . .'

There remained Balzac, the friend of women and their
supreme hope. She had heard about him from a sister of Zulma
Carraud, who lived in Limoges and was a great admirer of his
work. Indeed, she had even written him letters which she had
not ventured to post. But this was at the time when Sandeau
was lodging with Balzac, and so a meeting with the great man
was easily contrived. She was invited to dine in the Rue Cassini
and to contribute to the *Chronique de Paris*. Balzac, always

fascinated by provincial psychology, found her voluble, self-revealing talk amusing. He suggested that she accompany him on a trip to Touraine, to visit the châteaux of the Loire, but she refused.

Balzac to Émile Regnault, Saché, 27 June 1836: This, my old bird, is to tell you that a hundred francs, or fifty crowns, would be very useful to your old *Mar-à-sec*, because after finishing *Le Cabinet des antiques* and probably *Ecce Homo* I should like to relax by going to see Chenonceaux and Chambord, which are on my way. . . . How is Jules? Don't forget Béthune and Level. You may even risk the blush I perceive on the cheek of the fair Madame Marbouty, who, if she had consented to visit the châteaux of Touraine in my company, would have had no cause to regret the journey. . . .

But then came the chance of a journey even more suited to Caroline's romantic tastes, the trip to Turin. This time she accepted, and, moreover, offered to contribute five hundred francs to the expenses. To avoid scandal she proposed to go in man's clothes and pass herself off as Balzac's secretary or valet, George Sand having set the example of male attire. Balzac ordered the necessary garments from his accommodating tailor, Buisson, and on the day of their departure Caroline arrived at the Rue Cassini with a case containing one woman's dress and a week's underwear. The post-chaise was in the courtyard, and Sandeau and Balzac were awaiting her. She went upstairs to change, and when she came down in a tail-coat, with a riding-crop in her hand and a look of resolution on her face, both men found her enchanting. Sandeau may have felt a pang of jealousy as she and Balzac drove off together; but it was his destiny to envy the good fortune of other men while never contriving his own.

Caroline Marbouty to her mother, Turin, 2 August 1836: The heading of this letter will astonish you, my dear mother. You are far from supposing me to be in Italy, two hundred leagues from my accustomed surroundings. I will tell you how it has come about, but only you. You will keep this journey secret, because I count on your discretion . . .

To begin with, Balzac invited Nana ([Anna de Massac] and me, through Jules, to dine at his house. I had made up my mind

that the day I met him I would captivate him. I was absolutely
determined. I succeeded, and I have *magnetized* him. . . .
    A few days later he called on me. He was going to Touraine
and afterwards to Italy. . . . He missed me in Touraine, and when
he got back to Paris he proposed that I should accompany him
to Turin and from there to Genoa and perhaps to Florence.
After much hesitation I consented. What a wonderful journey!
We left Paris by post-chaise and reached Turin five days later,
having crossed the Alps at Mont-Cenis and stopped at the
Grande Chartreuse. I thought of you while I was there. You
too had made that journey. I remembered your account of it,
and I shared the exaltation it inspired in you. . . .
    I am alone with Balzac, with no servants. He has made me
dress up as a man, and the costume suits me very well and I am
delighted with it. It prevents me from being recognized and
permits me all kinds of charming and unaccustomed liberties.
It suits my original turn of mind. Here in Turin I pass as his
secretary. He is very fond of me and surrounds me with attentions. But by great misfortune I am not well. No happiness is
ever complete. My wretched ailment has returned, worse than
ever; I do my best to hide it, but it tired me greatly on the
journey. I suffered for a month before leaving Paris, and only
my habitual courage enabled me to endure this ignoble malady
which the fatigues of travel might well have rendered serious.
Fortunately they did not, and I am even a little better.
    Like all men of superior intellect, Balzac is very much pre-
occupied with his ideas and not very lovable. But he has such
intellectual force and vigour and there is such superiority in his
whole being that he pleases none the less. His physique is poor
and his face, though wonderfully expressive, is bizarre.
    We are treated like princes. He is charged with despatches to
the Embassy, which brings him into contact with all the best
people. This evening he is dining with a senator; I am to fetch
him at ten, two leagues outside Turin, and I look forward to a
beautiful evening in the open carriage. At other times the
carriage is at my disposal.
    I have a magnificent apartment and am admirably waited
upon. What makes it all the more remarkable is that Balzac has
not a penny and is overwhelmed by debts, and it is only by dint
of incredible labour that he is able to maintain his position
between luxury and the financial ruin that threatens him every
day.
    He says that I have 'great ability' and he wants to put me to
work to earn an income of twenty thousand *livres*. But I am

bound to tell you that he is a man full of day-dreams who is only to be reckoned with *in the present*. So I count very little on that. His idea is that we should write plays together. . . .

After Balzac's death Mme Marbouty produced a lively chronicle of their journey, which she claimed to have written 'at the spiritual dictation' of the departed. It contains a few added details. The monks at the Grande Chartreuse saw through her disguise and Balzac had to go in alone. Later there was a bathing episode, when she refused to undress in his presence. He tried to spy on her but, by her account, failed.

The strange pair occupied the most handsome suite at the Hôtel de l'Europe in Turin, where Caroline (as his male attendant she was called Marcel) had the main bedroom, with the bed on a dais, while Balzac slept in a smaller room with a communicating door. But this, according to what she told her mother, was as far as their intimacy went:

I have reserved for myself *the right to freedom*. I have accepted only friendship, pure and simple, as a bond between us. I consider myself the more fortunate in the kind of love I inspire inasmuch as it is rarer than ever in these days. Only the artist still understands it a little; the rest of the nation has no idea of it. Has the woman artist sufficient freedom to seek it—and to find it?

I have not been carried away. My ideas on love have undergone many modifications since I learned to know the real world and the character, the needs and the nature of superior men. One is only loved when one knows how to control one's senses, when the mind remains cool. . . . That is what has happened to me in this case. But shall I always be sufficiently mistress of myself? That is the question.

Balzac is very kind, even-tempered and frank, like all great spirits, but more concerned with the *future* and *ambition* than with the love of women. Love is necessary to him as a physical act. Except for this, his whole life is given to work. Should I be always content with this state of affairs? Above all, would it satisfy my needs? I fear not. But such is life; we have to accept it as it is. . . .

When Balzac published *La Grenadière* in 1842, six years after this excursion, he dedicated it 'To Caroline. To the poetry of the

journey, from the grateful journeyer.' To Mme Hanska he
wrote:

The *poetry of the journey* was poetry and nothing else. I will
tell you candidly how it was, and when you come to Paris I will
prove it to you for your punishment. You will see that I have
never had any taste for the women, like Madame de Lamartine,
who inspire the lines of the old comedy:

*Et parbleu! chevalier! je veux être un coquin
Si ce diable de nez n'est pas en bleu turquin!**

with which I set a whole salon laughing when someone asked me
my opinion.

She was, *cara diva*, an intimate friend of Madame Carraud.
I have not seen her since. As for her wit, it was charming. . . .

The truth as served up to Mme Hanska was seldom the
whole truth. Nevertheless Balzac and Caroline both affirmed,
vigorously and independently, that they did not become lovers
during the twenty-six days they were together. This 'Scipiones-
que' restraint, as Balzac called it, may have been due to the
lady's indisposition. However it was, they remained on gay
and friendly terms. 'Do you remember our charming luncheons
in the downstairs dining-room with its huge windows opening
on to a flower-decorated verandah? . . . The warm Italian sun
streamed over the luxuriously dressed table. Everything was
made ready for us in advance, so that we should be undisturbed
—delicious fish, figs, a little Italian white wine, so very sweet,
and magnificent fruit . . .'

Balzac revelled in this life of splendour and in the fuss that
was made of him by Piedmontese society. He had arranged
beforehand to be treated as a distinguished visitor and had
brought letters of introduction from Graf Apponyi, the Austrian
Ambassador in Paris, and the Marquis de Brignole, the Sardinian
Minister. Thanks to these and the good offices of a distinguished
writer, the Conte Frederico Sclopis, he had the entrée to all the
more agreeable salons, and here met a circle of amiable and distinguished people, among them the Contessa Sanseverino, who

*Upon my soul, Chevalier, may I be called a rogue
      If that devilish nose is not turquoise blue!'
The joke is obscure. Trs.

taught him a number of sixteenth-century Italian oaths, which he later used in his story *Le Secret des Ruggieri*.

Despite his denials, Turin insisted on mistaking Caroline for George Sand, and honoured her accordingly. The Conte Sclopis wrote in his parting letter: 'I beg you not to let your charming travelling-companion forget me. Our sex would not seriously venture to claim him for fear of losing him in the other. . . .' Balzac replied, 'As for my travelling-companion, he sends you a thousand messages. . . . She is a charming, witty and virtuous lady who . . . being able to escape for twenty days from domestic tedium, has flown to me for shelter in inviolable secrecy. . . . She knows that I love another, and has found in this the surest of safeguards. . . .' Caroline did, however, make one appearance as a woman, at an evening reception, 'in a ravishing toilette, simple, elegant and entirely Parisian . . . even to the tiny hat, called "*bébé*", which was being worn at the time.' She was an outstanding success.

Balzac did not lose sight of his mission. Sclopis put him in touch with the advocate Luigi Colla, who besides being an eminent jurist was also a collector of rare plants. Balzac's visit to his greenhouses, accompanied by Caroline in male attire, is generally held to have been the origin of the scene in *Le Cabinet des antiques* in which the Duchesse de Maufrigneuse, dressed as a '*lion*' and with a whip in her hand, is conducted by the old judge, Blondet, round 'his cherished flowers, his cacti and pelargoniums'.

Colla, working with his son, encountered great difficulties in the case of the Guidoboni-Visconti succession, which was complicated not only by the claims of the nephew, a minor, but by those of the Conte's half-brother, Laurent Constantin. Balzac corresponded for a considerable time with the two lawyers while they struggled with the slowly turning wheels of Piedmontese justice. The Guidoboni-Viscontis had chosen a zealous emissary. He would gladly have stayed longer in Turin, but, as he wrote sadly to Sclopis: 'The time-limit of twenty days is like the one for Cinderella's slipper. . . . "Marcel" must resume her woman's diadem and discard her student's whip. . . .' And he wrote from Paris, on 1 September:

My dear Count, Marcel and I had a very fatiguing journey,

because there was so much to be seen . . . that time was lacking and we went short of sleep. We looked for you in Geneva, but in vain. We walked along every street but 'No Sclopis!' exclaimed Marcel.

I have returned to my literary treadmill . . . eighteen hours' work a day are scarcely enough for all I have to do. The contrast between my laborious life and the *twenty-six days of dissipation* I allowed myself has had a curious effect upon me. There are moments when I seem to have been dreaming. I wonder if Turin exists; but then I think of your kindness to me and know that it was not a dream.

I beg you, in the name of this beginning of a friendship which will grow, to keep an eye on our little legal matter and on our good attorney, Colla, to whom I would like to be remembered less as a client than as an admirer of his high qualities. May he keep the interests of Monsieur and Madame Guidoboni-Visconti close to his left ear [he was deaf in the other]. . . .

If you write to me please address your letter, in a double envelope, to *Madame veuve Durand, rue des Batailles, 13, à Chaillot, Paris*. That is the secret of my hiding-place, where neither the Garde Nationale (which has sentenced me to ten days' imprisonment in my absence) nor anyone else knows where I am, and no one disturbs me. Oh, how I would love to travel down the Mont-Cenis again in six months' time! But I have to produce a great many volumes of pernicious compositions and painful phrases. . . . *Addio*.

The interlude had been brief but relaxing and delightful, a spell of sunshine between storms. It was described to Mme Hanska as follows: 'I took the opportunity of going to Turin to render a service to a gentleman with whom I share a box at the Italiens, a M. Visconti, who had a law-suit pending in Turin but could not go there himself. . . . I returned by way of the Simplon with a lady who is a friend of Madame Carraud and Jules Sandeau as my travelling companion. As you may guess, I stopped at the Piazza Castello, your hotel, in Turin, and in Geneva. . . . I looked again at the Pré-Lévêque and the Maison Mirabaud. . . . You alone, and the memory of you, could refresh an aching heart. . . .' The escapade had become a pilgrimage.

XXIII

The Death of Madame de Berny

TRAGIC NEWS AWAITED him on his return to Paris. Madame
de Berny had died on 27 July 1836. Her son, Alexandre,
wrote: 'This is a letter of mourning, my dear Honoré. After
ten days of acute nervous pains, choking spasms and dropsy,
our mother succumbed at nine o'clock this morning. . . .' We
cling always to the hope that those we love will outlast ourselves, even when we know them to be dying. Although she had
forbidden him to come to her after the death of her other son,
Armand, in 1835, Balzac bitterly regretted not having been
with her at the end. He had sent her a specially printed copy
of *Le Lys dans la vallée*, and perhaps her last happiness had lain
in re-reading the splendidly moving tribute he paid her in that
book: 'She was not only the beloved but the best-beloved. . . .
She became what Beatrice had been to the Florentine poet, the
spotless Laura of the poet of Venice, the mother of great
thoughts, the unwitting cause of saving resolutions, the mainstay of the future, the light shining in obscurity like a lily in the
leafy shade. . . . She taught me the steadfastness of Coligny that
I might vanquish conquerors, rise again after defeat, outweary
the strongest. . . . Most of my ideas were born of her, as scent
rises from a flower. . . .' The book was filled with her. Mme
de Mortsauf's 'apprentice letter' to Félix de Vandenesse consisted in essence of what she had tried to teach Balzac: 'Everything is fine, everything is good in you, so *be determined*! . . . Be
simple in your bearing, gentle in manner, proud without foolishness, above all discreet. . . .'

She had several times repeated her refusal to allow Honoré to
come to La Bouleaunière. She had not wanted him to see her

other than looking well and beautiful, and she affected a serenity which misled him as to the seriousness of her condition. It was a time, in any event, when he was desperately involved with his own affairs, the winding-up of the *Chronique de Paris*, negotiations with Mme Béchet, preparations for the Italian journey. But still she had longed for him, and when she felt that the end was near she sent Alexandre to Paris in search of him. He was away two days. Meanwhile, lying in her bed with a view of trees and sky, she re-read the *Lys* and asked for her mirror and rearranged her hair. Balzac had written of the 'touching and pathetic charm of a woman in pain'. She said to her doctor, 'I must live till tomorrow.' But Alexandre returned with the news that Balzac had left for Italy. She knew then that she would never see him again. She sent for Abbé Grasset, the curé of Gretz, and he administered the last rites that evening.

She said to Alexandre: 'I want you to look in my desk for a bundle tied with several strands of thick wool. They are Honoré's letters. You are to burn them. . . .' After her death he did so, putting the love-letters of fifteen years on the fire. One can imagine how Balzac regretted their loss. He wrote to his mysterious correspondent, 'Louise':

The person I have lost was more than a mother, more than a friend, more than any creature can be to another. . . . She sustained me through great tempests with words, with deeds and with devotion. If I am still alive, it is due to her; she was everything to me. Although for two years illness and circumstances have kept us apart, we were visible each to the other at a distance; she influenced me, she was a spiritual sun. Madame de Mortsauf in the *Lys* is but the pale expression of the least of her qualities, a distant reflection of her, for I have a horror of exposing my private feelings in public, and nothing that happens to me personally will ever be known. Well, in the midst of the new reverses that threaten to overwhelm me, has come her death. . . .

Family troubles were among the reverses. One of Laurence's sons, Alfred de Montzaigle, was destitute and had to be supported, and Madame Mère, having handed over the last remnants of her fortune to Henry, was appealing to Honoré for help. The Survilles were doing battle with officialdom as Balzac was with hostile reviewers. Laure, 'the little heretic', was very unhappy, and Madame Mère urged her to seek consolation in religion:

Religious people are happier and better, and therefore the religion which brings this about is good and necessary. . . . The great diversity and number of religions prove that men have always felt the need of one. . . . Yes, my angel, you have reached a phase in life when moral support is necessary. . . . Oh, yes, you know of the existence of prayer, but you do not know its power. . . . Your spirit has never yet been touched by our Lord's caress. . . . The calm and well-being which your body experiences when I magnetize you can give you but a faint idea. . . .

There was perhaps a hint of impiety in comparing the Lord's caress with magnetic passes, but the advice was well-intended. Madame Mère further sought to console her daughter by offering her one hundred francs out of the five hundred paid her monthly by Honoré, to buy 'eight metres of lace'; and proclaimed her fury with the opponents of canals, whose necks, were she not a Christian, she would twist.

Balzac besought Eve Hanska to take the place of Laure de Berny in his life:

I make you her heiress, you who have all her noble qualities, who might have written that letter by Madame de Mortsauf, which is but an imperfect echo of her invariable wisdom, and would at least have completed it. . . . But, *cara*, do not aggravate my distress with humiliating doubts; believe that calumny is easily visited on a man so heavily beset, and that now I must let anything be said about me without allowing it to trouble me. In your latest letters, you know, you have believed things which cannot be reconciled with what you know of me. . . .

He sealed this letter with the seal he had used when writing to Mme de Berny, remarking that he did not feel guilty of any sacrilege in doing so. But it was certainly a mistake. The mistrustful Eve could never play the part of the generous-hearted Dilecta. Zulma Carraud would have done better. She wrote on 7 October 1836:

I saw a deep wound in your heart and wept with you for the angelic being whose greatest sufferings you ignored. Has there been no reaction in you, Honoré, in your soul? I possess none of her right to speak to you, but on the other hand I am restrained by none of the diffidence which so often caused her to keep silent. Although you have begged me not to refer to the subject, I must ask you whether, on the day when you suffered this mortal blow, you did not realize that there are other things in life besides a pocket-knife costing eight hundred francs and a stick which has no other virtue than to attract notice. What celebrity for the author of *Eugénie Grandet*! . . .

She was very angry with him. When would he cease to be led astray by the chorus of adulation, the fashionable women, the precious fops? If he was ruined, as he said, whose fault was it but his own? He had earned an immense amount of money in the past eight years and yet was more in debt than ever. Did a thinking man need so much to live on? Must he be forever in search of material pleasures, and only write under compulsion? 'The life you have betrayed, Honoré—the talent you are stifling at its source! . . . When, *dearest*, shall I see you work for the sake of working? You would do such wonderful things!' She was right about the life, but wrong about the talent. He *was* doing wonderful things. Despite all the tribulations, all the excesses, his demon did not desert him. On 1 October he had written to Eve: 'To show you the extent of my resolution I must tell you that the *Secret des Ruggieri* was written in a single night. Think of this when you read it. *La Vieille Fille* was written in three nights. *La Perle brisée*, which concludes *L'Enfant maudit*, was written in a single night.' These were his victories in his 'battle for France'.

La Vieille Fille was intended for *La Presse* and marked his rather tepid reconciliation with Girardin, who wrote: 'Believe me, my dear Balzac, our rupture has not for a moment destroyed in me the old affection we had for one another. . . . I am sincerely attached to you; I think I have already proved it; and if I have been in the wrong I am only too ready to admit it. . . .' Editors cannot afford to lose valuable authors. It was the first time a work of fiction had been serialized in a newspaper. The practice had long been common in the weekly and monthly reviews, but Girardin was the first to attempt it in a daily, and he needed an author like Balzac, as popular as he was prolific, if the venture was to succeed.

The idea of the story had been in Balzac's head for a long time. He took a naturalist's interest in the 'elderly spinster' species, observing the torments of frustration they endured. The best of them sublimated their unavowable longings and desires in charitable work; but others turned malignant, like Sophie Gamard in the *Curé de Tours*, and Cousine Bette, who was still to come. The *vieille fille* in this case, Rose Cormon, daughter of a wealthy Alençon family, suffers to the point of obsession from her 'over-long virginity'. At the age of forty-two she still dreams of marriage and children, and the maid finds her bed in the mornings 'turned upside down'.

She is hesitating between two suitors, attracted by her fortune and her large bosom. One is the Chevalier de Valois, an elderly aristocratic libertine who still enjoys rumpling the laundry-maid and has a very big nose from which Lavater would have drawn conclusions. The other is du Bousquier, a former army contractor whose sexual excesses have left him bald and impotent. Mademoiselle Cormon, ignorant of all such matters and burning with desire and hope, falls for du Bousquier's toupee and broad shoulders. She marries him and finds that she has been cheated. There is a third contender, Athanase Granson, a misunderstood but talented young man who is genuinely in love with her. However, Rose, who has no wish to play Madame de Berny to this other Balzac, rejects him, and he commits suicide. Balzac says of the devout Madame du Bousquier, 'She will be a fool to her last breath.'

He wrote *La Vieille Fille* while he was mourning Madame de Berny and under great pressure. Madame Béchet was harassing him, he was writing two other tales at the same time (*L'Enfant maudit* and *Le Secret des Ruggieri*) and Girardin was in a hurry. Publication of *La Vieille Fille* began before he had finished it, and he received a number of letters from readers who were outraged by certain of the physical details, notably Rose Cormon's enormous breasts. Even Laure Surville seems to have been disconcerted. Eve Hanska, refusing to replace Laure de Berny as his literary conscience, said nothing. The critics derided Balzac's 'Lavaterism', the pseudo-science which claimed to interpret the human heart and its romantic fervours from physical indications. The other daily papers, fearing that Girardin's experiment with serialization might rob them of readers, attacked the serialist. Balzac knew he had written a good book. The picture of provincial society was striking in its truth, and Rose Cormon and her suitors were original, living characters. But in this 'battle for France' to which he was devoting such immense gifts he was alone and without allies.

Not to neglect any chance of extravagance, he was making improvements to the house in the Rue des Batailles, decorating an attic, 'white and coquettish as a sixteen-year-old *grisette*', and at the same time having a study furnished in black and red, with a circular divan with twelve white cushions. Antoine Fontaney, the poet, came upon him during that year in the studio of the painter, Louis Boulanger, posing in a white tail-coat with his arms crossed and vigorously discoursing.

From Fontanay's Journal: Description of his white gowns. He has not worn any other costume since he visited the Chartreuse. He has a gown washed only once. He never gets ink on them. 'He is very clean at work.' But one has to see the gowns against the furnishings; there are shades of pink. He got his tassels from church decorations. The Church does everything for a purpose. He got his famous white divan made when he was on the verge of having a lady out of the top drawer—dammit, he had to have something handsome, she was used to it! It seems that when she found herself on it she was not displeased. . . .

The lady, Fanny Guidoboni-Visconti, was so little displeased that she paid the divan frequent visits. To appease Eve Hanska, who heard of what was going on from her dangerously well-informed aunt, he had a copy made of the Boulanger portrait (at M. Hanski's expense). Its look of monkish celibacy seemed to him reassuring: 'What Boulanger has managed to depict, and what I like, is the tenacity—like that of Coligny or Peter the Great—which is at the root of my character; an intrepid faith in the future. . . .'

But with his faith in the future was mingled a great relish for the present. He drew a pathetic picture for Eve of creditors, malicious journalists, grief and exhaustion, and it was all true. But on the credit side there was his irrepressible vitality. He might seem to be defeated, but in his heart he was sure that all would come right. What was his life if not a novel in itself? He would correct it in proof. On the same day that he borrowed petty cash from Dr Nacquart and an elderly workman 'more trusting than men of the world', he bought himself a new stick for six hundred francs. The worse things were, the more he bought, to give himself the illusion of prosperity. And was it, after all, an illusion? Like Vautrin he felt that he had in him the strength to challenge society and conquer it.

His financial position in the early months of 1837 looked worse than ever. He owed 53,000 francs more than at the end of 1836, partly because of the failure of the *Chronique de Paris*; and he was threatened with legal proceedings, having rashly used certain of Werdet's notes-of-hand to buy out Duckett. Werdet could not meet them, and Duckett, a tough business-man, could only proceed against Balzac, who, having been registered as a *'commerçant'* at the time of the printing-works, was liable to imprisonment for debt. Such was the law. And Balzac was ill at the time. In spite of everything he managed to finish revising the first part of *Illusions perdues*. Although he knew now that it was only the beginning of a much larger work, he had to publish it at once to bring in money.

And he had to dodge Duckett's process-servers. Duckett had already impounded the tilbury with its flowered cushions, but he could not catch Balzac. The porter in the Rue des Batailles professed never to have heard of him; he only knew the 'Widow Durand', who was not at home. Eventually the porter produced another address, 22 Rue de Provence, where Balzac had rented a room—but he was not there either. The dun concluded: 'Everything goes to show that the Sieur de Balzac is seeking to escape from his creditors . . . by passing under different names.' Undoubtedly he was; and forgetful of all extravagances, recalling his kindness to people like Jules Sandeau and persuaded of the incompetence of his business associates, he was disposed to regard himself as a persecuted man, an injured innocent. But this hunted life was too much for him. He found himself 'without ideas, without strength, broken in spirit' and incapable of working. He had to get away somehow. At one moment he toyed with the idea of securing a passport for Russia and going to the Hanskis 'to take shelter for two years, abandoning my reputation to fools and enemies'. But once again the Guido-boni-Viscontis came to the rescue.

The law-suit over the succession was still proceeding, having been transferred to Milan. Balzac set off once more for Italy, this time alone but on the same terms as before. He had power of attorney, his expenses were paid and he was to receive a commission on the final settlement. It was another triumphal progress. If he was a debtor on one side of the Alps, he was a conqueror on the other. He reached Milan on 19 February, and found the whole of Italian society, particularly the ladies, anxious to meet him.

He was armed with more letters of introduction than he could use, among them one from the Contessa Sanseverino to her brother, Alfonso Porcia, and their friend Clara Maffei, a lady prominent in fashionable and artistic circles. She was young, cultivated and attractive, and since Balzac could never set eyes on a pretty woman without trying his luck he paid assiduous court to her; to the point, indeed, that she incurred a rebuke from her husband, who himself lived a life of celibacy:

All eyes are fixed on this celebrated foreigner; everyone knows that he spends a great deal of time at our house, both in the morning and at night. . . . You have read his novels, and you must realize how well he understands women and how subtle he is in the arts of seduction. . . . Add to this the fact that in dissolute Paris he has the reputation of a libertine. . . . You must not suppose that his ugliness will protect you against your inexperience. . . . Consider, my little Clara, that you are the beloved of Milan. . . .

Nothing serious came of it, but the flirtation added to the pleasure of his visit.

The Principe Porcia and his mistress, Contessa Bolognini, were kind to him, and he was touched by their affection for one another. 'If only I had the good fortune to be so loved by a woman that she would consent to live with me!' he wrote hopefully to Eve. Porcia lent him his carriage and his *loge* at the Scala. Stendhal has described the charm of that great theatre at the time. All the leading families had boxes, and the performance was a round of social exchanges. Spontaneous kindness and a capacity for enjoyment were the key-notes of life in Milan, and Balzac must have found it doubly attractive after his tribulations in Paris.

The press was wonderful: 'Have you seen the aurora borealis? And have you seen Monsieur de Balzac? These are the questions everyone is certain to ask you at present. But the aurora borealis is already almost forgotten, whereas the name of Monsieur de Balzac is still on everybody's lips.' His wit was praised, the liveliness of his conversation, even his modesty! A pickpocket stole his watch while affecting to embrace him as a friend, but it was recovered the same evening. A sculptor, Alessandro Puttinati, made a statuette of him. He signed countless autograph albums, writing in that of Clara Maffei, 'At twenty-three all is in the future!', and was taken to call on Alessandro Manzoni. This was not a success. He had not read *I Promessi Sposi*, the work which had occupied the great man for six years, and talked to him about criminology.

The Guidoboni-Visconti business did not turn out well. The amount involved was not large, a matter of 73,760 Milanese *livres*, and there were too many claimants. In the end Balzac secured a sum of 13,000, to be divided between the Conte Guidoboni and the nephew. From this 4,000 livres had to be deducted to pay the lawyers' fees and his own costs.

The settlement had to be endorsed by the boy's father, the Barone Galvagna, who lived in Venice, and Balzac decided that he would save time by going there to secure his signature, rather than attempt to do so by correspondence. It was raining heavily when he arrived at the Albergo Reale (nowadays the Hotel Danieli), where the handsome bedrooms were even furnished with pianos. Without knowing it he was given the suite which had been occupied by George Sand and Musset in 1834; but in spite of this he was at first not much taken with the town. 'I would give all Venice,' he wrote to Clara Maffei, 'for an evening, an hour, even a quarter of an hour at your fireside.' He liked the gondolas, but, 'I must confess that I am in despair at not having the lady of my thoughts to share one with me.' They were evidently on terms that were, at the least, cordial.

He liked Venice a great deal better when, after two days, the sun shone. But he was far less warmly received here than in Milan. The press was sarcastic and almost hostile because he had not sought to cultivate the minor men of letters, and the Conte Tullio Dandolo wrote an indecent account of a dinner with him for the *Gazetta di Venezia*. However, he accomplished his mission and paid Galvagna 4,500 *livres* for the benefit of his son. The next day he returned to Milan.

Balzac's ideas on Italy and the Italians were transformed by those two visits. Hitherto he had depicted Italian women as being of easy virtue, but after 1836 they became models of constancy, in love if not in marriage. He had a warm regard for Clara Maffei and Eugénie Bolognini: 'The Frenchwoman is intensely preoccupied with her skirts, whereas the Italian woman scarcely troubles about them or seeks to defend them with a stony gaze, knowing that she is protected by a single love, a passion sacred to her as it is to others. . . .' Here he was in agreement with his friend Stendhal.

On his homeward journey he was caught by a quarantine order at Genoa and had to spend some days in a sort of hostel 'unworthy to serve as a prison for brigands'. But here he met a Genoese trader, Pezzi, who was trying to promote a remarkable business venture. It seemed that the Romans, when mining the silver deposits in Sardinia, had abandoned huge slag-heaps of silver-bearing ore which they lacked the means to refine. There were millions there for the taking. The idea, with its romantic and historic associations, enchanted Balzac, and he promised himself that he would follow it up. He visited Florence, where he steeped himself in pictures, and had a bad time crossing the Saint-Gothard pass in fifteen feet of snow and twenty-five degrees of frost. 'In spite of eleven guides I nearly perished several times,' he told Eve, and perhaps there was some truth in it. On 10 May 1837, he wrote from Paris:

I am back at work. I am going to bring out *César Birotteau*, *La Femme supérieure* and *Gambara* one after another. I shall finish *Illusions perdues* and then *La Haute Banque* and *Les Artistes*. Then we will fly to the Ukraine where perhaps I shall have the good fortune to write a play which will put an end to my financial miseries. That is my plan of campaign, *cara contessina*. . . .

He had an idea for a play, to be called *La Première Demoiselle*, of which the setting was a tradesman's shop in the Faubourg Saint-Denis, on the lines of the Maison du Chat-qui-pelote. The *première demoiselle*, or head saleswoman, a sort of female Tartuffe, was to become the tradesman's mistress and rule the whole establishment, riding roughshod over his wife and daughters. It was a promising theme and, as Balzac said, a female Tartuffe is more deadly than the male because she has more effective weapons at her command. Another stage piece he had in mind was to be about M. Prudhomme, whom he had no scruple over borrowing, to the last detail, from the cartoonist, Henri Monnier. To Balzac, Joseph Prudhomme, the essence of bourgeoisdom under Louis-Philippe, the man of the Garde Nationale, of middle-class morals and hoarded savings, was an even greater comic character than Figaro or Turcaret. He had the plot neatly worked out and all that remained was to write the play, which was to be called *Le Mariage de Mademoiselle Prudhomme*. But in his heart Balzac preferred the novel; he only turned to the theatre, and always without success, when driven by financial necessity. At that moment, in May 1837, he had a little money in his pocket, his very small share of the Guidoboni-Visconti legacy. There was, of course, no question of using it to settle any of his debts—money paid to creditors was money lost to happiness. But his mother was by now in really desperate straits, and it must be said that during the past two years he had most shamefully neglected her. He found a letter from her (addressed to 'Madame veuve Durand') awaiting him when he got back to the Rue des Batailles:

Chantilly, April 1837. Your journey to Italy is a very long one, my dear Honoré, and it is a long time since I saw you or had news of you. I cannot grow used to this treatment.

Despite your promises it is more than two years since you last wrote to me, and I have to discover where you are, and what you are doing, from the newspapers which the Chantilly ladies bring me. If I do not complain you think I do not care, and if I do complain you think I'm a nuisance. Ho! it is sad to have become useless, my son, and not to be sufficiently loved....

My son, since you have been able to find money for friends like Sandeau, for mistresses, jewelled canes, rings, silver and furniture, your mother may, without presumption, remind you of your promise. She has waited until the last moment before doing so—but that moment has come....

Money is the last protection of the aging and unloved, a fictitious strength to compensate for all that they have lost. 'Oh!

my God!' exclaimed poor Madame Mère. 'Why did you not leave me a fortune?' All was gone from her, the power to terrify her children with her frosty gaze, almost the power to touch their hearts. The Survilles did what they could, but they, too, were in trouble. General and Mme de Pommereul, who had so often been generous in the matter of canals, had grown uneasy, and finally angry, when they found that the work was not even begun. 'The worst thing of all,' Laure ingenuously wrote, 'is that no interest on the money has been paid.' That was also the General's view. Laure sought to appease them by shopping for the Baroness in Paris and buying 'dresses, shawls, cloth, night-caps and hair-nets, things that can't be got in Fougères'.

She was putting a brave face on misfortune ('My husband is in no way discouraged'), but still, with two girls to bring up, a penniless mother, a wastrel brother (Henry) and not enough money coming in, she was understandably in acute distress. Anxiety had made her ill the previous year. Henry was such an embarrassment to them that Honoré was charged with the task of persuading him to return to Mauritius, which he did in December 1836 (but while waiting to embark at Paimboeuf he made a frantic appeal to Laure for funds to pay his account at the inn). Surville was aging, his hair white with worry, while he expressed his gratitude to the Pommereuls 'for their confidence in me'. But the confidence was wearing thin. Madame de Pommereul even went so far as to question Honoré's talent, at which the family pride rose up in arms. 'Honoré's aim,' wrote Laure, 'is to draw a complete picture of his time. . . . We cannot judge it except as a whole. . . .' It was bravely said. But after March 1837 Madame de Pommereul no longer answered Laure's letters. To maintain a friendship when material interests are seriously affected calls for great magnanimity.

The affection between brother and sister was constant as ever. On her birthday, in September 1836, Laure allowed herself the treat of paying Honoré a visit. 'Her husband's affairs are going slowly,' he wrote, 'and so is her own life; it is wasting away in shadow, and her splendid qualities are squandered in an obscure, inglorious struggle! . . . We celebrated her birthday in tears! And the poor child kept her watch in her hand, she had only twenty minutes. Her husband is jealous of me. That she should have to visit her own brother in secret!' He might perhaps have found in her the consoler and counsellor Madame de Berny had been, but 'my sister, who so dearly loves me, can never receive me in her home. A ferocious jealousy prevails there which prohibits everything.'

He could look for no financial assistance from the Survilles. In reply to his mother's letter he wrote:

My dear mother, it is as though I were on the field of battle, and the struggle is desperate. I cannot answer you with a long letter, but I have thought hard and considered what is the best thing to do. I think that to start with you should come to Paris and talk to me for an hour so that we may understand one another. It is easier for me to talk than to write, and I believe everything can be arranged to meet your needs. Call on me whenever it suits you to come. Here in the Rue des Batailles, as in the Rue Cassini, you will be with a son whose heart is torn, at this moment, by the least of your words. Come as soon as you can. I clasp you to my heart and wish I were a year older, because you must not fear for me, there is great certainty in my future. . . .

More brave words; but not much 'real money', as he himself would have said, for an elderly lady 'without hearth or home'.

XXIV

The Myth of Sisyphus

Il y a eu un moment où Sisyphe n'a plus ni pleuré, ni souri, où il a participé de la nature des roches qu'il soulevait toujours.

BALZAC

THE RETURN TO PARIS, after three months of the *dolce vita* in Italy, was terrible. Bills had been piling up in the Rue des Batailles, and financially he was in a worse state than ever. His debts now amounted to 162,000 francs, with little money in prospect because so much work that had been paid for in advance was still to be done. Duckett was proving the most unrelenting of creditors, and there was a real possibility that the literary lion of Venice would find himself in a debtors' prison. 'You must forget this abyss of sorrows where I have forbidden you to set foot,' he wrote to 'Louise'. 'To take any interest in me is to suffer. . . .'

His first need was to dodge the process-servers, who now knew both his places of residence. The Carrauds, at Frapesle, were also ruled out, because he would certainly be run to earth there. He besought his former assistant on the *Chronique de Paris*, du Belloy, to find him 'a room in secrecy, and bread and water'. Belloy presented him with an idea for a story, *Gambara*, but had nothing else to offer. Once again it was the Guidoboni-Viscontis who saved him. The Contessa took him in at 52 Champs-Élysées, braving public opinion and running considerable risks. 'Like many Englishwomen,' he wrote of Lady Dudley in *Le Lys dans la vallée*, 'she looked for what was startling and extraordinary. She wanted pepper and spices for the nourishment of her heart, just as Englishmen want fiery condiments for their palates.' Fanny Guidoboni was allured by all things romantic, unconventional and difficult. Balzac moved in secretly, and at once settled down to work.

His programme for 1837, all contracted for in advance, was

a large one. He had to finish *La Femme supérieure* for *La Presse*, to write *César Birotteau* for the new *Figaro* under Alphonse Karr, and to produce a number of shorter stories to complete the *Études philosophiques*. All were part of the vast and ordered structure of the *Comédie humaine* which he was now engaged upon, and it is characteristic of him that, despite the strain, the urgency, and the need to work like a day-labourer, all these tasks were admirably accomplished.

The visit to Italy furnished him with much material for the short stories. He was more than ever obsessed with the idea that any work of art risks being destroyed by the undisciplined fervour of the artist. When a musician seeks to reproduce the music of the angels he ceases to be understood by men. He had himself suffered this disaster with *Séraphita*, and in *Le Chef-d'oeuvre inconnu* he had sought to depict an over-gifted and aspiring painter, Frenhofer, who in his search for the Absolute ruins his work by divorcing it from nature. The first version of that story lacked any theory of artistic creation that a painter might conceive. Later Théophile Gautier, drawing on his experience as an art-student and critic, enabled him to turn it into a philosophical study.

Gambara returned to this theme. The central character this time is a composer of genius who fails to make himself understood because his music is incomprehensible. Auguste de Belloy had roughed out the idea and Maurice Schlesinger commissioned it for his musical journal. Balzac reshaped it entirely, and with the help of Jakob Strunz, a German composer, introduced lengthy analyses of the operas *Mahomet* and *Robert le Diable*. Balzac confessed his own ignorance of musical technicalities and in a letter described an orchestra as being to him 'an ill-assorted and bizarre assembly' of strangely shaped contrivances, heads, arms, lights and scores, 'wherein inexplicable movements take place, where they all seem to be blowing their noses or coughing more or less in time'.

The fact is that he understood all the arts, and delighted even George Sand when he talked about music. However, he left the technicalities in *Gambara* to Strunz, who obliged with truly German thoroughness. The digressions, ten pages long, on 'tonics' and 'dominants' would have killed the story, had it been by anyone but Balzac.

In *Massimilla Doni*, a novella which he wrote in 1837 although it was not published till 1839, Balzac applied the same idea to love as well as music. Just as excess of passion can kill a work of art, so can it kill male virility. The man who 'fails' with a mistress he adores may be the potent lover of a prostitute for whom he cares nothing, in the same way that an opera-singer may fail at the very moment when his musical feeling is most intense: 'When an artist has the misfortune to be carried away by the emotion he seeks to express, he cannot do so, because he has become the thing itself instead of being its instrument. Art proceeds from the brain, not from the heart. When you are dominated by a subject you are its slave and not its master. You are like a king besieged by his people. Over-intense feeling at the moment of execution is the rebellion of the emotions against the mind. . . .' In short, excess of imagination exhausts a man's strength, so that he cannot apply it in action. Just as an idea can kill, so can it emasculate.

This novella, one of Balzac's best and most 'daring', is developed on two levels. Emilio Memmi, Prince of Varese, who is madly in love with Massimilla Doni, Duchess of Cataneo, knows that if he seeks to possess her it will end in disaster; Genovese, a leading tenor, although he sings admirably when Clara Tinti (whom he loves, but who is in love with Emilio) is not on the stage, loses all his quality when she appears. A French doctor proposes a remedy. He suggests that Massimilla, a stainless beauty, shall occupy Clara Tinti's bed (by arrangement with her) and deceive her lover by herself playing the prostitute. 'Is that all?' she says, smiling. 'I will surpass Tinti if need be, to save my lover's life.' The scabrous theme may have been derived from Stendhal's *Armance*, but Balzac had always been obsessed with the physiological side of love. The distinctive touch is in the parallel between the impotence of the artist and that of the lover, both due to excess of passion. The novella is padded out with disquisitions on the art of Rossini, again the work of Strunz, and it is linked to *Gambara* by the character of Massimilla, who appears in both stories.

A few hours had always been all Balzac needed for the understanding of a town or a society. In *Massimilla Doni* he depicted the Venetian aristocracy, once the first in Europe but now almost completely ruined. There were gondoliers who were the sons of former doges, their lineage more ancient than that of kings. Emilio Memmi weeps for the Venice of the past 'and the days when the Palazzo poured out light from every window; when a hundred gondolas were tied to its mooring-posts, and on its terrace lapped by the waters the crowd of elegant masks surged . . . and its galleries, filled with music, seemed to contain the whole of Venice coming and going on stairways that echoed with laughter. . . . But now the walls, stripped of their hangings, and the dingy ceilings, were silent and wept. There were no more Turkish carpets or chandeliers festooned with flowers, or statues or pictures; no more happiness and no more money, the means of happiness. Venice, that London of the Middle Ages, was crumbling stone by stone and man by man. . . .'

Quick to sense the feelings of his Italian friends, he had understood the proud sadness of oppressed Italy. Describing a performance of Rossini's *Moses*, he showed how near to the hearts of the audience was that story of the Israelites struggling to escape from servitude. When the first chords on the harps announce the Hymn of Deliverance, the Duchess puts her elbow on the velvet arm of her seat and rests her head on her hand. The entire audience clamours for the hymn to be repeated. 'I felt as though I were witnessing the liberation of Italy,' reflects a Milanese. 'Sing!' exclaims the Duchess. . . . 'Sing and you are free!'

It is wonderful that Blazac in the midst of his own troubles, hounded as he was by duns and publishers, could yet find the strength to make such eloquent use of his Italian impressions. He had always loved music, but in Italy he learned how it speaks to the spirit, evoking the stir of emotions that cannot be defined and perhaps have never been experienced.

Yesterday [he wrote to Eve] I heard Beethoven's Symphony in C minor. Beethoven is the one man who has taught me to feel jealousy. I would rather have been Beethoven than Rossini or Mozart. There is in him a divine power. . . . No, the writer's gift does not afford any similar satisfaction, for what we paint is finite and determined, whereas what Beethoven flings at you is infinite. . . .

Besides the Italian stories, he wrote in one month (but not in four days, as he had hoped) *La Femme supérieure*, which filled seventy-five columns of *La Presse*:

I have got through the thirty nights of this damned month without, I think, having slept more than sixty-odd hours during the whole time. I haven't been able to shave and now I who am the enemy of all affectation, I have a goat's beard like the young men. After finishing this letter I am going to have my first bath, not without misgivings, for I am afraid of relaxing fibres strung to the highest degree of tension, and I must start work again on *César Birotteau*, which is becoming ridiculous because of all the delays. Besides, it is ten months since the *Figaro* paid me the money. . . .

La Femme supérieure had started by being to some extent the story of his sister, Laure; that of a lovable but ambitious woman who attempts to drive a husband less aspiring than herself to heights not easily scaled. Célestine Rabourdin is married to a civil servant, a section-chief in the Ministry of Finance, the details of whose life are mysterious. Like Surville he has never known his father, a powerful figure in the background who, after helping his son at the outset of his career, ceases to manifest himself, presumably because he is dead. The desirable but virtuous Célestine has difficulty in making ends meet. It is she who cleans the lamps and watches over the cooker in the morning, clad in a dressing-gown and an old pair of slippers, with her hair undone (this was probably a picture of Laure). She is caught in this state of undress by Clément des Lupeaulx, the Minister's permanent secretary, who nevertheless finds her attractive, catching a glimpse of bare flesh through a gap in her camisole. Des Lupeaulx, upon whom her husband's career depends, makes advances to her. Célestine hopes to preserve her virtue while at the same time helping her husband. Unhappily for himself, Rabourdin is a sort of administrative genius, than which nothing could be more dangerous in a government employee. Balzac knew all about that bureaucratic world; it had been described to him by Émile de Girardin and Henri Monnier among others. He brought the Ministry into the story and turned it into a brilliant comedy. The character of Rabourdin lacks depth and stature, but his colleagues, ten or more of them, are sketched with a master hand both in their professional and their private lives.

Balzac could never touch a subject without deepening it. What was to have been a drama of married life became a broad historical study. Under Napoleon the imperial despotism had restricted the power of the bureaucracy, 'that ponderous curtain set between the good that needs to be done and the man who can command it'. Under a constitutional government, ministers being of uncertain duration and mainly concerned with safeguarding their existence before Parliament, officialdom reigns supreme and creates a device of inertia known as the Report, which delays effective action: 'Every kind of lobbying springs to life. . . . The best things in France have been accomplished when there was no Report and decisions were spontaneous. . . . ' Wholly composed of narrow minds, bureaucracy obstructs the prosperity of the country, keeps a canal project (here we catch a nod to Surville) in its files for seven years, eternally drags out abuses and thus perpetuates itself.

These considerations move Rabourdin (and Balzac) to advocate a drastic overhaul—the number of ministries to be reduced to three, staff to be cut down, salaries to be doubled or trebled. Taxes will be on personal fortunes and property, and indirect taxation will be abolished: 'Personal fortunes are admirably represented in France by rents, the number of servants, horses and carriages, all easily assessable.' Taxation will be heavy, but no matter: 'The budget is not a vault but a watering-can; the more it collects and pours out, the more does a country prosper. . . . ' It may be noted that these very new ideas ran counter to those of the Legitimist Party. The author, like his character, was rowing against the stream. But Rabourdin in his inevitable downfall was to be consoled by the steadfast devotion of Célestine. Who was to console Balzac?

While he was elaborating the thoughts of Rabourdin the *gardes du commerce*, whose business was to effect the imprisonment of debtors, had found means of reaching him under the roof of the Guidoboni-Viscontis. The latter had instructed their servants to reply to inquiries that M. de Balzac did not live there, but there was a traitor in the camp: a jealous maid gave away the secret. An agent disguised as a messenger got into the house on the pretext that he had a parcel and a sum of money to deliver to Balzac—who came running. The man grabbed him by his gown and threatened him with arrest if he did not forthwith pay the sum of thirteen hundred and eighty francs, plus additional expenses. The house was surrounded. It was a matter of payment or imprisonment, and so Fanny Guido-boni-Visconti paid, although she herself was very hard up.

These recurrent crises were shattering to Balzac, but he was proud of what he had accomplished—*Gambara, Massimilla Doni, La Femme supérieure* — — 'I hope the labourer may be worthy of his hire.' But now that he was able to come out of hiding he found that there were still people who thought that he had published nothing. James Rothschild, meeting him on the boulevard, asked, 'What are you doing these days?'—and this when *La Femme supérieure*, published a fortnight previously, was filling the columns of *La Presse*. He was Sisyphus, for ever pushing his rock uphill. 'Must I, for the fifth or sixth time, describe the mechanics of my misery?' he wrote to Eve, and embarked on the familiar liturgy of his grievances—his family's refusal to support him in 1828, the double-dealing of Latouche, the collapse of Werdet, the money-lenders at twenty per cent, the fire that had destroyed the edition of the *Contes drolatiques*, the dreadful failure of the *Chronique de Paris*. He even defended his extravagance. For a man whose time was worth fifty francs an hour a carriage was an economy, and in any case a writer who did not make a show of prosperity was at the mercy of publishers:

If you do not respect a man who, bearing this burden of debt, writing with one hand and fighting with the other, committing no base act, bowing neither to the money-lenders nor to the press, begging favours of no one, neither creditor nor friend, has still held his ground in the most untrusting, egotistical and niggardly of worlds, where money is lent only to the rich; who has been, and is still being, pursued by calumny, and who was said to be in a debtors' prison when he was visiting you in Vienna—then you know nothing of the world! . . .

Indeed, Eve Hanska did know nothing of that Parisian world, and he sorely missed Laure de Berny, who had never hesitated to write in the margin of a manuscript, 'Bad . . . sentence to be rewritten.' He longed for Eve to take her place:

Carina carina, you must get it into that head which glows

with such sublime intelligence that I have the most absolute confidence in your literary judgement; that in this respect I have made you the successor to the angel I have lost; that whatever you write to me becomes the subject of lengthy meditation, and that therefore, *mail after mail*, I expect from you a criticism of *La Vieille Fille* such as the dear conscience I once had, whose voice still lingers in my ears, was accustomed to make. That is to say that you should re-read the story and point out to me in detail, page by page, the thoughts and ideas that shock you, telling me if I am to eliminate or replace or alter them. Show me no mercy or indulgence. Go boldly to work. . . .

But Eve, although she was not stupid or lacking in culture, possessed neither the generous capacity for admiration nor the affectionate frankness of Laure de Berny. In their correspondence as in all their dealings, despite their strong affection, there were constant disharmonies. She scolded, lectured and argued, and he sighed in reply that there were as many differences between them as there were miles.

His letters, with their torrent of present indicatives, sometimes recall the monologue in *Le Mariage de Figaro*: 'From having in 1827 rendered service to a working printer, I find myself in 1829 overwhelmed with a hundred-and-fifty-thousand francs of debts and driven penniless into an attic. . . . Having made some progress, I constitute myself the Don Quixote of the weak; I hope to restore the courage of Sandeau, and on this account lose four or five thousand francs which might have saved others! . . . I am thirty-eight; I am loaded with debts. . . . My hair is turning white. . . . Eveline, Eveline, how you distress me!'

In 1837 he had a spell of desperation. His brain would no longer function and one of his lungs was affected. Dr Nacquart sent him to Saché with orders to do no work, to relax and go for walks. Admirable counsel, but how could he not work when he had to finish *César Birotteau* and write *La Maison Nucingen*? And how go for walks when he was coughing like an old man?

I have reached the point where I no longer care for life; hope is too far removed and tranquillity too filled with toil. If I needed only to work in moderation I would accept my lot without a murmur; but I suffer too many disappointments and have

too many enemies! The third part of the *Études philosophiques*
has been published, and not a single paper has said a word about
it. . . .

Above all, Paris terrified him. Paris meant creditors. It also
meant the odious Garde Nationale, which had caught up with
him again and wrote derisively to 'Monsieur de Balzac, alias
the Widow Durand, man of letters, *chasseur* in the First Legion'.
And still Paris, with her tar-surfaced boulevards shining under
the bronze gas-lamps, her coming and going of crowds in
the market-place, was the unrivalled spectacle, the queen of
cities which he could never live without. However, he had to
put a little distance between them if he was to escape the Garde
Nationale.

In Saché this thought took more precise shape. He would buy
a house, a cottage near enough to Paris for him to be able to
reach the Théâtre des Italiens in an hour on evenings when he
felt the need of music, but still remote enough to be beyond the
reach of *gardes du commerce* and sergeant-majors. And where
was the money to come from? When Balzac passionately longed
for something he dismissed sober calculation. He treated life as
fiction, conjuring up wondrous events: For example, a stupendous transaction whereby the whole of his works would be
re-issued in a new, illustrated, subscribed edition, with a bonus
for each subscriber, financed on the lines of his father's beloved
Tontine Lafarge. Who could fail to subscribe when the survivors would secure an increasing income as well as the complete works of Balzac? In addition he would have a couple of
plays put on, or four or five, and everybody knew how much
money there was to be made in the theatre. And then again,
M. Hanski might die, and he would marry his widow and
become the master of Wierzchownia, rolling in wealth. Finally,
there were those abandoned silver-mines in Sardinia. With so
many strings to his bow, it was his plain duty to buy a house.

And he knew where to go for it. On the road to Versailles,
tucked away in a sea of greenery, was the charming village of
Ville-d'Avray where he had often visited Olympe Pélissier.
There he would be near Versailles, and therefore to the Guido-
boni-Viscontis, and within an hour and a half by coach of the
Italiens. To begin with he rented a lodging there (in the name

of Surville); but in September 1837 he found a plot of land and a cottage at a spot known as Jardy, the property of a weaver named Varlet. The price was 4,500 francs, plus legal charges. The next day he bought the adjoining plot at a price of 6,850 francs. By 1839 he owned four or five acres with a total value of 18,000 francs: 'The name of my modest hermitage is Les Jardies, that of the piece of land on which I have settled like a caterpillar on its lettuce-leaf. . . .' His plan was to reserve the weaver's cottage for the Guidoboni-Viscontis (who financed the transaction) and to get Surville, who being a civil engineer was also an architect, to build him a small house for himself. Thus he would be of Paris but not in it. He would pay no tolls or excessive taxes, and he would be sheltered from the importunities of the gutter-press. The house would not cost more than 12,000 francs, making 40,000 in all, with the price of the land and the furnishing and decoration. This represented only a small rent. He did not, it is true, possess the 40,000 francs; but the builder had agreed to start work for 1,500 on account. All he now had to do was to finish *César Birotteau* and write *La Maison Nucingen*. Sisyphus rolled up his sleeves and returned to his boulder.

XXV
Treasure Hunt

Balzac ne fut rien, que ce désir toujours renaissant du désir, cet élan vers l'avenir qui s'éprouve à la fois comme victorieux de tous les obstacles et sans cesse contraint de se mesurer avec eux—une vie perpétuellement en projet.

GAÉTAN PICON

BALZAC HAD MENTIONED *César Birotteau* to Zulma Carraud as early as 1833, and in 1834 he wrote to Eve Hanska, 'I am writing a major work, *César Birotteau*. He is the brother of the Birotteau you know, and like him a victim, but the victim of Paris civilization, whereas his brother [the Curé de Tours] is the victim of a single man ... the angel trodden underfoot, the honest man despised! It is a great picture!' At that time his intention had been to let Werdet have the novel as one of the *Études philosophiques*. But other books intervened, Werdet went bankrupt and *Birotteau* was put aside. Werdet sold his option on Balzac's future works to a consortium of booksellers for 63,000 francs. The consortium paid Balzac an advance of 50,000 francs and, in addition, a sum of 1,500 francs a month. He was to renounce all normal author's rights but was to be credited with half the profits. In 1836 the *Figaro*, which had come under new management, bought *Birotteau* from the consortium, to use it for the purposes of sales-promotion: 'All persons taking out a three months' subscription (20 francs) to *Le Figaro* will receive as a bonus *L'Histoire de la grandeur et de la décadence de César Birotteau*, perfumer, Chevalier of the Legion of Honour, deputy-mayor of the second *arrondissement* of the City of Paris, a new *Scène de la Vie Parisienne* by H. de Balzac. Two volumes in octavo, hitherto unpublished.'

Balzac to Mme Hanska, 14 November 1837: They are offering twenty thousand francs for *César Birotteau* if it's ready by 10 December; I have a volume and a half to do, and poverty has forced me to promise. I shall have to work twenty-five nights and twenty-five days. . . .

In fact, he already had first proofs of the book in the worn type that was used for the purpose, but it was destined to grow in all directions. Poverty had made him promise it; sheer creative urge made him expand it. *Birotteau* was a picture of Parisian commerce, first on the scale of the family shop, like that of the Sallambiers and the ironmonger Dablin, and then as it became when its centre of gravity 'had removed from the Rue Saint-Denis to advance prudently towards the Faubourg Saint-Honoré, where the large shopkeeper is no longer a *tradesman* but not yet a businessman . . . where the shop-fronts carry sign-boards and are bright with streamers; where the assistants have their meals in the back room and sleep in the attic; where the chief assistant, after ten years on probation, marries the daughter of the house: a hybrid phase of French economic life during which retail trading clung to its patriarchal habits while the monsters and prodigies of capitalist prosperity were appearing on the streets, the *Dames blanches*, the commercial banks and the public companies. . . .'* César Birotteau, a tradesman 'come up' to Paris, has established himself in the perfumery trade. He plunges into ruin when he abandons his craft to engage in speculation, the 'vice of the century'.

The change is also one of manners and morals. In Balzac's eyes Birotteau and his wife, their friends Ragon and Pillerault, and their chief assistant, Anselme Popinot, represent virtue, even if it is only a relative virtue. César knows perfectly well that his 'cephalic oil' does nothing to make the hair grow; he relies, when he first markets it, on the gullibility of the public, the discreet silence of scientists and the vanity of old men. Later he assists its sale with pseudo-scientific leaflets which are held by Judge Popinot to be 'a first step in knavery'. For this Balzac can forgive him. Business is business. But bankruptcy is another matter. To César, as to his author, it is an intolerable disgrace. Balzac's parents had ruined themselves in saving him from it. César Birotteau, with his bourgeois principles, is destined to be 'killed by the idea of financial probity as though by a pistol-shot'. Thus the novel is a study in morals, the picture of a world

*Maurice Bardèche

which Balzac knew from top to bottom because he came from it, a world in which 'invisible threads linked the Sign of the Reine des Roses with that of the Maison du Chat-qui-pelote', and also a philosophical study, inasmuch as it contrasts the tradesman's shop with the banking house, and old-fashioned 'honesty' with modern corruption, besides illustrating the power of an obsession, which in this case causes death to ensue from the very excess of happiness.

César's worst fault is that he is foolish, like his brother, the Curé de Tours. He naively trusts Nucingen, Claparon and du Tillet, just as the Abbé François Birotteau trusted the treacherous Troubert. He is incapable of foreseeing the ruin which his own vanity brings upon him, but he honourably reinstates himself at the cost of all his assets, instead of turning bankruptcy to profit, as Grandet or Nucingen would have done. In addition the story contains a 'Cato the Elder of the hardware trade', as Alain called him, in the character of Pillerault, for whom little '*père* Dablin' served as model: 'No fortune was ever more nobly earned or more legitimate or more honourable than his. He had never over-charged or gone out of his way in search of business.' This was true of Dablin, the 'great-hearted ironmonger' and Balzac's steadfast friend.

So we have on the one hand the traditional world of artisans and independent tradesmen, with its long-established, vigorous principles and customs, and on the other hand the rising and ruthless world of large-scale commercial bankers, discounters and usurers. The book is masterly, not only for the factual knowledge it contains (including Balzac's own bitter experiences as a debtor threatened with legal bankruptcy) but for the historic picture it presents and the simplicity of its construction. The curve of César's rise to fortune is completed by the curve of his rapid fall—greatness and decline. The climax of the first part is the costly and extravagant ball he gives to celebrate his Légion d'Honneur, and no doubt it contains echoes of the ball given by Dablin for the marriage of Mlle Pépin-Lehalleur. Balzac had written of this to Eve: 'Tonight I am going to a ball—*me*, to a ball! But, my love, I have to, it is given by the friend who has never failed me.'

Balzac evokes Beethoven for the expression of César's happiness, transposing the finale of the C minor symphony into visual images. At the very end of the book, when thanks to his own high principles and the devotion of his friends he is cleared of debt and his honour is restored, César recalls that last, triumphant passage and in doing so dies. 'The divine music shone and sparkled in all its moods, sounded its trumpet-call in the convolutions of that tired brain, of which it was to be the grand finale.' So great an epic of the bourgeois world, penetrating, precise and loftily conceived, had never before appeared in French literature. Yet there were moments when its author had doubts about it. 'I don't know what to make of *César Birotteau*,' he wrote to Eve. 'You will have to tell me before I shall be able to become my own audience and to read it. I feel profoundly disgusted with it and can only curse it for the fatigue it has caused me.'

And then he painted the other side of the picture in *La Maison Nucingen*—the art of making a fortune by putting oneself above the law. In contradistinction to the innocent and honourable César we have the financial tycoon who deliberately withholds payments in order to alarm his creditors into compounding for a lesser sum, the banker who dominates his world not by honourable toil but by astuteness. Nucingen rides the storms on the stock-market as a seaman rides a gale, knowing that prices rise and fall like the waters, and that the losses on the ebb will come back on the floodtide. Those who have understood this, ambitious men like Rastignac and du Tillet, grow rich, whereas others, like Beaudenord and Ragon, duped by the shifts of public opinion, are ruined. The tale is told in a private room in a restaurant, where four financial adventurers are dining together, Andoche Finot, Émile Blondet, Jean-Jacques Bixiou and Couture, a newcomer to banking but one who has already grasped the essentials. They cynically note that whereas a Birotteau dies of over-strain, a Nucingen acquires a barony. Blondet sums up in a saying of Montesquieu: 'The law is like a cobweb through which the big flies pass while the little ones are caught.' As for Balzac, different aspects of him are everywhere to be found in those two prophetic books. He has been Birotteau, he understands Nucingen, he would like to be Rastignac, and it is his spirit which brings Bixiou and Blondet to life. Was he not himself 'one of those intrepid cormorants born of the foam on the crest of the waves'? But his debts were crushing him. He feared to end like Birotteau, and compensated by creating Nucingen.

The year 1837 had been a very hard one. The immense task of revising and re-writing *Birotteau*, with its implacable delivery date, obliged him to work hours that were excessive even by his standards—with his feet in a mustard-bath as a precaution against congestion of the brain! He was utterly exhausted, his hair whiter than ever. On New Year's day he wrote to Zulma Carraud: 'Greetings to 1838 whatever it may bring! Who cares what trials may be concealed in the fold of its garment? There is a remedy for all things; that remedy is death, and I do not fear it.' When such thoughts assailed him he turned for refuge to Frapesle. He hoped to be able to work there, to write the second part of *Illusions perdues*, although in his weariness the idea of writing anything caused him to recoil. And he was sickened by the unfairness of the critics. He had produced one masterpiece after another, but they still refused to class him with Chateaubriand, Lamartine or Victor Hugo. They put him on the level of Eugène Sue, whose meretricious star was rising in the literary sky.

There was another thought in his mind. Why kill himself with this unrewarding labour when a great fortune lay ready to his hand in the silver-workings of Sardinia? He needed only to secure the concession, and liberty and wealth would be his. He was afraid to go to any banker for support, lest some Nucingen or du Tillet should steal the idea from him. He talked first to Major Carraud, who found nothing intrinsically improbable in the venture but was not prepared to share in it. The Major, Balzac wrote to Madame Hanska, was a man of inaction, one of those 'great mathematical minds' who accept life for what it is and, 'seeing no logical purpose in it, await death to be acquitted of their time'. In the end, to secure the funds necessary for the journey, Balzac had recourse to his two last resorts, Dr Nacquart and the tailor, Buisson.

Before leaving, since he was at Frapesle, very near Nohant, he wanted to see George Sand again. They had fallen out for a time over Jules Sandeau, but Balzac had finally come round to her way of thinking. 'He's an old man of the sea,' he said of him. Besides, Eve Hanska wanted to add George Sand to her collection of autographs. So in February 1838 he wrote asking for permission to make 'a pilgrimage to Nohant . . . I would not wish to leave without having seen the lioness of Berry, or the nightingale, in her den or her nest.' George Sand also did not like being on bad terms with a writer of genius and she responded with a warm invitation. He arrived there on 24 February.

Balzac to Mme Hanska: I reached the Château de Nohant at about half-past seven in the evening and found Comrade George Sand in a house-gown, smoking an after-dinner cigar by the fireside in a huge, lonely room. She was wearing pretty yellow slippers with fringes, fancy stockings and red pantaloons. So much for the general aspect. Physically, she has developed a double chin like a canon of the Church. She has not a single white hair, despire her terrible misfortunes; her swarthy colouring has not changed; her eyes are as beautiful as ever; she looks perfectly stupid when she is thinking, because, as I said after studying her, her whole expression is in her eyes. She lives almost exactly as I do. She goes to bed at six in the morning and gets up at midday, whereas I go to bed at six in the evening and get up at midnight. But naturally I fitted in with her arrangements, and during three days we talked from five in the evening, after dinner, until five in the morning, so that I got to know her better in those three long conversations, and reciprocally, than in the preceding four years, during which she came to see me while she was in love with Jules Sandeau, and later when she was with Musset. We met then because from time to time I visited her.

It was as well that I went to see her, because we compared notes about Jules Sandeau. I was the last to blame her for having left him, but now I have nothing but the most profound sympathy for her, as you would have for me, if you knew the person we had to deal with, she in love and I in friendship.

All the follies she has committed are titles to glory in the eyes of noble spirits. She was the dupe of [Marie] Dorval, of Bocage, of Lamennais, etc., etc. By the same token she is the dupe of Liszt and Madame d'Agoult; but she has now realized this, where that couple is concerned, as she has in the case of Dorval, for she is one of those people who are masterful at the writing-table but easily caught out in real life. . . .

The two great 'men', experts in feminine matters, talked through the nights of marriage and lovers and the state of women. Balzac believed he had converted George Sand and persuaded her of the social necessity of marriage. When he left Nohant he took with him the theme of a new tale, *Les Galériens de l'amour* (the story of Franz Liszt and Marie d'Agoult, which George Sand made him a present of, since she could not write it herself) and also a new vice—'She made me smoke a hookah with latakia; it has suddenly become a necessity to me. The change will enable me to give up coffee and vary the stimulants which I need in order to work. . . .

He found smoking a great aid to thought:

The most wonderful prospects pass and pass again, but no longer as illusions, they have acquired bodily form and dance like so many Taglionis, and with what grace! You know it, you smokers! The show improves on nature; all life's difficulties vanish; life is lighthearted, the mind is clear, the grey atmosphere of thought is turned to blue; but, strange phenomenon, the curtain falls on the opera when the hookah, the cigar or the pipe goes out. . . .

In fact, he needed no hookah to transform his hopes into certainties. The business of the Sardinian mines was to show him once again at grips with reality. It is a strange thing that a man of so much intelligence, so versed in practical affairs, capable of laying bare the financial stratagems of a Nucingen with the lucid precision of a prosecuting counsel, should have neglected even the most elementary precautions when he came to operate on his own account. The most subtle mind of his time, flawless in judgement where his fictions were concerned, he was never so in practice, but rather resembled those great lawyers who invariably mishandle their personal affairs. Yet there never was a venture which called more plainly for caution and prudence.

Guiseppi Pezzi, the Italian trader he had met in Genoa, who had started this hare in his eager mind, had promised to send him samples of the Sardinian ore. He had not done so, possibly because he had decided to keep the business to himself. In any case, where, exactly, were these mountains of slag? Balzac did not know. And possessing no technical knowledge, how was he to assess their value or that of the abandoned workings? He took no instruments with him; he did not know how to go about securing the concession, and he knew too little Italian to be able to obtain information on the spot.

In fact, he embarked upon another work of make-believe, a fiction, moreover, which he had already written. He had written it in 1836 for the *Chronique de Paris*, a novella entitled *Facino Cane*. The narrator in this tale falls in with an old clarinet-player who claims to be the last descendant of a Venetian senatorial family, and to know the hiding-place of the treasure of the Procurators, the hoarded millions of the Republic. But he is blind and cannot find it by himself. The narrator, thinking him to be mad, says nothing. Facino Cane picks up his clarinet 'and played with melancholy a Venetian song, a barcarolle for which he rediscovered his youthful talent, that of a patrician in love. It was something like the *Super flumina Babylonis* . . .

' "We will go to Venice!" I exclaimed when he stood up.

' "So I have found a man!" he cried, his face aflame.'

But Facino Cane dies after languishing for two months, and the narrator forgets about the Venetian treasure. Balzac the novelist thought Facino Cane mad; Balzac in real life let himself be carried away, as Cane had been, by the vision of untold wealth. It was no new phenomenon. 'He dreams of floods of gold and mountains of diamonds,' Théophile Gautier wrote. He employed clairvoyants to look for buried treasure. He claimed to know where Toussaint Louverture had hidden his booty after the Haiti uprising, and made the story sound so plausible that Gautier and Sandeau were talked into agreeing (at the moment) to buy pick-axes, charter a brig and set off secretly in search of it. It was all fiction: 'Need I say that we never unearthed Toussaint Louverture's treasure? . . . We had scarcely enough money between us to buy the pick-axes. . . .'

The narrator in Facino Cane never went to Venice; but Balzac went to Sardinia so ill-provided with funds that he had to make great haste. On 20 March he wrote to Zulma from Marseilles: 'Here I am on the verge of success, and let me tell you that you do not know me if you think I cannot do without luxury. I travelled five nights and four days on the top of an "imperial", drinking ten sous' worth of milk a day, and I am writing from a hotel where a room costs fifteen sous and dinner thirty. Yet if need be, as you will see, I can be unshakable.' He discovered in Marseilles that there was no direct boat to Sardinia and that he would have to go via Corsica: 'In a few days I shall have for my pains one illusion the less, because it is always when one is approaching the climax that one begins to lose faith. I leave for Toulon tomorrow, and on Friday I shall be in Ajaccio. From there I will see about crossing to Sardinia.' To his mother he wrote: 'I am in a hotel which would make you shudder, but with the help of baths one manages. . . .'

He was quarantined for five days in Corsica because of an outbreak of cholera in Marseilles. He spent the time visiting Napoleon's house, 'a wretched place', and reading *Sir Charles Grandison* and *Pamela* in the Ajaccio public library—'dreadfully boring and silly'. But he liked the country and its primitive inhabitants: 'There are no reading-rooms here, no prostitutes, no popular theatre, no society, no newspapers, none of the impurities which stand for civilization. The women don't like foreigners; the men pass their days strolling up and down and smoking. A state of unbelievable indolence. There are eight thousand inhabitants, great poverty, and excessive ignorance of current events. I am enjoying complete anonymity. . . .' He was, however, recognized by an officer and a student: 'How tiresome! I can no longer do anything, good or bad, without publicity!' Finally some coral-fishers took him over to Sardinia, with no other food than the fish they picked up on the way.

The journey to the mines was a rough one. There were no roads in Sardinia at that time, no vehicles and no inns. He had to go on horseback, although he had not ridden for four years. Virgin forests, gigantic oaks and nothing to eat. When at length he reached Argentiera he found that a Marseilles syndicate, acting in conjunction with Pezzi, had had the slag-heaps assayed, and finding that they came up to all Balzac's expectations had secured official sanction for the reopening of the mines. As in all his ventures, Balzac had seen clearly but failed in execution. The Société des Mines d'Argentiera was to bring its promoters the 1,200,000 francs he had hoped for; whereas all he got out of it was a loss of time and money. While the man of business, Pezzi, had been besieging government offices, the man of letters had been writing *César Birotteau*. The two vocations were incompatible, the one cancelling out the other. 'Do not scold me too much when you reply to this letter,' he wrote to Eve. 'The vanquished need to be comforted. I thought of you very often during the adventurous journey, and I imagined you saying more than once, "What the devil does he think he's doing?" '

He returned by way of Genoa and Milan, where he could count on the Viscontis' bankers. This visit to Milan was less agreeable than his first, but the kindly Principe Porcia saved him hotel expenses by putting a small room at his disposal where he could work in peace. Later he was to dedicate two of his finest works, *Splendeurs et misères des courtisanes* and *Une Fille d'Ève* to the Principe and the Contessa Bolognini. 'As you see, although the French are charged with frivolity and forgetfulness, I am Italian in my constancy.'

Splendeurs et misères des courtisanes was destined eventually to become a major work, but in 1838 Balzac had not thought of the title or the general plan. While he was in Milan, and a little homesick for the streets of Paris, he sketched out a first episode, *La Torpille*. It tells of the love of Esther Gobseck, a ravishingly beautiful girl in a brothel (nicknamed *torpille*, or sting-ray, because of her electrifying effect on men), for the handsome Lucien de Rubempré of *Illusions perdues*. She meets him on her day off, near the Porte-Saint-Martin, and falls violently in love with him. She leaves the brothel and lives happily with him for three months; but then she is recognized at an Opera ball, despite her mask, by some heartless young men who betray her secret. She tries to commit suicide but is saved by a priest who, realizing the depth and humility of her love, sends her to a convent-school to make a respectable woman of her. This narrative was to have appeared in *La Presse* in 1838, but Girardin was afraid of the reaction of his subscribers, who had already been shocked by *La Vieille Fille*. A prostitute in a convent-school was a bit too much! *La Torpille* was published by Werdet in the same volume as *La Femme supérieure* and *La Maison Nucingen*.

Balzac wrote only half of it in Milan, although his host left him free to work as he pleased. The truth was that he was not happy. Milan, where the Austrian Emperor was shortly to be crowned King of Lombardy, had less time for him than on his previous visit. The cloudless sky oppressed him, and he was homesick for the mists of France. He felt lost, and longed for his 'dear hell', the Paris of insults and ingratitude. On 20 May he had entered his fortieth year: 'I am beginning the year at the end of which I shall belong to the great and numerous regiment of resigned spirits, for I swore, in the days of misfortune, struggle and faith which made my youth so wretched, that when I reached the age of forty I would no longer fight against anything. . . .' At this crucial moment in his life he felt more than ever the need to be settled, to have a home of his own and live there with 'the woman of my dreams'.

But would he ever find her? The women who had sustained his youth were passing one by one. He had come back from Italy in 1836 to learn of Laure de Berny's death, and when he returned in 1838 it was to find that the Duchesse d'Abrantès had died. The poor lady's life had ended cruelly. After a few years of literary success she had met with reverses. Balzac had ceased to help her, and although she had been resigned to losing him as a lover she had hoped to keep him as a friend—and as a rewriter: 'My old friendship is not to be shaken. Heaven knows, old friendships and young loves touch the soul!' She had rented a ground-floor apartment in the Rue de la Rochefoucauld where she tried to establish a salon and where many of her friends visited her, among them Juliette Récamier, de Broglie and even Victor Hugo, faithful to the memory of the Empire. Théophile Gautier nicknamed her la Duchesse d'Abracadabrantès. For a time she managed a fashionable company of players for Comte Jules de Castellane, but she allowed too many well-to-do young ladies to join it, and the gossip columns talked about *la société des Polichinelles*.

The sad tale of advancing age and mischance ended in penury. Her publisher, Ladvocat, rejected her writings and refused advances. She had to move to a smaller apartment. The day came when her belongings were sold by auction to pay her debts, while she herself lay in bed with jaundice. She was moved to a nursing-home and put in the attic, since she had no money to pay for anything better, and here she died, at the age of fifty-four. Hugo, Chateaubriand, Dumas and Madame Récamier attended her funeral. They wanted her to have a tombstone in Père-Lachaise, but the Municipality refused the plot of ground and the Ministry of the Interior turned down the request for a marble slab, despite the touching verses which Hugo wrote in protest.

All this in Balzac's absence. At the moment of her death he was crossing the Saint-Gothard in fifteen feet of snow. Two months later he wrote to Eve: 'You will have read in the papers of the lamentable end of the poor Duchesse d'Abrantès. She finished as the Empire has done. Some day I will tell you about that lady. It will make a pleasant evening at Wierzchownia. . . .' So short a memory! The life of a mistress once ardently desired had become no more than a subject for discourse on 'a pleasant evening'. But he had never loved Laure d'Abrantès as he did Laure de Berny. The one had made use of him and the other had served him, and to the memory of the second he was always faithful.

To Eve, 15 November 1838: The spiritual is less satisfying than the physical; I am growing old, I feel the need of companionship, and every day I mourn the beloved being who now lies in a village graveyard near Fontainebleau. My sister, who so loves me, can never receive me in her home. . . . My mother and I do not agree. I shall have nothing but work to fall back on, unless I have a family of friends around me; and that is what I seek to attain. Alas, I despair of a good and happy marriage, although no one was ever more fashioned for the domestic life. . . .

For Balzac complete happiness in love was never to be more than a longing and a dream. His Dilecta, with her nobility of heart, her grace and exquisite manners, had given him many happy hours and much good advice—'But she was twenty-two years older than I, so that, if spiritually she was more than perfect, on the physical plane, which counts for much, there were impassable barriers. The limitless capacity for love that my soul contains has never found its full sustenance. One half has always been lacking. . . .' Mme Carraud was a noble spirit, but friendship could not take the place of love, 'the love of everyday . . . which causes one to take infinite pleasure in the sound, at any passing moment, of a voice or the rustle of a skirt in the house, such as I often knew, although imperfectly, during ten years. . . .' This was what Eve Hanska could give him, if she would believe in him; but she was mistrustful, she invented monsters, she made of him an imaginary being whom she scolded, lectured and accused.

Cara, I would like you to tell me what I have done to deserve the following phrase in your last letter: 'the natural frivolity of your character'. In what way am I frivolous? Is it because for twelve years I have laboured day and night to pay off an immense burden of debt inflicted on me by the insane mis-calculations of my mother? Because despite all my troubles I have not hanged myself, or blown out my brains, or flung myself in the water? Because I work incessantly and seek, by ingenious attempts which fail, to shorten the period of my enforced labour? Tell me what you mean! Is it because I avoid society, all other commitments, in order to pursue my purpose, my toil, my acquittal? Because I write twelve volumes instead of ten? Because they don't appear regularly? Because I write to you with passion and constancy, sending you a signed copy of everything, with incredible frivolity? . . . I beseech you, have no fear, tell me! . . .

Frivolity of character! It is as though a respectable citizen, seeing Napoleon turn left and right and all ways while he studies the field of battle, were to say, 'That man can't stay still; he has no fixed idea'!

Do me the kindness of going to look at the portrait of your poor mujik, wherever you have put it; note the breadth between the shoulders, the chest, the forehead, and say to yourself, 'That is the most constant, the least frivolous, the most reliable of men!' It will be an act of penitence. . . .'

The least frivolous of men, perhaps, but certainly the least easily satisfied. His life was given to an undertaking so vast that no amount of effort, even superhuman, could enable him to accomplish it. What did he want? He wanted everything. 'He was,' wrote Léon Gozlan, 'the human encyclopaedia by instinct and *par excellence*; he did not want any fact taken by itself; for him it was part of another fact, and that fact part of a thousand more. . . . Everything he wrote, articles, books, novels, plays, was but the preface to what he meant to write. . . .' So one might say of his life what he himself said of each of his works, that it was a preface to his life. That Sardinian treasure-hunt was to him no more than an episode in his search for the Absolute.

XXVI

Les Jardies

La vie n'est tolérable qu'à la condition de n'y jamais être.
GUSTAVE FLAUBERT

'A LITTLE HOUSE with the woman of my dreams . . .' While he was away the builders had completed the house, and Balzac described it in lyrical terms to the woman of his dreams. From the heights of Ville-d'Avray there stretched a superb view culminating in Paris, the 'dear hell', its smoky atmosphere shading the flank of the famous slopes of Meudon—'strangely magnificent and in ravishing contrast'. At the foot of his land was the stopping-place of the Paris-Versailles railway line, so that at a cost of ten sous and in ten minutes he could be in the heart of Paris, whereas from the Rue des Batailles it took at least an hour and cost forty sous. Because of this the property would always be of immense value: 'I shall live there until my fortune is made . . . and there I shall end my days in peace, renouncing, without any flourish of trumpets, my hopes, my ambitions and all besides . . .'

The house bore a black marble plaque with the name, 'Les Jardies', in letters of gold. In Balzac's imagination it was Marly, it was Versailles. To the less inspired eyes of his friends, and even to his own eyes when he opened them, it was a chalet with green shutters, a parrot-cage with three bedrooms one above the other, and with a highly inconvenient external flight of stairs dignified with the name of 'staircase'. 'A small, gloomy property,' Léon Gozlan called it. The land did not so much run down to the road as fall into it, its successive terraces tending to slide into the one below at every downpour. The retaining walls, built at great expense, showed an astonishing disposition to crumble. No tree of any size would root in that steep, ungrateful soil. Balzac had a notion of bringing timbers of aloe from Venice, those indestructible piles on which splendid palazzos had been built, but a sensible contractor managed to dissuade him. Gardeners spent months struggling, with ingenuity and gravel, to make the slippery top-soil less treacherous. The actor Frédérick Lemaître, when he was shown over the estate, carried a couple of stones to secure his foothold whenever they paused in their stroll.

But Balzac never slipped. Faith sustained him. The soil, he claimed, was the best in the world; famous vines had grown in it; the very steepness of the slope was an asset, since it caught the sun. He intended to build greenhouses and grow exotic plants, especially pineapples. Pineapples were then being sold in Paris at twenty francs each; he would sell his for five. Say 500,000 francs for the crop, deduct 100,000 for labour and expenses, and there you were with a profit of 400,000—'and not a word to write'. What bliss!

He went with Théophile Gautier to Montmartre in search of premises from which to sell the pineapples. The shop-front was to be painted black, with gold adornments, and the sign would read, in huge letters, ANANAS DES JARDIES. 'To Balzac,' Gautier wrote, 'the lacy plumes of those hundred thousand pineapples were already visible above their plump golden cones, arrayed in rows beneath huge vaults of glass; he saw them in his mind's eye, glowed in the warmth of the greenhouses and with nostrils passionately distended breathed their exotic scent; and even when he was back at home, leaning on the window-sill and watching the snow fall silently on that bare slope, he scarcely lost the illusion.'

The original dwelling at Les Jardies was a peasant's cottage situated in the same enclosure, about twenty yards from Balzac's villa. The Contessa Guidoboni-Visconti occupied it with her children. Balzac had equipped it with the best of his furniture and part of his library—a precaution against possible seizure. His own dwelling contained little besides a bed, a chair and a writing-table, but he wrote in charcoal on the walls—'Here a surface of Parian marble—Here a stylobate of cedar-wood—Here a ceiling painted by Eugène Delacroix—Here an Aubusson tapestry—Here a fireplace in Cippolino marble—Here a doorway in the style of Trianon—Here a parquet floor of rare woods from the Islands. . . .' On one shelf stood a row of volumes containing the progressive stages, manuscript and proof, of a single book, from the first draft to the final text. Not far from these Gautier noted a sinister-looking, black-bound volume. 'You can keep it,' said Balzac. 'It's an unpublished work, but it has its value.' The title was *Comptes mélancoliques*. It was a file of unpaid bills, tradesmen's reminders and summonses. Beside it were the *Contes drolatiques*—'to which,' said Balzac, laughing, 'it is not a sequel.'

He could still laugh 'with his Herculean joviality'. The 'melancholy accounts' would soon be settled; he was going to write plays. The theatre was not his natural medium; he had less talent for dialogue than for descriptive writing, character analysis and broad historical perspectives. But a successful play could bring in one or two hundred thousand francs, ten times as much as a novel, and he would soon master the technique. Besides, a play contained far fewer words than a novel and was soon written. He could knock off three or four, with a few friends to 'devil' for him, while still going on with his serious work.

He had plenty of ideas for plays. A whole page of his daybook, *Pensées et fragments*, was devoted to them. He had even roughed out one or two. There was a comedy to be called *Orgon*, a sequel to Molière's *Tartuffe*, of which the first act had turned out not too badly, and a drama of the early days of the Consulate, *Richard cœur d'éponge*, which was full of promising material. But since it was vital for him to produce something quickly he decided upon *La Première Demoiselle*, a drama of bourgeois life in the Marais which he had talked about to Eve Hanska, who did not much care for it, and later to George Sand, who was enthusiastic. The title was changed to *L'École des ménages*. His original idea, the conquest of the proprietor by his chief saleswoman, and the indignation of the family, seemed admirable. But when he came to write it the whole thing changed its shape. The Demoiselle, who was to have been a hard-bitten female Tartuffe, became a pure and tender-hearted young girl genuinely in love with her employer, and for his denouement Balzac had the lamentable notion of using a story told him by Metternich, about two lovers who went mad and did not recognize each other! The comedy of bourgeois life lapsed into deplorable melodrama. It was a great pity. If he had pursued his original idea it might have launched him in the theatre.

He brought as an assistant to Les Jardies a young writer named Charles Lassailly, whose talents he seems to have over-estimated. 'A big body dominated by a big nose. Forward march! The nose started off and the idiot followed.' Such was Ludovic Halévy's summing up of Lassailly, which may, how-ever, have been unduly harsh, because both Lamartine and Vigny thought well of him. In any event, he was horrified by his employer's habits of work. He would be got out of bed at one o'clock in the morning, served with a substantial meal and strong black coffee, and then Balzac, in his monk's robe, would march him into the study. 'Write this down—*L'École des ménages* . . .' Balzac would dictate until seven, roughing out scenes which Lassailly was to polish and complete. Such was life at Les Jardies. Like Borget and Sandeau before him Lassailly fled in terror. Ordinary men cannot co-exist with supermen.

Balzac's only genuine collaborator was the engaging Laurent-Jan, nine years his junior, whose real name was Jean Laurent. Tall, thin, bowed and bandy-legged, he hobbled along with a stick. 'His grey eyes darted flame,' and his mouth darted sar-casms. Professedly a black-and-white artist and a writer, he drew very little and wrote nothing at all. Gavarni remarked, 'Balzac kept him so as to be able to say, "I have a barren fig-tree at Les Jardies." ' The truth is that he amused Balzac and was loyal to him, Bohemian though he was. He had been one of the lively company, with Gozlan and others, who had feasted in the Rue Cassini, helping Balzac to forget his duchesses and 'let down his hair with pleasure and profit'. They were on terms of close famil-iarity. He used *tu* to Balzac, called him *chéri* and 'my loved one', and ended his letters, 'I press myself to your fat bosom'. Madame Mère bridled indignantly when addressed as *mon enfant* by Laurent-Jan. 'If he was talking to the Pope,' she snapped, 'he'd call him "my child".' But with all his quirks and his acid tongue he was the soul of devotion. He unobtrusively settled the bills that Balzac ran up at Frascati's and kept importunate visitors at bay. He offered to try to place *L'École des ménages* with the Comédie-Française, but by then Buloz had become manager and Balzac had nothing to hope for in that quarter. The piece was offered to the Théâtre de la Renaissance and refused, after long discussion. Yet it was not without merit. Gérard de Nerval considered that, in its bourgeois setting, it recaptured all the furies of the Atreidae. Balzac read it aloud on more than one occasion to audiences which included such writers as Stendhal and Gautier and other persons of distinction. He was not dismayed by its rejection, but noted without surprise that his career as a dramatist was proving as difficult at the start as his career as a novelist had been.

He finished *Le Cabinet des antiques* at Les Jardies, having begun it in Geneva. Like *La Vieille Fille* it was set in the town of Alençon, and Mlle d'Esgrignon was in some sort a pendant to Mlle Cormon in the earlier tale; Balzac enjoyed this mingling of parallel and contrast. It was in this story that he made use of his visit with Caroline Marbouty to the conservatories of Luigi Colla in Turin: he caused Diane de Maufrigneuse to visit an old judge, a lover of flowers, clad in a man's clothes and carrying a riding-crop. He never lost sight of the odds and ends stored away in his capacious memory, and could always lay his hand on the scene or incidents he needed.

His admirable preface conveys the theme of the story, the attraction of Paris for leading lights from the provinces:

Le Cabinet des antiques is the tale of impecunious young men, the bearers of great names, who come to Paris to meet with disaster—through gambling, or the desire to shine, or the allurements of Parisian life, or the attempt to increase their fortune, or through happy or unhappy love affairs. The Comte d'Esgrignon is the counterpart of Rastignac, the latter another type of provincial young man, but adroit and audacious, who succeeds where the former fails.

Then, being in a mood to write masterpieces, he embarked at once on the second part of *Illusions perdues—Un Grand Homme de province à Paris*. He brought into it the memory of his own beginnings, his own desire to shine, the cynical, needy hackwriters, the poisonous malice of a venal press. He had already begged Charles de Bernard for poems for Rubempré; now he applied to Delphine de Girardin, Gautier and Lassailly for more. ('I note in this,' wrote Alain, 'a kind of disdain which is in some sort professional.') Lucien's extravagances—canes, diamond studs, lavish repasts—were Balzac's own and led to the same disaster. But we must again remember that a good novel is never an autobiography. *Illusions perdues* is an account of the savage baptism of fire which every provincial undergoes who attempts the conquest of Paris. It was natural for Balzac to think of Le Poitevin, Raisson and Sandeau, as he did of Ladvocat, Canel and Werdet when describing the bookseller-publishers to whom Rubempré offers his wares. As for Lucien himself, he was drawn from a number of sources, including Sandeau and a young man from Grenoble named Chaudesaigues 'who came to Paris full of confidence in his talent and good looks, plunged recklessly into the fashionable world, became the lover of marchionesses and finally fell back to earth, penniless and near to suicide'. Living models were not lacking.

An examination of the book in manuscript shows more than one track which was later covered over. Finot's journal was first taken textually from the *Courrier des Théâtres*, and Finot himself was derived from Dr Véron, Amédée Pichot and Victor Bohain. But Balzac took care not to make his portraits too faithful. Blondet, Lousteau, Nathan and Rubempré were his own creations, more alive than the living. D'Arthez, the great man of the 'Cénacle', the literary circle, bore a resemblance to Buchez, the follower of Saint-Simon; but here again Balzac merged a number of real people into a single character, and Daniel d'Arthez is mainly the best of himself.

Illusions perdues is perhaps the finest of his novels. He was able to keep very close to his own life. Lousteau sponsors Lucien with publishers, as Latouche had done for Balzac; and Lucien's hovering between the 'Cénacle' and hack-writing was Balzac's own, as was his vague hope of uniting republicans and legitimists (Michel Chrestien and d'Arthez) against the self-seeking of the bourgeoisie. Coralie's love for Lucien, her death, and the passage in which her lover, seated beside her dead body, writes lively, popular songs to pay the funeral expenses, is deeply moving.

Meanwhile further novels were taking shape in his mind—*Le Curé de village*, *Qui terre a guerre a*, *Une Fille d'Ève*, *Béatrix*. Each of these was to become, as it has remained, a source of wonder and delight. The man knew everything. He knew the rivalries of Alençon, the undercurrents of Limoges, the separate worlds of the demi-monde, of journalism and book-publishing, the infatuations and repentances of women. He knew the great figures in the life of Paris and was finding it difficult to distinguish between these and his own characters. Which was real, and which fiction—Delacroix or Bridau?—Dupuytren or Desplein?—George Sand or Camille Maupin?—Gustave Planche or Claude Vignon? The real world and his works were joined by an umbilical cord that was never cut. Absolute master of the world contained within him, he needed only to survey his creation to select the protagonists of a new tale. Their past gave birth to their future.

That the choice should be determined by the private necessities of the moment, the requirements of a particular paper, the need to complete a volume, seemed to him natural and inevitable. He felt it to be a hypocrisy when a writer like Astolphe de Custine, whose inherited fortune permitted him to disdain the one he might have gained by his pen, spoke in praise of asceticism and the pride of Rousseau as opposed to the writers who commercialized their talents. Balzac replied that Rousseau's *Confessions* contain a lengthy account of the negotiations which finally brought him an income of 600 francs, and that Racine, like Molière and Boileau, had not been above accepting royal patronage. A writer in 1837, if he wished to earn a living, was obliged to take account of popular taste and the bookseller's convenience. An editor asks for a story of such-and-such a length, and the writer goes into his stock-room and comes up with *La Maison Nucingen*; but although this is all right for size and price, it contains matter which does not suit the policy of the paper, so he has to think again: '*Eh bien!* You who jeer at this state of affairs, do you think art loses by it? Art adapts itself to everything and fits in everywhere; in the corners of the room, at the back of the oven, in the segments of the vault; it can shine in all things, no matter what shape it is given. . . .' Chance is a good workman, as Leonardo and Michelangelo proved a hundred times over; a bare wall produced the Last Supper, and a block of shapeless marble the Chained Slave.

Balzac stated his position in the preface he wrote to a volume containing *La Femme supérieure*, *La Maison Nucingen* and *La Torpille*, published by Werdet in 1838. Things being what they were, a writer had to keep several works going at once, at the risk of not placing any of them. His brain was like a painter's studio, with, for example, a group entitled *Illusions perdues* in one corner. It was no use complaining because the group was unfinished; the publisher only wanted one volume. The second would follow in due course. If *La Torpille* had been slow to appear it was because editors were afraid of a story about a prostitute. That was why there were pictures in the studio with their faces turned to the wall. An artist without private means or patronage or an hereditary title (this was aimed at Custine) had to produce in order to live, and what did it matter if the work acquired a different shape when he came to take it in hand? If in *La Femme supérieure*, which he wrote on his return from Italy, there were many more male than female clerks, it was because he had had plenty of experience of the men but had to take more trouble with the women. *La Presse* was waiting for that story; the *Figaro* had paid 20,000 francs advance on *César Birotteau*, which needed revision; and he had to write a number of novellas and short stories to complete the *Études philosophiques*. We get a picture of the painter darting from one easel to another. But whatever Balzac might say, his work sometimes suffered under the tyranny of serialization. The daily public exercised its own censorship over fiction intended for the home. The readers of *La Presse* found *La Femme supérieure* too harrowing, and those of *Le Siècle* protested at the use, in *Béatrix*, of such words as *gorge* (bosom) and *volupté*. 'It's wildly funny,' Balzac wrote to Eve.

His methods of work did not change. His head was always teeming with subjects that could be jotted down in a few words. 'Human love leading to divine love' (this for a novel to be called *Sœur Marie-des-Anges*, which was never written); 'a worthy man, having ruined himself for his daughters, dies like a dog' (*Goriot*); and 'for *Scènes de la vie politique*, a minister who sacrifices his daughter, his son-in-law and his friends for the sake of a political manœuvre' (another unwritten work). Sometimes he repeated an idea but gave it a different ending. *Béatrix*, for example, is the story of the Comtesse d'Agoult, who abandoned her husband and daughter, and a brilliant worldly position, for the sake of Franz Liszt; and in *Une Fille d'Ève* Marie Vandenesse undergoes the same temptation but is saved by the adroitness of her husband.

With stories weaving through his mind like trout in an aquarium, he fished out the one he needed. Sometimes he could not bring it off at the first attempt, and then he would put it aside and go on to something else, to return to it later. *César Birotteau* was particularly obstinate, although eventually he wrote it with enormous speed. Or he might make an entirely fresh start, as in the case of *Béatrix*.

This was basically the story of Liszt and Marie d'Agoult, which George Sand had told him. His first thought was a novel with some such title as *Les Galériens de l'amour* (*The Galley-slaves of Love*); but he could not, for obvious reasons, stick too closely to the original. There were three people involved, the two lovers and Sand herself, the woman of genius who witnessed the drama and described it to him. How should he present them, and in what setting?

He started by setting the story in Paris, with an account of legitimist circles after the 1830 revolution. The Baronne Emma de Retzau, a young woman of good family, 'slender and erect, with a long, pointed face . . . pale blue eyes . . . a curved nose . . . the proud air of a princess, which well suited her . . .' (it is the portrait of Marie d'Agoult) falls in love with the writer Nathan (one of Balzac's gallery of recurrent characters, the friend of Rastignac, Blondet and Maxime de Trailles) and prepares to elope with him. But here that first draft ended (to be used later in *Une Fille d'Ève*). Balzac had decided upon another approach. He would make a fictitious Sand the narrator of the story, since she was better qualified than anyone to tell it—and indeed had only refrained from writing it herself for fear of offending Liszt.

Recalling his journey to Guérande with Laure de Berny in 1830, Balzac turned Sand's Château de Nohant into a Brittany manor-house. George Sand herself became 'Camille Maupin', a suggestive name, since Gautier had endowed his Mlle de Maupin with tastes attributed to Sand, and Camille is one of the three French christian-names which can be borne by either man or woman. Camille Maupin wears men's clothes, and loves riding and music. Her physical description, the small waist, the olive skin, the wonderful eyes and the air of vacancy at certain moments, is an exact picture of Sand, but so charming that it could not offend her. And Balzac gave her a lover, a noted literary critic named Claude Vignon, based on, but far sur-passing, Gustave Planche.

Guérande, an old fortified town, suggested a feudal society and so Balzac made it the home of an ancient feudal family.

The Baron du Guénic, who owed much to Lavater's *Physiognomie*, was an epitome of all Breton noblemen, a character seemingly more contrived than observed. As for the Baronne, she was Irish and partly derived from the Contessa Guidoboni-Visconti. Although she was older, but still a beauty at forty-two, both were fair-haired and pale-skinned, both had eyes of turquoise-blue and both were called Fanny. *Béatrix*, like *Le Lys dans la vallée*, affords an admirable illustration of the 'alchemy' of novel-writing. Although Balzac made great use of what George Sand had told him, no happening in real life can be reproduced exactly in a work of fiction. He re-organized the story, stressing certain lights and shades, heightening characters to lend them a wider significance, and bringing the episode into the context of its time by showing the antique world of Guérande in process of being destroyed by the modern world. And it can also happen to a novelist that, having reached a certain point in his work, he finds that life has not supplied him with all the material he needs. He can only put it aside until inspiration, or a chance encounter, enables him to finish it. *Béatrix* had to wait five years for her denouement, during which Marie d'Agoult and her fictitious double grew five years older. We shall see later how another woman came to be merged in the character, and how Calyste du Guénic, the simple-minded Breton who leaves his young wife for that perverse enchantress, has his 'illusions exorcized' and is brought home again by means of a benevolent conspiracy among his grandmother (the Duchesse de Grand-lieu), a priest and an adventurer, Maxime de Trailles. Balzac's company contained players for every occasion.

But wonderful though it is to carry a world in one's head over which one presides, godlike, selecting, arranging, disposing, there are still times when one has to come down to earth—to the slippery clay of Les Jardies. And here disaster was looming. Balzac's expenditure on the property in 1839 totalled 50,000 francs. He owed money, not only to all his friends, but to the portress in the Rue des Batailles, to the gardener Brouette (brought from Villeparisis) and even to the *garde-champêtre* of Ville-d'Avray. Léon Gozlan found him 'hiding in his garden like a hunted hare', afraid to show himself in the woods in case that humble functionary should see him! The *garde-champêtre* figured on the list of 'crying' debts—oversights, as Balzac called them—which amounted to 4,000 francs; and among the 'quiet' debts was the 10,000 francs which he owed Fanny Guidoboni-Visconti. His note of this is followed by the remark, 'To be repaid by the end of the year, *without interest*.' He later gave her the bound proofs of *Béatrix*, and the book itself was dedicated to her under the name of Sarah, which aroused the jealous misgivings of Eve Hanska.

But he still believed that the theatre would put everything right. Having decided to make a play of Vautrin, the character in the novels, he went to see Harel, the manager of the Porte-Saint-Martin theatre and coolly asked him to undertake to produce it, before it was even written. As it happened, Harel was in urgent need of a play, and he was as self-deluding as Balzac. Arguing that the public already knew the character through the success of *Père Goriot*, and that the part would be played by Frédérick Lemaître, which made success certain, he agreed.

Théophile Gautier, an honest and friendly witness, has described Balzac's methods as a dramatist. The man who re-wrote his novels ten times over did not write his plays at all. The day before he was due to read *Vautrin* to the company at the Porte-Saint-Martin he summoned Gautier, de Belloy, Ourliac and Laurent-Jan to meet him on the premises of the tailor Buisson, in the Rue de Richelieu, where he had a pleasant little attic room furnished with a blue-and-white carpet and tapestries on the walls. Gautier has given an account of the proceedings:

'So here's Théo at last!' he cried. 'Lazy and late as ever. You should have been here an hour ago. . . . I've got to read Harel a five-act play tomorrow.'

'And you want our opinion?' we asked, settling ourselves in our armchairs with the air of men preparing for a long session.

Perceiving from our attitude what was in our mind, Balzac said with perfect simplicity:

'It isn't written.'

'For Heaven's sake!' I exclaimed. 'In that case you'll have to postpone the reading for six weeks.'

'Not a bit of it. We're going to knock off this *dramorama* and raise the wind. Just now my arrears are pretty heavy.'

'But we can't do it between now and tomorrow. There wouldn't even be time to copy it.'

'This is how I've arranged it. You'll do one act, Ourliac another, Laurent-Jan the third, de Belloy the fourth and I'll do the fifth—and I'll read it at midday tomorrow, as agreed. One act of a play is only four or five hundred lines, and anyone can write five hundred lines of dialogue in a day and a night.'

'Well, if you'll tell me the subject and give me the scenario and let me know something about the characters, I'll get to work,' I said, not a little alarmed.

'Oh, Lord,' he cried, with a look of superb astonishment and magnificent scorn, 'if I've got to tell you what it's all about we shall never get it done!'

Needless to say, it was not done in time. The only one of the team to do any work on it was the devoted Laurent-Jan, who may have done more than Balzac himself. It was presented for censorship in January 1840 and at first rejected on moral grounds: the resemblance between Vautrin and the character, Robert Macaire, both notorious and successful crooks, and the fact that Vautrin is allowed to get off scot-free. But after a few minor alterations the permit was granted. The piece opened on 14 March in a hostile atmosphere. The gentlemen of the press were angry with Balzac because of the picture he had drawn of them in *Illusions perdues*, and he sought to exclude them by not issuing press-tickets. But his adversaries were in the majority. The first three acts were coldly received, and when, in the fourth act, Lemaître appeared in the uniform of a Mexican general, wearing a toupee like that of Louis-Philippe, there was a roar of protest. The Duc d'Orléans left the theatre, and returning to the palace woke up the King to ask him if he was prepared to tolerate this public derision. The play was promptly withdrawn, and Balzac, like Perrette in the story, was left with his overturned milkpail. He was haunted by that fable.

The failure of *Vautrin* was a severe blow to the whole Balzac family. Surville, already in low water and driven distracted by the canals he could not dig and the railways he could not build, became even more irascible and violent. His wife, when he abused her, would reassure her daughters by saying that he was in one of his 'bridge moods'; but although afterwards he would try to make things up, there was coldness between them. Poor ageing Laure, with the memories of her bright youth and missed opportunities! Fortunately her daughter, Sophie, was a consolation to her, and it must be said for Surville that he had much to contend with. He worked desperately hard, he was near to ruin, he was the son-in-law of Madame Mère and the brother-in-law of Honoré, not an easy position to sustain. Laure acknowledged his goodness of heart; but she had given up going to dances, evening parties and theatres, and was beginning to worry about her daughters' marriages. In short, she was growing more and more like Mme Bernard-François Balzac in Villeparisis.

Honoré was a cause of great trouble to them both. After the banning of *Vautrin*, Laure lent him sixty francs out of her modest monthly house-keeping allowance of five hundred. There would have been a terrible scene if Surville had known! But when his distress over that business made him ill she gallantly took him into her home, put him to bed and nursed him very well, even if he had to listen rather often to the words, 'I told you so!' Madame Mère wrote: 'You do not realize the effect *Vautrin* has had on me (apart from the money). There's the matter of reputation. He's done for if he does not make a brilliant recovery. . . .' They might have been back in Bayeux in 1820. The mother of the greatest living novelist was wringing her hands over her son as she had done in the days of *L'Héritière de Birague* and the *Vicaire des Ardennes*.

XXVII

Rearguard Battles

L'un des malheurs des hautes intelligences, c'est de comprendre forcément toutes choses, les vices aussi bien que les vertus.

BALZAC

IT IS NOT SURPRISING that Balzac, smarting under the rebuffs of critical opinion, which denied him the stature that was his due, should now and then have reflected on the apotheosis of Voltaire. To save an innocent man is surely as great an achievement as to create a master-criminal. In 1839 he believed he had found his own Calas affair. The case of Peytel attracted his notice because he knew the accused man. He had seen something of him in Paris between 1831 and 1832 when Peytel, then very young, had acquired an interest in *Le Voleur* in order to become its theatrical critic. Balzac had thought him vain and over-excitable but had found no other harm in him. After leaving Paris, Peytel had worked in lawyers' offices in Lyons and Macon and finally had set up as a notary in Belley. In 1838 he had married Félicie Alcazar, an 'undeniably attractive' young woman of Creole extraction with a passionate, uncertain temperament, whose family considered her 'false and dangerous'.

During the night of 1 November 1838 a Dr Martel, of Belley, was got out of bed by Peytel to attend to his wife, who had been fatally wounded by a pistol-bullet. They had been on their way from Macon in a carriage. Peytel's story was that the shot had been fired by his own servant, Louis Rey, and that when his wife was hit he went in pursuit of her attacker. He claimed that he always carried a miner's pick as a weapon of defence when travelling. He had used it on Louis Rey: 'I do not know how many times I struck him on the head as he lay at my feet.'

The police and magistrates did not accept this story. Public opinion in Belley proved very hostile to Peytel, a newcomer to the district. The preliminary hearing was tainted with political prejudice. The prosecution drew a highly-coloured picture of Peytel as a crafty and hypocritical individual who, after squandering his fortune in a life of dissipation in Paris, had married a plain but wealthy young woman in order to buy himself a legal practice. Balzac and Gavarni, who also knew him, could not credit this story. When he was sentenced to death at the Bourg assizes they visited him in prison, and Balzac, taking up the cudgels on his behalf, wrote a long memorandum headed *Lettre sur le procès de Peytel, notaire à Belley*.

He sought to draw a truer picture. 'Peytel received the education that all [well-to-do] families give their children. The family fortune amounts to 100,000 crowns. As a notary he belongs to the bourgeois class that is now nearly sovereign in France. As a young man he engaged in literature and journalism in Paris. Is it not a duty to defend him? . . .' Balzac went on to show, with the competence he possessed in such matters, that Peytel had had no need of his wife's dowry to buy a legal practice, since his family inheritance was intact in Macon. Further, Lamartine, the great Lamartine himself, had testified to 'the purity of his antecedents and his irreproachable private life'.

But Balzac's efforts were fruitless and may even have annoyed the Court. In his journalist days Peytel, under the pseudonym 'Louis Benoit, Gardener,' had written a piece entitled *Physiologie de la Poire*, with illustrations by Monnier, which was anything but respectful to the royal countenance—and this was something that King Louis-Philippe had not forgotten. Roger de Beauvoir wrote an unkind couplet:

> We must avoid, alas,
> Balzac seeking his Calas.

And Balzac's attire did not please the Bourg magistrates. 'My poor Balzac,' said Gavarni, 'why have you not got a friend, one of those stupid, affectionate bourgeois, to wash your hands for you and tie your tie? . . .'

Peytel was executed in October 1839. He was probably guilty, but for reasons less infamous than those advanced by the prosecution. He never disclosed the fact that his wife had been having an affair with the manservant (which may well have antedated the marriage, since Louis Rey had been in the service of her sister, the Marquise de Montrichard). In short, it had been a crime of passion, not a squalid murder for financial motives. Balzac wrote to Eve that Peytel could have saved himself if he had told the whole truth.

The circumstances were more than extenuating, but impossible of proof. There are noble impulses in which men will never believe. Well, it is over. Some day I will show you the letter he wrote me before he went to the scaffold. . . . He was a martyr to his honour. That which is applauded in Calderon, Shakespeare and Lope de Vega was guillotined in Bourg!

Balzac had given generously of his time, his pen and his money. Altogether the Peytel affair, including the journey to Bourg and the printing of the memorandum, cost him 10,000 francs—and, he said naively, put his work back by 30,000. And this at a time when he needed every penny he could raise. In June 1840 his total indebtedness (we have to keep account of that rising tide) amounted to 262,000 francs, of which 115,000 were 'friendly' debts, to his mother, Mme Delannoy, Dr Nacquart, the tailor Buisson and others, and 37,000 were *dettes tranquilles*, that is to say, not pressing, (for instance the money he owed the Vistontis). But there was at least one creditor who was anything but *tranquil*. This was Le Sieur Foullon, a landowner and species of Gobseck who had advanced him 5,000 against the rights in *Vautrin*, on extortionate terms. When repayment was not forthcoming he resorted, like Duckett before him, to every sanction provided by the law, including seizure of property. The old game of evasion began again at Les Jardies. The gardener, Brouette, told the bailiffs that the furniture in the cottage was the property of Count Guidoboni-Visconti. In Balzac's own house there was nothing worth impounding except a chipped Chinese vase and a few books. Accordingly Foullon put in a claim for the buildings themselves, and Balzac was faced by the prospect of hastily selling Les Jardies and going elsewhere. The Rue des Batailles was surrounded, and the furniture which he had stored with Buisson, in the Rue Richelieu, had already been sized by Foullon.

And Madame Mère was not being as *tranquille* as her son would have liked. She wrote to him on 22 October 1840. 'Today, my dear one, is my sixty-second birthday. . . . I started

the day with a prayer and a blessing on my children. . . . I pray
every day that Providence will sustain you in your struggle. . . .'
She had not been to see him for fear of 'an icy reception', but it
distressed her to be living on the charity of her son-in-law. Could
not Honoré give her lodging? The thought terrified Balzac. How
could he possibly work with his mother in the house? And he
had still so much to do. The more he produced, the farther off
did the final achievement seem. On one occasion he wrote to
Zulma Carraud: 'The end is coming into sight'; but a few
months later—'It's always the same, night after night and book
after book! What I am striving to build is so lofty and so
vast!' In truth, since he was trying to compete with the
Almighty he could not have hoped to complete the work if he
had lived to be a hundred.

And who, except Zulma, understood him? His relations with
the Guidoboni-Viscontis were becoming less cordial. Although
she had truly loved Balzac, the Contessa was growing tired of
this life of constant upheavals, unpaid debts, duns at every
corner. Moreover, Balzac himself seems to have been wearying
of the liaison. Fanny had never asked, or promised, fidelity. She
stuck to her principles and was in no way disturbed by his
affair with Eve Hanska, although she knew about it. But here,
too, a change seemed to be taking place. The correspondence
with Eve was falling off. Gradually the hopes so often disappointed were sinking into oblivion. Other women were appearing in Balzac's life. He could never resist temptation, and all
women, all living creatures, were grist to his mill.

In April 1839 he had received a letter in praise of *Béatrix*,
of which the first part had appeared in *Le Siècle*. The writer
declared herself to be a girl born in Guérande who had been
doubly interested in the tale because it dealt with her own
country and the heroine bore one of her own christian-names,
Félicité. Strange reasons, perhaps, for admiring a great novel,
but such readers are not uncommon. Balzac was happy to reply
because of the diffidence with which she wrote, as though over-
awed by the unapproachable great man. Upon learning that he
was laid up at Les Jardies with a sprained ankle she sent him
a piece of floral embroidery which he acknowledged as follows:

3 July 1839: Mademoiselle—I am still unable to walk, and

this painful circumstance will explain why I have delayed exchanging my poor flowers of rhetoric for your own charming bouquets, which express your delight in labour and resemble the work of an imprisoned fairy.

The sentiments expressed in your letter will surely excuse me in your eyes for being in the country and having fled Paris, which is fatal to certain spirits. I hope towards the end of this week to send the books to the address you have given me, if they are ready.

Since you follow the example of God, who bestows His gifts without showing Himself, I will tell you here what I would have wished to say to you in person—that I am touched by the feelings to which I owe your letter, and that in replying I make a distinction between yourself and the merely inquisitive correspondents an author attracts.

Your closing words, and what you convey by them, prove that there is indeed much poetry in your heart. True feeling is always wise, and although I am aware of all that I am losing, I think that you are acting rightly. But let me beg you to believe that I shall never think of Brittany and the beautiful country where you live without seeing your own mysterious face.

I have been the subject of calumny, but, although your godmother may in general terms be right, I beseech you to believe, Mademoiselle, that among—I will not say authors, but men— I am one of those who cannot but admire you wholly, even though I am not the object of what you call the romantic tendency of your nature. We authors, more than all others, know how rare is that noble frankness of heart which does not let itself be bound by convention. Reject, I beg of you, all bitter thoughts. I send you my thanks and the expression of my gratitude for all your consideration. . . .

The letters from this young woman were a curious mixture of truth and shameless falsehood. Hélène-Marie-Félicité de Valette was telling the truth when she proclaimed her noble birth, but not when she talked of her mother as being 'alive and at her side'. Mme de Valette had been dead for twenty-one years.

She also said that she was a Breton and unmarried. She had indeed been born at Rochefort-sur-Mer and educated at a convent at Vannes. But it was not true that she had never been married. The only child of a naval officer who had turned priest when his wife died, she had married, at the age of seventeen, a notary in his fifties, a widower and the father of an adolescent son. When she set about the conquest of Balzac, in 1839, she was thirty. Her letter-paper bore a coronet, and she did not care to be addressed as 'Widow' Goujeon.

Her married life had been short. She had married in January 1826 and lost her husband in the November of the following year. He had left her a quarter of his estate and a quarter-share in the income from his landed property, the rest to go to his son, with a proviso that if she married again—she was then nineteen—she would forfeit this. Not only did Helène refrain from mentioning her widowed state to Balzac; she said nothing of the fact that she had a lover and an illegitimate child, the son of the Comte du Moulinet d'Hardemare, born in 1831 and baptized Eugène: 'She treated the Comte as though he were her husband, having more esteem than love for him, and deceived him without compunction.' *

Moreover, she had another protector. The Baron Hippolyte Larrey, surgeon-in-chief of the Army like his illustrious father before him, and 'the most charming of men', was so devoted to her that the attachment endured throughout his life. In 1839 Hélène was living partly in Brittany and partly in Paris, where she had a permanent lodging in the Rue de Castiglione, a 'mere artist's garret'. At the end of that autumn she obtained Balzac's permission to visit him at Ville-d'Avray, but when she arrived there he was away from Les Jardies. She walked calmly into the house and helped herself to a souvenir: 'I was very conscious of the enormity of the "theft" I ventured to commit. But I was wild with joy, wild to the point of tears, at finding myself in the place it pleased you to create, and which you love. So you must forgive me, as one forgives those who take leave of their senses. . . .'

She seems to have gone off with Balzac's ink-stand, because she offered him 'in exchange' the one she had inherited from her godmother, Mme de Lamoignon. In letter after letter she recounted the mythical saga of her life. She had, she said, just got married, and she was distributing her 'girlhood belongings' among her women friends: 'Shall I be happier? Only God can tell. I do not leave my native countryside without regrets, although the only happiness I knew there came from you. This I shall find everywhere. . . .' So lofty an approach, when he was

*Maurice Regard

its object, could not fail to enrapture Balzac. Early in 1840
Hélène appeared to him in person, was generous in her offers of
financial assistance and not coy in other respects. By March he
was calling her 'Marie', an infallible sign, and had borrowed
10,000 francs from her which he promised to return after the
triumph of *Vautrin*. Being unable to do so, he made her a present
of the proofs of *Béatrix*, corrected with his own hand:

My dear Marie—Here are the proofs and the roughs of
Béatrix, the book which you have caused me to hold in greater
affection than any other, and the link which has joined us in
friendship. I never make such gifts except to those who love
me . . . and among all those on whom I have bestowed them I
do not know of a heart more pure and noble than your own. . . .
I send you a thousand tender messages. . . . *Addio cara*. . . .*

To Balzac, effusions of this sort, and gifts of manuscripts,
were simply part of the conventions of a love-affair. They did not
commit him. Nevertheless it pleased him to feel that he was
loved by an angel of purity, a daughter of the wild Breton
countryside. He informed Hélène a month later that he was
writing another play, *Mercadet*, which would redeem all the
losses of *Vautrin*: 'In October I shall repay everything advanced
against my plays. . . . I write this in haste to reassure you, my
treasure. Thank you for your letter, dear darling. . . .'

But the myth of Breton purity was soon to be dispelled. A
gentleman by the name of Edmond Cador (probably Roger de
Beauvoir, a journalist who wrote under a variety of names)
brought Balzac irrefutable and shattering evidence to the effect
that Hélène de Valette was in reality the Widow Goujeon, that
she had an illegitimate child, that she was being openly kept by
two rich men and that she had had a great many other lovers,
including Monsieur Cador himself. Balzac wrote to the lady, who
was spending the summer in Brittany, and asked for an explanation, to her great dismay:

Hélène de Valette to Balzac, Batz, 29 July 1840: Since I

*This letter, together with the proofs of *Béatrix*, is preserved in the Tours
municipal library, numbered 1742. Thirteen years after Hélène de Valette's
death her legatee, Baron Larrey, presented them to the town of Tours
because it was Balzac's birthplace, taking elaborate precautions to ensure
that 'Madame Marie X' could not be identified.

got your letter my life has been nothing but a nightmare, and when I answered it I did not know what I was doing. I had only one thought in mind, to assure you that I never loved M. Cador. Now you ask me for details and the truth about everything. . . . *I have never belonged to that man.* . . . He amused me; I put up with him out of fear and coquetry. He told me the first time I met him that he had been the lover of George Sand and that he had whipped her! I was appalled. . . . My dear, now you know as much as I do. . . . M. Cador is full of vanity. You might get my letters away from him, but you would not prevent him from talking. He would be delighted to find his name linked with that of a man like yourself. I don't want this to happen. I will accept the consequences of my culpable levity, but you, my dearest, must remain neutral. . . .

A mythomaniac, carried away by her own poetic fancy, she went on romancing about her life.

August 1840: I should have understood you better and had more trust in you. We will talk, since you are so kind as to be interested in my affairs. I will be prudent. . . . I wanted to preserve my independence. I am free for ten months in the year. I live alone. . . . My concern is for the most honourable man alive, who has made immense sacrifices of fortune and position on my behalf. . . . I am committed to him. I would not for the world cause him the least distress, and that is why I was terrified that the abominable E.C. would compromise me. . . . My feeling for the Comte is not all that I could wish it to be, and so I know that I must surround him with proofs of affection. . . . I did not want to tell you these things, but to be for you simply a vision—the untamed girl from untamed Brittany. . . . But this Monsieur Cador has spoken of me to you, he has told you about my child, and you have asked me to confide in you. Now you know the best and the worst about me. . . .

After all, Balzac himself had never been a model of fidelity, nor did he show any excessive regard for the truth. The two play-actors supplied a need in each other: Hélène was an agreeable travelling-companion, and Honoré owed her money; so why break it off? In April 1841 he went with her on a tour of Brittany, visiting Guérande, La Croisie and Batz, places he had last seen in company with Laure de Berny. He was hoping to finish *Béatrix*, of which the second half was still to be written.

In July he wrote to Eve: 'My state of mental and physical fatigue obliged me to spend a fortnight travelling in Brittany in April and the first few days of May. When I got back I was ill. I spent all the rest of May in a bath-establishment, taking daily three-hour baths to reduce the inflammation. . . .' There were unpleasant rumours concerning Hélène de Valette's state of health.

The character of Béatrix in the latter part of that novel is far closer to Hélène than to Marie d'Agoult. Balzac depicts her as an unbalanced, rancorous creature whose amorous propensities become suddenly harsh and spiteful. This seems to have been true of Helène. She was skilled in playing at love, but Balzac's view of her is summed up in the words of Maxime de Trailles to the Duchesse de Grandlieu: 'Love amounts to saying, "The woman I love is abominable; she deceives me and will go on deceiving me; she is a harlot; she reeks of all the roasts in Hell" and then to go running to her side, and there find the blue of the heavens and the flowers of Paradise. . . .' In 1841 Balzac dedicated *Le Curé de village* 'To Hélène'; but on a working copy which he revised in 1845 he removed this dedication. By that time they had quarrelled, and Mme de Valette was bitterly demanding the return of her 10,000 francs, with interest. A squalid little affair.

Meanwhile Zulma Carraud seems to have been entirely deserted. Not only did Honoré no longer go to Frapesle, but when she was in Versailles, so close to Les Jardies, he did not spare the time to pay her even a brief visit. The most generous spirits are always those worst treated, because they cannot bring themselves to complain:

You must realize that if I did not visit you at Versailles it was because I was absorbed in work which brooked no delay— I could scarcely even go to hear the *diva*! There is no pause, no bivouac, in my campaign. At the time I was writing the *Fille d'Ève*, *Béatrix* and the *Grand Homme de province*, in all five in-octavo volumes, and I was publishing *Le Curé de village*. You can imagine what my life was like. . . .

Zulma was more critical of Balzac's loves than of his work:

My dear, you are happy, I know; I have not wanted to say anything out of harmony with the pleasures of your present

life. . . . I knew you had published the *Grand Homme de province*
and I got a copy. It is a book that is all intelligence, but good
intelligence, simple and unpretentious; it is a long time since I
read anything of yours which gave me so much pleasure. . . . Our
paths have so diverged that it is not surprising if we cannot
clasp hands. . . .

Balzac to Zulma Carraud, November 1839: You think I'm
happy! My God! I have been in bitter trouble, intimate, deep
trouble which cannot be told. As for material things, sixteen
volumes and twenty acts written this year have not been enough!
The hundred and fifty thousand francs I have earned have not
brought me peace! . . . Les Jardies should have meant happiness
in many ways, but those hopes are in ruins. I don't want to lose
my heart any more, and so I am thinking seriously of marriage.
If you should come across a girl of twenty-two with a dowry of
two hundred thousand francs, or even one hundred thousand,
provided it can be used for my affairs, you must think of me. I
need a woman who can be whatever the circumstances of my
life require, an ambassador's wife or a general servant at Les
Jardies—but you mustn't tell her that, it's a secret. She must be
ambitious and intelligent. . . .

Zulma Carraud to Balzac, 2 December 1839: I do not know
of any girl with the qualities you demand, and, to tell you
the truth, if I did the words "I don't want to lose my heart any
more, and so I am thinking seriously of marriage" would put
me off. Marriage, in my eyes, has become more than ever a
serious matter. I have reflected on the *Physiologie du mariage*
and I so realize all the miseries of the married state, engendered
by the couple themselves, that I never attend a wedding without
feeling on the verge of tears. So you must allow me to take no
part in a transaction which may prove the disaster of your life. . . .

Why, knowing him so well, did she take his moods so
seriously? By the time she replied he had probably forgotten all
about the 'transaction', being absorbed in *Le Curé de village* as
well as in a number of short stories. Having long promised Eve
Hanska to write *Le Prêtre catholique* he did so now, but he gave
it a sombre background of love and crime (an echo of the Peytel
affair) which is not relieved by the light of the curé, Bonnet,
until after the first part. It is the story of Véronique Graslin, the

wife of the richest banker in Limoges, who, detesting her repulsive and overbearing husband, has a secret love affair with a pottery-hand, Jean-François Tascheron, who without premeditation murders him. Arrested and sentenced to death, he feigns madness to avoid compromising Véronique until the Abbé Bonnet, the curé of a nearby village, succeeds in touching his heart. He dies a Christian death.

The reader is told nothing about the love-affair but is the witness of Véronique's repentance. She retires in her widowhood to a country estate formerly owned by her husband, and under the guidance of the Abbé seeks to redeem herself by her works. The countryside is impoverished by lack of water and by bad farming methods, but with the help of a young civil engineer (in whom there is a touch of Surville) she brings about great improvements. Catholicism and philanthropic work are the saving of her, and she makes a public confession on her death-bed. In no other of Balzac's novels, not even the *Lys* or the *Médecin de campagne*, are his religious views so clearly manifest. He did not accept the literal truth of the dogma, but he did believe that the charity of priests like Abbé Bonnet could restore hope to souls believing themselves to be irretrievably lost; and that the priestly spirit, profoundly humble but overflowing with love, self-abnegation and charity, possessed the power to redeem even the most guilty, provided these were prepared to offer 'their collaboration in sacrifice'.

This high doctrine is sustained in *Le Curé de village* without any weakness of thought or style. Pictures of forest and plain, the splendours of the Limousin countryside, alternate with extensive technical descriptions of the joint work of Abbé Bonnet and Gérard, the engineer; and matters of irrigation and land-reclamation are gone into in such detail that the book has been called 'the *Georgics* of the polytechnician'. Like his country doctor, Balzac's village priest believes in the spiritual efficacy of action. 'Your prayers should be works,' he says. Here Balzac approaches the feeling of the end of the second part of *Faust*, which also exalts the spirit of the engineer. He was always closer to Goethe than he knew.

He himself made one further incursion into the sphere of action when he started the *Revue Parisienne*. The sorry lesson of the *Chronique de Paris* should have been enough; but in 1839

Alphonse Karr had started *Les Guêpes*, a small political-literary review which had at once sold 20,000 copies a month, rising to 30,000. Since Balzac possessed more ability than Karr, a greater capacity for work and certainly no less audacity, why should he not produce his own single-handed review? He set forth his policy in the Introduction—to depict 'the comedy of government' and disclose what was going on behind the political scenes; to tell the truth in the literary field, where criticism 'lacked sincerity'; and finally to print unpublished fragments of his own works. 'The Review does not merely promise the work of the greatest pens; it provides it.' In fact, it had only one great pen at its disposal, but this quill was at least the best cut.

The business manager was a man called Dutacq, who was responsible for production and distribution. The profits were to be divided equally between them. Balzac was hoping that the review would spare him the trials of newspaper serialization, where he now had keen competitors. Alexandre Dumas, Eugène Sue and Frédéric Soulié, less serious writers than himself, were better able to adapt their fiction to newspaper requirements. He was till regarded as one of the 'serial kings', but the sceptre was becoming shaky in his hand. The *Revue Parisienne* seemed to offer a way out.

Among its contents was an admirable tale by Balzac entitled *Z. Marcas*—a name which he had found when studying shopsigns in the Sentier quarter; an odd, outlandish name, but one that deserved to be made memorable, being easily pronounced and having the brevity which a celebrated name should possess. Moreover, it was rather like 'Balzac', and as for the Z, did not its shape suggest 'the stumbling and random progress of a tormented life'? Marcas, curiously enough, was a patriotic republican, although like Balzac he had a big, powerful head, a wide, spreading nose and an almost terrifying countenance relieved by dark eyes, infinitely gentle, calm, meditative and profound. Balzac had a particular esteem for him, as he had had for the character of Michel Chrestien: 'Like Pitt, who took England for his wife, Marcas carried France in his heart and loved her to idolatry. . . .' But it must be repeated that Balzac's admiration for Z. Marcas, the republican, did not conflict with his own monarchism. Both were opposed to the 'mediocracy' and the gerontocracy. The régime born of a revolution inspired by youth and intelligence, had thrust youth and intelligence aside. 'At this moment the entire younger generation is being driven into the arms of republicanism. . . .' The young had not forgotten the youthful deputies and generals of 1792, and in Louis-Philippe's Chamber there was not a single deputy under thirty. This was what Balzac and his fictitious character had in common.

He also wrote brilliant and explosive literary criticism for the review, unduly hard on the unfortunate Latouche and Eugène Sue, but wonderfully perceptive in the case of Stendhal, who was then very little known. He wrote of Latouche, 'A farrago of crimes and impossible ineptitudes is what you will find in the dreary non-magic lantern show entitled *Léo . . . Léo* proves that M. de Latouche cannot plan a scene or draw a character, or shape a contrast or sustain interest. . . .' The two men had not merely parted; they now hated each other. Latouche had plagued Balzac with too much advice, which is difficult to forgive; and Balzac had not followed it, which is unforgivable. 'Watch out!' he said to George Sand. 'You will find one of these days, without knowing why, that he has become your mortal enemy.' The truth is that Latouche liked his entries up to the moment when they started winning the races he always lost; but it must be admitted that the entries were very hard on the trainer.

Another writer whom Balzac attacked was Sainte-Beuve. Of his *Port-Royal* he wrote: 'M. Sainte-Beuve has had the petrifying idea of reviving this tiresome genre. . . . Tedium falls upon the reader like a thin rain which ends by penetrating him to the marrow. . . . But in one respect this author is deserving of praise: he does justice to himself; he goes little into the world and causes boredom only with his pen. . . . M. Sainte-Beuve's poetry always appears to me to have been translated from a foreign language by someone knowing the language only imperfectly.' *Port-Royal* was a fine book, and the criticism unjust.

The only excuse for this concentrated venom is that Sainte-Beuve himself had started it. He called Balzac 'a doctor of unavowable maladies': 'There is in him something of the over-familiar practitioner who creeps in from the back of the alcove, something of the seller of women's clothes, of the manicurist and of the entertainer. . . . This most prolific of our novelists has needed a dung-heap as high as a house to cultivate a few rare and sickly flowers. . . .'

But Balzac's articles on Stendhal are heart-warming. Here it was a matter of an established writer using all the weight of his authority on behalf of the author of the *Chartreuse de Parme*, which had been published ten months previously and largely ignored by the critics. 'I, who believe I know something of these matters, have just read it for the third time. I found it even better than at the first reading, and it gave me the feeling of happiness which is prompted by a good deed done. . . . M. Beyle has written a book which grows in greatness from chapter to chapter. In an age when noble themes are rarely found, after writing perhaps twenty extremely clever books he has produced a work which can only be appreciated by persons of true discrimination. Indeed he has written a modern *Principe*, the novel Machiavelli might have written if he had been exiled from Italy in the nineteenth century. . . . I know that my admiration will give rise to many pleasantries. . . .' To Eve Hanska he wrote: 'Beyle has just published what is to my mind the finest book that has appeared in fifty years.'

He knew Stendhal personally, having first met him in 1830 in the studio of the painter Gérard. When Stendhal, or Henri Beyle, was posted to the Consulate at Città Vecchia in 1840, he wrote to Balzac: 'I may confess to you now that when I read that astonishing review, such as no writer has ever written about another, I burst out laughing. Whenever I came upon a particularly warm word of praise, and they were frequent, I thought of my friends' expressions as they read it.'

Sainte-Beuve in 1857, fifteen years after Stendhal's death, was still amazed at 'the importance attached to his novels, which always fail although there are good things in them, and which on the whole are detestable. . . .' But two men had seen the truth about Stendhal, Goethe (in his *Conversations with Eckermann*) and Balzac; and the latter's gesture was the more magnanimous in that Stendhal, in his account of Waterloo, had successfully done what Balzac had dreamed of doing for ten years—in *La Bataille*, the Napoleonic novel he never wrote. It is moving to think of those three great men, so different in character, saluting each other above the heads of lesser men.

The *Revue Parisienne*, alas, died young, after only three issues, and the partners shared what was, in the event, only a trifling loss. Once again Balzac had failed in publishing, as he had in business and politics. And his love-affairs were in no happier state. His *Etrangère*, so far away, had almost ceased to write to him, and he reproached her for her neglect:

It is more than three months since I heard from you. . . . Oh, I find that you have turned out to be very petty, and it makes me realize how worldly you are. You didn't write because my own letters became infrequent. That was because I did not always have the money to frank them and did not want to tell you. Yes, my state of need went as far as that, and further. It is dreadful and sad, but it is true, as true as the Ukraine, where you are. Yes, there have been days when I proudly ate a roll of bread on the boulevards. . . . May God forgive her, for she *knows* what she does! . . .

She reproached him in return with Fanny Visconti and the dedication of *Béatrix*, 'A Sarah'. He insisted that there was nothing in it:

The friendship which I told you about, and with which you have mocked me in the matter of the dedication, is not what I expected. English prejudices are terrible, and they destroy everything that is necessary to the artist, all ease of conduct, all abandon. I realize more than ever how well, in very few words, I summed up the women of that country in the *Lys*. . . .

We may take this with a grain of salt; but the fact remained that both parties to that affair were tiring. The 'untamed daughter of Brittany' had turned out to be a tissue of lies, and Eve was remote and her husband seemingly immortal. Nothing was going well. Honoré was forty. Forty years of tribulation: 'I sigh for the promised land of a happy marriage, weary as I am of wandering in this arid desert, blazing with sun and full of Bedouins.' He talked of 'taking his bones to Brazil, in a mad enterprise'. He had striven for money, women and renown; but he had no money, the women were failing him and fools cast doubt upon his fame:

I shall burn all my letters and papers and leave nothing but my furniture and Les Jardies, and I shall set off after entrusting such small things as I value to the devotion of my sister. She will be a dragon in guarding them. I shall leave someone in charge of my literary works with full power of attorney, and go in search of the fortune I lack. Either I shall come back enormously rich or no one will ever know what happened to me. The venture is one that has been planned with the utmost care, and it will be carried out this winter, resolutely and without delay. My work will never pay my debts. I have to adopt other means. . . .

But in fact it was no more than another fiction, that might have been called *Voyage au Brésil*—like so many others, never to be written.

XXVIII

The Secret House

*Un écrivain ne confie tout ni à ses journaux intimes, ni à
sa correspondance; seules ses créatures racontent sa véritable
histoire, celle qu'il n'a pas vécue, mais a souhaité de vivre.*

FRANÇOIS MAURIAC

LIFE AT LES JARDIES was becoming impossible. Despite
the sturdy backing of his lawyer, Maître Gavault, Balzac failed
in his struggle to gain time. His principle creditors, especially
the remorseless Foullon, were pressing him hard while the small
fry, Brouette the gardener, the tradesmen and the gamekeeper,
patiently waited. The rich it was who pursued him without
mercy. But Balzac still had a trick up his sleeve. He had once
written a short story in which the dandified Maxime de Trailles
says blandly to a creditor: 'If you can extract the amount of
your debt from me, Monsieur, I shall be grateful to you. You
will have taught me what further precautions I need to take. . . .'

Like Maxime, Balzac regarded the tussle between debtor and
creditor as a state of war without quarter. Acting on Gavault's
advice, he went into liquidation and sold Les Jardies at a valuation price. It fetched 17,550 francs, although in building,
terracing and cultivation it had cost him 100,000. But the
purchaser, an architect named Claret, was his own proxy. The
sale was a fiction. His creditors were forced to compound for
this meagre sum and Balzac secretly remained the owner of the
property.

He had written two years previously to Eve: 'Thus Monsieur
de Balzac, aux Jardies, à Sèvres, is and will long remain my
address. I hope to end my days there in peace.' But in November
1840 everything was changed: 'Write to me as follows: "Monsieur de Breugnol, Rue Basse no. 19, à Passy, près de Paris." '
Passy was then a village on the outskirts of Paris, known for its
thermal springs and the charming estate and sugar-refinery of
Baron Delessert. This new arrangement had many advantages.

The house, discreetly tucked away on the steep slope running down to the Seine, was nearer to Paris than Les Jardies; it was rented under another name, and it had a double entrance. The financier who built it had later added an annexe on the lower side, so that the original ground floor, on the level of the Rue Basse, became the second storey when approached from the garden. The stable yard, on a lower level still, gave on to the steep and narrow Rue du Roc, and Balzac had access to it by means of a private stairway from his apartment. Nothing could have suited him better. If any bailiff called at the Rue Basse he could escape down the Rue du Roc to the river-embankment, whence a *patache*, an unsprung passenger-omnibus, would convey him to the Palais-Royal.*

Félix Solar, the editor of the newspaper *L'époque*, has left us an account of how he visited Balzac to discuss a serial. He was given a password. At the Rue Basse he had to ask for Mme de Breugnol. Unlike the 'Widow Durand' of the Rue des Batailles, this lady did exist. She was Louise Breugnol, a native of the Ariège, now aged about forty; an energetic and intelligent woman of peasant stock who seems to have made it her business in life to look after unmarried writers of mature years. Before going to Balzac, to whom she was recommended by Marceline Desbordes-Ralmore, she had been housekeeper and probably more to Latouche. Solar describes her as having a plump, placid face like that of a nun. A come-down, no doubt, after the great ladies Balzac had known, but he was tired of difficult women and hoped for peace with this one, whom Marceline nicknamed 'Terre-neuve' or Newfoundland. Balzac added a 'de' to her name, with the fondness for aristocratic style which he inherited from his parents.

She played a far larger part in Balzac's life than has been generally supposed. Besides running the house, in which he was ostensibly only a guest, she visited printers, publishing houses and newspaper offices on his behalf, and was shrewd in negotiating contracts. And she satisfied his physical needs. He

---

* The Rue Basse is now the Rue Raynouard, and no. 19, preserved as the Maison de Balzac, has become no. 47. The Rue du Roc has become the Rue Berton, but the courtyard of the Maison de Balzac (24 rue Berton) still retains its carriage entrance, all that remains of what was once a farm in the village of Passy.

even travelled with her, as she recalled ten years after his death in a letter to her lawyer. She mentions a visit to Baden-Baden, where she had last been in company with the great man: 'I heard the people around me saying, "Have you seen him? . . . I've seen him. . . . There he is!" Poor dear, he was annoyed by their importunities, but I was young and proud of my happiness. I felt terribly sad in Baden-Baden when I went to look at the house we had nearly rented, thinking to end our days there. . . .' Louise 'de' Breugnol was long devoted to Balzac, who showered on her the promises with which he was so lavish; she believed that she was to be his mistress-housekeeper for life.

It was she who showed Solar into Balzac's work-room:

. . . the first thing I saw was an enormous bust of the author of the *Comédie humaine*, a magnificent piece of work in the finest marble, standing on a pedestal in which there was a clock.

A glass-paned door, giving on to a small garden planted with meagre clumps of lilac, lighted the room, of which the walls were covered with pictures without frames and frames without pictures. There was a bookcase opposite this door containing, in a disorderly array, *L'Année litteraire*, *Le Bulletin des lois*, *La Biographie universelle* and Bayle's dictionary. To the left was another bookcase which seemed to be reserved for his contemporaries. I noticed Gozlan, between Alphonse Karr and Madame de Girardin.

In the middle of the room was a *small* table, the writing-table no doubt, on which lay a single volume—a French dictionary.

Balzac, clad in a voluminous monk's robe which had once been white, had a duster in his hand and was lovingly wiping a cup of Sèvres china. . . .

Balzac presently decided that, since his mother was now wholly dependent on him, it would be more economical for her to live under the same roof, whatever the disadvantages:

To Laure Surville: Tell Mother that she will have to leave her feather-bed, her clock, her candlesticks, two sets of sheets and her personal linen with you; I will have it all collected on 3 December. . . . If she chooses she will be very happy; but tell her that one must go to meet happiness and not frighten it away. She will have a hundred francs a month for herself, someone to keep her company, and a servant. She will be looked after in the way that best suits her. Her bedroom is as elegant as only I can make it. It has a Persian carpet which was in my own room in the Rue Cassini. . . .'

But despite good intentions on both sides, the experiment lasted only six months. There could be no peaceful co-existence between Mme Balzac and Mme Breugnol. The unequal humours of Madame Mère 'would drive any man mad, even if he ran no risk of it from the multiplicity of his ideas, his labours and his troubles'. She herself became anxious to get away, and she left, probably, in July 1841.

Mme Balzac to Honoré: When, my dear Honoré, I agreed to come and live with you, I believed I could do so happily. I soon realized that I could not endure the strains and daily tempests of your life, but I bore it, nevertheless, so long as I thought I was the only one to suffer. When I perceived from your coldness that my presence was tolerated only from necessity, and that far from being agreeable to you I was in a fair way to displeasing you, my position became even more painful! The situation caused me to utter words which hurt you. From that moment I resolved to leave your home. The truth is that old people cannot mix with the young! . . .

Mme Balzac to Laure Surville: I want to tell you again that I am blaming no one. Madame de Brugnole [*sic*] is a good woman. If she has failings, they are not intentional. She is the soul of honesty and delicacy. I yield my place to her without fear. She loves Honoré and will look after him well. . . . I think Madame de Brugnole will never be a danger to Honoré. The poor woman has had many troubles. . . . I assure you, she is to be pitied, and I hope that Honoré will make her life secure as soon as he can do so. It will be only fair, because she curbs his spending and restrains him from many follies. . . .

Madame Mère's mistake had been that she sought to play a part in her son's life. But, as he repeatedly told her, he had no life other than his work: 'To work is to get up at midnight, write till eight, breakfast in a quarter of an hour, work till five, dine, and start again at midnight! Out of these labours come five volumes in forty days!'

As for the volumes, at the time he was working simultaneously on a number of novels and novellas, putting them aside and coming back to them. The ones principally mentioned in his letters are the *Mémoires de deux jeunes mariées*, *La Fausse Maîtresse*, *Ursule Mirouët*, *La Rabouilleuse*, *Une Ténébreuse Affaire*. There are super-writers, just as there are supermen. Balzac was a super-novelist. His stock of material was inexhaustible; he accumulated and re-shaped it over the years. For example, *La Succession*, which figured in his programme as far back as 1833, for a time under the title of *Les Héritiers Boisrouge*, gave birth, when he was in the Rue Basse, to two novels—*La Rabouilleuse* and *Ursule Mirouët*.

Having decided upon a subject, he would place it in a setting which he knew well and people it with characters already conceived in his mind. *La Rabouilleuse* is situated in Issoudun, a town he had come to know during his visits to Frapesle. At the time of the Restoration the inhabitants had been terrorized by a gang of wastrels and half-pay officers known as the 'Chevaliers de la Désœuvrance' (the Knights of Idleness). But if he was to win the reader's interest in this grotesque crew, Balzac needed to include an outstanding character among them. He had only to look in his puppet-box to find what he wanted, a monster of outrageous energy, Philippe Bridau, the brother of a painter, Joseph Bridau. The other principal characters are Philippe Bridau's uncle, '*le bonhomme* Rouget', an elderly, amorous bachelor; Flore Brazier, '*la Rabouilleuse*,'* who physically enslaves him; and her lover, a scamp called Max Gilet.

Colonel Philippe Bridau comes to Issoudun to claim an inheritance; he kills Max Gilet in a duel, takes Flore away from his uncle, subdues both the old man and the girl, and robs his own mother and brother; but he so abuses his strength that he fails on the verge of success, 'because he goes too far'. To all this is added the circle of painters and writers who are friends of Joseph Bridau, and the actresses and strumpets at the beck and call of Philippe (characters already used by Balzac). The extravagant mixture had a success which astonished even the author. He had been afraid that the 'terrible tale', containing no element of tenderness, would be found objectionable. In the event the violence of Philippe, the senile collapse of Rouget, the billowing of Flore and the atmosphere of powerful sensuality proved much to the public taste.

---

* *A rabouilleur* (dialect) is someone who stirs the waters of a stream for the purpose of netting fish. *The Seductress* might serve as an English title. *Trs.*

Balzac himself preferred *Ursule Mirouët*, another story of a will, with elements of the telepathy and occultism in which he delighted to believe. A certain Dr Minoret learns at a distance, through a clairvoyant, of the love of his ward for a handsome young neighbour, and at the same time of her immaculate purity. He dies leaving a will intended to provide for her future. But one of the beneficiaries, the postmaster of Minoret-Levrault, fraudulently gains possession of his fortune. The dead man appears to Ursule and denounces the crime; the villain, a huge, bull-necked man, wastes away and dies when he realizes that his guilt is known, and it ends in restitution and marriage. Despite the improbability of the tale it is so solidly planted in real life—family relationships, details of the postal service, descriptions of a garden ('*Ursule Mirouët* is a story of the open air,' wrote Alain)—that disbelief is suspended. 'Balzac's improbabilities are more often probabilities which our own insufficiently penetrating gaze, less penetrating than the eyes of genius, have failed to discern. In the same way, in another field, phenomena which science can now account for were formerly only glimpsed by exceptionally gifted minds, or by seers.'* An act of faith is required; but Balzac claims and deserves it.

Une Ténébreuse Affaire was born of his youthful memories. His parents had heard the story of the senator, Clément de Ris, who was mysteriously kidnapped during the Consulate, from General Pommereul; and the Duchesse d'Abrantès, who knew all about the business, must have filled in the details for Balzac. Fouché's police had pretended to get to the bottom of the crime, and three young aristocrats had been executed, although they were undoubtedly innocent. As to the reason for the kidnapping, many people believed that the police themselves had rigged the whole affair, in the hope of securing certain documents which would have proved that Clément de Ris was involved with Pichegru and others who, at the time of Marengo, were plotting to overthrow Bonaparte if he was defeated. The episode was a novel in itself, but Balzac wanted a romantic element. To give his young aristocrats, the twin brothers Paul-Marie and Marie-Paul de Simeuse, a motive for the kidnapping, he caused Malin de Gondreville (the Clément de Ris of the

---

* The words are those of Marcel Bouteron, written on the margin of a manuscript entitled *Aimer Balzac* which Claude Mauriac had shown him.

story) to have secured possession of their estate, confiscated when they left the country at the time of the Revolution. To the brothers he is an usurper, and this explains the bitterness of all those who love and serve them, in particular the estate-manager, Michu, who is eventually guillotined. We are back in the atmosphere of *Les Chouans*, the horses galloping in the night, the sallow tinge of the sinister Corentin. It is history on the level of the actors, as obscure and baffling as a battlefield to the rank-and-file. Here and there we are afforded a glimpse of the men who know what it is all about—Napoleon before Jena, and, at the very end, the Minister, Henri de Marsay, who in a few sentences dispels the thick fog by which the affair is still enveloped. Behind the scenes of the drama of love and fidelity powerful interests are at work, those of the profiteers under the Revolution, who want to hang on to the emigrés' estates. History dictates the course of fiction, and in the words of Alain we see in this corner of the provinces 'how the Empire gained accept-ance, less by force than by the order it created and the per-manence it promised'. Stability inspires fidelity.

In *Une Ténébreuse Affaire* Balzac was again propounding the only politics in which he really believed, the politics of Nature, those dictated by the natural instincts of man. In his *Mémoires de deux jeunes mariées* he reaffirmed his ideas on marriage and took a hard look at 'romance'. It contrasts the lives of two girl-hood friends, Louise de Chaulieu and Renée de l'Estorade, one of whom chooses a life of passion, the other a life of orthodoxy. Renée makes a 'marriage of reason' with a man whom life has dealt hardly with, a good man but not easy to love. Yet a 'reasonable love' grows between the pair, based on conven-tional morality, the physical, economic and political links that unite them, their affection for their child, their common interests and the avoidance of excessive demands. The wife transforms her husband, bringing out the best in him. It is no wildly passionate love, but it is happiness, if we are prepared to agree, with Renée, that the secret of a successful marriage is contained in the words 'acceptance' and 'devotion'. Louise de Chaulieu, on the other hand, makes a love-match with a mysterious Spaniard, a marriage that achieves such heights of physical rapture that in the end the over-passionate woman destroys her husband. She remarries and finally herself commits suicide in a fit of insane jealousy. The stories are told in the letters exchanged by the two women, some of which were written by Laure Surville.

The moral of the tale is, of course, that family ties and common interests are the mainstay of marriage; but this did not prevent Balzac from writing to George Sand: 'Don't worry, we hold the same views. I would sooner be killed by Louise than live a long life with Renée.' It can certainly be said of him that in his own life he looked for passionate love, but is it altogether true? He would never have let Louise kill him. His relationship with Laure de Berny was based on common interests as well as passion; she was involved in his work, his struggles, even his business affairs. Marie du Fresnay, Fanny Visconti and Hélène de Valette were light loves rather than affairs of true passion, and he said more than once to Caroline Marbouty that he regarded love, if it was not physical, as a game of no importance. What he had longed for since 1833 was marriage to Eve Hanska and his unequivocal acceptance by the society of his time, which neither his birth nor his genius had procured for him. His life did not contradict his beliefs; but he never achieved the kind of life he really desired, which would have been in accordance with them.

There were two quite different men in Balzac: one the fat man seeming to exist in the everyday world, quarrelling with his mother and sister, hiding from the duns, pursuing a love-affair by correspondence with a Polish countess while at the same time he was living with a mistress-housekeeper; and the other, the creator of his own world, the lover of white shoulders and bright eyes whether they belonged to actresses or duchesses, the man of most delicate understanding and sensibility who lived sumptuously regardless of financial considerations. The human Balzac endured the members of his own bourgeois family while the Promethean Balzac mingled with the great families he had himself created. Involved as he was with the creatures of his own invention, he had no time to worry about others. He was not present at the death of Laure de Berny or Laure d'Abrantès, although he had loved both during his terrestial moments; but he watched lovingly over the dying hours of Henriette de Mortsauf, Esther Gobseck and Coralie, the daughters of his genius. He might seem graceless and heedless in the real world; but he was all tenderness and passion in his own, the only world in which he truly believed, and in which his heart and spirit were actively and intensely engaged.

What is astonishing is that the human Balzac, the hermit of Passy, who could turn out a novel in twenty days, living without sleep in a sea of proofs and printer's ink, still found time to escape down the narrow streets and see something of the world. On 15 December 1840, he watched the remains of Napoleon being conveyed in state to the Invalides:

The banks of the Seine were black with people all the way from Le Havre to Pecq, and they went on their knees when the boat passed. It was greater than any Roman triumph. He is recognizable in his sepulchre: the flesh is white, the hand eloquent. He was the man of marvels and Paris is the city of miracles. In five days a hundred and twenty statues were erected, seven or eight of them superb; a hundred triumphal columns, urns twenty feet high and stands for a hundred thousand spectators. The Invalides was hung with blue velvet embroidered everywhere with bees. My own embroiderer said in explanation: 'In a case like this, Monsieur, everyone is an embroiderer.'

Balzac must have been very happy that day, with his passionate love of Napoleon—and of embroidery.

In March 1841, he spent a happy evening in the drawing-room of Delphine de Girardin, with Lamartine, Hugo, Gautier and Karr: 'I hadn't laughed so much since the maison Mira-baud.' In June he attended the ceremonial induction of Victor Hugo to membership of the Académie. Hugo made a majestic entry, his great forehead well to the fore, but Balzac thought nothing of his speech. 'The poet deserted his supporters,' he wrote to Eve. 'He deserted the older branch and sought to justify the Convention. His speech was a bitter disappointment to his friends.'

Balzac himself had long aspired to join that illustrious com-pany, the Académie. He had been saying since 1836 that he meant to batter down its doors with cannon fire, and he had counted the profit that would accrue—the 2,000 francs annual salary, the 6,000 from the Dictionary Committee, the life-peerage which (he assumed) would naturally follow. In 1839 he had had his name put forward, but had withdrawn it in favour of Hugo, who had called to see him in Les Jardies. The story of that visit is worth repeating.

Balzac was taking the air in the steep, slippery garden, and Hugo walked with him, too intent on keeping his balance to say anything, until they came to the single walnut-tree.

'A tree at last!' Hugo remarked.

'And what a tree!' said Balzac. 'Do you know what it yields?'

'As it's a walnut-tree I suppose it yields walnuts.'

'I don't mean that. It brings in fifteen hundred a year.'

'The nuts do?'

'No, not the nuts . . .'

Balzac went on to explain that by an ancient feudal custom all the inhabitants of Ville-d'Avray were required to deposit the contents of their sanitary utensils under the tree. It meant a huge daily heap of human dung which Balzac could sell to the local farmers and wine-growers.

'The tree's a goldmine—or to be exact, a guano-heap.'

'Without the birds,' said Hugo with his Olympian calm.

They discussed the matter of the Académie Française at luncheon. Hugo promised little, but, as will later appear, was better than his word. After moving to the Rue Basse, Balzac continued to entertain Academicians from time to time: 'I do so simply to let it be known that I want to be elected, for this is a present that I would like to give my Eve. . . .' But membership of the Academy was also a decided social asset, a fact which even the most rapt visionary could not ignore.

Another writers' association, the *Société des Gens de Lettres*, took up a certain amount of his time. Balzac had long been concerned with the professional interests of his colleagues. In 1834 he had published a 'Letter to French Writers of the Nineteenth Century' in which he said: 'The Law safeguards the land; it safeguards the house of the proletarian who sweated for it; it confiscates the work of the poet, who thinks. . . .' The gross receipts of the Paris theatres amounted to 10,000,000 francs every year. What was the budget for serious writing in print, including the earnings of men like Hugo and Musset? It came to less than a million for the whole of France. The ten thousand wealthy families had not a franc to spare for the twenty outstanding books produced each year. They borrowed them from the library or bought cheap, pirated editions.

Balzac claimed that a writer's work should constitute an estate like any other (at that time literary copyright extended for ten years after the author's death); he demanded that literary property should be protected against theft abroad (he had lost a lot by being pirated in Belgium) and that the author should retain control over his work, so that it could not be adapted or in any way altered without his consent. This was all fair and reasonable, and eventually it became the authors' charter; but it took a long campaign to overcome the indifference of the legislators. A Société des Gens de Lettres was at length formed, in 1838. Victor Hugo, Alexandre Dumas and Frédéric Soulié were among the founder members. Balzac was away at the time, but he joined in December of that year and the following year was elected chairman, succeeding Abel-François Villemain, who had become Minister of Education.

Saint Beuve, his steadfast enemy, took advantage of the occasion to pour ridicule on *la littérature industrielle* and what he called 'the demon of literary property': 'The fountain of arrogance descends in a shower of gold. It may easily amount to millions; and one does not blush to display them or to beg for them.' He derided the Society of Men of Letters (*véritable compagnonnage ouvrier*) and the 'Marshals of French Literature' (Balzac's phrase), writing disdainfully '. . . men, as you must realize, who have a certain commercial gloss suitable for exploitation'. But it was all very well for Sainte-Beuve to talk light-heartedly of literary pirating as a vocational risk and an honour—he ran little risk and the honour was never to be his.

XXIX

La Comédie humaine (1)

La Comédie humaine, c'est l'Imitation de Dieu le Père.

ALBERT THIBAUDET

IN 1841 BALZAC signed an agreement with a group of publishers (Dubocher, Furne, Hetzel and Paulin) for the publication of his entire works under the all-embracing title, *The Human Comedy*. He had already made considerable use of collective titles for groups of novels and stories: *Scenes of Private Life, of Paris Life, of Provincial Life*, as well as the *Studies of Manners and Philosophical Studies*, to be completed by the *Analytical Studies*—which last, however, excepting the *Physiologie du mariage*, never came into being. That these were somewhat arbitrary classifications is evidenced by the transfer of novels from one group to another. But the effect he was seeking to produce, that of a single, immense structure, would be enhanced if the structure bore a name. At first he thought of calling it simply *Études sociales*; but with Dante in mind he finally decided upon *La Comédie humaine*, which is first mentioned in a letter to Hetzel in 1839.

It was not simply a publishing device. The vast panorama was intended to embrace every human type and activity. Whether Balzac would live to complete it was another matter; but by 1841 it had become an organized world, propagating itself, like the real world, by its own fecundity, by apposition and natural extension. *Un Grand Homme de province à Paris*, for example, called for its opposite, *Un Grand Homme de Paris en province* (the theme of *Modeste Mignon* and *La Muse du departement*) and *Le Contrat de mariage* was to have had a sequel, *L'Inventaire après décès* (settlement of the estate after death) although this was never written. This process of self-propagation added incalculably to the author's creative resources. Maurice Bardèche has shown that to grasp the full depth and density of the structure we need to take into account the stories Balzac planned, each as a contribution to the whole, but was never able to write. *Louis Lambert* is a case in point. This story of a man of genius destroyed in youth by the power of his own intellect was to have been complemented by *Le Crétin*, the man who lives to a great age through having no intellect at all.

Spoelberch de Lovenjoul has listed fifty-three titles of novels and stories which were planned but never written. We have details of some of these: *Les Héritiers Boisrouge, Les Grands, L'Hôpital et le peuple, Entre Savants, Le Théâtre comme il est, La Vie et les aventures d'une idée, L'Anatomie des corps enseignants.* In addition there are countless ideas jotted down in a few words: 'A penniless girl who tries to attract a husband by pretending to be rich, and finds that she has married a poor devil playing the same game . . .'; 'A girl deceived by a man's attentions into thinking he loves her, finds he doesn't and hates him, and then he falls in love with her. . . .' Two promising *Scenes of Private Life*. In the words of Maurice Bardèche, 'Imagination can run riot amid this profusion of titles, this mushroom growth of characters and themes which in its fruitfulness, prodigality and detachment resembles life itself. . . .' It is sad to reflect that if Balzac had lived to be seventy we should have been left admirable portraits of his characters in their old age.

Hetzel insisted on an Author's Preface to this uniform edition, which was to put the stamp of success on the huge labours of ten years. Balzac, in his overworked state, suggested that Davin's introductions should be used instead, but Hetzel would not have it: 'It is out of the question that a complete edition of your works, the biggest thing that has been done with them, should be offered to the public without a few words from you at the beginning.' Balzac gave way and in a long *Avantpropos* sought to explain how the *Comédie* had originated.

Its root, as we have seen, lay in his concept of social species corresponding to zoological species, the differences between the workman, the merchant, the sailor and the poet being of the same order as those distinguishing the lion, the ass, the shark and the sheep. But the human comedy is infinitely more complex than the animal comedy. Animals pair with their own species, the lion with the lioness, the fox with the vixen. It is quite another matter in the human world, where the lion may set up house with a ewe or a tigress. Moreover animals only evolve through millennia into more complex species, whereas in the human world the grocer may become a peer, or the duke a pauper, in a matter of years. Finally, Man, with his intelligence and his acquired skills, has the power to change his environment, so that the naturalist studying the human species has to take account not only of men and women but of things.

Walter Scott had raised the novel to the dignity of history, but it had not occurred to him to link his separate works in any way. This was Balzac's second inspiration, the idea of writing a complete history of manners in which every chapter would be a story in itself. Having compiled his own Social Register, so to speak, by bringing two or three thousand characters into the world, he proceeded to bind them together with the social cement of hierarchies and callings. The unity of the work is such that, if its full spell is to be experienced, the whole of it must be read.

Only by doing so can the reader discover the extent of that Empire on which intelligence never sets. 'I have learnt more from Balzac,' wrote Engels, 'than from all the professional historians, economists and statisticians put together.' The *Comédie humaine* is both the truest portrayal of the eternal man and the best picture we possess of manners and customs under the Bourbon restoration. It contains everything, aristocracy and bourgeoisie, the administration and the Army, the mechanism of credit and commerce, of transport, of the press and of judicial, political and fashionable life—not superficially sketched but drawn in depth, dissected, examined like the separate components of a huge machine.

His vast knowledge embraced houses and towns; he knew every district of Paris. 'A nocturnal Homer,' wrote Henri Focillon, 'he lights with an uncanny flame the cellars and by-ways of a feverish city where a sinister epic is taking place.' He penetrates into students' restaurants, the wings of theatres, the boudoirs of duchesses and the alcoves of courtesans, and everywhere clothes and invests his creatures with reality. The famous tailor Staub dresses Lucien de Rubempré, and Charles Grandet was dressed by Balzac's own tailor, Buisson. The beautiful Mme Rabourdin was supplied with bunches of grapes in jade by the jeweller Fossin, of 75 Rue de Richelieu. There was nothing he did not know about the social peculiarities of Angoulême, Le Havre, Limoges and Alençon, and no one understood better than he the implacable and shabby antagonisms created in towns like these by the social convulsions between 1789 and 1830. Restoration France would be unintelligible if the reader were not made to see how deeply it is rooted in the past: 'Real life is the life of causes.' And the use of recurring characters enabled Balzac to project his imaginary beings into a fourth dimension, that of Time.

But it was not enough for him to describe a whole society. What in his eyes made the writer the equal, if not the superior, of the statesman was 'a view of human affairs'. If Balzac knew himself to be the greatest of novelists, it was not simply because he had brought so many creatures to life (one can imagine an industrious, uninspired novelist creating endless characters), but because he had leavened the human dough he was kneading with his own personal myth—the power of will when it is concentrated upon a single purpose. This power of will has its enforced limitations. Nations, like men, have their ass's skin. A people can be assured of long life only if restrictions are imposed on its vital activities. Therefore Balzac favoured stable governments and discipline: 'I write by the light of two eternal truths, Religion and Monarchy.' He believed himself to possess a Mephistophelian cunning in matters of State. 'An honest-John policy,' he said, 'is like a steam-engine with feelings, or a steersman who makes love while he is at the helm—the ship sinks.' But George Sand, who knew him so well, replied to this: 'Confronted by saddened conviction, or by a reproach coming from the heart, all his diabolical power collapsed beneath the good and naïve instincts which were the essence of his being. He would clasp your hand and fall silent, and then talk of other things.' The Machiavellianism was born of intelligence; the generosity was innate.

Politics and Religion

The best form of government, so Balzac believed, was that which released the highest degree of national energy; and he further believed that this was best achieved by concentrating the authority of the State. We may recall the conversation he imagined between Catherine de' Medici and Robespierre. He acquiesced in those two instruments of State necessity, and he admired Napoleon for the same reasons. Like most men of his age he had grown up 'a child of Austerlitz', and he never lost that early ardour. He wrote of Napoleon in *Autre étude de femme*: 'A man who is depicted with his arms folded, but who did everything! The greatest power ever known, the most concentrated, the most incisive, the most astringent of all powers. . . . A man who could do everything because he willed everything . . . arbitrary or just, as the case demanded—the true King! . . .' And that is pure Balzac. Without a touch of arbitrariness there can be no justice. When the cause is hopeless, when the laws betray, the last appeal is to the King—or to a band of outlaws, the Thirteen.

After the 1830 revolution he might have accepted the Government of the 'bourgeois King' if it had shown itself to be strong. But 'we have made a big revolution and it has fallen into the hands of small men. . . . The worst fault of the July revolution is that it did not allow Louis-Philippe three months of dictatorship in which to put the rights of the people and the throne on a secure basis.' Absolutism (or the greatest possible concentration of power) was the only way of ensuring the well-being of the masses: 'What is called representative government is a state of incessant turmoil. . . . The essential quality of a government is stability. . . .' After two years of constitutional monarchy, whose weak ineffectiveness he found deplorable, Balzac turned to the 'legitimist' cause not for sentimental reasons, like Chateaubriand, or from self-interest, as Zulma Carraud thought, but because he believed that absolute rule by a legitimate monarch was the best system of government.

Flaubert and Zola were later to be scandalized by his political views. 'He was on the side of Catholicism, Legitimism and the landowners . . . A tremendous man, but second-rate.' Balzac second-rate! Alain, even more of a republican than Flaubert, understood his politics better. It was also said of him that he supported the Crown and the Altar without believing in either. This was true if it implied disbelief in their transcendental qualities, but false if it meant disbelief in their practical value. Balzac believed in tradition, in the family and in Monarchy *because they existed*, and because they safeguarded the national energies. To be constantly changing the leader of the Government, making Action as fluid and inconsistent as Thought, was, in his view, to weaken the State. Duration seemed to Balzac a virtue in itself. It might as easily lead to the dictatorship of the people as to monarchism, to Napoleon or Marat as to Louis XIV. Napoleon's great fault was that he had not achieved permanency. The true king might come from below or from above. What Balzac found intolerable was unstable government by mediocrities. He dreamed at moments of some form of collective dictatorship: 'If fifteen men of ability were to come together as the Government of France under a leader on the intellectual level of Voltaire, the nonsense which is called constitutional government, and which is based on the perpetual enthronement of mediocrity, would rapidly disappear.' Positive vigour conferred both power and legality.

But this vigour need not always spring from the same source. Balzac understood the radicals, Michel Chrestien and Z. Marcas, as well as he understood the Comte de Fontaine or Henri de Marsay. The doctor, Horace Bianchon, one of his favourite characters, says of the Marquise d'Espard: 'I hate people of that sort. I would like to see a revolution which would rid us of them for ever.' Balzac himself had had similar moods of fury with the Marquise de Castries, although these were due to wounded vanity. He has been called a revolutionary because he painted a corrupt society and encouraged the wish to transform it; but he was writing as a bourgeois, a son of the middle classes, who only wanted to make a place for himself in it.

So—Monarchy and Religion . . . But what was the religion? In his Preface to the *Livre mystique* he replied that it was mysticism—Christianity reduced to first principles. He held the Book of Revelation to be a bridge between Christian mysticism and that of the Indian, Egyptian, Greek and Hebrew mystics. This doctrine was passed on by Jakob Boehme to Madame Guyon and Fénelon. In the eighteenth century it found in Swedenborg an evangelist who is as towering a figure as St John, Moses or Pythagoras; and later it had its French prophet in Saint-Martin. It was the religion of Louis Lambert, and it was the one preached by Balzac. Writing to Charles Nodier in 1832 he recalled his philosophical studies at the age of twenty, when he was reading Leibniz and Spinoza in his garret. It had led him to the following dilemma: either God and matter are contemporaneous, in which case God ceases to be omnipotent, because He lives in co-existence with a power distinct from His own; or He pre-existed all things, in which case, since He created the universe out of His own essence, there can be no good or evil in society or in the world: 'As Bayle said, God is on both sides in every battle, fighting against Himself.' All scholasticism leads to an impasse.

So we must fall back on agnosticism, or embrace Christianity in a spirit of unquestioning love. As a young man Balzac adopted the former position: 'Every man has his passion, religion is simply the most sublime of them all' (1824); 'I am neither converted nor capable of conversion, because I have no religion' (1837). He chose in the end to embrace Christianity, but not that of the Catholic Church. He had been attached to the Church from childhood; he had written wonderful tales defending it; he had exalted its civilizing influence in *Le Médecin de campagne* and its evangelical tenderness in *Le Lys dans la vallée*. But all that did not make him an orthodox Catholic. 'The Catholic Faith,' he said, 'is a lie with which we deceive ourselves.'

Yet to the novelist presiding over the destinies of his characters the Church seemed the natural guardian of moral and social truth. If we are to understand the role he assigned to religion, sceptic that he was, we must remember the society he depicted, that ferocious world dominated by money in which the weak went to the wall and the criminal was honoured if he knew how to evade the law: 'What is France in 1840? It is a country exclusively concerned with material interests, without patriotism, without conscience, and where the governing power is without strength. . . .' In the face of Evil triumphant, Catholicism provided 'a complete system for repressing the depraved tendencies of Man'. Balzac did not accept dogma at its face value; he regarded it as an aggregation of sublime and fruitful myths—and what were men capable of understanding, except myths? 'You cannot get a whole nation to study Kant.' Faith and custom were of greater value to a people than study and reason.

'I do not forget,' François Mauriac has written, 'that if Balzac was a Catholic, it was on political and pragmatic grounds . . . which are certainly not the best. But a more authentic religious stream flows through the depths of his life, as it does through the depths of his work. . . . One has only to re-read *Louis Lambert* and *Le Médecin de campagne* to see that if he went very far in the recognition of Evil . . . he also had a perception of essential Good. . . .' It was not simply a matter of a specious and narrow Catholicism, useful to the middle-class householder as a means of keeping his wife in order and protecting his property. In the novels which were to complete the *Comédie humaine* Balzac proposed to allot a large place to Christian charity. The soul's salvation takes place silently and in secret, but charity performs visible miracles. Dr Benassis redeems himself by his work for others, as does Véronique Graslin.

The devout believer may be shocked by this attitude of intellectual condescension. But although Balzac did not himself swallow it whole he respected faith in others. In *La Messe de l'athée* the surgeon Desplein, who believes in neither God nor devil, has masses said for the soul of a poor water-carrier who did him a signal service. He says to Bianchon, his pupil: 'I say with the good faith of those who doubt, "My God, if there is a place where, after their death, you bestow those who have lived without fault, think of Bourgeat. . . ." That is all a man holding my views can allow himself. God must be a kindly devil, he won't hold it against me. I swear to you, I would give my fortune to have Bourgeat's faith penetrate my heart.' And Bianchon, who nurses his master during his last illness, cannot be sure that he died an atheist. There was in Balzac, mixed with Desplein's agnosticism, something of the noble priests he created.

Had he any kind of metaphysical beliefs? Evidently, since he did not believe that physical determinism could account for all things. He was both materialist and, in the broad sense, spiritualist. The spirit pervades all matter. The scale of created things rises from the minerals, whose consciousness is imperceptible, to Man, whose soul is bound to the body, and upward to the angels, which are all soul. Balzac believed, if confusedly, that the evolutionary process, extending from the rock to the saint, would eventually transform men into angels. He believed that the Universe was informed with a great secret, and that Life contained a principle more powerful than itself; and he was content that the secret and the principle should be called God. Man seeks to grasp them, but we can do so only by way of allegory, symbol and token. Though God remains silent, things and living creatures are charged with mysterious messages. There are secret relationships between matter and man, and what is of real importance in the universe is to be found at the level of the infinitesimally small. These were the thoughts moving in his mind, and they explain why he took such infinite pains to describe an article of furniture, a costume, a gesture. Everything is contained in everything. In terms of the Absolute, the commercial traveller is the equal of the emperor.

The world to him was one, and the physical and spiritual worlds both were engendered of a single substance. Balzac liked to evoke this unity by dwelling upon the interaction of body and spirit. Frustrated eroticism is transformed into paternal love, spiritual energy into charity, as heat is transformed into light. We all have a vital force within us; some convert it into useful achievement, others into crime. Pleasures self-denied reinforce the will, that powerful fluid that enables man to act upon the world. It was Balzac's dream to concentrate the will so as to make of it a magical force, even divine.

To be God, to create a world . . . it was the unavowed dream of Louis Lambert, Balthazar Claës, Frenhofer, all projections of Balzac. But there is a limit to human capacity, and madness lies in wait for Prometheus. Balzac himself at times confessed to this terror. He was saved by work and a few women: for the unity and balance of nature result from the fusion of two principles, the male, which seeks action and conflict, and the female, which imposes stability and continuance. The Saint-Simonians and later Auguste Comte professed the same doctrine. Balzac, as deep a thinker as Comte and a poet into the bargain, expressed his metaphysics in myths. Plato, Dante, Shakespeare—all were not far away.

Love and Marriage

Balzac wrote of love both as a mystic and as a physiologist. The vocabulary is always restrained, with no description of physical nudity and few scenes of sexuality; but there is a clinical boldness, proceeding from the principle that the secret humours of the body determine those of the heart. At his first meeting with Dinah de la Baudraye, Bianchon guesses her secret from the tone of something she says: her husband is impotent, and she is still virgin. And so she is at the mercy of Lousteau whenever he chooses to take her—Lousteau, the insignificant journalist, rather than Bianchon, the distinguished doctor: 'This is the reason. Women in search of love recoil instinctively from men whose lives are dedicated to exacting callings; whatever their qualities, they are always women in their desire to possess and be possessed.' It is the observation of a hard-pressed man for whom time was money. Balzac described with an expert eye the 'red look' exchanged by two people who desire each other. He knows the role which the senses play. He knows which caresses are refused by the Duchesse de Langeais, by what perverse means Béatrix, the mature woman, triumphs over the young and charming Sabine, whom Calyste has married, and how Valérie Marneffe, or La Torpille, keep their hold over old men. Had he not adored Madame de Berny, who was older than his mother, furiously desired Madame de Castries and shared with the plump Èveline the raptures of the 'unforgettable day'? He knew all the recipes in 'the cookery-book of love'.

But every love not endorsed by society seemed to him fore-doomed. He many times depicted the griefs and tragedies of clandestin love. A man needs to satisfy not only his senses, but his self-esteem and his material interests. He needs to love everything in the woman he loves, her body and her mind, her flounces and the adornments of her life. Eve Hanska pleased him not only because she was 'good to make love to' but because of her wide reading, her three thousand peasants, her title, her château and her religious faith. He defended marriage in argu-ment with George Sand because only in marriage could two lovers share everything, bed, success and fortune, besides having the support of religion, society and family ties. It was true, of course, that the marriage of reason, unless it became transformed into a marriage of inclination, did not lead to real happiness. Balzac wished his characters, as he did himself, not 'a cottage and a heart, but a palace with the beloved'. It was the opposite of the attitude adopted by the Romantics. In love as in politics he swam against the stream.

He always stressed the difference between sexual passion and love: 'Passion is a hope which may be deceived. . . . Both men and women may without dishonour know more than one passion—it is so natural to clutch at happiness! But there is only one love in life.' He himself had had his string of infatuations, but in theory, at least, he adhered to the doctrine of the heart: 'There are not two loves in a man's life; there is only one, deep as the ocean but without shores.' Erotic and spiritual life should grow together in a single person, two beings 'soaring on the wings of rapture' merging into an angel. It was an allegory in *Séraphita*, a dream of perfection in the eyes of Camille Maupin, a positive hope that he held out to Eve Hanska. But although he might paint the rarified picture, absorbed as he was in his work he could not live it. A great man cannot afford a great love, he cannot belong to any woman. He may be capable of such a love, but his first business is to create. This was something he did not mention to Eve.

There are many instances in his works of passionate love. Eugénie Grandet deeply loves her cousin; Louise de Chaulieu and Ursule Mirouët love their husbands; Henriette de Mortsauf's love for Félix de Vandenesse is a mingling of physical desire and maternal instinct. There are others; but most of the women in the *Comédie humaine* are in search of riches or worldly satisfactions. Rosalie de Watteville seeks to gratify her pride; Modeste Mignon manoeuvres her suitors as though they were pieces on a chessboard; Renée de l'Estorade amazes her husband with her calculations. All these virgins know that they are to be sacrificed to the Golden Calf, and that women are like slaves in the market-place, some selling themselves outright in marriage, others hiring themselves out in prostitution—but a loveless marriage is also prostitution. 'We bring up our daughters like saints,' wrote George Sand, 'and dispose of them like fillies.' Hard truths which society prefers to ignore: 'The feeling which prompts us to dress up the food we eat, to serve it on gold and silver and porcelain, is the same as the one which causes us to embroider and veil love.'

Balzac and his heroines were prepared to accept any bargain. Beautiful girls were ready to wed aged noblemen to keep their rank, or aged bankers to achieve riches, and handsome young men sold themselves to older women for money or power. Rastignac is installed in an apartment by Delphine de Nucingen, Maxime de Trailles by the Comtesse de Restaud. Lucien de Rubempré hopes to grow rich through Coralie and then through Esther. The *Prince de la Bohème* accepts a 'considerable sum' from his mistress. It was not a matter in which Balzac could afford to be self-righteous. In the *Comédie humaine* the men marry sometimes to further their ambitions, nearly always from some form of self-interest.

'Because there are money considerations there is competition,' André Wurmser has written in *La Comédie inhumaine*. 'The heiress, before she becomes the victor's stepping-stone to success, is the object of a relentless battle. Cruchot and Grassin fight for Eugénie Grandet, Bousquier and the Chevalier de Valois for Mademoiselle Cormon, Philippe Bridau and Maxence Gilet for Flore Brazier [la Rabouilleuse]. . . . Man battles with man to win a dowry, woman with woman to win a husband. . . . And because money, competition and the clash of interests are all involved in marriage, its rules have been codified. "You will see, dear foolish one," writes Renée de l'Estorade, "that we have studied the Code in its bearing on conjugal love!" . . . The bonds of matrimony are the bonds of property.'

To the critic expressing astonishment at the large part played by women in the *Comédie humaine* Balzac might reply that he has not sufficiently reflected upon the difficulties of producing a saga longer than the *Thousand and One Nights* and composed of more than a hundred separate works. In eastern fables, since women were segregated, the storyteller could only set his scene in the bazaar, the Sultan's palace or the cobbler's booth, and therefore needed marvels and enchantment to sustain the interest. In medieval Europe the springs of heroic action were to be found in warfare, in the uprising of the slaves against the masters and in the struggles between priesthood and monarchy. The only kind of romance possible in the recent past had been exhausted by Scott. The France of the nineteenth century had lost much of its picturesque quality. Caste no longer stamped its imprint upon every face. And so, as the Marquis de Custine wrote, 'since form is lacking, the novelist has to turn to the story of ideas, and seek out the most delicate feelings of the human heart'. No one did so with a greater penetration or understanding than Balzac. He exposed the souls of women without causing them offence. An unsparing witness, never fooled by the stratagems of love and money, he could when he chose depict the most exquisite shades of sensibility. Women remained his faithful readers because no writer ever understood them better. More than one, seeing her pretences stripped away, enjoyed it in her secret heart.

Having seen much of courtesans, he believed them to be capable of love as well as sensuality. He himself loved their flesh, their luxury, their knowledge of men and their acceptance of risk—in short, their poetry, born of what was ephemeral in their lives. In his works they form a world apart, having its own language, its laws, its young lovers and rich dotards, and its tragedies. As for men, 'love will never be anything to them but an appetite, a need embellished by our imagination'—or a necessary ally in their challenge to society. Rastignac needed Delphine de Nucingen for his worldly ambitions; Blondet owed his salvation to Madame de Montcornet. 'Love,' says Blondet, 'is the only chance fools have of rising in the world.' But why 'fools'? Where would Balzac have been without Laure de Berny, and did he not look to marriage with Eve Hanska to assist his own rise in the world? And why the *only* chance? The man incapable of inspiring love in women was still not without resources—friendship, association. The Balzac hero dreamed as much of a friend, or group of friends united in unreserved devotion, as he did of a wife. The aristocracy fascinated him because it was a closed circle which looked after its own. In his early days Balzac had been a young man alone, afraid of solitude. He sought companions in the struggle. The daily gatherings at the Café Flicoteaux, the Thirteen, the Cheval Rouge, Vautrin and his gang, all these partake of the mystique of the group, the surrogate of love.

Money

Money and the means of acquiring it, dowries, legacies, trade, banking, usury, the forging of wills, all forms of financial chicanery—these play as large a part in the *Comédie humaine* as does love. Indeed, larger, for many of Balzac's novels contain little or no love interest, and he was amazed that in the *Chartreuse de Parme*, of which he thought so highly, 'amid so many happenings' there was never any question of money. The major part played by Money-the-King in his own work may be ascribed to two causes, the author and the period.

First, the author. Balzac came of a family with a money-fixation. We may recall his mother's words: 'A fortune, a great fortune, is everything.' All those nearest to him were short of money, the Survilles, the Montzaigles, his parents, himself. Certainly it was their own fault. His parents had enough to live on; the Survilles might have lived in modest comfort on an engineer's salary; he himself could have earned a handsome living had he been less wildly extravagant. But then, he *was* extravagant—from frustration. He had started life in a lawyer's chambers breathing the rank air of money ill-acquired. It was there that he discovered the true relationship between Law and Justice. He saw honest men cheated, swindlers triumphant, judges who turned a blind eye. He found that justice was not always impartial: it might seek to save the forger, Esgrignon, because a pretty woman of high estate demanded it, or defer to the whim of Mme Camusot de Marville. Balzac wrote these things because he had witnessed them.

It was a corrupt time. Under the Ancien Régime honour had inspired as many actions as greed, and under the Revolution and the Empire there had been idealism and military ardour. But the purchase of confiscated estates, war profiteering, huge speculation on prospective changes of régime, the purchase of *rentes* at thirty francs—all this had produced a different climate. It had brought into being a new ruling class concerned only with personal enrichment. Where Bernard-François Balzac, volubly overflowing with ideas, had failed, the taciturn Grandet amasses a huge fortune. Taillefer raises himself in the world by a crime, others by false bankruptcies or shameful marriages. Society was contaminated by a spreading immorality. Philippe Bridau, who would have made a good soldier if the war had continued, commits murder for the sake of an inheritance. César Birotteau ruins himself by speculation. Gobseck, the usurer, can still be the most honest of men, because he is the most candid. 'If I died leaving children,' says the advocate, Derville, 'I would want him to be their guardian.' He knew that the trust would be honourably discharged, however many people Gobseck might ruin in the way of business.

It was under the July Monarchy that large-scale capitalism came into being (the word itself still unknown, although 'capital' and 'capitalist' both were used). Real estate in Paris acquired a fantastic value. James de Rothschild financed the Chemins de Fer du Nord, and Balzac, who believed in the future of the railways, encouraged Eve Hanska to invest in them —too soon, as usual. The popular press was growing and providing a new outlet for writers. Publishing was emerging from its infancy and adopting new methods which Balzac had foreseen. 'Enrich yourselves,' said Guizot. Balzac asked nothing better, but one cannot at one and the same time write the *Comédie humaine* and live it. Money governed the world; Balzac described the world.

He did so without passing judgement, and he has been blamed for his failure in this, as though it implied approval of what went on. But he felt instinctively that explicit judgements can only weaken a work of art. It was not for the author to praise or blame, but to keep aloof, leaving the reader to judge for himself: 'The moralist should conceal himself with skill in the cloak of the historian.' Balzac knew that it was not his business to dispense justice; he was the chronicler of a living society, not a crusader against it. The only charge that can be brought against him is that he did not know the whole of it. There are few, if any, industrial workers in the *Comédie humaine*, and when he wrote about peasants he seemed to be seeing them through the eyes of Wenceslas Hanski or General de Mont-cornet. It is the misfortune of writers in love with wealth that the people they consort with are generally wealthy. Victor Hugo owed *Les Misérables* to his plebeian mistress, Juliette Drouet. For Balzac, Madame de Berny, Madame Hanska, the Duchesse d'Abrantès and the Marquise de Castries lighted only half the stage.

XXX

La Comédie humaine (2)

*Il nous arrive quelquefois de condamner la condition
humaine, mais par comparaison à une perfection abstraite
qui n'existe pas. Au contraire la donnée doit être l'humanité
elle-même, campée comme elle est et vociférant comme elle
fait. Et si cela n'est pas l'ornement du monde, il faut aller se
noyer. Balzac guérit la misanthropie; c'est à cela qu'il est
bon.*

ALAIN

The Workshop

HOW DID HE WORK and what were his materials? He was
given to saying 'All is true' in English. He talked about his
'terrifying exactitude', and added: 'The worst horrors that
novelists think they invent are still less than reality.' Certainly
Nature is richer than Art, but Nature's truth is not Art's truth.
One can neither exhaust nor wholly grasp it. What is literally
true is seldom true-seeming. It lacks consistency and unity.
Unity of composition is what the writer seeks. Balzac liked to
call himself a poet, that is to say, a man who re-creates the
essence of things: 'What is Art? It is concentrated Nature.' The
imaginary reposes on the real, but by bringing it to order. The
creative writer has to simplify: to embody ideas in people,
create characters that can be believed to be alive, while at the
same time he simplifies. At the centre of a Balzac novel there is
a passion, an obsession; and the story is of the growth of this
passion, which sweeps everything before it, even to the point of
death.

Balzac's novels, and his characters, are both true to life and
larger than life. 'I like exceptional beings,' he wrote to George
Sand. 'I myself am one. Moreover I need them to throw my
more commonplace characters into relief, and I never sacrifice
them unnecessarily. But the commonplace characters interest
me more than they do you. I enlarge them, I idealize them in

reverse, their ugliness and their stupidity; I bring to their deformities an added dimension of the horrifying or grotesque.' In this process of enlargement he was akin to the Romantics; but whereas they drew grotesques without troubling about verisimilitude, Balzac took pains by the exactness of his detail to keep his characters human.

Three stages are to be discerned in the creation of a Balzac character. In the first he drew upon people he knew or characters in books. Dablin was the starting-point of Pillerault, and Marie d'Agoult of Béatrix. But then the original picture undergoes a change as he enriches it with elements borrowed from other models. In this second stage he was moved not by the desire to effect a literary transformation but by the requirements of the story. Like a painter standing back to survey his canvas and then adding a touch of line or colour, he took account of the whole to throw the part into greater relief. And then, at the third stage, as though in a vision, he reshapes the character to make it the embodiment of an idea. Gobseck becomes the Power of Money; Birotteau is Probity incarnate, Goriot is Paternal Love.

But even when he enters the field of abstractions he keeps his feet on earth. Nothing is more fascinating than to detect in his books the traces of his daily life. Grandet calls his wife *Ti-Mère*, as Laure Surville did their own mother; and he talks, like Bernard-François, about the Grand Mogul. Surville's canals are to be found in Rabourdin's green folders. The fragment of reality is taken apart and reassembled in a different shape. Inevitably Balzac made most use of himself, his own recollections and griefs. Many of his novels are novels of compensation. He gives himself what life has denied him. Through de Marsay he acquires good looks and power, through Rastignac a rich marriage and a great career, through d'Arthez purity. And again, by a process of magic as old as mankind, he rids himself of his own tribulations by inflicting them on some character whom he destroys. Rubempré relieves him of the burden of his unhappy youth, Birotteau of the bankrupt printing-works, Nathan of his creative agonies. He knows that his genius and capacity for work make him the master of those poor devils; he knows it, but takes pleasure in reminding himself of the fact—and in proving it. Z. Marcas and Albert Savarus play the part of redeemers—characters worthy of himself, his equals in genius, who yet fail. 'Thus,' wrote Gaétan Picon, 'every Balzac character is the double of his creator: he triumphs or meets with disaster, he succumbs to propitiate the Fates.'

To Balzac all the beings of his creation existed on the level of the real world 'wherein the characters seemed to him but a feeble copy of his own'. Securely installed in this reality at one remove, he could travel with them through time. He makes the point in his preface to *Une Fille d'Ève*: 'Here the huge figure of de Marsay appears as Prime Minister, whereas in *Le Contrat de mariage* he is only at the start of his career; and later, between the ages of eighteen and thirty, he appears as the most futile and idle of fops.' So it is in life. You run into a man you have not seen for twenty years and find that he has risen from poverty to riches, and someone takes you aside and tells you the story of how it came about. Balzac excels in conversations of this kind, and the seeming digression always has its significance. The same story may recur in different works—'Nothing is all of a piece in the world . . . ,' Balzac wrote in the preface to *Une Fille d'Ève*. 'The author's model is the nineteenth century, an excessively turbulent model, difficult to control. . . .' He had sometimes to wait years for the ending of a story, as in the case of *Béatrix*, and sometimes he forgot the past of his characters—or chose to ignore it. In *La Torpille*, written before *Un grand homme de province à Paris*, we find Lucien de Rubempré's friends and enemies talking of him as though they had lost their memories. . . . Later the author would put these things right, if he had time. What is magical is that he saunters through his world as we do through the real world, waiting for a chance encounter or unexpected revelation to tell him what happens next; and when he went into the real world he saw nothing but his own characters and continued to learn about them.

His approach and his methods were those of the historian. When he needed an instance to explain a situation, it was in the *Comédie humaine* that he sought and found it. When he wanted guests at a party he invited whichever of his own characters, from commerce, bureaucracy or the Faubourg Saint-Germain, were appropriate. His people's memories were, of course, of events described in earlier tales. The *Comédie humaine* is a history with History. He proclaimed jestingly, in the preface to *Une Fille d'Ève*, that one day someone would compile a biographical index to the *Études de moeurs*, and as a sample he wrote the article on Rastignac. He did it as a joke, but he was only anticipating.

One can see from this how it was that when a publisher called for sixty pages to fill out a volume he was able to produce a story of appropriate length at such great speed. He had only to assemble his company and select the players he wanted. And if need be he could draw on his innumerable scraps of journalism, the sketches of people and places scribbled to fill a hole in some newspaper. This padding might subsequently be removed. For example, the 'vignette' of the Bois de Boulogne which appeared in the original version of *L'Illustre Gaudissart* vanished from the reprint. He attached no more importance to the journey-work of the trade than a stage-director does to the spotlight he switches on and off as it suits him. Nor was he above borrowing from others—a civil engineer writing in a review of bridges and highways, a poem by Delphine Gay or Théophile Gautier. What did these trifles matter when his own spirit infused the whole and the story would soon start moving again?

Baudelaire found in his writing 'something diffuse, hasty and slapdash'. It is not true. In his letters and journalistic pieces Balzac wrote admirably, with vigour and style. As a historian of manners and a descriptive writer he is lucid and precise. Whether he is dealing with a cooper or a scent-manufacturer, the back-stage of a theatre or a chemist's laboratory, his technical vocabulary is flawless. As a moralist he scattered his work with aphorisms worthy of La Rochefoucauld or Chamfort: 'Only old men have time for love. . . . Resignation is a form of daily suicide. . . . Conflicting interests often end by swallowing each other; vices always come to terms. . . .' His knowledge of the seventeenth- and eighteenth-century classics is everywhere apparent. Except for his inspired phrases, of which there are many, he accepted *l'automatisme du style*, a pedestrian style; but he was an excellent writer of pastiche, whether of Rabelais or Sainte-Beuve. He was brilliant in the exposition of scientific or philosophical theory. He was not, as has been said of him, 'a pretentious popular novelist' stuffing his work with moralizing to produce an effect, but a man who from youth had been passionately interested in ideas.

It remains true that he lacked judgement and discrimination, and was sometimes absurd and overblown when he wanted to be sublime or merely pretty: 'She would have gilded mud with her celestial smile. . . . The chaste swelling of their veiled hearts. . . . Are you too in an abyss, my angel? . . .' There are altogether too many angels in his writings. But we have to take account of the period, the high-flown rhetoric of the Romantics and the taste of his readers. The language of a Massillon, admirable in itself, may sound ridiculous in a love-letter. Henriette de Mortsauf, like her creator, had read too much Saint-Martin. And because Balzac believed in the unity of all Creation he allowed himself metaphors that were sometimes striking and sometimes preposterous: Madame Matifat, 'that Catherine II of the shop-counter'; Nucingen, 'that elephant of finance'; Goriot, 'the Christ of paternity'. This was an addiction with him, as was his *Voici pourquoi*. But what writer is free of mannerisms—La Bruyère with his concluding flourish, Proust with his garlands of adjectives and flowing metaphors. . . .

The masters are a law unto themselves. 'They have no need to be stylish, those great ones,' wrote Flaubert. 'They are strong despite all their faults, and because of them. It is we, the small men, who must be judged by our felicities. . . . I will here venture upon a proposition that I would not dare to express elsewhere: it is that very great writers often write badly, and so much the better for them. We must not look to them for formal perfection, but to those of the second rank. . . .'

And despite this, no writer ever worked harder. 'It cost him infinite pains to express himself,' said Théophile Gautier; but he added, 'Balzac had a style and a very fine one, the inevitable style, mathematically suited to his way of thought.' Like Chateaubriand he collected rare words and archaisms to bring them back into currency; to say nothing of the magical names in the *Comédie humaine*—Gobseck, Birotteau, Sérizy, Gaudissart —which he culled from shop-signs and directories, or delved out of his memory. In the *Curé de Tours* he invented the 'sub-conversation'—the thoughts passing through a man's mind behind the spoken words which conceal them. It may be said that his letters (particularly those to Eve Hanska) are full of 'sub-conversations'. Reading between their lines one may discern the mixture of good faith, naïve dissimulation and literary artifice moving at the back of his mind as he wrote.

Observer or Seer

The Introduction to the *Comédie humaine* propounded a general philosophy which served Balzac as a useful springboard for his flights of imagination. 'He wanted,' wrote de Musset, 'to seize a thread which would unite and concentrate all things. . . . His ambition was to be the sole possessor of a unique key to his epoch. . . .' It was true: life, to Balzac, was a system of cause and effect, but in him genius preceded and was outside the system. A great creative artist does not know how he works; he tries to understand when he contemplates the finished work, and he seeks to explain by rationalizing a unity that proceeds from his own temperament. Balzac adapted the world to make it Balzac's world; but although he needed reality to relate his characters solidly to life, there was no single key to fit all that diversity of locks. Rastignac was not Thiers, or Bridau Delacroix; the Marquise de Castries was not the Duchesse de Langeais, and Laure de Berny was not Henriette de Mortsauf; but aspects of Thiers, and of the Delacroix brothers, have gone into the shaping of Rastignac and the two Bridaux. Rastignac, like Thiers, married the daughter of his mistress. Sandeau is neither Lousteau nor Rubempré, but both those characters owe something of their life to him. Camille Maupin could not have existed without George Sand; nevertheless she is not George Sand, and when Balzac told Eve Hanska that she was, he failed to realize his own power of invention. The true formula of all Art, said Gide, is 'God proposes and man disposes.' Nature supplies the materials; the artist shapes them.

It does happen, however, that life will now and then miraculously furnish an author with a character that can be turned directly into fiction, with very little re-touching. Anne-Marie Meininger has shown that in countless details the marriage and love-affairs of Cordelia de Castellane (Chateaubriand's mistress) resemble the adventures of Diane de Maufrigneuse, who first appears in *Le Cabinet des antiques* and later becomes the heroine of *Les Secrets de la Princesse de Cadignan*. Both were born of wealthy, aristocratic families, and both ended in disaster. Cordelia de Castellane, separated from her husband, lived in a small house in the Faubourg Saint-Honoré; Diane has a ground-floor apartment in the Rue de Miromesnil. They have the same charm, the same idyllic beauty, the same blue-eyed gaze. They are alike in their depravity, their string of elegant lovers openly proclaimed, their gift of brilliantly adorning 'soul and body', their liveliness of mind and courage in adversity.

Everything points to the resemblance. Just as the Princesse de Cadignan (Diane de Maufrigneuse) has a dangerous woman friend in the Marquise d'Espard, so was the Comtesse de Castellane on terms of close friendship with her rival, the Duchesse de Dino. 'Undoubtedly they knew weighty secrets concerning each other, and were not likely to quarrel over a man or a service to be rendered. . . . When two women-friends are capable of murdering each other, and each sees the poisoned dagger in the other's hand, they present a touching spectacle of harmony which is only dispelled when one in a moment of inadvertance lowers her guard.' Balzac's words could be applied as well to the two real women as to the two imaginary ones. The very name 'Cadignan' was no doubt adapted, after his fashion, from that of a certain Princesse de Carignan (whose dress caught fire at a ball, like that of Cordelia de Castellane). Diane keeps Rubempré's letters as Cordelia kept those of Chateaubriand; and one may find in Cordelia's circle the living prototypes of Michel Chrestien, Henri de Marsay and Daniel d'Arthez. In short, here it was Nature that created the work of art; genius merely perceived its existence.

But such chances are rare. When Balzac published *La Fille aux yeux d'or* he was asked if the story was true. He replied: 'The episode is true. . . . The historian of manners is obliged to seek out events prompted by the same emotion, things that happened to different people, and knit them together to make a complete drama.' But the novelist, the poet, transformed the rough notes supplied by the historian of manners. Just as Rembrandt caused the darkest interior to glow with his own especial radiance, so does Balzac, shedding his golden beam on the most melancholy and sordid dramas, evoke powerful contrasts of light and shade. He has been described as a realist and as a visionary. Taken separately, either designation is false; but both are right when they are understood to complement each other.

Baudelaire wrote in *L'Art romantique*:

It has always astonished me that Balzac owes his fame to the fact that he passed for an observer. To me it has always seemed that his chief merit lies in his having been a visionary, and an impassioned visionary. All his characters are endowed with the blazing vitality that he himself possessed. All his fictions are as highly coloured as dreams. From the peak of the aristocracy to the lowest level of the plebs, all the actors in the *Comédie* are more furious in living, more vigorous and cunning in conflict, more long-suffering in misfortune, more greedy in pleasure, more angelic in devotion, than the comedy of the real world shows them to be. In brief, every character in Balzac, even the hall-porter, is possessed of genius. Every soul is stuffed with will-power to the throat. They are all Balzac himself. . . .

This is only true if we add that the visionary derived his visions from reality. 'It has been repeated *ad nauseam*,' wrote Chasles, 'that M. de Balzac was an observer, an analyst; he was both more and less, he was a seer.' The verdict has become famous, but it calls for reservations. Balzac saw beyond reality, but he also saw reality. He listened to conversations in the street, questioned soldiers, lunched with the public executioner, made friends with an ex-convict and heard the confessions of decorous women. He read everything and often found the starting-point of a book of his own in one by some other writer which he held to have failed. His work is planted in a rich compost of classical culture, vast reading and astonishing knowledge of his own time. The superabundance of material still had to be converted into works of art, and the process of transmutation remained a mystery, even to him. The fusion was brought about during laborious nights passed in a state of exaltation, 'a sublime paroxysm of flogged intelligence in which the pangs of childbirth vanished in the delights of cerebral excitement'. An idea flashed in his mind, to be embodied in a human form or social type, and suddenly there is a living person: Michu with his neck awaiting the guillotine, Vautrin in his red cloak, Corentin with his frowsy perruque.

Houses and towns in the *Comédie* are a combination of masonry and ideas. Every scene must have its setting. Balzac used the towns he knew, but did not hesitate, if need be, to make a Saumur that suited him with bits of Tours or Vouvray. He took his players with him, shifting them about as he pleased. Philippe Bridau, the Parisian, stirs up trouble in Issoudun;

Bianchon, who comes from Sancerre, makes his career in Paris. From 1842 onward the Balzac world was so tumultuously alive that it created its own hazards.

Some of the tales are 'meeting-places' where characters already known to the reader for the parts they played in other stories are brought together for the first time. *Un prince de la Bohème*, *Un homme d'affaires*, *Les Comédiens sans le savoir* come in this category. The thing may be quite casually brought about, by elaborating an anecdote into a study of manners, and it is linked to the *Comédie* as a whole by the use of proper names. We first meet the Councillor of State, Claude Vignon, as a literary critic, and the celebrated painter, Léon de Lora, was originally the studio apprentice Mistigris. Balzac often points out the connection in brackets: ('See *Béatrix*. . . . See *Le Cabinet des antiques*. . . .') The story in these 'meeting-place' episodes may amount to very little, but they delight the lover of Balzac because they show his world in movement. The *Comédie humaine* evolves, like life, from day to day. Its creator was too much at the mercy of publishers and editors to be able to choose what he would do next—he had to hurry from one canvas to another. And no doubt it was better thus. The enforced disorder reproduces the disorder of life. At the beginning he had had to resort to artifice, changes of name and chronology, to fit the parts already written into the framework of the whole. But at the point we have now reached the Balzac world was a fact, a society breeding its own dramas, the whole infinitely greater than the sum of its parts.

Despite the antagonism of the Paris press, whose favourite target he remained, the Promethean work gradually asserted itself, both by its massive substance and by its beauty. Balzac the man continued to surprise and often shock his admirers. Although Baudelaire did not talk, like Sainte-Beuve, about 'commercial literature' he was astonished at the extent to which Balzac's visionary mind was cluttered with financial calculations, like a banker's office:

That is what he was, the man of mythical bankruptcies, of hyperbolical and phantasmagorical ventures in which he always forgot to light the lamp; the grand pursuer of dreams, ceaselessly *in search of the Absolute* . . . the 'character' as intolerable in life as he was magical in his writings, the fat child bulging with genius and vanity, with so many good qualities and so many bad ones that one hesitates to dwell upon either for fear of losing sight of the other. . . .

But Balzac's defects were also his virtues. If he made of the novel of manners 'that pedestrian genre, a great achievement, always surprising and often sublime, it was because he flung himself into it with all his heart and soul'. If he could invest a tussle between lawyers with the significance of a battle between nations, it was because he himself had been ground by the millstones of finance and law. 'His genius lay in his power of entering into the mediocre and rendering it sublime without changing it.' Those who find the *Comédie humaine* overdrawn are those who have not lived it. To Balzac it was all too true: it killed him. He saw around him his three thousand characters; beyond them a 'delayed Apocalypse'; and in the far distant future, 'when the globe turns over like a sick man in a dream, and the oceans become continents', the bones of twenty worlds, our own among them. What human mind could sustain such labours and such visions? He knew, in his furious bouts of industry, that he was sacrificing his life to his work. Like Raphaël in *La Peau de chagrin*, he could not cease to desire, or to create. With the mud of daily life clinging to his ankles, he soared in spirit over the world of which he was the demiurge.

The Wisdom of Balzac

The practical morality of the *Comédie Humaine* has two sides, of which one is to be found in the letter of counsel written by Henriette de Mortsauf to Félix de Vandenesse. She advised him to respect the rules of society but to admit no compromise on a point of honour. A very different philosophy of life is expounded by Vautrin in his lectures to Lucien de Rubempré and Eugène de Rastignac. 'There are two kinds of history,' says Vautrin. 'Official history, composed of lies, in which deeds are attributed to noble sentiments; and secret history, the only true one, in which the end justifies the means. Men in general are fatalists; they worship the event and rally to the side of the

conqueror. Succeed and you will be justified. Your actions are
nothing in themselves; they are what other people think them to
be. Keep up appearances; hide the seamy side of your life and
put on a brilliant show. Form is everything.'

Balzac endows the cynical Vautrin with as much eloquence as
the saintly Henriette de Mortsauf. He put his whole conviction
into those aggressive diatribes when the time came to write
them. It is true, in dialectical terms, that every idea calls for its
opposite; and it is true that a protagonist in a work of fiction
must talk in character; but this sharp clash of philosophies also
represents the conflict in Balzac himself—between the man he
really was and the man life had made him. He was by nature
generous and gentle-hearted. This is testified to by all those who
knew him (apart from his professional detractors) from Gautier
to Gozlan. Even the most cynical characters in the *Comédie* like
to become defenders of the right (Vautrin ends as Chief of
Police). We must repeat, with George Sand, that Balzac was
'naïve and good'. But he had two powerful reasons for pessimism, his personal misfortunes and the corrupt period he
lived in.

The picture he drew of contemporary society could not fail to
be a sombre one. He meant it to be: 'Great works live on the
passions they contain.' But passion 'is excess, is evil'. He
claimed now and then that the malefactors in the *Comédie* were
all punished for their misdeeds. That is not true; they were often
triumphant. 'It is a fact,' Pierre Laubriet has written, 'that the
terrifying scenes in Balzac, and the characters dedicated to evil,
achieve such a height of grandeur that they inspire us with
mingled feelings of admiration and horror, like Ulysses encountering the Cyclops, or Sinbad faced by monsters on the
strange islands where he landed.' He liked to shed this sul-
phurous light on his menagerie; and if he treated his angels as
harshly as, or more harshly than, his devils, it was because he had
seen life do the same. The happy ending, in his eyes, was a form
of 'the hypocrisy of beauty'. The malignant Madame d'Espard
seeks the indictment of her husband, a worthy man; she finds a
corrupt judge and wins her case. Rastignac and de Marsay,
fundamentally callous and frivolous, become rulers of France,
whereas the great and lofty spirits, Louis Lambert, d'Arthez,
Rabourdin, all fail.

The youthful, high-minded Laurence in *Une Ténébreuse Affaire* is appalled when the innocent Michu is condemned to death. Napoleon, on the battlefield of Jena, points to his armies and says to her: 'Here are three hundred thousand men, and they too are innocent. Well, tomorrow thirty thousand of them will be dead. . . . You must understand, Mademoiselle, that a man may have to die for the laws of his country just as he does for its renown.' Balzac does not judge but merely notes. To change the form of society is only to change the people in power; the species are changeless; there will still be workers, bureaucrats and rascals in carriages—another lot, that is all.

'Why be bitter about spies?' asks Napoleon. 'The spy is no longer a man. He can no longer have feelings, he has become a cog in a machine. That one did his duty. If instruments of his kind ceased to be what they are, government would become impossible.' Even Balzac's honest men, like the advocate Derville, are indulgent towards scoundrels. It is not a matter of condemning but of portraying them, if one is an artist; and of knowing them, to avoid or make use of them, if one is a man of action. 'There are virtues of which a man must rid himself if he is to govern.' And for the rest, the morality of a work of fiction is bound up with the morality of the reader. The young man reading *La Comédie humaine* who does not condemn Lousteau or Rubempré is himself condemned.

What is astonishing is that a writer more capable than any other of conjuring up monsters should have still so respected social values. In fact, Balzac only conceived his monsters in terms of society. The individual exists only in his relation to an environment, an economic situation; that is why Balzac is still approved of by Marxists. He supplies them with arguments. Royalist and political realist though he was, they prefer him to Eugène Sue, the utopian republican who appealed to 'the understanding of the benevolent rich'. Better Gobseck or Vautrin than Prince Rodolphe of the *Mystères de Paris*. To stage the social tempest, Balzac wrote, 'you need men of giant strength to work the machinery of the waves, hidden three floors below the boards'.

And how did he reconcile so many moral contradictions? The truth is that he did not try. He painted his pictures, like any other artist. It was the critics who later sought to assess his moral values. 'The true poet must stay hidden, like God, at the heart of his world, and be visible only in his creation.' Balzac transcended his characters who, at their best, rise high above human weakness and may readily be pardoned on the level of the sublime. The reconciliation, beyond passion and prejudice, makes of his Work, for all its sombreness, a source of strength and serenity. 'I have found,' said Alain, 'that to judge men truly we must love them in the rough fashion Balzac teaches us.'

Part Four

SWAN-SONG

Les caresses d'une femme font évanouir la Muse et fléchir la féroce, la brutale fermeté du travailleur.

BALZAC

XXXI

The Torment of Tantalus

*Il n'y a pas d'intervalles dans ma pensée où je sois seul;
je t'ai en moi comme j'ai mon chagrin, mon travail et mon
sang.*

BALZAC

ABSENCE MAY MAKE the heart grow fonder while its memories are still vivid; but separation too prolonged drains away the
substance of a love-affair. Balzac and Eve Hanska had not met
since his visit to Vienna in 1835. In 1841 he was still writing to
her at monthly or two-monthly intervals, sending her his books
and renewing his avowals, although with precaution, since
Monsieur Hanski might ask to see the letters. Eve wrote very
rarely in reply, being more concerned with the education of her
daughter, whom she adored, than with a lover who had receded
so far into the background of her life. She was bringing up
Anna on strictly religious principles; together they read
Massillon and St François de Sales. Balzac noted sadly that his
Étrangère was becoming ever more remote: 'I do not understand your silence. I have been waiting many days for a reply.
. . .' He consulted a clairvoyant and then 'a very famous
magician', Balthazar, who told him that his life thus far had
been a series of victorious battles and that within six weeks he
would receive a letter which would transform it.

Magicians are not always wrong. On 5 January 1842, a
black-sealed letter arrived from the Ukraine. Wenceslas Hanski
had died on 10 November. To Balzac it was a cause for rejoicing, but he wrote to the widow in suitable terms:

As for me, my dear adored one, although the event makes
possible the attainment of what I have so fervently desired for
nearly ten years, I can, in justice to myself, say to you and before
God that there has never been in my heart anything but complete acceptance, and that even in my unkindest moments I have

not sullied my thoughts with any evil wish. We cannot restrain an occasional involuntary impulse. I have often said to myself, 'How much happier my life would be with *her*!' One cannot preserve one's faith, one's heart, one's most intimate being, entirely without hope. Those motives which the Church holds to be virtues have sustained me in my struggle. But I deeply sympathize with you in your grief. . . .

What he did not realize, with all his perceptiveness, was that Eve genuinely mourned the elderly man who had been her watchful protector and understanding husband. His death confronted her with great difficulties. The estate did not run itself. M. Hanski had always allowed his wife a free hand in disposing of the income, but now his family intervened. A formidable uncle, a sort of feudal Grandet whom Balzac christened Uncle Tamburlaine, lodged a protest against the absolute transference of the property to the widow. The Tsar of All the Russias had no fondness for the Polish-Ukrainian nobility. A false step could lead to Madame Hanska's disgrace and ruin. Therefore (she wrote) Balzac must be in no hurry to come to her, since his precipitate arrival might prove disastrous.

She inquired anxiously about the letters she had written to him. Was that bulky correspondence kept in a place of safety, against the contingency of his sudden death? He replied that he had affixed, to the strong-box containing the letters, a note addressed to his sister Laure, instructing her 'to put them all on the fire without looking at them'. But why was she so perturbed, when now there was no one who had any right to be jealous? Life for the two of them would henceforth be simple; they would end up like Philemon and Baucis, a white-haired, adoring husband and wife seated at their own fireside. The thought of this felicity moved him to tears. What was she afraid of? That he was asking her to share a life of financial embarrassment? On the contrary, he had recently completed so many works that he could afford to pass four months in Russia *at his own expense*. He would bring to their marriage more than literary fame. All he needed, to become a member of three Academies and a deputy in Parliament, was 'financial independence', and this he would achieve by his labours.

But despite his commitments he worked badly during that month of January 1842, and largely because of Eve. At a time so

crucial for them both, and free though she now was of all super-
vision, she left him without news. 'It is nearly a month since I
received your welcome letter, and you have not written to me
since. . . .' She may perhaps have found his 'welcome letter' lacking in tact. And he was already writing to her like a husband,
advising her about the management of the estate and recom-
mending that she should get Anna married as soon as possible
(the girl was then just fourteen) to 'a man of intelligence, but
above all rich' and that in exchange for a fixed income she
should make over all her rights to her daughter, who was in any
case the eventual heiress.

Balzac's state of perturbation increased as the silence continued; and when at length a letter from Eve arrived, on
21 February, he was utterly dismayed. She wrote 'with icy
calm': 'You are free.' She said nothing about marriage; she
intended to devote herself entirely to Anna. Her terrible Aunt
Rosalie had put her on her guard against the French: 'Paris—
never!' Aunt Rosalie (she was in fact a cousin) had good reason
for hating and fearing France. Her mother, Princess Lubo-
mirska, had been beheaded in that country in 1794, and she
herself retained a hideous memory of weeks in prison under the
Terror. But above all the highborn family deplored Eve's
'vulgar' liaison. Her elder sister, Caroline Sobanska, had also
had lovers; but Pushkin, a Russian of authentically noble
lineage, was very much more acceptable than Balzac, whose
bourgeois and bohemian state was utterly to be condemned.

If Eve had written to say that they must wait a year or two, he
would have accepted the situation. As it was, he was moved to
bitterness: 'Disinterest, devotion, faith and constancy are the
four keystones of my character, and between those four there is
only tenderness and absolute good will. . . . So, after that cruel
letter, I shall wait. . . . I have always believed, for my part, that
Petrarch was greater than Laura. If Hugues de Sade had set her
free she would have claimed the protection of the author of the
sonnets, spinning a gossamer web into threads of steel and
finding pretexts to bring in all her relations. . . .' He had been
dealt a most wounding blow.

With what did she reproach him? She had said to him in
Vienna in 1835: 'Do not form any other attachment. I want
your constancy and your whole heart.' This injunction (so he

said) had been more easily observed than she believed. To an idiot who questioned him about his supposed good fortune with women he had replied as follows:

'Monsieur,' I said, 'during the past year I have written twelve volumes and ten acts for the stage, which is to say that I have worked three hundred nights out of the three hundred and sixty-five, ordained by God. Well, the year 1841 is in all respects similar to the ten preceding years. I do not deny that women have fallen in love with an imaginary Monsieur de Balzac, or that they have come to call upon the plump, round-cheeked warrior who has the honour to address you. But all women (the greatest and the least, the duchess and the trollop) claim a man's undivided attention; they cannot, without rebelling, allow him to concern himself with larger matters, even for ten days. That is why women prefer fools. The fool devotes all his time to them and proves that he loves them by interesting himself in nothing else. A man of genius may give them his heart and his fortune, but if he does not give them his whole time as well they will not believe in his love.'

Since the death of Laure de Berny, he had lived, 'the most tender creature on earth . . . in the solitude of the heart and the senses'. Certainly he had hoped at one moment to find a little peace and warmth with M. Visconti; but this (he claimed) had turned out as cruel a disappointment as the one he had suffered at the hands of M. de Castries. In any event, he no longer wanted mistresses; he wanted marriage, permanency, the assurance of living and dying together: 'I beseech you, think of this; you have still a whole life to live. . . .'

He wrote her a series of most touching love-letters, all perfectly sincere. The novelist was living his own romance. But it was not so easy for Eve to believe in his sincerity. She knew very well that faith and constancy had not always been 'the keystones of his character'. Deprived of all support by the death of her husband, she had to take into account the reactions of her family, so unshakeably opposed to any 'misalliance'. Above all she feared that if she remarried Anna would be taken from her. And also she was seven years older than when they had last met, no longer sure of pleasing a lover who seemed to be still so strongly physical in his demands. As a precaution she sent him a recent pastel portrait of herself. 'Clearly, my adored one, the sending of your profile was an act of coquetry, for it might be the picture of a young girl.'

But a major cause of misunderstanding lay in the fact that, familiar though he was with the workings of French society, Balzac knew little about the complexities of life in the Slavonic world. The Poles of the Ukraine lived in a state of harsh repression, both as potentially rebellious Russian subjects and as Roman Catholics. The Governor-General of Kiev, exercising a despotic rule, might if he chose, in the case of a family quarrel, issue an order sequestrating the property under dispute. The High Court in Kiev had refused to endorse M. Hanski's will, on the grounds that it was too favourable to his widow. M. Hanska appealed to the Senate and, through this body, to the Tsar. Eventually, finding that she could not rely upon her brother, the Tsar's aide-de-camp, to present her case adequately, she resolved to go to St Petersburg and do so herself. Balzac approved of this: 'Go to St Petersburg and apply all your intelligence and all your energies to winning your case. Use every means, see the Emperor, if possible use your brother's credit and that of your sister-in-law. Everything you have written to me about this matter is full of good sense.' He was ready to give her all the help he could: 'I will become a Russian citizen, if you see no objection, and go to the Czar myself and ask him to sanction our marriage. It's not a bad idea! . . .'

Russian citizenship! What had induced the most French of writers to pursue this latest and strangest of fantasies? The fact was that in France he had suffered a severe setback. For the past two years all his hopes of easy wealth had lain in the theatre. Victor Hugo, talking with 'the unction of a Père Grandet and the assurance of an accounting clerk', had told him of the money to be made out of plays. Inspired by this, Balzac had offered the Théâtre de l'Odéon a comedy in the Spanish manner, by no means without merit, entitled *Les Ressources de Quinola* (he owed the subject to Marceline Desbordes-Valmore). It dealt with the tribulations of Alfonso Fontanares (a Spaniard who invented a steamship before Fulton) and the stratagems of his valet, Quinola, a sort of Figaro. Balzac read the piece to the company; or, to be exact, he read them the first four acts, doing so admirably, but then announced that the fifth was not yet written; he would tell them how it ended. And here he came to grief. Obviously improvising on the spur of the moment, he stumbled badly and lost his way. When he had finished the actress Marie Dorval, on whom he was counting, said that she did not see a part in it for her.

Balzac to Marie Dorval: When I wrote to you about the terms I had extracted from the company of the Second Theatre, my dear Faustina [the name of the character he wanted her to create], Merle let fall a word which calls for the letter I now write [Jean-Toussaint Merle was her husband] '. . . I fancy,' said Merle, 'that Madame Dorval will not accept without having seen the part.' This would postpone the decision until your return, in ten days. If you have not the confidence in me that I have in you there is no point in waiting, for *they*, at the Odéon, cannot wait.

I ask you therefore to write and tell me if you accept my conditions, and to promise that, if we have a success, you will not allow yourself to be taken away from my play as long as the success lasts. Be faithful to me! If it were a matter of your heart I should not be so stupid as to say such a thing; but it is a matter of your talent.

If we have a great success you will receive about ten thousand francs, assuming an average of 2,500 francs for a hundred performances. If it's a flop you will go back to the Dutchmen of whom Merle has spoken to me. . . . We cannot leave the matter undecided. So I await word from you. Write to me at Rue Richelieu, 112.

You said to me 'I will go with you wherever you go', and I have counted on your word, not as a woman but as an actress, and, as you see, I have secured you excellent terms . . .

Despite the failure of the reading and the defection of Marie Dorval, Lireux, the manager of the Odéon, accepted the play and praised it warmly, talking of Calderon and Lope de Vega. He announced that it would go into rehearsal at once, despite certain preposterous stipulations made by Balzac, who insisted that there should be no 'claque' and that every seat in the house should be placed at his disposal for the first three performances, *to be sold by him*. Léon Gozlan has left us the following fragment of conversation:

'I want nothing but Chevaliers de Saint-Louis in the back stalls. . . . In the front stalls, only Peers of France. Ambassadors will have the stage-boxes, deputies and high officials will be in the dress circle.'

'What about the upper circle?'

'High finance.'

'And the gallery?'

'Carefully selected wealthy middle-class.'

'But what about the critics—where are they to go?'

'They'll have to pay for their seats if there are any left—and there won't be.'

A state of warfare with no holds barred had existed between Balzac and the critics since *Illusions perdues*. 'They want to scalp me,' he said, 'and I want to drink out of their skulls.' He pictured the first night as though it were a scene in a novel. It was to be the most brilliant occasion Paris had ever known, a dramatic triumph, a fashionable sensation—and financially rewarding. Not merely did he sell tickets, he used all the tricks of a black-market salesman. To quote Gozlan again:

If someone asked for a dress-circle box he replied from behind his grill, 'Too late! Too late! The last has been sold to the Princess of Modena.' . . . 'But Monsieur de Balzac, we're prepared to pay a very high price.' . . . 'Even if you were to offer me the earth you still couldn't have a dress-circle loge because there are none left.' The customer retired defeated. These methods worked for a few days. Seats were acquired with difficulty at exorbitant prices. But then the excitement died down. . . . During the week before the opening night Balzac was happy to sell seats at the normal price. . . .

The play eventually opened on 19 March 1842, to an almost empty house. Many people stayed away in exasperation, and the few who came did so to jeer. It was a disaster. 'To no avail,' wrote the critic, Hippolyte Lucas, 'had Monsieur de Balzac allotted the greater part of the seats to a selected public (at very high prices). Public opinion protested in the name of Literature, slighted by one of its most eminent practitioners.' But it was Monsieur Lucas himself, not Literature, who took offence.

'*Quinola* has been the subject of a memorable battle, like that over Hugo's *Hernani*,' Balzac wrote to Eve. 'For seven consecutive performances people booed the play from beginning to end without listening to it. Today is the seventeenth performance, and the Odéon is making money. . . .' But they were making very little money. '*Quinola* won't bring me in more than 5,000 francs. . . . All my enemies, and they are numerous, rushed in to attack me. With two exceptions the papers vied with one another in abusing me and condemning the play.'

The theatre emphatically did not suit him, and perhaps this failure was providential. He returned to his normal work, 'in order to live and fulfil contracts', he said; but in truth because he produced splendid novels as readily as an apple-tree produces apples. 'I'm going to do what I've been doing for the past fifteen years, to bury myself in the depths of work and creation, which has the advantage that its pangs cause you to forget other sufferings. I have to earn 13,000 francs by my pen during the next month.' Far from confessing to the pleasure he took in it, he talked as though he were condemned to a treadmill: 'To be for ever creating! Even God only created for six days! . . .'

He dreamed, in good faith, of escape from this endless travail, retreat with the beloved to some remote corner of Russia or France where he would forget all about creditors and publishers and the writing of books. It was a genuine longing, yet what would he have done in his corner except go on working? But still the pace was too great, even for him. 'Yesterday I finished *Le Voyage en Coucou.* . . . I'm finishing *Albert Savarus*; they're shouting for *Les Paysans*; and *La Presse* is asking for the end of *Les Deux Frères*, of which the first part appeared two years ago. It's enough to drive one mad. . . .'

But he did not go mad or leave anything unfinished. He owed *Le Voyage en Coucou* (*Un Début dans la vie*) to his sister Laure and her daughters, Sophie and Valentine. The girls' progress at school always interested him, and he liked to see their written work. When they earned his praises he told them that they were richly rewarded in gaining the approval of a man 'as distinguished as himself'; and sometimes he even did them the honour of borrowing their material. *Un Début dans la vie* was derived from a little tale written by Laure, based in its turn on a story her daughters invented, of which she later published her own version.

It is the story of some young people on a coach who indulge in high-flown and impudent conversation, not realizing that the person they are talking about is among their fellow travellers, an influential man capable of ruining their prospects in life. Oscar Husson, whose start in life it is, is a boastful youth, and those few minutes of foolish vanity wreck his career. There was something of Oscar in Balzac himself, as there is in every young man. But he expanded the trifling, adolescent tale by bringing in characters already known to the reader—the Comte de Serizy, the advocate Desroches and Joseph Bridau, the painter—and endowing it with the weight and substance of recent history. The lives of all the characters are linked by great events. The fact of having been born in 1799 was of immeasurable value to Balzac. His first-hand knowledge of three régimes enabled him to turn his spotlight not only on the past but on the future. Services rendered in times of trouble may lead later to unexpected favours, as Bernard-François well knew. The Serizy estates having been saved during the Revolution by their agent, the agent's son is able to rob the Count almost with impunity. Oscar Husson takes part in the street-fighting in July 1830, and eventually loses an arm in Algeria. The hero thus redeems the youthful liar; the novelist summons History to his aid.

Balzac dedicated the book to Laure: 'That the brilliant and modest spirit who gave me the subject of this Scene may be duly honoured—HER BROTHER.' In fact the brief tale is of value principally as a stone in the edifice, but it is an amusing, well-contrived detail and a further exposition of the Balzac morality: 'work, probity, discretion'. Oscar Husson is rather late in learning that those three words contain the secret of success. As for Balzac, in the matter of work he need fear no reproaches; but his views on probity were peculiar to himself, and for discretion he had no talent at all.

If in Oscar Husson there was something of the uncouth adolescent who committed so many *gaffes* in the home of Laure de Berny, in *Albert Savarus* we have a picture of the grown man. With *Louis Lambert*, *Le Lys dans la vallée*, and certain of the shorter tales, it is one of the fictions most nearly related to Balzac's personal life. The master-builder in erecting his cathedral was guided by no considerations save those of art, but he sometimes allowed his portrait to appear in a stained-glass

window. Albert Savarus is Balzac himself in the year 1842; it is
also a poignant appeal to the unpredictable Eve. He wrote to
her: 'Amid the thousand torments of this renewed battle, the
thought, "If she should grow weary!" has pierced me to the
heart, causing me more pain than all the stones they fling at
me. . . . There is a magnificent life within my life, and I have no
one to confide in except this sheet of paper.' No one? But a novel
is the most docile of all confidants.

'If she should grow weary . . .' The words contain the key to
Albert Savarus. An ambitious man of genius, having suffered
humiliating reverses, comes to live in Besançon, a 'secret' town
whose secret Balzac had penetrated, in one of his miraculous,
intuitive flashes, during a visit of a few hours, when he went
there to buy paper in 1833. The description of Albert Savarus
is Balzac's own portrait, as he saw himself at the age of forty-
three: 'A superb head: black hair in which a few white threads
were already mingled, hair such as we see in the pictures of
St Peter and St Paul, with thick, shining locks, stiff as horsehair;
a white, round neck like a woman's; a magnificent forehead
divided by that furrow that great undertakings, great thoughts
and profound meditation inscribe on the foreheads of great
men. . . .'

Savarus is deeply in love with a high-born Italian lady, the
Duchess of Argaiolo, and seeks to achieve a political triumph as
an offering worthy of her. He conquers Besançon with his
eloquence and his understanding of the town's complex social
life, and by winning the support of the profoundly wise Vicar-
General, whose friend he becomes. His triumph would be
complete had he not attracted the love of a young townswoman,
Rosalie de Watteville, a romantic but malicious creature with
a fondness for intrigue. Disdained by Savarus, who does not
even notice her, she revenges herself by intercepting and
falsifying letters between him and the Duchess. The outraged
lady impulsively marries someone else. Savarus in despair turns
to religion and enters the Grande Chartreuse, the realm of
silence. Broken in will-power he renounces all worldly ambition
and delivers himself into the hands of his Superior: '*Fuge, tace,
late.*' Balzac took pleasure in depicting those sudden shipwrecks
in which a man loses himself body and soul. How often, in his
own despairing moments, had he sighed for a similar end!

Albert Savarus was a cypher-novel, easily decoded and addressed to Eve. 'I'm at the end of my strength; if you should fail me I shall go down for good in one way or another. . . .' In writing to her he made no secret of his own affinity with Savarus. He set the beginning of the love-affair nostalgically in Switzerland. The lovers meet in Geneva, but 'I don't want to put the princess in the Maison Mirabaud, because there are people who would draw conclusions. . . .' Still less in Diodati: this would have been transparent, and the four syllables still caused his heart to beat faster. Like Balzac, Savarus always has the image of his *étrangère* in his mind, and a picture of her dwelling. The young woman who separates the lovers is called Rosalie, after Eve's dangerous aunt. Everything in the book helps the author to exorcize his 'black devils'.

There is a secondary theme which he pointed out to Eve:

I want to include in the first volume of my *Comédie humaine* an important lesson for the Man, as opposed to the Woman, and to show how, through excessive worldly ambition, and by over-straining heart and mind, he may reach the point of no longer desiring what was the first object of all his efforts. It will be *Louis Lambert* in another form. This small but great subject will be called *Albert Savarus*; I hope to make of it a noble and poetic page to enrage the critics. . . .

The lesson applied no less to Balzac, who had reason enough to shudder at his own huge programme. 'I have no longer the strength or capacity for anything save happiness,' says Savarus, 'and if it does not come soon to place its wreath of roses on my head. . . . I shall be a thing destroyed. . . . To die when one has reached the goal, like the runner of antiquity. . . . No longer to possess the power to enjoy when one has earned the right to happiness! . . . Oh, how many men have suffered that fate! . . .' And his author wrote: 'I'm afraid of being nothing but an empty sack when happiness arrives.'

It was an admonition to Eve, but she seems to have understood neither the lesson nor the novel. 'I'm surprised that you didn't like *Albert Savarus*,' wrote Balzac sadly. She replied that it was a 'man's book', in which she was right. It was the work of a builder in torment who stands contemplating his unfinished structure, knowing all that remains to be done, knowing that each day carries off another 'shred of his inner life' and of its duration; a man who feels in his bones the shrinking of the ass's skin, who longs to lay aside the too exacting task and rest in the arms of a loving woman, and who fears lest, robbed of this hope, he will no longer have the strength to live.

XXXII

Reunion in St Petersburg

L'espoir est une mémoire qui désire.

BALZAC

IN EVERY LIFE there are periods of pause. We await an event, a decision, and life goes on but living is supended. So it was with Balzac after Wenceslas Hanski's death. 'I now have a great mistrust of life and what it may bring me,' he wrote to Eve. The love which for some years had seemed to be fading was revived with a new hope, but overwork was beginning to affect his health: 'I have a constant twitching of the eyelids which greatly troubles me, for I see in it a portent of some nervous ailment.' Dr Nacquart, that firm believer in natural remedies, again sent him to bed for a fortnight: 'A fortnight without doing anything—I who am ceaselessly active! So I have amused myself by thinking about *us*, making plans, turning up "happy cards" as the fortune-tellers say.'

In bed and feverish he sought to visualize that rosy future. His lawyer and his 'man of straw' would contrive matters so that he could keep Les Jardies, and he would furnish and decorate the house for Eve. Given time, patience and money, it could be turned into a delightful retreat. 'With this and a Paris house, and 24,000 francs a year, we shall have an ideal life, for I shall be getting 15,000 from the Institute, and my pen, working only six hours a day, will bring me in 20,000 a year for another ten years, which will enable me to accumulate some capital. . . .' It was another pipe-dream. Far from seeking to keep Les Jardies, his lawyer, Maître Gavault, was asking for his authorization to sell it; indeed, was insisting that it must be sold:

He says that it is a ruinous expense, and he undertakes to find something better with the money he gets for it. . . . He's genuinely attached to me. . . . He has as much pride in me as I have in myself; but he's a dawdler. He wants to pay off some dreadful debts, and for my part I'm trying to pay off some terrible ones out of the money I need to live on. But earning money means creating and creating. I'm beginning to fear that my capacity for work will fail. . . .'

He was wrong in this. Despite worry and sickness his output was still very large and worthy of him. *Honorine*, which he claimed to have written in three days (he had his vanities), was an admirable novella, written with restraint but daring in its subject, as charming as *La Femme abandonnée* or *Une Fille d'Ève*. Honorine leaves the most estimable of husbands, Comte Octave de Bauvan, for an unworthy lover who promptly deserts her. She lives alone, trying to gain a livelihood as a florist, although her husband is only too ready to take her back. But he physically repels her, and she prefers an arduous, solitary existence to a life of fashion in which she would be obliged to submit to his embraces. He watches over her at a distance and, without her knowing it, helps her by buying at a high price the artificial flowers she makes. Between the lines we catch a glimpse of Balzac's personal apprehensions as he wondered whether the absent Eve would ever return to him. His account of Octave de Bauvan's tormented nights is a description of his own:

Can you see me calming the frenzies of my most violent despair by gazing at a miniature in which I contemplate and kiss her forehead, the smile on her lips, the outlines of her face, and breathe the whiteness of her skin, and can almost feel and touch the dark ringlets of her hair? Have you ever caught me transfigured with a sudden hope while I writhe beneath the thousand darts of despair and stride through the Paris mud to subdue my eagerness with physical fatigue? . . . There are nights when I hear the tinkling bells of madness. I fear these violent transitions from a weak hope suddenly gleaming and darting to an access of despair that brings me as low as man can sink. . . . Three days before the arrival of Marie-Louise, Napoleon lay in anguish on their marriage-bed at Compiègne. . . . All great passions have the same fury. I love like a poet and like an emperor! . . .

Yet Balzac had his doubts about the story, touching and poignant though it was: '*Honorine* is not bad, but the soberness of style is disturbing—only to me, for there are people who find

it superb, whereas perhaps it is really weak. . . .' He was uncertain because his critics were unsparing. *Albert Savarus* was
condemned for its 'heavy, congested style . . . with a feeling of
fatigue.' The new serial-king was Eugène Sue. All France was
awaiting the next instalment of the *Mystères de Paris*. The
Revue des Deux Mondes said that the author of *Louis Lambert*
and *Eugénie Grandet* was simply living on his reputation—a
monstrous injustice. Could he be said to be living on his
reputation when, within a brief period, he produced the second
part of *Illusions perdues, La Muse du Département, La Torpille*
and *L'Envers de l'histoire contemporaine*, all written hastily and
in fragments because one editor or another was crying out for
copy; while at the same time he spent two hundred hours a
month at the printer's in Lagny, reading the proofs of the
Comèdie humaine? However beset he might be, he still revised
his work ten or eleven times over, which Dumas and Sue
certainly never did.

He was like a mason building half a dozen houses at once, or
a chess-master playing a dozen simultaneous games and winning
them all. He had no difficulty in returning to a work laid aside
years before. *La Muse du Département*, for example, simmered
for a long time in his slow, mysterious furnace. At the start, in
1832, it was a cruel little tale entitled *La Grande Bretèche*. Round
about 1837 it was expanded into a novella, *La Grande Bretèche,
ou Les Trois Vengeances*, one of the *Scènes de la vie de province*,
in which the virtuous and disconsolate wife of a wealthy provincial landowner is in danger of being seduced by a high
government official. As a warning to her, two Parisians tell
horrific tales of marital revenge. Balzac here made some use of
the voluble revelations of Caroline Marbouty, but only to a
limited extent; and for the town of Limoges, of which she had
been 'the Muse', he substituted Sancerre, which he knew
through his friend, Dr Émile Regnault.

Then, in 1843, having had the idea of writing Benjamin
Constant's *Adolphe* 'in reverse'—that is to say, from the point of
the woman—he brought Caroline out of store to make her, with
modifications, *La Muse du Département*. Dinah Piedefer, of
protestant stock (like Caroline), is married off by her parents to
a wealthy and 'antlike' husband, La Baudraye. Like Caroline,
she forms a literary salon where she reads her poems, winning

the applause of the gentlemen, if not of the ladies; but, again like Caroline, despite her many admirers she remains faithful to her husband for a long time.

Then two gentlemen arrive in Sancerre, former citizens of the town who have become great men in Paris (like the surgeon, Dupuytren, when he stayed with the Marboutys, their visit has to do with a parliamentary election). They are Dr Horace Bianchon and Etienne Lousteau, an indolent but amusing hack-writer. Dinah falls for Lousteau's elegant talk and becomes his mistress, to find, after he has left, that she is pregnant. 'There is in Dinah,' Maurice Bardèche has written, 'a feminine quixotry which ordains her fate. . . . She has spent ten years of her life flirting with intellect. . . . She makes the same mistake with love. . . .' She rushes to Paris, to live there with Lousteau; and now the story becomes cruel. She has given her heart to a man unworthy of it, who seeks to rid himself of her by staging an ignoble farce with a troop of strumpets and hangers-on. But the noble-spirited Dinah (Lousteau calls her 'Didine'), who believes everything and understands nothing, is unshakable in her devotion. Not until six years have passed does she realize the worthlessness of her lover, and then, having read *Adolphe*, she refuses to play the part of Ellénore. Instead of giving way to despair she returns to her husband, who takes her back and accepts the paternity of Lousteau's two sons. The powerful, sardonic tale proclaims, in a manner very characteristic of Balzac, the inevitable degradation of any love that does not conform to the rules of society.

Caroline Marbouty was by no means pleased with *La Muse du Département*, which she feared would give rise to talk in Limoges. Her own daughters might be attributed to Jules Sandeau, and she herself might be suspected of having kept a second-rate writer in Paris on her husband's money. Fortunately this did not happen. The people of Limoges were not great readers.

Caroline might well have been touched by 'Didine', the gallant young woman who rises above misfortune and, even after the rupture, comes to the rescue of her former lover, the man who taught her the 'red gaze' of desire. But she was not. She chose instead to answer with a novel of her own, *Une Fausse Position*, written under the name of Claire Brunne, in which she depicted herself in two aspects—as a discontented provincial wife and a *déclassée* middle-class woman in Paris. She took the name of Camille and described herself as *une nature d'élite*, a rare spirit. Camille finds her way into the literary world of Paris and makes the acquaintance of Ulric (Balzac) whom she treats with little indulgence: 'Popular and sought-after, he was intoxicated with his long-delayed success, to the point that he did not know what to do with it, and his dreams, his plans, his ambitions became as vast as his opinion of himself. His vanity culminated in absurdity and monomania. It created meretricious needs. . . . A man of genius, Ulric acquiesced in the spirit of the time. He saw everything in terms of money, as belonging to money or deriving from money. . . . But he had the simplicity to admit it . . . and so he made many enemies. . . .' The publication of *Une Fausse Position* in 1844 cost Caroline the friendship of all those who, recognizing themselves in its angry pages, felt themselves insulted. She never saw Balzac again. She even lost the dedication of *La Grenadière*. But the great-hearted Dinah still keeps our esteem. The portrait infinitely excels the sitter. Balzac had never displayed a greater mastery; and yet . . .

And yet dissatisfaction and a profound lethargy were overtaking him. He had written in the past: 'The great events in my life are my works.' Now there was a strange reversal. His life was no longer wholly absorbed in literary creation; it was, as he repeatedly said to Eve, ruled by his heart, by the need to find a love as ardent as his own, by the memory of past happiness: 'I recall the path in Diodati, the pebbles of the alleyway through the garden of the Maison Mirabaud where we walked together; or a certain tone of voice, a pressure of the hands. . . . And other things that cause me to turn pale!' He burst out in an agony of frustrated love: 'Oh God, one day you'll realize my childlike nature, its truth and sincerity, my inexhaustible tenderness, the undying constancy of my heart, when you find me clinging to your skirts for the rest of my days. . . .' He breathed the scent of her letters for hours on end; he worked solely for her. *Una fides.*

He knew how to 'persuade others of many things and himself of anything'; and so he firmly believed that since 1832 he had had but one faith, one love, one single hope. Who had truly loved him, except Eve? 'If you knew what my mother is like! She's both a monster and a monstrosity! At this very moment she's engaged in *killing my sister* as she did poor Laurence and our grandmother. . . . I have come very near to breaking with my mother; it is almost a necessity. But I prefer to go on suffering. It is a wound that nothing can heal. We thought she was mad. We consulted the doctor who has been her friend for thirty-three years and he said, "Alas, she isn't mad, she's bad!" . . .' We may concede to this savage resentment a particle of truth, but it contains far more ingratitude and an insatiable desire to be pitied: 'I had neither mother nor childhood.' He forgot the gaiety of Villeparisis, the jesting of the 'most excellent family', the poor lady's devotion.

As for Madame de Berny—yes, she had been a mother to him, she had formed him; but how could she have given him what he really longed for, the love of a young and beautiful woman? And Countess Guidoboni-Visconti? . . . 'Versailles? Have no fear. . . . Versailles has long been condemned for ever. Ingratitude and heedlessness, that is the story of Versailles. Louis XIV took a fancy to Versailles, which is a chilly place without a heart. . . .' The untruthful words were simply intended to allay Eve's jealousy: he was still writing Fanny Guidoboni affectionate notes which he signed 'Bally', and even—supreme proof of friendship!—borrowing money from her. Yet he solemnly affirmed to Eve that any love between him and 'the English-woman' was a thing of the past. And Caroline Marbouty? He snubbed her when she wanted to visit him: 'Monsieur de Balzac does not forget the charm of Madame Marbouty. But Madame Marbouty has perhaps forgotten what it is to be a wretched writer, forced to work for a living. . . .'

No, nothing now existed for him excepted his angel, his 'dear darling', his flower of light. He christened her 'Madame l'Humble' because she desired neither celebrity nor notoriety. But he would compel her, whether she liked it or not, to share his fame and his honours. The Académie Française was now almost a certainty. He had run into Charles Nodier, a very influential Academician, who had said to him: 'My dear Balzac, you can be assured of unanimity in the Academy. But the Academy, although it will readily accept a scoundrelly politician destined to be pilloried by history, and even a rogue who has only escaped justice through his wealth, turns pale at the thought of a note-of-hand which may send its signatory to prison. It has neither kindness nor pity for the man of genius who is poor and whose affairs are in bad shape. . . . Make a position for yourself by marriage, by proving that you owe nothing, or by possessing a house of your own, and you'll be elected.'

And once elected, Balzac went on, 'I shall be appointed a member of the Dictionary Commission, which means 6,000 francs a year in perpetuity; plus 2,000 as an Academician, and I shall certainly be elected to the Académie des Inscriptions et Belles-Lettres and become permanent secretary. . . .' After which, as his habit was, he passed from the future tense to the present: 'So apart from anything the Government may do I have a permanent income of 14,000, dependent on no one. . . . Win your case! You will be winning mine. . . .'

Eve, on her side, wrote to him pathetically about her trials as a lonely woman beset by complicated affairs. 'Three years to wait, it means death,' she said, which sounded promising. 'But no,' he replied, 'I can answer to you for the future. Nothing will make me change, or you either. So let us trust in God!' Meanwhile the two sundered hearts were living not too unhappily in their separate worlds. Balzac dined at the house of Madame de Castries (now a duchess) in company with Hugo and Gozlan, a feast of reason and a flow of soul. Madame Hanska, in St Petersburg, was paid court to by an agreeable, cultivated elderly gentleman, a Monsieur de Balck, who even hinted at marriage. She soothed him gently, persuaded him of the impossibility of the match and sought to turn his thoughts to God; and he assured her that he felt better, more religious, every time he had the happiness of meeting her. Balzac, when she told him this, was highly alarmed: 'I dare not tell you how much I suffer at the thought of your making anyone happy, even the poor old man you mention. . . .'

He was guilty of an act of astonishing rashness. Despite his knowledge of men and women and the snares of love, he sent her a letter of introduction to Liszt, who was leaving for St Petersburg to give a series of recitals.

My dear Franz. . . . If you wish to do me a personal favour you will spend an evening with the lady who will send you this note on my behalf, and you will play something for an angelic child who will, I am sure, fascinate you—Mademoiselle Anna de Hanska. . . .

All Europe knew of the power over women which Liszt owed to his looks, his talent and his exalted conquests. Eve, who kept a diary, confessed in it that he had a disturbing effect upon her. She went with Anna to his first recital and was enraptured. Liszt visited her several times, and when he departed for Moscow bade her adieu with an air of affliction by which she was not unmoved. In a rush of 'Rzewuskian temperament'— that is to say, a love of taking chances, a love of great men and a love of lecturing—she wrote to him. With a man like Liszt the correspondence might have led anywhere, but by the time he returned to St Petersburg he had become involved with a deter- mined young lady in Moscow. The mortified Madame Hanska reminded him of past misadventures, of his flight with Marie d'Agoult and what came of it. 'Have no fear,' he replied gravely. 'I have learnt reason. This time if I abduct the lady I shall take her husband too.' He was, however, perfectly capable of accommodating both ladies, and he made pressing advances to Eve, who was far from sure of herself:

Liszt is of average height. . . . His nose is straight and well- chiselled, but the best thing about him is the shape of his mouth; there is something particularly sweet, I would even say seraphic, about that mouth. . . . He is an extraordinary mixture and I enjoy studying him. There are sublime things in him, but also deplorable ones. He is the human reflection of what is splendid in Nature—but also, alas, of what is terrible. There are sublime heights, but bottomless depths and abysses . . . which will bring more than one disaster upon himself and others. . . . The society of Liszt has its dangers—he makes reprehensible things seem attractive, and when he lets fall some remark which is really profoundly immoral, one smiles—one tells oneself that an artist of such genius has a right to disregard reason . . . one forgives, one even applauds, one loves him. . . .'

The flirtation became a skirmish. Eve kept him at arm's length, and Liszt accused her of prudery. When, before leaving Russia, he came to bid her farewell, 'he took my hand, kissed it and held it clasped in both of his. I withdrew it gently and said, "Believe me, Monsieur Liszt, you must not return. This must be our last meeting." ' Which was wise of her, and the terrified Balzac never referred to him again except as 'poor Liszt', whom Marie d'Agoult had left for Émile de Girardin after a liaison lasting ten years, during which she had borne him three children. He wrote: 'Be very careful what you say to Liszt if you write to him; you don't realize how discredited he is....' The great analyst of love could be remarkably ingenuous.

With jealousy an added spur, Balzac was more than ever anxious to go to St Petersburg, and not only in order to join Eve now that she was free. He believed that he could help her win her case. He had a great reputation in Russia, as he knew; he held himself to be a good advocate, and he imagined that his personal appeal to the Tsar would prove decisive. But Eve had no intention of letting her cause be pleaded by her lover: 'Stay quietly where you are and leave me to do things my own way.' Very much more Polish than Russian, she was little impressed by the despotism of the Romanovs, and in her private diary she talked about, 'the furtive gaze of the slave'.

Monday, 16 May 1843, was Balzac's forty-fourth birthday:

Oh, great St Honoré, after whom such a fine ugly street in Paris has been named, give me your special protection this year! Do not let the ship sink! Cause me to cease to be a bachelor, through the good offices of Monsieur le Maire or Monsieur le Consul de France, because you know that I have been married in spirit for nearly eleven years!

He had greater need than ever of the protection of his patron saint. Work was overwhelming him. He had to spend whole nights at the printing-works in Lagny, sleeping on a truckle-bed, while at the same time he was fulfilling other commitments to raise money for his journey to Russia.

I'm consuming three pots of black coffee a day and getting stomach-cramps as usual, and my blood's boiling and my skin's the colour of wood! Oh, how I mean to rest, to live like the animals and think about nothing, to become a 'cockney' of St Petersburg during this glorious June, July, August, September and October! Four months without newspapers, without books, without *proofs*, except such as you may require of me! I want to be very quiet, not to see too many people, to be within a yard of you and live like an oyster. . . .

In June 1843, he finished the third part of *Illusions perdues*, entitled *Les Souffrances de l'inventeur*: 'I have to show the tremendous contrast of the life of David Séchard and Ève Chardon in the provinces, while Lucien was committing all his blunders in Paris. The tribulations of virtue as opposed to the tribulations of vice.' It was a work of great difficulty. Balzac had sought to interest the reader in his account of the conflict between Séchard, the inventor of a revolutionary method of paper-making, and the brothers Cointet, wealthy and old-fashioned printers. He was not sure that he had succeeded. The picture of provincial life, and the noble-hearted David and Ève, seemed colourless after the full-blooded picture of Paris. He worked over the proofs fifteen or sixteen times.

Then there was *Esther*, the sequel to *La Torpille* (later to be embodied in *Splendeurs et misères des courtisanes*), with its harrowing account of the aged Baron Nucingen falling besottedly in love. He wanted to show 'the true Paris'; but, as always in Balzac, horror had its aspect of comedy (the obese banker, stuffed with aphrodisiacs, paying grotesque court to Esther) and also of pathos (the sudden dawning, in an old man, of the romantic illusions of youth): 'Love then flowers like a neglected seed from which a tardy sun draws splendid blossoms.' Balzac could no longer even say that he was tired: 'I've become a sort of word-machine, and I think I must be made of iron.' The printers in the 'abominable place' at Lagny were driven to distraction, but the author held out, and by July everything was done. And now another threat arose. The newspapers serializing the two stories, *David Séchard* and *Esther* were both in low water and there was a danger that he would not be paid: 'The attempt to live by one's pen is a monstrously silly undertaking.' However, thanks to Gavault he got enough to cover his expenses. Then he had to go to the Russian Embassy for a visa. He was interviewed by a secretary, Victor de Balabin, who noted in his diary, 'a little, fat, flabby individual with the face of a pantler, the general look of a cobbler, the girth of a barrel-maker, the manners of a hatter, the dress of an inn-

keeper, and that's him! He hasn't a penny so he's going to Russia; he's going to Russia so he hasn't a penny. . . .'
Sainte-Beuve wrote to Juste Olivier:

Balzac, penniless and worse than penniless, has left for St Petersburg after letting it be known in the press that he is going for reasons of health and has decided not to write anything about Russia. The hospitality of that country has been so often abused that no doubt he hopes by this promise to make himself welcome and win all kinds of small indulgences from its ruler. But do his promises count for anything in these days?

The Russian chargé d'affaires in Paris reported to his government:

Since this writer is always in financial difficulties, and at present is more embarrassed than ever, it is possible that some form of literary speculation is one of the objects of his journey. . . . In which case, having regard to Monsieur de Balzac's need of money, it might be possible for us to turn his pen to our advantage (since he still retains a certain popularity here, as he does in Europe as a whole) by getting him to write a refutation of the slanderous book by Monsieur de Custine . . .'*

However, the suggestion was not acted upon. Balzac reached St Petersburg on 29 July 1843, western calendar, and wrote in Eve's diary:

I arrived on 17 July (Polish style) and at mid-day had the honour to be received by . . . my dear Countess Eve in her home, the Maison Koutaizoff. . . . I had not seen her since Vienna, and I found her as beautiful and young as she was then. But there had been an interval of seven years during which she had remained in her desert of corn and I in the vast human desert of Paris. She greeted me like an old friend, and to me all the hours that I had spent away from her seemed wretched, cold and sad. Between 1833 and 1843 ten years have sped, during which all my feelings for her, contrary to the general rule, have been intensified by the pangs of separation and my many disappointments. We cannot remake time or affection!

To preserve appearances he did not stay at the Maison

* *La Russie en 1839.*

Koutaizoff but in lodgings, where his slumbers were disturbed by bed-lice. But what did anything matter, now that his Eve was ready to love him without restraint? They were back in the raptures of Geneva and Vienna, enhanced indeed, for now that she was widowed and free she welcomed the closest intimacy. Her legal affairs seemed to be going well and she was no longer afraid of losing her estate. The notes which Balzac wrote her testify to his happiness: 'Sweet *minette* . . . My adored *loulou* . . . A thousand caresses from *loulou* to *louloue* . . . I shall be with you in an hour. . . .' Her nearness so inspired him that he could even work without the aid of coffee!

He called daily at about midday, concerning himself little with 'the rest of the world'. However his presence in St Petersburg did not go unnoticed. Princess Rasoumowska wrote to Eve that she had heard *from the Emperor* that 'a certain personage, he who has best understood and portrayed the heart of Woman, has just arrived.' Another lady wrote: 'Shall we know how to appreciate and welcome this illustrious man? Please God that he will take away a favourable impression of Russia.' Eve was besieged by requests to meet him. Count Benckendorff had him invited to the military review at Krasnoye-Selo, where he had a close view of the Tsar: 'Everything that has been written about the Emperor's good looks is true. There is not another man in Europe . . . who can compare with him.' Balzac had a touch of sunstroke at the review, genuine as well as metaphorical.

A week after his arrival the wife of Chancellor Nesselrode wrote to her son: 'Balzac condemns Custine, as was only to be expected; we need not suppose him to be sincere.' A newspaper remarked: 'Russia knows her value and cares little for the opinion of foreigners.' In short, authority asked nothing of him, and Balzac himself had no thought of refuting Custine. He was not looking for official subventions or sops to his vanity. It was enough for him to see Eve, to have endless conversations with her, their only audience the samovar, the 'stupid elephant', the small rug, the Louis XIV screen, the armchair where she rested her adored head, the ivy decorating the chandelier, of which he took away a leaf, seeing in it a symbol of their destiny—'I die where I cling.' There was a double-backed lovers' seat in her boudoir, and a blue settee favourable to dozing while he awaited the rustle of a skirt, the creak of the door which sent a shiver down his spine. Ah, the blue and yellow dress of that first day! Anna Hanska later recalled, in a letter to her mother, how Balzac had read them *Une Fille d'Ève*, a short novel of great delicacy and charm in which he shows how the dangerous thoughts, the obsessions, which in men are a spur to action in women take the form of romantic fantasy. Marie de Vandenesse, the wife of Félix of the *Lys dans la vallée*, becomes infatuated with a gifted, unprepossessing writer, Raoul Nathan; but Félix, formed by Henriette de Mortsauf, proves himself a wise and skilful husband and averts disaster. The admirably told tale, with its shrewd, knowledgeable picture of people and society, delighted mother and daughter. Balzac had reconquered his Eve. She had recently read the correspondence between Goethe and Bettina Brentano (who had since become the wife of Achim von Arnim), and the episode of a romantic girl writing to a great man she has never met had reminded her of her own early correspondence with Balzac. Indeed, it had inspired her to write a novella she afterwards burnt. She told Balzac this, and he asked to see the Goethe-Bettina letters. He wrote a savage article about them. 'This book is for the pure in heart, not for the evil-minded,' Frau von Arnim had said in her Preface—in other words *Honi soit qui mal y pense*. Balzac took the part of the evil-minded, finding the letters self-conscious and artificial:

> If the expression of love (the *literary* expression, be it understood) is to become a sublime work of art—and in this matter only the sublime is tolerable—the love which is depicted must be complete; it must be revealed in its triple form, head, heart and body; it must be divine and sensual at the same time, expressed with insight, with poetry. . . .

Bettina, he said, had never loved Goethe; she had simply made him an excuse for writing letters. She had embroidered waistcoats and slippers for him. 'I hoped that in the process of dressing Goethe she— —But no! The waistcoats were as un-electrifying as the prose!' It was a way of saying to Eve, 'The only real loves are those like our own, not only of the heart but of the body.' But severe though he was with Goethe and

Bettina, he did not lose sight of the subject and later wrote to
Eve:

Your story sounded so charming that if you wish to give me
great pleasure you will write it again and send it to me. I'll
revise it and publish it under my own name. Thus you won't
have changed the colour of your stockings, and at the same time
you'll know something of the joys of authorship when you see
how much of your elegant and delightful writing I have preserved. You must first describe a provincial family, of which
one member, growing up amid the vulgarities of that way of life,
is an ardent and romantic girl; then, through the correspondence, you must *slide into* the description of a poet in Paris. The
poet's friend, who continues the correspondence, should be one
of those glib young men who become the hangers-on of a famous
man. There is a nice picture to be drawn of the gentleman-
lackeys who deal with the newspapers, run errands and so on.
. . . The denouement should be in favour of this young man, as
opposed to the poet, and should depict the quirks and humours
of a lofty spirit, which so alarm lesser ones. Do this and you will
have done me a great favour. You will have earned me a few
thousand-franc notes. What glory! . . .

Of this collaboration *Modeste Mignon* was born in 1844, the
last *Scène de la vie privée*: 'It is the conflict between poetry and
reality, between illusion and society; the last lesson before I
pass on to scenes of later life. . . .' Also, it was another instance of
Balzac's fondness for turning the tables on other writers. His
Lys had been a retort to Saint-Beuve's *Volupté*, and the *Muse
du Département* was a counter-blast to Constant's *Adolphe*. He
believed that his own way of living and loving was better than
Goethe's, because he would not have accepted a young girl's
homage with that famous Olympian calm but in a more humble
spirit, knowing the realities of suffering—and of physical
delight. The characters so hazily sketched in Eve's narrative
were lit with his own flame. Modeste Mignon became Eve
herself as a girl, with something of her cousin, Calixte Rzewuska.
He gave her Eve's countenance, 'in which the poetry that shone
on the almost mystical forehead was half-denied by the sensual
expression of the mouth'. Modeste's father calls her his *petite
babouche*, a nickname used by Eve's father. Like the youthful
Eve, Modeste aspires to be the companion of a great artist or

poet; she writes to the poet Canalis (possibly Lamartine) as Eve did to Balzac, and like Eve's her letters are inclined to be pedantic and affected. Eve's contribution somewhat weakens the vigour proper to Balzac; the drama at moments lapses into drawing-room comedy. But, as Alain has said, Balzac could not fail with a novel, and the character of Canalis is as real as that of d'Arthez. The dwarflike and mysterious Jean Butscha, the lawyer's clerk who looks after Modeste, resembles Eve's cousin Thaddeus, who was always devoted to her. The background was based on Le Havre, which, like Angoulême, had its upper and lower town. All the materials were to hand, all transformed.

Eve strongly disapproved of the scene between Modeste and her father in which the latter rebukes her for having written to a stranger: 'Surely reason and good sense must have told you, even if your natural modesty did not, that to behave in that fashion was to *fling yourself at a man's head*. Am I to assume that my daugher, my one and only child, is lacking in all delicacy? . . .' It sounded too like a reflection on Eve's own behaviour. Balzac defended himself unanswerably, pointing out that a novelist must get into the skin of all his characters, father as well as daughter.

But this was a trifling difference between them. Eve was left with golden memories of his visit to St Petersburg. She wrote in her diary: 'How sweet and swift they are, those moments in life when the heart, swelling with joy, reflects a serene sky that seems to radiate immortal youth! But how long the years preceding them, and how bitter and heavy with poignancy the hours that follow! . . . Transports, enchantments, true happiness, ecstasy of the Ideal, pure joys, innocent joys, inward and charmed voices which expressed them, echoes of the soul, deep and vibrant resonances of the beloved voice—these are the consolers of loneliness, the sustainers of hope. . . .' She went so far as to admit that she had for her lover one of the greatest men of all time.

He returned by way of Berlin and Frankfurt to Paris, dreaming of those St Petersburg nights: 'Wholly tender and voluptuous spirits foster their memories, and that of my dearest *minou* is for ever in my heart and on my lips. . . .' The separation dulled his wits, afflicting him with a 'spleen of the heart' and '*difficulty in existing*'. He felt so ill when he got home that he called in Dr Nacquart, who as usual diagnosed inflammation of the brain. Balzac considered that it was more likely 'longing for dear *minou*'.

I was deaf like Beethoven, blind like Raphaël and soldierless like Napoleon at Beresina; out of place, out of life, out of the sweet habit of my heart and thought. There had not been at Vienna, Geneva or Neuchâtel that constant flow of feeling, that long adoration, those hours of talk. . . .

He brought with him, out of that cloudless sky, the conviction that all life could be the same, deliciously sensual. The newspapers were predicting further persecution of the Catholics in the Ukraine. Let Eve settle her affairs without delay and come and join him!

Needless to say the story was still circulating in Paris that the Tsar had paid Balzac a handsome sum for a reply to the book by 'that infernal French marquis'. He wrote to Eve in November: 'They imagine, and it is infinitely flattering, that my pen was necessary to the Russian Empire, and that I have brought back a great fortune in payment for its services. To the first person who said this I replied that they did not know your great Tsar, or me.' And in the following January he returned to the subject: 'They say I refused enormous sums to write a certain refutation. . . . What imbecility! Your Sovereign is too intelligent not to know that a paid pen lacks all authority. . . . He will understand that I write *neither for nor against* Russia. Does one create *precedents* at my age, when one is innocent of all political opinions?'

Louise de Breugnol, his mistress-housekeeper, was patiently waiting in Passy, having occupied her time with embroidering a tapestry as a surprise for him. What did she hope for? She was on friendly terms with his family, passed on their mutual recriminations and generally contributed to the difficulties of their touchy relationship. But Honoré was less concerned with them than with Henriette Borel, Anna Hanska's former governess, a Catholic convert who was seeking to enter a French convent. This matter was to give him some trouble.

As for Les Jardies, no purchaser had yet been found, and he again toyed with the idea of having the house done up for Eve.

With all its drawbacks, it had some advantages. It was within a quarter of an hour by rail of the Chaussée d'Antin. The land might eventually be made productive, and at least its possession enabled him to argue to the Academy that he was a property-owner and therefore eligible for election. This thought was still very much in his mind, although he claimed that he wanted it only to please Eve:

Being still outside the Academy I have placed myself at the head of the excluded writers, and I would rather be that kind of Caesar than the fortieth immortal. Moreover, I do not want the honour before 1845. . . .

His friend, Charles Nodier, was dying: 'He said to me, "My dear fellow, you ask for my vote but I give you my seat. Death is grinning at me. . . ." '

Other Academicians continued to mutter preposterously about his debts, as though wealth could be equated with talent:

So I thought of writing to the four academicians I have seen, because I should be a fool to worry about the thirty-six corpses, and my job is to erect a Monument, not to go running after votes. I said yesterday to Mignet, 'I would rather produce a book than lose an election. I have made up my mind. I don't want to be elected to the Academy *because of* my wealth. I hold the Academy's view in this matter to be insulting, the more so since it is spreading to the general public. When I am rich, as I shall be by my own efforts, I shall not offer myself. . . .'

He wrote dignified letters to his four supporters, Hugo, Nodier, Dupaty and Pongerville, in which he 'washed the word Academy out of his mind'—but only for a few months. And then he went off and paid a very high price for an antique chest of drawers which, the dealer said, had belonged to Marie de' Medici. He was back in the life of Paris. But the *soirées de Saint-Petersbourg* had been a wonderful interlude.

XXXIII

Chorus of Wolves

*Quand un artiste a le malheur d'être plein de la passion
qu'il veut exprimer, il ne saurait la peindre, car il est la
chose même au lieu d'en être l'image.*

BALZAC

HE HAD KNOWN when he got back to Paris that there was a
difficult time ahead of him. Literature was becoming increasingly commercialized, and writers of fiction were looking more
and more to the sale of serial rights. The serial technique did not
suit Balzac, with his careful setting of the scene, his elaborate
descriptions and character analyses, and the rapid rise of Dumas
and Sue meant that newspaper editors no longer found him
indispensable. However, he was given a chance to reinstate
himself. Bertin, editor of the highly respected *Journal des
Débats*, which had published Sue's *Mystères de Paris*, contracted
with him for two novels, *Modeste Mignon* and *Les Petits
Bourgeois*. This in itself was a triumph; but since it would be his
first appearance in the *Débats*, and at a time when his enemies
were saying that he had written himself out, it was essential that
he should produce a masterpiece. *Modeste Mignon* began serial
publication in April 1844, and the fact that he owed it to Eve
gave him particular delight. It was dedicated: 'TO A FOREIGN
LADY—daughter of an enslaved land, an angel in love, a demon in
fantasy, a child in faith . . . a man in intellect, a woman in heart,
a poet in her dreams . . .' and so on. The implacable but ill-
informed Sainte-Beuve at once proclaimed that the lady was
Princess Belgiojoso and that the dedication had outraged her:
'Did anyone ever read such a farrago? Why are not writers of this
kind drowned in ridicule, and how can a self-respecting journal
open its columns to them with so much blowing of trumpets?'
Certainly the dedication was preposterous. Still under the
influence of the visit to St Petersburg, when for the first time he
had been able to enjoy without restraints the woman whose

temperament so exactly matched his own, Balzac could not contain his rhapsodies: 'I love as I loved in 1819, I love for the first and only time in my life.' When she sent him a strip torn from a gown she had worn he shed tears at the thought that he was to wipe his pen on it—'. . . something that for a time counted the beats of the most accomplished heart in the world, and that once covered——No; one must love deeply to dare so much! I shall think of this every time I use it.' The naïveté is hard to credit. But Balzac in love *was* naïve; it was his virtue and his charm. He was carried away by his own rhetoric, and if it was partly a game it was a game that intoxicated him. He had a miniature of her on his writing-table, a picture of Wierzchownia on the wall, and on his left hand he wore not only the jewelled ring she had given him but also a wedding-ring. He sat there pouring out his paeans: 'You are the light, the happy star. . . . You are honour and delight. . . .' There was further mention of *bengali* and *minou*, with assurances of the absolute fidelity of the former. 'Sweet, gentle *minou*! Does it know that by the very act of writing this letter *bengali* is aroused? . . . Is it, too, moved? . . .'

He complained of languors which for whole nights plunged him into dreaming, greatly to the hindrance of his work. Only *Modeste Mignon* progressed well, since she had inspired it. But it failed as a serial, being too lacking in incident for the newspaper public, and the *Débats* hastily began the publication of Dumas's *Monte-Cristo*. Balzac wrote to Eve, 'I am conscious of having created a masterpiece for me and for you, and who else matters?' *Les Petits Bourgeois*, a large-scale work with twenty-five or thirty characters, was stuck in the mud. Then there was *Les Paysans*, originally entitled *Le Grand Propriétaire*, which he had started eight years previously at the suggestion of Monsieur Hanski and put aside and returned to a dozen times—a huge and difficult and unrewarding task. Originally the 'great landowner' of the title had been the Marquis de Grandlieu, an extreme reactionary in conflict with a group of bourgeois liberals. Balzac had abandoned that first version, although he meant to return to that subject in an entirely different form. But before doing anything else he had to finish *Splendeurs et misères des courtisanes*.

The third part of *Illusions perdues*, it may be remembered, had dealt with the misfortunes of David Séchard and his wife; but its most important single episode, in terms of the *Comédie* as a whole, was the chance meeting between Lucien de Rubempré, desperate and on the verge of suicide after his failure in Paris, and Carlos Herrera, who passes himself off as a priest but is in fact the ex-convict Vautrin. The false Abbé, seduced by Lucien's physical attractions, conceives a passion for him and resolves to help him take his revenge on Paris. But first the young man has to learn the rules of the game and stop behaving like a child: 'If you had left Coralie with Monsieur Camusot and kept your relations with her a secret, you would have married Madame de Bargeton and by now you would be Prefect of Angoulême and the Marquis de Rubempré.' This sums up the cynical realism of Vautrin.

The theme of revenge is at the root of *Splendeurs et misères des courtisanes*. The long, untidy book was compiled between 1838 and 1847 in a series of parts—*Comment aiment les filles* (which absorbed *La Torpille*, already written), *A combien l'amour revient aux viellards*, *Où mènent les mauvais chemins* and *La Dernière Incarnation de Vautrin*. It is an extraordinary mixture of romance, melodramatic absurdity and realism. The prostitute redeemed and then compelled by love to return to vice; the demonic influence of Vautrin; his more than questionable love for Lucien, and his reflections as he passes the house where the young man lives ('the *Tristesse d'Olympio* of pederasty' as Proust called it)—all this is romance. The suicide of Esther is pure, if touching, melodrama; as is the battle between Vautrin and the policeman, Corentin, and the unnecessary death of Contenson, another policeman. But there is no lack of realism in the sardonic comedy of Nucingen, the ageing banker besotted with desire, or in the primitive despair of Léontine de Sérizy when she learns of Lucien's death, or in the picture of the gang-leaders of the underworld and the memorable description of the ancient prison of the Conciergerie. 'What I'm writing is pure Sue,' Balzac confessed to Eve, and certainly he was trying to compete, in the serial field, with Sue and Dumas, those dangerous rivals. But as he grew older he tended more and more to revert to his fondness for extravagant plots, mystery-making, the Thousand and One Nights of Paris, the shadowed world of Ferragus. He was infinitely superior to his competitors in the depth and accuracy of his setting, his sober condemnation of a corrupt society, the skill with which he showed prostitution to be a link between the highest and the lowest worlds, and in 'the whiplash with which he brushed aside the rags and tatters covering the sores'.* But he swamped Lucien in a world of melodramatic catastrophe beyond his stature, and the result is far less moving to the reader than the story of the young man's first human misadventures.

In *Splendeurs et misères* Balzac expressed his own duality in terms of the opposed characters, Lucien and Vautrin—Lucien, his feminine side, 'one of those incomplete geniuses who have a certain power to will and conceive, but lack the strength to execute', and Vautrin, his masculine complement; between them they constitute a single 'polity'. The young man lucidly perceives this in the letter he writes to Vautrin before hanging himself in his prison-cell: 'There is the heritage of Cain and that of Abel. . . . Cain, in the great human drama, is the rebel.' Cain's descendants, hard and malignant, dominate the sons of Abel: 'Endowed with immense power over gentler spirits, they attract and crush them. It is great, it is beautiful in its way. . . . It is the poetry of evil. . . . You have caused me to live that gigantic life, and now I have had enough of living. I can withdraw my head from the Gordian knot of your stratagems and thrust it into the slipknot of my cravate. . . .' Balzac himself was descended from both Cain and Abel. If he had some of Lucien's weaknesses, he also possessed the genius of David Séchard and the strength of Vautrin. A great writer needs not only talent (which Lucien possessed); above all, he needs will-power. The law of toil is always harsh. Balzac accepted this, and Lucien rejected it; hence their divergent destinies.

Although he had had the huge book in his head since 1843, his state of health did not permit him to finish it until some years later. He had jaundice after returning from Russia, followed by severe headaches. Dr Nacquart decided that his condition was not serious, although he was also suffering from colic and a form of dermatitis. His family were becoming more and more difficult. Madame de Berny had warned him long ago that Laure would end up by resembling her mother, and he noted with dismay that, as usual, she had been right. Brother and sister were seeing less of one another—a state of affairs which did

* Marcel Proust.

not altogether displease him, since it would simplify matters when he married Eve. He admitted to being terrified of what the great lady of Wierzchownia might think of his relations; not a pleasing attitude, but there it was, and the family bonds were loosened.

On the other hand, he was encumbered with Henriette Borel, the first go-between in his love-affair with Eve. Having, thanks to him, secured a special dispensation to enter a convent (she was over the accepted age), she arrived in Paris in June, 1844. He lodged her in the Rue Basse and even gave up his bedroom to her, a signal honour. But he soon found her tiresome. Although in her case the Church was prepared to forego the dowry, she insisted upon paying it, 'out of *humility*, the silly creature', and regardless of the fact that she needed to keep some money in reserve in case her vocation was not confirmed. Balzac straightened out her affairs in conjunction with James de Rothschild, and she was eventually admitted to the convent of an uncloistered Order, where he often visited her, mainly for Eve's sake.

When was he to see his love again? By now Eve had won her lawsuit. Her future husband's indifference to this news came as a shock to her; he announced magnificently that he wanted to owe his fortune to nothing but his own efforts. Nor was he impressed by the Tsar's verdict.

It is favouritism influencing justice. Madame de Sévigné also brought a case which came up before the Grand Council. When the documents were placed before Louis XIV he wrote: 'Since this affects Madame de Sévigné the decision must be favourable. I have no wish to examine it.' . . . No doubt, my dear Polish Sévigné, your spiritual ancestress told her daughter that Louis XIV was the greatest of all monarchs. That is my view. . . .

It was a view that was far from pleasing Eve, who considered that she owed her success to her tactical skill. And he went on to load her with advice. She should apply to the Kiev court for immediate possession. 'What a pair of lovers we are . . . our letters stuffed with figures and business matters. But, dearest *louloup*, figures are the foundation of our happiness.' She had left St Petersburg for Wierzchownia, and he advised her to take charge of the estate herself, in the manner of a Frenchwoman,

avoiding all extravagance and showing herself to be hard-bitten
from the outset:

Louis XVI brought about all the massacres of the Revolution
by not mowing down the riff-raff at the start of the States-
General. So *persist*, that is to say, demand your arrears of income, have the amount properly assessed, even if you don't
want the money immediately, and the same with your legal
costs and living expenses. Try to stir your uncle out of his
apathy, if you can. Do everything that a wife and mother as
great as yourself can do, without compromising herself, to
arouse him. He's old; he'll end up religious, you can be sure of
it; you don't know what the smell of the grave does to these
unbelievers. They brood on their sins and find themselves
defenceless. He'll send away his moujiks and recollect the harm
he has done you and his niece. Above all, collect capital and
imitate the lady who placed her funds out of danger. Become a
miser. What a wonderful page I'm writing!

But all she wanted, having won her case, was to escape from
Russia. Being unable to obtain a passport for France she went to
Dresden, which was full of Polish refugees. Balzac, in a fever to
join her, asked her to engage a room for him in the town. But
before he could leave he had at all costs to finish *Les Paysans*,
which had already started to appear in *La Presse*. After the first
few instalments he told Eve that it was a dazzling, unexpected
success; but Théophile Gautier, a loyal friend, reported that on
the contrary letters were coming in by every post from readers
who wanted the tedious tale to end. It was not suited to serial
publication, and Balzac worked on it without enthusiasm. He
had neuralgia: 'I wrote *Birotteau* with my feet in a mustard-
bath, and I'm writing *Les Paysans* with my head in opium.'

On 6 December *La Presse* announced the publication of
Dumas's *La Reine Margot*. Girardin wanted to make sure of his
January subscribers by serving up a more attractive serial.
Having succeeded in this he called for the rest of *Les Paysans*
(paid for in advance), but 'the machine had broken down'. The
first criticisms had been thoroughly unfavourable: 'Another
book begun and discontinued,' wrote the critics, 'to be concluded no one knows when or how. . . . It is Figaro slandering
the poor instead of decrying the rich. . . . He is bent on doing
dishonour to rural life. . . . He treats the peasants at the gates of

society as though they were savages. . . .' Balzac said himself that
he was disgusted with the book: 'I shall never cease to regret
having let myself in for *Les Paysans*.' He knew that Girardin
would insist upon his pound of flesh, but whenever he sat down
to work on it his face twitched like a monkey's.

He wanted to rush to Dresden to appease his physical
longings, and when Eve firmly forbade this he grew frantic with
frustration. She was driving him to suicide. Why was she so
afraid of his coming? Was it because of his enemies? But it had
been the same when he went to St Petersburg. Who were these
'Russian princesses' who were poisoning her mind against him?
And if she did not want him in Dresden why would she not join
him elsewhere?

Working little and badly, he spent hours every day searching
Paris for a house to shelter the two *louloups*. (This was a
whimsy that had crept in since the visit to Russia. He was the
loup, she the *louloup* and their joint wealth the *trésor louloup*.)
He had given up the idea of converting Les Jardies. Any
house worthy of the chatelaine of Wierzchownia (and the
Marie de' Medici chest of drawers) must be noble and dignified,
set between courtyard and garden, and standing on a site that
would *increase in value*. 'But why this fury of speculation?' she
asked. Because, he replied, wealth was required if his great lady
was to lead in Paris the life to which she was accustomed. He
would create for her the most wonderful setting in the world.
The Medici chest-of-drawers, with its gold and mother-of-pearl
inlay, represented a fortune in itself, enough to pay all his debts,
but he would only sell it to a Rothschild—or perhaps to Sir
Robert Peel in England, for £3,000.

He scoured fashionable Paris. The Champs-Élysées quarter,
he predicted, had a great future: land there would some day be
worth 100,000 francs the *toise* (about thirty-six square feet).
Reckoning the cost of their house at 200,000 francs, including
alterations and repairs, he soared off into hopeful calculations—
the sale of Les Jardies, the proceeds from *Les Paysans* and *La
Comédie humaine*, plus a contribution of 20,000 from Eve . . .
They would manage. It was a pity Eve had not brought more
money with her out of the Ukraine, where sooner or later her
possessions were certain to be confiscated. Why did she so
mistrust his financial planning? When it came to matters of

business he was a hardened veteran and she the merest child! He now suggested that she should come to Paris and see for herself. It would be quite simple. She and Anna would travel on his passport and he would pass them off as his sister and niece. They would explore the town incognito, and for Anna there would be the Exhibition, theatre, concerts, endless delights. A two months' stay would not cost more than 3,500 francs a month, with a cook, housemaid and a groom. Madame de Breugnol would see to everything. . . . But Eve must decide quickly and end this agonizing suspense: 'I can't drag a line out of my head, I've no more courage or strength or will-power. . . .' To keep his sanity he had taken to playing cards and going out in the evenings! There was truth, no doubt, in the high-flown picture he drew of his mental and physical state, but he made it larger than life, from force of habit and by design. He cannot have been so utterly exhausted when, having to finish *Béatrix* and portray the distress of a young woman deceived by her husband, he called on Delphine de Girardin and cross-questioned her at length about the stormy beginnings of her own married life. The bee was still gathering honey.

Eve's unresponsiveness was due in part to a domestic problem. Anna, a fervent Polish patriot, was resolved not to marry anyone but a Pole. There was a certain Count Georges Mniszech, an agreeable young man as wealthy as herself, who was interested in art and entomology. But as yet there had been no formal declaration, and Eve may have feared that he would change his mind when he learned that his prospective mother-in-law was proposing to marry a Frenchman. She may also have been shaken by Balzac's strong disapproval of the match. 'Being rich and Polish,' he wrote, 'your daughter is in an exceptional and dangerous position.' The Tsar was bent on uniting his empire, and this must entail the destruction of Polish nationalism and Roman catholicism (a procedure which Balzac, the Machiavellain politician, found entirely reasonable). Everything rich and Polish was thus imperilled. Safety for Anna lay in a foreign marriage, with a German or Austrian aristocrat. Was she really in love with the young man? 'She knows nothing of the physical repulsions which only marriage discloses,' wrote the expert author of the *Physiologie du mariage*.

His state of desperation was increasing: 'There's only one

word to describe my condition—*I'm wasting away.*' If he dared to reproach her she took offence. He called her a 'cossack' (which was not so far-fetched) and she bridled and talked about entering a convent, but then said, 'I forgive you' and he kissed the words on the paper.

Finally, in April 1845, the ban was lifted. 'I want to see you,' she wrote, and he hurried to Dresden with gifts of scent, 'a cloud of perfume'. She had reserved a room for him near the hotel where she and Anna were staying. He was ravenous for her—'Dresden is hunger and thirst, poverty amid happiness, a poor man flinging himself upon a rich feast of the rich.' While he was there his appointment to the Légion d'Honneur was announced, but he does not seem to have been much gratified. He was only made a 'chevalier'. It was too little and too late, but he could not affront his friend Villemain, the Minister, by refusing. The cartoonists, always fascinated by his doings, depicted him fixing the cross to the knob of his enormous cane.

He liked George Mniszech, although he found him a little gauche: 'He lacks the polished manners appropriate to his name and rank, the grace of a true nobleman. . . . He should have been educated by a woman, one of those mature ladies who instruct young men in the ways of the world and life and correct behaviour.' But since the young people were now engaged it was too late for him to find a Madame de Berny.

Before long the four of them left Dresden for Hamburg and Cannstadt, where Eve took the waters. There followed four months of travel and what amounted to wild dissipation, compared with Balzac's normal laborious life. The young couple, George and Anna, adopted him with genuine affection. At that time the troupe of travelling players known as the *Saltimbanques* (mountebanks) was widely known, and they adopted the name for themselves. Balzac became Bilboquet, Eve—Atala, George—Gringalet and Anna—Zéphyrine. Life was a round of gaiety, with Balzac leader of the revels. Finding release at last in the arms of a woman 'so good to love', he recovered all his zest and talent for living. In subsequent letters to Eve he recalled their stopping-places in discreetly erotic terms: 'Cannstadt—all the delicious trifles of dessert, the gourmet trying to accustom himself to a loaded plate but not being able to. . . . Carlsruhe—alms bestowed on the poor. But Strasbourg—ah, at Strasbourg it was expert love, a Louis XIV feast, the knowledge of shared happiness! . . .'

They reached Strasbourg early in July, and there booked three seats on the Paris mail-coach. Georges was to rejoin them later in Belgium. Madame de Breugnol received detailed instructions, accompanied by compliments—'I have just received your letter which, like yourself, is sweet and charming. You are always the same.' Dangerous praise by which the hopeful lady may well have been misled. She was to rent a furnished apartment near the Madeleine, at not more than 300 francs a month—'but in your own name, for the ladies will have no passport. . . . Madame Hanska now wants an extra room so that I can stay there. . . . It must be kept absolutely secret. . . . I have every assurance for the future, in every sense. Anna is very fond of me, and I am sure of a warm understanding between us. . . .' It seems, then, that at this stage his mistress-housekeeper unprotestingly accepted the idea of his making a rich marriage, and even of pre-marital relations. She was asked to instal a blue carpet in the ladies' bedchamber and to book seats at the play for Anna, who adored the theatre.

The rhapsody of love and towns continued, now with musical adornments: 'Passy and Fontainebleau—the genius of Beethoven, sublimity itself! Orléans, Bourges, Tours and Blois— concertos, beloved symphonies, all more or less light-hearted, but with graver notes interjected by the indisposition of one of the "wolves". Paris, Rotterdam, the Hague, Antwerp—flowers of autumn. But Brussels was worthy of Cannstadt and of us, the triumph of two unique loves. . . .'

The tour was indeed a period of almost flawless happiness, marred only by tiffs in Holland, where Eve took Balzac severely to task for his extravagance in the antique shops. She was particularly annoyed by his purchase, in Rotterdam, of an ebony cabinet for 375 florins. 'The only thing the "wolves" quarrelled about was furniture!' That is to say, there was no actual quarrel over Louise de Breugnol. There was simply a ukase, issued by Madame Hanska in her most cossack manner. From the moment of her arrival in Paris she had viewed the relations between Honoré and his housekeeper with suspicion. The two women did not take to one another, and she insisted that Louise must go. Balzac promised to deal with the ticklish situation upon his return to Passy, and in the meantime sought to appease Eve by referring to Louise as 'the female', 'the harpy' and 'that infernal creature'. When, in September, he gave her six months' notice, the unhappy woman wept.

By then the holiday was over, and Balzac, sundered from his beloved *Saltimbanques*, and in particular from Eve, was again plunged in melancholy, although the separation was only be to brief, since he was to rejoin her when he had attended to his affairs.

Never had I lived so happily, heart-to-heart with my Evelette; I was torn by the loss of the graceful elegances of life, all the unexpected joys that had been revealed to me. I suffered from that interrupted rebirth of my youth, an unlooked-for, adorable state of conjugal bliss which surpassed all my hopes.

It has been asserted, without evidence, that Eve was not really in love with him. Certainly we do not possess her letters, but we can judge of their nature from Balzac's replies: 'Your last three letters are wealth to my heart. You fulfil all my desires, all the dreams of my loving imagination. It so rejoices me to be loved like this. . . . Your letters, in our separation, were what my Eve was at Baden, a masterpiece of the heart! . . . Oh, *louloup* . . . a violent and lasting love binds us closely together.'

Nor was he forgotten by the other members of the party. George sent him a design for a medallion, his own work, inscribed, 'To Bilboquet from the grateful Saltimbanques', and accompanied by a charming letter from 'Atala'. So in the matter of love all was well; but life in Passy was less agreeable. Madame de Breugnol, not unnaturally resentful, demanded 7,500 francs compensation and a tobacconist's stall (a Government concession). Dr Nacquart, who knew the Directeur Général des Tabacs, set about getting her one, but when he was on the verge of succeeding she decided that she did not want it—tobacco was lacking in dignity, she said. She now wanted a stamp-bureau. Madame Mère and Laure sympathized, and supported her when she made a last effort to remain with Balzac. 'But,' he wrote to Eve, 'I said to her, "If you so much as utter a *name* which I venerate like that of God, you will leave this house instantly. I will pay for your lodging elsewhere and have my meals at the inn." She was silent, and she has said nothing since.' Not to him, perhaps; but she evidently said a good

deal to his family. She was growing increasingly bitter.
Balzac's lawyer, Gavault, was also found wanting—
'atrociously idle'. A new man of affairs was put in charge of his
debts, Auguste Fessart, who miraculously persuaded his
creditors to compound for a fifty per cent settlement—all except
the tailor, Buisson, whose faith in Balzac was so unshaken that
he accepted a renewed note-of-hand, gambling on his future
prospects. The conjugal dwelling was another problem. It
seemed impossible to find in Paris a house worthy of Eve. Once
again Balzac drew up his elastic balance-sheet. There was the
trésor louloup (the joint fund), banked with Rothschild. The
proceeds of the *Comédie humaine* he reckoned at anything from
100,000 francs to none, according to sales and his mood of the
moment. At least there was no lack of work in prospect.
Chlendowski, a Polish publisher, was crying out for *Les Petites
Misères de la vie conjugale*, but Balzac, in his present glow of
requited love, found this a tedious task. The series of pieces was
very inferior to the *Physiologie* of his youth.

In any case he was in no mood for work. The *Comédie
humaine* had been shelved for six months. After creating so
many imaginary hells, had he not a right to his share of paradise?
'I do nothing but think of you; I have no mind left.' Unfulfilled
desire may stimulate genius, but satiety turns it sluggish. At the
end of September he paid a quick visit to Baden, and returned
exhausted to Passy. Eve had arranged to spend the winter in
Italy with George and Anna, and he went with them, joining
the party at Chalon-sur-Saône, whence they travelled by
river-boat to Marseilles, and thence by sea to Naples. This trip
was to be the high-point of his love-affair: 'Lyons has shown me
my love surpassed by a grace, a tenderness, a perfection of
caresses and a sweetness of love which for me has made the town's
name one of those private shibboleths which, being spoken, are
like the sacred word that opens the gates of Heaven. . . .' In a
period of over six months, for the first time in his working life, he
had written nothing except the end of *Béatrix*, a few pages of *Les
Paysans*, and a rough outline of the last part of *Splendeurs et
misères*. 'I'll knock them off in no time. What do I care about
money? I want happiness, and I'm coming back.' The poor
great man! He had lost sight of the fact that happiness is fatal
to the artist, and that great men belong to their works alone.

XXXIV

Perrette and the Milk-Pail

*Nous autres femmes, nous devons admirer les hommes de
talent; en jouir comme d'un spectacle; mais vivre avec eux,
jamais.*

BALZAC

BALZAC WOULD GLADLY have stayed in Italy, in that *dolce
far niente* where he had nothing to do but make love to Eve and
visit antique shops; but after the many months of indolence he
had to get back to Paris to ward off financial perils, keep in touch
with Fessart, pacify the publisher Chlendowski, add to the
Comédie humaine, rehabilitate himself with the newspapers and,
above all, find a house.

He reached Marseilles on 12 November after an eight-day
sea-passage in atrocious weather (concerning which he made
the familiar claim that everyone on board was seasick except the
crew and himself) and in company with the Marseillais poet,
Joseph Méry, visited a curio-dealer's where he bought Eve a
handsome coral necklace—of priceless Indian workmanship, he
said. 'The red of victory, the purple of happy love. . . . My eyes
are damp as I write . . . in overflowing gratitude. . . .' The supreme
blaze of love is as sweet as the dawn of fame.

His homecomings were always catastrophic, and this one was
no exception. For a time there was no shortage of ready money.
Eve had entrusted him with a large sum (about 100,000 francs)
for the purchase and furnishing of the house. It was of course a
sacred trust, but the inveterate gambler felt himself entitled to
'make it bear fruit' by buying shares in the Northern Railway,
then under construction, which he believed were certain to rise.
His own Baron Nucingen could have told him that the Bourse
took a different view, but it is not the policy of the Nucingens to
enlighten investors. However, at the end of 1845 Balzac's affairs
seemed to be improving. Under the influence of Eve and Fessart
he was methodically reducing his debts, having repaid 40,000

francs. The generous '*petit père* Dablin' accepted five thousand in lieu of eight, and, according to Balzac, had even been prepared to lend him 200,000 francs to make him completely solvent, but Madame Balzac and Laure had prevented this. The story sounds improbable.

Madame Mère claimed that his debt to her now amounted to 57,000, including the unpaid interest. 'Fantastic!' said her son. 'Tragic ingratitude,' she retorted. By the good offices of Cousin Sedillot they reached an equitable agreement. Madame Delannoy, he knew, would never press him. As for the Guidoboni-Viscontis, far from demanding the return of their 10,000 francs, they lent him, in 1846, another 12,000. This did not prevent him, when he wrote to Eve, from referring to Fanny as 'the old English woman'. It was an awkward situation. He had handed over railway share-certificates as security, although these, strictly speaking, were the property of Eve.

But all things considered, and thanks to Eve and Fessart, the financial problem would have been far less acute if Balzac had shown a little reason. He seemed bent on self-destruction. He could resist no speculation, however precarious. A ship-builder named a new vessel *Balzac*, and he promptly bought a share in it for 10,000 francs, which would, he said, pay forty per cent.— but that was the last that was heard of it. He spent his days dickering over houses and sites, and since the hypothetical dwelling was to be furnished with oriental luxury he bought an antique Chinese dinner-service: 'I got it for 300 francs, although Dumas paid 4,000 for it and it's worth 6,000.' He went to Rouen in search of ebony panelling—'you can get it there for next to nothing.' He bought a set of chairs for the little sitting-room on the first floor which was to be called (when it existed) the *salon vert*, and a writing-desk for Eve and two charming cabinets with a floral inlay.

I spent three hours looking round and I bought: *primo*, a yellow cup (five francs) which is worth at least a hundred, it's exquisite. *Secundo*, a cup which was offered to Talma, blue Sèvres Empire, which is of incalculable value, because there's a bouquet of flowers painted on it which must have cost twenty-five louis (twenty francs). *Tertio*, six royally upholstered chairs . . . for the *salon vert*. . . . I shall leave four as they are and make two into a settee. A wonderful bargain . . .

And what did the cost matter? Anyone who could hang on to the railway shares for a year ('as *we* can') would make a profit of 300 francs per share, and since they held 150 shares this (said Balzac), would pay for everything.

But there were other problems to be solved, the most urgent being that of the wretched Madame de Breugnol, who could not make up her mind about anything. She had thought of marrying a sculptor, Elschoët, (this caused Balzac to christen her 'la Chouette', the 'screech-owl'), and wanted a dowry. But she reverted to the idea of a stamp-bureau when she discovered that her sculptor, besides being monstrously ugly, had a fondness for little girls. A stamp concession was not easy to secure, and Balzac invoked the aid of James de Rothschild:

Rotschild [*sic*] was 'regency' as he always is. He asked me if she was pretty, and if I had had her. 'A hundred and twenty-one times,' I said, 'and if you want her I'll give her to you.' . . . 'Has she any children?' he asked. . . . 'No, you must get her with one.' . . . 'I'm sorry but I only protect women who have children.' It was a way of getting out of it. If she'd had children he'd have said that he could not countenance immorality. 'My dear Baron,' I said, 'do you think you can outmanœuvre me? I'm a shareholder in Northern Railways. I'll give you a note-of-hand and you'll treat my affair as though it were a four-hundred-thousand-franc railway.' . . . 'Really?' he said. 'If you can get me to agree I shall admire you more than ever.' . . . 'You'll agree,' I said, 'or I'll tell your wife, and she'll keep an eye on you.' At this he laughed and sank back in his chair saying, 'I'm worn out, business is killing me. Give me the note-of-hand. . . .'

But that matter was still unsettled, and Louise de Breugnol, now with her blood up, was uttering threats.

The second problem was the family. Laure had badgered Surville into going to Spain to examine a new project on the spot, and in his absence the bridge he was building over the river Doubs was swept away in a flood. Poor Laure! With her large ambitions she committed nothing but blunders. And on 1 January 1846, there was a minor crisis. It was customary for Madame Mère, Laure and her two daughters to visit Honoré on New Year's Day, but this year only his nieces came.

I guessed it was my mother's doing and so I got dressed. I called on her to pay my respects and was most coldly received.... She wanted me to be in the wrong. She had said repeatedly to my sister the day before, 'You'll see, your brother won't come to pay his respects.' She was furious because I had not done what she expected.... I have resolved that, for my part, I shall only see my mother on New Year's Day, her saint's day and her birthday, for ten minutes each time. As for you, where my sister and mother are concerned there need only be an exchange of cards. . . .

There was also Henriette Borel, who was claiming her dowry and wanted Balzac to be present at her taking of the veil. The ceremony was a very long one—time enough to write at least four folios. 'These impudent nuns think the world revolves round them.' However he had to go, since his 'dear wife' and Anna must be represented at her 'burial', and in the event he did not regret it:

Since I had never witnessed a taking of the veil I watched and noted everything with a close attention that must have made me look extremely devout. . . . It is an impressive and very dramatic ceremony. I was deeply moved when the three recipients prostrated themselves, to be covered with a pall, while prayers were recited for the death of their worldly lives; and then they reappeared as brides crowned with white roses, and took their vows of marriage to Jesus Christ. . . .

He was able to talk to Henriette after the ceremony and found her as gay as a lark. 'So now you're Madame,' he said, smiling. But the biggest problem was his work. Once it had been his greatest happiness, but now his mind refused to function: 'I find it excessively difficult to write. My thoughts are not free, they no longer belong to me. . . . All day yesterday I had a dreadful sense of mourning in myself. . . . But I've got to do the six folios which will complete another volume of the *Comédie humaine*. . . .' His eyes twitched and were so tired that he had to replace his three-candle stick with a five-armed candelabra——— 'And it burns one franc fifty centimes' worth of candles in two nights—do you hear that, Madame? With two francs for heating and fifty centimes for coffee, that makes four francs a night. The

Tales of a Thousand and One Nights have suffered a serious rise
in overheads! . . .'

He could not get on at all with *Les Paysans* so he tried to write
the third part of *Splendeurs et misères des courtisanes*, entitled
La Dernière Incarnation de Vautrin. He rewrote the first page
twenty-five times without being satisfied. And the book was
expanding; it would have to be in four parts, the third being
Une Instruction criminelle (later *Où mènent les mauvais chemins*).
To obtain material for this he had to visit the prison of the
Conciergerie. This latter part of the very long novel was
destined to win high praise, but that came later. In 1846 Balzac
made painfully slow progress, and the gossip-writers talked of
him as a back-number. He wrote to Eve that he would only
recover his powers when marriage had put an end to his uncertainties: 'It is not just love, it is dementia.' It was undoubtedly an obsession, than which nothing can be more hostile
to creative work.

If he could be sure of the marriage! But there were stormy
passages in his correspondence with Eve. One of her sisters had
warned her that he was 'insatiably amorous, a lover of young
flesh' which prompted her to ask if she were not too old for him.
'That's a little hard,' he replied, 'when my one fear is that I may
not be young enough for you. I wish I were twenty-five. Be as
old as you like, but go on loving me. . . .'

Louise de Breugnol (now the 'Screech-owl'), infuriated him
with her mockery, which was on similar lines: 'She says, "You
love no one but yourself (she makes me out to be an egoist
because she's leaving) and if you were offered a girl of twenty
with a hundred thousand a year and a great name you'd marry
her—and you'd be right." ' This he denied hotly and with
heavy sarcasm, or so he reported the matter to Eve. And the
truth about his amorous propensities was quite otherwise.

The bird of Bengal is dead. It has succumbed to work, to
daydreaming, to errands, to anxieties and to coffee. That is
what happens to little creatures of that sort—a grand resurgence,
a period of singing, and when they find that it is unrewarded they
relapse and stir no more, like a dog that, after kicking up a great
row during the absence of a beloved master, lies down in
silence. . . .

In February 1846, Eve wrote: 'Come to Rome. From there we will go to Florence and cross our beloved Switzerland by way of Geneva and Neuchâtel. You can leave us to take the waters in Baden while you return to Paris to attend to your affairs.' He asked nothing better. 'There is always time to write a book *one can't write.*' But he was delayed by an accident. Leaving Buisson's tailoring establishment on the corner of the Rue Richelieu he jumped a gutter and tore a muscle in his leg. This wasted a fortnight; but at least it gave him time to dispose, as he hoped, of the Screech-owl, who got her stamp-concession. He set out for Rome late in March, with an outfit of new clothes. The party of *Saltimbanques* travelled by way of the Borromean islands to Switzerland, Heidelberg and Frankfurt, and he came to life again in the arms of love, while he and his 'wife' discussed their plans. She seemed now to have quite decided to marry him. They would buy a château in Touraine, where they would spend the greater part of the year, and rent an apartment in Paris, in the Faubourg Saint-Germain, for the winter.

Directly he got back to Paris Balzac set about putting their plans into effect. He bought more railway-shares and went with Jean Margonne to Vouvray, hoping to find a property where he might provisionally instal his bachelor furniture, keeping the handsome pieces he had recently bought for the Paris apartment. This would make him a landed proprietor, as well as part owner of two hundred railway shares. The Château de Moncontour was up for sale, a charming turreted manor-house overlooking the Loire which had been his dream for thirty years: 'Moncontour with its beautiful view, its shady walks, its fruit-trees and the river at our feet . . .' He was weaving new pictures of felicity. They would make Moncontour their home for six years in order to save money, but they would come to Paris in the winter so as not to lose touch. And since the railway station from Tours was near the Jardin des Plantes, their Paris *pied-à-terre* would need to be at that end of the boulevards. The Place Royale, for instance—a nice little apartment with three servants' bedrooms. How practical and sensible he was being!

Good news came from Germany. George Mniszech's father was dead. God rest his soul; but this was excellent for the young couple, since it would facilitate their marriage. Eve must lose no time in bringing that about, and then she would be wholly free. But the second piece of news was tremendous, and it filled him with pride and delight. Eve was pregnant! The child must have been conceived at Soleure during their journey across Switzerland. So Honoré de Balzac was to become father of a son (he had no doubt of its sex) who would be christened Victor-Honoré. He overflowed with jubilation and wise counsel: 'Love-children never cause morning-sickness, they are easily carried. But take great care. Poor little Victor-Honoré! . . .' The tremendous things he would do, now that he was working for three 'wolves'! (We must bear in mind the immense importance he had always attached to paternity.) The debts were nothing, he would get rid of them all: 'I've been considering what I must do in the way of writing, setting manuscripts against debts.' There was an item of 2,500 francs which could be covered by a short story, another of 7,500 francs which called for a serial for *La Presse*. If there was anything sordid in this balancing of creative work against material needs, the thought certainly did not trouble him. Who cared for the claims of Art? 'Does one worry about that when one has a living to earn? Was Rossini worrying about his reputation when he wrote the "Barber" for a hundred crowns? He did just what I did when I was writing the *Physiologie du mariage*—he thought about the next meal. We told each other so.'

It was important for the prospective parents to marry in good time, if they were to have a legitimate child and not 'a bastard subsequently legitimized by marriage': but for a variety of reasons, among them the continuing threat to Eve's property in Ukraine, the wedding would have to be held in secret. They would then pretend that it had taken place before pregnancy. Balzac had an idea. The Prefect of Moselle, Germeau, was an old schoolfellow from Vendôme, and Delacroix, the public prosecutor in Metz, was a personal friend. If they could find an ignorant, or obliging, mayor in Lorraine, it should be possible to bury the published banns under other documents. But legal documents of identity were indispensable. Accordingly Balzac applied for his papers in Tours. Eve's only identity-paper was a Russian passport. He told her to send to Poland for her husband's death-certificate, giving Anna's prospective marriage as the reason.

'Your parents' death-certificates are immaterial,' he wrote, 'but your own birth-certificate is essential. You must get hold of it at all costs. One can't marry in any country in the world without one.' And here a very delicate problem arose. Eve, born in 1800, had consistently knocked six years off her age. She could not bring herself to admit the fact to Balzac. It was a harmless fraud that a woman of forty-six does not lightly confess to, unless she is a great deal more hard-bitten than Madame Hanska. She recoiled from the prospect and resolved to bear her child in secret, to entrust it to Balzac and return to Wierzchownia.

The birth-certificate was not her only reason. When it came to the point, when the issue had to be faced of joining her life with his, for better or for worse, all her misgivings returned. That she loved him as a lover is beyond doubt; but she dreaded his irresponsibility as a husband. 'Am I not a good accountant?' he was always asking—and the answer was no. He talked repeatedly of the sacred nature of the *trésor louloup*, while making heavy inroads into it. He praised his sagacity in the matter of the railway shares, although they were plummeting down. He would proudly proclaim in one letter that he had settled all his debts, and they would crop up again in the next.

Everything, he insisted, would be paid for out of his own earnings, and their joint fund would make a handsome profit on the railway shares—or if these continued to fall he would buy at the bottom of the market and thus repair the loss. Count Ernest Rzewuski had long owed his sister 25,000 francs, and this would in due course accrue to the fund. By the winter Balzac, free of debt, would have 20,000 francs in hand, a state of affairs to gratify the most meticulous accountant. But in a moment of lucidity, he added, 'Oh, splendid La Fontaine! *Perrette et le pot au lait* is the most wonderful of fables'—which was charming in it ingenuousness, but scarcely reassuring.

I beseech you to have no anxiety, either of the heart or the head. I will undertake no business without giving you a chance to say, 'I approve', because your letter has grieved me for the lack of faith you have in me. I am so confident of the future that I laugh at your fears; but it distresses me that you should be needlessly distressed. . . .

She had reason enough. Having said prudently in August,

'We must postpone buying any property', he proceeded to buy a house in September—14 Rue Fortunée,* off the Faubourg Saint-Honoré. He liked the name 'Fortunée', which had been that of Fortunée Hamelin, the beautiful 'Merveilleuse', part-owner of the land on which the street was built. The owner was a Monsieur Pierre-Adolphe Pelletreau, and the transaction included a 'fiddle' which delighted Balzac:

'If the price is 50,000 francs M. Pelletreau and I will make it 32,000 in the deed, and I will pay him another 18,000 in three months. As a security for this, which will not figure in the deed, I will lodge fifty railway shares with him. . . .

He besought Eve to raise no objections, because it was a wonderful bargain. Repairs would only come to 10,000 francs. The whole thing would cost 60,000 and in four years it would be worth 150,000. He referred to it with mock-modesty as merely 'a love-nest', although it had a frontage of nine windows. And of course it was to be regally furnished: 'You will be able to receive your cousin the Princesse de Ligne in it. She will have nothing as handsome in any château of any *Ligne*. . . .'

The house, which backed on to the Chapelle Saint-Nicolas (in the parish of Saint-Philippe-du-Roule) had originally been one of the large cluster of buildings forming the Chartreuse Beaujon. Nicolas Beaujon, Receiver-General of Finances under Louis XVI, a philanthropist, a libertine, and already the owner of the Palais de l'Élysée had built it as a 'folly' wherein to hold his *fêtes galantes*, together with the chapel dedicated to his patron saint, which contained the mausoleum where he was now buried.

All Paris is moving to the Champs-Elysées. [Balzac wrote.] If I delay six months, what I can buy today for 50,000 francs will cost double, particularly if Louis-Philippe is still alive. There must be no hesitation. I have seen the chapel, which is charming, like a miniature Panthéon. . . .

A new 'Beaujon quarter' was springing up in the fragmented park, and its shade and greenery were attracting painters such as Gudin and Lehmann. The Balzac house was a decidedly odd

* The street is now the Rue Balzac, having been renamed in 1850.

one. Its two-storey façade extended along an enclosed courtyard, with only two windows giving on to the street. The
ceilings were low and the garden extremely small, but Balzac
was attracted by its romantic seclusion:

> It's as mysterious and hard to find as my apartment in Passy.
> A woman can live there incognito, for there is a secret suite
> contrived by M. de Beaujon for that very purpose. She can live
> there invisibly and see and hear everything that goes on. . . .

Moreover M. de Beaujon had liked to be able to pass in
comfort from the profane to the sacred. His own room had
direct access to a private gallery in the chapel where he could
hear Mass. Balzac was not slow to point out this advantage to
Eve:

> Your religious habits and your piety are to me the most
> beautiful qualities of your beloved soul, and the house I have
> bought stands back-to-back with the Chapelle Saint-Nicolas,
> a chapel-of-ease of Saint-Philippe-du-Roule. Beaujon built it
> and bequeathed it to the parish, reserving right of entry for his
> servants and a magnificent gallery for himself. . . . You can go
> straight to it from your bedroom. That, my angel, is what
> decided me to buy the house, which is situated between a garden
> and a pretty little church. The right is expressly reserved in the
> deeds, and it is the only house in Paris to possess anything of the
> kind. . . .

But Eve did not rejoice. The precipitate purchase of a house
before his debts were paid, and one which would cost a great
deal to put in order since its previous owner (Pelletreau was
simply a property speculator) had never lived in it; the need to
instal an expensive heating system to protect the charming
murals against damp; the absence of stables, outhouses and a
porter's lodge (these appurtenances of the Chartreuse Beaujon
having already been sold)—all this exasperated her; and Balzac,
in his efforts to soothe her, had to make great play with the
chapel:

> 8 December 1846: When I think that my beloved wife will
> be able to pass from her dwelling, upstairs or downstairs, on to
> her private balcony or into the body of the chapel, to hear the
> Holy Office, and that this is the only house in Paris to enjoy that
> royal or princely right, it takes my breath away. . . .

He was bound to admit that from the outside the house looked
'horribly like a barracks', but he would so load it with marvels
that the interior would be like an oriental palace. The appre-
hensive Eve, already horrified to learn that he was furnishing ten
rooms, was sent plans drawn up by the architect Santi and
endless lists of wallpapers, clocks, vases, chandeliers and pictures: 'It is the fantasy of one who wants to have all things
beautiful around him, just as all will be beautiful in his heart
and in his wife, his Eve, who has been his dream for fourteen
years! . . .'

All things beautiful! . . . A woman might well hesitate to cast
in her lot with a man so given to impulsive, immoderate
actions. And would he even be faithful? He had not always been
so in the past. Eve was astonished to learn that Louise de
Breugnol was still living in the Rue Basse. Balzac explained that
she was merely there as housekeeper, although she was also
useful in business matters. It was certainly true that she was
threatening to do him untold harm, but to dispose of her for
good and all he needed to pay her 7,500 francs, which he had not
got. 'I shall never get married, I'm at the bottom of your list,'
the 'Screech-owl' complained. And then she contracted
typhoid, with extensive haemorrhages, and he had to nurse her.
A bachelor-life has its horrors. But Eve was unjust in her reproaches. Working day and night, as he was now doing, he was
like a child dependent on a nurse. That was why he needed the
'wretched woman', and not for the reason Eve suspected: 'I
want her married and off my hands, and I shall see to it when I
get back.'

He meant when he got back from Germany, where he was to
attend the marriage of George and Anna. But before leaving
Paris he had literary commitments to fulfil. The last part of *Les
Paysans* was due to *La Presse*, and to obtain a delay he paid
court to the plump Delphine de Girardin. She invited him to
dine, with Lamartine, whom he congratulated on his political
success— —'But what a physical wreck he is! He's fifty-six and
looks eighty. He's worn out, done for; he won't live more than
a few years. He's consumed with ambition and corroded by his
sordid affairs . . .' Lamartine, at the time, had another twenty-
three years to live; Balzac had four.

His literary programme would have terrified any other writer:

This is what I have to write. First, *L'Histoire des parents
pauvres*—*Le Bonhomme Pons*, which will make two or three folios
of the *Comédie humaine*, and *La Cousine Bette* which will make
sixteen; then *Les Méfaits d'un procureur du roi*, which will make
six—a total of twenty-five folios, or 20,000 francs, serial and
volume sales included. Then I have to finish *Les Paysans*. All
this exceeds my expenses. . . . Besides, I like the subjects and will
write them extremely quickly. I'm out for money. The book-
trade is in a bad way. . . .

There were also family obligations. His relations with Madame
Mère were much improved, Cousin Sedillot acting as a buffer
between them. When he ran into her in the Rue Vivienne she
publicly embraced him, an act of unaccustomed warmth. And
Laure came to tell him that they had found a paragon of husbands for his niece, Sophie.

He is content [Balzac wrote to Eve] that the dowry should
take the form of shares in the Jura bridge which Surville is just
finishing. He's rich and he thinks Sophie wonderful. He is also
a big timber-merchant owning land, houses and capital. I said,
'Grab him! In this bourgeois age they're more likely to elect
oak-beams to the Chamber than Lamartines. But be quick
about it. Delayed marriages don't come off.' . . . So there are
four of them! First the Screech-Owl; second, Anna; third, us;
fourth, Sophie. What a year! . . .

A year indeed—rich in marriages but poor in work. Balzac's
enemies rejoiced in his silence. There had always been enemies,
those who were jealous of his success, those who took offence at
his manners, those who envied his immense gifts. They liked to
think that he had drained himself dry with overwork and too
many serials: 'M. de Balzac has exhausted, in this commonplace
and unrewarding labour, the gift of bold and penetrating
observation which atoned for many lapses of taste and imperfec-
tions of style; he has reduced himself to impotence. . . .' There
could be only one sufficient answer to this, a masterpiece—if he
still had the power to write one.

XXXV

The World Around Him

Le monde est un tonneau garni de canifs.

BALZAC

HE HAD LONG POSSESSED the faculty of burying himself in work for weeks on end, to the exclusion of all else. In moments of particular stress he had fled for refuge to Saché or La Bouleaunière or Frapesle, there to write happily and with phenomenal speed. But now, as the year 1846 drew to a close, he found that this resource was failing him. The torrent of ideas, of words, had become no more than a trickle. 'We need to be together,' he wrote to Eve. He had *une brume sur l'âme*, a misting of the spirit. And there were too many distractions, the thought of approaching fatherhood, with its grave responsibilities; above all, the house in the Rue Fortunée, 'Beaujon's Folly', which was now in the hands of builders and decorators. This called for constant attention. He spent whole days which should have been devoted to the *Comédie humaine* poring over estimates and architects' plans. It seemed that, allowing for everything, it was going to cost about 77,000 francs—a trifle, of course, for the most elegant house in Paris, particularly when one reflected that in a few years it would have doubled in value; but still, more than he had originally reckoned.

Its internal elegance, to compensate for that barrack-like exterior, was what chiefly preoccupied him. Fortunately there were all the expensive items he had picked up on his travels, furniture, pictures, glass and pottery—'the things you called foolishness are now shown to be wisdom'. He was 'too sensible' to order a lavish bookcase; but on the other hand he found himself 'compelled' to buy Smyrna carpets—'Good, lasting stuff is always an economy, as I had the sense to realize.' The words economy, good sense, prudence were constantly on his lips, and were used to justify all manner of extravagance: 'We need curtains for nineteen windows, and think what that costs, at 300 francs a window! But a makeshift job would cost only a third less than doing it properly.' In short, the curtains had to be such as would last for ever, and if that was foolishness it was at least better than spending the money on riotous living. There had to be household linen: 'If you can find some nice pillow-cases, we want a dozen for each bed, embroidered at the corners and round the edges. They do that sort of thing better in Germany than in France, but yours can be edged with lace here.' Sheets, towels, dish-cloths—the earnest paterfamilias thought of everything and bought everything—even a grip for the lavatory chain, of green Bohemian glass.

He could not understand Eve's misgivings. In Heaven's name, why? They could be married and settled in two months. He had been to Metz, and all was well. There was a discreet, obliging mayor, and the civil ceremony would take place in his house at night. Dr Nacquart's son and Germeau, the Prefect, would be witnesses, and the married pair would then ask the blessing of the Bishop of Metz or the Curé of Passy. 'But if you knew the difficulties that have had to be overcome, and how many kind people I have met! . . . The irregularities will be trifles, and the marriage-certificate perfectly valid. . . .' Of course, if she could arrange for them to be married in Wiesbaden or Mainz, that would be more secret still. What was she afraid of? Her letters were filled with hints of disapproval, and this made him very unhappy. Was she worrying about money? A month's work would take care of everything.

Thus he kept up his spirits, while the facts remained obstinately facts. The books went unfinished; publishers insisted upon seeing manuscripts before paying for them; contractors would not wait for their money, and Madame Mère was complaining again and the Screech-owl was screeching. He had had to draw on the *trésor louloup* to pay for the house, and there was now nothing left of it except the railway shares, which persisted, most infernally, in falling. In this matter Balzac was not wholly at fault. The shares were, in fact, an admirable long-term investment; but, like everything else, they were involved in the general financial crisis. There was a threat of war, and Louis-Philippe was a sick man. Balzac had never had a high opinion of that monarch, but he feared, with many people, that his death would lead to catastrophe. In any event, the shares were not fully paid-up; he needed to raise another 28,000 francs or else sell at a heavy loss. He besought Eve's help, sending her a statement of the account, but she replied bluntly that she could do no more. There was nothing for it but to borrow from Rothschild, handing over shares as collateral. Life was hard.

The sad truth was that Eve had lost all faith in his practical ability. She wrote, 'Scatter what I have given you to the winds, dearest Noré [Honoré], but do not devour my patrimony.' The unfairness! He could see nothing to regret in his many transactions: 'Scold me when I'm wrong, but not when I have acted rightly.'

She now did nothing but scold him, and the thought of marrying him, whether in Metz or Mainz, terrified her. She determined to postpone the wedding for at least a year. She would bear her child in secret, and they would acknowledge it later in the marriage-settlement. This came as an appalling shock to him: 'Your decision strangely alters my plans. My dream of happiness is now fifteen months distant, or at least a year. . . .' Certainly there were all kinds of legal, family and social difficulties; but the real impediment was Balzac himself. In the midst of financial disaster he told her that he was thinking of buying a collection of books on the theatre at a cost of 24,000 francs. It was (as always) a wonderful bargain, and to be paid for in annual instalments of 6,000 francs, the merest nothing; but it was a nothing that he did not possess. He wanted her to bring a bedspread of Russian ermine for their bed, but she refused. Wealthy though she was, his recklessness made her shudder. 'Do you know,' he wrote, 'that I am going to possess the fountain which Bernard Palissy made for Henry II?' Did he want to turn the place into a museum?

Everything conspired against them. In October Germeau came to warn Balzac that no marriage contracted in Moselle could long be kept secret. Well-disposed though he was, he had no doubt reflected on his own position if any infringement of the Code should become known. And anything might happen if the Tsar came to learn of Eve's secret marriage to a foreigner. All her legal advisers agreed that she must return to Poland to get her affairs finally straightened out before marrying again.

Balzac was forced to acquiesce: 'It is your opinion; it is now mine as well.'

The whole problem would be solved, he told her, if she made over her property to her daughter:

> As for me, I care nothing for that estate. . . . I repeat, I shall have enough money for both of us. I shall earn 100,000 francs in 1847, with first, *La Fin de Vautrin*; second, *Les Vendéens*; third, *Le Député d'Arcis*; fourth, *Les Soldats de la république*; and fifth, *Une Famille*. *La Comédie humaine* will be reprinted. In six years' work I shall earn as much as I have done in Passy, 500,000 francs. . . .

But he had to interrupt his labours for a few days to attend the wedding of George and Anna in Wiesbaden. It enabled him to spend another 'unforgettable night' with his *blanche et grasse volupté d'amour*. When he got back to Paris he sent reports of the wedding to the *Messager* and five other newspapers.

> Wiesbaden, 13 October.
> The wedding today took place, in the Catholic church in this town, between one of the richest heiresses in the Russian Empire, Countess Anna de Hanska, and the representative of the ancient and illustrious House of Vandaline, Count George Mniszech. Monsieur de Balzac was among the witnesses. . . .
> On the side of her mother (née Countess Rzewuska) the bride is a great-grandniece of the Queen of France, Marie Leczinska; and Count George, a grand-nephew of the last King of Poland, is a direct descendant of the father of the celebrated and unfortunate Tsarina, Marina Mniszech, whose life-story has been written by the Duchesse d'Abrantès.

This news-item, so highly gratifying to its compiler, moved Aline Moniusko, Eve's sister who was then in Paris, to exasperated sarcasm. 'She told me,' Balzac wrote, 'that you were a ruined family, destroyed, fallen, etc. etc. and that it was quite unsuitable. . . . It is terrifying how *your* family resembles mine. . . .' Aline wanted to know if it was true that Eve intended to remarry, and he cautiously replied that this was what he hoped for, although nothing was yet settled; but that if it did happen he would bring 300,000 francs to the marriage, entirely unencumbered by debts, and a further 10,000 a year earned by his pen. Whereupon Aline said with a sigh, 'So she'll be doing very well!' A perfect scene of comedy with the prospective husband at his wits' end to find the money he urgently needed, and the railway shares still falling!

But there were happier moments. George and Anna wrote to him, to his delight.

To the Count and Countess George Mniszech, 23 October 1846: My excellent, adorable lovers, dear, sweet little *saltimbanques*, *père* Bilboquet herewith tenders his resignation. Gringalet has grown up and Zéphyrine is emancipated. In the play she married the awful Ducantal, but we have changed all that, as Molière says. She is happy with Gringalet, a sphinx-lepidopterous Gringalet, an ante-deluvian coleopterist, but not a fossil, I hope. . . .

I must tell you how deeply touched I am by the affection to which your letter bears witness, at a time when two such charming creatures can have little thought to spare for anyone but themselves. . . .

Rothschild advanced him the money to meet his most pressing commitments, another ray of light. But most important of all, Balzac suddenly recovered his power to write. *La Cousine Bette* and *Les Deux Musiciens* both made good progress, and *Les Paysans* and *Les Petits Bourgeois* were to follow. He began to work really well, inspired by the tremendous thought that he would soon have settled all the debts, paid for the house and saved the *trésor louloup*; but it was an arduous business:

Ah, *mon loup*, you don't know what it is to fill volumes! They're delightful to read when they're good; but to produce eight of them is a bigger job than the whole Jena campaign! . . . Pray to God for me, that ideas may flow as readily from my pen as the ink does. If it were only a matter of ideas: but there has to be style as well. . . .

Neither was lacking. The collected reprint of the *Comédie humaine* brought him back into the public eye, and *L'Instruction criminelle* (later to be incorporated in *Splendeurs et misères des courtisanes*) added to his reputation. Suddenly the wind had turned in his favour. When *Cousine Bette* began serial

publication it was acclaimed as a masterpiece, at first to his
surprise: 'I did not realize how good *La Cousine Bette* is. You will
find in it the finest scenes I have written in my whole literary
career. . . . There is an immense reaction in my favour. I have
won! . . .
He no longer doubted that all would now be well, and that Eve
and he would be rich and happy. 'Oh, 1847 will be a tremendous
year!' After being absorbed for some months in the correction
and revision of the *Comédie* he was free to devote his whole time
to fresh work. He would write twenty volumes and two or three
plays.

But then came a shattering blow. Eve fell ill in Dresden. Her
child was born prematurely and died. Balzac wept, a frustrated
Goriot. His first thought was to hurry to her side, but it was
impossible. There had been another fall in the railway stock, and
he was pinned to his desk. He had lost a most cherished dream:

I so longed for a child by you! It was a whole life. Believe me,
the setback to our affairs is nothing! But . . . our coming
together, all the rewards of a life of toil and privation, the
beginning of happiness, all checked, delayed, perhaps lost! Still,
you remain to me; you are still there, and loving. For this I must
thank God, and go back to my work and wait. Go on waiting!
. . .

He had been waiting for thirteen years, and now he reproached
himself with having caused the disaster, first by getting her with
child and then by advising her to travel with the Mniszechs to
Dresden:

I shall never forgive myself, for there can be no doubt that
it was the jolting of the train which caused the calamity that has
put an end to so much hope and happiness, to say nothing of
your own suffering. Take great care of yourself, for these dreadful maladies are the most dangerous, those which lead to the
most cruel consequences, the most difficult to abate! Obey your
doctor, don't go out, don't excite yourself, don't worry about
anything. . . .

It was advice that he himself could not follow: 'Nothing
interests or distracts me, I can't concentrate on anything. I did
not know I could so love an unborn being. But it was you, it was

us.' He was so afflicted that, having decided not to go to Dresden because it would entail the loss of twelve days' work, he spent the time in a state of stupor, his mind incapable of working. Anna wrote on Eve's behalf to tell him that 'the emotion of seeing him would be fatal'. He sat brooding over the fire into the small hours, wondering why he did not hear from her. When at length Eve wrote it was to offer one small shred of consolation. He need not mourn for Victor-Honoré. The child had been a girl.

You have not weakened my grief at your own suffering . . . but you have lessened my sorrow, for I so hoped for a Victor-Honoré. A Victor-Honoré does not leave his mother, and we should have had him with us for twenty-five years. That is what we have to bear. . . .

Eve now talked of returning to Wierzchownia, to save money and restore their fortunes. He replied that she was his only fortune, and that if they did not marry soon (July 1847, he said) he would not be answerable for his actions: 'Grief will destroy me or I'll make an end of this wretched life.' Grief was undermining his health and he had become alarmingly thin.

To make things worse, malicious rumours concerning Eve and himself were going round Paris. The world was 'a barrel lined with knives', like the one in the tale by Perrault. The Duchesse de Castries, 'with one foot in the grave, looking like a dressed-up corpse', gave a twist to one of these knives by referring slyly to a certain Countess Mniszech who had entertained on the grand scale in the days of the Empire and had had an affair with the Duc de Maillé. Did Balzac know her? He pretended complete ignorance, and exclaimed, when she mentioned Madame Hanska, 'But she's fifty-eight years old and a grandmother!' So then Henriette de Castries asked him about his new house:

'They say it's awful.' . . . 'Horrible,' I replied. 'It looks like a barracks, and there's a garden in front, thirty feet by a hundred, which is like a prison-yard. But no matter. It gives me solitude and silence, and it's cheap.' . . . When I had convinced her that I was badly housed, never going to marry and likely to plunge into new follies, she became charming. And that is an old friend. . . .

Delphine de Girardin's reaction to the rumours was of quite another kind. The report of Balzac's foreign conquest added greatly to his interest in her eyes. When (at the time when he was gathering material for *Béatrix*) he had called upon her and they had talked at length about the problems of married life, she had put her own interpretation on the visit. However, Balzac assured Eve, there was no cause for alarm: Madame de Girardin had become hideous. But this did not prevent him from escorting her to the theatre, where she, too, inquired about his marriage to Madame Hanska:

This is what I said to her: 'Madame, it would be so wonderful for me that I hope for it without believing in it. For fourteen years I have loved that lady exclusively, nobly and purely. I am above all things her friend, prepared to travel fifteen hundred leagues to satisfy her least whim, and I would that she had many more. If I do not marry her I know that she will not marry at all. To be her friend is the pride of my life. If she were to tell me (for I should learn it only from her), "I am going to marry such and such a prince", in ten days I should be dead. . . . This is no empty utterance. She has been my whole life for fourteen years. . . . For a long time past wealth, reputation, etc.—all the things that commonly attract men—have played no part in it. I love chivalrously and nobly, and I believe my love is returned. The deep piety of the lady is my guarantee. If she should betray my friendship God would cease to exist for me. That is the truth behind the tales the world is inventing, for I know the matter is discussed by people who know nothing about it.'
She was overwhelmed. She looked strangely at me.
'I may seem gay and witty, light-headed if you like, but that is a mask hiding a soul unknown to all the world, except to *her*. I write *for her*, I want fame *for her*. She is everything, the public, the future!'
'You have explained the *Comédie humaine* to me,' she said.
'So great a work could be written in no other way.' . . .

Such was the report of the conversation he sent Eve; we may surmise that it was carefully edited. He had reasons for wanting to keep in with Delphine, who, with *La Presse*, was agitating for his election to the Academy. But he feared indiscretions which might attract the notice of his creditors. When Théophile Gautier came to inspect the house and marvelled at its contents,

he said with a hang-dog show of modesty: 'I'm worse off than
ever, none of it belongs to me. I've furnished the place for a
friend whom I'm expecting. I'm simply the caretaker and hall-
porter.'

With Eve's announcement that she was returning to the
Ukraine inspiration again forsook him and he could not write a
line: 'I pray every instant that the cork which is holding up the
flood will suddenly burst out. . . . .' He was lost without her.
Would she not come to Paris before going to Russia, to live
privately in a furnished apartment, since she could not stop in
the Beaujon house? But she could talk of nothing but his extravagance. A 'shattering' letter from Dresden caused him to
wonder what knaves and fools were poisoning her mind against
him:

Oh, *louloup*, if in your letter you were not so deliciously a
mother, and a loving mother, I would reproach you for your
wounding lack of trust in me. I am forty-eight, and my hair is
turning white. I seek a fortune and am working to achieve it. I
don't mean to repeat Les Jardies or any other blunder, but you
think I'm heading blindly for the same mistakes! You make me
out to be a grown-up child, a deluded poet. . . . Be calm, beloved
loup; more people think me miserly than think me extravagant.
. . .

She was not convinced: 'After Beaujon it will be Montcon-
tour; it will start all over again. I am in love with an incorrigible
squanderer!' To which he replied, 'And I am in love with a
person very ready to believe the worst and very quick to scold.
But I shall be revenged: in future I shall become a hoarder. . . .'
If she insisted on returning to the Ukraine he would follow her.
What was there to keep him in Paris? Neither fame nor furniture.
He would get rid of everything in a month, and leave with
profound happiness, profound indifference to everything that
was not her: 'I won't even finish *les Paysans*; by God, I won't
write anything more at all, not so much as a line. I'll live and
dream, the happiest man in the world, your dog, your moujik,
always near you, never to leave you. . . .' Why would she not
come? Was she waiting for him to grow old? But it would be a
pity for her not to see the house.

Everything is taking shape. . . . They're doing the carving

outside. . . . We shan't be as ugly as I thought. We're going to plant and sow and grass, and put green trellises up the walls, to make Eve's paradise complete so that she will not be able to say I have overlooked anything. The painter is doing the cupolas; Hédouin is restoring the washed-out murals. In three weeks the place won't be recognizable. . . .

If you knew what our linen amounts to! It's terrifying— twenty-four sets of sheets, a hundred clothes, twelve dozen towels, etc. etc. . . .

But she must not worry about the cost. By 1850 everything would have been made good, the debts, the *trésor louloup*, everything, and he would have a settled income of 16,000 a year, 6,000 from the Academy. She had so often shaken her head over his financial forecasts, but this time it was *mathematically certain*. Two newspapers, *La Siècle* and *Le Constitutionel* had plans for serializing some of his better-known novels, and the new *Comédie humaine* was selling splendidly. The only flaw in the tale of triumph was his present inability to work, and for this Eve was responsible. His state of uncertainty was doing him untold harm: 'I need to know if I am to live in Russia or if you will live in Paris.'

At which point Eve abruptly changed her mind. She decided to come to Paris for two months before going to the Ukraine. The effect on Balzac was electrifying: 'That is all I need! Let me perish afterwards! Nothing will matter if my dream can be made *real* for two months. I'll work; I'll write *Les Paysans* under your eyes!' The cure operated immediately. He wrote twenty or thirty folios a day. *La Dernière Incarnation de Vautrin* was finished. By 25 January he had finished *Le Cousin Pons*, which the great Veron, the most difficult of all the critics, held to be an even greater masterpiece than *La Cousine Bette*. And it was all her doing!

Do you realize the happiness you have given me? You will be neither ruined nor tormented if you will follow my advice, that is to say, live quietly in your apartment in the Champs-Élysées and never leave it except to go out with me after dark. . . . It will be Paradise, the Garden without the intruder and with know-ledge. . . .

By February 1847, everything was arranged, and he went to

meet her in Frankfurt. He had rented a handsome ground-floor apartment in the Champs-Élysées quarter—entrance-hall, drawing-room, dining-room, three bedrooms and a maid's room, with access to a garden. She was to have a 'superb carriage, from a leading hirer':

It is like a dream. . . . To be together for two months! Married for two months, tucked away in a corner, secret and happy, with mild debauches at the Conservatoire, the Opera, the Italiens. . . .
Be calm: 300 francs for the apartment, 370 for the kitchen . . . Allow 500 for amusements, carriage, etc.—a total of 1,200, or 2,400 for two months. Allow another 2,400 for your journey home, and that makes 5,000. Allow 2,000 more for emergencies and you have a grand total of 7,000 for the months of February, March, April and May. Is that too much? You expected it to be double. God, how I hunger and thirst for you! . . .

XXXVI

Swan-Song

L'amour et la haine sont des sentiments qui s'alimentent par eux-mêmes, mais des deux la haine a la vie plus longue.

BALZAC

THE THEME OF a great man so overwhelmed by obsessions—sexual desire, marriage, collector's mania—that his work is brought to a stop, is one worthy of Balzac himself. Yet his creative powers remained unimpaired, his mind as lucid as ever. Directly his uncertainties were in some degree resolved the flame sprang again to life and a string of masterpieces followed. He was even able to go back to *Les Paysans*, which he had found so obstinate, and give that book its true dimensions.

As we have seen, the idea for it had originally been proposed to him by Wenceslas Hanski in 1834, but after making a first attempt he had put it aside. It was to become a work of particular historical importance which deserves to be studied in some detail. Balzac had had a number of opportunities of observing rural life at first hand—in Touraine, with Jean de Margonne and Joseph de Savary; at L'Isle-Adam, when he went to stay with Villers-la Faye; round Villeparisis, and perhaps even at Les Jardies. He had seen that it presented one of the gravest social problems of the time. The French Revolution had placated a section of the bourgeoisie by affording them access to power, but it had done nothing for the peasantry. The big landed estates were soon reconstituted, sometimes as a reward to Empire generals, but later, under the Restoration, for the benefit of their original owners. This backward step was one that the farming population was not prepared to accept, and Balzac, the historian of manners, had been quick to perceive the numerous links between them and the petty bourgeoisie of the countryside—notaries, dealers, bailiffs, mayors—who were urging them to revolt against the new feudalism.

Although Monsieur Hanski had suggested the book, and although Eve herself was a great landed proprietor, Balzac was too much of a novelist not to enter into the feelings of his characters and sympathize with the peasants' grievances. 'The bourgeois does his stealing at his own fireside,' one of his characters, *le père* Fourchon, remarks. 'It is more profitable than picking up trifles in the woods. . . . I saw the old days, my good learned sir, and I see the new ones. The label has changed, but the wine is still the same.' What difference did it make if the new owner was a bourgeois instead of a lord? 'Haven't you noticed that the bourgeois turns out worse than the lord? . . . What would they do if we all got rich? . . . Would they plough their own fields and harvest their own crops? . . .' Balzac predicted that a dissatified working population, born of the Revolution, would one day swallow up the bourgeoisie, as the bourgeoisie had swallowed up the aristocracy.

If the owner was prepared to turn a blind eye when his neighbour poached his land, he might be tolerated; but not otherwise. Balzac drew an imaginary estate, the Château des Aigues, near La Ville-aux-Fayes (somewhere in Burgundy, in the region of Joigny, where his friend Lautour-Mézeray was sub-prefect). After being acquired by a beautiful 'impure', Sophie Laguerre, at the time of the Directoire, it passes into the hands of an Empire general, the Comte de Montcornet, a hero of Essling and a choleric giant of a man whose frail wife is the mistress of Émile Blondet, a good-looking and amusing literary free-lance. The estate-manager, Gaubertin, believes at the time of the transfer that life under the General will go on much as before—that is to say, that he will be able to pursue the profitable and illegal sidelines which were winked at by his former employer. But the General, an exemplary soldier and staunch believer in discipline, with little knowledge of country matters, insists on enforcing the letter of the law.

'You're living on my land,' he says to Gaubertin.

'But do you expect me to live on air?'

'Clear out, you dog! I'm dismissing you!'

Gaubertin is replaced by a more honest man, Michaud. But the General has stirred up a hornet's nest. Gaubertin, the dealer in goods and land, has relatives and associates throughout the region. The chief magistrate is his cousin and ally. The law does not operate in remote country districts where rapacity (whether for women or for land) is without scruple and the *garde-champêtre* knows when to turn a blind eye. The amateur landlord will always be beaten. He may win a case in the local court, but he will lose it on the land itself, where a network of covert interests surrounds him. The honest Michaud is murdered, and the murderer goes free because no one will give him away. The sub-prefect advises Montcornet to sell the estate and invest his money.

'What! Surrender to the peasants, when I didn't retreat even on the Danube?'

'Ah, but where are your cavalrymen now?' asks Blondet the journalist.

A week later the sale is announced. A local moneylender buys the estate, keeps the vineyards for himself, puts the woodlands in Gaubertin's charge and disposes of the rest. Once again the label has changed, but the wine remains the same.

Long after all this, Blondet, reduced to penury and near to suicide, receives a letter from the Comtesse de Montcornet telling him of her husband's death. She is his heiress (and also the daughter of a French viscount and a Russian princess). Now aged forty, she offers her former lover 'a fraternal hand and a considerable fortune'. So Blondet marries her—and Balzac achieves the happy ending he so desired for himself.

But the book presented great difficulties. Peasant society, as secret and enclosed as that of the Faubourg Saint-Germain, was no less difficult to know. It was true that he had touched on the subject in *Le Médecin de campagne* and *Le Curé de village*, but these were studies of country life seen from a different angle. In a pamphlet entitled *Catéchisme social* he had discussed the problem of agricultural prices, arguing that it was in France's interest to keep them as low as possible—'in order that industry may be better able to compete with England, which is the great regulator of prices'. He conceded that French prosperity could only be founded on the 'excessive sobriety' of the peasant population, a euphemism for the state of appalling squalor in which they lived. At the time he had seen this as a social fact, to be accepted as the existence of a condemned species is accepted as a zoological fact. But the peasants themselves could not be expected to view it in this light, and he came to realize that the problem was a crucial one, calling for deeper study than he had given it.

This explains why, after all, he never finished *Les Paysans*. Girardin, who had published the beginning in *La Presse*, paid him an advance of 9,000 francs for the conclusion, but Balzac eventually repaid a part of this sum. *Les Paysans* was not published until 1855, five years after his death. Eve, by now his widow, asked first Champfleury and then Rabou to finish it, and when both refused she contented herself with the outline of the ending which Balzac had sketched in 1838, only adding 'a few grains of sand and gravel'. In which she was wise. The book is a very fine one, inexhaustible in its truth and as sound today as it was over a century ago. Its message is clear: no peasantry and no people can be governed by a system of law founded purely on reason. Every Montcornet will meet his Gaubertin out in the fields. Here, as everywhere, Balzac's realism is manifest: he sought to legislate for men and women as they truly are.

Balzac's swan-song—that of a still-young man worn out before his time by personal suffering, disappointment and sleepless nights—is contained in the two novels forming the diptych, *Les Parents pauvres*. He knew that he was playing for high stakes. On 16 June 1846, he wrote to Eve:

The time has come for me to produce two or three major works which will overthrow the false gods of this bastard literature and prove that I am younger, fresher and greater than ever. *Le Vieux Musicien* [*Le Cousin Pons*] is the male poor relation, cruelly treated but gentle of heart. *La Cousine Bette* is the female poor relation, cruelly treated, living on intimate terms with three or four families, and revenging herself. . . .

The symmetry pleased him. At first he thought of making them into two novellas, of which one, *Le Cousin Pons*, was to be based on a short story entitled *Les Deux Bassons de l'Opéra* by Alberic Second. 'You will see,' he said to the youthful author, 'what I will make of your idea.' In the event he put so much of himself into it that it grew into a long novel.

Old Pons's art collection is the one Balzac would himself have liked to possess (and, indeed, believed he possessed). Pons's passion for antiques was his own, as was his terror of callers who might cast profane eyes on his treasures. And there were other

models for Pons. Little *père* Dablin was a collector; and there
was a first violin at the Opera, Sauvageot, with whom Balzac
corresponded, who was also a collector as well as a musician.
As the story developed the 'poor relation' theme receded into
the background, becoming only one of many. There is the
tender devotion to Sylvain Pons of the German, Schmucke (the
former music-teacher of the de Granville sisters in *Une Fille
d'Ève*); the tragedy of Pons, the parasitic gourmet suddenly
deprived of his elegant dinners and turned away in disgrace from
the home of his cousin, Madame Camusot; the ruthless and
elaborate stratagems of the concierge (the abominable, yellow-
eyed Madame Cibot) and Remonencq, two monsters of the
deep; the undeserved good-fortune of the Camusots, who after
their shameful treatment of Pons fraudulently obtain possession
of his property upon his death, at the expense of the heartbroken
Schmucke. In short it is a drama of innocence assailed on all
sides, appalled by the greed and malice that surrounds it and
finding no defenders. What is most striking is the use that a
writer of genius, sustained by the resources of his own imaginary
world-in-being, has made of Alberic Second's slight anecdote.
'To me at least,' Balzac wrote to Eve, 'it is one of those masterpieces of extreme simplicity which contain the whole human
heart. It is as great and even more clear than *Le Curé de Tours*,
and it is fully as heartrending. I am delighted with it. . . .' He
had reason to be. *Le Cousin Pons* still overwhelms its readers.

The book is also of interest because it deals mainly with a
lower level of Paris society than the one Balzac was accustomed
to depict, that of the well-to-do quarters which he had enviously
contemplated from the slope of Père-Lachaise in 1822, and into
which he eventually thrust his way. There are more duchesses
than grisettes in the *Comédie humaine*, although *César Birotteau*,
Les Employés and *Les Petits Bourgeois* are exceptions. The
writers and artists in *Illusions perdues* live on the fringe of the
Restoration half-world. *Le Cousin Pons*, which takes place in the
reign of Louis-Philippe, opens at the home of the Camusots de
Marville, but very soon moves to a shabby street in the Marais,
and to the dismal third-floor apartment which Pons's art
collection has transformed into a museum. This is a very
different world, a jungle in which dark figures prowl, the
fortune-teller with her toad, the seedy man of affairs who tran-

sacts the business of the poor; but all is relieved by the deep and tender friendship (one of Balzac's lifelong dreams) between the two elderly men. He had indeed proved to his detractors that he was greater than ever.

La Cousine Bette also expanded enormously in the writing. Its starting-point (not for the first time) was a short story by Laure Surville, *La Cousine Rosalie*, which appeared in 1844 in *Le Journal des enfants*. But whereas Laure had flatly narrated 'a simple tale, full of good intentions and worthy sentiments', Honoré turned it into 'a complicated intrigue, scabrous and cruel'. Bette, a diabolical creature, writhes 'like a creeping plant' in the flames of hatred. She may be said, indeed, to have escaped from the control of her author, who in a last blaze of inspiration added a group of new characters to the cast of the *Comédie humaine*: Bette herself (Lisbeth Fischer), Valérie Marneffe, the Brazilian Montès, and the two Hulots.

The process was the same as in *Illusions Perdues*: an idea embedded in reality, but so imaginatively enriched that it gave birth to monsters. Balzac wrote of Bette that she was compounded of his mother (whose show of affection for himself he believed, quite wrongly, to conceal a secret hatred), Marceline Desbordes-Valmore and Eve's formidable Aunt Rosalie. He might well have added Louise de Breugnol to the list. Her bitter campaign against Eve differed only in degree (and success) from the tortuous intrigues whereby the unbeautiful, humiliated Bette contrives the ruin of the Hulot family.

Baron Hulot, brother of the Marshal Hulot who figures in *Les Chouans*, himself a high-ranking army officer, a Councillor of State and grand-officer of the Légion d'Honneur, is an elderly libertine who sinks by stages into a hell of sexual squalor. It has been suggested that the Hulots—Hector Hulot, whose wife's maiden-name was Adeline Fischer—are a transmutation of Victor Hugo and his wife, Adèle Foucher. Apart from the striking similarity of names, Hugo had been surprised *in flagrante delicto* with Léonie Biard, as Hulot was with Valérie Marneffe. There had always been something equivocal in Balzac's attitude to Hugo. Hugo defended and admired him; but Balzac, although he praised the writer, unjustly denigrated the man. Anyhow, he made use of the Biard episode, as he did of everything that came his way.

Bernard Guyon considers that Balzac, a prey at the time to his own erotic obsessions, found much of Hulot in himself; and it has also been suggested that the character owes something to a certain Comte d'Aure, a Councillor of State who had died the previous year. None of this need be ruled out: men, women, friends, mistresses, debauches, physical delights, the author himself, all go into the author's pot. Balzac may well have had himself in mind when he wrote, of Hulot: 'Seeing ourselves from day to day we end, like the Baron, by believing that we have not greatly changed, that we are still young, whereas others see the hair turning white, the wrinkles on our forehead, the thick folds in our stomach.'

The central theme of the book recalls that of *Goriot*, *Grandet* and *La Recherche de l'Absolu* in that it depicts the ruin of a family by an obsession, in this case an old man's eroticism. The Hulot family puts up a long and devoted resistance, but in the end passion 'in rebellion against Nature' swells 'like a monstrous wave' and sweeps everything away. After Valérie Marneffe's death Hulot takes up with a chorus girl, then with a working woman and finally with a young girl, scarcely more than a child, who is sold to him by her parents. The family strive to keep him at home, but he creeps out at night to visit his doxy in a garret. Not only does he degrade himself but he drags his noble-hearted wife into the same pit of degradation: 'Tell me what those women do to gain such a hold on you. I'll try . . .' But 'the obsessed are happy in their own filth'. Balzac had never written anything more atrocious or more moving, but he did so at a heavy price. The superhuman effort which *La Cousine Bette* cost him (he wrote the whole long book in two months) completed his physical and mental exhaustion.

The time had come at last for Eve's visit. Thanks to this great burst of work he had a little money in hand. The collected edition of the *Comédie* was reprinting, and he had been paid for *Cousin Pons*, *La Dernière Incarnation de Vautrin* and *Le Député d'Arcis*, although the last was scarcely begun. Eve was to pay her household expenses in Paris, and he would provide her with linen and silver. The two months' rent of the apartment had to be paid in advance, a cook engaged and Madame de Breugnol disposed of, with compensation—but these were trifles.

'I have only one thought in my mind,' he wrote, 'that I shall see you this week, breathe your breath, fling myself on your dear person, feel the touch of your dress. . . .' But he added: 'This is the first time we shall have been alone together, with no one else. Being free of restraint we shall both show the worst side of our character. You will be beaten and I shall be scolded! . . .'

He left for Frankfurt on 4 February 1847, and returned in triumph with his 'plump, tender and voluptuous' Eve. Voluptuous she certainly was, but the tenderness was less to be relied on. She nearly broke his heart when he took her to inspect the house in the Rue Fortunée. He had expected cries of delight, but she criticized everything—too much marquetry, too many bronzes, too much marble, too many cupboards inlaid with tortoiseshell and brass. Why spend a fortune on this 'sinister and comical' place? Was this the reward of so many years' devotion? How could she judge it in any case, when it was smothered in scaffolding and rubble?

During her stay he gave up work almost entirely so as to take her about Paris—to Véry's, to the Palais-Royal (where Lucien de Rubempré, soon after his arrival, had given a dinner-party which had cost as much as a month in Angoulême) and other fashionable restaurants. They visited the Exposition des Beaux-Arts and the Théâtre des Variétés, where she laughed her head off. But their domestic fare, to judge by what he wrote to her later, was of the plainest: 'Day after day I watched an enchanting creature eat ragout made of the remains of yesterday's meat, leaving the fresh meat for her lover—and I never said a word in gratitude! But I saw it, I was touched. . . .'

It lasted two and a half months. Then he took her back to Frankfurt, and returned like a body without a soul.

Farewell, my dear, beloved treasure! We must hope, as you say. This will be our last crisis, our last trouble. . . . I love you more than ever. I must have you for my wife, or life will mean nothing to me. . . .

That issue was still in the balance, and all his latter works were clouded by the uncertainty. From 1829 to 1842 he had lived on memory and dreaming; he had written of his youth and rejoiced in his revenges. But after Monsieur Hanski's death all this was changed. The cloudy aspirations, the dreams of fame and love which had sustained him, were transformed into a single, plain objective: marriage to Eve. The novels *Honorine* and *Albert Savarus* reflect the torments of a man unsure of being loved, and *Les Paysans* and *Les Parents pauvres* are pervaded with the melancholy of disillusion. He still hoped to complete his *Comédie humaine.* 'I have been sixteen years at it, and I still need another eight to finish it,' he wrote to Zulma Carraud. It must eventually be rounded off with the *Études analytiques*, which were to supply the moral and philosophical key to the whole great structure. But would he have the strength to write them—or the time?

XXXVII

Body Without Soul

Avez-vous jamais vu bâiller le lion du Jardin des plantes?
C'est un spectacle navrant.

BALZAC

IT MAY BE admitted that there was a good deal of Baron
Hulot in Balzac deprived of his mistress. He suffered physical
torments which prevented him from working. Eve's stay in
Paris had not been all that he had hoped. There had been painful
scenes between them which he never forgot. But he could no
longer live without her, and his state of loneliness was un-
endurable. While tidying his room he came upon a pair of
embroidered slippers with a pencilled note attached: 'I did
these during the times when you went out and left me alone.'
He burst into tears and wept for two hours. These were not
tales invented to win Eve's compassion; they were the reactions
of a sick man rendered sentimental by nervous exhaustion.

But he had to deal with practical matters, the first being
Madame de Breugnol, the Screech-owl, who was still making
trouble. She had gone off with Eve's letters to him when she
left the Rue Basse. Now she was demanding a heavy price for
their return, and threatening that otherwise she would send
them to Anna and her husband—which, considering their
nature, would be horribly mortifying to Eve. Both the police
and his lawyer advised Balzac that it would probably come
cheaper to settle with her than to take legal action, which would
also entail unsavoury publicity. To have to visit the venomous
creature, and bargain with her, made him physically ill. At
length, in July, she handed back the bulk of the letters in return
for 5,000 francs in gold; but she kept one or two referring to
Eve's child. Balzac, for his part, kept the document in which she
confessed to having stolen the correspondence, and thus had
a hold over her. After a last look at those yellowed sheets which
had reached him over the years from Russia, Switzerland, Italy

and Germany he put them on the fire and wept as he gazed at the ashes: 'To think that fifteen years should occupy so small a space! The fire of the spirit wrote them, the fire of earth has consumed them! . . .'

He removed to the house in the Rue Fortunée and busied himself with arranging his treasures on the shelves—the countless pieces of glass and enamel, the bronze and porcelain. If this mechanical labour wearied him, at least it occupied his mind. And nothing could be more perfect than the silence of the Rue Fortunée; one might have been in the depths of the country. He had promised Eve that he would buy nothing more, and he did his best; but still there were things that *had* to be bought, kitchen equipment for instance, and bargains so sensational that they simply could not be ignored. For example, he had seen a Riesener chest with a movable marquetry top which would come in very handy as a table, but it was so exquisite that he had felt sure the price would be well over a thousand. When he inquired, however, he found that it was only 340 francs. How could anyone resist? Moreover, having bought it he discovered (he said) that it had belonged to Élisa Bonaparte!

But Eve must not be perturbed; he had become wise and prudent—too much so, perhaps. He saw two beautiful vases which were just what he wanted for his study; but he refrained. Instead, he bought a portrait which looked like a sketch by Titian, an old Chinese vase, a Boulle pedestal and a caryatid carved in wood: 'You think I'm ruined and done for? I got them for 350 francs. . . .' They also needed a few trifles for the water-closet. That water-closet!

For the secret room we needed: *primo*, a pretty couch; *secundo*, a console at fifty francs to enclose the little box you know of and to carry a basin; *tertio*, another console to put the candle on; *quarto*, three rosewood consoles for flower-vases. You asked in Mainz what I meant to do with the Chinese porcelain-top box. It serves as a draining-board for the brush in the corner. That room is a pleasure-resort, as pretty as a boudoir; and you see how little it has cost! . . .

This brought a furious lecture from Wierzchownia. 'That's *enough*!' wrote Eve, and he meekly bowed his head. Very well, then. He badly needed a new alarm clock, since his own no longer worked; but although he had seen a particularly good one for a mere hundred francs, he had not bought it. Since she insisted that with him buying was a vice, and not a matter of foresight and prudence, he would adopt principles of 'quakerish austerity' and never enter a shop:

'Is Your Majesty prepared to make an exception in the case of an article of cheap mahogany to keep my shoes in, and another for my linen? . . . If this is an infraction of the rules I will continue to put my shoes in the window-boxes on the stairs, because I deny myself flowers, which cost too much. I'm not writing or earning anything; I have no right to spend money. . . .

There was, in fact, no money to spend. Their loss on the railway shares, at the current market quotation, was now 60,000 francs, on a total investment of 130,000. Sooner or later the shares would certainly recover, and the loss might have been turned into an eventual profit by further buying and waiting: but that was a policy for the rich, not the poor. It was maddening. 'I cannot be philosophical in this matter,' he wrote. He was beginning to regret the house (in the Rue *Infortunée*, as he now called it), which was still eating up money, despite its 'excessive modesty'. Only the best would do for it: 'The two ermine bed-spreads are indispensable. . . . Nothing else would be in keeping with its Babylonian, even oriental, artistic splendour. . . .' He would have to write ten books to pay for all that was needed, and he proposed to do so that winter at Wierzchownia.

In the meantime he was writing very little: 'I can't fix my mind on anything. I try all kinds of ideas and grow disgusted with them. . . . I sit for hours lost in my memories, quite besotted.' Yet there were commissions to be fulfilled, promises to be kept—the last part of *Les Paysans*, the *Député d'Arcis*.

God, how difficult it is to get down to work! And I've got to earn enough to bring in 16,000 a year, besides paying off 55,000 of debts, altogether a capital sum of 600,000 francs. Work, little author of the *Comédie humaine*, write *L'Education du prince*, write novels, plays. . . . Pay for your luxuries, expiate your follies, await your Eve in a hell of ink and paper! . . .

He needed to get *Les Paysans* off to *La Presse*, but even to read the manuscript sickened him. Only the letters he wrote Eve gave him any pleasure, and these became voluminous: 'How can I help it? My thoughts obey my heart, so how can I write *Les Paysans?* . . .' He had thoughts of another play, *Orgon*, a sequel to Molière's *Tartuffe* in which Tartuffe, mourned by all the household, would make a triumphal reappearance. But it would have to be written in verse, and Théophile Gautier refused to collaborate: 'So I'm thinking of giving an act to Charles de Bernard, two acts to Méry and the last two to two other poets.' This system of farming out did not work; he found that he must do it himself if it was to be done at all. . . . So he went back to coffee, drank enough in a week to write a book on—and wrote nothing. The flood of mocha had no effect. He was a sick man, literally wasting away for lack of the happiness he could no longer live without. Laurent-Jan, worried by his state of apathy, brought him a copy of *The Cricket on the Hearth*: 'The little book is a flawless masterpiece. Dickens got 40,000 francs for it. They pay better in England than they do here.' An offensive letter came from Girardin, saying that he wanted the end of *Les Paysans* only because Balzac owed it to *La Presse*: 'If you can repay the advance I will gladly drop it.' *La Presse* had recently published a serial by Marie d'Agoult, who since the publication of *Béatrix* had become his bitter enemy. Girardin's letter produced a prompt reaction: 'Contrary to your view, I consider the work excellent.' But the only convincing reply was a good book, and he could not write one—'my house is odious, literature is stupid and I sit with folded arms when I should be working.'

Servants were another problem. He had engaged an Alsatian manservant, François Münch, a cook-housekeeper, Zanella, and a housemaid. For a man of his age and standing it was a reasonable establishment; but their wages, at 90 francs a month, and their food came to 12,000 a year. And when he thought he had disposed of that matter, he found that Zanella was not to be trusted. She privately promised to show his neighbour, the painter, Gudin, over the house in Balzac's absence—just as, in *Le Cousin Pons*, Madame Cibot showed Rémonencq the dealer over Pons's collection. Once again life was imitating art, and to Balzac it was an act of sickening disloyalty: 'I no longer believe in anything but God and my dear girl.'

A further distraction was Eve's sister and lifelong enemy, Aline Moniuszko. She was still in Paris and found Balzac charming now that Eve was not there. Eve had indeed commanded, 'You must dazzle my sister.' But Aline was more than dazzled, she was amazed. Her behaviour, when she visited the Rue Fortunée, was worthy of Cousine Bette. Balzac wrote to Eve:

She was furious that this *palace* as she called it (where, she said, even the nails showed that it was made ready for a beloved woman) should be destined for the one whose nose she had punched when they were children. 'What is Wierzchownia,' she asked, 'compared with this enchanting home? I have seen nothing like it anywhere. Wierzchownia, my dear Monsieur de Balzac, is a model of bad taste, for that was my poor brother-in-law's great weakness.'

I had to burst out laughing, because the way she said it made everything clear. How could a man who had preferred Eve to Aline be credited with good taste in anything?

In the library she said, 'But this alone must have cost a hundred thousand francs. The libraries at Neuilly and Saint-Cloud are nothing to it.' . . . 'I'm fond of books,' I said. She went off overflowing with admiration, and quite convinced, simply from the look of the house, that I was a millionaire.

She had started at the sight of two pillows on Balzac's bed. As the people who knew him were aware, he always slept with two pillows; but she jumped to the conclusion (and no doubt hoped) that he had a woman hidden in the house: ' "Why the two pillows?" she asked. "Oh, I see—it's for emergencies." '

But all these things put together are not enough to account for Balzac's state. He was genuinely ill. His friend Frédéric Soulié died of heart disease, his legs swollen with dropsy: 'It gave me a shock because I think I am suffering from the same thing.' Gavault, his lawyer, besought him to leave Paris—'or you're a dead man'. He was not dead yet, but he was a man mentally afflicted and he had always believed in the influence of the mind on the body. He took a gloomy view of everything. The French bourgeois monarchy seemed to him on the verge of collapse;

revolution was brewing in Italy and threatening to set all Europe on fire. 'You don't realize,' he wrote to Eve, 'how communism is gaining ground, the doctrine that wants to overthrow every-thing and share everything, even food and goods, between all men, whom it holds to be brothers. . . .' Eve knew what he thought about this; but no one could alter the set of the tide.

He paid a visit to L'Isle-Adam, where he had stayed with Villers-La Faye, hoping to find refreshment in a return to the scenes of his youth:

I looked over the gulf of thirty years at the forest and the valley; but that familiar country which at eighteen had restored me to health now did nothing for me. It was a like a dream. I went there by train, walked for seven hours like a soldier on sentry-go and then caught the train back. It had no effect on me. I saw it all without emotion, with none of the stir that I expected. If you had been there, so that I could have said to you, 'I sat under that tree dreaming of fame, and there I dreamt of the woman who would someday love me, and there I recovered from maternal tyranny. . . .'—then there would have been some sense in it. . . .

He was a child again, longing to rest his head on a maternal bosom, longing for the tenderness of Laure de Berny. But Eve was no *Dilecta*. She was behaving like a stern judge, and a not very enlightened one, unmoved by sufferings not her own. He felt her resentment, acute and almost hostile, and was tempted to abandon everything and hurry to her: 'But then I realize that you don't want me and I fall prey to a double despair, that of not being expected and of not having written a line. . . . Oh, what has happened to my spirit? It is at Berditcheff, on those Russian plains of Beauce which I see without having seen them! . . . Be gentle to the absent; try to know him better than you do. . . .'

He could not discover why she would not let him join her. Was she afraid of gossip, or too busy with her own affairs? Was it because she was growing old (as she said) and felt that he needed younger, prettier women, or because she feared the Tsar's disapproval? Finally he wrote to Anna:

Your dear Mamma writes to me very seldom and bans me from the Ukraine. These things seem to me against nature. . . .

I have grown so accustomed to the three of you that life without you has become intolerable. . . . I am like a dog without a master, looking only for what it has lost. . . .

In the end, whatever her misgivings, Eve let herself be touched by his tragically unhappy state. She loved him, when all is said, and was not hard-hearted. She wrote telling him to come. At once he shook off his lethargy, had his passport visaed, started to make ready for the journey. Souverain, the publisher, would let him have the money he needed, or at a pinch he could earn it by publishing a few short stories. 'I shall take sixteen rolls of rye-bread and a tongue to keep me going between Cracow and Wierzchownia.' His happiness was indescribable: 'With you everything is possible, without you everything is impossible and I give up. I am worn out with waiting. . . . Mark you, I don't complain, for no man on earth has been happier. . . . You contain infinity within you. . . .'

So he hastened to the infinity, and he could not have travelled faster. Leaving Paris on 5 September (by the Northern Railway which had cost them both so much!), and travelling by *schnell-post*, *extra-post*, and *kibitka*, he reached Wierzschownia on the 13th. He had been warned that he must expect to meet with all kinds of difficulties in that country where he was entirely ignorant of the language, so he took with him a picnic-basket containing (besides the rolls) *biscuit de mer*, coffee-concentrate, sugar, a tongue and a bottle of anisette. In the event his great reputation caused him to be made welcome everywhere. The head of the Russian frontier-post received him in person and invited him to take pot luck, and he was delighted by the richness of the pot.

Following this mark of esteem, he was treated with great deference by the customs officials, against whom he had been particularly warned, and was accordingly much impressed by Russian discipline. But he did not enjoy the *kibitka*, a wooden vehicle which 'transmits every rut in the road to your bones. . . . The evening was superb, the sky like a blue veil held in place by silver nails. The profound solitude was relieved by the tinkling of the bell on the horse's neck, whose clear, monotonous note in the end is infinitely pleasing. . . .'* Finally, by way of the

* Balzac: *Lettre sur Kiev.*

illustrissime town of Berdichev, he entered the Ukraine: 'It is emptiness, the kingdom of wheat, the rolling plains of [Fenimore] Cooper and their silence. This is where the humus of the Ukraine begins, dark, rich soil, fifty feet deep and often more, which is never dunged. . . .' He fell into a deep sleep and was aroused by a shout: 'I saw a sort of Louvre, a Greek temple gilded by the setting sun.' It was Wierzchownia.

XXXVIII

Wonderland

*Un fait digne de remarque . . . c'est comme nous sou-
mettons souvent nos sentiments à une volonté, combien nous
prenous une sorte d'engagement avec nous-mêmes et comme
nous créons notre sort.*

BALZAC

HE HAD EXPECTED a great deal but was still dumbfounded.
The castle in the Ukraine surpassed all the castles in Spain he
had ever built.

To Laure Surville: This mansion is indeed a Louvre, and the
estate is as big as one of our departments. It is difficult to grasp
the extent and fertility of the land, which is never manured and
where wheat is sown every year. Although the young Count and
Countess have something like 20,000 male peasants between
them, making 40,000 souls, they would need 400,000 to cultivate
all this land. They only sow as much as they can reap. . . .

Having dreamed for thirty years of the delights of being a
Marquis de Carabas he now found himself the prospective
husband of the Marquise.

It was a time of enchantment. The three other *saltimbanques*, Atala, Zéphyrine, and Gringapet, welcomed their
Bilboquet with genuine affection. He was given a charming
suite of rooms, bedroom, sitting-room and study; and the
opulence of the silver, the china and the carpets—those thick
luxurious rugs!—satisfied even his exacting taste. From every
window there was a view of cornfields stretching to the horizon.
And 'five or six other suites like this are available for guests!'

The country is remarkable in the sense that the utmost
magnificence goes hand in hand with a lack of the most ordinary
aids to comfort. This is the only estate in the whole region that
possesses a Carcel lamp and a hospital. There are mirrors ten
feet high but no paper on the walls. . . . The house (and it is the

510

size of the Louvre) is heated with straw. They burn as much in a week in their stoves as you would see at the Saint-Laurent cattle-market. . . .

The kindness of his hosts made it easy to forget the discomforts of the Russian winter. Exalted beings though they were, they lived a quiet family life. Anna ploughed through the ten volumes of Capefigue's *History of Europe in the Time of Louise-Philippe* while her mother did embroidery and Balzac talked to George about business matters. In the Ukraine, as everywhere, he saw dazzling commercial possibilities.

Jointly with his brother André, George Mniszech owned the estate of Wisniowiec, near Brody, one of the finest in Russia, which includes 20,000 acres of oak-woods. At the time there was a great demand for oak in France, for use as railway sleepers. Transport was the problem, with railways still in their infancy, bridges unbuilt and rivers to be crossed. One would have to allow 20 francs per sleeper for this, and the cost of tree-felling and rough-hewing (with Russian serf-labour) might be reckoned at another 10. So, 60,000 sleepers at a cost of 30 francs each. Even if one priced them as low as 50 francs in Paris, there would be a profit of 120,000 francs, without counting the enormous supply of firewood that would be left behind.

The astonishing thing, said Balzac, calculating like Père Grandet, was that nothing of the kind had yet been done, and this was only to be explained by the heedlessness of Russian landowners. He wrote to Surville for his professional opinion, asking for a prompt reply because Eve was proposing to take him on a tour of the Crimea and the Caucasus:

The amount of accumulated wealth in Russia, neglected for lack of transport, is unbelievable. . . . The other day I visited the *folkwark* of Wierzchownia, the place where the corn is threshed by machinery, and in that single village there were twenty ricks thirty-six feet high, fifty feet long and twelve feet wide. . . . But the estate-manager's pilfering and the overall expenses make great inroads into the revenue. . . . The estate has to provide itself with everything. There is a baker, a weaver, a tailor, a shoemaker, etc.—all attached to the house. I can now understand the reason for the three hundred servants which Monsieur de Hanski talked to me about in Geneva. He had his own orchestra. . . .

The estate contained an admirable textile mill, producing 10,000 pieces a year. The 'colossal riches' of which Balzac wrote are still astonishing to a Frenchman. But it was all to be made over by Eve to her daughter in return for an annuity. 'I knew of her intention,' Balzac wrote to Laure, 'and I am delighted that my life's happiness is to be independent of material considerations.' The fact was that the property-transfer was essential if the marriage was to take place. And there were other obstacles. The Tsar's approval had yet to be secured and family opposition overcome: 'You need to be here to realize all the difficulties that lie in the way. . . .'

It has been said that the frivolous ladies of Wierzchownia prevented Balzac from working while he was there, but the facts prove otherwise. Certainly he only completed the second episode of *L'Envers de l'histoire contemporaine*, (*L'Initié*), published in 1848; but he also worked on *Le Député d'Arcis*, a vast novel with a hundred characters, *Les Petitis Bourgeois*, *Le Théâtre comme il est* and *La Femme auteur*, of which the very promising beginning suggested that he was henceforth to depict 'an evolutionary process in the Balzac world akin to the evolution of French society'. *La Femme auteur* contains a number of characters whom the reader has already met at earlier stages in their careers. Claude Vignon, secretary to the Minister of War in *Cousine Bette* and a professor at the Sorbonne in *Les Comédiens sans le savoir*, is now a Member of the Institute while still remaining a Councillor of State. Joseph Lebas, one-time senior apprentice at the '*Maison du Chat-qui-pelote*' and later owner of the business, is president of the Chamber of Commerce and a peer. The 'illustrious' Gaudissart, a theatrical manager in *Cousin Pons*, and now a banker and railway-manager, has clearly forgotten that he started life as a commercial traveller; just as Andoche Finot has forgotten the young jackals of journalism who once showed him so little respect. This kind of forgetfulness is a fact to be noted in society no less than in individuals. The world of Balzac's imagination was, as Maurice Bardèche has said, 'both autonomous and consistent with historical truth'.

Far from preventing him from working, Eve urged him on. During his return journey he wrote to her: 'Do not reproach me with having worked so little. Think rather that in writing

L'Inité I achieved a miracle. . . .' The story certainly deserves to be looked at.

The theme of *L'Envers de l'histoire contemporaine*, of which it was the second part, is charity—the opposite of that of the *Histoire de Treize*, the group of rich and ruthless men who perform arbitrary acts of justice. The first part, *Les Méchancetés d'un saint*, had appeared in 1842 in a Catholic magazine. The work as a whole comes in the same category as *Le Médecin de campagne* and *Le Curé de village*, a book deserving of the Prix Montyon. But *L'Initié* presented difficulties: 'To make a story interesting without a single wolf in the fold calls for a *tour de force*.'

Balzac solved the problem by introducing a penitent wolf, Godefroid, a young man of fashion who, after running through his money, makes the acquaintance of the elderly Baronne de la Chanterie, living in the shadow of Notre-Dame. The old lady has four anonymous associates, four men 'as unshakable as Buddhist priests', who are held in high respect by the Arch-bishop of Paris and the higher aristocracy. They have large funds at their disposal, which they use for the relief of the distressed. In short, this is a conspiracy of virtue, not the most promising subject for a dramatic tale; and Balzac wanted it as enthralling as the corruption of *La Torpille*. So he livened it up with a true story of the *Chouannerie*.

Under the Empire a certain Marquise de Combray had been condemned to twenty-two years in chains for having harboured conspirators against Napoleon. Her daughter had died on the scaffold. Balzac modelled his Madame de la Chanterie on the Marquise, making her a *mater dolorosa* haunted by atrocious memories. He had secured a copy of the indictment from the Court of Appeal in Rouen, and this he adapted to his purpose, keeping very close to the original. But there are countless details pointing to the influence of Eve. The four unnamed men are all readers of Thomas Aquinas, whose *Imitation of Christ* was the first present she had given him, and Madame de la Chanterie presents the neophyte, Godefroid, with a copy. 'For with Balzac,' writes Maurice Regard, in his Introduction, 'religion, like politics, was essentially sentimental and romantic.' During the family evenings at Wierzchownia he read aloud what he had written during the day, and even the prosaic

George, so much more interested in insects than in novels, seems to have been impressed—'one of Bilboquet's greatest triumphs'.

Although it is the work of a tired man, *L'Initié* has considerable merit. Balzac heightened the drama by causing Godefroid (the Initiate) to be entrusted with the mission of saving the family of Bourlac, the Public Prosecutor, who was responsible for Madame de la Chanterie's imprisonment and the execution of her daughter. Bourlac himself is modelled on the official prosecutor at the Criminal Court in Rouen, and the figure of pathos indispensable to a popular romance is his daughter Wanda, afflicted with a mysterious malady known as the 'Polish scurvy'. For details of this disease Balzac applied to the Hanski family physician, Dr Knothé, and he also made use of him in creating the fictitious doctor who cures it. Wanda, 'the laughing, spoilt child, musical, a devourer of novels, extravagant and coquettish', is Anna Mniszech.

Living in a Polish household, Balzac made use of whatever it had to offer. The very door-curtain which Wanda embroiders in the story was the work on which Eve was engaged. He must have enjoyed the notion of making Bourlac, the savage prosecutor, a father of the Goriot type who surrounds his invalid daughter with the illusion of luxury while the room next door to hers is a picture of destitution. It was not so very different from the Rue des Batailles, where the visitor had to pass through a dilapidated hall and several empty rooms before reaching that Arabian Nights boudoir. The ending of the novel may appear ridiculous or sublime, according to how the reader looks at it. At the moment when the former prosecutor, overwhelmed by benevolence, sinks to the floor, the ghost of Madame de la Chanterie appears, and raising his eyes he murmurs, 'Thus do the angels revenge themselves.' Even religion, in Balzac, acquires a look of magic and becomes the instrument of a vast, occult power. But in terms of the *Comédie humaine*, the novel is less a drama of persons than a picture of charitable work in Paris, as secret as the town's depravities.

We may imagine the ladies of Wierzchownia being moved to tears, and perhaps they were caused to think more highly of their friend Bilboquet, whom they sometimes treated as a mere entertainer. To him, forgiveness was something that went without saying, men being what they were. They must be painted without indulgence, as he so often did, but with respect for the nobler qualities which were never lacking, even in the worst of them.

The ladies took him to Kiev, and he wrote to Laure:

So I have seen the Rome of the north, the Tartar city with its three hundred churches. . . . It is a good thing to have seen once. I was overwhelmed with attentions. Do you know, there is a rich moujik who has read all my books and burns a candle for me every week at St Nicholas, and he promised the servants of one of Madame Hanska's sisters that he would pay them if they would warn him of my next visit, so that he could see me. . . .

Madame Mère wrote to him for New Year's Day. She had paid a visit to the Rue Fortunée:

I found everything in perfect order and clean enough to satisfy the most exacting woman. You have two splendid caretakers; I think they are very honest; they look forward to your return. They said that there had several times been talk of your returning, and they quite understood that this was to keep them up to the mark. They told me that your architect calls once a week.

As always, my dear one, I am at your disposal, very happy, as you know, to be of service to those I love. You may count upon me in all things, at every moment of my life.

Following ancient custom, I will speak of the New Year. My first visit was to God, and after worshipping in His temple I had only one thought—for yourself—and only one favour to ask Him—the happiness of my dear children. . . .

Balzac must certainly have been tempted to stay longer at Wierzchownia, in that haven of rest and security, and in the company of his beloved *saltimbanques*; but another payment was due on the railway-shares, and this obliged him to leave for France in January, at the height of winter. Eve gave him a cloak of fox-fur, but the cold was so intense that he wore an overcoat beneath it. She also gave him 90,000 francs to cover the payment and other requirements.

It is pleasant to think of his happiness during that visit. For the first time in his life he had been privileged to live in the kind of palace he had dreamed of since his childhood, waited upon by countless attentive servants. It did not trouble him that their obsequiousness was due to the harsh penalties which any lapse would incur. Zulma Carraud had vainly reproached him with his indifference to the sufferings of the common people. She had been astonished, and with reason, brilliantly imaginative as he was in depicting people of his own class, at his inability to evoke the depths of poverty and oppression. During those four months he had been absolved from the daily burden of work to be delivered, the corroding misery of contracts and unpaid bills. It was an unspeakable relief to the man, but a source of weakness in the author. The fact that at Wierzchownia he never achieved the productive rhythm of his great days was certainly due in part to that easing of the pressure.

This was not the only reason. The *Comédie humaine* was beginning to present new problems. His characters were growing older, as he was himself; and many were dead. A splendid tombstone now adorned the grave of Esther Gobseck and Lucien de Rubempré at Père-Lachaise. Vautrin was now Chief of Police, Rastignac a Minister for the second time. Certainly it would be wonderful to bring them to life again, those shades that, like Homer's dead, clustered insistently about him, filling the pages of unwritten books. He rejoiced in them, knowing what he could make of them; but he did not know if he still possessed the strength. Such were his thoughts as, with Eve's cloak about his shoulders, he crossed the bleak and icy plains.

XXXIX

Alarms and Excursions

FRANCE IN FEBRUARY 1848 was a political volcano. It was the time of 'reformist' banquets, with after-dinner speakers vehemently demanding universal suffrage. Thiers likened the Government to a leaky ship that was visibly sinking. Lamartine proclaimed that the revolution of liberty would be followed by the revolution of contempt. Even the Garde Nationale bellowed, 'Vive la Réforme!', and bourgeois disaffection was gravely threatening the bourgeois régime. Balzac had never liked the July Monarchy, feeling the need of something stronger; but he feared the convulsions which must follow any radical change.

He dined on 22 February with Jean de Margonne, who had an apartment in Paris. Such was the disorder in the town that half the guests failed to arrive. Balzac himself had to walk home, his nervous carriage-hirer having refused to come and fetch him. The crowds were carrying corpses by torchlight through the streets. On the following day the King bowed to public opinion and dismissed his ministers. 'It is Louis-Philippe's first step on the way to exile or the scaffold,' Balzac wrote to Eve. His own apprehensions were such that he ranged himself on the side of the 'ultras': 'Policy must be ruthless in maintaining the social order, and I must say, after what I have seen, that, as always, I approve of the Austrian *carcero duro*, of Siberia and the methods of absolute power. My creed of absolutism is steadily gaining ground; even my brother-in-law is coming round to it.' Poor Surville was equally terrified.

On the 24th Balzac followed a crowd of rioters out of curiosity and watched them smash mirrors and chandeliers in the palace of the Tuileries, tear down the gold-fringed, red velvet window-curtains and burn books. These saturnalia disgusted him, he said; but he nevertheless came away with some ornaments and draperies from the throne room, and some school exercise-books belonging to the young princes. The collector seems to have prevailed over the upholder of law and order.

Victor Hugo and his associates were hoping to save the monarchy by making the intelligent and liberal-minded Duchesse d'Orléans regent. But an armed mob besieged the Chamber, and a republican régime was set up which, Balzac believed, would pave the way for anarchy. The fact that his friend Lamartine was a member of the provisional government did not reassure him; he thought him honest but mistrusted his lyrical outbursts. Money was disappearing. The Northern Railway shares touched their lowest level; the three per cent. Funds were still falling. A Grandet would have bought; Balzac wrote to the Mniszechs asking for more capital, but this was not forthcoming. Such was the state of panic that he found it impossible to market his own wares: editors and publishers were afraid to commit themselves.

At the Tuileries Balzac had fallen in with a young writer named Champfleury, also a contributor of fiction to the newspapers. He invited him to call at the Rue Fortunée, and received him there on the 27th in his famous white robe. Champfleury was greatly impressed: 'His bright, dark eyes, his thick hair shot with white, the vivid tints of pure yellow and red which alternated sharply on his cheeks, the odd tufts of hair on his chin, gave him the look of a good-humoured wild boar. . . . He laughed often and loudly, his paunch quivering with mirth, and behind the full-blooded lips one saw a few scattered teeth, as solid as fangs. . . .'

Champfleury stayed three hours while Balzac loaded him with advice. He was a writer of short stories. 'Short stories get you nowhere,' said Balzac. 'They're too limiting; in the end they narrow the mind.' He recalled having known a man from Cambrai, Berthoud, who had contributed a short story a week to *La Presse*: 'He kept it up for a year or two—but what has become of him since? . . . Write novellas and short stories since you enjoy it, but not more than three a year. Write them for your own satisfaction. At the rate of three a year you will have written thirty novellas in ten years, and if twenty of them are masterpieces you may count yourself happy. And you should devote the other ten months in the year to writing for the theatre to earn money, a lot of money. An artist should live splendidly.' By way of illustration he showed his visitor round his art collection, saying that M. de Rothschild was very jealous of it. The young man kept wondering, where have I seen this before? Suddenly he realized that it was the collection of Cousin Pons.

Champfleury had had the luck to catch Balzac in a cheerful mood, but this was soon damped by the course of public events. A trial of strength between the middle classes and the workers —tail-coats versus smocks—seemed unavoidable. A parliamentary election on a basis of universal suffrage was to be held in April, and Balzac wrote to *Le Constitutionnel* announcing that he would stand as a candidate. No one, he wrote, could hold back 'at a moment when France has need of all her strength and intelligence'. But he had no illusion as to his prospects. 'Since most men are mediocrities,' he said to Alexandre Weil, 'they generally vote for mediocrities. . . . You think Lamartine is head of the Republic? He'll stay there just so long as he allows himself to be dragged in the wake of the real leaders; but the moment he tries to enforce an idea of his own, or to put in one of his own men, they'll smash him.' For his own part Balzac proposed to leave France if he was not elected. But whether this would be possible, with revolution spreading in Germany, Austria and Poland, was another matter.

He sighed for Wierzchownia. What could he do in Paris, with his two sources of livelihood, literature and the theatre, both drying up? In any case, he refused to become citizen of a republic. While Lamartine was in the Government he would have no difficulty in obtaining a passport; but he needed first to settle his debts—and where was the money to come from? A theatre management proposed to revive *Vautrin*, banned under Louis-Philippe. But they wanted to turn it into a political satire, with Frédérick Lemaître burlesquing the dethroned monarch: 'It's a monstrous idea and I would never agree, even if it were to bring me in 80,000 francs! . . .' But one good thing happened. Louise de Breugnol finally got married—not to her sculptor but to a wealthy industrialist, thus becoming the sister-in-law of a Peer of France. 'Is the man mad?' wondered Balzac. But he rejoiced on Eve's account, since it might be presumed that a lady moving in fashionable circles would give them no further trouble.

The resilience of Paris was astonishing. Early in March the Girardins held a brilliant reception. Everyone Balzac knew was speculating in land- and house-property, buying at the present rock-bottom prices and prepared to hang on until things improved: 'Since the Republic can't last longer than three years, at the outside, we must try not to miss any chances. . . . We are bound to have a dictator, or some form of dictatorship, after which we shall return to a hypocritically constituted monarchy. . . .' In the meantime Balzac needed work.

The theatre began to revive. Marie Dorval wanted a play for the Théâtre Historique, and Balzac had the beginning of one in his bottom drawer, *La Marâtre*, which seemed suitable and which he could quickly finish. With the book-trade still in the doldrums, the stage was his best hope, and by now he was so short of money that he made a *boeuf à la mode* last a whole week! 'I feel old,' he wrote to Eve. 'Work grows increasingly difficult, and I have at the most only enough oil left in the lamp to light the last things I want to write. Five or six plays are all that is needed, and I have still enough in my head to do them. But these last efforts will be bathed in my tears and my farewells. Yes, I no longer hope for anything good. . . . There are beings born to know only the bitterness of life, others on whom everything smiles; and I accept my destiny. I thank you, and I thank God, for all the happiness you have given me.'

If he could do as well in the theatre as he had done in literature he would be wealthy and secure; but how was anyone to work amid the present disorders? 'We're heading for a clash which the republicans will lose.' And then shares would rise. If only George would let him have 100,000 francs! Railway stock that had once stood at 120,000 could now be had for 27,000! A counter-revolution was certain—'We are not merely sitting *on* a volcano, we're *inside* one.' As he wrote this he could hear a crowd in the distance singing the *Marseillaise*.

Although his eyes were troubling him (he was suffering from a form of double vision, and Dr Nacquart feared that the optic nerve might be affected), *La Marâtre* made progress and he hoped to read the play to the company on 9 April: 'We shall open on the 29th. . . . If it succeeds all will be saved. I shall become another Scribe and make 100,000 a year.' But the troubles continued, and the Baroness Rothschild, a noted political barometer, wore 'the air of calm which precedes a tempest'. Balzac believed that the election would be followed by civil war, although he did not withdraw his candidacy on this account, being incapable of watching a lottery without buying a ticket. His view of the situation was profoundly pessimistic. It seemed possible that in six weeks not a throne would be left standing in Europe: 'And make no mistake about it, the King was the symbol of property. I'm afraid that before long property itself will be attacked. . . .' This would be the end of everything; and Eve must get it well into her head that even Russia was not immune. But if she was forced to flee from the Ukraine a refuge awaited her in Paris: because in three months Paris would be the safest city in the world, the revolt having given birth to a dictatorship.

On 9 April he read the first two acts of *La Marâtre* (*The Stepmother*) to Marie Dorval and the manager of the theatre, Hippolyte Hostein, both of whom seemed delighted with it. He read them the third act a week later, and Hostein asked him to write in a part for his mistress. That was the theatre for you; nothing but fiddles, a mad world—and he was planning six plays altogether! 'But they'll bring me in the five or six hundred thousand I need, if they don't kill me!' However he was learning the tricks of the trade and would soon be able to turn out plays as easily as novels. Paris meanwhile was bubbling with rumours. The Carlists, the idiots, imagined that Henri V would be brought back by Madame Lamartine, 'that old Englishwoman, the daughter of a cheese-merchant. It's madly funny!' Yet who could tell? Anything might happen. And then Balzac would become Préfet d'Indre-et-Loire, or director of the Beaux-Arts, or a tobacconist.

The air was heavy with foreboding. There were only fifty vehicles on the Champs-Élysées, where the year before there had been ten thousand. The Government was muzzling the press. 'We have *liberty* to die of hunger, *equality* in misery, the *fraternity* of the street-corner.' The road and railway navvies marched in procession through the boulevards. On 19 April, just before the election, Balzac published a letter in the *Constitutionnel* calling for stable government:

Between 1789 and 1848 France, or Paris if you prefer, has changed its constitution every fifteen years. Is it not time, for the honour of our country, to devise and institute a form, an empire, a durable system of rule, so that our prosperity, our commerce and our arts, which are the life-blood of our commerce, our credit and our renown, in short, all the fortunes of France, may not be periodically imperilled? In truth our history during the past sixty years explains the ancient mystery of the disappearance of thirty Parises, of which only relics remain, in different parts of the globe, to be dug up by travellers, the adornment of museums, and which are the ancestors of the Paris of today!

May the new Republic be powerful and wise, for we need a government which will sign a longer lease, by fifteen or eighteen years, for the benefit of the lessee! That is my desire, and it is worth any number of professions of faith. . . .

France went to the polls on 23 April. Balzac got 20 votes, whereas Lamartine got 259,800 in Paris alone. It is scarcely surprising that his absolutist creed should have met with no response. The election passed off smoothly, but he found the outlook still disquieting. Paris would never accept the National Assembly which the provinces had elected. He was more than ever anxious to leave France. Lamartine promised him a passport, but he still had to obtain a Russian visa. Meanwhile he finished *La Marâtre*, dined at the home of the Duchesse de Castries ('She's hideous, a corpse!') and was visited by his future sister-in-law, Aline Moniuszko, who brought her daughter Pauline, a very beautiful girl. He also attended an amateur performance, at the Duchesse de Castries' house, of Musset's *Un Caprice* and thought very little of it. He had to return home on foot from the Rue du Bac to the Rue Fortunée, and all the way he dreamed of Wierzchownia: 'I would give all my plays to be able to drink tea off the glazed canvas of the big table in your salon, instead of raising canvases for a public of idlers who will hoot me!'

On 16 May, the feast of St Honoré and the day *La Marâtre* opened, a general call-to-arms was sounded in the Paris streets. Marie Dorval, whose grandson had just died, had given up the leading part, which was played after all by Hostein's mistress. Despite all this the piece had a brilliant success, the

first Balzac had achieved in the theatre: He had at last succeeded in endowing a play with the compulsive force of his
novels.

The story may be briefly told. Gertrude de Meilhac ('*la
marâtre*') has been governess in the home of the Comte de
Grandchamp, a former Empire general and now a textile
manufacturer at Louviers (which seems a strange end to a
military career!). Having brought up the General's daughter,
Pauline, she succeeds in marrying her distinguished, if anti-
quated employer, but then falls in love with the same young
man as her stepdaughter and tries to poison her. Balzac has
told us how the play originated. On an occasion when he was
visiting an ostensibly united family he caught a furious exchange
of glances which caused him to realize that the lady of the house
and her stepdaughter were bitterly hostile to one another. He
made no attempt to find out more about the two women, as a
novelist of the realist school might have done, but developed the
situation according to his own ideas. In the best tradition of the
Comédie humaine he gave his domestic drama a historical
context. Pauline's suitor is also the son of an Empire general,
one of those who deserted Napoleon in 1818; and therefore
Grandchamp, the fanatical Bonapartist, will never consent to
the match. It is Montague and Capulet.

Théophile Gautier gave the play an enthusiastic notice:
'Despite the heat and other adverse circumstances, the Théâtre
Historique has had a success which gives us particular pleasure,
because it will encourage a man of genius to apply to the drama
the gifts he has already displayed in the novel. . . .' Gautier went
on to ask why those prodigious gifts had not hitherto been
successfully employed in the theatre, and to volunteer an answer.
The real reason, he suggested, was far less the censorship, now
abolished, than the difficulties inherent in any theatrical production, the number of people involved, the differences of opinion,
secret antagonisms, snares and pitfalls of every kind which were
exasperating to a man of genius. 'The sole thought of the
manager, the producer, the actors [and everyone concerned] . . .
is to turn the play into something other than the one you wrote.
. . . You give way to them and are blamed for their combined
idiocies.'

This time Balzac had been allowed greater freedom, and the

result was a unanimously favourable reception. Jules Janin, a critic who, unlike Gautier, was often hostile to him, wrote: '*La Marâtre* is a complete success. Once again this admirable novelist has shown that he possesses in the highest degree the art of uniting grace with strength . . . nature, art and talent.' But political convulsions are fatal to the theatre. There was rioting in the streets and many people were afraid to leave their homes. The house at the second performance was two-thirds empty. Hostein decided to take his company to England and to shelve *La Marâtre* until things were quieter. It had earned Balzac less than 500 francs! But, encouraged by its reception, he planned a series of other plays—*Les Petits Bourgeois*, *Mercadet*, *Orgon*, *La Folle Épreuve*, *Richard cœur d'éponge*, *Pierre et Catherine*—telling Eve that he intended to write them to acquit his conscience: 'If by December my heart and my life are in the same state I shall give up the struggle and let myself drift on the tide, like a drowned man. . . . You will hear no more of Bilboquet. . . .'

His present mood of melancholy was due to renewed anxiety on her account. The warmth and tenderness of Wierzchownia seemed to have been transformed into indifference, even harshness, since his return to Paris. A highly sensual woman, she needed his physical presence, whereas his own feelings were intensified by separation. He wrote volumes to her, and received only brief notes in return. She even advised him to marry a young woman! Aline Moniuszko, to whom he showed this unbelievable letter, promptly offered him her daughter Pauline, which he found even more unbelievable. To thrust a beautiful young girl into the arms of a man nearly fifty! . . . It was a case of rivalry between sisters.

Finding him lonely and deeply depressed, Jean de Margonne, with his habitual offhand courtesy, invited him to come and work at Saché. Balzac was anxious to finish *Les Petits Bourgeois*; he was feeling crushed by Eve's unaccountable silence, and so he accepted.

Saché at first did him good, the familiar Touraine countryside of woods and valleys and small manor-houses which had been the setting of *Le Lys dans la vallée*. With the thought of Wierzchownia never absent from his mind he compared himself to Louis-Philippe, who in his English exile must be pining for the Tuileries. The February revolution had not affected the daily life of the house. Although Madame de Margonne, the sad, hunchbacked woman, was dead, there was still the invariable game of whist after lunch and dinner with the neighbouring country gentlemen. But in this sociable atmosphere, and amid the mists of Vouvray wine, *Les Petits Bourgeois* made little progress. Margonne, although thrifty in other respects, still kept a good table, too good for Balzac, whose palpitations and shortness of breath were growing worse. To walk up a slope, and still more to climb the steep stairs of the château, cost him a great effort. He believed he was suffering from an oedema of the lungs, and that his distended heart was 'pouring blood'.

Nor did events in the outside world afford him any comfort— the bloody 'Days of June' in Paris, with 25,000 dead; the fall of Lamartine 'in the depths of disgrace'; the theatres closed. Margonne made preparations for leaving Saché, which would not be safe in the event of a general uprising. Paris looked even less safe, but Balzac had no alternative but to go back to the Rue Fortunée. He could at least be thankful that he had not been there during the insurrection, when as a member of the Garde Nationale he would have had to attack the insurgent barricades, his round shape offering an admirable target for bullets. Fortunately for him he had left during a period of relative calm, and so could not be accused of having run away from his duties as a citizen-soldier.

And in Paris a wonderful surprise awaited him—several long letters from Eve. He had wrongly accused her of neglecting him; it was the post that was responsible for the delay. And what letters they were! 'I have been reading them for the last ten hours! . . . Have you ever seen a blackbird at the *vendange*, drunk on grapes? . . . It is Heaven. To be able to slake one's thirst without pause, drink in your spirit, live two months of your life in two hours—it is indescribable. . . .' He went on to answer her 'scoldings'. How could she possibly have taken Aline's *monstrous* offer of her daughter seriously? Since he had first set eyes on a certain gown of pansy-coloured velvet, seventeen years ago in Neuchâtel, he had had no thoughts for any other woman: 'We shall live and rest side by side *in aeternum*, even if I'm scolded through all eternity by my fellow-corpse! . . . In a mournful, empty Paris, deserted by a third of its inhabitants, I am gay. You know why. It is because I know that you love me as much as I love you. . . .'

But things in the Rue Fortunée were in great disorder. Zanella, the housekeeper, was slovenly as well as a bad cook: 'If you knew how I need a wife!' In the meantime he got his mother and his nieces, Sophie and Valentine, to put the house to rights, and it was arranged that when he returned to the Ukraine Madame Mère would come and live there. A little money was coming in. The Comédie-Française paid him an advance of 5,000 francs on *Les Petits Bourgeois* and the Odéon was offering 5,000 for *Richard coeur d'éponge* (*Richard the Sponge-Hearted*). Perhaps, if he lived long enough, he would be able to produce a new *Comédie humaine*, this time for the theatre. It was a wonderful thought. And Eve sent him 10,000 francs to cover the next payment on the railway shares, which had to be hung on to at all costs, because the Northern network was now nearly completed, and then the shares would rise to 1,000 francs. These happy events cured his palpitations. Eve enclosed a flower in one of her letters, a pink periwinkle. Suddenly he felt young again, and afraid of nothing.

On 4 July Chateaubriand died. 'Paris was still stupified by the Days of June,' wrote Victor Hugo, 'and the din of fusillades, tocsins and cannon-fire still echoing in its ears drowned the sort of silence that falls when a great man dies. . . .' Balzac walked in the funeral procession with people chattering around him: 'That procession was a lesson to me. It was cold, rehearsed, indifferent. One might have been at the Bourse.' He dined that night with the Survilles, and while they played whist they listened to the sounds in the street: 'Keep to the centre of the road! . . . Squad, attention! . . . Who goes there?' Deaf people and those who failed to answer a challenge were liable to be shot.

Balzac at once resolved to offer himself for Chateaubriand's seat in the Academy, and Hugo promised him his vote. Hugo also asked him for a serial for the new paper he was starting, *L'Événement*, a gift from Heaven in those chaotic days. The editor was a young man called Auguste Vacquerie, with whom Balzac became friendly. He had written a drama in verse, *Tragaldabas*, and invited Balzac to a rehearsal. They walked back together from the Porte Saint-Martin to the Faubourg Saint-

Honoré. Although Balzac had not at all liked the piece ('Terrible
. . . a sort of comical Hugo . . .), he unburdened himself to the
young man. He was beginning to believe in the possible return
of Henry V, in which event he proposed to apply for an
embassy, either London or St Petersburg. 'What a pity it is,'
he said, 'that Victor Hugo has compromised himself by
supporting the Republic. Otherwise everything would have
been open to him.' Vacquerie remarked that Balzac, too, had
stood for Parliament. 'Ah,' said Balzac, 'but that's quite
different. I wasn't elected.'

On 17 August he read his play *Mercadet* (later *Le Faiseur*)
to the Comédie Française company. He did so admirably.
Théophile Gautier, who had already heard the piece, marvelled
at his histrionic powers:

He roared and cooed and wept and raged and thundered in
every conceivable tone of voice, while Debt sang a solo supported
by a huge choir. Creditors appeared from everywhere, from
behind the stove, under the bed, out of the chest of drawers;
they poured down the chimney, crept through the keyhole and
climbed in at the window like lovers; . . . they popped up like
jacks-in-the-box; . . . it was a riot, an invasion, a flood-tide.
Mercadet might settle with a few, but there were always more.
One had a feeling of the dense army of creditors stretching to
the horizon and pressing forward like termites to devour their
prey.

'Never,' said an actor who was present, 'have I better understood the meaning of that irresistible force which is genius.'
The play was accepted without a dissentient vote. But Balzac,
regardless of his prospects in the theatre and at the Academy,
had only one thought in mind—to return to the Ukraine. It was
due less to the fear of revolution than to his simple need to be
there: 'My thoughts so dwell in Wierzchownia that I can
picture it to the smallest detail. In spirit I open the cupboard of
sweetmeats below the window-sill in your bedroom, near the
mahogany door leading to the *cabinet de toilette*; I count the
splashes of candlegrease on the velvet board on which we
played chess. . . . I look in your wardrobe and count the handker-
chiefs. . . . I drink tea at half-past eight in Madame Eveline's
bedroom. Upon my honour, because I love you, I live with

you. . . .' Truly it was love. His distant countess was no longer immensely rich and she was forty-eight years old: 'And so, since I have an inextinguishable desire to be with my *loup*, since I live only to feel her in my arms, to hear your voice, to be scolded by you—since I am consumed with the wish to sit waiting for the rustle of your skirts—it must be true. . . .'

He was already preparing for the journey and for his marriage. He called on his parish priest, the curé of Saint-Philippe-du-Roule, who was kindness itself and gave him the *demissorium* which would enable the wedding to take place in a Polish diocese. The Russian Embassy granted him a visa, but at the same time sent private instructions to the Governor of Kiev: 'His Imperial Majesty has graciously deigned to permit the French writer, Balzac, who was there last year, to enter Russia again. . . . I have the honour to request Your Excellency to keep him under strict surveillance and to furnish me with a full report of his activities.'

He left on 19 September, resolved to abandon everything and even to become a Russian citizen, if the Tsar insisted. Laurent-Jan was put in charge of his literary affairs and Madame Mère moved to the Rue Fortunée. He left the house without regrets, 'worthy of two angels' though it was, feeling himself a stranger in the new world that was coming to life in Paris and throughout France. He had been too close to it; he needed a greater degree of detachment if he was to describe the transformation that was taking place. How could he work, in any case, while his thoughts were obsessed with the marriage, so long delayed, which he believed would be his salvation? A sick man is always something of a child. He needed mothering, and his mistress-mother might scold him to her heart's content, she could never destroy his love. But above all, with his faculties still unimpaired (the novels he began at the time are proof), he needed strength to carry out all that he had in mind; and this he hoped to recover in the Ukraine.

XL

A Ship Befogged

Je fais partie de l'opposition qui s'appelle la vie.

BALZAC

BALZAC SPENT THE end of 1848 and the whole of 1849 at Wierzchownia, in refuge from the storms and tribulations of Paris. He had a handsome suite of rooms and a personal attendant, the gigantic Thomas Gubernachuk, who sometimes went down on his knees before him. A log-fire blazed in his study when he entered it in the morning. Wearing slippers of fur and a robe of 'termolama', a wonderfully warm and light Caucasian cloth, he felt 'clad in sunshine'. Silver sconces lighted his work-table. Thus equipped he worked sporadically on *Mademoiselle du Vissard, ou La France sous le Consulat*, or *La Femme auteur*, or *Le Théâtre comme il est*, but with no real energy. The stimulus was lacking, the frantic pressure of Paris, where a bill to be paid might compel him to produce a short story in a single night. Now when he was confronted with an urgent demand for money he applied to his hostess, whose Russian bankers transmitted the sum to Rothschild in Paris. This was certainly agreeable, but it did not make for literary productivity.

Nor was Eve always prepared to accommodate him. Having made over the estate to her daughter she now had nothing but her annuity. The last resort was George Mniszech, but he too had his problems. Anna was a free spender, and the estate, vast though it was, produced an absurdly small income. Both the young people were troubled by the thought of their mother's marriage to an extravagant Frenchman with a huge load of debt. They loved Balzac and were happy to have him with them; but they did not want to see Eve in the position of having to meet demands which were beyond her means. The house in the Rue Fortunée, about which Balzac talked with so much pride, was by no means wholly paid for: large sums were still owing for furniture and decorations. It seemed, moreover, that the future Madame de Balzac might find herself having to keep her husband's entire family. Her prospective mother-in-law was penniless, and she had already promised her an allowance of 1,200 francs a year. Surville's affairs were in bad shape, as usual, and Sophie's very eligible suitor had changed his mind, so that Laure had both her daughters on her hands, both needing dowries. These considerations were certainly not absent from Eve's mind. The bond of affection and sympathy between Honoré and herself was as strong as ever, but she was still reluctant to marry him. He should at least first settle his debts. And the ever-present doubt remained: how trust a man who had never known the difference between fact and fiction?

Thus there were reserves between them which did not always go unspoken, and Balzac was deeply afflicted. In his exhausted state he could see no future or prospect of happiness except in the marriage. The Academy turned out to be a forlorn hope. He had instructed his mother to leave cards on all the 'immortals', the members; but this was a poor substitute for his active presence. 'Should you not have done something more?' Madame Mère diffidently asked. The election of Chateaubriand's successor took place on 11 January. When Victor Hugo entered the room Empis and Pongerville (two immortals destined to be mortally forgotten) murmured in his ear, 'Balzac, of course?', to which he replied, '*Pardieu!*—By God, yes!' The only other candidate was the Duc de Noailles. The Duke received twenty-five votes and Balzac four, with three abstentions. A week later there was another election, for the empty chair of another since-forgotten member. This time Balzac received two votes, those of Hugo and Alfred de Vigny. If votes had been weighed he would have been elected, but they were only counted; and the seat went to the Comte de Saint-Priest. The author of the *Comédie humaine* was passed over in favour of the author of a history of the conquest of Naples. *Toute assemblée est peuple*, Cardinal de Retz had once said—'All public bodies are second-rate'—and Laurent-Jan wrote to Balzac: 'It would seem that bad counts [*comtes*] make good Academicians. . . .'

Madame Mère, in the Rue Fortunée kept an eye on the servants, François and Zanella, and did battle with the notary, the tax-collector and the tradespeople. She received instructions to speed up the upholsterer and buy crystal candlesticks; to get *one* silver dish out of pawn and take it to the silversmith, Froment-Meurice, to serve as a pattern for the dinner-service he was making for them; to order two very pretty Boulle cabinets on which to stand two Chinese vases which must be lifted from the bottom, not the top, because otherwise they would break. A thousand tasks were assigned to her, calling for considerable exertion on the part of an old lady of seventy-two; but all were faithfully performed. In compensation she was authorized to travel by cab, instead of taking the far cheaper omnibus; she was warm and well-fed, and greatly enjoyed the elegance and luxury of the house, after the shabby poverty she had so long been accustomed to.

But if Honoré now showed her some consideration—no more than was her due, in view of all she did for him—he did not spare her errors. He arranged for Eve to send her 31,000 francs to meet a further payment on the railway shares and various other expenses. The sum was to be conveyed by messenger from Rothschilds to the Rue Fortunée, where it was to be paid to 'Madame Sallambier'. This was because Balzac owed the bank money and did not want the remittance, or any part of it, to be retained by some over-zealous clerk against his overdraft. But when the messenger arrived at the house he was turned away by the servants, who had never heard of Madame Sallambier. Rothschilds thereupon got in touch with Eve's bankers, who applied to Wierzchownia for fresh instructions. To Balzac it was a most mortifying occurrence: 'So many dagger-thrusts. How I suffered!'

And why, he furiously asked his mother, had she been so foolish as to talk openly in her letters about Laure's money-troubles, even going so far as to say that if Surville failed in his present venture (it had to do with the draining of marshlands in the department of Hérault) he would be ruined? Had she no conception of what life was like in a place as remote as Wierz-chownia, where the mail was brought from Berdichev by mounted courier, the eagerly-awaited letters opened and dis-cussed in the family circle? He had unthinkingly started to read her letter aloud, and so was forced to confess that Surville was hounded by creditors, as he himself had been for twenty years.

This had called forth great lamentations and reproaches: 'If we had squandered less money on the house we might have something in reserve to help the poor man.' . . . And another thing, his mother must on no account mention the money owed to the Guidoboni-Viscontis, or if she was obliged to do so she must refer to it as the 'Fessart account'. How could she be so lacking in imagination as to make these blunders?

The poor lady, whose evenings were spent in reading the *Imitation of Christ* and knitting a bedspread for her grand-daughter, wrote indignantly back, saying that she prayed for his peace of mind, her own being a more difficult problem. She was answered by a tirade which deserves to be quoted at length, since it contains the ghost that haunted Balzac all his life:

Wierzchownia, 22 March 1849: My dear Mother—If anyone was ever astonished in this world it is the child of fifty to whom your letter with its mixture of *vous* and *tu* was addressed, dated the 4th of this month and received yesterday. . . . At the risk of receiving another of the same kind let me tell you that I should have laughed at it had it not so deeply distressed me by its complete injustice and cruel ignoring of our respective positions. You should have learnt at your age that if one does not catch flies with vinegar, still less does one catch women with that unpleasant acid. As it happens your letter, with its studied formality and extreme coldness, reached me at the very moment when I was saying that at your age you should have every comfort and Zanella should stay permanently with you; and that I should be very happy for you to have your rent paid, in addition to your allowance of 100 francs a month, and a further 300 francs for Zanella. . . . And at this moment, referring to matters of which you yourself admit the truth . . . along comes a letter from you which, morally speaking, is the equivalent of the angry glare with which you terrified your children when they were fifteen, but which now, since I have unhappily reached the age of fifty, leaves me quite unimpressed.

Moreover the person to whom I look for all my happiness, the *only happiness* in a stormy, laborious and fevered life, pervaded from end to end with constant hardship, this person is not a child; she is not a girl of eighteen dazzled by fame, allured by wealth or attracted by manly beauty. I offer her none of that. She is a person over forty who has undergone many trials. She is very mistrustful, and the events in her life have increased her mistrust. . . . It is perfectly natural that, knowing her attitude for the past ten years, I should have said to her that *she will not be marrying my family*, and that she will be entirely free to see or not see them as she chooses; for honesty, delicacy and good sense all required me to do so. Nor have I ever sought to conceal this from you or from Laure. But natural though it is, you have already chosen to take offence at it, and to see it as an excuse and an indication of something bad in me—excessive ambition, snobbery, disdain for my own family, etc. . . . But what I have said is the pure and simple truth. . . . Do you think that these letters of yours, written to someone you should be proud of but containing only a brief, perfunctory word of affection, and above all the letter I received yesterday—do you think they are calculated to inspire a woman of the character and experience I have described with any *desire* to cultivate a new family?

I am certainly not asking you to profess sentiments you do not feel, for God knows, and you know, that you have not smothered me with caresses since I came into this world. And you were right not to do so, because if you had loved me as you loved Henry I should doubtless be where he is now, so in that sense you have been a good mother to me. But what I do ask of you is an *intelligent perception of your own interests*, which you have never had; and not to go on hampering my future prospects, for I will say nothing about my happiness. . . .

The family's attitude astounded Balzac. There he was, with every hope of marrying a wealthy, aristocratic and infinitely benevolent lady, the desired of all Russia, who when she came to live in Paris would be in a position to ensure good matches for the two Surville girls—and his mother, from sheer perversity, seemed bent on ruining everything! And Laure, could she not see how easy it would be for Madame Hanska to drop the whole thing if she felt like it? That she did not do so was due to the great and growing esteem in which she and her children held him, Balzac; and this being so, how could they fail to be shocked by his own family's lack of respect?

To Laure: Do not be hurt by what I am saying. It is written in all kindness from a desire to show you how we must behave in the matter of this marriage. Dear child, we must tread lightly as though on eggshells, weigh every word and every action. If I have said anything wrong in the course of this long letter you must not hold it against me; you must take note of what is right, and above all burn everything and let us not talk about it any more. That is what I would also advise Mother to do. . . . Above all, get it well into your head that I have no desire to dictate to the family, to be *absolute* or *obeyed*. . . . I want to avoid errors, and if good sense condemns me it cannot be helped. . . . All that I long for is absolute tranquillity, a private life, and work in moderation to finish the *Comédie humaine*.

I think I see things clearly and I hope, if all goes well, to make a good home, as the saying is. If it all goes wrong I shall remove my books and personal belongings from the Rue Fortunée and philosophically resume my life and fortunes. . . . But in that case I shall live in a boarding-house, in a single furnished room, so as to be independent of everything, even furniture. . . . For me this present business, sentiment apart (failure would morally destroy me), is all or nothing, double or quits. With the game lost I should no longer think of living; I should be content with the garret in the Rue Lesdiguières and a hundred francs a month. My heart, mind and ambition have no other aim than the one I have pursued for sixteen years; if this great happiness fails me I shall need nothing and want nothing.

You must not think that I love luxury for its own sake. I love the luxury of the Rue Fortunée for the sake of what goes with it, a beautiful, well-born woman, a comfortable life and distinguished connections; apart from this I care nothing for it. The Rue Fortunée was created solely *for* her and *by* her. . . .

He had another grievance, this one more trivial. Since he had been in the Ukraine his nieces had written him a number of gay, amusing letters which had greatly pleased the Countess Anna. But then they had stopped writing because, said Madame Mère, he did not reply. 'My dear mother, do you really think that at the age of fifty I am under any obligation to my nieces? They should consider themselves honoured if I even send them a message! . . .' Madame Mère deferred to this, and Sophie and Valentine's letters were resumed.

Sophie also kept a diary. That family had ink in their veins. She has left us an account of dinner *chez grand-mère* in the Rue Fortunée on 1 January 1849: 'Poor Grandmamma! It was such happiness to her to receive us, to be able to play the great lady *as in the past*. . . . There was a big fire burning in the big, carved fireplace. Such a good little dinner, which we all enjoyed, with François and Zanella waiting on us so attentively. Only father seemed gloomy and depressed. . . . Our uncle is in Russia. He has not even written to us! He is living in the midst of wealth and luxury, but he does not give a thought to his poor little nieces. . . . 'Sophie was attracted by Ivan Carraud, Zulma's son, but this came to nothing. And when *père* Dablin visited them on New Year's Day he brought them no presents: 'How horrid! An old bachelor with forty thousand a year and a passion for collecting, and all he brought was a china cup worth two francs. Still, at his age one can forgive a little stinginess. . . .'

At length Uncle Honoré did write, but it was a melancholy letter. He was still not certain of his marriage 'to the beautiful and noble Countess Hanska. Will he be happy? She is very proud and she thinks him beneath her, famous though he is. Perhaps I am wrong. So I earnestly hope that everything will turn out as he desires. Yet this will separate us. We shall be humiliated, but what does that matter? I shall pray tonight for my uncle's marriage. . . . I want to love him as he is. . . . He has promised Grandmamma an allowance of a hundred francs a month. What happiness! . . . It must be admitted that when he is with his great lady his sentiments improve and his heart grows warmer. He becomes kind. He must truly love her. . . .' The youthful Sophie was not lacking in perception; she had already discovered that true love engenders benevolence. She pitied her parents and forgave them for having ruined their lives: 'It is terrible to see a brave father so discouraged! He has worked so hard. . . . He goes to bed but does not sleep. . . .' To distract her father she took him on outings to the Tuileries and Neuilly: 'How beautiful Paris is! How beautiful the sunshine is! The air was so fresh and soft. . . .'

It is interesting to note the Balzac family characteristics reappearing in the next generation. Both Sophie and Valentine had a fondness for writing, a touch of vanity and an underlying goodness of heart. Middle-class though they were, in upbringing and in manners, they had nevertheless inherited from their grandparents an instinctive respect for aristocracy and a disdain for people who were 'in trade'. Dablin was an exception; he had a genuine love of art and music. He enjoyed hearing Sophie play

the piano: 'I esteem him highly but my pride does not allow me
to show it. He is rich, and I do not want to be one of the crowd
of people who are hoping to get something out of him. . . .'
Besides, when Dablin was 'surrounded by his satellites, he lets
his common side run away with him and makes big, coarse
jokes and laughs like a shopkeeper . . .'. The Balzacs, let it be
borne in mind, were artistic and preferred to overlook the fact
that their forebears had also kept a shop in the Marais. Mamma
had even written a play, *La Femme heureuse*, and Papa had read
and criticized it. 'In matters of art,' noted Sophie, 'one must
never pay attention to the opinions of one's family; when they
are not too flattering they are too severe.' It might have been
Villeparisis in 1820.

Balzac to Laure, 25 June 1849: The girls' letters have
given me the utmost delight. One can read their characters, and
discern their especial kind of beauty, their manners and
qualities of mind, in the style and the handwriting. *Their* letters
are always the ones that are called for when a packet arrives
addressed in your hand. If ever Countess Anna comes to Paris
she will take them frequently to the Italiens, the Opéra and the
Opéra-Comique. But I fear that Capestang* will take them away
from Paris. What you tell me about this is balm to my heart.
Surville has steered his ship very well. . . .

Balzac's own ship was still befogged. The riotous but competent Laurent-Jan was acting as his literary agent in Paris,
negotiating contracts with publishers and editors which
Madame Mère was empowered to sign but not to discuss. But
despite all his efforts Laurent-Jan could not persuade any
management to produce *Le Faiseur*. He reported to Balzac
the state of the Paris theatre. Hostein was filling his Théâtre
Historique with Dumas's 'sempiternal Musketeers', but his was
the only theatre on the boulevards that was steadily making
money. Another had had some success with a little propaganda-
piece directed against the Republic, which Laurent-Jan considered a shabby way to behave: 'To put up for a year with a
government one abominates, pay it lip-service all day, dish out
money galore, and think honour is saved because one jeers at it

* The reference is to Surville's marsh-draining operation.

a little at night, is a hollow mockery of courage.' He begged
Balzac to send him a masterpiece: 'I make no reproaches, but
France has been widowed of your genius for six months and, like
sister Anne, I see nothing coming. Your valet, Laurent-Jan.'

Eve and the Mniszechs were 'sublime' in their affection for
Balzac and their desire to smooth his path, but the marriage was
now subjected to other and exasperating delays. Eve was greatly
dependent on the Tsar. The transference of the estate to Anna
and the formal agreement of Eve's annuity, even the church
wedding ceremony, called for imperial sanctions which had not
yet been granted, although they had been repeatedly applied for.

*Balzac to His Excellency Count Ouvaroff, Minister of Public
Instruction, at St Petersburg, 5 January 1849*: For nearly sixteen years I have loved a noble and virtuous woman. . . . She
is a Russian subject whose perfect loyalty cannot be questioned.
. . . This must certainly be appreciated, for you know everything in Russia. . . . She does not wish to marry a foreigner
without the consent of her August Sovereign. Accordingly she
has deigned to authorize me to solicit this. Far from complaining
of her obedience, I find it natural.

It is against my political principles ever to criticize, still less
to contravene, the laws of any country. The fate of those who
fail to observe this rule would be sufficient in itself to make me
obey it, even if I were not already disposed to do so. Nor does it
cause me any misgiving to find my life's happiness wholly
dependent on His Majesty the Emperor of Russia, and my
confidence in a happy issue is almost joyous, so profoundly do
I believe his chivalrous bounty to be the equal of his power. . . .'

The youthful Balzac might well have exclaimed, 'Ta-ta-ta!'
But would he live long enough for the marriage to take place?
He was now seriously ill. His heart had been troubling him for
a long time, and in 1849 it gave rise to acute anxiety. He could no
longer walk or even comb his hair without losing his breath,
and he had had several attacks of severe strangulation. The
medical attendants attached to the Wierzchownia estate were
Dr Knothé and his son, both pupils of the celebrated German,
Dr Franck, and Balzac had great faith in them. They diagnosed
a simple enlargement of the heart, and their treatment consisted
in 'the re-establishment of the arterial blood-circulation, which

has sensibly diminished, and its purification' (since the blood had thickened). But when he was made to swallow lemon-juice on an empty stomach Balzac had a terrible fit of vomiting and thought that he was at death's door: 'Only my bull's constitution enabled me to hold out against the Sovereign Ruler of mankind. I am a member of that opposition which is called Life. . . .' Madame Mère reminded him that neither she nor her mother had been able to tolerate lemon-juice.

His state of health made it impossible for him to return to France. He had thought of doing so in September 1849, but was too ill to travel: 'It will take another six to eight months of treatment before the valves of my heart have recovered their elasticity. . . .' He was fond of Dr Knothé, who compounded secret nostrums and collected violins. The Mniszechs raised no objection to his prolonging his stay—by then he had been with them for more than a year—and they even welcomed it, although they had been having misfortunes—two fires, three lawsuits, the collapse of some buildings and a bad harvest. George, who had hitherto farmed the estate himself, with five hundred hands, now proposed to rent it out in farms, only retaining the house and park.

Balzac had bronchitis nearly every winter. His attack in January 1850 was exceptionally severe:

I had to keep to my room all day without leaving it, and even in bed, but the ladies had the adorable kindness to keep me company without being repelled by my spitting, which was as bad as if I were being seasick. In fact I suffered a great deal, but I'm over it now and have even become acclimatized. . . .'

The outlook for the 'grand affair' was improving, although it would call for self-sacrifice on Eve's part to marry a sick man who could no longer be her physical lover, and a writer who, to all appearance, would do little more writing. Moreover the political situation in France was confused and alarming, with Louis-Napoléon now President of the Second Republic. Balzac and his mother had no high opinion of him:

As for the poor President, everyone notices his mental fatigue and preoccupied manner. He does not seem to know how to wear the impenetrable mask which every politician must adopt, and is so visibly confused that he answers *yes* for *no* and half the time does not know what is said to him. There is still ingratitude in the air. Everyone is asking, 'How is it going to end? . . .'

Eve may well have reflected upon the unwisdom of leaving that Ukrainian fastness, where she lived like a minor royalty, for the perils of the Paris mob and the duties of a sick-nurse.

At length, in March 1850, the imperial sanction was secured, the papers put in order, the last obstacle to the marriage removed. Balzac bombarded Madame Mère with instructions against his return to Paris with his bride. The window-boxes were to be filled with flowers, there must be briar roses in the tubs and all the books were to be rebound. He was as meticulous over the household details as he was in the descriptive passages in his novels.

But still he was uncertain. Three days before the wedding he wrote to his mother: 'Everything is now prepared for the matter you know of, but I shall not write to you about it until it is over. Here as elsewhere these things are never concluded until one has left the church.' Eve's doubts persisted to the end. It was charity, as much as love or fame, which finally turned the scale.

They were married at seven in the morning, on 14 March, in the parish church of St Barbara at Berdichev, 'gleaming with snow and resounding with bells', the officiating priest being the Abbé Count Ozarowski, who had been delegated for this function by the Bishop of Zitomir. George Mniszech was one of the witnesses and Anna escorted her mother, 'both in a state of extreme joy'. The party returned to Wierzchownia on the same day, arriving home completely exhausted at ten o'clock that night. Bitter winds were blowing round the house. Balzac could scarcely breathe, and Eve (she was fifty) had an attack of gout: 'Her feet and hands are so swollen that she cannot walk or move her fingers. . . .' Dr Knothé's treatment for this was strange and barbarous: 'Every other day she has to thrust her feet into the body of a sucking-pig which has only just been slit open, because it is necessary that the entrails should be quivering. No need to describe the agonized squeals of the little pig, which does not realize the honour that is being done it. . . .' Neither husband nor wife was in a condition to travel, and they decided to postpone their departure until the latter half of April: 'I hope to be in Paris before the end of the month. Alas, my state of health is such that I have great need of my native air, and I very much hope that it will benefit my wife, whose state is also deplorable. . . .'

Balzac wrote four personal letters after the wedding, to his mother, to Laure, to Dr Nacquart and to Zulma Carraud. To the last of these he wrote:

17 March 1850: We are such old friends that you must learn from no one but myself of the happy outcome of this great drama of the heart which has lasted sixteen years. Three days ago I was married to the only woman I have ever loved, whom I love more than ever and shall continue to love until I die. This union is, I believe, the recompense God has held in store for me for so many adversities, so many years of toil, so many difficulties encountered and overcome. I had neither a happy childhood nor a fruitful springtime; I shall have the brightest of summers and the most mellow of autumns. . . .

In his letter to Dr Nacquart he talked about his brilliant new connections and his health. What would the envious say when they learned that he was the husband of a great-niece of Marie Leczinska, brother-in-law to an aide-de-camp of the Tsar and a nephew by marriage of the Tsarina's first lady-in-waiting? But what would the doctor say when he found his patient incapable of walking up a flight of twenty stairs and liable to fits of suffocation even when he was sitting down? Delighted though he was at the success of his plans, Balzac had no illusions regarding the future. The ass's skin was shrunken almost to nothing. The *Bedouck*, his magic ring, had brought him the dearest dream of his life, but he knew that the marriage-bed would be his death-bed as well. He could say, with Marie de Verneuil in *Les Chouans*, 'Six hours to live'. He had written in 1834: 'It will be strange if the author of *La Peau de chagrin* dies young.' It was not strange; it was inevitable. How can any man be longlived who night after night consumes his life? But at all costs one must 'die in one's lair'. He was desperately anxious to bring his wife to the Rue Fortunée.

Before he could do so, however, they had to go to Kiev for Eve's name to be inscribed on her husband's passport and to secure an exit-visa from Russia. This trip brought on an attack of ophthalmia, and he could not read or write. Dr Knothé, after treating it, finally allowed them to leave for Paris on 25 April. The journey from Cracow to Dresden was a nightmare. Their covered carriage, a 'berlin', sank deep in the mud, and Balzac, gasping and half-blind, had to sit by the roadside while peasants levered it out with poles. He sat with his hands pressed to his heart, fighting for breath. On 30 April Eve wrote from Brody to Anna:

I am not at all happy about his health; the fits of suffocation are becoming more and more frequent; he is extremely weak and has no appetite and suffers from heavy sweats which weaken him still more. At Radzivilov they found him so changed that they scarcely recognized him. . . . I had no idea how adorable he is. I have known him seventeen years, but every day I discover qualities in him that I had not known he possessed. If only his health would improve! Do, please, talk to Dr Knothé about it. I cannot tell you how bad he was last night. I pray that his native air will do him good, and if this hope fails I shall be much to be pitied, I assure you. It is so good to be loved and protected like this. His poor eyes are very bad too. I don't know what it all means, and at moments I am very unhappy and perturbed. . . .

She ended the letter on a more hopeful note: 'Bilboquet says that he will get well directly his feet touch the soil of France.' They reached Dresden on 10 May, and Balzac wrote to Laure, without being able to see what he was writing, 'Here we are at last, still alive but sick and tired. A journey like this takes ten years off one's life, for think what it means for two people who adore each other to feel that they are killing one another. . . .' He insisted, both to Laure and to his mother, that Madame Mère should *not* be there to receive them when they arrived at the Rue Fortunée. It would be incorrect: 'My wife must call on Mother and pay her respects. Once this has been done she can show herself to be as devoted as she is; but her dignity would be compromised if she helped us to unpack.' The dowager Madame de Balzac was to leave the keys with François, the Alsatian manservant, and return to her own lodging in Suresnes.

The travellers spent a few days in Dresden, where they were entertained by Eve's acquaintances. They went shopping, and Honoré bought a magnificent toilet-set and Eve 'a pearl necklace fit to drive a saint mad'. Eve wrote to her children: 'Monsieur Bilboquet embraces you.' They seemed as happy as any couple can be, with death in the background.

At last they reached Paris. That morning an old lady had left the house in a fiacre, after carrying out her instructions in the matter of flowers and shrubs. In the evening a carriage drew up in the Rue Fortunée, and a breathless, half-blind man, exhausted by two days of travel and sleeplessness, got out, followed by a woman who was still beautiful. The postilion rang the bell but there was no reply. Yet the house was clearly occupied, for lights were to be seen in the rooms. They rang again and hammered on the door, but no one came. The triumphant arrival which Balzac had looked forward to was turning into a bad dream. Despite the lateness of the hour a locksmith had to be fetched from the Rue du Faubourg-Saint-Honoré. When finally they were able to enter the house that had been so lovingly made ready for them they found that François, who was there alone, Zanella having been dismissed, had suddenly gone beserk. He had turned the place into a shambles and then barricaded himself in his room. They had to wait till dawn before he could be removed to an asylum. After paying and dismissing the locksmith and postilion, Eve retired to the red bed-chamber, Honoré to the blue. The shred of ass's skin was now no larger than the petal of a flower.

XLI

The Race to Death

When the house is finished Death enters.
TURKISH PROVERB

'BILBOQUET HAS ARRIVED here far worse than you have ever seen him,' Eve wrote to Anna. 'He can't see or walk and he has constant fainting fits.' Since he could not leave his bed she nursed him. Dr Nacquart was so shocked by his condition that he insisted on calling in consultants. After an examination on 30 May the doctors ordered bleeding or heavy cupping, purges and diuretics. The patient was to avoid all emotional disturbance and to talk as little as possible and only in a low voice.

Dr Nacquart has left us a note of his personal opinion. He considered the case hopeless. The change in Balzac's countenance was plain to everyone, the more so to a doctor who had treated and loved him from his infancy. Nacquart found that the heart disease had taken a new and fatal turn. The patient was gasping and could speak only with difficulty. Nevertheless it seemed for a few days that rest and the treatment prescribed might at least effect a temporary improvement.

The new Madame de Balzac preserved an Olympian calm that matched her Junoesque forehead. In a letter to Anna, written on 7 June, she complained with a strange detachment of not being able to escape from 'this state of suspense which takes up all my time in a most annoying manner'. Since Balzac could not see to write he dictated his letters to her; and what with this and nursing him and running the house she could scarcely spare a moment to walk up and down the tiny garden, 'between the syringa which is blossoming, and the laburnum which is falling' there to seek comfort in the thought of her children by 'burying her mind in the depths of the future'.

Did she already realize, when she talked about 'taking refuge with her two darlings', that her husband could not live? 'The treatment,' she wrote, 'has had excellent results. The bronchitis has cleared up, the eyes are improving, the fainting attacks have ceased and the gasping fits are growing fewer.' But she could not leave the bedside, even to visit Henriette Borel in her convent. She was the most devoted of nurses.

Faithful and robust, gallantly enduring her changed way of life, its fatigues and anxieties, 'Never,' she wrote, 'has my health been better. The air-baths of France are all I need. . . . I have at last made the acquaintance of *Mother-in-law*. Since my duties as a nurse prevent me from going out she came here to see her son. Her health is entirely restored. As for herself, let it be said in confidence she is an *elegantka zastarzela*; she must have been very beautiful. . . . Fortunately she will not come here too often to claim our respects, because she has left to spend the summer in Chantilly. I prefer her daughter, who is a round little ball but intelligent and warm-hearted. The husband is an excellent man and the girls are charming. . . .'

Friendly letters were exchanged between Eve and Laure. Eve wrote on 1 June: 'Poor Honoré was bled this morning. . . . Our adorable doctor came to see him. . . . We talked a lot about you this morning, and Honoré did so with great affection. . . . I shall be telling you nothing new when I say that he is the noblest spirit ever to have left the hands of the Creator.' Sophie took a great liking to her new aunt, whom she referred to as *l'Adorable*, and both nieces considered that she was having an excellent influence on her husband: 'Our uncle, ill and married, has become kind and tender to his family.' The family and their friends were filled with pride when they heard that the President himself, Louis-Napoléon, had asked for news of Balzac.

But Eve found life a sad business in that *maison infortunée*: 'When will God take pity on us? Have we not suffered enough?' Balzac himself was still hopeful, the famous gold-flecked gaze still bright; but this last flicker of youth was denied by his ashen colour. 'He was nothing but the shadow of himself,' Laurent-Jan noted in despair; and Théophile Gautier wrote after his death: 'Nothing is more to be feared than a dream fulfilled. . . . The marriage so long desired had taken place; the house was furnished; the *Parents pauvres* were universally acclaimed. It was too much; there was nothing left for him to do but die. . . . Yet no one expected his death. . . . We had been convinced that he would see us all out. . . .' He had talked so often, and with such eloquence, of the longevity promised by the magician Balthazar that they had ended by believing it.

Gautier, who was leaving for Italy, called at the Rue Fortunée on 19 June, but Balzac was out. He had very rashly gone in a carriage to the customs-office to collect the things he had bought in Dresden. Like Pons, the collector defied illness to safeguard his treasures. He was heartbroken at missing Gautier and dictated a few lines to Eve: 'The fact that I was out does not mean that I'm better. I had simply dragged myself to the Customs against doctor's orders. They hold out great hopes of my recovery, but in the meantime I have to go on living like a mummy, denied speech and movement. I owed this note to your friendship, which I find even more precious in the solitude to which the Faculty has condemned me.' At the bottom he scrawled in an almost illegible hand: 'I can no longer read or write.' If that scene of living death and tragic impotence had figured in one of his novels, how wonderfully he would have described it!

On several occasions he and Eve believed that he was improving, but to Dr Nacquart, who had now diagnosed serious kidney trouble, these were only temporary lulls. The old doctor had formed a high regard for Eve—'a noble, generous and lofty spirit'. Balzac received Paul Meurice and Auguste Vacquerie in his dressing-gown, half-reclined in a big armchair. 'Talk to my wife,' he said to them. 'I'm not allowed to talk today, but I can listen.'

Victor Hugo came, masterful, friendly, bursting with health. He caught Balzac on a good day, in high spirits and confident of recovery, laughing as he displayed his swollen legs. Later Hugo described the visit:

We talked a lot and argued about politics. He accused me of 'demagogy'. He himself was a Legitimist. 'How could you so easily give up the title of Peer of France?' he asked. 'It is the greatest title after that of King of France.' He also said: 'I have the house of Monsieur de Beaujon minus the garden but with a private gallery in the little church at the corner of the street. There is a door from my staircase which leads to the church. A turn of the key and I am at Mass. I value that gallery more than the garden.' When I left him he went with me as far as the stairs, walking with difficulty, and showed me the door; and he called to his wife, 'Make sure you show Hugo all my pictures!'

He had often talked unjustly and even acrimoniously of Hugo, but in his heart he loved and admired him. They were the two greatest men of their time, and both knew it.

Anna's letters from Russia at that stage seem to echo more hopeful medical bulletins: 'May God be a thousand times praised and blessed that my beloved father's precious health is sensibly improved. . . . Oh, beautiful Rue Fortunée, a million times fortunate! . . .' She reported Dr Knothé as saying: 'If only I could have kept Monsieur de Balzac another month, and above all if I could have persuaded him to eat a lemon a day, he would be almost cured by now! . . . ' *Sancta simplicitas!*

But in July there was a sharp deterioration. One of the specialists said to Hugo, 'He has not six weeks to live.' His dropsical swelling became enormous. Laure wrote to their mother: 'The doctor bravely put a hundred leeches on his stomach, in three instalments. . . . But amid the gaiety that never deserts them, amid Honoré's puns and jesting in the face of death, he was so weak that my sister-in-law said quietly to Sophie, after the night when peritonitis set in, "I thought I had lost him." ' Eve soon recovered the saintly and miraculous confidence which seldom deserted her and in the morning she unflinchingly attached the last thirty leeches. 'My sister-in-law is to me an enigma. Does she realize the danger or does she not? If she does she is heroic.'

She must certainly have realized it. Nacquart was not the man to mislead a woman whose courage and steadfastness he so admired. There was nothing to be gained by lamentations. It was better to go on conscientiously applying leeches, and not undermine the confidence of a man whose mind, in his better moments, was still as clear as ever. Balzac talked about future books, reckoning the time it would take him to write them. 'God alone knows,' wrote Dr Nacquart, 'how much we have lost by not preserving the new ideas, the characters created, the themes conceived . . . which, for the first time, his pen could not execute.' He also wrote:

In his state of organic disorder Monsieur de Balzac, who at

all times had understood the whole destiny of man, wished to converse with a worthy minister of God in whose mouth religion was the highest expression of the intelligence of the universe. How heartrending was the serenity of this man who, still young, faced the loss of the renown he had so painfully acquired in thirty years of sleepless labour, the hope of seeing his work completed, and, more than all this, the personal happiness he had only just won. . . .

The priest was the Abbé Ausoures, the curé of Saint-Philippe-du-Roule who also officiated in the chapel. There are many death-bed scenes in Balzac's novels, those of Goriot, Madame de Mortsauf, Pons, Valentine Graslin and others. We may be sure that his last conversations with a priest were lofty and worthy of him. The doctors had now given up draining him since his dropsy was thickening, although when he bumped his leg against a piece of furniture a flood of liquid was released. On that day, 5 August, Eve wrote a letter to Fessart at his dicta-tion: 'I now have a painful abscess on my right leg. This will tell you how much my suffering has increased. I believe that it is all part of the price exacted by Heaven for the inexpressible happiness of my marriage.' He signed the letter himself, and beneath his signature Eve wrote: 'You may wonder, Monsieur, how the unhappy secretary has found the strength to write this letter. It is because she is at the end of her strength, and in that condition one is nothing but a machine which goes on functioning until Providence, in an act of mercy, breaks the spring.'

Clearly she no longer had any illusions, if indeed she had ever had any, even on the day of their wedding. That had been an act of heroism, as Laure said; she must have known that she was undertaking the care of a dying man and would be faced by a disastrous situation in her second widowhood. Balzac's mind was now beginning to wander, although the fits were still infrequent and 'astonishing to himself, for he wondered what had happened when he recovered his wits'. Then gangrene set in and the odour of decomposing flesh became intolerable. The doctor's last orders, after prescribing absolute quiet and a draught of henbane and digitalis, recommended that all doors and windows should be opened and bowls of phenicated water 'set at a number of places in the death-chamber'. Nacquart's use of that word, while his patient was still breathing, shows that it was all over. Balzac is reported to have said before he finally lost consciousness, 'Only Bianchon can save me', and it is likely enough that in the delirium preceding the final coma he strayed into the world of the *Comédie humaine.*

On Sunday, 18 August, at nine in the morning, Eve sent for the Abbé Ausoures. Balzac received the last sacrament and showed by faint signs that he understood. At eleven the death-agony began. Eve, worn out by the strain of the past months, had brought in a nurse. Madame Victor Hugo called during the afternoon, and in the evening Hugo left his dinner-table, where he had guests, and came to take leave of the only man who was his peer:

I rang the bell. There was a bright moon veiled by clouds. The street was empty. No one came. I rang again and the door opened. A servant appeared with a candle.

'What does Monsieur want?' she asked.

She was in tears. I told her my name. I was shown into the salon on the ground floor, in which, on a pedestal opposite the fireplace, there stood David's huge marble bust of Balzac. A candle was burning on a handsome oval table, in the middle of the salon, which in place of legs had six gilt statuettes, in admirable taste. Another woman came in, also weeping, and said to me:

'He is dying. Madame has retired to her own room. The doctors gave him up yesterday. . . .'

Eve was resting. The death-agony might last a long time, and there was nothing to be done. Hugo's narrative continues:

'Monsieur has not spoken since nine o'clock this morning. . . . The death-rattle began at eleven and he no longer sees anything. He will not survive the night. If you wish, Monsieur, I will fetch Monsieur de Surville, who has not yet gone to bed.

The woman left me and I waited a few moments. The candle scarcely illuminated the splendid furniture of the room and the magnificent paintings by Porbus and Holbein on the walls. The marble bust rose dimly in the shadow, like the ghost of a man about to die. A smell of death filled the house.

Monsieur de Surville entered and confirmed what the servant had told me. I asked if I might see Monsieur de Balzac. We crossed a hall and went up a red-carpeted flight of stairs on which there were a great many *objets d'art*—vases, statues,

pictures, cases of enamel ware—then along a passage, and I saw
an open door. I heard a loud and ominous rattling sound. I was
in Balzac's bedroom.

A bed stood in the middle of the room. A mahogany bed
with supports and straps at either end belonging to an apparatus
for moving the patient. Monsieur de Balzac lay in the bed, his
head propped against a heap of pillows to which red damask
cushions borrowed from the bedroom sofa had been added. His
face was purple, almost black, and turned to the right; he was
unshaven; his hair was grey and cropped short, his eyes open
and staring. I saw him in profile, and seen thus he resembled the
Emperor.

An old woman, the nurse, and a manservant were standing
on either side of the bed. A candle was burning behind the head
of the bed, on a table; another stood on a chest of drawers near
the door. A silver vase stood on the bedside table. The man and
woman were silent, in a sort of terror, as they listened to the
loud, rattling breath of the dying man.

The candle at the head of the bed brightly illumined the
portrait of a young man, pink-cheeked and smiling, which hung
on the wall by the fireplace.

An intolerable odour rose from the bed. I drew back the
coverlet and took Balzac's hand. It was damp with sweat. I
pressed it, but he did not return the pressure. . . . The nurse
said to me:

'He'll die at daybreak.'

I went downstairs again with the picture of that darkened
face in my mind. Passing through the salon I glanced at the
motionless bust, proud and faintly glowing, and compared
death with immortality.

When I returned home—it was a Sunday—I found a number
of people awaiting me, including Riza Bey, the Turkish chargé
d'affaires, Navarrete, the Spanish poet, and Count Arrivabene,
an exiled Italian. I said to them:

'Gentlemen, Europe is about to lose a great spirit.'

Balzac died that night. The devoted Laurent-Jan was the
first to arrive. Eve was not fond of that disorderly character; she
deplored his disreputable appearance and 'bad form'; but at
this tragic moment he did her great service. It was he who
attended to the formalities and sent the announcement to the
papers. He fetched the painter, Eugène Giraud, who did a
pastel of Balzac on his death-bed. The skilful, affectionate

portrait depicts a noble head, powerful and at peace. A moulder called Marminia also came and made a cast of Balzac's hand, subsequently addressing the bill to 'Madame Balsaque'. Such is fame.

Balzac's life ended like a chapter of the *Comédie humaine*. How often had he evoked the dreams of love and happiness pursued by a man throughout his life, only to elude him at the moment when they seem to be within his grasp! It was the ending of *Les Chouans, Louis Lambert, Albert Savarus*: 'To die when one has reached the goal, like the runner of antiquity! To see fortune and death come together in the doorway. To win the woman one loves at the moment when love is extinguished. No longer to possess the power to enjoy when one has earned the right to happiness. Oh, how many men have suffered that fate!'

The fate was his own, as he had long foreseen that it would be; and to his lucid intelligence, which so rejoiced in throwing light on the secret causes of events, the springs of his life must in those last days have been apparent in their stark simplicity. He died burnt out by his desires, drained dry by the acts of his imaginary world, the victim of his own works. The frustrations of his childhood and youth had fostered in him ambitions too great for any man. He had wanted everything, love and wealth, genius and fame; and despite the seemingly impassable distance between the starting-post and the finish, he had achieved them all. He lay on that night of 18 August 1850 in a setting of his own creation that resembled his dreams of a Thousand and One Nights, close to the miraculous Foreign Lady who had left a petty kingdom for his sake, and in the heart of the world he had peopled and made alive, which was to live on after him. But Death, after so long dogging his heels, had breasted the tape at his side. He belonged now to darkness and eternal rest.

Epilogue

L'amitié et la gloire sont les seuls habitants des tombeaux.
BALZAC

THE CURÉ OF Saint-Philippe-du-Roule allowed the body to lie in state in the private chapel for two days. In Hugo's words, Balzac in death 'passed through that doorway of which the key was more precious to him than all the pleasure-gardens of the former minister'. The funeral service took place on Wednesday, 21 August, with little display. The greatest novelist of the century was not entitled to any official pomp. There were no insignia on the black drapery of the coffin, no muffled drums, uniforms or embroidered tunics; but at eleven o'clock 'all those who thought and marvelled' gathered round the church and the Chapelle Saint-Nicholas. Among the crowd were many of the compositors who had wrestled with Balzac's manuscripts and proofs. The Government was represented by the Minister of the Interior, Pierre-Jules Baroche, who with Victor Hugo, Alexandre Dumas and Francis Wey held the tassels of the canopy on its way from the chapel to the church. 'He was a distinguished man,' the Minister remarked to Hugo. Hugo replied: 'He was a genius.'

The funeral procession followed, moving with an interminable slowness along the whole length of the boulevards to the cemetery of Père-Lachaise. It was late in arriving. Dumas and Hugo followed it on foot, and at the cemetery Hugo, who narrowly escaped being crushed between the hearse and a monument, delivered an oration which was listened to in profound silence. 'While I was speaking,' he noted afterwards, 'the sun went down. All Paris was spread out before me, wreathed in the splendid mist of the sunset. A part of the wall of the grave collapsed almost at my feet, and I was interrupted by the thud of earth falling on the coffin.' On that hillside consecrated to the dead, where Rastignac had once uttered his challenge to Paris, Paris now honoured Rastignac's creator:

Monsieur de Balzac [said Hugo] was one of the first among

551

the greatest, one of the highest among the best.... All his books together make one book, living, luminous and profound, in which the whole of our contemporary civilization is to be seen in movement, coming and going upon its affairs, with an element of awe and of the terrible mingled with its reality. A book which the writer called Comedy although he might well have called it History, embracing all forms and styles, reaching beyond Tacitus to Suetonius and through Beaumarchais to Rabelais ... overflowing with the truths of daily life, its privacies, commonplaces and trivialities, but at moments ... suddenly disclosing the most sombre and tragic of visions. . . .

That is the work he has left us, lofty and enduring, built solidly on rock—a monument! Henceforth his renown will radiate from its heights. Great men lay their own foundations, but it is for posterity to erect the statue.... Alas, that powerful and unwearied worker—philosopher, thinker, poet, genius— lived with the rest of us in the world of storm and struggle that is common to all times and all great men. Today he is at rest, escaped from controversy and beyond the reach of enmity. On one and the same day he enters glory and the tomb. Henceforth he will shine above the clouds that hide our heads, among the brightest stars in our country's sky. . . .

Barbey d'Aurévilly wrote on the same day:

This death is an intellectual disaster to which only the loss of Byron can be compared, amid all the deaths that we mourn in our time. Byron, like Balzac, died at the end of his youth, in the full maturity of his powers, and like Balzac left his work unfinished. *Don Juan* is no more complete than that other and perhaps greater epic, *La Comédie humaine*, of which we have scarcely half.... Walter Scott sank like a peaceful sun at the end of a long and limpid day. . . . Goethe, that darling of the gods, became a legend in his own time, in an old age that was a foretaste of immortality. But Balzac was struck down in the midst of life, in the still expanding empire of his talents and his plans. . . .

Sainte-Beuve, that most constant of enemies, announced in his 'Monday' article of 2 September that he proposed to assess Balzac's work in a spirit of detachment free of all personal bias:

Who has painted better than he the old men and beautiful

women of the Empire? Above all, who has caught more delightfully the duchesses and vicomtesses of the end of the Restoration, those women of thirty who, being posed, awaited their
painter with a vague disquiet? . . . Who, finally, has better
grasped and depicted in all its amplitude the bourgeois society
triumphant under the dynasty of the weak? . . . Great and rapid
though M. de Balzac's success was in France, it was perhaps
even greater and less contested in the rest of Europe. . . . There
was a time, for example, when Venetian society amused itself by
adopting the names of his principal characters and playing their
parts. During a whole season Rastignacs and Duchesses de
Langeais and de Maufrigneuse were to be met everywhere, and
it is said that more than one actor and actress in that social
comedy carried their role to its full conclusion. . . .

But having thus, as he considered, done his duty in the matter
of praise, Sainte-Beuve could not restrain himself from adding
a drop of venom. He could not, he said, admire Balzac's literary
style, 'so often prolix and formless, slack, rose-tinted and shot
with every colour, delicious in its corruption, quite asiatic, as
our masters used to say'; nor could he share his avowed fondness
for Swedenborg, Mesmer, Cagliostro and others of that ilk. He
felt obliged to say these things, Sainte-Beuve continued, 'so
that our admiration and mourning for a man of marvellous
talent may not go beyond permissable bounds'. And he
remarked in passing that George Sand was a greater writer than
Balzac. We may hope—and believe—that George Sand herself
was shocked by this.

Some brief account must be given of the other actors in the
play.
    Madame Mère lived another four years to cosset her daughter
and harass her son-in-law. She preferred to visit the family in
Surville's absence—'The old cat's away so the little old mouse
can dance,' she wrote in her lively style. She continued to work
herself into fevers of indignation, to play whist, to eat heavily-
sugared oranges, to remember anniversaries and to write to Eve,
'Say that you will always love your poor mother-in-law in
memory of him who was so dear to us both. . . . I have to pay the
doctor, firewood and rent, and I've only just enough to see me

through till 1 February. . . .' The truth is that Eve never let her go short of anything. She died on 1 August 1854, and her last letter was to Laure, 'with a big mother's kiss on her dear daughter's forehead'.

Laure maintained the family tradition of nervous crises. The pleasant little tales she wrote sold badly, and her over-aspiring husband was always biting off more than he could chew. Their finances went from bad to worse. Surville (Eugène Midy de la Greneraye) died in 1867. He left a quite substantial sum, but evidently his liabilities were greater, for his widow and daughters did not accept the legacy. Sophie, the elder girl, married a widower twenty years older than herself who deserted her; she then became a governess. Valentine, who lived till 1897, married a lawyer who became private secretary to the President of the Republic (Jules Grévy). The unhappy Henry de Balzac never learned that his natural father had made a will leaving him 200,000 gold francs; he died in a military hospital exactly two months before the death of Jean de Margonne.

Little 'père Dablin', the great-hearted ironmonger, remained throughout his life a friend of the Survilles. When he died he left Laure a silver soup-tureen and fifty miniatures; to Sophie a casket of Saxon porcelain and (as she had foreseen) a China cup; and to Valentine two enamel vases which Balzac had greatly liked. Perhaps a little hard cash would have been more welcome; but Dablin had thought of everyone, the poor of the district where he lived, those of Rambouillet, former servants, numerous cousins, countless friends and the Louvre Museum. His name will be linked with that of Balzac as long as books exist and people read them; and in particular with Les Chouans: 'The first work to the first friend'.

The silent and ruminative Major Carraud died in 1864. Zulma, much impoverished, was obliged to leave Frapesle. She moved into a small cottage at Nohant-en-Graçay where she wrote a number of children's books that had some success. She lived until 1889, surviving both her sons.

Balzac's will constituted his widow his sole heir and acknowledged a debt to her of 130,000 francs. She had in fact lent him more than twice that sum. To Marie du Fresnay he left a Girardon 'Christ', which was not by Girardon, in a Brustolone frame which was not by Brustolone, and Dr Nacquart,

Alexandre de Berny and Zulma Carraud all received tokens of his affection.

Eve might well have refused the succession of an estate so heavily encumbered, but she elected to pay off all the debts. Although she kept her mother-in-law free from want, she did not neglect to remind her of the fact. To a request for a larger allowance she replied coldly: 'I have not, I think, promised anything more than the exact payment of the interest due to you, and I can assure you that this is not easy. You know better than anyone that my whole fortune has gone to your son's creditors. . . .' She also wrote to a notary, Maître Delapalme: 'During four months I was not the wife but the *sick-nurse* of Monsieur de Balzac. In nursing my husband's incurable malady I ruined my health, just as I have ruined my private fortune in accepting the inheritance of debts and embarrassments which he left me. . . .' All this was true.

Eve's grief was nevertheless sincere and acute. She wrote to Dr Nacquart that she was no more than 'a body without a soul', a phrase which was itself a part of her legacy. ' . . . Despite your great and sensitive intelligence you cannot realize how it is with me. You do not know the courage it takes to live when life is nothing but suffering. . . .' She gave him Honoré's turquoise-studded cane as a souvenir.

The young Mniszechs were stunned by the news of 'dear Bilboquet's death. ' . . . This dreadful, unexpected blow,' Anna wrote to her mother. 'We shall devote our whole lives to consoling you in the bitterness of your loss.' They sold the greater part of their Polish estates, only retaining Wierzchownia, which they placed under the management of Dr Knothé. Having come to visit Eve in Paris they decided to settle there, and built themselves a handsome house on a site which they bought from the painter, Gudin, next door to the *maison infortunée*. Among its contents were glass cases of butterflies.

At the age of fifty Eve de Balzac was still both desirable and susceptible. 'So much so,' wrote Barbey d'Aurevilly, 'that she was worth of any folly. . . . Her beauty was imposing and noble, somewhat massive, a little fleshy, but even in stoutness she retained a very lively charm which was spiced with a delightful foreign accent and a striking hint of sensuality. . . .' Among those to be struck by it was the youthful Champfleury, who was away from Paris at the time of Balzac's death but later called upon his widow. Eve received him all too kindly and asked him to help her sort her husband's papers:

I had a headache, and while we were talking I kept putting my hand to my forehead. 'What is the matter?' she asked. 'Nothing—a slight neuralgia.' 'I'll make it go away.' Standing behind me she put her hands on my forehead. There are certain magnetic effluvia, in such situations, of which the effect is that the matter does not stop there. . . .

Thus began a brief and consoling liaison. Champfleury was twenty years younger than Eve, who wrote to him in May 1851: 'I go to cafés-chantants every night. . . . The night before last I laughed as I have never done before. . . . Oh, how wonderful it is not to know anyone or have to worry about anyone, to have one's independence, liberty on the mountain-tops, and to be in Paris!' She must certainly have fallen in love with Paris, because she never went back to her own country.

But she did not neglect her duty to her husband's memory. She charged Armand Dutacq with the task of preparing an edition of the Complete Works—or rather, the completed works, because she intended to publish *Le Député d'Arcis* and *Les Petits Bourgeois*, both of which had been left unfinished.

She asked her youthful lover to finish them anonymously, but Champfleury refused. In fact it was not very long before he was trying to escape from her. The mixture of 'cossack', mystical fervour and sensual ardour, which had so appealed to Balzac, had come to terrify him. Eve was both dictatorial and furiously jealous. She held him for a time, partly with financial inducements, but in November 1851 there was an open quarrel which brought the affair to an end.

Champfleury having failed her, Eve applied to Charles Rabou to finish the two novels—solely, she wrote to Dutacq, 'because my husband himself suggested him in the course of our talks about his uncompleted work, during his last fatal illness . . . .' As to the truth of this, we have no means of knowing.

Part of *Le Député d'Arcis* had been serialized in *L'Union*

Monarchique during April and May 1847, and although no continuation was to be found among Balzac's papers, Eve considered that she knew enough about it to be able to tell Rabou how it should end:

I have lived more with the characters in *La Comédie humaine* than in the real world. Anyone wishing for details concerning the habits, morals, relationships, acts and gestures of any member of the numerous and imperishable family created by that great mind and powerful will, must always apply to me. . . .

Rabou went to work under Eve's guidance. The novel grew to such an extent that when it was published in *Le Constitutionnel* in 1852 it ran to 101 instalments, of which only the first 31 were the work of Balzac. This first part had been entitled by Balzac, *L'Élection*. The whole novel, *Le Député d'Arcis*, as it appeared in *Le Constitutionnel* was in three parts—*L'Élection*, *Le Comte de Sallenauve* and *La Famille Beauvisage*. There was no mention of Rabou.

Rabou also finished *Les Petits Bourgeois* and again Eve told Dutacq that this was at her husband's express desire. The first part, published in 1856, was divided into 27 chapters of which the first 22 were by Balzac. The whole of the second part, published in 1857, was by Rabou. The publisher De Potter, who brought out the first volume edition of *Le Député d'Arcis* (before the Completed Works in 24 volumes published by Michel Lévy) had the courage to print 'concluded by Charles Rabou' on the title-page.

In 1851 the painter Jean Gigoux, whose dramatic historical canvases were highly commended for their 'virile talent' when they appeared, as they regularly did, in the Salon, made a portrait of the Countess Mniszech. Anna took her mother to his studio, and Eve was conquered by the virile talent. The relationship between them was virtually marital, since it lasted until Eve's death in April 1882. Gigoux survived her by a dozen years, 'a veteran loaded with years and fame' and with a large Gallic moustache. They lived together at the Château de Beauregard, at Villeneuve-Saint-Georges, which Eve bought not long after she became a widow.

Eve's last years were overshadowed by her children's mis-

fortunes. Anna, in whom Balzac had noted an irresistible fondness for jewels and expensive clothes, so succumbed to the
attractions of Paris that she ruined herself by her extravagance.
In 1875 George had a stroke from which he never recovered.
He lost his reason and died in 1881. Wierzchownia had long
since passed into the hands of Count Adam Rzewuski, Eve's
brother. After the death of her husband and mother, Anna sold
the Château de Beauregard and entered the convent of the
Dames de la Croix in the Rue de Vaugirard, having shown
herself to be 'as charming and good in times of misfortune as
in her days of opulence, and with the same birdlike innocence
that had delighted Balzac'. She lived until 1915.

A word may be said about Caroline Marbouty, Balzac's
romantic travelling-companion on his first journey to Italy. She
continued to write autobiographical novels under the name of
Claire Brunne and became the mistress of the Marquis de
Pastoret, a supporter of the claimant to the throne, Henry V,
who inspired her to write *Le Marquis de Precieux, ou Les Trois
Époques*. The liaison gave rise to a scandal, an obscure and
involved business in which compromising documents largely
figured. Whether or not Madame Marbouty was guilty of
attempted blackmail, she was thoroughly discredited and banned
from the Paris salons. The gallant 'Didine', in *La Muse du
Département*, has come off better.

Caroline now lies in the cemetery of Père-Lachaise, in
company with Balzac and his Foreign Lady, Anna and George
Mniszech, Hélène de Valette and so many others who figured
in the Balzac story.

Having buried the dead it is right that we should turn to the
living. They are imperishable—Goriot, Grandet, Hulot, Bette,
Pons, Rastignac, Rubempré, Popinot, Vautrin, Birotteau,
Gobseck. . . . They surround and haunt us, teaching us to know
men and women, who do not change. The Princesse de Cadignan
and the Marquise d'Espard still enact their subtle, cruel scenes;
the Goriot daughters have never ceased to batten on their
father; there is more than one Benassis fighting today to save a
French village, while in the next parish a General de Montcornet sells his estate. Gaubertin the dealer will buy it.

Year by year, in every country in the world, the host of readers grows in constancy and numbers. Every publisher who reprints *La Comédie humaine* sees it rapidly sold out. Balzac's fame shines far more brightly now than it did on that evening when Hugo, gazing into the mist of the setting sun, paid him eloquent homage. 'The time of impartiality has not yet come for me,' Balzac wrote in 1842. It was slow in coming. Until long after his death he was treated coolly by the critics. 'Every great monument throws a shadow, and there are people who see nothing else.' Writers of the realist school regarded him, wrongly, as their own forebear, although Zola thought he perceived 'a streak of genius' in Balzac's mysticism and political philosophy. Émile Faguet, in 1887, accused him of having the outlook of 'a provincial lawyer's clerk' and deplored the uncouthness of his style.

But the greatest writers were the first to recognize his greatness. After Hugo came Baudelaire, then Dostoevsky, Browning, Marx and Strindberg; then Proust and Alain; finally, the world. The academic critics, such as Faguet and Brunetière, ended by admitting their error. Taine, and after him Paul Bourget, showed that the thinker in Balzac matched and guided the observer. History was on his side. He had lived in an age of disenchantment. The tremendous energies that had been generated in men's souls by the Revolution and the Empire were never marshalled and put to use by the unheroic régimes of the Restoration and the Bourgeois Monarchy. In part they were absorbed by the explosion of 1830 and 1848; but the great surplus found its outlet in great matters of another kind—the industrial revolution and the *Comédie humaine*.

The latter half of the nineteenth century, smugly confident of progress through the growth of science, either denied or disregarded the hard truths preached by Balzac. Our own age, after living through two wars and experiencing so many upheavals, so many astonishing reversals of accepted values, is very much nearer to him. How could Émile Faguet, for example, understand the character of Philippe Bridau, when he had never known anyone like him? But in our time we have seen it all happen, the half-pay soldiers, the assassinations, conspiracies, *ténébreuses affaires*. Our scientists have confirmed Balzac's theory of the unity of matter and are in search of the Absolute. They believe, with him, that the mind acts upon the body; the whole study of psychosomatic medicine bears out the intuitive beliefs of Louis Lambert. And we read in César Birotteau: 'Hazards following in series constitute a providence'; it is a foreshadowing of statistical law.

Proust, who was as great as Balzac and familiar in detail with the *Comédie humaine*, would have been the last to find it surprising that the huge work could be accomplished in a short, difficult and often mediocre lifetime. Villeparisis was not so unlike Illiers; Tante Léonie might well have been a member of the 'most excellent family'; and the garret in the Rue Lesdiguières was no more solitary than that cork-lined room on the Boulevard Haussmann. 'Those who produce works of genius are not those who live in the most refined surroundings.' From the day when Honoré de Balzac set out to give to the world, transforming them in the process, the stern, chilly gaze of his mother, the sorrows of his neglected childhood, his reading under the stairs at Vendôme, his first 'scent of woman', the vicissitudes of his brother-in-law, the squalid stratagems of usurers, his lost illusions and his creative ecstasy, he sustained a multitude of living people with his own substance. He gave them his life, and so died young. But who would not wish to be Balzac?

BIBLIOGRAPHY

CHRONOLOGICAL LIST
AND INDEX OF WORKS

INDEX OF NAMES

Bibliography

Alain: *En lisant Balzac* (Paris, 1935)
  Avec Balzac: (1958), etc.
Arrault, Albert: *Madame de Berny, éducatrice de Balzac* (Paris, 1945)
Arrigon, L.-J.: *Les Débuts littéraires d'Honoré de Balzac* (Paris, 1924)
  Les Années romantiques de Balzac (Paris, 1927)
  Balzac et la Contessa

Bardèche, Maurice: *Balzac romancier* (Paris, 1940)
  Notes on individual works
Barrière, Pierre: *Les Romans de jeunesse d'Honoré de Balzac* (Paris, 1928)
Baudelaire, Charles: *Curiosités esthétiques*
Béguin, Albert: *Balzac visionnaire* (Paris, 1946)
Bertault, Philippe: *Balzac et la réligion* (Paris, 1929), etc.
Billy, André: *Vie de Balzac* (Paris, 1944)
Bouteron, Marcel: *La Véritable Image de Madame Hanska* (Paris, 1929), etc.
  Editor: *Les Cahiers Balzaciens* (Eight volumes, Paris, 1927-8)
Brunne, Claire (Caroline Marbouty): Published and unpublished writings, the latter in the collection of Madame Simone André-Maurois
Brunetière, Ferdinand: *Balzac* (Paris, n.d.)

Castex, Pierre-Georges: Prefaces to individual works
Chasles, Philarète: *Mémoires* (Paris, 1876-7)
Curtius, E. F.: *Balzac*

Davin, Félix: Introduction to the *Études philosophiques*
Descaves, Pierre: *Les Cent-Jours de Monsieur de Balzac* (Paris, 1950)
  Le Président (Paris, 1951)

Faguet, Émile: *Balzac* (Paris, 1913)
Fargeaud, Madeleine: Notes on Laurence de Balzac, Dablin, Henry de Balzac contributed to *L'Année Balzacienne*

Gautier, Théophile: *Honoré de Balzac*, etc.
Goncourt, Edmond and Jules de: *Journal* (Vol. 1)
Gozlan, Léon: *Balzac en pantoufles*
Green, F. C.: *French Novelists from the Revolution to Proust* (London, 1931)
Guyon, Bernard: *La Pensée et sociale de Balzac* (Paris 1947)

Hannotaux, Gabriel, and Vicaire, Georges: *La Jeunesse de Balzac; Balzac imprimeur; Balzac et Madame de Berny* (Paris, 1921)
Hugo, Victor: *Choses vues*, etc.

Le Breton, André: *Balzac, l'homme et l'oeuvre* (Paris, 1905)

Lovenjoul, Vicomte de Spoelberch de: *Histoire des oeuvres de H. de Balzac* (Paris, 1888), etc.

Marceau, Félicien: *Balzac et son monde* (Paris, 1955)

Maurice, Claude: *Aimer Balzac* (Paris, 1945)

Meininger, Anne-Marie: 'Eugène Surville', etc., contributed to *L'Année Balzacienne*

Picon, Gaétan: *Balzac par lui-même* (Paris, 1956)

Regard, Maurice: 'Balzac et Laurent-Jan', contributed to *L'Année Balzacienne*. Introduction to *Béatrix*. 'Documents sur Hélène de Valette'

Risch, Léon: *Balzac et sa famille à Villeparisis* (Vesoul, 1936)

Royce, William Hobart: *A Balzac Bibliography* (Chicago, 1929)

Sainte-Beuve, Charles-Augustin: *Causeries du Lundi*, etc.

Sand, George (Aurore Dudevant): *Histoire de ma vie* (Paris, 1851)

Silver, Mabel: *Jules Sandeau, l'homme et la vie* (Paris, 1936)

Surville, Laure: *Balzac, sa vie et ses œuvres d'après sa correspondance*, etc.

Turnell, Martin: *The Novel in France* (London, 1950)

Wurmser, André: *La Comédie inhumaine* (Paris, 1964)

Zweig, Stefan: *Balzac*

Other major sources

Balzac *La Comédie humaine* Standard edition in eleven volumes (Bibliothèque de la Pléiade)

General correspondence, in three volumes, edited by Roger Pierrot

Correspondence with Zulma Carraud, edited by Marcel Bouteron

Letters to Madame Hanska (*Lettres à l'Étrangère*), in five volumes, the fifth not yet published in volume form.

Hommage à Balzac, a collection of contemporary writings on Balzac issued in 1950 under the auspices of UNESCO to commemorate the centenary of his death.

Les Cahiers Balzaciens, in eight volumes, edited by Marcel Bouteron, containing further correspondence, unpublished fragments, letters from women to Balzac, etc. (Paris, 1927–8)

L'Année Balzacienne: an annual collection of new writings and research on Balzac.

Chronological List and Index of Works

The chronology is approximate for reasons which the reader of the book will understand. Titles are listed under the year to which they may be said to belong; and where, as so often happened, the title was changed, the final one has been used. The figures in brackets indicate the major reference or references to the work in the text.

1819 *Cromwell* [65–8]   A tragedy in blank verse, unproduced and unpublished during the author's lifetime

1822 *L'Heritière de Birague* [81] ⎫ Written in collaboration
     Jean-Louis [81]   ⎬ under the pseudonym Lord
                                    ⎭ R'Hoone

     Clotilde de Lusignan [92–4 *passim*] ⎫ Written   under   the
     Le Centenaire [102]   ⎬ pseudonym   Horace
     Le Vicaire des Ardennes [101]   ⎭ de Saint-Aubin

1823 *La Dernière Fée*   Horace de Saint-Aubin

1824 *Annette et le criminal* (*Argon le Pirate*)   Horace de Saint-Aubin
     Du droit d'ainesse   ⎫
                                        ⎬ Both anonymous
     Histoire impartiale des jésuites ⎭

1826 *Wann-Chlore* [121–2]   Horace de Saint-Aubin
     Code des gens honnêtes   Anonymous

1829 *Les Chouans* [141]   By 'Honoré Balzac'. The first work to be published under his own name, later incorporated in *La Comédie humaine*
     La Physiologie du mariage [155]   By 'a young bachelor'

1830 *La Vendetta*   ⎫ First *Scènes de la vie*
     Gobseck   ⎪ *privée*, novellas and
     Le Bal de sceaux [163–4]   ⎪ short   stories   of
     La Maison du chat qui pelote [158]   ⎬ varying length. He
     Une Double Famille [158, 163]   ⎪ now signed his
     La Paix du ménage   ⎪ works 'Honoré *de*
                                                ⎭ Balzac'

     Les Deux Rêves [164–5]   ⎫ First of the *Contes philoso-*
     L'Élixir de longue vie [181]   ⎬ *phiques*

565

1831 *La Peau de chagrin* [173–5, 177–80]
      Jésus-Christ en Flandre [183–5]
      Les Proscrits ⎫
      Le Chef-d'oeuvre inconnu ⎬ Further *Contes philosophiques*

1832 *Le Colonel Chabert*
      Le Curé de Tours [163, 194–5]
      La Femme de trente ans [159]
      Louis Lambert [199–201, 437]
      Les Contes Drolatiques [204–6]   The first ten. Tales in the
      manner of Rabelais, outside the *Comédie humaine*

1833 *Le Médecin de campagne* [226–8]
      La Femme abandonnée [202] ⎫
      La Grenadière [318–19]   ⎬ Among the first *Scènes de*
      L'Illustre Gaudissart [232] ⎬ *la vie de province*, the last
      Eugénie Grandet [233–5]   ⎭ a full-length novel

1834 *La Recherche de l'Absolu* [251–3]
      Histoire des Treize

          1. *Ferragus*   ⎫ Among the
          2. *La Duchesse de Langeais* [223, 242, 246]   ⎬ first *Scènes*
          3. *La Fille aux yeux d'or* [265–7, 272, 419]   ⎬ *de la vie*
                                                           ⎭ *parisienne*

1835 *Le Père Goriot* [256–61]
      Melmoth reconcilié
      Le Contrat de mariage [285]
      Séraphita [239, 288]

1836 *Le Lys dans la vallée* [282–5, 310, 437]
      L'Interdiction
      La Messe de l'athée [280, 405]
      Facino Cane [352]
      L'Enfant maudit
      La Confidence des Ruggieri

1837 *La Vieille Fille* [325–7]
      Illusions perdues (first part) [298–300]
      César Birotteau [345–8]

1838 *Les Employés* (*La Femme supérieure*) [339–40]   Play
      La Maison Nucingen
      La Torpille [354, 443]   First part of *Splendeurs et misères
      des courtisanes*

1839 *Le Cabinet des antiques* [320, 362]
Gambara [336]
Une fille d'Ève [453]
Massimilla Doni [337–8]
Béatrix (beginning) [366–7]
Les Secrets de la Princesse de Cadignan [418–19]
Illusions perdues (second part) [362–3, 443]
L'École des ménages [360] ⎫
Vautrin [368–9]   ⎭ Plays

1840 *Pierrette*
Pierre Grasson
Z. Marcas [382–3]
Un Prince de la Bohème

1841 *Le Curé de village* [380–1]
Le Martyr calviniste

1842 *Mémoires de deux jeunes mariées*
Albert Savarus [437–40, 501]
La Fausse Maîtresse
Autre étude de femme
Ursule Mirouët [392]
Un Début dans la vie [436]
La Rabouilleuse [391]
Les Ressources de Quinola [433–4]   Play

1843 *Une Ténébreuse Affaire* [392–4, 424]
La Muse du Département [443–4]
Honorine [442–3, 501]
Illusions perdues [450, 459]   The completed work, in three parts
Les Martyrs ignorés [104–5]
Pamela Figaud   Play

1844 *Modeste Mignon* [454–5]
Les Paysans [463]   (beginning)
Béatrix   The completed work
Gaudissart II

1845 *Un Homme d'affaires* [421]
Les Comédiens sans le savoir [421]

1846 *Petites misères de la vie conjugale*
L'Envers de l'histoire contemporaine [443, 513] First
episode
La Cousine Bette [486–7, 498–9]

1847 *Le Cousin Pons* [496–8]
La Dernière Incarnation de Vautrin [491, 499] Comple-
tion of *Splendeurs et misères des courtisanes*

1848 *L'Initié* [514] Second episode of *L'Envers de l'histoire
contemporaine*
La Marâtre [522–4] Play

Le Député d'Arcis [504, 512, 556–7] ⎫ Completed after
Les Paysans [493–6]   ⎬ Balzac's death by
                                          ⎪ Charles Rabou and
                                          ⎪ published in 1854
                                          ⎭ and 1855

Splendeurs et misères des courtisanes [460–1] First published as a single work (in four parts) in the Collected
Edition of Balzac's works issued by Michel Levy (later
Calmann-Levy) between 1869 and 1876. This edition
included the dramatic works and thirty *Contes drolatiques*

Index of Names

Alain, 402, 425, 455

Allain, Catherine (mother of Eugène Surville) 62, 63, 69

Arago, Étienne, 75, 103, 113, 252

Ausoures, Abbé, 547, 548

Balssa, Bernard (grandfather of Honoré), 19

Balzac, Bernard-François (father of Honoré), 18–20, 21–4 *passim*, 26, 28, 29, 38–40, 43–8 *passim*, 51–4 *passim*, 79–82 *passim*, 86, 98–100, 108, 112, 120, 122, 126, 127, 134, 144–5, 148, 222

Balzac, Henry (illegitimate son of Mme Balzac), 41, 45, 98, 111, 158, 173, 249–50, 280, 333, 554

Balzac, Laure (*née* Sallambier; mother of Honoré), 21–2, 24–8 *passim*, 36, 40–3, 45, 47, 52–5 *passim*, 66–70 *passim*, 77, 79, 86, 89, 90, 92–5 *passim*, 98, 99, 108–12 *passim*, 122, 123, 127–9 *passim*, 145, 172, 189, 195–8, *passim*, 203, 208, 211, 214–16, 232, 245, 250, 261–2, 287, 323, 324, 332, 333, 353, 361, 370, 373–4, 389–90, 445–6, 468, 471–3 *passim*, 481, 483, 515, 528, 530–1, 533–5, 538, 540, 541, 544, 553–4

Balzac, Laure (sister of Honoré), 24–5, 27, 28, 40–2, 43, 45, 49, 55, 56, 59, 60, 62–8 *passim*: *see also* Surville, Laure

Balzac, Laurence (sister of Honoré), 25, 27, 28, 41, 52–3, 56–7, 64, 65, 72, 75–8 *passim*: *see also* Montzaigle, Laurence

Balzac, Louis-Daniel (brother of Honoré), 24, 98

Barbier, M., 123, 125, 127

Baudelaire, Charles, 416, 419–20

Béchet, Mme Charles, 232, 250, 251, 265, 276, 280, 286, 291, 294, 295, 298, 323, 326

Belloy, Auguste de, 335, 336, 368, 369

Bernard, Charles de, 301, 362, 505

Berny, Alexandre de, 126, 322, 323, 555

Berny, Gabriel de, 82, 83

Berny, Laure de, 82, 83–90 *passim*, 93, 95–7 *passim*, 99, 110, 114, 116, 118, 123–6 *passim*, 129, 134, 137, 146–8, 152, 165–8 *passim*, 176, 189, 194–8 *passim*, 200–1, 202, 205–6, 217, 220, 232, 242, 245, 263, 282, 284–7 *passim*, 299, 301, 322–3, 324, 341, 355, 356, 394, 461

Berny family, 82, 83–4, 89, 112

Beyle, Henri: *see* Stendhal

Boisgelin, Monseigneur de, 17, 24

Bonaparte, Napoleon, 17, 29, 38, 42, 44, 104, 213, 246, 395, 402, 403, 424

Borel, Henriette, 228, 229, 240, 456, 462, 473

Bra, Théophile, 238

Breugnole, Louise de (the 'Screech-owl'), 388–90 *passim*, 456, 467–9, 472, 480, 483, 484, 499, 502, 519

Buloz, François, 287, 291, 297, 361

Canel, Urbain, 116, 117, 121, 124, 131, 138, 142–3, 175, 186, 187

Carraud, Major, 144, 168, 189, 203, 204, 248, 282, 349, 554

Carraud, Zulma, 144, 165, 168, 169, 188, 189, 193, 194, 201, 203, 206, 208–10, 213–16 passim, 221, 222, 225, 227, 229, 235, 245, 248, 261, 267, 275, 282, 285, 289, 299–301 passim, 321, 324–5, 345, 352, 356, 374, 379–80, 402, 501, 516, 540, 554, 555

Castries, Marquise de (later Duchesse de), 190–2, 195, 201, 202, 204, 207–11 passim, 214, 223, 225, 232–3, 246, 248, 253, 256, 262–3, 273–4, 278, 312–13, 488, 522

Champfleury, 518–19, 555–6

Chasles, Philarète, 118, 151, 168, 177, 181–2, 268, 420

Chlendowski, M., 469, 470

Comin', Mère, 54, 55, 62

Dablin, Théodore ('petit père'), 46, 53, 54, 59, 61, 65, 68, 69, 93, 126, 128, 286, 301, 346, 347, 471, 497, 535–6, 554

d'Abrantès, Duchesse, 118–21 passim, 123–4, 145–7, 150, 158, 165, 189, 195, 202, 278, 300, 355–7 passim

Daminois, Marie-Louise-Françoise: see Du Fresnay, Marie

Dassonvillez de Rougemont, Jean-Louis, 115, 116, 118, 123

Daumier, Honoré, 292

Davin, Félix, 255–6, 399

Delannoy, Josephine, 46, 98, 118, 123, 203, 204, 286, 292, 301, 373, 471

Delécluze, Étienne, 150

Desbordes-Valmore, Marceline, 238, 433, 498

Dessaignes, Jean-Philibert, 29, 34–6

Deurbroucq, Baronne, 195, 197, 202

Dilecta, La: see Berny, Laure

Dorval, Marie, 267, 434, 520–2 passim, 524

Du Fresnay, Marie, 233, 394, 554

Duckett (publisher), 295, 298, 328, 335

Dudevant, Aurore: see Sand, George

Dumas, Alexandre, 83, 460, 463, 551

Dutacq, Armand, 556, 557

Ellenborough, Lady, 277, 308

Étrangère, l': see Hanska, Èveline

'Fanny': see Guidoboni-Visconti, Contessa

Fessart, Auguste, 469, 470

Fitz-James, Duc de, 190, 192, 196, 210, 214, 253, 262

Flaubert, Gustave, 402, 417

Gautier, Théophile, 267, 268, 281, 291, 292, 336, 355, 359, 362, 368, 463, 489, 505, 523, 527, 544–5

Gavault, Maître, 381, 441–2, 506

Gay, Sophie, 151

Gigoux, Jean, 557

Girardin, Delphine de, 187, 189, 194, 195, 206, 225, 248, 271, 362, 395, 465, 480, 489, 520

Girardin, Émile de, 187, 194, 225, 248, 325, 326, 339, 354, 496, 505, 520

Gosselin, M. (publisher), 175, 181, 206, 225, 251

Gozlan, Léon, 434, 435, 447

Greneraye, Midy de la: see Surville, Eugène

Guidoboni-Visconti, Conte Emilio, 306, 307–8, 321, 328, 330, 340, 344, 375, 532

Guidonboni-Visconti, Contessa ('Fanny'), 275, 305–13 passim, 327, 328, 330, 335, 340, 344, 359, 368, 374, 385, 446, 471, 532

Guillonnet-Merville, Jean-Baptiste, 48–9, 158

Hammer-Purgstall, Baron Joseph von, 278–9

Hanska, Anna de, 228, 448, 453, 465, 466, 469, 475: see also Mniszech, Countess Anna

Hanska, Èveline (L'Étrangère), 218–22, 224, 227, 228, 229–33, 238, 239, 240–5, 246, 247, 249, 252–4 passim, 257, 263–4, 267, 269, 270, 274–8 passim, 285, 288–90, 293–5 passim, 297, 308–9, 311, 319, 321, 324–9 passim, 331, 338, 341–2, 345–6, 348, 349, 353, 355, 356, 360, 365, 368, 374, 379, 380, 384, 385, 387, 395, 407, 408, 418, 429–33, 438, 439, 441, 446–9 passim, 451–7 passim, 459, 460, 462–70, 474–92, 496, 499–500, 502–4, 506–8, 512, 515, 520, 521, 524–31 passim, 534, 535, 537–50 passim, 554–8 passim

Hanski, Wenceslas, 219, 230, 231, 245, 253, 277, 327, 429, 430, 459, 511

Hautefeuille, Comtesse, 92, 202

Hugo, Victor, 149, 159, 224, 236, 240, 292, 355, 395–6, 397, 412, 433, 447, 457, 498, 518, 526, 527, 530, 545–6, 548–52 passim

Jacquillat, Mme Jean-Brice: see Béchet

Karr, Alphonse, 292, 297, 336, 382, 395

Knothé, Dr, 533, 538–9, 541, 546, 555

Lamartine, Alphonse, 480, 519, 522, 525

Lassailly, Charles, 361, 362

Latouche, Henri de, 121–2, 126, 130, 131, 133, 137–40, 142–3, 238, 341, 383, 388

Laurent-Jan, 361, 368, 369, 505, 528, 530, 536, 544, 549

Lautour-Mézeray, 187

Lavater, Johann, 103–4, 110

Le Poitevin, Auguste (Vieillerglé), 74–5, 81, 102–3, 105

Lefebvre, Père (schoolmaster), 31

Lemaître, Frédérick, 368, 369

Liszt, Franz, 447–9

Lovell (Frances) Sarah ('Fanny'): see Guidoboni-Visconti, Contessa

Lovell, Julia, 305–6

Lovell family, 305–6

Maffei, Clara, 329, 330, 331

Malus, Édouard, 95, 96, 98, 99, 101

Mame, Louis, 197, 216, 225–6

Marbouty, Caroline, 314–19, 320, 443, 444–5, 446, 558

Mareschal, Lazare-François, 29, 36
Margonne, Jean de, 26, 27, 28, 42, 43, 189, 253, 475, 517, 524, 525, 554
Margonne, Mme, 26, 196, 253, 525
Mauriac, François, 404–5
Metternich, Prince Clément von, 278
Metternich, Princess Mélanie von, 278
Metternich, Count Victor von, 190
Michelet, Jules, 44, 45
Mniszech, Countess Anna, 485, 486, 488, 507–8, 511, 514, 529, 534, 536, 539, 546, 555, 557, 558: *see also* Hanska, Anna de
Mniszech, Count Georges, 465, 466, 468, 469, 475, 485, 486, 511, 529, 539, 555
Moniuszko, Aline, 485–6, 506, 522, 525
Monnier, Henri, 103, 161, 292, 295, 332, 339, 372
Montzaigle, Alfred de, 323
Montzaigle, Amand-Désiré de Saint-Pierre de, 79–80, 81–2, 86, 112
Montzaigle, Laurence (*née* Balzac; sister of Honoré), 79–80, 81–2, 86, 116, 117, 120: *see also* Balzac, Laurence

Nacquart, Dr Jean-Baptiste, 46, 65, 78, 80, 103, 172, 188, 195, 248, 253, 286, 296, 328, 342, 373, 441, 456, 461, 468, 520, 540, 543–7 *passim*, 555
Nodier, Charles, 446–7, 457

Orvilliers, Comte d', 52, 76

Passez, Maître (notary), 46, 47, 53
Pélissier, Olympe, 175, 179, 189, 343
Penhoën, Barchou de, 35, 45, 235
Peytel murder case, 371–3
Planche, Gustave, 291–2, 296, 366
Pollet, Charles-Alexandre (publisher), 97, 98
Pommereul, General de, 17–19, 24, 38, 44, 135, 141, 173
Pommereul, (Gilbert), Baron de, 135–6, 142, 176, 333
Pommereul, Mme (Gilbert) de, 136, 137, 249, 333
Porcia, Alfonso, 329, 354
Potocka, Countess Marie, 242, 247, 305

Rabou, Charles, 182, 556–7
Raisson, Horace, 103, 107, 110
Ratier, Victor, 161, 166–7
Récamier, Mme, 150, 237, 355
Rothschild, Baron James de, 210, 277, 280, 341, 412, 469, 472, 484, 486, 531
Rzewuska, Countess Rosalie, 239, 288, 498

Saint-Aubin, Horace de: pseudonym of Honoré Balzac
Saint-Hilaire, Geoffroy, 47–8, 288
Saint-Martin, Louis-Claude, 106, 199
Sainte-Beuve, Charles-Augustin, 262, 268, 284, 308, 315, 383–4, 397, 421, 451, 458, 552–3
Sallambier, Joseph (grandfather of Honoré), 22, 27, 28

Sallambier, Laure (mother of Honoré): *see* Balzac, Laure (mother)

Sallambier, Sophie (grandmother of Honoré), 21–2, 27, 28, 37, 40, 52, 62, 77, 82, 95, 96, 101

Sallambier family, 22, 46, 98, 108

Sand, George, 143, 175, 206, 252, 267, 269, 299, 315, 316, 330, 336, 349, 350–1, 360, 366, 378, 383, 394, 401, 407, 408, 423, 553

Sandeau, Jules, 175, 180, 252, 267–70 *passim*, 274, 291, 296, 299, 315, 316, 321, 342, 349, 350

Sautelet, Auguste, 45, 48, 74, 105, 124, 167

Savary, Anne de: *see* Margonne, Mme

Savary, Henri-Joseph de, 26–7, 72, 235

Sclopis, Conte Frederico, 319, 320–1

'Screech-owl', the: *see* Breugnol, Louise de

Scribe, Eugène, 59–60

Sedillot, Charles, 127, 129, 135, 143, 471, 481

Sedillot family, 21, 46

Solar, Félix, 388, 389

Sorel, Agnès, 18

Stendhal, 167, 329, 331, 383, 384

Sue, Eugène, 186, 216, 220, 222, 349, 383, 443, 458, 460

Surville, Eugène, 62–5, 69, 70, 89, 90–3 *passim*, 97–101 *passim*, 108, 112, 118, 120, 129, 144, 172, 173, 229, 245, 250, 251, 254, 296, 323, 333–4, 339, 369–70, 472, 481, 517, 526, 530, 531, 535, 536, 548, 554

Surville, Laure (sister of Honoré), 25, 27, 69–70, 72, 74–83 *passim*, 89–99 *passim*, 101, 102, 108–9, 112, 113, 118, 120, 127, 130, 145, 158, 172, 173, 198–9, 230–1, 245, 246, 249, 250, 254, 261–2, 279, 286, 290, 292, 323, 324, 326, 333–4, 339, 369–70, 386, 389–90, 394, 430, 436, 437, 461–2, 468, 471, 472, 481, 498, 510, 512, 515, 526, 530, 536, 540, 541, 544, 546, 554: *see also* Balzac, Laure

Surville, Sophie, 481, 526, 530, 534–6 *passim*, 544, 554

Surville, Valentine, 534, 535, 554

Thiers, Marie Joseph, 293, 517

Thomassy, Jean, 105–7, 115, 288

Trumilly, Mlle Eléonore de, 177

Valette, Hélène-Marie-Félicité de, 374–9

Vieillerglé: *see* Le Poitevin

Villers-La Faye, Louis Philippe de, 67–8, 72, 111, 155

Werdet, Edmond, 250–1, 276, 280, 286, 287, 289, 295, 296, 297, 328, 341, 345

Zanella (caretaker), 505, 530, 532, 535, 542

Zola, Émile, 402, 559